France,
1800–1914

A Social History of Europe

General Editor: Raymond Pearson

France, 1800–1914 is the fourth volume to be
published in this major Longman series. Wide-ranging both
geographically and chronologically, it will explore the history
of the peoples of Europe in an ambitious programme of
analytical surveys, each examining a nation, state or region
in a key phase of its development. The books will be written
by leading experts; and each, while synthesizing the latest
scholarship in the field, will be invigorated by the findings
and preoccupations of the author's original research.

The series is designed for a wide audience: the volumes will be
necessary reading for serious students and fellow scholars, but
they are also written to engage and interest the non-specialist
coming to the subject for the first time.

Inaugurated by the late Harry Hearder, the series is under the
General Editorship of Professor Raymond Pearson, Professor of
European History at the University of Ulster at Coleraine.

Titles available in the series:

A Social History of the Russian Empire 1650–1825
Janet Hartley

France, 1800–1914
Roger Magraw

French Society 1589–1715
Sharon Kettering

Spanish Society 1400–1600
Teofilo Ruiz

Forthcoming titles in this series:

Twentieth Century Italy
Jonathan Dunnage

French Society 1700–1810
Gwynne Lewis

Modern Spanish Society 1939–2000
Michael Richards

A Social History of the Russian Empire 1810–1917
David Saunders

France, 1800–1914

A Social History

Roger Magraw

University of Warwick at Coventry

An imprint of **Pearson Education**

London · New York · Toronto · Sydney · Tokyo · Singapore · Hong Kong · Cape Town
New Delhi · Madrid · Paris · Amsterdam · Munich · Milan · Stockholm

Pearson education limited

Head Office:
Edinburgh Gate
Harlow CM20 2JE
Tel: +44 (0)1279 623623
Fax: +44 (0)1279 431059

London Office:
128 Long Acre
London WC2E 9AN
Tel: +44 (0)20 7447 2000
Fax: +44 (0)20 7240 5771
Website: www.history-minds.com

First published in Great Britain in 2002

© Pearson Education, 2002

The right of Roger Magraw to be identified as Author
of this Work has been asserted by him in accordance
with the Copyright, Designs and Patents Act 1988.

ISBN 0 582 22816 6

British Library Cataloguing in Publication Data
A CIP catalogue record for this book can be obtained from the British Library

Library of Congress Cataloguing in Publication Data
A CIP catalogue record for this book can be obtained from the Library of Congress

10 9 8 7 6 5 4 3 2 1

Typeset in 9.5/11.5 pt Stone Serif by Graphicraft Limited, Hong Kong
Produced by Pearson Education Asia Pte Ltd.
Printed in Malaysia, LSP

The Publishers' Policy is to use paper manufactured from sustainable forests.

This book is dedicated to my daughter Nathalie, to my mother – and to the memory of my father.

Contents

General editor's preface

For far too long 'social history' was regularly, even routinely defined dismissively and negatively along the lines of 'history with the high politics, economics and diplomacy left out'. Over the latter decades of the twentieth century, however, a virtual revolution in the sub-discipline of 'social history' gathered momentum, fuelled not only by historians but also by specialists from such established academic disciplines as anthropology, economics, politics and especially sociology, and enriched by contributors from burgeoning cultural, demographic, media and women's studies. At the cusp of the twenty-first century, the prime rationale of the recently launched 'Social History of Europe' series is to reflect the cumulative achievement and reinforce the ripening respectability of what may be positively yet succinctly defined as nothing less than the 'history of society'.

Initiated by the late Professor Harry Hearder of the University of Wales, the 'Social History of Europe' series is conceived as an ambitious and open-ended collection of wide-ranging general surveys charting the history of the peoples of the major European nations, states and regions through key phases in their societal development from the late Middle Ages to the present. The series is not designed to become necessarily either chronologically or geographically all-embracing, although certain pre-eminent areas and periods will demand a systematic sequence of coverage. Typically, a volume covers a period of about one century, but longer (and occasionally shorter) time-spans are proving appropriate. A degree of modest chronological overlap between volumes covering a particular nation, state or region is acceptable where justified by the historical experience.

Each volume in the series is written by a commissioned European or American expert and, while synthesizing the latest scholarship in the field, is invigorated by the findings and preoccupations of the author's original research. As works of authority and originality, all contributory volumes are of genuine interest and value to the individual author's academic peers.

Even so, the contributory volumes are not intended to be scholarly monographs addressed to the committed social historian but broader synoptic overviews which serve a non-specialist general readership. All the volumes are therefore intended to take the 'textbook dimension' with due seriousness, with authors recognizing that the long-term success of the series will depend on its usefulness to, and popularity with, an international undergraduate and postgraduate student readership. In the interests of accessibility, the provision of notes and references to accompany the text is suitably restrained and all volumes contain a select bibliography, a chronology of principal events, a glossary of foreign and technical terms and a comprehensive index.

Inspired by the millennial watershed but building upon the phenomenal specialist progress recorded over the last quarter-century, the eventually multi-volume 'Social History of Europe' is dedicated to the advancement of an intellectually authoritative and academically cosmopolitan perspective on the multi-faceted historical development of the European continent.

Raymond Pearson
Professor of Modern European History
University of Ulster

Acknowledgements

Since this is essentially a work of synthesis, my first debt is undoubtedly to hundreds of fellow historians whose research has been ransacked and whose ideas and insights have been appropriated – in some cases disputed!

I would like to express my thanks to the University of Warwick whose generous sabbatical leave policy has allowed me the time to visit Parisian archives and libraries and to plan and write this book.

Professor Raymond Pearson has not only been a helpful and considerate editor, but also made real sacrifices beyond the call of duty to permit the publication of this work in its present form.

The staff at Pearson Education, in particular Heather McCallum, have been approachable and efficient. Caroline Ellerby, who checked the manuscript, exhibited patience and good humour in dealing with the countless bibliographical errors and omissions which it originally contained!

Colleagues Colin James, Hilary Marland and Gert-Reiner Horn offered valuable comments on individual chapters. Alan Bainbridge read the entire manuscript and made many useful suggestions. I thank him for his friendship and support across the decades.

Stephen and Jane Magraw and Mick and Angie Wilson have consistently made me welcome in their homes when I have sought escape from Coventry!

Finally, my warm thanks to Sue Webb who taught me sufficient word-processing skills to prepare and revise the manuscript – whilst understandably despairing of my unwillingness or inability to become fully computer-literate in order to cope with the brave new world of electronic signs and pulses which humanity is now entering and which feels to this ageing Luddite more dystopia than utopia.

The publishers are grateful to the following for permission to reproduce copyright material:

Maps 5 and 6 from *Revolutionary France 1788–1880* (The Short Oxford History of France, 2000), © Oxford University Press, 2002, published and reprinted by permission of Oxford University Press (Crook, M. 2000).

In some instances we have been unable to trace the owners of copyright material, and we would appreciate any information that would enable us to do so.

Map 1   French Speakers in the mid-nineteenth century © Oxford University Press, 2002. Reprinted from *Revolutionary France 1788–1880* by Malcolm Crook (The Short Oxford History of France, 2002) by permission of Oxford University Press.

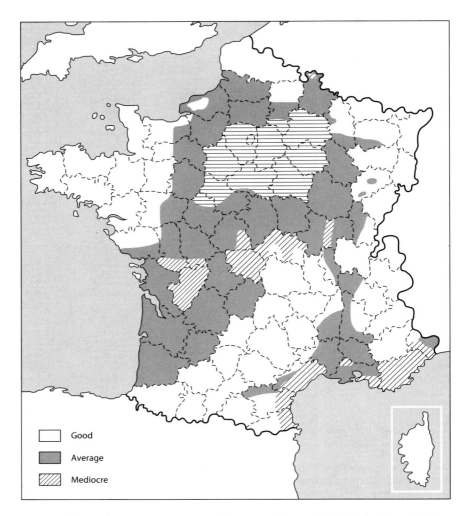

Good

Average

Mediocre

Map 2   Religious practice in nineteenth-century France © Oxford University Press, 2002. Reprinted from *Revolutionary France 1788–1880* by Malcolm Crook (The Short Oxford History of France, 2002) by permission by Oxford University Press.

Introduction: writing the social history of nineteenth-century France

Social history was once a marginal discipline, ranking well below established fields such as diplomatic or economic history. By 1970, however, Eric Hobsbawm confidently proclaimed that its day was dawning. Three decades later it is widely researched and written about – and taught in dozens of undergraduate courses. Its scope has expanded steadily to embrace 'new' topics such as women's history and gender, medicine, crime and consumerism – all discussed in the later sections of the present volume. And yet writing a general social history synthesis of the type envisaged by this series is a more difficult, not to say problematic, enterprise than before. This is not only – even primarily – because the range of subject matter and the sheer scale of research makes it impossible for any one historian to 'master'. It is because the *discipline itself* is in question. Certainly it now lacks any clear, accepted definition. In 1970 the structure of a volume such as this would have been suggested by one or other of the dominant paradigms.

The *Annales* school, then at its apogee, emphasised geography and climate, statistical analysis of long-term demographic structures and economic cycles, and deep-seated *mentalités*. It favoured 'hard', quantitative data from price lists, censuses, tax registers and inheritance declarations. Its concerns were with continuities, with very gradual – almost imperceptible – processes of change, with impersonal forces and with structures – economic, demographic, even mental. It allowed little scope for individual actions, politics or 'events'. Men did not really make their own history. Even the impact of 'revolutionary' upheavals on the scale of 1789 was downplayed. 'Politics' was discussed more in terms of long-term attitudes – political temperaments – than short-term decision-making. Culture and *mentalités* were considered as phenomena of the 'third level', much as Marxists consigned them to the 'superstructure'.

From such perspectives French society in the 'long nineteenth century' (1789–1914) might be conceptualised in terms of a gradual transition from an *Ancien Régime démographique et économique* towards 'modernity'. In the early nineteenth century birth *and* death rates remained high, life expectancy was barely forty – although the population was growing steadily. Agricultural yields, outside a few regions, were low. France remained vulnerable to classic Labroussean crises of harvest failures, grain shortages (and food riots), falling consumer purchasing power, textile/clothing sector unemployment, vagrancy, and sudden rises in mortality rates. Poor transport systems locked many regions into subsistence polyculture. Demographic and economic 'immobility' was mirrored in the cultural sphere. Schooling was patchy, literacy rates rose only slowly, a variety of regional patois were spoken and religiosity and superstition were rife.

The watershed came around 1850. The advent of the railways opened up regional economies, encouraged market agriculture, and stimulated expansion of coal-mining, metallurgy and heavy engineering. Improved agricultural yields – and food imports – eliminated the threat of famine. 'Surplus' rural populations migrated to growing industrial towns or found employment in an expanding tertiary sector. Overall annual economic growth rates were 2 per cent in the 1850s and 1860s, as against barely 1 per cent between 1815 and the 1840s. A modern demographic pattern of lower birth and death rates established itself. School attendance and literacy rates rose. A rational, secular mentality weakened the hold of religion and superstition. In time these processes moulded a France of strong regional identities and linguistic diversity into a French-speaking national community. The weight of *longue durée* factors meant that these changes were gradual and uneven. Climate, soils and mental structures continued to mould regional temperaments. Regional dialects and cultures proved tenacious in peripheral regions. Catholicism retained powerful bastions. A sizeable traditionalist peasantry slowed agricultural modernisation, and the pace of urbanisation and industrialisation remained slower than that in Britain or Germany.

Roger Price's (1987) volume is essentially constructed on this *Annaliste* model (Price 1987). Opening chapters on the economy and demography establish the mid-nineteenth century as the turning point. They are followed by chapters on social classes – conceived in largely structuralist terms – and then by a cultural section on religion and education. A postscript on the State gestures towards the importance of the political. Very different in style, but similar in underlying conception, is Weber's classic *Peasants into Frenchmen* (1976). Though treated with suspicion by some French historians as too impressionistic – and perhaps too witty and well-written – it is based on assumptions that a traditional rural France persisted until the 1860s until pushed towards modernity by the transport revolution. Among recent French studies, those of Dupâquier (1988) remain dominated by the *Annaliste* emphasis on the primacy of long-term demographic structures and trends.

The Marxist paradigm shared with the *Annales* a concern with economics and social structures and the relegation of culture and ideas to the superstructure. E. Labrousse was a pivotal figure straddling the two schools. A classic Labroussean thesis would begin with a section on geography, soil, climate, and demographic and economic structures of a region before moving on to sections on social groups and then political *mentalités*. Neo-Marxist 'new social history' of the 1960s and 1970s sought to jettison some of this positivist structural determinism by accepting the complex inter-relationship of base and superstructure, and the importance of class consciousness and experience. Where Marxism differed from *Annalisme* was in its emphasis on the centrality of class conflict as the 'motor' of historical change. Marxists saw the key issues of nineteenth-century society as the 'working through' of social conflicts of the French Revolution – a bourgeois revolution which had challenged and overthrown a feudal ancien régime. By 1830, they argued, the bourgeoisie had supplanted the aristocracy as the hegemonic class. Revolutionary legislation had swept away both aristocratic privilege and the obstacles to the functioning of a free-market capitalist economy – guilds, internal tolls – and cleared the ground for the (eventual) development of capitalism.

However, the Revolution had wider socio-political consequences. It had mobilised and raised the consciousness of a broad strata of the popular classes, both urban and rural. It was the anti-seigneurial peasant revolution of 1789–93 which swept away the ancien régime. Though the highly diverse peasantry failed to achieve many of their aspirations, for example access to more land and a world without taxes, they had at least fought for their right to remain on the land and posed an obstacle to the development of English-style agrarian capitalism. The mobilisation of the urban popular classes – the *sans-culottes* – saved the Revolution in 1793–94. If their aspirations for an egalitarian, 'small man' republic were thwarted after the fall of the Jacobins, the myths and memories of the 'Year II' survived to nurture and inspire Europe's most militant artisanal movement whose periodic insurrections challenged successive nineteenth-century regimes.

Marxists portrayed French society as dominated by complex, ongoing class struggles. Bourgeois 'beneficiaries' of the Revolution sought to consolidate their dominance by achieving political stability, preferably within a parliamentary system. But stability proved elusive. When threatened, the bourgeoisie ditched constitutional scruples and legalistic niceties and turned to quasi-authoritarian Bonapartist government, as in 1799 or 1851. Initially it faced a challenge from old aristocratic elites who, with allies in the clergy, remained nostalgic for the Ancien Régime. Urban artisans, whose aspirations had been raised by the Revolution, remained volatile and, at least in cities like Paris or Lyon, politically radical, and in the countryside millions of small peasants struggled to survive in an emerging capitalist market economy. Ongoing social conflict made it difficult for the bourgeoisie to take full advantage of the economic possibilities opened up by the Revolution. The civil war of the 1790s and the disruption of overseas and colonial markets during the Napoleonic wars created short-term economic dislocation. France had only modest, poorly located coal deposits and, until the advent of the railways, a poorly integrated transport network.

But many of the constraints on capitalist development were social and cultural. Craftspeople who feared the advent of factories and machines espoused socialist ideologies. Peasants clung tenaciously to communal rights. Many aristocrats – posing as paternalist social Catholics – wooed a populist clientele by denouncing the iniquities of the 'heartless' free-market system and laissez-faire ideology. Some bourgeois appeared more wedded to *rentier* or professional than to capitalist values. Of the major general studies of French society, that of C. Charle (1994), though not really 'Marxist', structures its narrative around class and class relations, including intra-class frictions, while that of P. McPhee (1992) is written from a broadly Neo-Marxist perspective, although one sensitive to issues of gender.

However, recent historiography has exposed the lacunae and inadequacies of *Annaliste* and Marxist paradigms. Revisionists criticised the Marxist interpretation of the Revolution – taking delight in discovering progressive, pro-capitalist aristocrats and *rentier* bourgeois who were flourishing in the Ancien Régime and in claiming that the Revolution had proved a disaster for the French economy. They insisted that this was not a *social* revolution, but rather the product of a new *political culture* – nurtured in Enlightenment salons – shared by bourgeois, aristocrats and clerics alike. Such views fitted neatly with the approach of younger *Annalistes* who were suggesting that culture should not be relegated to the 'third level' but could play a quasi-autonomous role. Meanwhile Zeldin's (1973–77) massive work sought to disaggregate the classes who had been the protagonists in Marxist narratives. In place of a newly hegemonic bourgeoisie his *pointilliste* empiricism disclosed a class fractured along lines of religion, politics, region, and economic and professional interest. Yet these were not the most fundamental challenges to social history orthodoxies.

The rise of first women's and then gender history suggested the possibility of a new paradigm in which gender was (at least) as important as class, and questioned the relevance of existing narratives of progress/change to women. Some feminist historians characterised the culture of Enlightenment and Revolution as constructed not just *without* but *against* women. Similarly the working class could be seen as constructed around the figure of the militant skilled male worker, and against that of the 'docile' woman worker portrayed as an 'objective' ally of the capitalist employer. Gender historians – who claimed that gender was a discursive construct not a biological given – used post-modernist theories and discourse analysis which raised fundamental questions about the status of the discipline of (social) history itself. Both Marxism and *Annalisme* were heirs of the Enlightenment – and of Positivism. Both assumed that there was a real society out there that had certain structures – possibly even 'laws' or observed frequencies – which could be observed and studied.

Post-modernists insisted that 'society' was a fictive totalising entity. 'The social' was simply a field constructed by positivistic historiography or social science. Indeed, ironically, it was 'invented' precisely by French bureaucrats and 'experts' in the early nineteenth century. By sweeping away the corporate world of the Ancien Régime the Revolution had ushered in a world of atomised individuals, free markets, poverty, unrest and flux. To understand, categorise, control and reform this new world governments needed 'experts' whose detailed surveys could define and quantify social problems. Sadly their reports were no more accurate representations of social realities than are the texts of social historians! They were essentially 'stories' – ideological constructs designed to serve particular purposes and interests. Post-modernism thus questioned whether it was possible for a historian to ever 'get at' the realities of a past society. At most he or she could study *discourses about* or *representations of* the past. It denied that class was an obvious 'given', an objective 'thing' with structures measureable by quantitative analysis. It doubted that one could ever retrieve the lived experiences of a class – as E. P. Thompson had sought to do – or that classes could be coherent actors. A recent study (Stuart 1992) of the Marxist *Parti Ouvrier Français* treats it not as a movement standing for the 'real' interests of Nord textile workers in the 1890s but as purveyor of a discourse about such workers designed to construct a particular image of the world.

Post-modernism also problematised issues of identity. Earlier social history paradigms (generally) assumed, in their naive Positivism, that an individual had a given class identity which could be 'read off' from his or her occupation, income and relationship to the means of production. Now it was claimed that class identity was discursively constructed *and* that one had multiple and shifting identities, of which class was but one and not necessarily the most significant. Social definitions were essentially contingent. Individuals belonged simultaneously to a range of 'imagined communites', built around workplace, religion, ethnicity, family, sex, community, region or consumer taste. Thus a German-speaking maintenance engineer in a textile mill in Mulhouse in 1850 might be a worker vis-à-vis the millowner, a skilled male in relation to unskilled mill girls, Alsatian when confronted with a French bureaucrat, French when dealing with Swiss immigrant workers, Protestant when in contact with Catholic neighbours. Such complex identities were, perhaps, particularly prevalent in a society where 'pluri-activity' was widespread – where rural proto-industry still flourished, where many industrial workers retained plots of land and many landowning small peasants spent part of their time as day labourers or carters.

Inevitably historians have been influenced by Foucault's insistence that 'power' in post-Revolution society did not just lie with the capitalist bourgeoisie or the bourgeois state but also in the multiple discourses of a range of professionals and 'experts'. The ubiquitous nature of power rendered problematic the underlying emancipatory narratives of Marxist historians in which the popular classes struggled to overturn first seigneurial then capitalist oppression. Historians began to focus on the perennial subordination of a range of marginal groups – convicts, the insane, hospital patients – to the projects and discursive strategies of criminologists, penologists or psychiatrists. Once, social historians had eagerly sought collaboration with sister disciplines, particularly those in social sciences such as economics and sociology. However, by the 1980s and throughout the 1990s they were not so much working with as being overrun and colonised by cultural anthropology, discourse analysis, literary theory and cultural history. Attempts to analyse – in a 'scientific' way – the structure, class system and long-term evolution of a 'society' were replaced by a focus on cultures and mentalities of sub-groups and on meaning. Rather than analysing 'popular protest' as a form of proto-political mobilisation, which potentially might challenge elite hegemony, it was viewed as 'violence' with its own complex rituals – to be understood by insights derived from anthropological studies of 'primitive' tribes. This approach distinguishes S. Schama's notorious *Citizens* (1989) which portrayed the 'popular movement' of the Revolution as driven by savage blood-lust. This type of ethnographic approach viewed rituals, symbols and festivals as holding societies together, making them very difficult to change.

The metamorphosis of Alain Corbin, the leading socio-cultural historian of nineteenth-century France, is fascinating and instructive. Corbin now insists that the historian can never find out how things 'really were' but, at most, how people *thought* that they were. His focus is now on social representations.

5

His first work (Corbin 1975) was a Labroussean study of the peasantry of the Limousin which moved from detailed analysis of demographic and economic structures to explore the mentalities of the peasantry of a region marked by seasonal migration, anticlericalism and oscillations between rural radicalism and Bonapartist populism. He then moved on to a study of Parisian prostitution – a women's history topic on a marginal social group (Corbin 1990). Subsequent areas of research have included the bourgeoisie's increasing intolerance of foul odours, changing responses to the ringing of village church-bells and the emergence of the vogue for the seaside. In *Village of the Cannibals* (1990) he located a gruesome murder of an aristocrat in 1870 by a crowd in a Dordogne market-town in the context of Bonapartist populism and peasant anti-seigneurialism, but with an awareness of anthropological studies on rituals of violence. The *Life of an Unknown Man* (2001) – an imaginative tour de force – attempts to retrieve the life and experiences of a 'nobody' chosen at random, a rural clogmaker from the Orne who left no diary or letters, joined no party or union, took part in no insurrection and was never charged with a crime. This could be construed as an extension of the 'history from below' championed by the 'new social history' of the 1960s. But Corbin deliberately turns his back on those militants and autodidacts whose role could be fitted into a Marxist narrative of 'popular protest'.

This approach is typical of much recent writing, which focuses on isolating the individual or the specific event, providing 'thick description' as favoured by cultural anthropologist C. Geertz, and extracting cultural meaning and significance rather than exploring structural social trends. The historian of the French bourgeoisie is now likely to study the symbolism and representation of household pets or the forms of middle-class sociability, not the evolution of the structures of capitalist firms. A study of La Villette butchers is less likely to be concerned with their geographic and social origins or their pay levels than with the symbolic meaning of blood and meat – or how butchers were represented and represented themselves. While the vogue for cultural anthropology and micro-history has undoubtedly produced much fascinating work, it has scarcely made things easier for anyone engaged in the quaint, outmoded task of providing an overview of social developments. The jettisoning of the classic social history paradigms has not been accompanied by any suggestion for an alternative model. Indeed post-modernists deny the validity of any such attempt at synthesis. For the 'coherence' of any such narrative would be no more than that of a neat, tidily plotted story constructed by a novelist – a fictional story told in ironic, tragic or heroic modes.

It is only by remaining resolutely untouched by post-modernism, discourse analysis and gender history that Charle succeeds in presenting a structured narrative. While willing to analyse sub-groups such as intellectuals who do not fit neatly into Marxist class models, and to emphasise – à la P. Bourdieu – socio-cultural distinctions and tensions which are not economic class conflicts, Charle is critical of the impressionism of Anglo–American empiricist historiography and the *pointillisme* that disaggregates every social grouping into a myriad of idiosyncratic individuals. Equally he takes issue with another modish approach to the history of France which downplays the significance of economics and 'the social' and prioritises issues of political culture and ideology.

Just as socio-cultural historians were abandoning attempts to offer a coherent structured narrative, so F. Furet – leading revisionist historian of the French Revolution – insisted that the central feature of the nineteenth century were the political and ideological struggles to establish the liberal/constitutional regime promised in 1789 but delayed by the disastrous lurch offcourse taken by the Revolution after 1792 when it was hijacked by Jacobin ideological fanatics and savages of the popular movement. Ironically, the neo-liberal Furet discarded the class analysis of politics which was a distinctive characteristic of one of his heroes – nineteenth-century historian and statesman Guizot (Furet 1992). Yet there is clearly plausibility in his claim that France experienced a surfeit of politics. It was a veritable laboratory of European politics, 'discovering' liberalism, socialism, nationalism and Bonapartism, and 'inventing' the division between 'left' and 'right' and the concept of 'revolution'.

France's unique volatility and instability stemmed from the lack of consensus about political legitimacy. Each successive regime suffered a legitimacy deficit. In eight decades France had twelve Constitutions, and passed through three monarchies, two Empires and three Republics! Perhaps a sense of French identity existed only because a variety of mutually antagonistic groups all agreed that 1789 marked a major watershed? There were five main political 'families'. Catholic-Royalists, known as Legitimists after 1830, aspired to return France to the world of the 1780s, dominated by 'natural' leaders – Catholic king, clergy and landed aristocracy. They disagreed among themselves whether the best strategy to achieve this goal was via insurrectionary or parliamentary methods, or even through an alliance with strata of the popular classes. Liberals – Orleanists or, later, moderate Republicans – sought a parliamentary, constitutional system with safeguards to ensure the influence of men of property and education. Bonapartists developed a distinctive synthesis of monarchism, authoritarianism, nationalism and populism. They guaranteed gains made by the bourgeoisie and peasantry in the Revolution at the expense of clergy and aristocracy, while insisting that order, stability and economic growth required a tough, powerful state – albeit one with the capacity to make populist gestures, to manage a mass electorate and consult opinion via plebiscites. Republicans favoured a parliamentary democracy, and the more radical of them were willing to envisage concessions to labour, some interventionist social reform and some of the egalitarian projects of the Jacobin Republic of 1793. Finally, a variety of socialist groups – some reformist some revolutionary, some advocating electoral strategies others direct action and industrial militancy, some keen on nationalisation others on workers' cooperatives – sought to build a social republic. One legacy of the Revolution was that France possessed a vigorous popular/plebeian 'public sphere' outside the propertied/educated elites. France's tumultuous history stemmed from ongoing, complex conflicts between these rival ideological groups, and these were made more complex and ferocious because the Revolution had left a legacy of religious conflicts. Supporters of 1789 became involved in a *Kulturkampf* against Catholicism. The concern of Republican activists was often less with issues of material prosperity of the masses – popular Bonapartism pandered to those – than with the creation of a world of dignified, free, independent citizens capable of self-determination and civic virtue.

Only the consolidation of the Third Republic after 1876, Furet argued, allowed the liberal revolution of 1789–92 to 'come home to port'. Political stability at last consolidated democratic, constitutional government, despite the persistence of challenges from the far right and the socialist left. In Furet's Neo-Whig narrative, political culture is invoked to explain why endless political turmoil and upheaval occurred in an essentially static French society where socio-economic changes were gradual and uneven, petty-bourgeois and artisan production persisted and the pace of urbanisation and industrialisation was slow. Marxists might seek to explain the political/ideological conflicts which Furet describes by ongoing, complex class struggles. However, social historians must acknowledge the importance of the state. Although space precludes a detailed analysis of its role, its presence pervades the whole of the present volume. The state was often resented for taxation and conscription, and sometimes acted in ways that provoked local/regional resentments and resistance. But it was the state that held together a France of atomised individuals, divisive memories of the 1790s, religious hatreds, disparate regional cultures and warring social classes or cultural groups. Bourgeois hegemony was often complex and sophisticated. It created long-term stability by manufacturing popular consent – or at least acquiescence – via economic growth, cultivation of consumerist values, education, religion, tactical political concessions, career opportunities and the nurturing of patriotism. But in the last resort it was the army and bureaucracy that reimposed order and ended revolutionary upheavals in 1799, 1848–51 and 1871. The system of departmental prefects and sub-prefects and state prosecutors (*procureurs généraux*) gave France its structure. The Bonapartist regime relied on military, police and bureaucratic systems – which were largely taken over by the Third Republic. For much of the century French jails housed at least a hundred thousand convicts.

Despite liberals' calls for minimal government and decentralisation, the state bureaucracy expanded steadily. Its upper levels were always monopolised by sons of the elites, and it provided employment at middle and lower levels for sizeable strata of the middle and lower-middle classes. Unsurprisingly the social composition of the state machine led it to act in a generally conservative way, defending order and property, seeking to deter or repress protest. Apart from a flirtation with free trade after 1860, French governments – heirs to a dirigiste tradition – generally acceded to demands of textile, metallurgical, coal and agricultural interests for protective tariffs. Technocratic civil servants, trained in the *grandes écoles*, helped to plan the rail network, state subsidies helped finance the rail infrastructure, and the state guaranteed profit levels for investors in the six private rail companies. State engineers inspected coal mines, *Ponts et Chaussées* officials the transport network, and forestry officials state woodlands. The education system, which helped erode regional particularism and linguistic diversity, was largely a state creation. After the Concordat of 1802 the *Police des Cultes* kept close surveillance of the clergy.

The growth of welfarism after 1880 was inspired by the concerns of bureau-crats and the military with France's declining birth-rate. Social history clearly can never be history with the politics left out.

Any total history of nineteenth-century France would need to incorporate the role of the military. Millions of Frenchmen were conscripted into the Revolutionary and Napoleonic armies – and memories of their experiences in Italy or Spain informed their subsequent worldview. Between 1815 and the 1870s the army relied on a narrower conscription system. An annual lottery (*tirage au sort*) selected those who would serve a seven-year term, and who were then given financial incentives to re-enlist. The reintroduction of uni-versal conscription after 1870 meant that experience of military service was shared by most of the adult male population. The army did, however, play a role in internal politics. Three army officers – Napoleon I, Cavaignac and McMahon – became heads of state. Military repression put down workers' revolts in 1848 and 1871. The army had a key role in the Bonapartist coup of 1851 – albeit claiming to be following presidential orders. However, France did not experience Spanish-style military juntas, nor was the army as inte-gral a part of the state structure as in Prussia. The political career of General Boulanger, who sought to ingratiate himself first with the Radicals then with Royalists before making a bid for power, proved very brief. The officer corps was too heterogeneous – socially and ideologically – ever to share a single political project.

During the Bourbon Restoration the influx of aristocratic ex-émigrés into the officer corps caused real resentments among existing Revolutionary and Bonapartist cadres, many of whom had risen from the ranks before 1815. Some sympathised with the liberal opposition in the 1820s and refused to defend the regime in its 1830 crisis. The Soult Laws (1832–34) sought to establish an 'apolitical' officer corps by guaranteeing tenure and a salary struc-ture. Subsequent expansion of the army, under Bonapartist *and* Republican regimes, and the need for technologically competent officers meant that the corps always recruited from the professional middle-class and from non-commissioned officers (NCOs). A sizeable minority of officers were Catholic aristocrats with royalist sympathies. Some flirted with ideas of a coup during the Dreyfus crisis of the late-1890s or resigned their commissions rather than enforce anticlerical policies against the religious orders. A suspicious Repub-lican government kept surveillance files (*fiches*) on Catholic officers, but did not feel the need to purge these since few allowed their crypto-Royalist sympathies to influence their actions. Most recognised that the Republic was a patriotic regime which was spending heavily on national defence – or perceived their loyalties to be to France, the *patrie* and the flag rather than to any specific regime.

Popular perceptions of, and attitudes towards the army were complex and ambivalent. There was hostility towards, and evasion of, conscription in peripheral regions of the West and the Southern Massif. Fear of a peasant electoral backlash persuaded the Bonapartist regime to delay plans for universal conscription in the late-1860s. Peasants resented the loss of a son's labour on the farm, and often viewed troops as rowdy, brutal and untrustworthy. Yet study of popular almanachs, songs and lithographs suggests that, at least

9

in frontier regions such as Lorraine, families took pride in having a son in the army; a soldier's macho image and uniform had a real appeal, not least to women! After the 1870s the Republic sought to nurture the image of a citizens' army and used schools to inculcate a pride in fulfilling one's military duty and a willingness to fight for the soil of the Republican *patrie*. Many working-class and peasant conscripts looked back on their years in the barracks with nostalgia, as a period of escape from factory or farm and from family controls and responsibilities, of camaraderie and drunken escapades. Labour militants remained suspicious of the army's role in strikebreaking and of the 'reactionary' attitudes of the officer corps, and a residual resentment at conscription persisted in the Midi (south of France). But on balance the army clearly became a force of social integration. It brought together conscripts from diverse regions and taught them that they were French with a duty to defend France against foreign 'others'.

Military combat which gave officers a chance to show initiative, and secure promotion, occurred largely in the colonies. With France's military prestige in tatters after defeat by the Germans in 1871, and falling birth-rates threatening future supply of conscripts, military strategists looked to Empire for a reassertion of military *gloire* and as a source of manpower. The role of 'the colonial' in French society deserves more extensive coverage than can be afforded within the scope of the present study, although it is not easy to measure its importance. Despite occupation of Algeria after 1830 and expansion into Indo-China during the Second Empire, France's Empire remained relatively modest until the 1880s. Demographic stagnation meant that there was less pressure than in Britain for white settler colonies. Though France became the world's second largest exporter of capital, much of this went to Europe, Latin America and Turkey. Only around 10 per cent of foreign trade was with the colonies. Hence some argue that Empire was of modest importance to the French economy, and of little significance to the masses who knew little and cared less about it. Yet it would be misleading to minimise the impact of colonialism on French culture by evoking supposed public ignorance or indifference. Empire was championed with vigour by pressure groups such as the Union Coloniale and Geographic Societies, was backed by business firms and secured parliamentary support. Mercantile and shipping interests in major ports were dependent on colonial trade. Marseille's varied industries were reliant on colonial raw materials. Textiles, clothing, shoes, hardware, cigarettes and jewellery were all exported to the colonies, as were iron and steel construction materials for public works projects. Key colonial imports included rubber and raw silk from Indo-China – for the Lyon textile industry – nickel from New Caledonia for the steel industry, phosphates, cocoa, coffee, rice and a variety of oils, as well as wine and cane sugar which competed with domestic production. Although a more systematic economic *mise en valeur* of the colonies was to occur in the inter-war years, it is evident that certain firms and sectors were heavily involved in Empire before 1914.

If there was no wild public enthusiasm for Empire, the impact of the colonies on popular culture and consciousness should not be underestimated (Chafer and Sackur 2002). From the 1880s government propaganda, aided by mass-circulation newspapers, sought to integrate workers by arguing that jobs were dependent on colonial markets and raw materials. Many perceived colonies as the potential site of economic or career opportunities. Inhabitants of west coast ports aspired to posts in the colonial administration or ventured to the colonies to set up small businesses. Peasants from barren, overpopulated regions looked on the colonies as a reservoir of fertile farmlands. Governments subsidised the outward passage of colonists to Indo-China and New Caledonia. The new Republican regime struggled to establish itself in the midst of a prolonged economic depression and in face of attacks from the Right and the socialist Left. It was desperate to restore France's international standing after the disasters of 1870–71, and in the face of a powerful German rival Empire became an obvious symbol around which national pride and a new national consensus might be constructed. School textbooks and official colonial exhibitions and museum displays projected the imperial message. A French identity was constructed in juxtaposition with a colonial, often Oriental, 'other' through music-hall songs, iconography, commercial adverts and travelling colonial fairs. The popular culture of Imperialism – as opposed to its 'official mind' – was also nurtured by cheap novels and the literary fantasies of authors like Pierre Loti portraying an exotic colonial world of adventures, heroic legionnaires and erotic encounters with brown-skinned, sensual native women. The French *colon* emerged as a tough, macho figure well-suited to survive in a harsh, social-Darwinian world – tanned, resourceful, capable of making deserts bloom and spearheading France's struggle for survival. Even those who were made uneasy by the naked racism of such popular literature could develop their own myths. Some Catholics rallied to a Republic whose expanding Empire might facilitate the global spread of christian missions. Some socialists espoused a 'civilising mission' which would rid Africa of feudalism and obscurantist religions and spread the values of the Enlightenment, the Revolution and the secular Republic.

The present volume is in many ways an old-fashioned work from an ageing Marxist reluctant to learn – or who is incapable of learning – new tricks. The narrative of the opening section is structured around the evolution of class and class relation. The middle section considers traditional areas of social history – religion and education. The final section offers an overview of the current state of research into the 'new' fields of crime, medicine, consumerism, gender and women's history. This final chapter discusses issues such as domesticity, women's work, women workers and the labour movement and feminism. However, an attempt has been made to avoid ghettoising women into a specific chapter and to draw on gender analysis throughout the text. I have been willing – in a piecemeal, unsystematic way – to borrow the insights of fellow historians who have been inspired by discourse analysis, the 'linguistic turn', cultural anthropology and Foucault. The net result is doubtless eclectic, not to say incoherent. It is clearly difficult to combine a Labroussean approach with a history of representations which sees a social group as constructed by discourses or sociability. I remain unrepentently convinced that there was/is a real society out there which social historians can and should attempt to analyse.

The main body of the text consists of nine thematic chapters, each covering the entire period. There is no introductory chapter outlining the nature of society in *c*.1800. Instead each chapter starts with both a brief, schematic outline of eighteenth-century developments and the impact of the Revolution and a discussion of key historiographical and theoretical issues. Given inevitable restrictions of space a number of important topics and themes have not been afforded the attention they would deserve in a total history. There are no separate chapters on economy or demography, though the chapters on class and gender do attempt to outline the peculiarites of the French economic model. Treatment of minority communities – Protestant and Jewish – and of immigrants, is thin. So too, despite the brief discussion above of their role in creating French identity, is coverage of the military and of colonialism. Childhood, the family, the evolution of welfare from paternalist charity towards state provision all really deserve separate chapters.

Bibliography

Aldrich, R. *Greater France: A History of French Overseas Expansion* (London: Macmillan 1996).

Chafer, T. and Sackur, A. (ed.) *Promoting the Colonial Idea: Propaganda and Visions of Empire in France* (Basingstoke/New York: Palgrave, 2002).

Charle, C. *A Social History of France in the Nineteenth Century* (Oxford: Berg, 1994).

Chevalier, L. *The Labouring and Dangerous Classes in Paris: 1800–50* (Princeton, NJ: Princeton, University Press, 1973).

Corbin, A. *Archaisme et Modernité en Limousin: 1845–80*, 2 vols (Paris: M. Rivière, 1975).

Corbin, A. *Women for Hire: Prostitution and Sexuality in France after 1850* (Cambridge, Mass: Harvard University Press, 1990).

Corbin, A. *Village of the Cannibals: Rage and Murder in France 1870* (Oxford: Polity Press/Blackwell, 1990).

Corbin, A. *The Life of an Unknown: the Rediscovered World of a Clogmaker in Nineteenth-Century France* (New York: Columbia University Press, 2001).

Crook, M. (ed.) *Revolutionary France: 1788–1880* (Oxford: Oxford University Press, 2002).

De Tocqueville, A. *Recollections* (New York: Garden City, 1971).

Dupâquier, J. (ed.) *Histoire de la Population Française* Vol. 3 (Paris: PUF, 1988).

Furet, F. *Revolutionary France 1770–1880* (Oxford: Blackwell, 1992).

Gemie, S. *French Revolutions: 1815–1914* (Edinburgh: Edinburgh University Press, 1999).

Heywood, C. 'Society and People in the Nineteenth Century', in M. Alexander (ed.) *French History Since Napoleon* (London: Arnold, 1999).

Lequin, Y. *Histoire des Français: XIX/XX Siècles* 3 vols (Paris: Armand Colin, 1983–4).

McMillan, J. 'Social History, New Cultural History and the Rediscovery of Politics', *Journal of Modern History* 1994.

McPhee, P. *A Social History of France: 1780–1880* (London: Routledge, 1992).

Porch, D. *The March to the Marne: the French Army 1871–1914* (Cambridge: CUP: 1981).

Price, R. *A Social History of Nineteenth-Century France* (London: Hutchinson, 1987).

Prost, A. 'What has happened to French Social History?' *Historical Journal* 1992.

Schama, S. *Citizens* (London: Viking, 1989).

Stuart, R. *Marxism at Work: Society and French Socialism 1882–1905* (Cambridge: Cambridge University Press, 1992).

Tombs, R. *France 1815–1914* (London: Longman, 1996).

Weber, E. *Peasants into Frenchmen* (Stanford: Stanford University Press, 1976).

Zeldin, T. *France 1848–1945* 2 vols (Oxford: Clarendon Press, 1973–77).

Chapter 1

Social elites

Introduction: a 'bourgeois century'?

The bourgeoisie has dominated French society for the past two centuries, emerging largely unscathed from successive changes of regime. The state system – bureaucratic, military and judicial – which it has controlled since 1830, has remained intact and capable of repressing popular challenges such as those of 1848 or 1871. Nineteenth-century law consistently favoured individualism and property rights, and juries were composed of male property owners. Trade unions were banned until 1884, while employers' associations received de facto toleration. There was no progressive income tax until the First World War. This was precisely *because* bourgeois influence was so pervasive, whether in education, the bureaucracy, the press, or in the framing of economic policies; it is difficult to discuss the bourgeoisie without involving the whole of society. Yet it is notoriously difficult to define 'the bourgeoisie'. What, if anything, did an industrial magnate like Schneider have in common with a corner-shop grocer? Were not the bourgeoisie's political, religious, regional, sectional and economic interests so diverse that any attempt to locate common features would be doomed? Or did most bourgeois – *grand* or *petit*, Catholic or Voltairean, conservative or liberal – share certain common interests and values (Daumard 1987)?

Analytical clarity is not helped by the multiplicity of usages of the term 'bourgeois'. Originally it meant the inhabitant of a town (*bourg*). Hence it referred to urban civilians who were neither nobles, nor peasants nor soldiers. Yet peasants called the local landowner '*le bourgeois*' – and historians have identified a 'rural bourgeoisie' of agrarian capitalists, rentiers or grain merchants. Confusions in debates over the French Revolution derive from the fact that after 1789 different uses of the term were in operation. It referred to non-noble rentiers and members of the professions and bureaucracy. However, dissemination of the discourses of Sieyes or St Simon led to an emphasis on 'productive' industrialists or businessmen as the typical 'bourgeois' (Sewell 1994). Older usages had not disappeared. The term '*vivre bourgeoisement*' still usually evoked a leisured, rentier lifestyle. And in the 1840s a *nouveau riche* businessman could be dismissed as lacking the requisite culture and manners to be 'authentically' bourgeois.

Marxists concentrated attention on the 'capitalist bourgeoisie'. *Annalistes* utilised inheritance and tax records – hard, quantitative data – to map structures of the bourgeoisie and chart the evolution of hierarchies of wealth and income. Cultural historians have been more willing to use soft data from diaries or etiquette books. Focus has shifted to the construction of collective professional or cultural identities or the role of voluntary associations in creating a bourgeois public sphere, an approach pre-figured in older studies which portrayed the French bourgeoisie as distinguished by its *savoir*, competence and cultural capital rather than by control of the means of production. Recent neo-liberal discourse has sought to equate bourgeois values with those of modern civilisation – freedom, economic dynamism, rule of law, probity, tolerance, initiative and independence (Daumard 1987).

Concern with lifestyle and personal values has also encouraged emphasis on domesticity and gendered separate spheres as central to emerging bourgeois identity. Photographs of the bearded paterfamilias surrounded by wife and children emphasise the importance of family values to the bourgeoisie's self-image. As Davidoff and Hall (1987) have shown for Britain, middle-class wives were agents in the construction of domesticity. They authored etiquette books, more prescriptive than descriptive, which defined qualities to which all bourgeois should aspire – efficiency, respectability, moderation, reasonableness. A *habit bourgeois* came to denote smart but unostentatious clothing. A *maison bourgeoise* was clean and orderly. *Cuisine bourgeoise* provided wholesome, tasty but unpretentious food. Bourgeois speech was distinguished by its grammatically correct use of the subjunctive, but also by its ability to adapt flexibly to the different contexts of home, business or social gatherings. Bourgeois *politesse*, through avoidance of both vulgar familiarity and aristocratic disdain, permitted one simultaneously to show respect, avoid embarrassment and maintain a certain distance. It was good manners and *savoir vivre*, not mere wealth, which defined bourgeois identity.

It is modish to argue that class is 'imagined' – that classes should be viewed not as objective social structural formations but as constructs of discourses about them. Whereas the term 'middle class' was used tentatively and infrequently in Britain before 1830, in France the *classe moyenne* was already portrayed as a heroic agent of an emancipatory revolution against feudalism and absolutism, custodian of universal 'rights of man' and guardian of civilisation against mob rule. Alternative discourses imagined the middle class in more critical ways. Radicals argued that the bourgeoisie was creating a 'new feudalism' to exploit the people. The middle class once '*was* generous, it has *become* corrupt, it *was enlightened*, it has become boorish. It would like to see the people as greedy and as servile as itself' (Wahrman 1995). A defining moment came in 1848 when, faced with socialist workers, the middle classes discovered an unprecedented unity. However, even if most bourgeois agreed on the need to defend property, they rarely agreed on *how* this might best be done. Moreover, some petty bourgeois viewed themselves as victims of 'financial feudalism' and as part of the 'people', while some lawyers and doctors espoused radical neo-Jacobin ideas.

The bourgeoisie had many critics. Aristocrats, disdainful of the *parvenus* who had displaced them, blamed bourgeois materialism and selfish individualism for declining moral standards. Marx was torn between admiration for a Promethean class re-making the world in its own image, and hatred of capitalist economic exploitation. Dominant images of the bourgeoisie were unflattering. Daumier's cartoons portrayed cigar-smoking financiers with bloated stomachs and spindly legs, rack-renting landlord Monsieur Vautour and swindler Robert Macaire. Eugène Sue's serialised novels portrayed a Paris of virtuous poor exploited by evil bourgeois. Such stereotypes appealed to some who were themselves objectively bourgeois – those excluded from the narrow property franchise of the 1840s, students, bohemians and writers. Flaubert, the son of a wealthy surgeon, lived off his family's *rentes* and had no Left-wing sympathies. Yet he used 'bourgeois' as a term of abuse, as 'all who think basely'. His typical bourgeois was boring, philistine, cowardly, materialistic, hypocritical, banal, pompous and self-satisfied. Unsurprisingly, the (bourgeois) city fathers of Rouen refused to dedicate a square to their famous native son! French novelists' reluctance to portray an authentic 'bourgeois hero' stemmed from their resentment at being forced to survive in the marketplace, to depend on commercial publishers who treated literature as a commodity, and on philistine middle-class readers. Contemporary dictionaries confirm that the adjective 'bourgeois' came to mean 'prejudiced', 'lacking in dignity'. Yearning for something more heroic, some bourgeois aped the refinements of aristocratic style – or even developed a taste for duelling as an affirmation of their masculinity (Girard 1969)!

The survival of aristocratic power?

The aristocracy and the Revolution
Until 1789, the 'Second Estate', some 1 per cent of the population, owned 25 per cent of the land and monopolised posts in Army, Administration and Church, giving aristocratic bishops and monastic heads access to income from church lands and tithes. Exempt from the land tax, it enjoyed lucrative seigneurial rights and controlled seigneurial courts. Critics denounced these as the privileges of a 'parasitic', corrupt class. Even Tocqueville, son of an aristocratic Normandy family, was later to admit that the nobility had become an object of hatred because it had ceased to perform useful social functions which once justified its hegemony. Opponents portrayed aristocrats as obstructing new economic ventures and squandering seigneurial dues squeezed from the peasantry on conspicuous consumption. They were accused of blocking the access to commoners to the officer corps and of preventing tax reforms, the prerequisite for successful state modernisation. Revisionist historiography rejects all this as liberal and Republican mythology. Nobles, some now claim, constituted an educated audience for the Enlightenment ideas, participating in political debates in Masonic lodges, *salons* and coffee-houses – the emerging 'public sphere'. Imbued with a 'service' ethos, many engaged in reform projects reflecting utilitarian or free-market ideas, or directly in economic activities – as *agronomes* maximising yields from their estates or as partners in trading or industrial ventures. Nobles owned 80 per cent of Franche-Comté forges. Bordeaux nobles often originated in trading dynasties and possessed libraries of Enlightenment books. No clear contrasts between feudal aristocrats and dynamic bourgeois

can be made, for they shared a common culture and a fusion of elites was occurring. The Revolution was neither inevitable nor necessary, but a disaster which created anti-aristocratic sentiments and polarisations that wrecked the chances of gradualist political and fiscal reform and economic modernisation. Yet, in the longer term, the Revolution did surprisingly little damage to the nobility. It survived, with most of its property intact, to form the nucleus of a stratum of landed *grands notables* which, allegedly, dominated French society into the following century (Figeac 1996; Cobban 1967; Tudesq 1964). Older orthodoxies may require modification, but revisionist re-evaluation of the aristocracy rests upon thin empirical evidence. Abbé Sieyes's classic assault on aristocratic privilege, *What is the Third Estate?*, came from a gifted cleric whose career prospects were thwarted by aristocratic control of the church. A few nobles accepted the need for fiscal reform. Most clung obstinately to tax privileges. Forster's (1971) study of a Burgundian aristocratic dynasty, the Saulx-Tavanes, shows that a 'seigneurial reaction' was occurring in the countryside, and its proceeds were spent on conspicuous consumption not agricultural investment. Similarly, the Marquis de Castries's use of Court influence and seigneurial powers to obstruct the mining of coal deposits in the Gard suggests that entrepreneurial nobles remained the exception not the rule. Seigneurialism remained a real obstacle to capitalist development (Sewell 1994; Forster 1971; Lewis 1994).

The aristocracy were the net losers of the Revolution; 1158 were executed. Six such martyrs in Franche-Comté were the last males of their line. At least 16,000 spent time as émigrés. Estimates of the size of the pre-Revolution aristocracy vary from 400,000 to a mere 120,000, but a significant proportion of the 25,000 noble families contained at least one émigré. Revisionist assumptions that for every noble who emigrated there were dozens who remained quietly in France tending family estates is problematic. Most of the 25,000 who received compensation in 1825 for losses sustained in the Revolution were nobles, suggesting they had been severely affected by expropriations and sales of émigré property. Aristocrats lost their monopoly of bureaucratic, military and church posts and were now subject to the 16 per cent land tax. The loss of seigneurial dues had a variable impact. Larger nobles with diverse sources of income were less dependent on these, and the seigneurial burden had been relatively light in Brittany. But in the southern Amienois (Somme) smaller nobles lost 30 per cent of their income. The Revolution both exemplified and accelerated the erosion of peasant deference. Peasants fought aristocrats' claims for redemption payments for loss of seigneurial dues. Aristocratic woodlands were invaded, seigneurial records burned. A quarter of commons confiscated from villagers by seigneurs before 1789 were reclaimed. Châteaux were destroyed, armorial insignia vandalised. Anti-seigneurial revolts occurred from Alsace to the Pyrenees, and anti-seigneurial hatreds persisting in some regions across the nineteenth century. At least one-fifth of aristocratic land was lost. Mayenne nobles eventually re-acquired 40 per cent of lost lands, yet re-purchasing alienated land could jeopardise a family's subsequent financial stability. In the Somme, the Béry family, émigrés to Prussia, found their château acquired by Amiens merchant Dotin – now the department's second-richest man. Four major noble families had liquidated all their assets in the

Somme by 1800. In Toulouse seventy-two aristocratic town-houses (*hôtels*) were acquired by bourgeois.

In 1825 the Bourbon regime compensated aristocrats with the *milliard des émigrés*. Some large nobles secured generous handouts. In Franche-Comté the Duc de Choiseul received 1.5 million francs and 2000 hectares of forest. But the process created difficulties. The average handout was only 46,000 francs. Smaller nobles often felt aggrieved and not all émigrés could substantiate their claims. In Franche-Comté, only 273 of 450 émigré families were compensated. Debtors swarmed round to claim their share of the windfall. Quarrels over distribution of compensation worsened intra-family feuds already provoked by egalitarian inheritance laws. Attempts to restore primogeniture and strict entails, abolished by Revolutionary legislation, proved abortive. A law of 1806 – repealed in 1833 – authorised *majorats*, which gave the largest share of an inheritances to one son. But families such as the Saulx-Tavanes became embroiled in squabbles over distribution of inheritances. Although there were examples in Franche-Comté of families collaborating to prevent one branch 'going under', older aristocrats lamented the weakening of family solidarities. Wives who had secured 'tactical' divorces in order to shield lands of émigré husbands sometimes refused to surrender the property! Although some discerned a 'new domesticity' within aristocratic families, there were signs that the active role of aristocratic ladies during these crisis years bred a female assertiveness disruptive of family cohesion (Forster 1967; Wiscart 1994; Brélot 1992).

Claims that the nobility emerged virtually unscathed from the Revolution are unsustainable. By 1830 a quarter of noble lineages in the Somme had been extinguished. Analysis of 1830s electoral lists suggests that 40 per cent of the noble families of the 1780s were either extinct or no longer sufficiently wealthy to pay the 200 francs annual direct taxes to qualify for the franchise. According to Beck (1981) 'There appears to have been either a substantial decline in the number of nobles or the creation of a *noblesse pauvre* of sizeable proportions'. Only 50 per cent of ancien régime families were still active in the Bordelais after 1815. Many suffered psychological blows from Revolutionary experiences. Franche-Comté noble Terrier de Loray began his 1811 diary by evoking the 'terrifying void that filled (my) days, the painful nullity of life'.

The aristocracy re-invented?
Nevertheless, the aristocracy had survived, retained considerable assets – and found imaginative ways of re-inventing itself to adapt to the new society. Napoleon sought compromise with the old élites. The Concordat facilitated reconciliation with Catholic-Royalists. Émigrés were encouraged to return. If the new Napoleonic aristocracy was the butt of snobbish jibes from the old nobility, many of the latter tacitly accepted the regime. In Touraine only 24 of 150 aristocratic families openly rallied to Bonaparte, but few voiced pro-Bourbon sympathies in public. Resort to the courts to recover lost lands was implicit recognition of the legitimacy of the post-Revolution legal system. Nobles sent sons to the *École Polytechnique* to train for the military. By 1812, 10 per cent of *Grande Armée* officers were nobles, as were 28 per cent of

Prefects. Some nobles felt reluctant admiration for Napoleon's genius and disliked the glee shown by ultra-Royalists at French defeats after 1812. Patriotism could outweigh atavistic class prejudice. 'Better to die on the scaffold of one's own country', insisted one ex-émigré, 'than to owe one's existence to foreigners'. Some *bien-pensant* bourgeois had never accepted the Revolution, and some former liberals, alarmed by revolutionary extremism, were now eager to bolster social hierarchy. The 'politics of inegalitarianism' appealed to bourgeois who aspired to the trappings of aristocratic culture and rentier lifestyle (Higgs 1987). In Balzac's *Eugénie Grandet*, the public prosecutor marries a nobleman's daughter and metamorphoses into *Cruchot de Bonfous*. 'New' nobles created by Napoleon sought to jettison their specific identity after his fall, rallying to the Restoration and hoping that possession of a title would obscure their origins as army contractors or *Biens Nationaux* purchasers and, in time, permit them to blend with the old nobility.

Aristocratic revival was underpinned by a strong landed base. Their estates covered some 20 per cent of French land. By comparison with their British counterparts, who owned 80 per cent of the land, their hold on the countryside was rather patchy. Weak in the Limousin or the Alps, their bastions included the West, Southern Massif, Flanders, the South-West and the Morvan. In the Somme two-thirds of the richest notables were still nobles in 1806. In Franche-Comté several nobles prospered from speculation in church lands, and those retaining iron forges prospered from war orders. Confiscated woodlands were returned en bloc. Some families had relied on female members to negotiate with Revolutionary authorities. In the Mayenne the Marquise de Hauteville, mother of three *chouan* sons, divorced her émigré husband and repurchased the family château from a former Jacobin. Many became experts on legal technicalities to defend or reclaim estates. Family meetings planned strategies to restore family finances to an even keel and seek new sources of income (Wiscart 1994; Denis 1977; Brélot 1992).

There was no necessary correlation between aristocratic landholding and local hegemony. In Burgundy, the Dordogne or Dauphiné, peasant anxieties about the return of seigneurialism nurtured rural populism, which could be manipulated by Republican or by Bonapartist politicians. In *Jacquou le Croquant* by Jacobin novelist E. Le Roy, the peasant hero takes his revenge against the cruel Périgord ex-seigneur Comte de Nansac who jailed his father for poaching rabbits by burning down the château! There was prolonged conflict between aristocrats and villagers in the Corbières, near Carcassonne, for control of common lands and *garrigues*. The Revolution gave the peasants the chance to assert their 'right' to woodlands and grazing resources, despite alarm at deforestation and environmental degradation. As the commons became denuded of trees, peasants planted disputed lands with vines and developed small-scale commercial wine production. The Restoration tilted the balance towards the nobility and peasants were prosecuted. However, the 1830 Revolution gave villagers a window of opportunity. When two aristocrats, accompanied by gendarmes, confronted peasant 'intruders', both were shot dead. In short large estates could fuel resentments, hierarchies could be contested (McPhee 1999).

Yet aristocrats could wield power over tenants, sharecroppers, agricultural workers and local tradesmen. 'With his tenants', Napoleon commented, 'the Prince de Boffremont can form an entire battalion.' *Resident châtelains* usually controlled 'their' villages. After 1815, 25 per cent of Somme aristocrats spent the year on their estates, embracing frugal lifestyles and developing self-sufficient home farms. Such austerity was an expiation for the excesses of their absentee ancestors. By 1824, 11 per cent of all mayors were nobles. They financed church repairs, used their influence to secure construction of local roads, and gave château reconstruction work to local craftsmen. The image of aristocrat as paternalist protector of local communities was strongest in regions where carefully cultivated and embroidered counter-revolutionary memories and myths permeated popular culture. In Brittany and the Vendée, hostility to the Revolution was fuelled by the intrusion of bourgeois outsiders who bought up church lands or threatened communal rights. In the Midi, beneficiaries of the Revolution included the Protestant bourgeois of Nîmes. The Revolution had politicised latent tensions between Catholic artisans and peasants, and Protestant financiers and merchants, allowing aristocrats to pose as defenders of 'little people' against domination by ruthless, 'heretic' exploiters (Lewis 1978). There were limits on potential aristocratic power. Unlike their British – or Magyar or Prussian – counterparts, their landholdings were rarely sufficiently extensive to ensure dominance at the departmental level. Many minor Somme nobles, chastened by Revolutionary experiences, kept a low profile even after 1815 (Wiscart 1994). However, there were examples where the benevolent paternalism eulogised by the aristocracy's defenders looked like neo-seigneurial arrogance. In Acquitaine in the 1830s, the curé would read out at Mass names of men expected to move stones from the *châtelain's* quarry! On the eve of 1914 in Chanzeau (Anjou), tenants were required to walk behind the aristocrat's coach to Mass, and answer questions on the sermon before being allowed to return home! Economically dependent villagers accepted such impositions without protest. Whether they did so without resentment is difficult to determine.

Aristocrats faced a fundamental dilemma in the post-Revolution world. To retain popular support they might pose as paternalist defenders of communities against exploitation by intrusive bourgeois and harsh laissez-faire capitalism. This was the message of ultra-Royalist de Bonald, whose denunciation of 'satanic' Revolution and calls for a hierarchical, theocratic order were allied to nostalgia for an 'organic', corporate social order. Such rhetoric might strike a chord with craftsmen struggling to survive after the abolition of the guilds. In Toulouse, which had boasted a large resident aristocracy, the Revolution undermined noble patronage. As employment prospects for artisans and servants deteriorated, along with donations to charity, so selective nostalgia for the 'good old days' nurtured popular Catholic-Royalism (Higgs 1973). Yet if there was a certain logic in becoming defenders of the 'little man', there were also dangers. If aristocrats set their face against the market economy, portrayed industry as 'unnatural' and refused to adapt to agrarian capitalism, they risked becoming dinosaurs. To take advantage of the still extensive resources, and to compete with the bourgeoisie, was it not imperative that they become efficient estate managers, exploit forests or mineral resources, erode remaining communal rights? Yet to do so risked alienating populist supporters mobilised during the Counter-Revolution. There were protests in the South-West in 1816–17 when aristocratic land-owners cashed-in on grain shortages by raising prices. Conflicts between nobles and village communities over control of forest resources became endemic in Provence, Burgundy and elsewhere.

Adapt and survive?

The Restoration saw the last sustained attempt to reinstate the aristocracy as the dominant political class. The Charte of 1814 signalled a compromise between the Bourbons' aristocratic and clerical supporters and the Revolutionary bourgeoisie. It guaranteed constitutional monarchy, parliamentary government, legal and religious freedoms, maintenance of the Napoleonic Codes, and the property rights of purchasers of church lands. Yet ultra-Royalists had no interest in accepting a modus vivendi. Alarmed by their intransigence, bourgeois and peasants in eastern France rallied to Napoleon's 'Hundred Days' in 1815. Returned from Elba, Napoleon claimed to stand between France and a return to seigneurialism and the tithes. In the aftermath of Waterloo, ultra-Royalists launched the 'White Terror' in the Midi. Gangs of Catholic artisans and peasants, directed by aristocrats or their agents, murdered hundreds of Protestants, *Biens Nationaux* holders and former Revolutionary officials. After a phase of moderation between 1817 and 1820, the assassination of the Duc de Berry provided a lurch to the right. The accession of Charles X – crowned provocatively in medieval pomp in Rheims Cathedral and claiming the power to cure scrofula sufferers with the 'royal touch' – promised a style of government calculated to offend bourgeois liberals. A Sacrilege Law, a financial indemnity for émigrés, press censorship and clerical controls on education led inexorably to the 'Polignac Decrees' of 1830 which, by threatening the Charte itself, finally drove the middle classes to rediscover their revolutionary heritage.

It is doubtless reductionist to claim that all reactionary policies were conceived by the aristocracy or that all opposition to them was bourgeois. Liberal aristocrat Chateaubriand defended press freedoms. *Bien-pensant* bourgeois such as provincial lawyers with traditions of service to noble families were staunch royalists. Nevertheless, Restoration politics was dominated by aristocratic attempts to restore their lost hegemony. The ultras' goal was to return France to a golden age before Bourbon centralisation when the aristocracy flourished as 'natural' provincial leaders. Such decentralist sympathies did not preclude recolonisation of the state. By 1829, 75 per cent of prefects and 45 per cent of sub-prefects were aristocrats. Fusion was attempted within the army between Bonapartist veterans and Royalists. But ex-Bonapartist officers living on modest pensions (*demi-soldes*) and non-noble officers and non-commissioned officers (NCOs) resented the favouritism shown to aristocratic officers; 50 per cent of entrants to St Cyr officer training college came from aristocratic Catholic schools. Bonapartist veterans figured prominently in Carbonarist conspiracies against the regime (Richardson 1966; Spitzer 1987).

Nobles combined loyalty to the king and religion with a cult of family heritage and an obsession with genealogy. They failed to restore primogeniture, portrayed as essential for preservation of the integrity of family estates. But the *milliard des émigrés*, even if it failed to provide full compensation for aristocratic losses, gave an indication of the regime's class sympathies. The electoral system, which enfranchised only the richest 90,000 who paid 300 francs per year in direct taxation, was already highly elitist. In 1819 a second vote was given to the largest taxpayers – mostly aristocratic landowners. The 'reactionary' mentality of ultra-Royalist aristocrats was caricatured by their opponents. The plots hatched in aristocratic secret societies such as the *Chevaliers de la Foi* or the *Congrégation* portrayed in Stendhal's *Le Rouge et le Noir* reflected the paranoia of liberal anticlericals and mirrored the Masonic conspiracy theories of the Catholic Right.

Revisionists deny that '1830' was a bourgeois revolution provoked by the spectre of an aristocratic revival. Yet contemporaries perceived the aristocracy to be the net losers. Their dynasty was exiled – this time permanently. Extension of the franchise to 200-franc taxpayers doubled the electorate, diminishing the aristocracy's weight within it. Aristocratic bureaucrats, magistrates and army officers were dismissed, or resigned, unwilling to serve the new regime. The percentage of aristocratic mayors fell from 11 per cent to 4 per cent, and from 80 per cent to 20 per cent in Catholic-Royalist Sarthe. Ultra-Royalists sought to mobilise popular protest and launch armed counter-revolution, but this attracted minimal support even in heartlands such as the Vendée. '1830' was a key moment in the aristocracy's political decline. Never again – except momentarily after 1870 – would they have a chance of controlling national politics or the state machine. Yet their economic, social and cultural power survived – 64 per cent of all aristocratic electors in the 1830s paid above 1000 francs in direct taxes, and 238 of the wealthiest 512 *grands notables* were nobles (Beck 1987; Tudesq 1964; Gibson 1981). Internal emigration – aristocrats' return to their estates after abandoning state posts – allowed some to become gentlemen-farmers and leaders of rural society. They faced strategic choices. Should they remain 'Legitimists' – French Jacobites loyal to the deposed Bourbons – or compromise with the new regime? Should they be paternalist critics of harsh free-market ideology, or diversify into urban and industrial investment and accept that their future depended on capitalist profits? Should they remain socially exclusive, or merge with Orleanist *grands notables*? Was it possible to synthesise tradition and modernity, to devise ways of performing the quintessentially noble feat of belonging to one's race without ceasing to belong to one's age (*'d'être de sa race sans cesser d'être de son temps'*)?

Balzac's cycle of novels, the *Comédie Humaine*, captures the complexities of aristocracy. He portrayed Bourbon loyalists who rallied to the 1832 rebellion as quixotic, none too intelligent, blind to new social 'realities'. Yet Balzac's aristocrats are highly diverse. Some aspire to the role of an Italian patriciate, others admire English country gentlemen. Some espouse ostentatious ultramontane piety. Impoverished *hobéraux* cling obstinately to fading silk breeches as a symbol of their ancien régime status. The younger generation are often frivolous, fashion-obsessed, hedonistic escapists who seek to forget the traumas of 1830 by hurling themselves headlong into the frenzy of Parisian *bals populaires*. De Soulas, the 'handsomest man in Besançon', dresses with *'exactitude Anglaise'*. Legitimist duc de Caraman insists that he has no wish 'to sacrifice a whole generation' to his own dynastic loyalties. But Legitimist 'ultras' sought revenge on the bourgeois *parvenus* who had displaced them. Poitou aristocrat Le Châtre in *Le Cabinet des Antiques* raises his children to hate the Revolution. Some Midi legitimists flirted with a *politique du pire* – forming tactical alliances with Republicans. During the 1846–48 economic crisis they stirred up social unrest and popular protest in order to destabilise the hated Orleanist regime. During the Second Republic, legitimist populists – the 'White Mountain' – mobilised newly enfranchised Gard Catholic peasants and workers against local liberal bourgeois elites. Although such populism was restricted to a few regions, the advent of mass suffrage allowed aristocrats elsewhere the chance to manipulate peasant electors.

Many aristocrats' legitimism was confined to nostalgia for the ancien régime and pilgrimages to visit exiled Pretender Chambord in his Austrian *Schloss*. H. de Kergolay's loyalty to his father's beliefs led him to abandon his bureaucratic career, condemning him to a futile life poisoned by corrosive bitterness and 'fatal *ennui'*. Comtesse Dash insisted that while she wept for an ancien régime that she had never known, aristocratic friends 'solicited posts from the usurper (Louis Philippe) whilst dreaming of the *fleur de lys'*. Tocqueville's visit to the USA deepened his conviction that democracy was an unstoppable force. If his class retained any useful function it was to moderate democracy's dangers – cultural mediocrity and tyranny of the majority. Before 1789 the aristocracy had betrayed its historic role as defender of provincial liberties against centralisation. By retaining privileges without serving a useful function it had become hated. Sadly France lacked the habits of local participation and religious pluralism which underpinned American democratic culture. Nevertheless, the best traditions of the aristocracy might be revived – the ethos of service and the role of buffer between state and society. Tocqueville's aristocratic liberalism led him down an idiosyncratic political path. He rallied to Orleanism, yet despised its bourgeois corruption. He supported repression of workers in 1848, yet unlike fellow aristocrats refused to concede that the Bonapartist coup was necessary to save society. Among other liberal aristocrats, Montalembert, a Franche-Comté landowner, urged Catholic aristocrats to work within the system of constitutional government and religious pluralism (Fiette 1997).

Aristocrats were persuaded to compromise with Orleanism by a number of factors. The return to Catholicism of strata of the bourgeoisie facilitated collaboration in the charitable *oeuvres* which characterised this 'age of the philanthropists'. Aristocratic officers in eastern garrison towns imbibed the military patriotism of the Lorraine borderlands and were relatively moderate in their political views. Since aristocrats and *grands bourgeois* shared common economic interests – as property owners whose income derived from a combination of land, state bonds and industrial investment – their shared fear of socialism might provide the basis for cooperation. Before 1848, aristocrats in industrial Lyon or Lille had forged a common front with businessmen. The scale of popular unrest in 1848–51 convinced liberal Vaucluse aristocrat de Cambris to prioritise 'anything that protected him against revolution'. Such men subordinated Legitimist sympathies and residual caste prejudices to the requirements of a broad 'Party of Order' to protect property.

Provincial nobles pursued various adaptation strategies. In Franche-Comté the aristocracy proved quite successful at reinventing itself. Nobles' estates comprised 10 per cent of the land, despite the loss of vineyards and forests, but were generally too small to ensure local hegemony. They faced active rivals in a liberal bourgeoisie of lawyers and wealthy forge-masters. Peasant communities had participated in the *jacqueries* of 1789–93 and remained suspicious of a revival of seigneurial pretensions. However, aristocratic families determined not to lose their specific identity by merging into an hetero-geneous elite of *grands notables*. Brélot's (1992) use of private papers exposes the limitations of quantitative, 'serial' history which, by emphasising income and wealth, fails to discern the specificity of aristocratic cultural values. Their lifestyle remained exclusive. Few bourgeois were admitted to their châteaux or to Besançon *hôtels*. They rarely married outside their class – a pattern in line with Tudesq's (1964) survey which found that only 7 per cent of aristocratic marriages between 1800 and 1860 were with bourgeois partners. Tensions between *épée* and *robe* dynasties had largely disappeared since their common struggles against the Revolution. They struck a balance between conspicuous consumption and adoption of rigorous domestic budgeting. Erudition in local history or genealogy was highly valued. Their 'culture of order' was tinged with narcissism. Codified good manners were designed to exclude bourgeois intruders. Children were raised to respect honour and duty, and revere the *patrimoine familial*. Marriage contracts included commitments to support poorer relatives. Those obliged to sell land tried to do so *within* the family.

Yet they were also flexible. Legitimist sympathies did not preclude tactical compromises with Orleanist or Bonapartist regimes. Adapting to mass electoral politics, several became deputies during the Second Empire. Trading on their cultural capital, aristocrats acquired *baccalauréats* and secured meritocratic entrance to state service, particularly in the magistracy, diplomatic corps and army, which saw a modest aristocratic comeback after 1850. This was ration-alised by invoking a tradition of state service, of loyalty to France rather than to a specific regime. Between 1815 and 1870, the region's nobility provided 30 prefects and sub-prefects, 15 diplomats, 60 magistrates and 80 army officers. State salaries underpinned their lifestyle, as did investment in state bonds, industry and commercial farming. The Marquis de Vaulchier's château and *hôtels* in Besançon and Paris were financed by Jura vineyards, iron-forges and rail directorships. Capitalist farming led to conflicts where aristocrats eroded communal rights or evicted inefficient tenants. Yet the logic of their agrarian strategy was as much socio-political as economic. They tolerated rent arrears in difficult years, and arranged cheap credit for tenants. Relationships with peasant communities did not deteriorate markedly. They posed as 'protectors' of the village, although not of individual villagers. De Vaulchier criticised his family for fleeing from their village in 1854 to escape the cholera. By transmitting a message that the wealthy could save themselves they were betraying their duties as Christian gentlemen. Aristocrats now placed their tombs in parish churchyards rather than adjacent to the château, financed roads or fountains, subsidised *Bureaux de Bienfaisance*, even attended the occasional peasant wedding. Multifaceted but informal patronage achieved a degree of *proximité consentie* between legitimist aristocrats and peasants often Republican in their sympathies and unwilling to become subordinate 'clients' (Brélot 1992; Tudesq 1964).

Such examples have prompted a re-evaluation of Legitimists. No longer dismissed as dinosaurs, they are now credited with some political sophistication. Aware that state repression of popular protest might sometimes be necessary, they argued that a stable social order required 'natural' elites engaged in the battle for minds against those who fostered insubordination. Recapturing the initiative required distinctive solutions to the 'social question'. Relationships between landed elites and peasantry had to be rebuilt by addressing problems of rural depopulation and defending local identities threatened by centralisation. This would exonerate Legitimists from accusations of desiring to return to a world of privilege and deference. As Catholic-Royalist Albert de Mun insisted, the ancien régime 'is *dead*, along with its merits and its abuses. If it is true that, after a century of revolution, we need social reorganisation, it is no less true that this is only possible through an . . . accord between traditions and the *actual* condition of society'. Legitimism was never just 'aristocratic'; 39 per cent of Legitimist notables in the 1860s were middle class – magistrates, industrialists, Midi *négociants*. One Legitimist claimed that 'the bourgeois who fears that (Legitimism) prefers titled gentlemen . . . is no less credulous than the peasant who fears that . . . it will send him to silence the frogs in the *château* moat at night!' Chambord advocated an 'aristocracy of merit' – its sense of duty forged in Catholic colleges where aristocrats and bourgeois pupils mixed. The 'enemy' was neither bourgeoisie nor proletariat but false doctrines of secularism. Nevertheless, there were correlations between Legitimist bastions and aristocratic estates. High religious practice, myths and memories of the counter-revolution and resident aristocrats provided the milieu for Legitimism in the West and Southern Massif. Legitimism was weak in the Vosges, de Mun claimed, because aristocratic landowners were hedonistic, business-orientated absentees. Legitimism made a cult of residence, urging *châtelains* to renew ties of 'vertical integration'. This ideology was bolstered by the post-1830 internal emigration which saw aristocrats resign from state posts and return to their estates. As 'gentlemen-farmers' aristocrats could raise agricultural productivity, make profits, boost the local economy and rebuild social relations with tenants. Many aristocrats, Balzac observed, became 'more preoccupied . . . with their Normandy cider than with the fate of the Monarchy'. Comte de Diesbach managed a 'progressive' dairy farm in the Pas-de-Calais, Bouillé introduced the Dombasle plough into the Nièvre. The prominence of aristocrats in the *Société des Agriculteurs de France* alarmed Bonapartist prefects, who viewed it as a legitimist front organisation (Kale 1994; Locke 1974).

Many aristocrats remained rentiers or traditional *hobéraux*. Balzac's Adolphe de Saintot, though president of Angoulême's *Société d'Agriculture*, was as 'ignorant as a carp' about farming! In Ile-et-Vilaine support for the *Société Agricole* came from bureaucrats and bourgeois landowners rather than from aristocrats, few of whose tenancy contracts contained clauses about the introduction of fertilisers, market crops or modern ploughs. However, Mayenne nobles did seize opportunities opened up by railways to develop commercial livestock rearing, while seeking to preserve an idyllic rural backwater uncorrupted by *frénésie capitaliste*. They eulogised harmonious, face-to-face relations with their villagers. Leasing land to sharecroppers maximised electoral influence. By financing the reconstruction of churches and châteaux they provided employment for local craftsmen and slowed the rural exodus (Denis 1977; Cocaud 1996). Reconciling preservation of semi-autarchic rural societies with agricultural efficiency was not easy. Having inherited a debt-ridden family estate, de Falloux was obliged to evict some of his sharecroppers. Calvados landowner de Chaumontel confessed to the 1867 agricultural *Enquête* that 'we are guilty of contradictions'. Legitimists, keen to halt the rural exodus, distrusted urban construction projects – and even conscription – which took young men from the villages. Yet they did not mistrust *everything* in the modern economy, for some now had portfolios of shares. They favoured a 'sincere fusion' of progressive agriculture with conservative elements in industry. Some financed farm-schools and sought to preserve rural industries.

One lesson of 1789 was that the monarchy had become too centralised. Versailles nobles had lost their influence in the regions. Jacobin and Bonapartist centralisation exacerbated the problem. Haunted by the spectre of Paris sapping the vital forces of the 'real' France, Legitimists championed decentralisation, sponsoring regionalist organisations such as the *Association Bretonne* (1843), and collected folk-tales and songs. Support for decentralisation united liberal nobles like Tocqueville with Legitimists. They insisted that the department was 'unnatural', and that historic regions ought to be revived under their 'natural' elites. Class conflict, crime and alienation could only be avoided if these protected the poor against the excesses of the free market. Traditional charity was no longer adequate. Hence, despite disquiet about socialist state interference, aristocrats sponsored housing projects and schemes to protect apprentices and female workers. The *Saint Vincent de Paul* society, which spearheaded such activities, had several hundred branches. Its aristocratic leadership alarmed Bonapartist authorities who saw it as a front for legitimist politics (Kale 1994).

Such activities suggest an urban role for aristocrats. The model of the *châtelain* was not the only one available. Wealthier aristocrats divided their year between estates, town-houses in departmental *chef-lieux*, Parisian *hôtels*, and the cosmopolitan world of spas and the Riviera. This super-elite had diversified investments; 55 per cent of Parisian nobles' investment was in land in 1820, and only 20 per cent by 1914. Some were sent abroad for their schooling, others studied for the *baccalauréat* in urban colleges or state *lycées*, whose former pupils' associations, containing both aristocrats and bourgeois, were active in Catholic urban social *oeuvres*. Lyon aristocrats tried to act as an urban patriciate on the Italian model, and had close ties to Rome. Aristocrats, 9 per cent of the city's 540 leading families, were active in the magistracy and the university faculty. They adopted a bourgeois household style, keeping financial accounts and avoiding waste. Their *salons* admitted a few commoners, and there was some intermarriage with rich bourgeois. Their spokesman attributed the city's success to its resident Catholic aristocracy. 'Just as . . . Vendée peasants follow their *gentilhommes*, so in Lyon people and bourgeoisie support the efforts of the aristocracy on the city's behalf.' *Le Tout Lyon* guide to the city's elite included nobles alongside bourgeois. Nobles figured prominently in *Sociétés Savantes*, a feature of elite urban culture with some 200,000 members at their peak. However, it is doubtful whether this was evidence of the acculturation of the aristocracy to modern society. They specialised in local history, archaeology or genealogy. *Sociétés Savantes* provided an intellectual façade for antiquarian activities and created an appearance of aristocratic cultural hegemony. In reality aristocrats were becoming marginal to the life of French cities (Brélot 1995).

There was little intermarriage between aristocrats and bourgeois. An analysis of 500 Parisian aristocratic marriages found only 1 per cent in this category. Balzac described aristocratic *salons*' 'ferocious resistance' to the influx of *nouveaux riches*, though one duchess dubbed fellow aristocrats mad for wishing to 'remain in the fifteenth century when we are in the nineteenth. There *is* no longer a nobility. Napoleon's *Code Civil* killed it off – just as cannon killed off feudalism! You will be a lot more noble when you have some money!'. Commenting on an unfinished inscription on a bourgeois tombstone, one aristocrat speculated that 'the widow's grief had expired before the work was completed!'. The incomplete epitaph symbolised the bourgeois family. The deceased was 'one of those Revolutionary *parvenus*, abandoned children of our century, who grew rich by dubious means and left nothing after them – neither establishment, heirs nor reputation. They are merely a point between two abysses, an existence between two voids of forgetfulness'. Nobles' inability to secure a foothold in urban administration rendered fanciful their claim to be a 'patriciate'. Nobles provided 30 per cent of departmental *Conseils Généraux* members in 1870. But in the Somme their rural influence was not replicated even in Abbeville, with its 60 aristocratic *hôtels*, let alone in Amiens which was dominated by businessmen (Wiscart 1994).

In 1900, half of Lyon aristocrats described themselves as rentiers, only 28 per cent declared a profession. Most lived in Place Bellecour, away from the city's commercial hub. Their disdain for economic activity provoked the resentment of business leaders. Banker Aynard insisted that *his* family's nobility lay in remaining bourgeois and proud of it! Parisian nobles remained ill-at-ease in a 'Babylon' of crime, atheism and undeferential proletarians. Their memoirs, typified by the Marquis de Bonneval's *La Vie de Château*, were replete with formulaic nostalgia for childhoods spent on family estates. Their self-image was that of *terriens*, rooted in the soil of their native regions. The most prestigious charity among Faubourg St. Germain aristocrats was one which raised funds for rural clergy (Brélot 1995).

Nevertheless, the aristocracy was not entirely divorced from modern capitalism. For example, 30 per cent of Bank of France regents in 1860 were nobles. Prince d'Arenberg's presence on the Suez Canal board suggests the eagerness of corporate enterprises to secure prestigious aristocratic directors. Many Somme nobles were suspicious of large-scale capitalism, but a few sat on bank and rail company boards. In Franche-Comté, de Grammont flourished as a forge-master, although several local industrial nobles suffered spectacular crashes. Benoit d'Azy's hands-on role in heavy metallurgy in Alais was almost unique. Aristocratic entrepreneurs sought to reconcile industrial involvement with the ethos of their class by running paternalist enterprises – seeking to create neo-feudal enclaves of loyal company workers. But only one of Balzac's large gallery of aristocrats participates in industry. In the 1840s, 28 per cent of bourgeois electors were involved in industry, a mere 4 per cent of aristocrats. Diversification of aristocratic investments was mainly into state bonds rather than industrial shares (Locke 1974; Brélot 1992; Wiscart 1994).

Decline and fall? (1870–1914)
If Balzac is the chronicler of the dilemmas of the post-Revolution aristocracy, Proust and Maupassant serve this function for the Belle Époque. Maupassant's aristocrats conform to stereotypes of a decadent, declining class. Two-thirds are rentiers, seeking consolation for political marginalisation in the Jockey Club, spas and the Riviera. The young are obsessed with fashion, cards, and the correct handling of the monocle. Two-thirds of aristocratic ladies portrayed have extra-marital affairs. Maupassant juxtaposes aristocrats' religious moralising with their eagerness to fight duels! Proust's analysis is more nuanced. Aristocratic opulence and the façade of stability can no longer hide signs of decline. His final volumes tell of the death of aristocratic officer St. Loup in the Great War, the crumbling of the exclusive *salons* of the Faubourg St Germain and the disgrace of Charlus, whose homosexual infatuations symbolise the aristocracy's biomedical degeneration. On the eve of the war, Gervaise married St. Loup, believing that his title would guarantee her status. This 'was an error, for the value of a noble title, like that of stocks and shares, rises with demand and falls when it is on offer. Everything that seems to us imperishable tends toward decay. A position in society is not established once and for all . . .'. Yet Proust's world is one where, despite loss of political hegemony and relative economic decline, aristocrats have retained cultural and social prestige. There is little overt class-conflict with the bourgeoisie, but rather tensions charted in anxieties over (subtle) changes in social status (Sprinkler 1994).

Aristocratic political influence fell sharply after the 1870s. Although many aristocrats rallied to Bonapartism for protection against socialism, the regime had gradually eroded their rural power base. Resources were channelled into villages via prefects and mayors, accustoming peasant electors to look to the state machine rather than to notables for patronage. In the crisis of 1870–71, with German troops occupying much of France, many peasants turned to aristocrats as 'protectors'. The 1871 elections produced the highest number of aristocratic deputies for fifty years. Comte de Maillou exulted that 'his' Anjou peasants elected him 'because I used to be their seigneur!'. Intoxicated by this resurgence, Legitimists demanded that the capital be moved from godless 'Paris/Babylon' and support for Catholic family values. However, Republicans exploited peasant alarm at the threat of the return of seigneurialism. Their electoral victories of 1876–77 meant that henceforth they could manipulate state patronage. Now there was no *political* way back for the aristocracy. From 33 per cent in 1871 the proportion of aristocratic deputies fell to 9 per cent by the 1900s, all in classic heartlands such as the West

(Gibson 1981). They lacked a coherent political strategy. Chambord's death undermined prospects of a restoration. Legitimist ultras flirted with the anti-semitism of the proto-Fascist New Nationalist Right – though this was largely an urban, populist movement outside their control. Others were persuaded to compromise with the Republican bourgeoisie either by papal endorsement of the Ralliement, or because they saw the need for a broad anti-socialist alliance. Meanwhile, aristocratic control began to unravel. *Abbés démocrates* challenged Royalist landowners for the votes of Breton and Flemish peasants and petty bourgeois. Proust's Charlus is aware that his Legitimist loyalties make him an anachronism. St. Loup reluctantly rallies to the Republic, but his uncle 'through hatred of the tricoleur . . . would rather serve under the red flag . . . !'. The son of one Mayenne aristocratic family, despairing for the future of his class, died fighting for the Boers (Denis 1977; Sprinkler 1994).

Political decline was influenced by deterioration in the aristocracy's econ-omic position. Some were hit by the 1882 collapse of the Catholic Union Générale bank, ascribed to machinations of Jewish finance capital! This obliged Comte Jean de Monbello to cancel orders for Worth fashions and take brisk walks instead of coach rides! More serious was the reluctance to diversify investment. In 1900, land comprised 2 per cent of bourgeois in-come, but 30 per cent of aristocratic wealth. This became a problem once the Agricultural Depression ended an era when returns on landed investment had been consistently high. The fall in agricultural prices, profits and rents hit landowners who had borrowed from the *Crédit Foncier* to finance estate refurbishments. Some sold-off land and moved into urban real estate. In one Niortais village an aristocrat elected as mayor in 1872 but burned in effigy after Republican electoral victories in 1877, sold-off his château and 600 hectares of land. French aristocrats lacked the landed power of their British counterparts and their lucrative ties with the 'gentlemanly capitalism' of the City of London.

Construction of local railways opened up the aristocracy's rural bastions such as the Southern Massif, allowing their Republican rivals – grain and wine merchants, small town lawyers and doctors – to cultivate a peasant clientele. Nevertheless, the 1884 Associations Law opened up new possibil-ities for aristocratic influence on the peasantry. The *Société des Agriculteurs de France* claimed 2000 local *syndicats* by 1900, many in Republican strong-holds such as the South-East, Champagne or Franche-Comté. These provided peasants with a range of services – bulk purchasing and marketing, insur-ance, and access to credit. Two-thirds of regional *syndicats* were established by aristocrats. 'Cruel' electoral defeats in the Vivarais, observed the Marquis de Melchior, did not remove his 'obligation' to play an active role in farm-ing. Such involvements permitted aristocrats to combine pragmatic agri-cultural projects with fantasies about an 'agrarian corporatism' which might undercut the hated Republic, with its 'artificial', individualistic electoral sys-tem, by rallying peasants behind 'natural' elites. Nobles involved in *syndicats agricoles* cultivated a populist stance, inviting peasants to fétes in château grounds, attending *boules* after Mass. They funded agriculture classes in Catholic schools, sponsored Marian pilgrimages and weekend retreats to train future peasant cadres. Some aristocrats thus reacted positively to the challenge of falling landed incomes and the rise of rival Republican elites. Moving beyond the paternalism of the traditional *châtelain*, they developed a discourse blending corporatism and rural populism which had the potential to build a 'countryside alliance'of *agrariens* (Brélot 1996).

Proust's portrayal of a resilient aristocracy unwilling to surrender without a struggle is, thus, quite convincing. Aristocrats became adept at trading their status on national and international marriage markets – marrying American heiresses or marrying their daughters to industrialists like Schneider. Proust's St. Loup makes his marriage with Gilberte Swann to replenish the family coffers. Even dynasties such as de Noailles were prepared to cash in on bourgeois obsession to gain access to society. Meanwhile, a belated diversification of aristocratic investments occurred. Land comprised 66 per cent of aristocratic wealth in 1860, only 38 per cent by 1900, when 16 per cent of all company directors were nobles. Nor did the Republic remove the aristocracy's footholds in state service. Some magistrates were purged in the 1880s. Some aristocratic officers resigned their commissions rather than enforce Republican measures against the religious *congrégations*. However, aristocratic officers set the tone of the officer corps in the 1890s and were favoured for promotion; 25 per cent of the diplomatic corps were still nobles. By 1900 economic power lay with the *grande bourgeoisie*. Political control of the Republic lay with the professional middle-class. In 'compensation', the Faubourg St Germain cultivated an image as the exclusive, fashionable milieu whose cultural and social hegemony remained intact. It continued to set the tone for *Le Tout Paris*, as in the 1830s after the disappearance of the Bourbon Court. Codification of manners asserted the aristocracy's singularity and distinction. Comtesse d'Agoult's etiquette books discussed 'correct' times at which to dine, avoidance of bourgeois faults of ostentatious clutter, and how to blend simplicity of manners with intimations of *richesse cachée*. But true *bon ton* was indefinable. Those requiring etiquette books to learn *savoir-vivre* were, by definition, incapable of so doing, for one needed to inherit this from one's family upbringing and breeding! The rare bourgeois admitted to aristocratic *salons* were those, like Proust's Swann, with refined cultural tastes. 'Money capital', Sprinker (1994) observes, 'will only become a bourgeois entrance ticket into the Faubourg St Germain late in (Proust's) novel. Cultural capital allows select bourgeois to enter the forbidden realm (earlier).' Reactionary aristocrats like Charlus, who flirt with antisemitic New Nationalism, are nevertheless worried that the 'Dreyfus business' might 'destroy society by the influx of "unknown" people just because they belong to the Patriotic or Anti-Jewish League or I don't know what! As if a *political* opinion gave one a right to a *social* qualification!'.

Proust's 'profound account of a profoundly frivolous world' is that of an observer 'situated at the decisive site of the Republic's class struggle prior to the Great War . . . at the point where aristocratic social power and bourgeois social ambition met'. Many bourgeois both resented and envied aristocratic lifestyle. Proust introduces a radical engineer who laments the Jacobins' failure to guillotine the entire aristocracy, and who metamorphoses into Legrandin de Méséglises and tries to pass as a noble! In short the aristocracy could still partly set the terms on which the bourgeoisie could obtain the

29

outward signs of social acceptance. It was a society of struggles over status, in which class identity was constructed by perceptions. Proust, unlike Balzac, rarely analysed the sources of aristocratic income. It remains a class defined by style, manners and consumption, whose surviving power includes an apparent capacity to keep 'the economic' at arms' length. The seaside resort of Balbec is the site of an uneasy modus vivendi, typical of the *Ralliement* period of the 1890s, between aristocrats and Republican bourgeois. But in Paris it is still the aristocracy who set the tone of society, dominating the Jockey Club and *Académie Française*. Few bourgeois could match the 'multiple acculturations' of a Marquis de Vaulchier, moving seamlessly between Franche-Comté château, Besançon town-house, Parisian *hôtel*, and the London and Riviera 'seasons' (Sprinkler 1994; Brélot 1995).

Arno Mayer's (1981) thesis that Europe remained dominated by a landed aristocracy lacks plausibility when applied to France. Its aristocracy was weaker than its British and Prussian counterparts. The House of Lords' powers were curtailed only in 1911. Tory cabinets in the 1890s were dominated by aristocrats, whose class owned huge areas of rural Britain, urban real estate and coal mines, and was integrated into City of London 'gentlemanly capitalism'. Prussian Junkers remained a distinct legal order, retaining primogeniture and strict entail to preserve their estates. In 1907 they held 11 of the 12 provincial governorships and dominated bureaucracy and army officer corps. In France, the political power of the aristocracy was broken by 1830. Its economic power was steadily eroded. Elements of its social and cultural influence lingered until 1914. Only at the end of Proust's novel, charting the post-1918 world, has aristocratic society become permeable and the prestige of its salons faded. 'Thus in the Faubourg St Germain the apparently impregnable position of the Duc and Duchesse de Guermantes had lost their inviolability. Thus the shape of things in the world changes: thus the Charte of social prestige, the *cadastre* of fortunes all that seemed to be definitive, is perpetually being re-modeled' (Mayer 1981; Sprinkler 1994).

The France of the bourgeoisie

A bourgeois revolution? (1789–1830)

The French Revolution was once interpreted as a 'bourgeois revolution'. A 'middle class', emerging with the expansion of Atlantic trade and articulating its aspirations in the language of the Enlightenment, burst asunder the fetters of a 'feudal' Ancien Régime. Victorious in the struggle with the aristocracy, it framed the legislation of the 1790s and the Napoleonic period to re-make society in its image and prepare the path for capitalist development. This interpretation was seen as Marxist – though Marx always remained cautious about reading the Revolution unambiguously as capitalist and borrowed his concepts from French liberal historians. Britain's seventeenth-century revolutions largely disappeared from public discourse. The American revolution was assimilated into an anodyne national consensus. But the French Revolution remained too central to the mythology of the (French) Left for conservatives to permit the above interpretation to go unchallenged. Hence in years of sustained revisionist assault, Anglo-American empiricist historiography relentlessly chipped away at – and claims to have demolished – the stereotypes of a revolutionary, capitalist bourgeoisie and a feudal aristocracy, and even came close to denying that the Revolution constituted a significant social rupture. In France, renegade ex-Marxist Furet accepted that it constituted a seminal moment in Western political culture, but insisted that the rise of the bourgeoisie was a long-term process which could not be compressed into a few years, and that it was misleading to portray the Revolution as a 'class war'. Furet's concern with political discourses was extended by post-modernist approaches which questioned all teleological historical meta-narratives in which rising and falling classes are presented as coherent actors.

Revisionists insist that the Revolution emerged from a specific *political* and *financial* crisis, not from a fundamental *social* crisis. There were individual bourgeois, but no bourgeoisie with an awareness of common identity, common grievances or sense that its interests were being systematically thwarted. At most there were 'stress zones' within the elites. Some bourgeois were deeply embroiled in the system as seigneurial lawyers or purchasers of seigneurial rights. Many derived their wealth from landed rents or government bonds, and aspired to live as *rentiers* or to purchase offices which gave tax exemptions and, in time, noble status. Peasant revolt overthrew seigneurialism. The emerging public sphere within which reform had been debated included aristocrats, clergy and enlightened bureaucrats alongside members of the professional middle class. Sadly the Revolution's net impact was to delay implementation of reformist projects. The chaos of the 1790s allowed the intrusion into politics of violent mass direct action and ideologically fanatical Jacobins, whose Rousseau-inspired projects anticipated twentieth-century totalitarianism. The net economic impact of the Revolution was overwhelmingly negative. Far from being the prerequisite for industrialisation, revolution set back economic growth for decades. Peasant revolution entrenched millions of small-holders, who were an obstacle to the continuation of agrarian modernisation underway before 1789. Civil war disrupted internal investment. Revolutionary and Napoleonic wars led to the loss of colonial markets and a naval blockade which cut France off from world trade. The populations in Nantes and Bordeaux fell by 15 per cent, as their mercantile, shipbuilding and industrial elites retreated to purchase estates in the hinterland. The 'new'social elites differed little from those of the 1780s. The aristocracy formed a composite class of *grands notables* with rentier, landed, bureaucratic and professional strata of the middle class(es).

Revisionism landed a few telling blows. It obliged Marxists to accept that it was difficult to discern a self-conscious bourgeoisie with a clear project, although politicians such as Barnave had come close to articulating one. Merchants and industrialists were rarely the most prominent actors in the conflicts of 1789–1830. When contemporaries began, eventually, to talk about a 'middle class', their focus was often on lawyers or civil servants. But revisionism proved better at empirical dissection of the Marxist model than at replacing it with alternative coherent interpretation. Its propositions were derived largely from systematic negation or inversion of Marxist theses. Its claim that the Revolution left the composition and nature of the elites largely unchanged is simply unsustainable. It contradicts the perceptions of contemporaries, including liberals who are the revisionists' heroes, who *were* convinced that they were living through an era of fundamental social change. The voice of the early Revolution was Abbé Sieyes. He identified the enemy 'other' as aristocratic 'privilege', and called for rights for the 'Third Estate' on the grounds of their utility and productivity. It took time for this image of the bourgeoisie to become dominant. Jacobins preferred to portray model citizens as exhibiting the classical republican quality of *virtu*. But by the 1820s the audience for the writings of St Simon, or of economist J. B. Say, suggest that many had come to recognise themselves in a productivist economic mirror (Sewell 1994).

There is a central contradiction in revisionists' portrait of eighteenth-century France. On the one hand they present a traditionalist, undynamic rentier bourgeoisie. On the other, to emphasise that the Revolution was disastrous for emerging capitalism, they evoke an economy flourishing as a result of Atlantic trade, vigorous 'proto-industry', commercial vineyards and rapid growth in internal markets. By 1789, the bourgeoisie, with 2.3 million members, had trebled in size since 1700. There is evidence of a growing consumerism. Bourgeois homes were increasingly well-furnished. Newspapers featured advertisements for piano-tuners, cosmetics, medical services and products. Within weeks of its fall the Bastille was acquired by an entrepreneur who grew rich on the proceeds from the sale of stones from its demolished walls, miniature replicas and guided tours of the dungeons! (Jones 1991). Even if the bourgeoisie did remain more a class of professionals than of businessmen, it does not follow that their mentality remained traditional. The spread of birth-control and the emerging ideology of 'separate spheres' hint at changes within the middle-class family. The private papers of the Lamothes are revealing. They remained pious Catholics, convinced that individual autonomy should be subordinated to the 'good of the family'. The women had already imbibed the values of family duty, domesticity and charity viewed as typical of the nineteenth-century bourgeoisie. The men – lawyers and doctors – were proud of their competence. A profession was a calling which had its own ethos and provided a public service. They were open to Enlightenment's discourses of reason, toleration and science and utility, were active in Bordeaux's cultural life and had a strong civic sense. Though they were scarcely revolutionary, their family papers reveal a sense of class identity – a pride in *not* being 'frivolous', 'idle' aristocrats (Adams 2000). Nor were such professionals cut off from the emerging commercial culture. Doctors were seeking access to lucrative city practices and active in a medical marketplace. Lawyers practised commercial law. Masonic lodges acted as a meeting place for professionals seeking a wider civic role.

Bourgeois strata were emerging who resented aristocratic privileges and pretensions. Such men were prominent in the revolutionary project which abolished those privileges, introduced 'equality before the law', emphasised 'careers open to talent' and abolished corporate controls and monopolies. Such reforms appealed to their dignity as much as their material interests. Both self-interest and cultural background gave government officers and lawyers a professional commitment to the victory of the rule of law over violence and caprice. However, one should not underestimate the significance for the economy, and the interests of the economic bourgeoisie, of the 1790s reforms. Cobban's (1967) claim that the Revolution's impact on the economy was 'astonishingly small' is astonishing. Revisionists underestimate the perform-ance of French capitalism in the nineteenth century. Despite short-term dis-ruptions caused by internal conflicts and war, the longer-term development of the economy was shaped by the abolition of guilds and internal tolls, confiscation of church property, abolition of seigneurialism, banning of trade unions, introduction of uniform currency and weights and measures, and a commercial code, and the creation of the Bank of France. A unitary national state now presided over uniform legal, taxation and bureaucratic structures. None of these changes occurred without problems. Strengthening of private property rights initially hindered capitalist coal-mining because it distrib-uted rights to sub-soil minerals among thousands of small peasants (Lewis 1994). Only in 1809 did the Bonapartist regime rationalise this by conced-ing mining rights to those with the necessary capital and expertise. Post-Revolutionary regimes remained ambivalent on the issue of free trade in grain, which had provoked popular unrest when briefly introduced by Turgot in 1775. The Jacobins, under popular pressure, reimposed controls in 1793–94. Even the Napoleonic regime, concerned about disorder if food supplies were disrupted, regulated grain markets after 1810. Not all businessmen welcomed abolition of the corporate system. Some Lille textile merchants saw it as a protection against intrusive interlopers and a guarantee of quality produc-tion on which the city's reputation rested (Bossenga 1991). After 1791 they pressured governments to restore the corporate order, and discovered that prefects and ministers were themselves torn between free-market ideology and nostalgia for the virtues of regulation.

Revisionists cite the evidence that only 13 per cent of deputies in the 1789–90 Assemblies were businessmen as indicative of the marginal role of the economic bourgeoisie in the Revolution. However, all parliaments are domin-ated numerically by lawyers! The paucity of industrialists in the 1848 Frank-furt Parliament gives a misleading impression of their importance in German liberalism. Analysis of the 1790s 'municipal revolution' shows that business-men dominated urban politics, though their strategies varied according to local circumstances. In Rheims, a weak local aristocracy compromised with a powerful textile bourgeoisie confident of its ability to control local workers. In Lyon, recent weavers' revolts meant that merchants were initially too scared to launch their own municipal revolution and compromised with the old oligarchy. In Elbeuf, the trajectory of the Revolution followed a recognisably Marxist path. In 1789 its *cahiers de doléances* complained of an iniquitous tax system, internal tolls and a regime which systematically ignored grievances voiced by the Chamber of Commerce. By 1814 the town had grown by 50 per cent, its textile mills had been mechanised and its business community was consulted by government (Hunt 1984).

Even if a self-conscious bourgeoisie had not made the Revolution, by 1830 it was evident that the Revolution had made the bourgeoisie. The experi-ences lived through by middling strata of French society forged both a class identity and political discourse about the middle class which were stronger and more coherent than in Britain, where in objective, structural terms the economic bourgeoisie was substantially larger. In 1789 supporters of moderate reform found the monarchy unable or unwilling to implement these. Aristocratic counter-revolution was defeated only by tactical alliance with a popular movement whose aspirations were dangerously radical. The Napoleonic regime then offered relative internal stability which allowed gains of the Revolution to be consolidated. The Bourbon Restoration raised the spectre of an aristocratic revival which many found threatening. In short, it was in the crucible of prolonged struggles with aristocratic and popular 'others' that middle-class identity was forged. Indeed, the classic thesis of bourgeois revolution was not Marx's invention but, rather that of 1820s liberal historians, in whose writings 'the middle class retrospectively recognised itself' (Hobsbawn 1989).

In 1830 Guizot proclaimed that 'the middle class has arrived in power'. Tocqueville insisted that 'our history from 1789 to 1830, viewed from a distance and as a whole, affords the picture of a struggle to the death between the Ancien Régime – its traditions, memories and hopes as represented by the aristocracy – and the new France, led by the middle class'. A history was constructed for the middle class in an era when history provided the language of politics. A narrative was provided in which the Revolution became the logical and necessary culmination of processes which had seen a middle class rise with the growth of trade and towns. Historians insisted that '1789' marked a 'rupture' in French society. Revolutionary legislation was, Mignet insisted, 'the work of the middle class for – *as everyone knows* – the dominant power *always* seizes control of institutions'. Their rule was justified because they incarnated culture, reason, moderation, initiative and hard work. Above the middle class, Royer-Collard insisted, 'one finds the need for dominance, *below* lies ignorance, habit and lack of independence'. By 1830, Tocqueville claimed, middle-class triumph was 'so thorough that all political power . . . was confined within the limits of one class. Not only did they rule society – but it may be said that they formed it'. This discourse would have been unthinkable in 1789. The insights of such contemporary liberals are a better guide to the lived realities of post-1815 France than the claims of modern revisionists. They were not simply offering a Sorelian mobilising myth about the middle class, but were convinced of the gulf between the society of the 1830s and that of 1780 – the France of Balzac and that of Beaumarchais. The Revolution, Tocqueville insisted, was 'in the process of destroying everything in the ancient society derived from aristocratic institutions'.

Some saw the middle class as so diverse as to be impossible to define. H. Fonfriede insisted that 'the present day bourgeoisie is *in no way a class*: it is a strange compound, lacking cohesion and homogeneity. The word "middle class" is a misnomer . . . This supposed middle class is a confused jumble of *twenty different classes*, each having moral and individual interests that are sometimes contradictory'. Such observations are echoed by revisionists who dismiss claims that '1830' was a bourgeois revolution. They view the Restoration's opponents as ideologically eclectic and sociologically diverse. They ranged from moderate future Orleanists via neo-Bonapartists to radical Republicans, and included ex-officers and NCOs, students, journalists, lawyers and provincial businessmen. Their grievances included patriotic resentment at France's diminished international status and alarm at Restoration clericalism. None of this adds up to a coherent bourgeois move-ment. Though industrialists were concerned about the late-1820s depression, there was no concerted campaign to blame this on the regime. Business interests were divided on issues such as free trade. Responses to the econ-omic crisis were essentially regional and sectoral. Hence 'in no sense did the liberals of 1830 simply represent capitalist, bourgeois France at odds with a regime of right-wing noble landowners'. Moreover, the 1830 elites were virtually indistinguishable in social composition from those of the 1820s (Pilbeam 1991).

However, class consciousness happens precisely when specific groups perceive themselves to have interests in common which outweigh real dif-ferences, and feel those interests to be challenged. The political discourse of the 1820s was moulded by perceptions of a threat to '1789' from a resurgent aristocracy. This nurtured a sociological approach to political theory, locating support for liberalism in specific social strata. Under Napoleon, the young began to take for granted equality before the law, 'careers open to talent' – in an expanding bureaucracy and army – educational opportunity and consoli-dation of the professions. Guizot claimed that his faith in the *Charte* waned as he came to regard the Restoration as a threat to the gains of 1789. His perceptions were shared by students and *lycéens*, the generation of 1820 with no experience of the ancien régime. Their collective mentality was shaped by educational institutions established by Bonaparte. Lacking the Voltairean anti-clericalism and the passionate revolutionary commitment of their fathers' generation, they found an improbable guru in Victor Cousin, whose eclectic philosophy sought to synthesise faith and reason. A professor at twenty-three, Cousin incarnated the new meritocracy. Taking the Revolution for granted, young bourgeois experienced a culture shock in the 1820s. Returning émigrés, as alien as figures from the Carolingian age, competed for bureau-cratic and army posts, much reduced in numbers since the collapse of the Napoleonic Empire. As successful *baccalauréat* candidates rose from 2200 to 3000 per annum, there were dangers, particularly in Paris, of overcrowding in bureaucracy and professions. Stendhal's Julien Sorel was typical of his genera-tion in his nostalgia for Napoleon who incarnated the promise of careers open to talent. Education became a battleground as students found university lecturers dismissed, 'suspect' courses in economics suspended. Theatres were censored and prosecutions of liberal newspapers threatened journalists. Frus-trated youthful aspirations fuelled student protests. 'We, the young', were 'victims' of Bourbon gerontocracy and aristocratic reaction. 'We need jobs, we need status; as we are human, we are ambitious, calculating . . .'. This uneasy blend of liberal idealism and self-interested careerism was underpinned by a discourse, derived from St Simon and J. B. Say, contrasting the useful, productive middle class with the parasitic aristocracy attired in silks and finery. There was little sign of that desire *épater le bourgeois* which typified later rad-ical, bohemian protest. Many youthful protesters secured lucrative posts after the 1830 Revolution. Liberal defence lawyers metamorphosed into public prosecutors of the new regime. Only a minority became radical Republicans or, like the disillusioned writers in Balzac's *Illusions Perdues*, realised that the problems of French society stemmed less from an ephemeral aristocratic reaction than from the logic of an expanding capitalist culture which reduced everything, including their youthful literary talents, to commodities and the cash-nexus (Spitzer 1987).

Some rebellious students came from provincial families, or attended provincial faculties. But many were sons of Parisian families whose bourgeois identity was in the process of formation. For them the overthrow of the ancien régime had meant abolition of restrictions which had obstructed their career prospects. The Revolution offered opportunities for men of talent and enterprise in business and administration. Obstacles placed in the path of 'outsiders' with wealth but of modest origins were to be swept away (Garrioch 1996). Before 1789 there had been no Parisian bourgeoisie – merely propertied, educated men influential within their *quartiers*. But changes had already been underway as Paris became a thriving commercial and artisanal centre. Growing centralisation and standardisation of city administration forced businessmen to look beyond their locality for contacts and access to power. They were drawn into debates on free trade, absorbed the rhetoric of 'rights', 'utility', 'virtue' and 'talent', and participated in coffee shops and Masonic lodges. One tannery employer died in the 1790s leaving a library of 500 books on economics, science and philosophy. Experiences after 1789 deepened their self-consciousness. Popular radicalism inculcated a fear of mass politics. Both the Directory and the Bonapartist régime relied on modest lawyers and local businessmen, not just on financiers and senior bureaucrats, to run local administration. Such men were active in the National Guard, on municipal councils and welfare bureaux. Most welcomed the end of guild controls. The sale of church property allowed acquisition of valuable buildings for warehouses and workshops. Warfare led to army contracts. Their sons found career opportunities in an expanding bureaucracy. Such families readily identified with liberal historians' 'foundation myth' of a bourgeois revolution, and took seriously the threat of an aristocratic revival. A grain merchant's son was amongst those killed during an 1820 demonstration against the franchise law which gave large landowners a double vote. Threats to disband the National Guard were viewed as deliberate insults to their class. By 1827 they were forming citywide electoral associations.

Such activity was not limited to Paris. Army officers angry at the promotion of ex-émigrés, journalists alarmed by press censorship, holders of *biens nationaux* worried by growing clericalism were potential recruits to the liberal cause. Limoges industrialists denounced an aristocratic mayor keener to build a road to his château than to improve the town's transport system! In Alsace, Protestant industrialist Koechlin dominated liberal politics, in a region which regretted the loss of Imperial markets after 1815. There were regional and sectional divisions within the economic bourgeoisie on the issue of protectionism. But the economic crisis of the late-1820s strained relations between business and the regime. Bankruptcies rose 75 per cent between 1826 and 1828. In the Gard obstacles were placed in the way of emerging industrial capitalism by Catholic-Royalist aristocrats. Until 1789 local coal resources had been available to small-scale peasant-miners who, protected by the Marquis de Castries, used the coal for local needs. Castries used his influence at Court, and even violence, to obstruct efforts of entrepreneur Tubeuf to introduce deep-mining and a disciplined labour force, and to export coal. The Revolution allowed Protestant textile merchants and financiers, hitherto denied religious freedom or access to local administration, to challenge the power of the Catholic aristocracy and, after a period of sectarian violence, to dominate economic and administrative life. They acquired municipal office and church lands. In 1810 a new mining law ensured that mining concessions would henceforth go to those with requisite capital and technical expertise. The Restoration threatened this bourgeois hegemony. The 'White Terror' of 1815–16 saw returning émigrés organise Catholic gangs to kill hundreds of Protestants. 'Ultra' prefects gave coal concessions to Catholic landowners who regarded coal as simply another crop, and ultra-Royalist populists appealed to Catholic 'little men' by denouncing free-market capitalism. 1830 proved a watershed. The new prefect gave mining engineers a free hand and mining concessions were granted to large companies such as Grand Combes. Parisian capital came into the region and rail links were constructed. It is difficult not to represent this as a historic victory for the, largely Protestant, bourgeoisie of the region from which Guizot had originated (Lewis 1994).

The structures of bourgeois society
The vogue for quantitative analysis of class structures has passed. Yet one should offer some estimates of the size of the bourgeoisie, its sources and levels of wealth and income, and its 'openness'. Daumard (1973) used two criteria for membership of the Parisian bourgeoisie. Between 12 per cent and 15 per cent of the population could afford the expenses of a funeral service and an individual grave. The remainder were transported to the cemetary in a *convoi des pauvres* and buried in communal graves. In the 1840s 12 per cent of Parisian households had a servant – as did 15 per cent of those in Rouen. There, 10 per cent of the population might be classified as authentic bourgeois, a further 18 per cent had incomes placing them above the popular classes. Such estimates correlate with statistics which suggest that 70 per cent of urban dwellers across the century died leaving virtually nothing (Daumard 1973; Chaline 1982).

Analysis of bourgeois occupation, wealth and income is difficult. Reliance on inheritance records – wealth left at death – may identify as rentiers elderly men who had spent their active lives in business or the professions. Since income tax was not introduced until 1916, taxation records give a less accurate assessment of 'mobile' than 'immobile' wealth – land and real estate. The former grew rapidly after 1850. Land, perceived as a guarantee of prestige and security, remained a major source of bourgeois fortunes. 'For as long as you *only* have money', A. Belot warned his brother, 'you will always be on the eve of owning nothing.' Annual returns on land remained above 5 per cent until the 1870s; 80 per cent of all electors during the July Monarchy held some land – and 50 per cent of Parisian electors. However, the proportion of Parisian bourgeois wealth derived from land fell after 1850. This trend began earlier in Alsace, but elsewhere gathered pace only with the fall in returns on land triggered by the 1870s agricultural depression. State bonds offered another 'safe' investment. De Franqueville, director of the Ponts et Chaussées corps in the 1860s, refused to play the stock market. Instead he accumulated 300,000 francs in bonds via monthly purchases, which he used to fund his daughter's dowry.

Urban real estate became more profitable. Haussmann's rebuilding of the capital allowed building contractors and speculators to benefit from the provision of bourgeois apartments in central Paris. Rents rose as the city expanded from one million inhabitants in 1850 to four million by 1914. And 8 per cent returns on capital tempted small shopkeepers to acquire properties to rent out to workers. Comparable returns occurred in expanding provincial towns, though in Rouen, where the economy was sluggish, annual profits were barely 4 per cent and the proportion of bourgeois wealth in real estate fell from 20 per cent to 11 per cent (Chaline 1982). Provincial bourgeois calculated that lack of contact with and knowledge of the Paris Bourse made heavy investment in stocks and shares risky. Many consulted *notaires*, whose investment advice was notoriously cautious. Deposit banks, which developed after 1850, did encourage modest clients to diversify their portfolios, and shareholders quadrupled to two million by the 1900s. In Rouen, 'mobile' wealth comprised 48 per cent of bourgeois fortunes in 1840, 67 per cent by 1900. Here 40 per cent of such investments were in 'safe' sectors, particularly railways, popular among small investors. By 1900, 50 per cent of Rouen 'mobile' investment was in foreign bonds, and only 10 per cent in industrial shares. It was larger city investors who showed an interest in industrial shares. In Lille in 1900, 50 per cent of business families' inheritances included shares in their own firms. Colonial investment grew only gradually to 8.8 per cent of French overseas investment by 1914 – a proportion which rose sharply after 1920. The balance of bourgeois wealth and income thus shifted gradually. Fortunes at death nearly quintupled between 1830 and 1914, despite sluggish expansion during the 1880s depression. 'Mobile' wealth finally overtook landed income in 1890. Although capitalist farming regions were affluent, the wealthiest departments – Rhône, Seine and Seine-Inférieure – were those with concentrations of urban bourgeois wealth. Wealth rose fastest in industrial cities such as Lille. By 1900, industrialists such as Schneider of Le Creusot were much wealthier than the largest landowners.

Laissez-faire ideologue Leroy-Beaulieu claimed that an expanding market economy led to wider wealth distribution and a narrowing of income disparities. He cited rising real wages and falls in returns on land and industrial shares in the 1880s depression as evidence. Yet statistical surveys reveal startling inequalities both between bourgeoisie and popular classes and within the bourgeoisie. In Rouen, 10 per cent of inheritances accounted for 70 per cent of the city's wealth in 1830, 80 per cent by 1910. In 1900, 95,500 died leaving a total of 25 million francs, an average of 250 francs each. But 660 died leaving 1600 million francs – 2.6 million per capita! In some cities economic development expanded 'middling' bourgeois incomes. But in Paris 30 per cent of wealth was bequeathed by the richest 1 per cent of the population in 1830 – by a mere 0.4 per cent by 1900. In Rouen, the median fortunes of the mercantile elite rose four times faster than those of the liberal professions (Daumard 1987; Chaline 1982). Wealth and income were not the only criteria for bourgeois identity or for rankings within hierarchies. New speculative wealth was suspect. Family reputation and connections, culture and profession were all significant. A modest lawyer, even one lacking the franchise, was more securely bourgeois in 1840s Paris than *nouveau riche* millionaire charcutier Véro. Senior bureaucrats came from established families who had paid for their higher education. Many had private means. But their salaries – usually under 20,000 francs – were substantially lower than incomes of many *négociants*. Nevertheless, state service conferred prestige, and their homes contained libraries, musical instruments and other symbols of assured cultural status.

Official discourse eulogised the bourgeoisie as an 'open' class into which anyone with talent and initiative could enter. Orleanist ideologues, while resisting demands to extend the franchise, insisted that only incorporation of new men guaranteed long-term social stability. The Revolutionary era had witnessed an expansion in army and bureaucratic posts and had enriched war contractors. '1830' led to a renewal of political and administrative elites. Economic expansion offered opportunities for upward mobility which lent credence to the Orleanist *Journal des Débats* boast that 'the bourgeoisie ceaselessly recruits amongst the people, and every day there are fresh bourgeois families'. The modest capital required by early textile mills allowed the clerk Lagage to enter the Roubaix *patronat*; 50 per cent of Paris merchants in 1840 had modest origins. The numbers paying the *patente* rose at a faster rate than the population. Parisian construction projects allowed skilled building-workers and subcontractors to become building entrepreneurs. The expansion of Marseille allowed migrants – *bourg* artisans or literate sons of peasants – to succeed as small businessmen or *fonctionnaires*. It was possible for shop-keepers' sons to acquire some secondary schooling and aspire to professional or bureaucratic careers. Yet there is persuasive evidence that the bourgeoisie was a class that was essentially reproducing itself and becoming increasingly 'closed' at its upper levels. Even in 1840 there was truth in socialist claims that the *grande bourgeoisie* was an hereditary caste. Orleanist *grands notables* came from families which had risen before 1814. Such 'dynasties' inter-married and consolidated their power (Tudesq 1964; Lhomme 1960).

Although the success of a Berliet in automobiles showed that ascent into the *grand patronat* was possible later in the century, levels of capital required by the industries such as steel were too high to permit the access of self-made men. The relatively undynamic Rouen textile sector became dominated by large mills utilising costly self-acting mules and owned by a few inter-marrying dynasties. The city's elite hardened into a patriciate; 80 per cent of its bourgeoisie were heirs of established families (Chaline 1982). Parisian workers might rise into the world of boutique or café, but the gulf between that milieu and the world of business, where over 90 per cent of *négociants* now inherited family capital, widened. In 1810, 15 per cent of Bank of France regents had lower-middle-class origins. By 1860 this was true only of maverick former *aubergiste* Dablay. The remainder were recruited from established financial and business dynasties and provincial industry (Plessis 1985). Around one in ten of the bourgeoisie at any given time – under 2 per cent of the overall population – had risen from the popular classes.

One paradox of bourgeois ideology was the coexistence of a cult of the 'self-made man' and myths of 'careers open to talent' alongside emphasis on the importance of family. Successful careers were built around family networks. To enter the magistracy required years of costly secondary and higher education, a stage as an unpaid *juge suppléant* and nepotistic family influence to secure the appointment. Self-made men were viewed as *parvenus*, liable to fall as rapidly as they had risen unless seen to be providing their sons with cultural and financial capital and their daughters with dowries. Bourgeois dynasties survived because of careful strategies and willingness to make sacrifices to fund education, dowries, or business ventures for sons. Parisian sugar refiner Lebaudy set up his sons in cotton-spinning, banking and sugar-refining and gave business advice and loans to nephews and sons-in-law. The family remained major industrialists down to 1914 (Daumard 1987).

Constructing bourgeois identity?

A firmer sense of bourgeois identity was emerging by 1830 as the Revolution's gains were defended against aristocratic revival and popular radicalism. Orleanist rhetoric identified the middle class(es) with a range of values and virtues – reason, respectability, hard work, moderation, and a sense of civic duty. But it took the threat of proletarian 'mob-rule' in Rouen in 1848 to persuade liberal, Voltairean free-marketeers and Catholic critics of 'modern materialism' that they shared a common identity or interests. Once order was restored after the upheavals of the Second Republic, underlying fissures within the bourgeoisie reappeared. The Rouen bourgeoisie has been likened to a kaleidoscope – its image endlessly dissolving, then reforming in ever-changing patterns (Chaline 1982). The collapse of the corporate Ancien Régime had left a world of atomised individuals and social fluidity. The self-interest of each individual made all men, particularly fellow bourgeois, potential competitors. Once interest became particular and fragmentary and an ideology of competitive individualism turned all men into rivals, what chance was there of constructing a sense of bourgeois solidarity?

Nevertheless, a bourgeois cultural identity *was* being consolidated. This occurred in the spheres of domesticity and consumption, which permitted considerable space for middle-class women. Central to the construction of bourgeois *male* identity were networks of urban voluntary associations which specifically excluded both female and working-class 'others'. Such associations had a problematic legal status. Article 291of the Code required police authorisation for public assembly. In 1849 controls over political clubs were tightened. Bonapartist authorities used these powers to monitor Masonic lodges, suspected of Republican sympathies, and Catholic St Vincent de Paul societies. Yet bureaucrats and members of middle-class voluntary associations 'ultimately saw themselves as collaborators in a project of civic order and prosperity' (Harrison 1998). Hence most such associations were tolerated, and some even received modest official subsidies. Most avoided divisive political issues and distanced themselves from the competitive ethos of the marketplace.

Within *Sociétés d'Émulation* competition was reconfigured as 'emulation' – a striving for excellence in a spirit of mutual encouragement, esteem and camaraderie. Just as bourgeois schoolboys aspired to prizes for academic or sporting achievements, so later in life they would do so within cultural societies. A member was defined not by his economic activity or income but by his interest in and contribution towards culture, science or local history. Homais, the pharmacist in *Madame Bovary*, appends 'member of several learned societies' to his surname. Voluntary association became a 'site' for regular performance of bourgeois masculinity. Ladies favoured decorative flowers. Bourgeois horticulturists emphasised the 'manliness' of field trips, developed scientific taxonomies of plants, evolved rational growing techniques, lectured to market-gardeners and developed strands of useful vegetables. However, their rhetoric was not uniformly utilitarian. It praised pursuits such as archaeology, with no market application and cultural institutions – museums, zoos, libraries – whose primary justification was development and ordering of knowledge. Expositions sponsored by Mulhouse's *Société Industrielle* were described in terms of 'emulation' and scientific innovation, for 'the principles of free-trade only create (businessmen aiming) to sell and to increase their wealth. *Expositions* inspire more elevated thoughts, they make manufacturers into *artists* sensitive to praise from fellow citizens'.

Such associations fused disparate elements of the 'middling' strata into a class. Whereas Besançon Académie was dominated by traditional notables, the *Société d'Émulation* brought together Catholic magistrates, government officials, university lecturers and Protestant businessmen. Mulhouse's *Société Industrielle* blended together the Calvinist industrial patriciate with 'new' engineers and managers, some destined to become their sons-in-law (Harrison 1998; Hau 1987). *Cercles* – male clubs more democratic than *salons*, less socially promiscuous than cafés – played a similar role. In 1843 there were 2000, with 120,000 members. Prospective members were proposed by sponsors and promised to accept rules, enforced by fines. A few offered space for Republicans, but most avoided sectarian politics and subscribed to a range of newspapers. They provided a refuge from female-dominated homes for husbands keen to spend leisure time in an atmosphere of male sociability – smoking, playing cards or billiards. Fathers introduced their sons as members (Agulhon 1977). Urban shooting clubs, which emerged after 1850, allegedly embodied bourgeois civic principles, and their patriotic utility was contrasted with futile aristocratic field sports. Middle-class daughters developed their piano skills within the home, but public music was dominated by male orchestras and choral societies, specialising in military marches and symphonic and choral excerpts featuring male singers in roles written for women.

Voluntary associations' rhetoric of inclusiveness could not disguise the fact that the bourgeoisie remained a club worth joining precisely because of its exclusiveness. There remained barriers between bourgeoisie and the lower-middle-class, as well as fissures within the bourgeoisie itself. Most sections of the bourgeoisie sponsored charities. However, Catholics favoured paternalist rhetoric and professed concern for the souls of donors and recipients alike. Liberals preferred a secular, 'scientific' approach, viewing excessive generosity towards the poor as distorting the free market. Nor was it possible in the climate of the 1860s – when the Syllabus of Errors put Catholicism on a collision course with 'modern' intellectual trends – to view science as a neutral meeting-ground above the middle class's political and religious divisions. Besançon's older Catholic elites proved reluctant to join the same societies as Protestant watch manufacturers. A Mulhouse *curé* refused permission for Protestant choral society members to hold a concert in his church. Jewish businessmen were refused entry to some *cercles*. The growing army of clerks, accountants, industrial draftsmen and textile designers were keen to establish their identity and status by founding professional associations and to assimilate with established bourgeois sociability by forming their own voluntary associations. Musical groups and sports and gymnastic associations multiplied, allowing clerks the thrill of parading with uniforms and banners in civic fêtes. They, too, claimed that voluntary societies produced fit, civic-minded, patriotic citizens who prized culture and the values of order, discipline and emulation. Yet their efforts met condescension from their betters. The textile *patronat* was aware of its reliance on the skills of its designers, but had no intention of mingling with them as equals. Dreams of equal access to the public sphere or to bourgeois culture thus proved illusory. Petty bourgeois associative culture remained largely distinct from that of their social superiors (Harrison 1998).

Parisian bourgeois identity and self-confidence strengthened after mid-century. The middle class had appeared private and inward-looking. Men wore dark suits, austere uniforms setting them apart from the finery of the aristocracy. The burgeoning cult of domesticity confined wives to the home, though there were fears that Parisian apartment blocks with shared corridors and stairways, outward facing windows – unlike those of aristocratic *hôtels* which opened on to internal courtyards – and prying concierges were insufficiently 'private' (Marcus 1999)! Bourgeois *cercles* were open only to members. But the bourgeoisie colonised the boulevards constructed by Haussmann's projects which evicted workers from the inner city. Police cleansed the streets of traders, knife-grinders, s*altambanques,* clowns, dancing bears, beggars and boisterous carnival crowds – anything or anyone that threatened to disturb the symmetry and order of the new city. Having crushed the 1848 revolution, the bourgeoisie, Rémusat claimed, felt a yoke lifted from its shoulders and at last at ease in 'their' city. An inner-directed culture assumed an expansive opulence. As bourgeois hegemony stabilised, affluence could be displayed in the theatre, department store or boulevard café. Restaurants witnessed displays of public eating – exhibiting the arrogance and gastronomic taste of the rich. Omnibuses allowed easy access to the city centre, with little danger of social mixing on most routes. The bourgeois lovers in Zola's *La Curée* treated the boulevards as an extension of the corridors of their hotel. Unlike the English bourgeoisie, which retreated to leafy suburbs, the French middle-class favoured life in a 'sanitised' inner city space (Burton 1994).

One figure ridiculed in Daumier's cartoons was the urban pedestrian proudly walking his pet dogs. Bohemians parodied this new ritual by walking turtles on leads! However, the house-trained domestic pet became a symbol of bourgeois civilisation, the antithesis of filthy mongrels who roamed among the 'dangerous classes' of the *faubourgs*. The Society for the Protection of Animals (1846) linked eradication of cruelty to animals with wider projects to control lower-class brutality. The faithful pet dog was eulogised as a loyal companion to those disturbed by the heartless anonymity of the city. It guarded the home, played with children and mourned its dead master. Distraught owners of dogs that had 'passed away' had them stuffed, or buried in the Asnières pet cemetery! Shops supplied bourgeois pets with special biscuits, flea powders, manicures. Maison Ladoube specialised in fashionable dog clothes. Dogs were fetishised, deodorised, trained with the aid of etiquette books – *Le Chien d'Appartement* – and selectively bred for Kennel Club exhibitions which, 'figuratively expressed the desire of the middle-class fancier for prestigious rank in an hierarchical society' (Keele 1994). The Commune showed that removal of the poor from central Paris was no guarantee that the city was 'safe'. Pet-owners exhibited anxieties, central to bourgeois culture, about the impossibility of isolating oneself from a threatening outside world. What if servants introduced fleas to the apartment which contaminated one's pet? An 1855 Act authorised impounding of mongrels – the poor canine 'lower orders' who posed a sexual threat to one's pedigree bitch and were a source of 'contamination' – potential vehicles for transmission of rabies into the household. In the pre-Pasteur years rabies still killed several dozen annually. But it was symptoms associated with the disease which were peculiarly disturbing to the orderly bourgeois home. In pets and humans alike it appeared to generate an uncontrollable sexual voracity. Experts were so struck by similarities with behaviour patterns of a bitch on heat that they developed a theory of 'spontaneous rabies' generated by a pet's suppressed sexuality. Such thinking generated disturbing reflections on dangers of over-civilisation and suppression of passions within bourgeois society itself. Equally disturbing for pet lovers was a dawning awareness of contradictions between their claim that concern for animal welfare was a sign of bourgeois civilisation and evidence that science, civilisation's great achievement, relied on vivisection and animal experiments!

A capitalist bourgeoisie?

Recent historiography has questioned the 'Marxist' stereotype of a bourgeoisie dominated by business interests and tied to the development of industrial capitalism, claiming that both numerically and in terms of power and prestige *rentiers*, bureaucrats and professional strata remained dominant. Many industrialists aspired to escape from business. Those who did not do so were deficient in qualities of entrepreneurial dynamism exhibited by British, German or American counterparts. Orleanist Anglophiles in the 1830s admired British landed gentlemen more than Lancashire mill-owners. In 1840s Paris, 15 per cent of electors under sixty were *rentiers*. Some held legal or medical qualifications but did not practice. However, the numbers of such affluent idle – *oisifs* – should not be exaggerated. Towns such as Amiens contained few rentiers. By 1906–11 there were 300,000 rentiers, but 90 per cent were over 50. The lure of the land did seduce some industrialists. In Rouen the most dynamic textile dynasties were Protestant outsiders, often Alsatians. As growth of the cotton industry slowed after 1860, mercantile and textile dynasties bought estates in the Normandy hinterland where they controlled 15 per cent of the land, and sent sons into the army or bureaucracy. Those remaining in industry pursued cautious strategies, investing in 'safe' government bonds. Mill-owner Le Poitevin married a ship-owner's daughter, purchased country estates and married his daughter into the aristocracy. Sons of Dutoit, the largest cotton-spinner of the 1840s, became rentiers and art-collectors (Chaline 1982).

Some businessmen hoped that their sons' education would secure prestigious bureaucratic posts. Bureaucratic dynasties often had little contact with the economic bourgeoisie. The Brières were *notaires* before becoming magistrates. One son became a *conseiller* at the Cour de Paris. The next generation included a magistrate who married the daughter of a War Ministry official – dying in 1872 with a fortune of 2.9 million francs. The extended family included a *conseiller d'État* and several *notaires*-rentiers. Such dynastic profiles evoke a world whose contours were shaped by law, magistracy and upper bureaucracy (Daumard 1987). Yet it is misleading to view the bureaucracy as somehow divorced from the economy. The classic critique of the French economy as 'too dirigiste' clearly implies that state officials played a role in economic decision-making. '1830' proved a watershed because Orleanists were prepared to provide state subsidies for modern mining projects and the bureaucracy now recruited figures like Legrand – *École Polytechnique*-trained technocrats capable of planning the rail system. The Grandes Écoles, apogee of the Napoleonic higher-education system, have been criticised, with some justification, for producing theoretical graduates ill-suited to the practical requirements of industry and snobbishly condescending towards provincial businessmen. Nevertheless, complex interrelationships between the *Grandes Écoles*, bureaucracy, industry and public utilities developed. They trained engineers for the *Ponts-et-Chaussées* corps, which supervised French transport, bridges and highways, and for coal-mine inspection. By mid-century *patrons-techniciens* who headed leading industrial firms, Cail locomotives or Fourchambault metallurgicals, were *Grandes École* graduates.

So, too, were managers in rail companies, gas and steel mills, some of whom had moved sideways from bureaucracy into the private sector. Between 1825 and 1871, 50 per cent of *École Centrale des Arts et Métiers* graduates became industrial managers. There was closer contact in France than in Germany between professional and bureaucratic strata of the bourgeoisie and industry. In the Reich there was a gulf between bureaucrats and the professional and academic middle-class and industrialists – *Bildung und Besitz*. In France, 35 per cent of senior civil servants were sons of businessmen; 25 per cent of entrepreneurs were sons of professional or bureaucrat fathers, as against 10 per cent in Germany. If 31 per cent of children of large businessmen married into bureaucratic or professional families, 40 per cent of senior bureaucrats themselves married into the world of business or finance. It is misleading to claim either a one-way tendency for sons of businessmen to abandon industry or to suggest that the industrial and bureaucratic worlds were hermetically sealed from each other (Kaeble 1993).

An influx of technocrats revitalised the iron and steel industry of eastern France. Forge-masters had often been tenants of the aristocracy. Growth in Lorraine iron had been slow. Charcoal-smelting survived until railways and free trade during the Second Empire made competition fiercer. The de Wendels – ennobled before 1789 – defined themselves as landowners and took pride in their military tradition. Some forge-masters owned châteaux and hunted. In the 1870s one rose at noon, drank several glasses of wine, visited the works to sign a few papers – before imbibing more wine! Yet Lorraine became one of the Continent's major steel regions. Precocious utilisation of Thomas processes for removing phosphorous from iron-ore permitted the Briey basin deposits to supply an industry which came to produce 75 per cent of French steel. Use of immigrant labour, paternalistic labour strategies and tough anti-union policies kept the wokforce fragmented and relatively docile. The market share of France's ten largest steel firms rose to 70 per cent. They became joint-stock companies and imported technocratic managers, who married into the *patronat* and sat on boards of directors. Cavillier of Pont-à-Mousson insisted that his wish was 'to *act* incessantly, to *create*, to build companies'. An admirer of colonial administrator Lyautey, he incarnated the leadership principle. 'In a large business there is a need for a man who personifies senior management – a man who will be the *Chief*.' He refused to install a sofa in his office. A steel mill was no place for a siesta! He arranged his Paris honeymoon to coincide with the national steel trade-fair! His epitaph reads – in Latin – 'Born, Worked, Died'.

French steel firms' production costs did remain higher than those of their German competitors, but their problems stemmed from objective difficulties – high coal costs and sluggish domestic demand – rather than from a Malthusian strategy of protecting inefficient plants via excessively high tariffs. Company histories portray the *barons de fer* in hagiographic terms – dynamic pioneers of an industry vital to the sinews of France's military revival. The Left spread a 'black legend' of ruthless authoritarians who refused to recognise unions and kept blacklists of militants. Their patriotism was suspect. They imported foreign labour to undercut wage levels, invested in coal and metallurgy across the German frontier and welcomed a war which allowed them massive profits as 'merchants of death' – supplying the armaments industries of both sides! They funded far-Right parties and exerted lobbying pressures on governments. In short the Lorraine steel-barons epitomised the oligarchy – the '200 families' – which dominated the bourgeois Republic. This portrait was not implausible. Emphasis on the power and economic success of steel magnates provides a necessary corrective to current orthodoxies about the French bourgeoisie. But neither their coherence nor wealth should be exaggerated. The *Comité des Forges* and *Comptoir de Longwy* cartel were fragmented by rivalries between individual firms. Although Wendel owned a Paris *hôtel* – and was prominent in the Jockey Club – most steel barons were regional rather than national notables, ill-at-ease in Paris. Their wealth, no higher than that of successful Bordeaux merchants or Lille textile-owners, did not approach that of a Krupps (Moine 1989).

The Paris Gas Company was a public utility run by technocratic managerial cadres. Established in the 1850s it secured, thanks to contacts with Bonapartist financiers, a fifty-year monopoly of supply to the capital with guaranteed minimum prices. For thirty years it maximised profits by supplying high-priced gas to a limited number of commercial and industrial consumers. Despite complaints from small consumers and from Republican politicians of 'monopolistic profiteering', it ignored all but the wealthiest domestic consumers. However, the challenge from electricity forced a strategic change. It campaigned to woo domestic consumers with offers of free installation of cheap gas cookers. The founder of the Paris Gas Company (PGC), son of a Rouen mercantile family, was a landowner in the Seine-et-Oise – an interesting example of symbiosis between commercial capitalism, landownership and corporate industry! Company advisors included a former Mines Inspector and a Sorbonne chemistry professor. Like the railway companies, the PGC. recruited managers from prestigious state corps. Senior personnel, often lawyers' sons, had trained as managerial engineers at the *École Centrale des Arts et Métiers*. Middle management came from the *Écoles des Arts et Métiers*. They had 'deficiencies'. Like many French managers they treated workers as children and lacked empathy with their aspirations. They viewed the emerging mass consumer market more as problem than an opportunity. Their education inculcated a typical French ambivalence towards 'the market'. Although accepting that 'self-interest' was the prime motivator, they remained wary of unfettered free markets. Yet they were industrious, committed and self-disciplined. Most existed on modest salaries, although eventually they were awarded company shares. They proved technically highly efficient. Proud of their 'vocation', they joined the *Société des Ingénieurs Civils*. They conducted laboratory experiments, solved technical problems of gas piping or high-temperature distillation. Flexible and adaptable, they quickly adopted innovations such as the Siemens oven. Net costs of gas production were lower than in London. They boosted profits by developing subsidiary markets for waste products of gas production, selling ammonium sulphate to farmers and coke to Parisian consumers (Berlanstein 1991).

This was one of many corporate businesses that mushroomed after mid-century. It is often claimed that France lacked a sizeable corporate sector and that its few large businesses lacked entrepreneurial dynamism. Company law allegedly inhibited joint-stock companies (*sociétés anonymes*: SAs), while banks proved unresponsive to domestic demands for investment capital. Such accusations are exaggerated. Until company law was liberalised in 1867, SAs were only established at the rate of 11 per annum. Yet enterprises such as Le Creusot functioned successfully as *sociétés en commandite par actions*, in which a *gérant* with unlimited liability exercised control, while 'passive' shareholders enjoyed limited liability. By the 1900s SAs were emerging at the rate of 400 annually. France had 6000 – more than Germany, even if the average size was smaller. Nor was industry starved of capital. Even the 'old' *Haute Banque*, often portrayed as obsessed with government loans, invested in Le Creusot in the 1830s. Industrial banks established in the 1850s by the Pereires ran into trouble in the slump at the end of the 1860s. But surviving joint-stock banks such as *Société Générale* ignored the advice of Henri Germain of *Crédit Lyonnais* and took the risk of investing in domestic industry. Banks were involved in massive capital exports during the Third Republic, which made France the world's second largest creditor nation. But interest rates were lower than in Britain, suggesting that modest domestic demand for capital was being met. Some large firms remained self-financing – a chosen option made possible by the high profits in mining and metallurgicals. Sectors such as steel, which equipped itself with Bessemer furnaces requiring major injections of capital, found little difficulty in securing these. Vaunted German *Grossbanken* proved less supportive of local industry than French regional banks such as those in Nancy which serviced eastern metallurgical and chemical sectors (Freedman 1993).

Nor was French industry entirely dominated by family firms. France did avoid the 'merger mania' which affected American industry. Concentration levels remained modest in construction and the automobile industry. But they were high in glass, chemicals and electrical equipment. And France had high levels of cartelisation. The steel cartel and Lorraine pig-iron consortium (*Comptoir de Longwy*) secured protective tariffs which maintained domestic price levels, and allowed producers to dump excess production on foreign markets. Sugar-beet, glass, aluminium and northern coal were other cartelised sectors. The *Syndicat Cotonnier de l'Est* was the largest textile cartel in Europe, throwing doubt on classic critiques which took textile dynasties to epitomise the lack of dynamism of French family firms. The Mottes of Roubaix were portrayed as anxious about excessive growth, reluctant to abandon 'auto-finance' lest external capital erode family autonomy, more concerned to protect domestic markets via tariffs than seek new market opportunities. However, the backwardness of the French textile sector cannot be attributed to the entrepreneurial deficiencies of such families. Although Britain established an early lead in mechanised factory production, after 1820 French mill-owners had access to British technology and know-how. Alsace mill-owners had ample investment capital, from local merchants or Swiss banks. However, technology transfers only made sense if these fitted into a matrix of related capacities. Whereas Lancashire cotton-masters in the 1780s had expanding overseas markets, labour supply bottlenecks and access to cheap coal, their French nineteenth-century counterparts faced conditions of sluggish domestic demand, abundant rural labour and scarce, scattered coal resources. In such circumstance it made sense not to copy the British model slavishly but to play to their strengths. They used proto-industrial rural labour and water power, and targeted quality markets for calicoes and indiennes, printed cottons – items which reflected French design skills. From 1780 to 1850, French textile production expanded at an impressive rate of 5 per cent per annum. Textile dynasties – Catholic in the Nord, Protestant and Jewish in Alsace – were proud of their industrial calling and showed no inclination to become rentiers. The Mottes educated sons in the *Grandes Écoles* and introduced technocratic managers in the 1870s. Careful marriage strategies built alliances with other textile dynasties. Sons-in-law were set up in subsidiary factories. Equally important was the political flexibility and skill shown by industrial dynasties like the Mottes, or their engineering and metallurgical counterparts in the St. Etienne region. Such employers faced the challenges of adjusting to the advent of a democratic Republic and to the rise of the labour movement in the context of prolonged economic depression and intense international economic competition (Heywood 1972; Landes 1976; Chassagne 1991; Hau 1987; Gordon 1996).

The cultural values of bourgeois elites evolved. In the 1830s the model for Anglophile liberals were the England Whig 'gentlemen' – incarnations of the values of constitutional liberties, religious toleration, decentralised local government and efficiency, and admired for blending tradition with modernity. Some Anglophilia survived. Liberal economist Leroy-Beaulieu preferred British laissez-faire to French dirigisme. Taine praised British elites' practical education and public schools' use of sports to develop character. The cultural model for younger bourgeois came from across the Atlantic. America was a democracy, but one prioritising individual freedom, federalism not Jacobin centralisation, free markets and competitive individualism not dirigisme. Family training in individual self-sufficiency and active involvement in a mobile, free-market economy equipped Americans for participatory citizenship. The future belonged to societies which cultivated a ruthless, conquering, entrepreneurial spirit. France's rising generation of industrialists looked to American 'scientific management' as the key to future success in a world of industrial Darwinism. To survive, France needed to jettison those Latin chimeras of equality and fraternity which the US despised and Darwinian laws did not recognise.

The political consolidation of bourgeois hegemony?
The elusiveness of political stability complicated the consolidation of bourgeois hegemony. Only the Third Republic, Furet argues, brought the moderate liberal project of 1789 finally 'home to port'. Most bourgeois favoured constitutional government on the British model. A limited franchise would allow men of property, education and 'reason' to retain control. In time, as prosperity and schooling spread and revolutionary passions faded, piecemeal franchise extension might be contemplated. However, instead of this gradualist path towards liberal democracy, they faced constant political upheaval. Sections of aristocracy and the popular classes proved reluctant to accept the bourgeois order, and fragmentation of the middle class itself precluded political consensus. Such 'fault lines' reflected economic, regional, cultural and religious tensions. Protectionist metallurgical, mining and cotton employers were at odds with free-trading silk and wine producers and port merchants. High interest or freight rates incited provincial industrialists against the financial feudalism of banks or rail companies. Liberals – some from minority Protestant or Jewish communities in Alsace or the Gard – favoured the post-1830 Orleanist constitutional monarchy or moderate Republicanism. But many *bien-pensant* Catholics – not just rentiers or magistrates but some businessmen too – favoured Legitimism. Socio-political upheaval might persuade hitherto liberal bourgeois to rally, as in 1799 or 1851, to semi-authoritarian Bonapartism. And France had a minority of radical bourgeois – 'neo-Jacobin' lawyers, doctors and journalists – who provided the cadres for egalitarian/democratic mobilisations.

Those who claim that the bourgeoisie became the ruling class after 1830 offer two possible narratives about the subsequent evolution of bourgeois power. One shows consolidation of the democratic Third Republic after 1877 shifting effective political control to middling strata of the bourgeoisie – the *classes moyennes*. Hence Lhomme's (1960) study of the *grande bourgeoisie au pouvoir* ends in 1880. The alternative narrative suggests that behind a façade of democratisation, upper-middle-class dominance persisted, even if the Republic required this elite to make tactical concessions. Lhomme, echoing

Marx, portrayed the July Monarchy as a period of undiluted *grand-bourgeois* dominance. Louis Philippe was crowned not in Rheims Cathedral but in parliament. Liberals distanced themselves from a revolutionary reading of '1830' – rejecting a Republic because it evoked the extremism of 1793. By 1835 controls on public meetings, trade unions and the press had been tightened. The franchise was extended only marginally, from those paying 300 francs annual direct tax to those paying 200. Initially this doubled the electorate to 160,000, but economic growth increased this to 230,000 by 1847 – barely 3 per cent of adult males. With bankers occupying 40 per cent of seats in its first cabinet, the regime began 'veritably under the auspices of Mammon' (Lhomme 1960).

Casimir Périer, the prime minister, was from one of those bourgeois dynasties that dominated nineteenth-century France. His family were Dauphiné lawyers who acquired church lands, diversified into mining and textiles, and became directors of the Bank of France. The proportion of deputies with business interests rose 20 per cent between 1829 and 1831, but land remained central to Orleanist elites' wealth and status; 50 per cent of the (narrow) electorate were landowners, 23 per cent businessmen, 10 per cent professionals and 8 per cent bureaucrats. However, it is misleading to suggest that little had changed since the 1780s other than a fusion of nobles and a rentier bourgeoisie into a composite stratum of conservative *grands notables*. Many aristocrats shunned the new regime, kept aloof from bourgeois 'upstarts'. Bourgeois landowners included agrarian capitalists engaged in commercial farming in the Île de France or Picardy. Many deputies were lawyers, acting as parliamentary lobbyists for industrial or commercial interests. Bureaucratic deputies included technocrats involved in planning the rail network. The central bureaucracy had expanded from one thousand to over twenty-five thousand since the Revolution. The state employed 'experts' – military officials, civil and mining engineers and statisticians who collected data, measured resources, compiled land surveys and tax registers. Such men were central to the projects of emerging capitalism. A significant symbiosis of landed, industrial and financial capital was occurring. Directors of large industrial and commercial enterprises also held landed investments. In *Education Sentimentale* (1867), Flaubert describes the death, in 1850, of the banker Dambreuse. 'Now that turbulent life of his was over. How many times had he flattered ministers . . . For he had acclaimed Napoleon, the Cossacks, "1830", the workers – worshipping authority so fervently that he would have paid for the privilege of selling himself . . . *Yet* he left behind three factories, a farm in Picardy, the forest of Crancé in the Yonne and a fortune in stocks and shares' (Lhomme 1960; Beck 1987; Cobban 1967; Johnson 1975; Tudesq 1964).

The 'Dambreuse syndrome' illustrates the *grande bourgeoisie's* political flexibility. Most Orleanists lacked fixed political loyalties, metamorphosing into moderate Republicans in 1848 or Bonapartists by 1851, backing any regime which promised law-and-order and security for property and investments. Orleanism had directly represented the interests of a thin stratum of landowners, financiers, big industrialists and merchants, senior bureaucrats and wealthy lawyers. Such men, incarnating qualities of reason, enterprise and culture, allegedly spoke for the *classes moyennes* who had only to demonstrate through economic success that they possessed the requisite qualities to earn the vote. Such arguments were tolerated in years of economic expansion. But economic crisis in 1846–47 provoked discontent among the professionals, modest businessmen, students and petty bourgeois. Despite Guizot's personal financial probity, the regime was wracked by corruption scandals, and Daumier's cartoons portrayed it as a joint-stock company run for the benefit of a narrow oligarchy. Its fatal weakness was loss of credibility among the middle classes, whose demands for modest franchise reform were rejected by Guizot, an admirer of the Whigs who failed to learn lessons from the 1832 Reform Bill.

During the Second Republic (1848–51) France teetered on the brink of class war as many newly enfranchised workers and peasants rallied to the Left. Bourgeois who had supported electoral reform and called themselves Republicans recoiled from the threat of social upheaval. Liberal lawyers metamorphosed into tough law-and-order public prosecutors. In June 1848, bourgeois National Guards converged on Paris to suppress a workers' insurrection. They indulged in shooting of prisoners with such fervour that Flaubert claimed that the middle class had discovered its 'true religion' – defence of property. Projects for secular education were jettisoned as Voltairean liberals found hitherto unsuspected virtues in Catholic schooling which offered workers' children the consolation of an afterlife to compensate for resigned submission here below. Briefly the threat of socialism persuaded the fragmented elites to unite in a 'Party of Order'. But Orleanists, Legitimists and moderate Republicans could not easily forget their ideological and cultural differences. With no coherent conservative party capable of defending 'order', many bourgeois lost faith in their own politicians and turned – more or less reluctantly – to Louis Napoleon who manipulated his uncle's myth to fashion an idiosyncratic blend of authoritarianism and populism attractive to elites and masses alike.

Relationships between the Bonapartist state and leading strata of the bourgeoisie were complex. Many acquiesced to abandonment of the 'principles of 1789' – press freedom, parliamentary control of the executive, rule of law. Thousands of Republicans were arrested in the aftermath of the Bonapartist coup. Police powers were increased. Male suffrage was maintained, but elections controlled and constituencies gerrymandered. A neutred parliament lacked a say in ministerial appointments or government policy. The state appeared 'above' class interests and outside direct control of the bourgeoisie. Yet such a regime was not necessarily inimical to bourgeois interests. In Wilhelmine Germany the middle class tolerated a semi-authoritarian regime, indeed one which preserved Junker military and bureaucratic power, because it controlled the working class, stimulated industrial development and allowed the growth of a bourgeois public sphere. In Bonapartist France the bourgeoisie found similar compensations. The stock market rose sharply in the aftermath of a coup which was to demobilise popular radicalism for a generation. Middle-class sons found ample career opportunities in an expanded bureaucracy. There was extensive interpenetration of the state and financial elites. With rare exceptions such as Education Minister Duruy, ministers, prefects and senior bureaucrats were recruited exclusively from the upper bourgeoisie. Construction of the rail network nurtured a sustained boom in mining, metallurgy and engineering. Parisian and provincial urban renewal provided lucrative public works contracts and stimulated a real estate bonanza. Well-lit boulevards, department stores and restaurants came to symbolise a newly self-confident bourgeois culture of consumption. A significant shift occurred in the balance between rentier and industrial fractions of the bourgeoisie. Industrial banks were established and joint-stock company law liberalised. After 1860, free-trade policies were pushed through by Bonapartist bureaucrats and economic advisors, in the general interests of modernisation of French capitalism, though against the wishes of some industrialists. Paris Expositions of 1855 and 1867 displayed France's economic dynamism and growing involvement in international trade. The role of a semi-dirigiste state in these processes was not inconsiderable. Long-term operating franchises and guaranteed returns on capital were granted to six rail companies and to public utilities.

Bonapartists calculated that economic expansion would erode historic divisions within the elites. Yet by the mid-1860s Catholic Legitimists, liberal neo-Orleanists and Republicans were all expressing open opposition. By then economic prosperity was faltering as rail construction slowed and the American Civil War disrupted French exports. Haussmann's Parisian projects became mired in accusations of financial irregularities and the construction boom ended. Tensions within the bourgeoisie resurfaced. Coal and factory textile employers criticised free-trade policies which exposed them to British competition, and wooed workers with calls for tariffs to protect jobs. Smaller businessmen criticised pricing policies of monopolistic public utilities. Provincial industrialists protested at rail freight charges. Around St. Etienne armaments firms reliant on state contracts remained Bonapartist, but medium-sized engineering employers questioned the long-term viability of the regime. Working-class unrest persuaded them that democratisation was necessary if social control was not to break down. Progressive employers – some Protestant – argued that Catholic schooling, encouraged by the regime, was ill-suited for the training of a modern labour force. Similar 'fault lines' emerged in Rheims, where mercantile families who dominated the Chamber of Commerce were challenged by newer textile employers, allied to the liberal professions, espousing moderate Republicanism and demanding parliamentary controls over tariff policies. Urban bourgeois elites demanded autonomy in the running of municipal affairs – education policy, policing, public hygiene, allocation of taxes.

Rather than (just) viewing Republicanism as a manipulative strategy of progressive bourgeois class control, recent historians discern a groundswell of middle-class opinion genuinely alarmed at excessive centralisation, the power of Bonapartist police and prefects, the weakness of French associational life and absence of participatory local democracy. 'Republican municipalism' was portrayed as a step towards class conciliation and cooperation. Participation in local politics, Ferry claimed, would make 'the rich more benevolent, the poor less bitter'. Pelletan insisted that an elected – rather than appointed – mayor would attract popular respect. 'This man, in general a doctor, a *notaire*, a merchant – independent in his situation, liberal by character – has no other ambition than to bring up his family, nurture his inheritance.' Municipalism combined democratic, participatory rhetoric with emphasis on the 'natural' influence of the local bourgeoisie. It offered an incremental strategy designed to build coalitions of industrialists, lawyers, petty bourgeois and workers. It won local, then parliamentary, elections in the late 1860s. In most towns the tone was set by moderate businessmen and lawyers. In 1865 Le Havre elected a Republican municipality – and for decades thereafter its politics were dominated by wealthy merchants such as Jules Siegfried. Atlantic trading links opened the port to American-style Republicanism. The bourgeoisie sponsored public libraries and cultural, musical and gymnastic societies. Workers were wooed with housing projects and educational schemes such as the *Cercles Franklin*, and endlessly reminded that their jobs depended on colonial trade. The labour movement remained weak until the 1890s, and no socialist was elected until the 1920s (Gordon 1996; Elwitt 1975; Cohen 1998; Hazareesingh 1998; Ardaillou 1999; Nord 1995).

The collapse of Bonapartism and the defeat of the Paris Commune gave the Republican bourgeoisie its chance to achieve its progressive form of hegemony – more complete and sustainable than that of Orleanism, which relied on a narrow property-franchise, or Bonapartism, which had depended on a quasi-authoritarian state machine. The Republican bourgeoisie deployed democratic rhetoric. Insisting that class terminology was outmoded, it appealed to the *nouvelles couches sociales* – new social strata. The Republic was portrayed as an alliance of useful, productive bourgeois – industrialists deploying 'active, working capital' – with professionals and experts dedicated to public service. Peasants and workers could trust such men. The Republican coalition defined itself against 'parasitic' notables of the old France – aristocrats, obscurantist clergy, idle rentiers and the forces of 'financial feudalism' (Elwitt 1975). Daniel Halévy, contemporary social commentator, claimed that the Republic's consolidation signified the *'fin des notables'*. Lhomme's (1960) analysis of the 'upper bourgeoisie in power' ends in 1880 – on the assumption that thereafter the ruling group were modest strata of the middle classes. This was the official narrative of the Republic. It should not be dismissed merely as myth. Openly reactionary magistrates were purged. By 1900, 10 per cent of prefects were recruited from middle-class *capacités*, as against 3 per cent in the 1860s. Whereas almost all ministers before 1870 had come from the *grande bourgeoisie*, between 1877 and 1899 29 per cent had modest origins. Radical Republican deputies were often small-town lawyers and doctors. The *Annuaire des Élites* now included engineers and modest professionals alongside established *notables* (Charle 1987).

The 'Republican moment' emerged from changes within middle-class culture and institutions taking shape in the last years of the Empire, which witnessed revolts of younger groups against conservative oligarchies. Parisian smaller businessmen challenged plutocratic control of the Chamber of Commerce. Within the Protestant and Jewish communities the hold of neo-Orleanist dignitaries and financiers was challenged. In Masonic lodges, a refuge for liberals after 1851, the leadership's deism was challenged by those demanding the jettisoning of the 'Supreme Being'. Republican lawyers such as Gambetta sought to make the Bar a bastion of liberalism. Paris Medical Faculty students challenged powers conceded to the clergy in the *Université* since 1850. Even Impressionism represented a democratic revolt by artists keen to replace the repertoire of battles and landscapes favoured by the *Académie* with the 'painting of everyday life'. Some Republican bourgeois even envisaged a shift from the patriarchal family – older husband, submissive wife, obedient children – towards 'companionate marriage' within which the wife would have educational opportunities in order to become a fit partner (Nord 1995).

Was this a genuine watershed, a moment when bourgeois elites became ideologically more liberal and socially and culturally more open? Or were these changes largely cosmetic? The 'real' foundation of the Republic, critics claim, occurred not with the 1876–77 defeat of Royalism but with the construction of a socially conservative, pro-capitalist bloc in the following decade – designed to combat economic depression and dangers of a socialist revival. Introduction of flexible tariff policies was sold to popular voters as essential to safeguard employment and peasant farming. But it also cemented a deal between Republican provincial industrialists, large paternalist employers – Bonapartist or Royalist in sympathy – and Catholic landed notables, a bloc similar to Wilhelmine Germany's 'Alliance of Iron and Rye'. Ferry's 'new Imperialism', presented as essential for securing markets and guaranteeing French jobs, found support among Republican and Catholic elites. The Republican order was also consolidated, Elwitt (1986) argues, via 'para-political' groups which debated social reforms designed to preserve social peace. These recruited Republican politicians and bureaucrats, 'experts', philanthropists, industrial managers and large employers. In short a modus vivendi was constructed between bourgeois Republicans and sections of the *grande bourgeoisie* and older *notables*. Although Elwitt underestimates ongoing antagonisms between secularist Republicans and the Catholic – and New Nationalist – Right, he does illuminate the strategies of capitalist defence and the ability of the *grande bourgeoisie* to fight its corner in the new 'democratic' world (Elwitt 1986; Lebovics 1998).

Analysis of the power structures indicates that it remained inflential. Continued recruitment of civil servants from elitist *Grandes Écoles* may suggest that the mythical '200 families', alleged by the Left to run France, were constituted less by financial and industrial dynasties than by a self-perpetuating bureaucratic oligarchy. Republicans failed to revive the 1848 project to ensure a meritocratic civil service by establishing a training college for future bureaucrats. The new *École Libre des Sciences Politiques* was designed to strengthen the cadres of an administrative elite capable of holding back the tide of egalitarianism. The growing interchange of personnel between bureaucracy and private sector solidified the coherence of a composite elite. Civil servants with prestigious but modestly salaried posts now ended their careers in lucrative business positions. By 1900, 50 per cent of *Inspecteurs des Finances* – as against 20 per cent in 1870 – transferred to the private sector. Diplomats found second careers in import/export firms. Even in parliament, where the *nouvelles couches* had some impact, control rested with the wealthier strata; 70 per cent of ministers were drawn from the wealthiest 2 per cent of

the population, 30 per cent from big business. The 1893 parliament contained 90 senior bureaucrats and deputies from major industrial dynasties –
Motte, Schneider, Siegfried. Rouen saw no change in the social composition
of deputies between 1876 and 1914, with 53 per cent from big business, 14 per
cent rentiers and 14 per cent well-to-do professionals. Such men attracted
votes by posing as defenders of the city's economic interests, capable of
securing rail links, protective tariffs, access to capital to modernise the port
(Charle 1987; Chaline 1982). The crucial battle of the 1890s was less defence
of the Republic in the Boulangist and Dreyfus crises, rather the ferocious
campaign waged by the *grande bourgeoisie* to defend their economic hegemony.
They scuppered progressive income-tax projects proposed by Radicals by
exploiting their control of a venal press, well-funded lobby groups, employers'
associations and the Senate – an upper chamber deliberately constructed to
over-represent conservative France. Waldeck-Rousseau headed the 1899–1902
government of Republican unity which 'saved' the Republic from the threat
of the far-Right during the Dreyfus crisis. He was also a conservative business
lawyer who aimed to 'tame' the radicals by diverting them from social and
tax reform with the 'plums of patronage' and the cheap fix of anticlericalism
(Kaplan 1995).

The large capital requirements of Second Industrial Revolution industries
made access to the economic elite ever more difficult. By 1900, under 10 per
cent of leading industrialists were of modest origins; 50 per cent of presidents
and vice-presidents of banks and joint-stock companies had inherited millions.
French business, notoriously individualistic, was now adept at defending
its interests through organisation. Membership of employers' associations
trebled in the years before 1914. The *Comité des Forges*, under the vigorous
leadership of R. Pinot, was one of many business lobbies whose views on
tariffs or tax-reform governments ignored at their peril. Radical-led governments of the 1900s remained 'business friendly' not just because they were
alarmed by the labour unrest but because they depended for parliamentary
majorities on Centre-Right parties who represented provincial industrial and
commercial elites such as the Nord textile dynasties. These adapted to mass
democracy by making their peace with the Republic and emphasising that
local prosperity and jobs relied on their business expertise and commitment
to the region (Gordon 1996).

Analysis of Chambers of Commerce provides revealing insights into business politics. The 'twenty-five families' of shipowners and merchants who
ran Bordeaux's Chamber were an 'oligarchy of cousins'. In Rouen, large
merchants held two-thirds of seats in 1900. Existing members secured seats
for sons and nephews. Membership opened the door to bank directorships,
seats on electrification commissions, and places on education or welfare
boards. The Senate obstructed attempts to curb the power of such patriciates
by enfranchising small businessmen until 1908. Even then big business
resisted dilution by mediocre elements, restricting the vote to those who
had paid the *patente* for five consecutive years. The threat from labour made
some capitalists aware of the need to woo the petty bourgeoisie – 'fellow
property owners' with a stake in the social order. However, the arrogance of
Chambers of Commerce was not conducive to this alliance, since it provoked

resentments among many petty bourgeois – sentiments which made the politics of this stratum particularly volatile (Moine 1999).

The petty bourgeoisie and the politics of anxiety?

In 1900, the 'authentic' bourgeoisie comprised some one million people. 'Below' them were eight or nine million who were neither peasants nor workers. This 'petty bourgeoisie' remains a neglected class, but its significance should not be underestimated. In an age of mass democracy the bourgeoisie – Republican or Catholic – eyed them as potential electoral allies. Social Catholic Le Play called them a *'classe tampon'* whose function was to protect the elites' flanks – to be the 'glue' holding industrial society together. In contrast to feckless workers they shared 'our' values of thrift, hard work, responsibility. Small (work)shops were family enterprises, where patriarchal fathers supervised wives and children and aspired to transmit the property to their heirs. Familial labour relations – with employees supplied with board and lodgings – were a model of intimacy which avoided the industrial conflicts of large firms. They represented a rung on a ladder of upward mobility, essential stepping-stones on the path of sons of the people making their way in the world. However, these strata were not easily co-opted as tame allies. They had their own grievances, and did not necessarily identify their interests with those of the bourgeoisie. Their politics proved volatile and diverse. The terms *classes moyennes* or *petite bourgeoisie* were catch-all categories encompassing retailers and small master craftsmen and businessmen – some solidly established, many ephemeral and precarious – and 'newer' strata of white-collar employees and minor civil-servants. Discourses about them imagined them variously as part of the bourgeoisie, as sui generis – or as a *bourgeoisie populaire*, which was really part of the people. In 'normal' times their subjective level of class awareness was fairly low. A sense of collective identity emerged more clearly in crises such as the depression of the 1880s/1890s (Crossick and Haupt 1995).

Marx offered a classic analysis of petty bourgeois consciousness and political volatility. Acutely vulnerable to the threat of large-scale capitalism, they were capable of perceptive analysis of the disastrous consequences for the 'little man' of the growth of monopolies, division of labour and disruption of communities. Their protests could – as in 1848 – draw them into 'broad-Left' coalitions. But in their 'doomed' attempts to prop-up small-scale enterprises they were more likely to espouse reactionary populism than to ally with the emerging proletariat. 'Ultimately they are not revolutionary but conservative. Nay more, they are reactionary, for they are trying to roll back the wheel of History.' Their role in inter-war fascist movements may confirm the perceptiveness of this analysis. Marx failed to predict the rise of a 'new' lower-middle class of white-collar employees. But their status anxieties and reluctance to identify with blue-collar workers made them, too, a potential audience for the radical Right. Marx's approach is open to three main objections. Firstly his teleology of rapid, inexorable economic decline proved misleading. Second his prediction of a *general* shift in petty bourgeois politics to the populist Right was too sweeping. Finally, the *tone* of his writing about them is too scathing – even if his view of them as blinkered, banal and bigoted has been shared by a range of observers from Flaubert to Brecht. Indeed, the petty bourgeoisie's champions were often less than flattering! 'Its qualities (of order and frugality)', claimed one Lyon Catholic in 1909, 'are not always the most attractive, and its egoism and narrowness of spirit are faults that are all-too-common'(Crossick and Haupt 1995).

Until 1850, petty bourgeois politics could, with local exceptions, be located towards the radical end of the spectrum. They belonged to that *menu peuple* which sustained the Revolution and remained loyal to its memory. *Sans-culotte* politics was the politics of urban 'little men'. The Revolution had swept away the corporate world of the guilds and some craft employers and retailers felt nostalgia for the lost world of corporatism which had guaranteed quality and provided control over labour and protection against intruders. However, attempts by Social Catholics to revive corporatism aroused little response. This was a sharp contrast with Germany, where some guilds survived until 1848. The Wilhelmine Reich encouraged neo-corporatist yearnings and used the rhetoric of 'orders' (*Stände*) to woo mastercraftsmen and retailers. The lower-middle class felt excluded from the world of the Orleanist *grande bourgeoisie*. One minister identified them as 'part of those classes which should *never* be allowed to join the electorate'. They felt no loyalty to the regime. Around 27 per cent of Parisian small *patente* payers 'disappeared', many through bankruptcy, in 1846–48, just as a range of financial scandals involving Orleanist politicians was disclosed. Analysis of Parisian *cabinets de lecture* and of the personal libraries of the lower-middle class suggest a taste for 'radical' authors such as Sue or Hugo. In 1847–48 the National Guard – its rank-and-file dominated by small shopkeepers – refused to suppress reform demonstrations. Clearly there *were* tensions between small businessmen and the emerging labour movement. National Guards units helped suppress workers' revolt in June 1848 and in popular *quartiers* there were conflicts between petty bourgeois landlords and tenants. Yet many activists in the *démocrate socialiste* movement of 1849–51 were from the urban and rural petty bourgeoisie. A Mulhouse police report claimed that small traders 'hate the factory owners *because they are rich*'.

Thereafter this 'old' petty bourgeoisie survived longer than Marx predicted, for the 'French path' of gradual economic change permitted the survival in niche markets – both foreign and domestic – of 'quality' craft production. It is difficult to calculate the precise size of the small-business sector. The *patente* was subject to political manipulation, occupational categories used by censuses changed constantly, and no census could capture the fluidity of a world of 'little men' – many of whom oscillated between being employers, self-employed and wage workers. But the rise in *patente* payers from 1.3 to 1.8 million between 1845 and 1896 scarcely suggests a widespread decline. Urban growth provided opportunities for small construction firms and butchers and bakers. Industrial firms subcontracted work or relied on small firms to cope with high seasonal demand. Trades adapted flexibly to changing opportunities. Tinsmiths metamorphosed into plumbers as piped water entered bourgeois homes. When the bicycle ceased to be a luxury item, cycle repair shops mushroomed. Small firms – in Paris's Xe arrondissement or in St. Etienne – pooled resources and shared the use of electricity generators.

Nor were Parisian small retailers necessarily undercut by department or chain stores. These attracted customers to the city centres who might also use smaller stores in the side streets of the Arts et Métiers *quartier* (Nord 1985). In Lyon, the number of butchers rose at a faster rate than the city's population.

Claims that the petty bourgeoisie provided a ladder of upward mobility into the bourgeoisie did not fit easily with assertions that it symbolised stability in a world of flux. But most social mobility was in and out of the lower-middle class. It could take one of several forms. Unemployed journeymen might be obliged to try to 'make it' on their own. A Paris engraver asked about his social identity replied 'wait until tomorrow, perhaps I'll be able to answer. The biggest employers in the trade have four workers for a few days. After which they become workers again themselves'. For others, 'promotion' proved more durable. Auvergnat migrants to Paris tapped the resources of their peasant families to set up wine-shops, or used wives' dowries to acquire the initial capital. Grocery assistants secured loans from wholesalers to establish their own stores. There was a sizeable rural petty bourgeoisie adept at combining roles of miller or wheelwright with the exploitation of small plots of land. Despite the depression, one-third of all *patentes* in 1900 were rural. A wife was chosen for her retail experience – her skills keeping accounts and serving clients was crucial to a business's success. Yet such active roles for wives – and daughters – and the absence of clear distinctions between home and workplace implicitly questioned the cult of separate spheres endorsed by those who praised the petty bourgeoisie for epitomising family values. Small businesses were regarded, in the wake of the Revolution's abolition of guilds and formal masterships, essentially as *family* enterprises, as resources for husband *and* wife, as possessions to be inherited. Family photographs taken outside the shop paid homage to the domesticity ideal by portraying husband and male assistants in working clothes, and wife and daughters in Sunday best at an upstairs window! Small enterprises often relied on credit from the extended family and employed cousins and nephews. However, family labour was often a form of self-exploitation. Sadly for its Catholic admirers, the petty bourgeoisie became the most Malthusian social group in France – practising birth control to avoid subdivision of inheritances and reduce education costs. Many petty bourgeois remained close to the culture of popular *quartiers*. Small shops were a meeting place providing seats for gossiping women. Parisian *faubourg* shopkeepers acted as marriage witnesses for artisans, or as 'bankers of the poor', providing 'tick' for clothing. Auvergnat wine-sellers retained customers by providing credit. The café remained the focus of largely male working-class sociability, a place to relax, to find jobs, discuss politics, organise strikes. Many café owners shared, even encouraged, their clients' politics. Decazeville miners in the 1870s boycotted the company-store and used small shops run by their own relatives. Small retailers were, thus, often petty *notables* whose stores gave identity to a neighbourhood. In Paris's Quartier de la Gare in 1900 there was a rapid turnover of workers and small businesses, yet a nucleus of retailers retained their shops in the same locations (Haine 1996; Faure 1986).

However, after 1880 structural changes and prolonged depression threatened small businesses. Anxieties fuelled hostility to alien and exploitative 'others' and forged a greater sense of identity, although this rarely generated real unity of action. With prices and profits falling, and access to credit poor, many feared bankruptcy. Before the depression only 11 per cent of small businesses in Niort lasted more than a decade. Now annual turnover in Parisian groceries rose to 20 per cent. A quarter of all bankruptcies in 1903–05 were of grocers and bakers. Competition from chain-stores grocers Félix Potin compounded the problems, as did the spread of consumer cooperatives which attracted 'reliable' working-class customers. Small retailers denied cooperatives' insinuations that they adulterated food or gave short measure. The small-business sector became overcrowded as unemployed journeymen, migrant traders from the depression-hit countryside and Jewish immigrants all sought to establish themselves. The petty bourgeoisie became resentful that *they* would foot tax bills to pay for welfare schemes which benefited workers, but ignored the distress of small businesses. Resentments were fuelled by bureaucratic inspection to enforce regulations on health and hygiene, food standards and weekly rest-days for employees – denounced as prohibitively costly for marginal small enterprises which survived only by long hours and low wages. Many disputes before industrial tribunals came from the retail sector.

Despite such problems, *some* petty bourgeois remained loyal to their 'progressive' political heritage. P. Marcelin's account of his father, a Nîmes lampmaker, is a moving depiction of a 'small man' who stayed staunchly radical. He read the anti-clerical *Petit Méridional*, but also Cervantes. Sympathetic to the workers, he felt that they should concentrate on mutual aid societies rather than strikes. Some petty bourgeois entered municipal politics to ensure that municipal taxes were kept low, 'illicit' traders were checked and 'excessive' regulation was curbed. This could bring conflict with organised labour. The new working class of the Second Industrial Revolution tended to live in segregated proletarian neighbourhoods rather than heterogeneous *quartiers* that had nurtured earlier populist politics. Marxists of the *Parti Ouvrier Français* (POF) lacked sympathy for the plight of small retailers – doomed victims of the capitalist juggernaut who 'can whine and petition, but . . . will continue to be devoured'. In Paris *faubourgs* there were tensions between petty bourgeois landlords and working-class tenants. Retailers resorted to debt collectors to retrieve money owed by customers. In St. Etienne ribbon-weaving the alliance of masters and journeymen, once cemented by a shared café-culture, fragmented. When the masters provoked strikes by resisting wage claims they were denounced by journeymen as 'as much exploiters as the merchants' (Crossick and Haupt 1995).

Such tensions allowed Catholic politicians to pose as champions of the interests of small employers. Nord textile magnate Motte defeated the Marxist POF in 1898 with the slogan 'For God, the small shopkeeper and Liberty!' (Gordon 1996). Big business appealed to the petty bourgeoisie as 'fellow property owners', with a shared interest in resisting socialism, welfare reform charges and health and safety regulations. By 1913, two-thirds of Paris shops had secured exemption from the law on the weekly rest-day. However, as in Wilhelmine Germany, the anxious petty bourgeoisie was no tame ally of conservative business elites. It might resent socialist cooperatives, Marxist trade unions or intrusive state bureaucrats, but its instincts remained populist. Enemies of the 'little man' included financiers charging usurious interest rates, big chain stores, large merchants in Chambers of Commerce who excluded small traders lest they 'drown the representatives of capital'. Some retailers were receptive to the rhetoric of the radical Right of the 1890s – Boulangist, anti-Dreyfusard, anti-semitic. The Jew could evoke not only Marx but also parasitic financiers who denied the 'little man' credit and immigrant store-holders who stole his customers. *La Croix* reminded lower-middle-class Catholics that Jews were responsible for the crucifixion. Catholic retailers attacked Jewish shops in the 1898 riots and made up 30 per cent of the membership of the ultra-Nationalist *Ligue des Patriotes* (Nord 1985). After 1890 a *Ligue Syndicale* recruited 130,000 small retailers and campaigned for boycotts of chain stores. It portrayed the small shopkeeper as heart and soul of the community, a holder of local capital. In Lille the bourgeoisie held 36 per cent of its wealth in stocks and shares – the petty bourgeoisie a mere 4 per cent. There are similarities here with the German *Mittelstand*'s emphasis on the 'home town' (*Heimat*). However, links between French small-business associations and the radical Right should not be exaggerated. By 1906 the *Ligue Syndicale* was closer to the orthodox conservatism of the republican Centre-Right than to proto-fascism.

'New' intermediary strata were emerging. In Paris white-collar employees increased from 126,000 to 352,000 between 1866 and 1911. State employees – minor *fonctionnaires*, teachers and postal workers – doubled between 1858 and 1896 to reach 416,000, many recruited from the offspring of small businessmen who railed against the bureaucratic state! Private-sector employees included commercial clerks, sales assistants, rail clerk, office staff in public utilities and industrial firms. There were 50,000 bank clerks in Paris by 1880. Across Europe novelists such as Gissing and Arnold Bennett portrayed this new stratum as 'conformist', desperate for status and security, eager to ape the lifestyle of the increasingly suburbanised bourgeoisie. Although 'really' wage workers, they distinguished themselves by their clean hands, smart attire and greater literacy. They married late and valued the education of their few offspring. Their jobs required respectability. Department-store employees were given elocution and etiquette lessons. Paris's 11,000 rail clerks had company lodgings and wore smart uniforms. More than the 'old' petty bourgeoisie they copied bourgeois lifestyles. Their homes were private spaces, with pianos, symbols of 'culture', and furniture from department stores. Children were forbidden to play in the streets with proletarian urchins. *Le Journal* pandered to their aspirations and anxieties. Voluntary associations which mushroomed after 1880 – sports clubs, shooting and gymnastics societies, music and choral groups – were dominated by (male) white-collar employees and retailers (Crossicks and Haupt 1995).

Harsh realities often punctured their dreams. Two-thirds of Parisian employees and minor civil servants earned less than skilled workers. Promotion prospects were poor and dependent upon favouritism and nepotism. To 'keep up appearances' – on dress or decoration of the apartment – many had to skimp on food. The spread of mass literacy eroded their cultural capital. In the Post Office male employees faced 'dilution' by women employees introduced by management to reduce salary bills. The Wilhelmine Reich proved adept at dividing white-collar and civil service workers from the blue-collar working class. Conformist elements were not absent in France. The *Fédération des Employés de France* in 1901 explained its 'no-strike' policy by invoking the 'platonic' relations between employees and management. Social Catholic organisations recruited among these groups. And yet many petty bourgeois or artisan families from which they were recruited – and the Republican state itself, which employed the *fonctionaires* – retained loyalties to '1789'. Civil servants who petitioned against authoritarian management invoked their Republican 'rights' against Bonapartist practices. Postal workers enquired how a *Republic* could grant unionisation rights to industrial workers denied to its own employees. However, the 1900s postal strikes were treated as 'heresy' by radical prime minister Clemenceau, who sought to sack the militants and to restore order via encouragement of status rivalries and bonus payments for loyal employees. Strikes were not common among private-sector employees but they did occur in department stores in 1907.

Did the petty bourgeoisie function as a bulwark of the social order – providing a buffer to protect capitalists from the working class and acting as a ladder of individual upward mobility from the popular classes? The answer is 'yes' – but a nuanced, qualified 'yes'. Many were more *petit* than *bourgeois*. There was a stratum of relatively secure small businessmen and retailers – drapers, family butchers in affluent quartiers. But many retailers operated on the edge of insolvency. It was difficult to pass one's position on to one's children, so there was much inter-generational downward mobility. In Rouen it was easier for a grocer to marry into the bourgeoisie in 1820 than in 1900. Many felt despised and used by the bourgeois elites. Crisis years brought fine rhetoric from Republicans or Social Catholics flattering the *classes moyennes* as 'salt of the earth', the repository of healthy national values and the backbone of the social order. Yet the bourgeoisie was unwilling to acknowledge even those lower-middle-class voluntary associations constructed in direct imitation of bourgeois models. Thus many felt a greater sense of separation from the interests of the bourgeoisie than of identification with them. However, if this generated a reluctance to be manipulated by the elites, a firm sense of class identity emerged only sporadically and briefly. Even in the depression of the 1880s and 1890s, only a minority of retailers and small businessmen joined associations like the *Ligue Syndicale*.

In Britain, where guilds were long dead, there was a striking *absence* of discourses about the lower-middle class. Despite local ratepayers' associations and attempts by small grocers to cling to retail price maintenance to compete with Sainsburys, their interests appeared to be represented by the Tory party. The German *Mittelstand* – both 'old' and 'new' – was central to political debate. Guilds survived in some regions until 1848, and the Reich flirted with plans to revive them. The rhetoric of 'orders' – *Stände* – appealed to some master craftsmen who were more distant from their journeymen than their French counterparts. German civil servants were employees of a quasi-authoritarian monarchical state, and German governments highlighted the gulf between white-collar employees and the working class. The *Mittelstand* was drawn to the politics of conservatism or, when asserting its autonomy, to the populist radical Right. Unlike its German counterparts, the French petty bourgeoisie was heir to a 'revolutionary heritage' and Republican tradition, and was often anti-clerical. This served to inoculate it against the lure of the reactionary Right – whether Catholic or proto-fascist.

Bibliography

General
Beck, M. *French Notables* (New York: P. Lang, 1987).
Charle, C. 'The present state of research into the social history of elites', *Contemporary European History* 1992.
Daumard, A. *Les Fortunes français au XIXe Siècle* (Paris: 1973).
Daumard, A. 'Wealth and affluence in France', in W. Rubinstein (ed.) *Wealth and the Wealthy in the Modern World* (London: Croom Helm, 1980).
Davidoff, L. and Hall, C. *Family Fortunes: Men and Women and the English Middle Class 1750–1850* (Chicago: University of Chicago Press, 1987).
Howorth, J. and Cerny, P. (eds) *Elites in France* (London: F. Pinter, 1981).
Mayer, A. *The Persistence of the Old Regime* (London: Croom Helm, 1981).
Mitchell, A. and Kocka, J. (eds) *Bourgeois Society in Nineteenth Century Europe* (Oxford: Berg, 1993).
Pilbeam, P. *The Middle Classes in Europe in the Nineteenth Century* (London: Macmillan, 1990).
Pilbeam, P. *The 1830 Revolution in France* (London: Macmillan, 1991).

Aristocracy
Beck, T. 'The French Revolution and the nobility: a reconsideration', *Journal of Social History* 1981.
Brélot, C.-I. *La Noblesse Réinventéé: Nobles de Franche Comté 1814–70* (Paris: Les Belles Lettres, 1992).
Brélot, C.-I. (ed.) *Noblesse et Villes: 1780–1950* (Tours: University of Tours, 1995).
Brélot, C.-I. 'Le Syndicalisme Agricole et la noblesse en France 1884–1914', *Cahiers d'Histoire* 1996.
Brélot, C.-I. 'Savoir-vivre, savoir-être: Attitudes et Pratiques de la Noblesse française au XIX siècle', *Romantisme* 1997.
Charle, C. 'Noblesse et Elites en France au Début du XXe Siècle', in *Les Noblesses Européennes au XIXe Siècle* (Milan and Rome: Ecole Française de Rome, 1988).
Cocaud, M. 'Les cadres de la rénovation agricole en Ile-et-Vilaine', *Révue d'Histoire Moderne et Contemporaine* 1996.
Darrow, M. *Revolution in the House: Class and Inheritance in Southern France* (Princeton NJ: Princeton University, Press, 1989).
Denis, M. *La Noblesse de la Mayenne et le Monde Moderne* (Paris: Klincksieck, 1977).
Dunne, J. 'The nobility's new clothes: revisionism and the survival of the nobility during the French Revolution', in J. Jeanneney (ed.) *The French Revolution and its Impact* (Westport, CT: Greenwood Press, 1996).
Fiette, S. *La Noblesse française des Lumières à la Belle Époque* (Paris: Perrin, 1997).
Figeac, M. *Les Destins de la Noblesse Bordelaise: 1770–1830* 2 vols (Bordeaux: 1996).
Forster, R. 'The nobility in the French Revolution', *Past and Present* 1967.
Forster, R. *The House of Saulx-Tavanes* (Baltimore: Johns Hopkins University Press, 1971).
Gibson, R. 'The French nobility in the nineteenth century', in J. Howorth and P. Cerny (eds) *Elites in France* (London: F. Pinter, 1981).

Higgs, D. 'Politics and landownership amongst the French nobility after the Revolution', *European Studies Review* 1971.

Higgs, D. *Ultraroyalism in Toulouse: 1789–1830* (Baltimore: Johns Hopkins University Press, 1973).

Higgs, D. *Nobles in Nineteenth-Century France: the Politics of Inegalitarianism* (Baltimore: Johns Hopkins University Press, 1987).

Kale, S. *Legitimism and the Reconstruction of French Society: 1852–83* (Baton Rouge: Louisiana State University Press, 1994).

Lewis, G. *The Second Vendée* (Oxford: Clarendon Press, 1978).

Locke, R. *French Legitimists and the Politics of Moral Order* (Princeton, NJ: Princeton University Press, 1974).

McPhee, P. *Revolution and the Environment in Southern France: Peasants, Lords and Murder in the Corbières* (Oxford: Oxford University Press, 1999).

Richardson, N. *The French Prefectoral Corps: 1814–30* (Cambridge: Cambridge University Press, 1966).

Sprinker, M. *History and Ideology in Proust: 'A la Recherche du Temps Perdu' and the Third Republic* (Cambridge: Cambridge University Press, 1994).

Wiscart, J.-M. *La Noblesse de la Somme au XIXe Siècle* (Paris: Bock, 1994).

Bourgeoisie

Adams, C. *A Taste for Comfort and Status: a Bourgeois Family in 18th-Century France* (Pennsylvania: Pennsylvania State University Press, 2000).

Agulhon, M. *Le Cercle dans la France Bourgeoise: 1815–48* (Paris: Colin, 1977).

Ardaillou, P. *Les Républicains du Havre: 1815–89* (Publics de l'Univ. de Rouen et du Havre: 1999).

Barral, P. *Les Périer dans l'Isère au XIXe Siècle* (Paris: PUF, 1964).

Beck, T. *French Legislators: 1830–34* (Berkeley, CA: University of California Press, 1974).

Berlanstein, L. *Big Business and Industrial Conflict in 19th Century France* (Berkeley, CA: University of California Press, 1991).

Bossenga, G. *The Politics of Privilege: Old Regime and Revolution in Lille* (Cambridge: Cambridge University Press, 1991).

Burton, R. *The Flâneur and the City* (Durham: University of Durham, 1994).

Carter, E. (ed.) *Enterprise and Entrepreneurs in 19th and 20th Century France* (Baltimore, MA: Johns Hopkins University Press, 1976).

Chaline, J.-P. *Les Bourgeois de Rouen: Une Elite Urbaine au XIXe Siècle* (Paris: Presses de la FNSP, 1982).

Charle, C. *Les Elites de la République: 1880–1900* (Paris: Fayard, 1987).

Chassagne, S. *Le Coton et ses Patrons: France 1760–1840* (Paris: Editions de l'EHESS, 1991).

Church, C. *Revolution and Red Tape: 1750–1850* (Oxford: Oxford University Press, 1978).

Cobban, A. 'The "middle class" in France 1815–48', *French Historical Studies* 1967.

Cohen, W. *Urban Government and the Rise of the French City* (New York: St. Martins Press, 1998).

Daumard, A. *La Bourgeoisie Parisienne: 1815–48* (Paris: Flammarion, 1970).

Daumard, A. *Les Bourgeois et la Bourgeoisie en France depuis 1815* (Paris: Aubier, 1987).

Duprat, C. *'Pour l'Amour de l'Humanité': Le Temps des Philanthropes* (Paris: 1993).

Elwitt, S. *The Making of the Third Republic: 1868–84* (Baton Rouge: Louisiana State University Press, 1975).

Elwitt, S. *The Third Republic Defended: Bourgeois Reform in France* (Baton Rouge: Louisiana State University Press, 1986).

Freedman, C. *The Triumph of Corporate Capitalism in France: 1867–1914* (Rochester, NY: University of Rochester Press, 1993).

Garrioch, D. *The Formation of the Parisian Bourgeoisie: 1690–1830* (Cambridge Mass: Harvard University Press, 1996).

Geison, G. (ed.) *Professions and the French State: 1700–1900* (Philadelphia, University of Pennsylvania, 1983).

Girard, R. *The Unheroic Hero* (1969).

Gordon, D. *Merchants and Capitalists* (Alabama, 1985).

Gordon, D. *Liberalism and Social Reform: Industrial Growth and 'Progressiste' Politics in France* (Westport, CT: Greenwood Press, 1996).

Harrison, C. *The Bourgeois Citizen in 19th-Century France: Gender, Sociability and the Uses of Emulation* (Oxford: Oxford University Press, 1998).

Hau, M. *L'Industrialisation de l'Alsace: 1803–1939* (Strasbourg: University of Strasbourg, 1987).

Hazareesingh, S. *From Subject to Citizen: the Second Empire and the Making of Modern French Democracy* (Princeton, NJ: Princeton University Press, 1998).

Heywood, C. *The Cotton Industry in France: An Interpretive Essay* (Loughborough: Loughborough University Press, 1972).

Hobsbawm, E. 'The making of a "bourgeois revolution"', *Social Research* 1989.

Holt, R. 'Social history and bourgeois culture in 19th-century France', *Comparative Studies in Society and History* 1985.

Hunt, L. *Politics, Culture and Class in the French Revolution* (Berkeley, CA: University of California Press, 1984).

Johnson, C. 'The revolution of 1830 in French economic history', in J. Merriman (ed.) *1830 in France* (New York: F. Watts, 1975).

Jones, C. 'Bourgeois revolution revivified: 1789 and social change', in C. Lucas (ed.) *Re-writing the French Revolution* (Oxford: Clarendon Press, 1991).

Kaeble, H. 'French bourgeoisie and German *Bürgertum* 1870–1914', in A. Mitchell and J. Kocka (eds) *Bourgeois Society in Nineteenth Century Europe* (Oxford: Berg, 1993).

Kaplan, R. *Forgotten Crisis: the Fin-de-Siècle Crisis of Democracy in France* (Oxford: Berg, 1995).

Keele, K. *The Beast in the Boudoir* (Berkeley, CA: University of California Press, 1994).

Landes, D. 'Religion and enterprise: the case of the French textile industry', in E. Carter and R. Forster (eds) *Enterprise and Entrepreneurs in France* (Baltimore, MA: Johns Hopkins University Press, 1976).

Lebovics, H. *The Alliance of Wheat and Iron in the Third French Republic* (Baton Rouge: Louisiana State University Press, 1988).

Lewis, G. *The Advent of Modern Capitalism in France: 1770–1840* (Oxford: Oxford University Press, 1994).

Lhomme, J. *La Grande Bourgeoisie au Pouvoir: 1830–80* (Paris, 1960).

Marcus, S. *Apartment Stories: City and Home in 19th-Century Paris and London* (Berkeley, CA: University of California Press, 1999).

Moine, J.-M. *Les Barons de Fer: Les Maîtres de Forges 1850–1939* (Nancy: Nancy University Press, 1989).

Nord, P. *The Republican Moment* (Cambridge, Mass: Harvard University Press, 1995).

Peiter, H. 'The consolidation of the business community in bourgeois France: 1880–1914', *Journal of Social History* 1976.

Pellissier, C. *Loisirs et Sociabilités des Notables Lyonnais au XIXe Siècle* (Lyon: Lyon University Press, 1999).

Plessis, A. *Régents et Gouverneurs de la Banque de France* (Geneva: Droz, 1985).

Reddy, W. *The Invisible Code: Honor and Sentiment in Postrevolutionary France 1814–8* (Berkeley, CA: University of California Press, 1997).

Sewell, W. *A Rhetoric of Bourgeois Revolution: Abbé Sieyes' 'What is the Third Estate?'* (Durham: University of North Carolina, 1994).
Spitzer, A. *The French Generation of 1820* (Princeton, NJ: Princeton University Press, 1987).
Tudesq, A. *Les Grands Notables en France: 1840–49* (Paris: PUF, 1964).
Wahrman, D. *Imagining the Middle Class: 1780–1840* (Cambridge: Cambridge University Press, 1995).

Petty bourgeoisie

Crossick, G. and Haupt, H.-G. (eds) *Shopkeepers and Master Artisans in 19th-Century Europe* (London: Methuen, 1984).
Crossick, G. and Haupt, H.-G. (eds) *The Petite Bourgeoisie in Europe: 1780–1914* (London: Routledge, 1995).
Faure, A. 'Petit Atelier et modernisation économique au XIXe Siècle', *Histoire, Economie, Société* 1986.
Haine, W. Scott *The World of the Paris Café: 1789–1914* (Baltimore, MA: Johns Hopkins University Press, 1996).
Moine, J.-M. 'Les Chambres de Commerce au XIXe Siècle', in C. Petitfrère (ed.) *Patriciats Urbains* (Tours: University François Rabelais, 1999).
Nord, P. *Paris Shopkeepers and the Politics of Resentment* (Princeton, NJ: Princeton University Press, 1985).

Chapter 2

The making of the French working class

Writing the social history of the French working-class

Labour historiography has undergone two major paradigm shifts since the 1960s. In the first, historians located the origins of the 'working class' in the resistance of artisans to threats to their skills, job autonomy, communities and lifestyle posed by the advent of the factory system. Labour movements – reformist or revolutionary – were viewed as key agents in the creation of a more just egalitarian society. Workplace and community solidarities, the cooperative ethos and job pride were all celebrated. Artisans were portrayed, even in defeat, evolving from craft to class consciousness and transmitting to subsequent proletarian labour movements a heritage of pride in working-class identity, combativeness and stubborn refusal to submit to the inexorable logic of the laws of the market. After 1980 de-industrialisation of heartlands of organised labour undermined trade-union power. The global triumphs of the free-market Right provoked a crisis of welfare states, of social democracy and – in France – of the Communist Party. As confidence in the 'forward march of labour' faded, a second paradigm shift occurred within the historical profession. The 'new social history' had sought to recover the experiences of workers whose identity was assumed to be rooted in the workplace. Influenced by post-modernism and cultural anthropology, historians now claimed that workers had multiple, shifting identities, of which class position was not necessarily the most significant. Instead of workplace solidarities, endless ethnic, religious, sectional, generational, gender and regional divisions were now emphasised. Images of the worker as male craftsman or coalminer were, it was claimed, constructed against numerous 'others' – women, unskilled, immigrants. As the working class of the 1980s disappeared before our eyes, so its past – the 'history of the working class' – was being deconstructed. Perhaps it had never existed except as a discursive construct of radical intellectuals or aspiring labour leaders?

How was the *French* working-class distinctive? One paradox appeared central to analysis of French labour in the 'long nineteenth century' (1789–1914). French workers exhibited precocious militancy and political consciousness. Yet the labour *movement* appeared numerically weak and ill-organised. In 1914 there were one million union members, whereas Germany and Britain both claimed four million. The French Socialist party (SFIO) had under one-tenth of the German SPD's one million members. Several explanations have been suggested. The first emphasises the structures of the labour force. Because craft products maintained niches in domestic and foreign markets, artisans constituted a high proportion of the labour force. Struggles to defend crafts in the face of industrial changes radicalised many artisans. Their movement exhibited distinctive style and priorities. It was concerned with skills. Its projects, whether cooperative or syndicalist, emphasised direct action and worker control rather than nationalisation. It mistrusted bureaucratic trade unions and centralised political parties (Berlanstein 1992).

However, a crucial watershed occurred with the rise of 'new' industries after 1870. Transmission of the values and experiences of the artisanal movement to a proletariat of rural migrants, women and immigrants proved difficult. The latter two groups lacked the vote. Company paternalism and scientific management strengthened employers' control and inhibited the development of unions (Noiriel 1990). An alternative approach emphasised the 'primacy of politics'. Involvement in the Revolution raised French workers' levels of consciousness. But the political lessons remained ambiguous. Was worker emancipation to be achieved via alliance with the 'progressive' Republican bourgeoisie, or through further popular insurrection? Workers alternated between hopes of a 'social' Republic, which would finally fulfil the promises of 1789, and anger and frustration when, as in 1830, 1848 and 1871, (sections of) the liberal bourgeoisie appeared to betray them. Ambiguous perceptions of the Third Republic explain oscillation between reformist and revolutionary sentiment in workers' discourse. It was *both* 'theirs', an instrument of capitalist social control, and yet *simultaneously* 'ours' – a regime with the *potential* to emancipate labour. Workers who denounced the use of troops against strikers might rally to defend the Republic against the far Right (Judt 1986). A final explanation emphasises the role of *local, informal* protest networks among 'unorganised' workers. Levels of unionisation in Nord textile mills were generally low. Yet there was a factory culture of ruses and symbolic protests – everyday forms of resistance which mocked managerial authority. The 'pragmatic of direct action' is typified by the stokers of the Paris Gas Company. Migrants without craft traditions, they developed a strategy of wildcat strikes at opportune moments to win concessions. When a union was formed in the 1890s, after pressure on management to normalise industrial relations from the Radical Paris municipal council, stokers mistrusted it as a ploy designed to tame their militancy – claiming to prefer the 'healthy' French model of confrontation to the British model of large but moderate unions. Many French workers who were not members of unions participated in strikes (Berlanstein 1992; Reddy 1984).

The making of the working class

The structures of the labour force (1800–70)
A genuine 'industrial proletariat' of factory workers, miners and forge-workers did emerge in a few regions. But it co-existed with a sizeable artisanate and rural proto-industrial workers. The industrial workforce rose from 2 to 4.5 million between 1800 and 1876. Textiles was the largest employer, followed

by 'traditional' construction and wood sectors. Artisans, 30 per cent of the workforce in 1860, dominated 'quality' export sectors – silks, porcelains, furniture, fashions and jewellery. Women made up over 30 per cent of the labour force, children under 16, 10 per cent. Child factory labour horrified social observers. But it has been argued that children had always worked, that working alongside kin in a mill was better than labouring in a cramped, filthy artisan workshop – in short that this was not a 'dark age' of unprecedented exploitation. Yet things probably got worse before they began to improve. Infant and child mortality, particularly from TB, was very high in textiles. Many conscripts from mill towns proved unfit for military service. Children were injured cleaning machinery and deformed by repetitive tasks. Factory jobs did not give opportunities to run errands in the fresh air which had made earlier types of child labour tolerable. Millowners, claiming that competitiveness depended on cheap child labour, evaded hours limitations imposed by the 1841 Child Labour Act. After 1860 technological changes made children less essential in textile mills, while paternalist or 'progressive' employers argued for regulation of child labour because French industry required a healthy, literate workforce. By 1870 children comprised only 7 per cent of the work-force.

Migration into industrial centres was steady rather than rapid. Many moved initially to a nearby town, then later along paths established by relatives or fellow villagers to a city or industrial region. Urbanisation was quite slow. By 1848, when 50 per cent of Britains lived in towns, only 25 per cent were urban dwellers. Only 4 of the 25 largest towns were industrial. Alsace, the Nord and the Stephenois were miniature versions of Lancashire and Yorkshire. Heavy industry was located in isolated, single-industry, company towns such as Decazeville. Rural industry proved resilient. It required less fixed capital investment. Wood and water power provided alternatives to scarce coal. Peasant-workers could be paid low wages because they produced some food, and could be laid-off in a slump without provoking dangerous unrest. Hopefully they were sheltered from the corruptions of city life. Many survived by 'pluri-activity' – using earnings from domestic weaving or clog- or glove-making to supplement those from agriculture or carting. Looms dominated villages around Rheims or Mulhouse and cotton outwork the Pays de Caux (Normandy). Charcoal forges flourished in Champagne and Périgord into the 1850s, as did watchmaking near Montbéliard or glove-making around Grenoble. Life in a proto-industrial village or an artisan quartier offered a degree of autonomy absent from a mill town. One could work irregular hours, rest on 'Saint Monday'. Pluri-activity allowed flexibility. During an economic slump not all one's eggs were in one basket. Reluctance to submit to the discipline of the factory, known in popular parlance as *bagne* (prison), combined with falling birth-rates to create recruitment difficulties for heavy industry. Proto-industrial workers developed 'informal' strategies of resistance not available to proletarianised urban workers. Fougères shoeworkers fell back on agricultural resources when in dispute with merchant capitalists. Paternalist strategies were designed to break such habits of independence by luring workers into the 'security' of reliance on company housing and pensions (Noiriel 1990; Berlanstein 1992).

Real wages stagnated until 1850 and rose only gradually thereafter. Food prices rose sharply after bad harvests in 1816–17, 1826–31 and 1845–47. Many conscripts from industrial regions were rejected because of diet deficiency diseases. Rising food prices reduced purchasing power and triggered industrial slumps and unemployment. Welfare relief from *Bureaux de Bienfaisance* was patchy, and many were reliant on private charity or the benevolence of notables or paternalist employers. The working day remained long – above fifteen hours in some sectors. Only a few 'progressive' employers, such as Alsace's Protestant mill-owners, accepted that shorter hours could reduce accidents and increase productivity. Disparities in wealth and income distribution widened in industrial areas. Under 10 per cent of the inhabitants of Lille controlled over 90 per cent of inherited wealth. Upward social mobility remained negligible, although some building craftsmen did become construction contractors.

'Before the making . . .': workers and protest *c*.1780–1830

The term 'working class' – *classe ouvrière* – emerged only in 1830. But the roots of working-class identity may be discerned in the corporate artisanal world and in popular mobilisations of the Revolution. Marxists portrayed eighteenth-century crowd protests, particularly grain riots, as resistance to an emerging free-market economy and argued that the popular movement was a key actor in the radicalisation of the Revolution. Parisian crowds stormed the Bastille, installed the Jacobins and forced them to introduce price controls. Rudé (1973) identified activists as craftsmen – skilled, rooted in their *quartiers*, fiercely egalitarian. Possibly this rather idealised narrative underplayed the role of the unskilled, 'floating' population – navvies, river dockers, porters. Revisionist historiography, reviving themes of nineteenth-century reactionaries such as Taine, reasserted the centrality of violence to the Revolution, allegedly stemming from a brutal urban popular culture. The apparent delight of Parisian crowds in mutilating the corpses of the Bastille's defenders has been correlated with the taste for cruelty revealed in artisan autobiographies. Such 'primitives', it is implied, are best studied by social anthropologists trained to observe strange tribes! Yet the *sans culotte* movement was a precursor of the artisan-based labour movement of the 1840s. Its rhetoric linked the social condition of the 'little man' with a radical political stance. It advocated an egalitarian Republic, direct democracy and direct action. Its perceived enemies were aristocrats and the '*gros*' – big merchants, speculators, middlemen and financiers. It advocated taxes on the rich and price controls. It drew on Republican discourses about the 'independent citizen' and an idealised discourse of the workshop contrasting the integrity of productive craftsmen – masters *and* journeymen – with the vices of parasitic elites. This was not yet the class discourse of an embryonic proletariat. Some *sans culottes* were small employers whose emphasis on independence made them suspicious of servants and day-labourers. Jacobin concessions to their demands were largely tactical, since popular support was needed to 'save the Revolution'. Eventually Robespierre clamped down on the popular movement and imposed wage as well as price controls. However, a myth of the Jacobins was later nurtured by Buonarrotti and Blanqui which, by 1848, transformed them into embryonic social democrats. After 1794 the popular movement itself disintegrated, its activists hounded and arrested, their workshops ruined. Yet memories of the Year II lingered on in popular cafés and Parisian *faubourgs*.

The 'radical artisan', defending his independence against industrial capitalism, has become the culture hero of early labour movements. Yet myths of a golden age of the craft workshop may bear little relationship to the realities of the world of work. Soboul assumed that *sans culotte* political ideology emerged from master/journeyman solidarities and shared pride in craft labour. Yet stable workshops with amicable master/journeyman relations were already rare. Rural proto-industry was undercutting guild producers. Many Faubourg St Antoine workers made cheap furniture outside guild controls. Division of labour was emerging in tailoring. Most journeymen stayed only briefly in a given workshop. Masters wanted strengthened guild controls to discipline insubordinate journeymen, who welcomed Turgot's 1770s attempt to abolish guilds as a measure against hierarchy within the trades – unaware that the logic of a free market would produce a world in which craft skills, apprenticeship and quality production would all be in jeopardy (Truant 1994).

Journeymen's *compagnonnages* were strong in central and southern France, particularly among single workers in construction trades. Older, sedentary workers tended to join *confrèries*. Since *compagnonnages* found lodgings and jobs for 'tramping' journeymen and organised boycotts of 'bad' employers, one might view them as embryonic trade unions. However, their division into three *devoirs* – each with a foundation myth claiming origins in Solomon's Temple! – suggests that they accentuated rivalries within the world of work. *Devoirs* had initiation rituals involving blindfolds and oaths. *Compagnons* had sobriquets, often of a warlike nature, and carried staves, adorned with coloured ribbons, used in brawls (*rixes*) with members of rival *devoirs* or different trades. *Compagnons* participated in regular drinking rituals. This was a culture prizing virility and violence. Rather than being 'traditional' organisations, *compagnonnages* were a response to a world of labour in transition. Corporate structures were disintegrating, the distinctiveness of individual skills increasingly blurred. Membership of a *devoir* allowed journeymen to construct a symbolic 'pecking order', to assert in ritual forms their differences from other, almost identical, workers in order to claim job monopolies in specific locations. Hence the survival of semi-clandestine *compagnonnages* after 1800 could be viewed as an *obstacle* to solidarity which a nascent 'labour movement' needed to overcome (Truant 1994).

Between the 1790s and 1830, workers participated in strikes, Luddism, food riots and inter-*compagnonnage rixes*. But prefects, armed with the Le Chapelier Law (1791) banning workers' associations, rarely viewed labour unrest as a major threat. It lacked coherent ideology or leadership. Labour policy during the Restoration was ambiguous. Pressure from business lobbies ensured that the Ministry of Commerce remained faithful to free-market ideologies introduced by the Revolution. However, ministers made neo-corporatist gestures to woo artisans, lending an ear to masters who wanted guilds restored to guarantee the quality of French craft production and restore order to the workshops. Policy towards *compagnonnages* proved ambivalent. Their clandestine existence and brawls were generally tolerated, but prefects intervened if they organised boycotts of employers. Less ritualistic and bellicose were mutual aid societies, whose Parisian membership quadrupled to 30,000 during the 1820s. These insisted on sobriety and 'dignity', disapproved of brawling and, unlike *confrèries*, were largely secular. Societies recruited from a single trade sometimes played a role in strikes, as in the Paris furniture trade in 1820–21 (Sibalis 1989).

This was a world in transition. Corporate structures were recalled with nostalgia by some craftsmen and paternalist officials. Free-market ideology was increasingly dominant, yet often resented. Authorities wavered between tolerance and repression of vestiges of workers' corporate organisations. Workers' oscillated between discourses of neo-corporatism, 'moral economy' and Revolutionary rights. Introduction of machinery provoked Luddite out-bursts – if fewer than in Britain. There were a hundred major incidents, fifteen involving serious violence. Many occurred in 1816–19 and 1830–31. Woollen towns such as Vienne were favoured locations. Employers admitted that machines would free them from the 'tyranny' of labour by undermining skilled workers' control of production processes. Threatened wool-croppers or handloomers appealed to the King, describing themselves as loyal family men. Such deferential rhetoric was often combined with threats against employers. In southern mill-town Lodève there were undercurrents of Republicanism. The Hérault prefect voiced the authorities' ambivalence. Describing cropping machines as an 'inevitable evil', he promised charity to redundant workers but threatened to prosecute the 'factious'. Nord prefect Villeneuve-Bargemont lamented that free-market policies both increased national wealth and denied workers bread (Perrot 1978).

The year 1830 was a watershed. A new consciousness was generated by political experiences rather than by any transformation of the structures of the labour force. In the 1820s bourgeois liberals sought popular allies for their struggle against the Bourbons, persuading printers that censorship posed a threat to their jobs. This 'alliance of "*blouse*" and frock-coat' rapidly disinte-grated once victorious Orleanists failed to offer political or social concessions. But during the political upheavals of 1829–31 city workers came into contact with 'advanced' elements of the middle class – St Simonian students and radical Republicans. Workers appropriated from St Simonian discourse the contrast between productive industrial and parasitic rentier classes, giving it a populist twist by identifying workers as the truly productive class. Soon the working class was described as the source of the nation's wealth, its mission one of self-emancipation. Lyon silkweavers who sent funds to aid striking St. Etienne miners addressed them as 'fellow workers'. Workers were no longer 'the mob' or the 'rabble' (*canaille*) – nor *gens de métier* linked to members of the same craft. The invention of the working class allowed workers in differ-ent cities and trades to claim that they shared a common identity and simi-lar grievances and interests.

The July insurrection was dominated by artisans, notably from the building trades. However, popular insurgents, lacking a coherent ideology or programme, were easily seduced by 'fine liberal phrases'. When an auton-omous workerist consciousness eventually surfaced, the window of political opportunity was already closing. By 1831 artisans were demanding the franchise, association rights, checks on the introduction of machinery and job-creation programmes. To the Orleanist elites 'liberty' meant something different – the franchise for men of property, freedom to introduce new machinery and work practices. As the new regime clamped down on popular militancy it became clear that participation in the Revolution had transformed many workers' mentality. Thousands of artisans joined the Republican *Société des Droits de L'Homme* (SDH). A. Colin's *Le Cri du Peuple* (1831) articulated the sense of 'betrayal' by bourgeois who had posed as friends but now revealed themselves as a new 'financial aristocracy'. Workers, the 'useful' class, should put aside craft divisions and stand together. Colin articulated a metanarrative in which the revolution was completed with a 'happy ending' in which workers secured the fruits of their labour. Workers would struggle against bourgeois oppressors whose pious law-and-order rhetoric was shamelessly hypocritical, since they themselves had come to power via insurrection! Scornful of bourgeois depiction of the 'criminal', 'dangerous' mob, Colin's discourse portrayed workers as imbued with the dignity of labour, 'proletarians' and proud of it (Judt 1986; Faure and Rancière 1976).

The radical artisan?
The decades after 1830 marked the apogee of artisan radicalism. Handloom-weavers faced competition from factory-based machine production. Tailors and shoemakers were threatened by a division of labour which enabled merchants to employ female labour to produce ready-made goods for an expanding petty bourgeois market. Craftsmen were forced to work longer hours for lower rates. Merchant capitalists were increasingly dominant, providing orders and raw materials, marketing finished items, supplying credit for weaving masters to purchase Jacquard looms, and dominating industrial disputes tribunals (*Conseils des Prud'hommes*). Young workers' chances of an apprenticeship were receding, as were journeymen's prospects of establishing their own workshop. Industrialisation also multiplied opportunities for skilled metal workers and engineers, while urban renewal projects provided employment for building craftsmen in a construction sector little affected by technological changes. However, even 'threatened' artisans possessed a range of resources which could be mobilised. Their skills remained essential in the production of fancy silks, fashions, decorated porcelains or furniture. Many adapted flexibly to innovations such as Jacquard looms or metal printing presses. Ownership of workshops and tools gave a degree of independence. Artisan quartiers such as Faubourg St Antoine, where 72 per cent of Paris furniture-makers lived, provided neighbourhood solidarities and allies among small shopkeepers and café-owners in whose establishments artisans spent work breaks. Semi-clandestine journeymen's *compagnonnages* survived from the ancien régime. Most artisans were literate, and artisan-run newspapers proliferated. Martin Nadaud ran classes for fellow Limousin migrant building workers, teaching both basic literacy and 'love of the Republic'. Many militants were autodidacts who, like locksmith Gilland, graduated from cheap *romans-feuilletons* to Rousseau and Socrates! Activists read aloud in cafés and workshops from Cabet's pioneering socialist *Le Populaire*, whose circulation figure of 5000 thus

disguised a much wider audience. Literate artisans were respected by fellow workers who used them as scribes and interpreters of official documents.

Some moved from narrow craft consciousness towards an inclusive class awareness, recognising that artisans in different trades faced similar problems and that mobilising the unskilled was essential since it was among this reserve army of labour that capitalists recruited to undercut craft workers. Artisan radicalism took a variety of forms. Parisian insurrections from 1789 to 1848, and beyond, were dominated by artisans. After 1830 producer and consumer cooperatives and mutual aid societies emerged, some acting as fronts for strike organisation, as with Parisian tailors in 1840. As many as 90 per cent of strikes in 1830–48 were artisanal. Strike leaders such as shoemaker Efrahem had contacts with the Republican SDH. Use of troops to arrest pickets exacerbated workers' sense of injustice. The role of lawyers such as Cabet as defence counsels for arrested strikers strengthened ties between artisan militants and bourgeois radicals. Denied access to electoral politics and freedom of association or assembly, the embryonic labour movement was driven to employ a range of less orthodox outlets. Some militants flirted with Blanquist secret societies which dreamed of a revolutionary coup. Others found opportunities to express egalitarian sentiments in popular song-groups (Prothero 1997; Sewell 1980; Moss 1976; Johnson 1974; Rudé 1973).

Artisanal cities were more militant than factory towns. The 'Rome of socialism' was Lyon. Praising its 'enlightened fanaticism', Proudhon lamented that he would 'never find a second city like it'. After suppression of worker insurrections there in 1831 and 1834, a worker-run press and mutualist and cooperative projects emerged. In 1844 there were strikes against targeted employers. Weavers were the key figures in a city which was the capital of the European silk industry; 40,000 of the city's 190,000 population worked in the industry, 400 merchants provided orders and raw materials for several thousand master weavers (*canuts*) who were assisted by 25,000 journeymen and auxiliary workers. International competition pushed merchants to cut costs by moving 'plain' weaving to peasant-workers in the hinterland. By 1847, 47 per cent of looms were outside the city. Silk preparation and spinning was done by peasant girls in convent workshops, supervised by nuns. Government rejection of demands for the restoration of fixed wage rates levels (*tarifs*) had provoked the 1831 revolt. Radical culture in Lyon was distinctive. Master *canuts*, the key cadres, were small employers yet were obliged to carry the *livret*, the workers' pass-book introduced by the Napoleonic Code. They *identified themselves* as workers. Joseph Benoît, a master who was a socialist deputy in 1849, entitled his autobiography *Confessions d'un Prolétaire*. A united front with journeymen was possible because they faced a common threat from the merchants. Journeymen lodged with masters in the Croix-Rousse weaving district. They both participated in flourishing consumer cooperatives, the purpose of which was to maintain the viability of small workshops by reducing food expenditure. Their newspaper, *Echo de la Fabrique*, portrayed weavers as sober craftsmen whose 'artistry' provided France with quality exports (Bezucha 1974; Stewart-McDougall 1984).

Tailors were hit by the rise of the ready-made clothing sector (*confection*). While 74 per cent of workers in Parisian bespoke tailoring in 1848 were workshop-based male craftsmen, 60 per cent of *confection* employees were seamstresses working from home. Tailors, shoemakers and handloom weavers provided the activists in Cabet's Icarian socialist movement (Johnson 1974). Although artisans had a range of strategies and idioms available, the dominant discourse was that of 'associationist' socialism. 'Associations', lamented Thiers, 'are the malady of the age' (Vincent 1984). Producer cooperation offered the prospect of introducing new technology under the control of workers themselves. Associationists accepted private ownership of workshops by working masters but denounced a free-market system which eulogised ruthless competition, treated labour as a 'commodity', undermined skills, reduced wages and generated overproduction crises. It demanded *tarifs*, controls on new machinery and hours reductions to redistribute employment more equitably. It developed through interaction between artisan activists and ideologists who articulated ideas circulating in the workshops, made explicit strategic choices available and coined slogans such as 'social workshops', 'organisation of work', and 'right to work' which popularised the movement's message. Louis Blanc urged alliance with bourgeois radicals to build a democratic Republic which would supply orders and credit facilities to large producer cooperatives in each sector. Buchez gave lower priority to politics and the state. He attracted support from the ex-artisan journalists who ran *L'Atelier* – who equated associationist values with a Christian fraternity neglected by a hierarchical Church. More pluralistic than Blanc, they envisaged a multiplicity of small cooperatives. They helped publicise strike petitions and articulate opposition to private job agencies and employer domination of *Prud'hommes*. Their insistence that to win respect of, workers must appear sober and industrious, was shared by P.-J. Proudhon. Trained as a printer, Proudhon was a prickly maverick who delighted in paradoxes. Although virulently anti-clerical, his views on women were traditionalist – even misogynistic. Despite coining the phrase 'property is theft', he supported small artisan and peasant property, articulating the concerns of a stratum of (master) artisans such as Lyon *canuts* desperate to defend their work-cultures and avoid the factory. Suspicious of Blanc's state cooperatives and of Republican politics, he favoured apolitical mutualism and a worker-run People's Bank. He viewed skilled labour as the prerequisite for workers' dignity and morality, but feared that workers, corrupted by capitalism, lacked the *virtu* to construct a better society (Berenson 1984; Fitzpatrick 1985).

Urging scepticism about linking 'professional situation, militant practice and ideological statements', Rancière (1989) claimed that the 'radical artisan' was a *construct* of two groups – intellectuals and autodidact former craftsmen such as *L'Atelier* journalists now remote from workshop realities. They *invented* the figure of the proud craftsman in order to refute bourgeois slanders about 'lazy', 'immoral', drunken workers. This myth was misleading. Their image of the austere artisan risked confirming conservative assertions that the mass of ordinary workers were hedonistic and feckless. Militant trades such as shoemaking or tailoring were increasingly 'vile' – their workers 'sweated', deskilled, demoralised. Radical tailors, viewing the workshop as a 'hell without poetry', dreamed less of reforming than of escaping from it. Few wished to spend their lives sewing *petit point*! Militants yearned to travel, write poetry. Worker poets were advised by intellectuals to write 'authentic' verse about their trades, but they wanted to write Romantic poetry about love! The memoirs of decorative painter P. Deruneau tell of visits to museums and art galleries and of drowning sorrows in taverns, but are silent on workplace experiences. Agricol Perdiguier found his furniture job fatiguing and stultifying and dreamed of hills and fresh air. Artisans' aspirations were not confined to the worlds of work. They wanted to be citizens, to be treated with dignity and to have wider cultural opportunities (Rancière 1989; McWilliam 2000).

Rather than seeking the seeds of radicalism in artisanal culture, some emphasise French workers' unique *political* relationship with a neo-Jacobin bourgeoisie. Both London and New York had tens of thousands of artisanal workers. If French workers aspired to be equal Republican citizens it was their *political* experiences of Parisian insurrections which provided the explanation. But the path from craft to class awareness was not smooth. Rather than viewing artisans as an embryonic working class, one might categorise them as 'reactionary radicals' – their militancy nurtured by a hatred of industrial capitalism and a desire to *avoid* becoming industrial proletarians. Such passions gave their mobilisations real ferocity, but were of limited relevance to workers in mills and mines or to the mass of casual and female labour. Artisans who valued 'manly independence' worried about the reactionary consequences of enfranchising 'dependent' servants, unskilled workers and women (Judt 1986; Calhoun 1983; Moss 1993).

There were tensions within the artisan world. Master/journeyman solidarity could be strained even in the Lyon silk industry. Many master-weavers were mature men – cautious, sober, eager to refute bourgeois slanders about 'feckless', 'immoral' workers. They were involved in mutualist and cooperative projects and in the workers' press, and aspired to enter electoral politics. Their journeymen, single and more volatile, enjoyed the hedonistic culture of cafés, song groups and Carnival, and were keen on direct action and violent confrontation. Benoît saw the 1848 revolution as premature, because most journeymen, even in Lyon, lacked the maturity and education to sustain a viable popular Republic. Tensions erupted where cost-cutting pressures obliged masters to reduce wages, as in Paris tailoring. Many industrial court cases involved disputes between masters and journeymen. Similar tensions in the construction industry are revealed by the complex Parisian career of Martin Nadaud. Though a radical Republican, active in strikes, Nadaud was a skilled mason with aspirations to become a building contractor. He sometimes acted as a *tâcheron* – a subcontractor who organised workgangs. Yet in 1848 building workers demanded the abolition of this hated subcontracting system. The workplace was often a site of conflict and divisions. Many artisans were doubtful that producer cooperatives could really emancipate them from the wage system. For some they were simply a refuge in periods when, as after 1834, repression closed off other outlets for labour politics. Others resorted to them as pragmatic responses to unemployment, or as a form of collective subcontracting. Associationism also also offered a convenient discourse for bourgeois Republicans keen to woo worker allies. Cooperatives could appear an anodyne alternative to more militant forms of popular mobilisation – strikes or insurrections (Prothero 1997; Stewart-McDougall 1984). There were other divisions within the artisanal world. If many artisans were anti-clerical, there were enclaves of popular Catholicism in towns like Nîmes and Marseille. Mutual aid society regulations excluded the unrespectable and the alcoholic, and often women. The radical artisan was quintessentially male. Tailors blamed 'sweating' on the influx of seamstresses into their trade and advocated the return of women to the home. One response of Lyon silkworkers to competition from female workers employed in the convent workshops was to burn them down! Many family workshops only survived by 'sweating' wives and daughters.

Yet one cannot dismiss the radical artisan as a myth. The artisan movement had its divisions, flaws and myopias, partly defining itself against unskilled and female 'others'. Yet France *did* possess Europe's most radical popular culture. Factory workers were more militant in towns like Rheims with a sizeable artisan presence. The qualities of the 'ideal type' artisan – pride in skills, a desire for autonomy in the workplace and for respect as a citizen, and willingness to take direct action – were prerequisites for the development of a radical public sphere distinct from that of the liberal bourgeoisie. The 'location' of this was often outside the workplace. Cafés were centres of occupational and neighbourhood solidarities, sites for discussion, newspaper reading rooms, job agencies, strike headquarters. They housed song-clubs (*goguettes*) which featured the radical songs of Pierre Dupont and which were, socialist jewellery-engraver Vinçard claimed, a 'powerful school of patriotic education'. Paris artisans were theatregoers, delighting in political innuendo, hissing upper-class and clerical villains. There was no unbridgeable gulf between the 'serious' culture of artisanal self-education and politics and a wider, hedonistic culture of cafés, *bals* and popular sociability. Nadaud won a reputation among fellow masons for his work skills, for running evening classes, and for being handy with his fists! Workers who read cheap popular novels – *romans-feuilletons* – could read into them a critique of a society where poverty and exploitation led inexorably to crime. *Goguettes*, which rejoiced in names such as 'Sons of the Devil', mixed the Rabelaisian with the political (Prothero 1997).

Rancière's scepticism is exaggerated. Canuts were fiercely protective of their reputation for quality silks. Furniture-makers took pride in their 'artistry'. Perdiguier claimed that a cabinet-maker shared Michaelangelo's concern to combinine mathematics and beauty. Sadly, Vinçard observed, artisans, like artists, were obliged to prostitute their talents to the crass commercialism of market society. Rather than accepting the factory system and then fighting for lower hours, artisans emphasised that one's integrity depended on producing only goods which satisfied professional standards. Concern with the aesthetics of labour, and to express symbolic rejection of market values, led some to spend time completing their 'masterpiece' (*chef d'oeuvre*). Possibly artisans' passion for labour was a morbid pathology which unwittingly made them complicit with capitalism. Perhaps it was a defiant assertion of identity. Many clearly viewed pride in 'quality', threats to their trades and dreams of an egalitarian Republic as interconnected issues. A letter from Lyon to Parisian tailors expressed alarm at threats to the 'artistry of the craft . . . , that superior elegance which brings honour to French industry. You are . . . aware of the catastrophe besetting our industry. It was in Paris that those soulless speculators – who see nothing in life but money, who push us towards concentration of commerce and who reject all sentiments of humanity – first saw the light of day'. Such capitalists represented a total denial of the motto 'Liberty, Equality, Fraternity' which adorned public buildings (Auslander 1993; McWilliam 2000; Liebmann 1980).

Beyond the artisanate

Militancy was low among proletarians in large-scale industry. Comprising 30 per cent of the labour force, they were involved in under 10 per cent of strikes, and rarely formed mutual aid societies or political groups. But there were variations within and between sectors and regions. The image of textile mill-towns was established by bourgeois 'experts' whose reports permutated a stock litany of phrases, combining 'miserabilist' tropes about the horrors of factory and slum life with a pervasive moralism which blamed workers' conditions on their own 'immorality'. Long hours in unhealthy mills exposed workers to industrial accidents and TB. Female factory labour weakened family ties. Child labour led to low school attendance. Alcoholism and prostitution were rife. Fatalism was more prevalent than revolt, as wills bowed to the trinity of 'factory regulations, boss and machine'. Low literacy limited the influence of radical propaganda. Recent migrants were disorientated, lacking community or corporate solidarities. With the exception of those involving male engineers or textile printers, strikes were brief and unorganised. Unskilled machine-minders were easily replaced if they did strike. The requirement to carry the *livret* facilitated blacklisting of activists.

Historians' reliance on such stereotypes has been questioned. Millworkers with experience of 'protoindustrial' textile work may have been closer to artisans than usually assumed. Perceiving themselves as 'paying' mill-owners for raw materials, heat and light and 'selling' them the finished cloth or yarn, they behaved more as independent producers than as waged proletarians. Measuring their militancy via strike levels is problematic. Some disputes did reveal a degree of sophistication. When 8000 Rouen workers withdrew their labour in August 1830 they contrasted 'freedom' proclaimed by the Orleanist regime with the draconian discipline in the mills. During the Lille spinners' strike in 1839 against fraudulent measurement of their yarn, they were supported by a solidarity fund from neighbouring mills. The leaders were jailed, but the issue of fraud was revived by a Republican Union of Spinners in 1848. Employers congratulated themselves on the relative 'calm' of mill towns in the post-1845 depression. Yet a report by liberal economist Blanqui, commissioned by Rouen employers, suggested that beneath workers' 'docility' lay resentment at speed-ups, rising accident rates and falling wages. In Midi towns woollen mills were established in the 1770s, spinning and carding mechanised in the 1800s. Third-generation millworkers developed solidarities. Some disputes in Lodève involved resistance to mechanised power looms, but even wage strikes showed signs of planning – with strikers targeting mills with full order books, then trying to extend wage concessions to neighbouring mills. The town became a 'red' bastion in 1848 (Reddy 1984; Johnson 1995).

During the July Monarchy annual coal production quintupled to five million tons. Deeper mines with heavy capital investment developed. Yet many miners remained quasi-peasants. Decazeville managers saw this as a mixed blessing. Such workers were immune from radical urban ideologies. But their disappearance at harvests and *fêtes* constituted an 'annual tribute that we pay to the farm'. Paternalist schemes – company housing, free medical provision – were used to construct a reliable, loyal labour force and reduce labour turnover. Anzin offered coal-sorting employment to miners' wives and daughters. Yet even paternalist companies were not immune to labour disputes. In 1833 troops were used to break an Anzin strike against tough labour discipline imposed in new, deeper pits. Protest was more organised in the Loire coalfield in 1844, where the monopolistic *Compagnie des Mines de la Loire* (CML) – employing 70 per cent of the region's 5000 miners – was blamed for escalating accident rates caused by increased work-pace. Miners' demands to control their own mutual aid society won local community sympathy. Strike leaders received heavy jail sentences because the authorities were alarmed by the political influence of local radical silk-weavers and glass-workers on the miners' anti-monopoly discourse (Reid 1985; Hanagan 1989).

Towards 1848
In the 1840s, government rejection of electoral reform encouraged a tactical alliance between Republicans, disaffected strata of the petty bourgeoisie and workers. If some workers remained suspicious of Republicans, others welcomed their provision of defence lawyers for arrested strikers. Nadaud felt flattered when congratulated by a Republican student for reading a radical paper in a *cabinet de lecture*. In Toulouse, once a bastion of popular Catholic-Royalism, Republicans played upon workers' growing anti-clericalism, adopted associationist rhetoric and tapped resentments at neglect of the region by Parisian economic elites. In Toulon, Republicans' 'democratic patronage' was crucial for the emerging labour movement. The insular conservatism of native Provençal workers was eroded by the influx into the naval dockyards of northern metal- and wood-workers. Defeat of the 1845 dockyard strike failed to disrupt close relations between worker militants and progressive bourgeois strata – Republican lawyers, St. Simonian naval engineers – who advocated an alliance of the 'productive' classes of the town. In Nantes, Republican doctor Guépin won workers' gratitude through medical work in the slums (Aminzade 1993; Agulhon 1970).

After 1845, France experienced a combination of a 'new' overproduction and 'traditional' – Labroussean – crises. Poor harvests triggered rising grain prices, a consequent fall in consumer goods' sales and rising unemployment. Mortality rates rose sharply, as did petty theft and vagabondage. Crowds attacked grain convoys, forcing traders to sell grain at a 'just price'. Calls for vengeance on 'hoarders' and 'speculators' mingled with cries of 'down with the bourgeoisie!'. Protesters included textile and mine workers, rail navvies, quarrymen and proto-industrial workers. With 25 per cent of the Nord population dependent on poor relief, the crisis highlighted the inadequacy of a welfare system in which a patchy network of underfunded *Bureaux de Bienfaisance* had to be supplemented by Catholic charities, subsidy of grain purchases by paternalist employers and improvised governmental provision of food coupons. Much protest was inchoate and 'apolitical'. There were attacks on Belgian immigrants in the Nord, and Luddism. But workers condemned charity as 'demeaning' and insisted on their 'right' to welfare – evidence, some argued, of the influence of pernicious socialist ideologies. With National Guard units reluctant to intervene, the army was used. Shootings in Lille and Mulhouse further weakened the regime's already shaky legitimacy.

Workers and the Second Republic (1848–51)

The Second Republic was a defining moment in the 'making' of the working class. Insurgents who overthrew Orleanism in February 1848, remembering the 'betrayal' of 1830, demanded a Republic with male suffrage, the right to work and an 11-hour day. National Workshops were established for the jobless – 60 per cent of the Parisian workforce. A 'workers' parliament' – the Luxemburg Commission – was established to debate labour problems. Unions were legalised. Cooperatives and mutual aid societies mushroomed. Workers joined political clubs which organised the April 1848 election campaign. Workers entered the Limoges National Guard. Election in 1848 proved disappointing. But in 1849 workers were prominent in a broad-left *Démocrate-Socialiste* coalition which secured 36 per cent of the vote in the May elections. Its programme of rail and mine nationalisation, state support for cooperatives, progressive income tax and free secular education, made it Europe's first mass socialist party. Its deputies included silkweaver Benoît and stonemason Nadaud. But conservative notables shrewdly manipulated peasant fears of the 'red peril'. In April 1848 radicals won barely 100 of 800 parliamentary seats.

Faced with a conservative government and continued unemployment, workers vented their frustrations in direct action. Troops suppressed riots in Rouen and Limoges, where radical urban voters had been 'swamped' by conservative ballots from the surrounding countryside. Parisian artisans grumbled at demeaning navvying jobs in the National Workshops, but their closure provoked a June insurrection, suppressed by troops, National Guards and paramilitary *Gardes Mobiles*, which left 1500 dead and 11,000 arrested. Historians have provided nuanced analysis of the forces on either side of the barricades, but contemporaries as diverse as Marx and Tocqueville saw this as a class war. Workers were now on the defensive. Clubs were banned, co-operatives harassed, cafés subjected to curfews. In the December 1851 coup, Lyon workers awoke to find cannon trained on the Croix-Rousse. But the city had existed under a state of siege since mid-1849. Workers grew cynical as hopes faded. Some had the edge of their discontent smoothed by falling food prices and improving job prospects, although recovery remained fragile until the coup reassured worried investors.

French workers had mobilised on an unprecedented scale. Thousands who attended Paris clubs had their consciousness raised by a crash course in political education (Amann 1975). However, defeat was not just due to coercive state power or *notables'* manipulation of rural voters. Fault lines of gender, religion, ethnicity, age and skill in the embryonic working class had been exposed. Anti-Belgian xenophobia disfigured popular protests in the Nord. Catholic workers in the Gard retained legitimist loyalties. Male tailors demanded exclusion of 'docile' seamstresses from the clothing industry. Most activists were skilled, male workers in artisanal towns. Sustained militancy was rare among factory workers, miners or metallurgy workers who often proved ideologically naïve, vulnerable to seduction by Bonapartist populism or company paternalism. Activists disagreed over strategy. Should one ally with bourgeois radicals who headed the *Dem-Soc* electoral coalition, aim for an autonomous workers' party or put faith in Proudhonist mutualism – or in insurrection? Nevertheless, labour did pose a challenge to bourgeois hegemony. Marx came to argue that immature workers had allowed themselves to acquiesce to bourgeois leadership, seduced by utopian chimeras of salvation of petty production through cooperatives and cheap credit. Further industrialisation was the prerequisite for successful revolution. Some portray 1848 as a watershed between 'archaic' modes of protest – tax and food riots, Luddism – and 'modern' electoral or union mobilisation. Hence the Second Republic constituted an 'apprenticeship' in political democracy. Others question Marx's assumptions of the primacy of the industrial proletariat, emphasising that the real revolutionaries were not factory workers whose jobs and identity were dependent on industrial capitalism, but artisans – 'reactionary radicals' who were fundamentally threatened by it (Tilly 1972; Calhoun 1983).

Patterns of mobilisation

Applicants for compensation for injuries sustained in the February rising were provincial-born craftsmen. Their profile resembles that of the 1830 insurgents, but their average age – thirty-five – was higher. They constituted a 'revolutionary generational cohort', with memories of earlier insurrections, in which 14 per cent of them had participated. But 11,000 June Days insurgents offer a broader base for analysis. Unskilled and 'lumpen' elements constituted under 3 per cent; 3000 were metal and building craftsmen – 4 per cent of the workforce in these trades. Most worked in small firms, though some engineers came from the La Chapelle locomotive works; 2230 were furniture makers and tailors. Print and luxury trades were less heavily represented, as were small masters. Of petty bourgeois insurgents, 191 (9 per cent) were winesellers. Cafés remained central to the sociability of popular quartiers. Many insurgents were arrested after tip-offs from landlords with whom they were in rent disputes. Conversely some arrested insurgents received character references from employers! (Tilly and Lees 1983). Analysis of the *Gardes Mobiles* who helped suppress the rising questions straightforward correlations between artisans and militancy. Rejecting Marx's claim that these were drawn from 'lumpen' elements – that the bourgeoisie recruited the 'dangerous classes' to restore order! – Traugott (1985) claims that they belonged to the very trades which supplied the bulk of insurgents. 'Organisational experience' supplied the link between class position and class identity. *Gardes* were recruited, isolated from Parisian politics and supplied with guns, uniforms, training and indoctrination. One could also explain the *gardes'* conduct in terms of their youth. Their average age was around twenty. Possibly government recruited them precisely because they had weaker family or workplace loyalties and were more malleable. Many had been laid off or had apprenticeships curtailed in the economic slump. Few were yet socialised into the cultures of their crafts. Some nursed resentments at bullying meted out to workshop newcomers by established artisans (Traugott 1985).

Debates among the 669 Luxembourg delegates illuminate artisans' grievances. Sewell (1980) detected in these a transition from craft corporatism to class consciousness and an associationist vision of emancipation of workers from the wage system. Judt is more sceptical, arguing that they still mobilised under craft banners. By entering candidates from each trade they split the workers' vote in April 1848. Many concerns were pragmatic – enforcement of hours limitations and of a minimum wage in each sector. They denounced competition from prison labour and subcontracting, and advocated public labour exchanges. But cooperative production was central to their vision of a 'federative trade socialism' in which state credit and orders would allow cooperatives to eliminate middlemen and to share out work. Cooperation was not merely a pragmatic response to unemployment nor simply a 'retreat' by labour after the setbacks of 1848. Throughout the spring, workers from varied ideological backgrounds debated an associationism which would cover most trades. The June Days weakened hopes of state support, though *L'Atelier* collaborated with Cavaignac's government which offered subsidies for mixed employer/worker cooperatives. Others sought to reverse the electoral disasters of 1848, arguing that cooperatives needed the backing of a social Republic. Some shared Proudhon's disillusionment with politics and urged workers to focus on mutualist projects. During 1848–49, 50,000 Parisian workers from 120 trades participated in 300 cooperative ventures. But with even apolitical mutualism viewed as 'subversive', police harassed and prosecuted dozens of associations. Others collapsed because of internal frictions or financial problems. The large Clichy tailors' cooperative ran into difficulties because of shortage of capital and disputes over labour discipline and distribution of dividends (Sewell 1980; Judt 1986; Moss 1976).

Solidarities between silk masters and journeymen were central to Lyon labour politics. Both felt threatened by big merchants, and residential solidarities of the Croix-Rousse underpinned their strength. As many as 74 per cent of weaver households had co-resident members in the silk trade. By contrast artisans in other sectors were dispersed throughout the city, with only 28 per cent of co-residents from their trades. In 1848, Lyon had 150 clubs with 8000 members. Their disciplined electoral tactics led to success for worker candidates. Cooperative and mutualist ventures multiplied in the aftermath of the June Days – many 'fronts' for political clubs. But political violence was always close to the surface. In 1848 a workers' paramilitary, *Les Voraces*, patrolled the city and occupied the fortifications. In June 1849 a rash assault on the town hall by 15,000 workers led to 25 deaths and 800 arrests, providing an excuse to introduce a state of siege and dismiss radical councillors. This lapse reflected generational and cultural tensions within the silk-weaving community. Older masters favoured careful planning, electoral strategies, mutualism and self-education. Younger journeymen, despairing of establishing their own workshops, were volatile and sympathetic to direct action. Though labour was now on the defensive, the prefect reported a defiant popular mood. 'To be a socialist here . . . is a sort of profession of faith – in conformity with which one regulates relationships from the workshop to the secret society to the barricade. Strong class and party discipline reigns due to 20 years of conflict' (Stewart-McDougall 1984; Liebmann 1980).

Patterns of mobilisation in Marseille reflected the fragmentation of its working population. Unskilled immigrants participated in riots, rarely in organised politics. Those in 'closed' trades such as stevedores had secure niches in the port and passed on jobs to their sons. Native-born Provençal speakers, suspicious of 'outsiders', had their own *confrèries* and a tradition of Catholic-Royalism. Only 30 per cent in 'open' trades such as shoemaking or tailoring were local-born. They were receptive to 'outside' ideologies and their religious practice was lower. Comprising 28 per cent of the labour force, they made up 47 per cent of club or cooperative activists or those arrested for political militancy. However, mobilisation during the Second Republic did produce discernible shifts in attitudes. Dissemination of discourses about the 'working class' led to a questioning of identities. Stevedores in the National Guard proved reluctant to fire on fellow workers. By 1851, 5 per cent of militants under police surveillance were dockworkers (Sewell 1988).

Ideological militancy among proletarian workers before 1848 was rare, but the circumstances of the Second Republic facilitated the contagious spread of popular protest. Textile mill-towns witnessed increased militancy as the fatalism with which workers had responded to the 1846 slump had shattered. Rouen workers denounced 'demeaning' charity and blamed 'arrogant' employers for mechanisation which led to overproduction and unemployment. There were Luddite outbursts, attacks on jails to release prisoners and post-election riots in April 1848. Denunciation of industrial *seigneurs* mingled with calls for a social Republic. In 1849, socialists won 32 per cent of the vote. However, Rouen had few artisans to act as intermediaries between the *Dem-Soc* leadership and the rank-and-file. Sporadic violence by mill-workers pushed the city's middle class towards the Right. Cooperative/associationist discourse had little appeal to a proletarianised labour force. Republicans utilised classic tropes about immiserated workers existing on subsistence wages and dwelling in foul slums. This discourse was not fully congruent with actual grievances and aspirations of cotton operatives who still perceived themselves as quasi-independent producers 'selling' their product to the mill-owner, and resented their lack of influence over hiring and fraudulent measurement of yarn and cloth which they produced. Alongside unorganised protests – food riots, Luddism – in the Nord, there were signs of a politicised unrest. Embryonic unions emerged, particularly among skilled mill maintenance engineers, textile printers and wool-combers. Strikers attempted to coordinate actions in Lille, Roubaix and Tourcoing. Consumer cooperatives multiplied. However, workers proved vulnerable to the seductive populism of Louis Napoleon, political clubs were rare and Left-wing voting modest. Imprisonment of a handful of militants after 1849 was sufficient to break resistance to imposition of new piecework payments systems (Reddy 1984; Aminzade 1993).

Labour's prospects in Alsace did not appear promising. Protestant textile employers were tough paternalists practising divide and rule strategies. Alongside the 'usual' divisions of skill and gender, labour was fragmented along ethnic, linguistic and religious lines, between French and German speakers, natives and Swiss immigrants, Protestants and Catholics. Yet, aided by votes from radicalised peasants and petty bourgeois, the Left dominated the 1848–49 elections. Alsace had rallied to the French Revolution and had a developed sense of French Republican identity. It sheltered German radical exiles and was acutely aware of the proximity of reactionary forces across the frontier. Alsatian textiles specialised in upmarket products and employed a high percentage of skilled workers – textile printers, machine-makers – who, together with tavern-keepers and teachers, supplied the socialist cadres. They took advantage of the weakening hold of paternalist projects, which employers found prohibitively costly during the slump, to assert control over mutual aid societies. Radical secret societies mushroomed in 1850–51. Alsatian electors voted 'no' in the post-coup plebiscite (Harvey 2001).

In April 1848, Decazeville's manager warned workers that revolutionary upheaval threatened their jobs, ran militants out of town and told Republican authorities 'I am the master here, more so than the Provisional Government in Paris'. Similar management tactics in other company towns did not always prevent trouble. A radical engineer was elected in Le Creusot in 1849. But Schneider soon exacted revenge, sacking militants and calling in troops to break strikes. Anzin followed a similar trajectory of radical electoral victory followed by punitive sackings. The most sustained coalfield militancy occurred in the Loire, where a coalition of radical lawyers and ribbon-weavers helped mobilise support for miners' struggles against the oppressive CML coal monopoly. Miners demanded control of their own mutual aid society, electing safety delegates and independent doctors, and eventual nationalisation (Reid 1985; Hanagan 1989).

The politics of democratic socialism
After the June Days, workers had the options of retreating into apolitical mutualism, developing secret societies or seeking to build a workerist party. However, the significant development was their involvement in the *Dem-Soc* movement. Led by neo-Jacobin lawyers and journalists, this sought to channel 'archaic' and anarchic local protest into electoral channels, to achieve a social Republic via the ballot box. Marx criticised its naïve faith in cross-class alliances, its 'parliamentary cretinism', its 'utopian' illusions about rescuing doomed artisanal and peasant petty production. Others are less dismissive of a movement which, in the face of bureaucratic repression and entrenched notable power, made impressive electoral gains and mobilised a broad populist coalition. Fears of *Dem-Soc* election victory in 1852 led conservatives to support the coup. Its appeal was increased by imaginative propaganda which used songs and *Almanachs* as well as newspapers, distributed by migrant workers and *colporteurs*. The movement suffered from internal social and ideological tensions. Some suspected that bourgeois leaders' rhetorical support for associationism masked a desire to divert workers from industrial militancy. Nîmes artisans were uneasy at the role of Protestant businessmen in local leadership. Faced with police harassment, rumours of Right-wing coups and daily clashes with Catholic-Royalists they grew impatient with electoralist strategies and flirted with secret societies. In a region with a history of bloody

sectarianism, activists' invocations of the 1793 Terror when one played *boules* with the heads of the royalist 'whites' sat uneasily alongside the leadership's fraternalist associationist rhetoric (Berenson 1984; Huard 1982).

Yet France *was* unique in possessing a radical middle-class stratum open to the egalitarianism of 1793, willing to restrict free markets, endorse workers' rights and embrace socialist discourse. *Dem-Soc* success was greatest where there was collaboration with cadres of literate artisans. Such alliances, impossible to construct in northern mill-towns, flourished in cities like Toulouse where barely 10 per cent of workers were in factories. Artisans and Republican bourgeois shared a distrust of 'northern' capital and a fear of Catholic-Royalism. The key to variations in local labour politics and class consciousness lay not *simply* in labour force structures or in workshop experiences but in the types of worker/bourgeois political alliances which were constructed. Radical Republicanism was not an ideology *imposed upon* the rank-and-file by manipulative bourgeois leaders. Two-thirds of urban Republican activists in 1849–51 were workers (Aminzade 1993).

The years 1849–51 witnessed the protracted 'agony of the Republic'. Police repression provoked resentment and resistance, but could also disrupt *Dem-Soc* organisational networks as newspaper editors were prosecuted, cafés placed under curfew, jury trials suspended, cooperatives hounded, radical councillors dismissed and activists prosecuted. In Limoges the porcelain cooperative faced police harassment, workers were ousted from the National Guard and the garrison was supplemented by a bourgeois militia to patrol workers' quartiers. But repression alone cannot explain Labour's defeat. Some workers felt that socialist agitation threatened the business confidence required for economic recovery and employment. The absence of a secret ballot and paternalist benevolence posed obstacles to the Left in company towns. Portrayal of socialists as atheists, men of blood eager to return France to the Terror, influenced conformist and Catholic workers. Finally Bonapartist propaganda, which used songs, lithographs and *Almanachs* to portray Louis Napoleon as the workers' friend, a ruler not tied to the economic elites, appealed to less sophisticated workers in regions such as the Pas-de-Calais (Merriman 1985; Ménager 1988).

Bonapartism and French labour (1851–71)

Bonapartism – between authoritarianism and populism
The Second Empire provided political stability which encouraged industrial expansion. This accelerated changes in the structures of the working class. Completion of the rail network threatened the livelihoods of river boatmen but quadrupled the number of railway workers – to 138,000 – and stimulated metallurgical and coal sectors. The Pas-de-Calais coalfield was opened up. Around St. Etienne heavy engineering, steel and coal ousted ribbons and hardware as the dominant sectors. The balance in textiles shifted from rural industry and southern mill towns like Lodève towards the north and north-east. Wool-weaving was mechanised in Roubaix and Rheims. Rouen cotton-mills fell from 233 to 185, but their average size rose. Coke-fuelled iron-forges

undercut charcoal forges. The balance of the labour force changed only gradually. Paris flourished as *the* European artisan centre, its craft industries adapting flexibly to changing consumer tastes and technological advances. Urban renewal projects benefitted small and medium building contractors. By 1870 France employed 121,000 miners and quarrymen, and 49,000 workers in heavy metallurgy, but 825,000 in textiles – many in small workshops or rural proto-industry. However, the labour movement was influenced as much by state policies as by structural changes. A regime adept at populist gestures began by repressing the Left – and retained authoritarian tendencies. Activists arrested in the coup were jailed or exiled, urban constituencies gerrymandered and municipal autonomy in major cities ended. Unlike in Britain, where mid-Victorian prosperity and liberalism fostered a reformist labour movement, police surveillance of activists and the ban on unions perpetuated a sense of alienation. Workers' viewed the state as the repressive arm of the economic elites. Restrictions on political activities limited workers' contacts with Republicans and pushed some craft workers towards Proudhonist mutualism. This sought to ignore (unpleasant) realities of state power to focus on mutal aid societies, whose membership trebled to 800,000, and producer cooperatives. These now functioned more as petty capitalist enterprises than as ventures aspiring to emancipate workers from the wage system.

Workers' relations with Bonapartism passed through three phases. Until 1857 prefects warned that absence of overt militancy signified fear of repression not support for the regime. Limoges workers boycotted elections. In Lyon thousands stayed off work on the anniversary of the Second Republic. After 1857 attitudes 'improved'. Economic expansion multiplied job opportunities and the regime's Italian policy attracted support. Thereafter prefects' reports became gloomier. The fading of the rail and urban reconstruction booms fuelled industrial unrest and the re-birth of radical politics. By 1869, the opposition vote reached three million (42 per cent) – five times higher than in 1857 – and industrial militancy reached unprecedented levels. However, if Bonapartism 'lost' the urban vote, it had enjoyed support among sections of the working class. Limousin migrant peasant-masons were seduced by the Paris building boom, to the despair of exiled radical Nadaud, now reduced to teaching French in a Wimbledon private college! Mulhouse Catholic workers voted Bonapartist as a gesture against liberal Protestant employers. The populist nationalism of a frontier region explains working-class Bonapartism in eastern France. Bonapartism's idiosyncratic blend of authoritarianism and populism had genuine appeal. Workers were assured that Bonapartism guaranteed political stability and full employment. Napoleon III was the 'people's Emperor' – sympathetic to workers' grievances, not beholden to the elites. He toured industrial regions. During the 1857–58 crisis of the Lyon *fabrique* the court increased orders for silk dresses. Public works projects provided employment. In 1854 the emperor responded to Loire miners' petitions by breaking up the CML coal conglomerate. State subsidies were available for mutual aid societies which adopted an apolitical stance, and for housing projects such as Paris's *Cité Napoléon*. As the regime alienated Catholic and business support by its Italian and free-trade policies, it stepped up propaganda to workers. Strikes were legalised (1864). Article 1781 of the Penal Code, which accepted employers' word in court, was abolished. Such populist strategies enjoyed only modest success. In the last resort the regime could never refuse Schneider's request to send troops to break a strike at Le Creusot. Concessions, as conservative Bonapartists had warned, produced not a grateful working class but encouraged further demands. By 1869–70 the regime drifted back into alliance with Orleanist business and Catholic elites, and cracked down on strikes and workers' organisations (Kulstein 1969; Ménager 1988).

The provincial proletariat

Pierrard (1965) claims that 'fatalism' was the overriding response of Lille mill-workers to appalling working and housing conditions. With typhoid and cholera frequent visitors, and infant and child mortality stubbornly high, life expectancy was twenty-four. Families spent some two-thirds of their income on food. Enforcement of child labour regulations remained lax. Low school-attendance kept literacy below 40 per cent. Observers lamented the fragility of family life, with 20 per cent illegitimacy rates, domestic violence and alcoholism. The rare organised strikes were by skilled male textile-printers. Possibly such analysis draws too heavily on the 'miserabilist' discourse of social commentators recycling the rhetoric of Villermé's 1830s reports which attributed workers' plight to their immorality. The café was a place of warmth and sociability, not (just) of dissipation. It housed both mutual aid societies and a vibrant song-culture which voiced forms of oblique, indirect 'resistance' – albeit in a world where open protest remained dangerous. Songs exhibited stoicism and self-deprecating humour. Lille was a 'dirty old town', but it was home. Workers were unimpressed by grandiose Bonapartist urban renewal projects. Customs such as 'St. Monday' were cherished. Strike statistics were inadequate indicators of industrial protest. In 1856 skilled *batteurs* faced arrest when they organised slow-downs to resist new machinery. They resorted to symbolic protests – mimes and pranks within the mills drawing on well-known phrases and jokes borrowed from street puppet theatre. And by 1867–70, 30 per cent of all French strikes were in the textile sector. Troops were sent to Roubaix to suppress protests against a new work system obliging weavers to operate two looms. In 1869 Republicans captured 80 per cent of the Lille vote. But employers proved adept at directing workers' anger against government free-trade policies, portrayed as a threat to jobs (Reddy 1984; Pierrard 1965). The fate of the Midi town of Lodève, a radical bastion in 1848, is instructive. Government orders for army uniforms, upon which its woollen industry depended, were transferred to regions with more 'docile' labour forces. This blow was compounded by the refusal of rail companies – dominated by financiers close to the regime – to construct rail links direct from Lower Languedoc to Paris via the Massif Central. By reducing a once-thriving textile region to an industrial backwater, capitalism illustrated its capacity – all too evident in our age of globalisation – to play 'hopscotch', to undermine pockets of worker resistance by shifting investment and production (Johnson 1995).

The strike in Zola's *Germinal* (1884) is based on two incidents in 1869 when troops shot striking miners in La Ricamarie and Aubin. Republicans claimed that Bonapartism's populist mask was slipping as it resorted to repression to contain workers' protest. Yet miners were scarcely in the vanguard of labour militancy. The dominant discourse *about* miners portrayed them as oscillating between volatility, stoicism and docility. They were portrayed as coarse, often drunken. Annual per-capita beer consumption at Denain was calculated at 330 litres! Underground work was viewed as brutalising, the youth of mining villages as ill-educated and immodest. Yet miners were also seen as quasi-rustics whose narrow horizons protected them from urban vices and radical ideology. The perils of pit work made them more God-fearing than urban artisans, though they were hedonistic 'festive' christians whose religiosity was heavily tinged with superstitious fear of underground ghosts! Coalfields exhibited diverse characteristics. The Pas-de-Calais had many isolated mining villages. The established Loire coalfield was more closely integrated with industrial towns. Full-time Loire miners worked 14-hour shifts, whereas isolated pit-towns like Carmaux employed 'peasant-miners' who worked eight-hour shifts before tending their farms. Paternalist firms like Anzin provided company housing and encouraged high fertility to create a 'hereditary' work-force. Girls were offered jobs as pithead coal-sorters. Grand'Combes (Gard) recruited from the surrounding Catholic peasantry and used nuns to run schools and charities and help with labour discipline. Even striking miners exhibited little ideological awareness. At Carmaux they blamed individual managers rather than the company for imposing stricter timekeeping, and chanted *'Vive l'Empereur!'*. Solidarities of Aubin miners were essentially those of Aveyron rural parishes from which they were recruited. Their grievances focused on fines for poor-quality coal and the lack of company housing provided at nearby Decazeville. Aubin strikers were, Reid (1988) observes, the type of 'archaic' Catholic protesters with whom labour history remains ill-at-ease. They, too, viewed their quarrels as with an individual manager rather than with the coal company – let alone capitalism or the Bonapartist state! Only at Ricamarie, where troops shot into a crowd seeking to free arrested strikers, were there signs of politicisation. Conflict was triggered by attempts to wrest control over mutual aid funds from management – a sensitive issue in a coalfield where there were few jobs for women and where accidents among male breadwinners were increasing. Hopes of support from the prefect proved unfounded. Strike leader Rondet – a sacked activist who ran a café – subsequently became a union leader. Loire miners had links to ribbon-weavers and skilled metalworkers in a region with an active Republican tradition (Reid 1988; Hanagan 1989; Trempé 1974).

Provincial cities
Provincial cities offered an environment better suited to labour politics than mill towns or pit villages. By 1870–71 Marseille had a branch of the First International and staged a brief uprising in support of revolutionary Paris. The city's population grew by 60 per cent to 312,000. Industrialisation and the influx of migrants altered the balance of the labour force and the nature of popular politics. Engineering, chemicals, soap, oil-pressing, tobacco and food-processsing expanded. Literate, skilled migrants – northerners and Cévenol Protestants – were drawn to the city by prospects of upward

mobility in the service sector. Italians became unskilled labourers. The expansion of the port and the resilience of artisanal sectors suggest that popular radicalism cannot be ascribed to impoverishment. Migrants exposed the city to wider cultural and ideological currents. They were less devoted to local religious *fêtes*. Mass attendance fell, delays between birth and baptism lengthened. French replaced Provençal as the lingua franca. Reconstruction of the docks threatened stevedores' work-culture – for direct hiring replaced gang-subcontracting, mechanical cranes were introduced and enclosed warehouses curtailed traditional 'perks' of pilfering from cargoes. Protest petitions to Napoleon III went unanswered. Resentment at domination by outside capital intertwined with hostility to centralisation to fuel demands for municipal autonomy in the political mobilisations of 1869–71. Yet the working class remained inchoate. Relations between Provençals, French migrants and Italian immigrants remained tense. Xenophobic discourse labelled the latter a volatile, criminal underclass. In new industries French workers did skilled and supervisory jobs, Italians dirty, unskilled tasks. Italian women worked in the sweated clothing sector and sugar factories, better-paid posts in the state tobacco works went to stevedores' daughters (Sewell 1985).

Lyon was kept under tight surveillance. There were 800 arrests during the 1851 coup. Lyon workers were egalitarian socialists just as eighteenth-century bourgeois had been *philosophes*, claimed the *Procureur Général*. After 1860, strike militancy revived and a branch of the International was established. However, the social basis of Lyon radicalism was in transition as industrial changes altered the balance of the workforce. Developments within the silk *fabrique* strained relations between masters and journeymen. By 1870, 70 per cent of plain weaving was done in the rural hinterland. Lyon became an entrepôt and a centre for upmarket fancy weaving and design. These were hit by declining American markets, fashion tastes which favoured mixed silk/cotton fabrics and pebrine disease which destroyed local raw silk supplies. The *fabrique* resorted to resilient Asiatic silks, which proved more suitable for power-looms. Forced to improvise survival strategies, masters intensified exploitation of family labour, employed female auxiliary workers and cut journeymen's wages. Relationships within the workshops deteriorated, and disputes between masters and journeymen now dominated the *Prud'hommes*. Masters feared that militancy would jeopardise the industry, and blamed journeymen's 'insubordination' for the *fabrique*'s 'moral crisis'. Producer cooperatives were now essentially petty-capitalist enterprises which distributed dividends. Consumer cooperatives were used to reduce food costs in order to hold down journeymen's wages. Journeyman Norbert Truquin saw masters as a labour aristocracy who no longer wore workers' blouses and who now favoured moderate Republicanism or Proudhonist mutualism – an analysis confirmed by the later chapters of Benôit's autobiography where this master-weaver and former socialist firebrand denounced 1860s strikers as 'agitators' with 'evil passions'. Journeymen, often reduced to casual jobs on building sites, now identified with the wider working class of engineering and chemical workers in suburbs of Oullins and La Guillotière. By 1870 only one of nineteen *Association Internationale des Travailleurs* (AIT) leaders came from the Croix-Rousse. Younger activists abandoned mutualism. Some favoured Bakuninist insurrectionism, and participated in an abortive rising in September 1870. Others sought to construct a workers' party with links to the (underground) trade unions, while collaborating with Republicans against Bonapartism. The strike wave of 1867–70 encompassed silk journeymen, a few plain masters, female *ovalistes* and workers from heavy industry. Barely 10 per cent of participants in the brief Lyon Commune of May 1871 were silkworkers (Sheridan 1986; Lequin 1977).

Workers and Republicans

By 1869, Bonapartism's hold on industrial France was waning. Workers were voting for opposition candidates and an unprecedented strike wave involved broad strata of the labour force. Wider implications of this mobilisation remained unclear. Would it be channelled by moderate Republicanism? Was a re-emergence of the democratic-socialist coalition of 1849 possible? Or would an autonomous workers' party emerge? Paris and Lyon militants were hostile to the Bonapartist state and large capitalism, and wary of cooption by bourgeois Republicans who 'betrayed' them in 1848. Elsewhere Republicans dominated opposition politics, either in the absence of strong labour traditions or because industrial changes had marginalised artisans who had been the cadres of earlier radicalism. Lawyers and businessmen constructed electoral coalitions which wooed workers by tapping grievances against free trade, domination of local economies by Parisian finance, excessive centralisation and clerical education. In eastern France or the Gard, workers signed Republican petitions for secular education. Republicans rejected the violence and 'utopianism' of 1848. They included 'progressive' industrialists who defined themselves against older Orleanist and Bonapartist elites – big merchants or large landowners – who favoured state repression, clerical education and authoritarian paternalism to impose social control. The only basis for a viable socio-political order was a democratic regime led by productive strata of the bourgeoisie – offering opportunities to aspiring *nouvelles couches* and association rights for workers. Such strategies succeeded in Rheims where handloomers, the militants of 1848, had been undercut by weaving mechanisation. Republicanism was led by mill-owner Holden – 'autocratic by instinct (but) democratic by ambition' – who denounced Bonapartist mercantile dynasties and offered workers the prospect of free schooling. Although a few militants joined the International, most acquiesced to such 'democratic patronage'. A similar pattern of class relations prevailed around St. Etienne. Here ribbon-weavers, once in the vanguard of labour politics, were threatened by new looms, operable by less experienced workers, which produced patterns automatically from perforated cards while a single bar moved multiple shuttles. If the outward form of industry – small workshop production – changed little, weavers' control was eroded. The balance of the regional economy was moving towards heavy industry. In big armaments plants and steel mills at St. Chamond workers were subordinate to authoritarian/paternalist Bonapartist employers. But medium-sized engineering employers such as Dorian criticised such styles of labour control, and the 'brutality' of a regime which shot miners at nearby La Ricamarie. Dorian dominated elections in 1869, insisting that *his* Republic stood not for disorder but for 'liberty, progress, security'. Radical weavers protested that 'progressive' employers were making St. Etienne their 'fief', for they were 'no different from the conservative bourgeoisie, since they live at the expense of the working class'. Despite a brief uprising in sympathy with Paris, the scope for independent labour politics had narrowed (Gordon 1985; Elwitt 1975).

Class structures and relations established fields of possibilities for progressive politics, but political alliances were required to realise these. In Toulouse, neo-Jacobin lawyers reassembled a coalition similar to that of 1849. Emphasising neglect of the regional economy by 'northern' Bonapartist elites, they appealed to shoemakers, furniture craftsmen and tailors who still dominated the labour force, though clothing masters had declined by 30 per cent since 1850, and flirted with associationist socialist rhetoric. Republicans were less influential in 'red' Limoges, where the working class was led by shoemakers and porcelain workers who lived alongside and mobilised the unskilled in their industry. In 1869 the prefect claimed that workers shared 'Parisian' ideas. Whereas it was often the municipalist strand of the Paris Commune that attracted provincial support, in Limoges it was its socialism. Local militants joined the International. In 1871 workers attempted to control the National Guard and prevent troop trains setting out for the capital (Merriman 1985). In 1870–71 most provincial industrial towns sought a third way between revolutionary Paris and reactionary Versailles. They desired a Republic which offered social and educational reforms and a degree of regional and municipal autonomy. Most provincial 'communes' of 1871 were ephemeral, relatively bloodless and thinly supported. Usually the uneasy alliance between bourgeois Republicans and workers held firm and accurately reflected local realities. The particular character of each movement was largely determined by the evolution of the structures of the local labour-force and by patterns of bourgeois-worker relations (Aminzade 1993).

Parisian workers between Haussmann and the Commune

Some view the Commune as the accidental outcome of the unique circumstances of the siege of Paris in the winter of 1870–71. Others locate its roots in grievances already fuelling unrest in Bonapartism's declining years. Marx is often portrayed as labelling the Commune an attempted socialist revolution and the first working-class government – a glorious harbinger of the future. Yet Marx constructed a heroic myth of workers 'storming the heavens' in order to salvage something from a bloody defeat. At the time he warned that a bid for power would be suicidal, and he subsequently intimated that the Commune had been merely the rising of a city under exceptional wartime circumstances. Ironically it was the contemporary Right which portrayed it as a proletarian rising masterminded by the International – a class interpretation contested by modern liberal/conservative empiricists. The Commune is now viewed more as 'dusk' than 'dawn' – less herald of an age of proletarian revolution than last gasp of artisanal radicalism or Parisian insurrectionism – or as part of of a wider municipalist revolt supported by sections of the middle class, against Bonapartist centralisation (Tombs 1999).

Haussmann's project was to accelerate the circulation of capital by construction of rail stations, goods yards, markets and boulevards, and relocation of heavy industry to the periphery. New sewers and water systems improved hygiene in the wake of cholera epidemics. Real estate speculators grew rich as central Paris was transformed into a space for bourgeois apartments and leisure culture. To render governable a hitherto ungovernable city, Faubourg St Antoine was surrounded by wide boulevards along which to move troops from newly constructed barracks. Construction projects, and the economic activities which they stimulated, were meant to generate jobs to defuse social tensions which had fuelled the upheavals of 1848. At its peak the construction boom provided employment for 20 per cent of Parisian workers. Migrant masons appeared reconciled to the regime by unprecedented prosperity, which also benefitted trades such as upmarket tailoring, bronze-working and *articles de Paris*. However, if *some* artisans survived in central Paris many were among the 350,000 displaced by Haussmann. Their sense of alienation ensured that a strategy designed to control and integrate workers ultimately nurtured popular resistance. Artisan delegates to the 1867 *Exposition* talked of 'Napoléonville' – a Paris of luxury and leisure – surrounded by *faubourgs* of squalor and deprivation. Demolition of inner city housing, and an influx of migrants which swelled the population by 65 per cent to two million, created a housing crisis and rising rents. Conflicts between tenants and landlords became endemic. Lacking access to transport and amenities, *faubourg*-dwellers resented the imposition of the *octroi* (consumption tax) to pay for Haussmann's projects. *Geographical* segregation influenced the 'social imagination'. Conflicts acquired *spatial* as well as class dimensions. However, if *faubourgs* did present a depressing blend of slum housing, railway sidings, gasworks, warehouses and refuse dumps, their residents developed a certain sense of community identity based both on a sense of exclusion from central Paris and on aspirations for improved amenities and municipal autonomy. Solidarities built a round *quartier*, street and café emerged as displaced artisans, and recent migrants and petty bourgeois intermingled. Around 75 per cent of working-class grooms and brides had small employers or shopkeepers as marriage witnesses. Radicalisation of such *quartiers* was rooted in such popular networks, not just in those of the workplace (Gould 1995; Shapiro 1985; Gaillard 1977). Where anxieties once focused on workers in inner city basements or attics, now it was to the heights of Belleville that bourgeois eyes were turned. Its population rose 67 per cent in 1851–56 alone. Its indices of crime, illegitimacy and mortality were rising; 85 per cent of inhabitants died leaving 0.8 per cent of inherited wealth. By 1869 it was identified with a re-emerging popular radicalism involving both skilled metal- and wood-workers and migrants drawn to the city by employment prospects but victims of the economic slump and rising rents and prices (Jacquemet 1984).

Despite relative prosperity for building trades and upmarket Parisian crafts, problems deepened in other artisanal trades. Sewing and leather-cutting machines allowed clothing and shoemaking entrepreneurs to use unqualified female operatives. Many apprentices lacked written contracts and failed to complete their training. Observers linked this to juvenile delinquency and advocated funding of formal, broad-based training programmes. Porcelain and hatting industries were leaving Paris in the quest for cheaper provincial labour. Other trades survived by accepting long hours and lower wages. Furniture makers increasingly produced shoddy goods unworthy of their 'artistry'. Free trade and railways created wider, 'faceless' markets. Haussmann's bright new world of bourgeois consumption was one of competitive pressures on declining trades, subdivided labour processes and sweated outwork. Yet artisan resistance was not yet broken. Denis Poulot, a 'progressive' engineering employer, dreamed of improving productivity within a moderate Republic and an industrial relations system where workers cooperated in the introduction of new machinery and payments' systems. His journeymen (*sublimes*) obstructed such projects. They were undeferential, moved regularly between small workshops (*bôites*) and resisted piece-work bonus systems. Sadly their skills were still needed, and their indiscipline was a role model for fellow workers. Politically aware, they attended the mass meetings which became a feature of Parisian public life after 1868. Held in the dance-halls and theatres of Belleville which they frequented, these attracted crowds of thousands. Alarmed at the tone of debates, police arrested some speakers. Blanquists and Internationalists denounced Bonapartism as the guard dog of capitalism – using troops to break strikes and the law to dispense class justice. The state apparatus was 'parasitic', existing on the back of workers' labour. Many repudiated Proudhon's criticisms of strikes and, in line with the strategy of the International, urged coordinated industrial and political strategies (Cottereau 1980; Dalotel *et al.* 1980; Auslander 1993; Berlanstein 1980).

This discourse, together with opposition election gains and the International-coordinated strike wave, prompted Dalotel *et al.* (1980) to argue that the Commune was 'born under the Empire'. The scale of worker disaffection *already* threatened Bonapartist hegemony. Such claims require qualification. Though Varlin insisted that 90 per cent of activists now accepted 'communist' ideas, successful opposition candidates in 1869 were mainly bourgeois Republicans whose emphasis on anti-clericalism, secular education, abolition of the standing army and municipal decentralisation enjoyed popular support. Labour was fragmented between Proudhonists, Blanquists and Varlin's wing of the International – itself disrupted by arrests in 1869–70. Much Parisian violence was ritualised street brawling, posing no serious threat. Nevertheless, Paris clearly did alarm the regime. Unrest was fuelled by the ending of the construction boom, alienation of those displaced by Haussmannism and the anger of threatened artisans. Social tensions were exacerbated by popular awareness of the city's history. Proud of their revolutionary heritage, Parisians were angered by the lack of municipal self-government. Uniquely Paris was a centre of government, an intellectual and academic capital and Europe's largest centre of artisanal production. The population of this 'laboratory of ideas' had a clear awareness of how political debates and ideological conflict could escalate into direct political action, access to a revolutionary repertoire of demonstrations and barricades and a sense that regimes could be overturned (Tombs 1999).

Clearly the Commune *was* a response to wartime experiences. After military defeats in the east had triggered the overthrow of Bonapartism in September

1870, Paris was subjected to a prolonged siege which caused food shortages, disease and high casualties. The male population was mobilised into the National Guard. The Armistice of January 1871, followed by national elections in February, dealt a double blow to Parisians' Republican patriotism. Surrender of Alsace-Lorraine appeared to render the city's heroic resistance futile. Royalist electoral victories raised the spectre of the new Republic's overthrow by reactionary rustic hordes. Hitherto support for the Left in Paris had remained modest. Blanquist coups attempted in October 1870 and January 1871 ended in fiasco. Only five socialists were elected in February. However, the reluctance of Republicans to support popular resistance to army seizure of National Guard cannons in Montmartre on 18 March allowed the Left to seize the initiative, proclaim a 'Commune' – a name evoking the patriotic resistance of 1792 – and win 80 per cent of votes in the ensuing elections. The Commune held out against military assault for nearly two months, making abortive efforts to solicit support from provincial sister movements. Although its leadership was preoccupied with defence, a range of imaginative social and cultural projects were debated and attempted at a local level.

Rather than interpreting this episode as the outcome of pre-existing class hostilities and community tensions, some argue that it is explicable in terms of short-term, 'contingent' experiences linked to the siege. The war stimulated the city's Republican patriotism and allowed the population to be armed. The key to the Commune perhaps lies in the experiences of 300,000 National Guardsmen. Service in the Guard provided 1.50 francs per day, food and a sense of camaraderie which many were reluctant to give up. The solidarities of guard battalions stemmed from recruitment from within *quartiers*. Officers tended to be white-collar strata or shopkeepers, NCOs craftsmen. Many guards fought doggedly for the Commune because of a sense of loyalty to neighbours, or for fear of being branded a 'shirker'. Most Communards *were* working-class. But the *language* which they used to identify themselves was not (merely) that of class. As *Republicans* they insisted that only a Republic represented France's general will, even if ignorant rustics voted for a monarchy. They were *patriots*, heirs of citizens of 1792 who resisted Prussian invasion and elite treachery. They constituted 'the *people*' – a category which encompassed strata of the middle class. And they were *Parisians*, heirs to the city's proud heritage asserting their right to municipal self-government. In their 19 April appeal to provincial cities for support they included such 'sisters of liberty' in this call for municipal rights. These discursive self-definitions were asserted against specific 'others' – Royalists and Bonapartists, police and bureaucrats, clergy, stupid reactionary peasants, the 'Prussians of Versailles'. 'Parasitic' financiers were reviled, as were landlords. The Commune froze rents and has been described, half seriously, as history's largest rent strike. There was relatively little denunciation of industrialists, indeed some Communards called for the marriage of productive industrial bourgeois to the people! The Commune's socio-economic programme was ad hoc and populist, not socialist. It left the Bank of France untouched and worked with big engineering firms like Cail willing to continue production for the defence effort. Much of its energy went into anti-clerical gestures and school secularisation (Gould 1995; Tombs 1999).

Yet to define the Commune *simply* as populist, 'Parisian', municipalist, patriotic and Republican is insufficient. Marx emphasised that half of its 80-man executive were workers. For thousands of workers in clubs and vigilance committees the short weeks of the Commune represented a springtime of hope. It was at *local* level that initiatives for wider social transformation were debated. Many insisted that workers must emancipate themselves, destroy and replace – not merely take over – the state apparatus. Certainly the International's role was subsequently exaggerated. Initially it appeared ideologically fragmented and marginalised. But 34 of the Commune executive *were* members and they headed key education, food and police commissions. Varlin was a leader aware of the need to combine political and industrial strategies. Sectarian divisions between Proudhonists, Blanquists and neo-Jacobins produced less feuding than might have been expected. Mâlon, who attended meetings of these diverse groups, claimed to have learned tolerance by finding men of 'good faith' in all of them. Even if Communards did not choose to identify themselves only as 'workers', most activists were artisans. In 1869–70 the International had militants in all trades with active *chambres syndicales*. The typical Communard was a skilled worker in his thirties, married, a migrant to the city but not a recent one. Among insurgents killed, arrested or tried, 15 per cent were from the liberal professions or petty bourgeoisie, a further 15 per cent unskilled. Printers and woodworkers provided the cadres, the building and metal trades a disproportionate share of fighters. Shoemakers and tailors were less prominent than in 1848, skilled workers from large engineering plants more involved.

One could interpret the Commune as a last chance to fulfil the cooperative dreams of 1848. Some activists dismissed cooperation as 'archaic' and anodyne – capable of delivering only a form of petty capitalism. The economic viability of cooperatives during the siege was always problematic. A successful ironfounders' cooperative with 250 workers was a pragmatic enterprise which employed a former patron as manager, set wages below the norm and traded with large private suppliers – who vouched for the members' reliability at their post-Commune trial! Yet many artisans still viewed cooperatives as offering a chance to maintain skills and dignity and to introduce new machinery under workers' control. A recent claim that the Commune represented a 'paradise of associations' is, perhaps, hyperbolic. But abandoned factories were taken over, some 2000 tailors worked for six cooperatives supplying National Guard uniforms, and encouragement was given to women's cooperatives (Johnson 1996; Tombs 1999).

The Right *behaved as if* the Commune was a workers' revolution and a real threat to bourgeois hegemony. It was they who contributed most to the subsequent myth, even if their depiction of Communards as drunken brutes from the 'criminal and dangerous classes', led by ambitious *déclassés*, was scarcely hagiographic. In 1848 repression targeted the leadership of the popular movement. Now it was all insurgents. 'If I had my way', said one police chief, '*everyone* who stayed in Paris would be punished.' 'The horrible sight of corpses', Thiers insisted, was a 'useful lesson' to keep workers' in their place. Thousands of prisoners were shot in the streets in a display of naked class vengeance for once lacking in any legal or patriotic fig-leaf. Worse than a crime, these massacres were a strategic error. They transformed Communards into martyrs, bestowing on the Commune a heroic grandeur in defeat. Pilgrimages to the *Mur des Fédérés* in the Père Lachaise cemetary, followed by clashes with the police, became an annual labour ritual. Many of the 4000 per year arrested in Paris cafés in the 1880s for disturbing the peace were metal and building workers who mixed denunciation of police brutality with threats to revenge the Communards. Songs such as *L'Internationale* or *Le Temps des Cerises* kept the Commune's memory alive in workers' song groups (Haine 1996).

The Commune complicated subsequent efforts to integrate labour. Syndicalists and Marxists evoked the repression to illustrate the brutality of the capitalist state. Certainly some ex-Communards metamorphosed into radical Republicans, moderate reformist socialists or, indeed, into quasi-fascist Boulangists! Yet repression of the Commune, by exorcising the 'threat' of Parisian revolution, served as the Republic's great 'foundation massacre', reassuring provincial France that a Republic could defend law-and-order. With one hundred thousand Parisian militants dead, exiled or jailed, the Commune marked the swansong of the age of artisan revolt and urban insurrections, less the dawn of a new era of working-class politics than the twilight of older traditions of popular mobilisation.

Workers and the bourgeois republic (1871–1914)

The re-making of the working class? Changing structures of the labour force

Complex changes occurred in the composition of the working class in the decades after 1871. There was a good deal of stability. In 1896, 36 per cent of non-agricultural workers were still employed in units of five or less. During the subsequent economic boom the number of self-employed working on their own rose from 223,000 to 356,000. Textiles, a heterogeneous sector employing 40 per cent of workers, remained the largest industry. Construction, a 'traditional' industry with 13.6 per cent of the workforce, was the third largest. But exposure to wider competition due to the railway revolution led to a decline in such rural industries as Troyes bonnet-making, Normandy textiles and Lyonnais gloves. After stagnation in the 1880s the workforce in coal, steel, chemicals, heavy engineeering and automobiles expanded rapidly. So, too, did employment in the tertiary and service sector and in transport. Of greatest significance for the labour movement was the decline – at first relative – of the craft sector. Lyon silk-weavers had adapted to the advent of Jacquard looms and electric power, to Asiatic silks and mixed or artificial fibres. Paris had remained a centre of diverse quality production. But by 1900 only 5 per cent of Parisian workers were apprentices, as against 18 per cent in 1860. Few had written contracts. Two-thirds failed to complete their training. There remained 4000 'quality' furniture craftsmen in the Faubourg St Antoine, but the 20,000 reduced to performing 'subdivided' tasks – making chair legs or table tops – lamented the decline of 'artistry' and urged their sons to quit the trade for the tertiary sector. *Métiers d'art* employed 29 per cent of Belleville workers in 1871, 14 per cent by 1891. By

1902, 56 per cent of building craftsmen's sons followed their fathers into the trade, compared with 77 per cent in 1869.

The new world of work was typified by Lorraine, now a major iron and steel region. By 1900, 86 per cent of miners worked in firms employing over 500. The rail workforce doubled between the 1870s and 1914. The automobile industry, Europe's largest, employed 33,000 in 50 firms. Chemicals, rubber and aluminium all expanded, often located in 'new' areas. Hydroelectric projects developed in Alpine valleys. As the city centre was bourgeoisified and artisanal Croix-Rousse stagnated, dynamic industries of the Lyon conurbation were those of Oullins or outer *banlieues* such as Vénissieux. During the Depression the industrial labour force hovered below the five million reached in the 1860s. It rose to seven million by 1910, not without recruitment difficulties in certain sectors. Some seasonal migrants settled into permanent urban employment. Peasant-workers, as at Carmaux, became full-time miners. But birth rates fell, and peasants or artisans were reluctant to enter heavy industry. Annual labour turnover at Anzin reached 33 per cent in 1900. Literate Protestants from Cévenol villages sought white-collar jobs in Nîmes. Catholic migrants were more likely to become blue-collar rail workers, yet once in the city their birth rate fell and their children, in turn, sought tertiary-sector employment. By 1914 there were a million immigrant workers, and women comprised over 35 per cent of the labour force. Retaining their role in textiles, clothing and tobacco, women were increasingly visible in hatting, printing and even engineering, which employed 43,000 by 1910. Belgians had long worked in Nord textiles. Now Italians were found not merely in the South-East but in Lorraine and, alongside Poles, in northern pits. In the Marais in Paris, hatters and tailors were Jewish refugees from Tsarist pogroms. Immigrants performed heavy jobs which French workers shunned, their presence allowing natives to occupy skilled, supervisory and clerical posts. But they were the target of xenophobia, some of it from unionised French workers who viewed them as undercutting established wage levels or as blacklegs.

Restructuring of the labour force had implications for working-class identity and consciousness and for the labour movement. Noiriel (1990) discerns a 'brutal rupture' as craft communities, bedrock of earlier popular protest, crumbled before coherent 'proletarian' identities or solidarities had been forged. Processes of 'class formation' should be viewed not as unilinear, but as marked by endemic discontinuities as old trades and communities dissolve, new identities emerge and 'class consciousness' has to be re-made. Artisans lamented that their skills were now redundant, their know-how was no longer being transmitted to the young who failed to appreciate the significance of past struggles and solidarities. Some spoke of a 'crisis' of worker culture as the young drifted into delinquency or were seduced by the lure of an emerging commercialised mass culture (Noiriel 1990; Lequin 1977; Berlanstein 1984).

Such rhetoric was too pessimistic. The strike wave of 1869–70 had hinted at emerging militancy in large industry. Some artisans found niches as skilled factory workers and were able to transmit their experience, organise the semi-skilled and sustain memories of past heroic struggles. In popular *quartiers* populist hostility to the *gros* was voiced by a *petit peuple* comprising a blend of small employers, shopkeepers, 'self-employed' artisans and journeymen. New industrial workers developed workplace and community solidarities – now clearly those of class not craft. In artisan quartiers of Lyon, marriage had been within the same trade. Now workers' children found partners from the wider working class. Moreover, production became concentrated into a limited number of industrial regions. Over 50 per cent of output was now in fourteen departments. Nevertheless, the labour movement, its cadres decimated by repression of the Commune, struggled to secure footholds in a changing industrial landscape. The 'rounded' skilled Parisian metal-workers of the small *boîtes* – Poulot's *sublimes* – were giving way to narrower 'specialist' workers (*ouvriers spécialisés*) such as millers or turners. In Britain the engineering craft union (ASE) was strong enough to offer protection from such technological threats. In France, where unions remained illegal until 1884, there was little organised resistance to these processes. Heavy engineering was located in outer banlieues, miles from city artisan quartiers. Many semi-skilled workers were migrants. Bretons who came, with their priests, to Paris's north-western outskirts to the rubber and cable industries were impervious to Parisian radical culture, voting, if at all, for employers' candidates. Glass-blowers' skills were rendered redundant by new Siemens gas-ovens. Resistance strikes in the 1880s were unsuccessful, though Carmaux glassworkers established a cooperative at Albi which survived until 1920. Chambon-Feugerolles file-cutters carved out a niche in production processes and mobilised unskilled workers to elect socialist deputies to speak for them in parliament. But elsewhere in the St. Etienne region, heavy engineering and steel relied increasingly on semi-skilled labour as crafts such as puddling were undermined by new technologies. St. Chamond militants lamented that workers 'bowed their heads in shameful apathy', voted for management candidates and raised wage issues only in humble petitions which disclaimed any intention of strike action! (Hanagan 1980; Scott 1974; Berlanstein 1984; Lequin 1977).

Although socialists appealed to the 'working class', one might argue that France had several 'working classes'. Processes which eroded artisans' skills and status simultaneously created semi-skilled posts promising higher wages and stable employment to casual labourers. The 'ideal type' class-conscious worker was male, skilled, a union activist, anti-clerical and a believer in a social Republic. Yet in 1914 over 80 per cent of workers were outside the trade unions. Many were female or immigrant. Some aspired to becoming small employers, put faith in the bourgeois Republic, or were loyal – or deferential – to paternalist employers. Some were Catholics – offended by the labour movement's anti-clericalism – or populist nationalists, vulnerable to the xenophobic anti-Marxist and anti-immigrant rhetoric of 'yellow' company unions. The co-existence of so many types of worker offers one explanation for the weaknesses of 'organised labour'. However, the decline of earlier patterns of popular mobilisation also owed something to rising living standards and to the policies of Republican elites and of employers.

The rise in workers' living standards?
Did rising living standards erode working-class radicalism? Unemployment was high from the late-1870s until 1896. Prolonged agricultural depression

increased 'vagrancy' and accelerated migration to the cities. But agricultural imports reduced food prices and diets became more varied. The *vie chère* riots which swept industrial France in 1911 were a protest at the price of former luxuries like butter and meat. Calculation of average wages remains difficult. Many industries had seasonal lay-offs. Workers were involved in pluri-activity. There was a variety of payment systems and complex subcon-tracting practices. Le Play's data on 'family budgets' must be treated with caution. Nominal wages were highest in Paris, but housing there was ex-pensive. Nevertheless, estimated average wage rises of 25 per cent in Lyon and 33 per cent in St. Etienne in the period 1881–1911 were probably not untypical. Family life was altered by the decline of child labour due to com-pulsory schooling, Child Labour Acts (1874, 1892) and technological change in textile mills. In the clothing sector, where child labour was still 'useful', employers and parents colluded to evade regulation. Factory inspectors were too few to police small-scale industry. Wary of offending Republican em-ployers they imposed nominal fines. The shift from temporary to permanent migration helped to stabilise family life, and children's health improved. Between 1869 and 1900 the percentage of Belleville conscripts unfit for mili-tary service fell from 30 per cent to 10 per cent. The average workday fell steadily, from 14 hours to 11 hours in the Lyonnais. A shorter working week and rising real incomes generated an embryonic 'leisure culture'. Although fashion historians emphasise French workers' loyalty to class-specific dress – the blouse and cap – falling clothes' prices allowed younger workers to dress up for the weekend.

Workers began to show interest in sports – as participants and spectators. Nord employers strengthened company loyalties by subsidising works' football teams. Midi landowners aped their Andalucian counterparts by financing commercial bullfighting for vineyard labourers. Bicycle and tyre manufac-turers sponsored cycle races in urban velodromes and the Easter Paris–Roubaix race became a feature of popular culture in the Nord. Sportshops emerged specialising in cycling gear and fishing tackle (Rougerie 1964; Noiriel 1990; Cross 1983; Lequin 1977). Dance and music-halls multiplied, the latter less dominated by jingoistic and conservative songs than their London counter-parts. Reduction of wine taxes encouraged the spread of the ubiquitous café. Its critics, including sober labour leaders, accused it of corrupting popu-lar culture by encouraging male workers to neglect family responsibilities and consume excessive amounts of alcohol. However, some cafés welcomed workers' family groups and acted not merely as the focus of quartier soci-ability and solidarity but also as unofficial job-centres, strike headquarters and centres of political debate (Haine 1996). Some welcomed greater family stability and cultural and leisure opportunities, but others claimed that commercial-ised leisure was a sop to offset loss of workplace skills and job control. Decline of apprenticeships accentuated generational divisions within the working class. The visibility of gangs of working-class youths allowed the mass press to play on the fears of settled, middle-aged workers. Anodyne music-hall songs were replacing political ballads once favoured by workers' singing groups. Literacy simply exposed workers to the seductions of cheap *romans-feuilletons* and social-imperialist newspapers such as *Le Petit Journal*.

Any optimistim must be qualified by the persistence of glaring social inequalities. 'We *must not* fool ourselves', insisted Dr E. Rey in 1900, 'the poor are becoming impatient with a Republic which has *not* (relieved) their sad situation. It would be *dangerous* to continue to deny them legitimate satisfaction.' Family budgets were squeezed when children were young or as ageing workers' earning powers were reduced. Periodic lay-offs or short-time working made survival dependent on charity, 'tick' from local grocers or pawnshops – whose custom rose 66 per cent in Lyon during the 1880s. Workers felt it futile to adopt bourgeois virtues of thrift and planning. Miners died prematurely of bronchial diseases or injuries. Millworkers were vulnerable to TB. Housing remained cramped, dirty and damp, and urban rents high; 33 per cent of court cases in Belleville involved rent arrears and evictions. Polluted water and poor sewage were endemic in workers' quartiers. By 1900 a socialist vote in eastern Paris was a vote against chemical companies whose pollution of water supplies went unchecked by complacent Republican authorities. *Faubourgs* like Belleville suffered multiple deprivations. Between 1860 and 1900 the percentage of the population dying propertyless rose from 79 per cent to 88 per cent; 85 per cent were buried in pauper graves. Statistics on social immobility must be handled with care, since workers who 'succeeded' were not classified as 'workers' at death. Yet 63 per cent of conscripts in the 1900s belonged to the same social class as their father, and 14 per cent had 'fallen'. In Lille in the 1900s, as in 1850, 90 per cent of the population died leaving under 10 per cent of wealth. In Lyon, income disparities widened (Berlanstein 1984; Shapiro 1985; Jacquemet 1984; Stone 1985).

Workers and the Republic

Workers' relationship with the Republic was complex. Some, particularly Catholics, deferentially accepted their place in a hierarchical social order. Others' visceral hatred of the bourgeois social order led them to favour workerist direct action. But many welcomed the Republic as fulfilment of a long-held dream – although hoping that it would metamorphose into a social Republic. Republicans introduced laic schooling for workers' children and legalised unions (1884). There were attempts to integrate a hitherto alienated working class into electoral politics and normalised industrial relations. Hopefully concessions would nurture a reformist labour movement on the British model. Yet by 1914 there were Marxist and syndicalist strands in organised labour, and strike levels were higher than in 1880. Did inadequate social reform and use of troops against strikers perpetuate worker alienation? Or did the relatively pro-labour stance of Republican politicians and bureaucrats, reliant on working-class voters against the Right, permit the (radical) labour movement greater 'space' than that allowed to its counterpart in the US, where repression of labour was more systematic? (Friedman 1998).

Working-class electors, who contributed to decisive Republican electoral victories in 1876–77, hoped that prefects would side with them against authoritarian employers. Yet the Republic's 'honeymoon' with labour risked being brief. Depression threw thousands out of work and exacerbated social relations, and the return of exiled Communards stimulated a socialist revival. Republicans realised that steps were needed to retain workers' electoral support. Thus, Elwitt claimed, attempts were made to weld 'disparate and otherwise antagonistic forces of the . . . bourgeoisie' into a flexible ruling bloc aware that the 'best defence against socialism (was) social reform'. Republican politicians, bureaucrats, academics, businessmen and Catholic paternalists from Royalist or Bonapartist backgrounds participated. Fearing labour unrest this coalition overcame ideological differences to establish parapolitical groups to frame social policies. Republicans toned down their anti-clericalism, conservatives hid their distaste for the Republic. 'Normalised' industrial relations were a priority. Strike militancy was spreading – both defensive strikes against wage cuts caused by the Depression and revolts against authoritarian employers. Use of troops risked eroding the fund of goodwill which the Republic enjoyed among workers. In 1884 unions were belatedly legalised in the hope of encouraging pragmatic labour leaders and marginalising revolutionary hotheads. Militants viewed with suspicion provisions in the Act banning 'political' debate and requiring membership lists to be deposited with the police! Perhaps the Act was part of a 'technology of power' through which aliberal regime was adjusting the mechanisms of social control – an analysis applicable also to municipal funding of *Bourses du Travail* as headquarters for local labour organisations and labour exchanges. If a *Bourse du Travail* flirted with revolutionary politics, municipal subsidies could be withdrawn. Conciliation and arbitration procedures involving JPs were introduced (1900) and Commerce Minister Millerand suggested 'tripartite' machinery to facilitate negotiations between employers, bureaucrats and union officials to head-off industrial conflicts (1900). Compulsory arbitration and strike ballots were envisaged. Industrial accident compensation (1898), an obligatory weekly rest day (1906), hours limitations for miners and railmen and workers' pensions (1910) were measures designed to conciliate labour. Parapolitical groups encouraged workers' savings banks, profit-sharing to give workers a 'stake' in capitalism, and mutual aid societies which by 1900 boasted two million members.

The *Musée Social* provided a forum for such ideas. It brought together social Catholics, technocratic managers and Radical Solidarists who sought a 'third way' between socialism and free-market capitalism, arguing that workers' marketplace inferiority made them unable to negotiate as equals or enjoy the independence necessary for citizenship. Society was an organic whole, not a collection of atomised individuals. 'Social diseases' had to be treated by 'experts' – doctors, sociologists, criminologists – consulted by the state. Through enlightened self-interest, the bourgeoisie should support reforms to strengthen capitalism by defusing working-class unrest. The quest for a viable bourgeois order, Elwitt (1986) claims, forged consensus among disparate ideological groups. Faced with falling profits, import penetration, rising unemployment and labour unrest, elites negotiated a 'second founding of the Republic' uniting industrialists and landowners around strategies of tariff protectionism and social imperialism. Royalist textile-magnate Motte rallied to a 'moderate' Republic which played down its anti-clericalism. As strike levels trebled between 1889 and 1893, and Nord textile workers turned to the Marxist *Parti Ouvrier Français* (*POF*) in the aftermath of the massacre of strikers at Fourmies (1891), Méline 'sold' tariff protection to workers as the guarantee of job preservation – trumpeting the 'solidarity of employer and worker' in the battle for *'travail national'*. Normandy employers gathered workers' signatures on protectionist petitions. The Marseille colonial exhibition, organised by shipping magnate Charles-Roux, linked the port's prosperity with colonial trade, forcing socialists to tone down anti-imperialist rhetoric lest it appear to threaten employment (Elwitt 1986; Lebovics 1988; Schneider 1982; Schöttler 1985).

Such strategies had limited success. Socialist voting and strike militancy increased. Elwitt's (1986) analysis conflates solidarist statist reform with paternalistic strategies designed to minimise state intervention and underestimates the strength of laissez-faire ideologies. As the Boulangist and Dreyfus crises suggest, it overestimates elite consensus. Not all conservatives accepted the Republic, nor did all employers accept the need for social reform or union recognition. Housing reform was never effectively addressed. Population growth in Paris drove up rents and pushed workers into shanty towns in *banlieues* lacking transport and basic amenities. Exploitative landlords remained bogeymen in popular culture. Anarchists organised tenants' groups and arranged 'moonlight flits' for those seeking to change apartment without paying rent arrears! Reformers dreamed of housing projects which would transform workers into conservative homeowners. But reluctance to commit taxpayers money or to allow municipalities financial freedoms to build council housing meant that the 1894 Housing Act was an anodyne measure – merely offering private builders tax concessions to construct cheap housing. Endless debate generated 'a voluminous literature but minimal advancement', since most reformers remained wedded to market solutions (Shapiro 1985).

Adult male unemployed faced harsh treatment. *Bureaux de Bienfaisance* resources were withheld from able-bodied unemployed – viewed less as victims of the Depression than as 'professional indigents', morally responsible for their fate. 'Vagabonds' – whose numbers swelled to 400,000 – were demonised. In 1890, 51,000 were arrested and 20,000 convicted. Unemployment was treated as a penal, and punitive 'workfare' scheme, based on 'scientific' American programmes, spread to 110 towns. Cities imposed residence qualifications for welfare claimants eliminating migrants and immigrants; 67,000 were pruned from Paris welfare rolls in the 1890s. Lyon abandoned welfare schemes hitherto operated to retain skilled weavers in the city during periodic slumps. By 1903 it had no adult males on relief! Private charities concentrated on mothers, children and the elderly, and imposed religious eligibility criteria. Reluctant to appear 'soft', radicals allowed debate to be dominated by hardliners who denounced welfare claimants as parasitic members of a degenerate, alcoholic sub-class. *Le Petit Journal* and Right-wing populists seized on the 'scientific' rhetoric of 'experts' who classified the jobless as 'social garbage' and advocated deportation of 'recidivist' beggars to penal colonies. In 1902, 10,000 such transportations occurred. *Office du Travail* reports on the structural roots of unemployment failed to influence policy-making. The lack of a national system of labour exchanges meant that the jobless were forced to rely on exploitative private agencies (Smith 1999, 2000).

Management, paternalism, industrial discipline – and the state

Strategies for 'incorporating' workers required employer co-operation. Waldeck-Rousseau introduced socialist Millerand to his 1899 cabinet and blamed intransigent employers for provoking strikes. He secured support from an employers' group, the *Comité Mascuraud*, founded by a Paris jewellery employer who was president of the Seine Industrial Tribunal. It included provincial industrialists who saw themselves as a productive class with roots in the people – heirs of that 'hard-working petty bourgeoisie, keen on reform, which made '89'. They sought a modus vivendi with labour and welcomed Millerand's tripartism. Some advocated a high productivity/high wage economy and job-creating public works projects. They urged fellow employers to accept the new Ministry of Labour (1906), the weekly rest-day and old-age pensions. The 'contradictions' of their position became clearer after 1906 when they supported Clemenceau's tough stance against syndicalist strikes. Their support for progressive income tax was premised on absence of 'inquisitorial' prying into company accounts! (Moss 1993). If France was unique in possessing some committed Republican businessmen, most industrialists were suspicious of state intrusion into industrial relations. 'I accept the intervention of *no one* outside the factory in contacts I have with my workers', Schneider insisted. The mining and metallurgy employers' association (UIMM) was founded to resist Millerand's reforms. Employers boycotted conciliation and arbitration machinery and refused to participate in collective bargaining. Only 1 per cent of strikes between 1899 and 1914 were settled by direct negotiations with unions. Factory inspectors' attempts to enforce industrial regulations were obstructed. Faced with the guaranteed weekly rest-day – introduced to head-off syndicalist demands for the Eight-Hour Day – big business mobilised small employers to secure a range of exemptions. Service-sector strikes against employers who flouted this Act prompted one Radical to enquire 'what shall we say to workers when every time a law punishes them it is respected – and when (one) benefits them, there is always someone to wreck it?' (Stone 1985).

Company paternalism produced workforces which oscillated between docility and sporadic protest. Zola described Anzin as a 'new type of Bastille' where miners, under incessant surveillance, lacked civil liberties. Large firms portrayed the patron as benevolent father figure – an image difficult to sustain if they became *Sociétés Anonymes* with boards of directors and technocratic managers. To create the 'tireless little worker' involved treating workers as children. Le Creusot installed a statue of workers, caps in hand, gazing up in admiration at their patron. The company ran the *mairie* and provided schools, stores, housing, allotments and a hospital. Schneider dreamed of a town with deserted streets, and no cafés where workers might hold subversive discussions. Such projects originated in efforts to build a stable labour force where peasants were reluctant to enter heavy industry. Anzin, aspiring to become a 'family of 15,000 souls', praised miners' wives as breeders and spiritual directors of the next generation, and awarded prizes to fathers whose sons entered the pit. Houses were open to surveillance, with fines for lack of cleanliness. Religious congregations ran schools and welfare agencies and compiled dossiers on the workforce. 'What we lack *at present*', lamented

Grand' Combes manager, 'is *complete* surveillance of workers' behaviour.' The ballot box was rarely secret.

But workers were not rendered deferential by the mere existence of paternalistic discourses. The 1880s saw violent strikes at Decazeville, at Montceau – where a church and pithead were dynamited – and at Anzin. Around 2500 strikers sacked in 1899 by Schneider left Le Creusot by train waving red flags. Many workers were grateful for company welfare, accepting the Faustian bargain of trading independence for relative security. Yet there were numerous contradictions. Companies which praised allotments for preserving workers' healthy ties with the soil forced peasant-miners to abandon smallholdings in order to create full-time workers with better time-discipline! With the priority given to creating a self-perpetuating 'race' of loyal employees, the steep fall in birth rates in company towns could be read as a form of resistance. Paternalism sought to cocoon infantilised workers, but only functioned effectively where workers lacked alternative job options or were remote from wider democratic currents (Reid 1985b; Noiriel 1984).

The labour movement remained feeble in Lorraine iron-mining and steel-manufacturing. Unions found difficulties in coping with technological change, a massive influx of immigrants and ruthless paternalism. The steel industry had relied on skilled men who passed on know-how to younger workers. However, the Bessemer process undercut puddlers' skills and production processes became controlled by supervisory staff. Employers developed a full range of paternalist tactics, supplying housing for long-time workers, financing *fêtes patronales*, spying on polling booths and cutting off water from cafés which offered meeting places for union organisers! By 1900, 70 per cent of iron miners were Italian. As one manager said, 'I prefer Italians rather than migrants from central France where strikes are endemic'. They lacked the vote and were not covered by the 1898 accident compensation legislation. Strikers risked deportation. Employers implemented a divide-and-rule strategy, an industrial apartheid. Images of knife-wielding Italian bachelors were invoked to arouse the xenophobia of 'decent', family-loving native workers who held skilled and supervisory jobs and enjoyed housing and welfare provision. Employer hegemony was challenged by strikes after 1900. An alliance formed between Italians – resentful of fines and company stores – and French skilled workers hostile to speed-ups and technological changes. Organisers came from the Italian socialist party and the *Fédération des Métaux* to address mass rallies. The employers' *patrie* was defined as 'that which makes the biggest profits'. But unity proved fragile. Xenophobia was never far beneath the surface. The *patronat* subsidised Biétry's anti-immigrant 'yellow' union, which recruited 'French' strikebreakers disgusted by 'violent' Italians and 'unpatriotic' Marxist agitators. Militants were sacked and the *Comité des Forges* drew up blacklists. Residential segregation widened the gulf between French and immigrant workers. Technological changes and rationalisation of space in the steel mills further eroded skilled workers' autonomy. With trade-union membership pitifully low, resistance was reduced to daily ruses and subversive café songs (Noiriel 1984).

Faced with the Depression and foreign competition, employers sought to cut costs by eroding the collective work practices of skilled workers. Taylorism

– 'scientific management' – was more an imported American ideology than a widespread practice, but it attracted technocrats and industrialists such as Renault who combined concern for industrial efficiency with authoritarian political views. It offered a vision of a future where skilled workers' autonomy could be curbed, though full-scale Taylorisation would be expensive and shift power from patrons towards engineers. The ad hoc, piecemeal elements of scientific management that *were* introduced provoked as much shopfloor protest as they quelled. Parisian engineering firms witnessed a 'revolt against work' – wildcat strikes against speed-ups, domineering foremen, piecework schemes and the introduction of machines such as 'universal millers'. Such disputes flared up sporadically until 1914, with time-and-motion study projects particularly resented in car firms such as Berliet. In the 1880s, 12 per cent of strikes had involved job-control issues – by 1910–14, 25 per cent. However, in the face of tough employers' associations, willing to use lock-outs and blacklists and to replace skilled workers with semi-skilled machine operators, strike success-rates fell (Berlanstein 1984; Humphrey 1986).

In the 1880s the Republican state responded positively when workers sought protection from prefects against intransigent employers – Bonapartists or Royalists – whose authoritarianism was perceived as provoking protests. Yet having created the space for the reviving labour movement, Republicans allowed the army to shoot strikers. Such 'proletarian massacres', critics argued, revealed the iron fist of a bourgeois regime. Fourmies (1891) boosted workers' support for the Marxist POF. Villeneuve-St-Georges (1908) confirmed the image of prime minister Clemenceau as France's 'top cop'. Police personnel and strategies changed little in the transition from Bonapartist to Republican regimes. Informers infiltrated labour organisations. Agents provocateurs instigated 'outrages' which 'justified' police clampdowns. Clemenceau flooded the coalfields with troops to smash a strike called to protest at 1100 deaths in the 1906 Courrières pit disaster. The 1910 rail strike emphasised the deteriorating relations between the regime and its sometime working-class supporters. Hitherto rail unions had been grateful to governments for interceding to secure shorter hours. However, the autocratic railway companies responded to cuts in the working week by imposing speed-ups, tighter schedules and fines on the drivers. The drivers' union, evolving from craft particularism towards wider class solidarity, applied to join the syndicalist Confédération Générale du Travail (CGT). Portraying the strike as a threat to national security, Briand's government threatened to conscript strikers and court martial any who did not resume work; 3300 were sacked. Although the strike crumbled, many railmen shared the verdict of one spokesman that the rail companies' authoritarianism 'should not exist in a Republic' – and that the 'Opportuno-Radical' regime was no better than a monarchy (Stein 1979).

Around 40 per cent of the really violent strikes of the Third Republic occurred in just three years – 1904, 1906 and 1911. Was this evidence that workers were losing patience with the inadequacy of Republican reforms and that the bourgeois Republic was revealing its true colours by backing the *patronat*? The reality is more nuanced. In the US there *really was* an alliance between government and ruthless union-busting employers which forced the American Federation of Labor to adopt a cautious stance. By contrast the

French Republic appears relatively progressive. It still faced real threats from the far Right, with which sections of big business had links, and held intransigent employers responsible for labour discontent. To win elections and preserve the Republic it still needed working-class votes. Even Clemenceau made no real effort to outlaw the syndicalist CGT. Possibly syndicalism was permitted to survive because Republicans treated it with some leniency (Friedman 1998).

Socialism, syndicalism and French labour 1880–1914

The labour movement took years to recover from the tragedy of the Commune. Municipal election gains preceded a breakthrough in 1893, when socialists won 750,000 votes (8 per cent) and 50 parliamentary seats. Progress was then retarded by internecine ideological splits until, in 1905, a united Socialist Party (SFIO) was formed which captured 100 seats and 1.4 million votes by 1914. Perhaps the depth of labour's ideological and organisational divisions should not be exaggerated. Many activists proved capable of holding both reformist *and* revolutionary views, emphasising one or the other depending on circumstances. Rival groups often collaborated within local *Bourses du Travail*. Nevertheless, the existence of several socialist groupings reflected real ideological and strategic differences. 'Possibilists' envisaged progress via reforms in alliance with the progressive Republican middle class and hoped to achieve meaningful local reforms through control of municipalities. At times anarchists, and even Marxists, shared such hopes. Marxism gained ground through the POF from the 1880s. Less influential – and less ideologically sophisticated – than in Germany, it was much stronger than in Britain. Though Marxism was denounced as an alien 'German-Jewish' implant, its insights were close to those of the historic French Left – unsurprisingly since Marx's emphasis on the working class's political capacity derived from his French experiences. The POF did well in Nord mill towns whose factory workers approximated to a Marxian proletariat. Its enthusiasm for scientific management failed to endear it to craftsmen. Outside the POF, Vaillant urged a blending of Marxist insights with France's Republican and anti-clerical traditions to appeal beyond a minority working class to peasants and petty bourgeois, and to coordinate party strategies with workers' shopfloor grievances. Similar concerns made groups such as Allemane's Parti Ouvrier Socialiste Révolutionnaire (POSR) sympathetic to syndicalism. Anarchists' influence was greater than its estimated 5000 activists might suggest. A police clampdown of 1893 curtailed their campaign of 'propaganda of the deed' – although not before Ravachol, who killed a judge, had become the 'hero' of a popular song performed in the bars of the Paris *faubourgs*. Anarchist groups were active in anti-landlord tenants' groups and moved into trade-union activity in the mid-1890s in order to strengthen syndicalist resistance to party control.

Prospects for socialist unity ebbed and flowed. Electoral successes in 1893 gave even Marxists illusions about the ballot box. An agreed minimum programme was constructed. Control of over 100 urban councils raised the profile of municipal socialism and worthy programmes of crèches, school meals and health clinic provision were introduced. Projects for council housing or 'gas and water socialism' foundered on the hostility of prefects and court judgements ruling it illegal to spend local taxes on such schemes. The scope for municipal projects proved narrower than that permitted to Chamberlain's contemporary Tory council in Birmingham! The inability of elected councillors to reform public amenities contributed to the souring of workers' attitudes towards the Republic. In the 1890s elections were lost because of sectarian feuding. After 1898 socialists were divided by the Dreyfus Affair. Some argued for defence of the Republic against the threat from the Right, others dismissed it as a capitalist regime like any other. Such splits proved damaging. In Bourges (Cher) the socialist candidate won 38 per cent of the vote in 1898, two rival socialists only 18 per cent between them in 1902. The vote was divided along occupational lines. The reformist attracted support from postal workers and arsenal workers reliant on state orders for their jobs, the 'revolutionary' from porcelain workers and lumbermen. The SFIO was a broad church seeking to hold together a disparate collection of reformists, Marxists, quasi-syndicalists and anti-militarists. By 1914 it attracted 1.4 million votes. Since many of these were from teachers, petty bourgeois and peasants, clearly many industrial workers voted for Republicans or even the Catholic or populist Nationalist Right.

The labour movement suffered from unresolved demarcation disputes between political and industrial 'wings'. Radical political mobilisations long preceded legalisation of unions in 1884. The POF sought to control the emerging union movement, but by the 1890s unions had asserted their autonomy. The CGT, established in 1895, was soon dominated by syndicalists who insisted that the overthrow of capitalism required industrial rather than political/electoral strategies. In 1902 the CGT united with the Fédération des Bourses du Travail (FBT). Bourses du Travail coordinated local labour activities, bringing together workers – skilled and unskilled – from different sectors. The CGT emphasised autonomy of local unions, but urged craft unions to amalgamate into industrial federations. After a slow start, union expansion gathered pace. There were 139,000 members in 1890, nearly a million by 1914. Only half affiliated to the CGT, which was shunned by some reformists. French unionism appeared numerically and organisationally weak alongside British or German counterparts, each boasting four million members and impressive bureaucracies. Workers joined during strikes, often to quit once these finished. Dues paying was erratic. New industries and some regions had minimal union presence. Yet labour militancy, measured by strike levels, was often higher than in neighbouring countries.

Varieties of labour experiences

Within the confines of the present study one can, at most, illustrate diverse labour strategies which evolved in specific industries and regions. Labour movements derive their distinctive characteristics from the nature of the labour force, the policies – liberal or authoritarian – of state and employers, and the availability of ideologies. But the French working class was so heterogeneous that strategies which appealed to some strata made little sense to others. And whereas one can categorise Tsarism as authoritarian, both the Republic and the *patronat* were Janus-faced – sometimes liberal, sometimes repressive. And France, Europe's most politicised society, had a veritable superfluity of ideologies on offer. Unsurprisingly no single style of labour politics was dominant.

Marxism in the Nord

One-third of the electors, and half the members, of the Marxist POF lived in the Nord, a department little touched by artisanal radicalism and rarely prominent in earlier labour militancy. However, textile strikes took off after 1880 and the Fourmies massacre (1891) proved the catalyst for socialist gains. POF activists, many sacked former mill-workers who ran cafés, dominated the textile union whose membership largely comprised unskilled, female and Belgian immigrant workers. The party's relationship with women workers deteriorated in the 1890s as electoral ambitions led to a concentration on concerns of male voters. Gains in national and local elections led, briefly, to dreams of achieving socialism via the ballot box. Control of municipal councils permitted the party to offer crèches and school meals for working-class families. In 1898 the POF's electoral momentum was lost as local industrialists exploited socialist divisions. Many workers were confused by the POF's sectarian insistence that the bourgeois Republic was not worth defending against the anti-Dreyfusard Right. Mill-owner Motte defeated Guesde by posing as a moderate Republican, wooing small retailers alarmed at high local taxes which municipal socialism implied, and by threats from socialist consumer cooperatives. He emphasised the role of employers in providing jobs and charity, and labelled the Marxist POF a 'foreign' party concerned more with immigrant Belgian workers than with native French. Although these electoral losses were eventually reversed, POF electoral support levelled off at one-third of the Nord vote. It was a revolutionary party which, like the German SPD, had no revolutionary strategy. It failed to use Marxist analysis to develop strategies appropriate to France's 'peculiarities' – the durability of artisanal and peasant strata and the historic importance of Republicanism. It ran a network of consumer cooperatives, but its lack of enthusiasm for industrial militancy made it insensitive to millworkers' shopfloor grievances and ensured that it made little headway among the region's miners and metalworkers (Stuart 1992; Gordon 1996; Willard 1965; Hilden 1986).

The song culture of Roubaix provides insights into workers' mentalities. In woollen mills where skill levels were already modest, Northropp mules finally eroded the relative job autonomy hitherto enjoyed by weavers. Hence songs reflect little joy in work or pride in skills – for machines do everything, the factory is a *bagne* (prison), workers *bagnards* (convicts). What makes life tolerable is the café where one meets friends, plays billiards. Songs by socialist activists reflect hostility to Catholic charity and disillusionment with a Republic which reneged on its promises to improve workers' lives. But textile workers read less and were less ideologically aware than city artisans. Their insular patois culture expressed localised solidarities. Even a trip to nearby Lille was a rarity. A 'frontier' patriotism made Guesdists wary of espousing anti-militarism, and an undercurrent of anti-Belgian xenophobia was expressed in resentment at immigrants' role as strikebreakers and cheap labour. Songs were male and misogynistic. Women workers were too docile towards employers, frivolous gossips who wasted family resources on dresses and made married life an endless sequence of petty disputes. The culture revealed by these songs has humour, vitality and warmth, but is introverted, fatalistic, and tinged with ethnic and sexual tensions. There are few aspirations to pro-letarian cultural autonomy. It was a culture the fragility of which would be revealed by exposure to Republican patriotism or to the lure of commercial-ised mass media (Marty 1982).

Miners and reformism

Concentration of miners in particular constituencies gave them a precocious capacity to elect their own deputies, while the role of state mining engineers in supervising the pits led miners to look to the state to regulate safety. Miners' long-term goal was nationalisation. In the interim, introduction of mine-safety delegates (1890) or the Eight-Hour Day (1905) were evidence that parliamentary reformism delivered results. During the 1880s – when Zola wrote *Germinal* – an unprecedented strike wave transformed the image of miners from culturally isolated quasi-rustics into archetypal proletarians. This militancy was provoked by management attempts to turn peasant-miners into full-time workers in order to improve labour discipline, timekeeping and productivity. Deprived of supplementary agricultural resources, miners became increasingly sensitive to wage issues and pit conditions. But strikes were also triggered by hopes that Republican prefects would support miners against authoritarian employers. The Nord/Pas-de-Calais coalfield emerged as the heartland of miner reformism. Employing 100,000 miners, it produced 75 per cent of French coal. The key figure was Basly, the 'Tsar of Lens'. His strategy was to use the union as an electoral machine to deliver deputies whose function was to lobby parliament. An admirer of the pragmatic union-ism of the British and Ruhr coalfields, he lobbied alongside employers for tariffs to protect French coal, urged wage restraint to win government approval and kept his union aloof from the syndicalist CGT. In the Arras Convention (1891) he secured collective bargaining rights for northern miners. Critics in other coalfields resented his indifference to national bar-gaining. Within the Pas-de-Calais, union officials – café-owners whose role appeared to be to maximise sales of alcohol – became resented as out of touch with pit-face grievances such as hated piecework wage systems. A quasi-syndicalist breakaway union emerged in the 1900s, briefly securing 20 per cent support (Michel 1974).

In the Loire, the second-largest coalfield, Rondet, was a miniature Basly. Isolated mining towns of the Centre and the South often had difficult seams and low productivity. Their management were often intransigent. In the Gard the influx of miners from outside the region eroded the introversion of local Catholic miners, paving the way for violent May Day strikes in the 1890s – virtual guerrilla wars with the sabotage of pits and militants taking refuge in the hills! Strikes were defeated and the union broken. When labour organ-isation revived it was more cautious and worked, in conjunction with radical *vignerons*, for the election of socialist deputies. Jaurès, the SFIO leader, was deputy for the Carmaux mining constituency. Here miners got support in the 1880s from anti-clerical Republicans against the Catholic-Royalist coalowner, before turning to socialism under the influence of local glass-workers. The path of Carmaux labour was scarcely smooth. Jaurès lost his seat, briefly, in 1898, and a company union gained ground. Local miners' leaders were repelled by Basly's 'repugnant egoism', favoured national bargaining and flirted with revolutionary rhetoric when the local prefect sided with management. Yet they shared Jaurès' faith in the Republic as a progressive regime which offered the framework for necessary reforms (Trempé 1974).

Syndicalism and labour protest: the rebels behind the cause

Revolutionary syndicalism was the ideology that best expressed the mood of militant workers. Syndicalists' attempts to challenge capitalism via industrial mobilisation rather than electoral politics made them heirs of traditions of popular direct action – and precursors of hauliers, fishermen and railworkers who still blockade Channel ports! Repression of the Commune suggested that urban insurrection was no longer viable in Western Europe. But disillusionment with the bourgeois Republic nurtured mistrust of politicians – an *ouvrièriste* sense that workers' autonomous actions were the only means for changing society. Syndicalists argued that workers could unite around shared experiences of exploitation at work. Concessions won by struggles strengthened consciousness and solidarities more than did passive receipt of reforms 'from above'. Syndicalism's emphasis on job control reflected the aspirations of surviving artisans and skilled workers. Dreams of producer cooperation appeared utopian after the Second Industrial Revolution. But syndicalists' 'socialism' was not that of bureaucratic nationalised industries but of federations of independent producers. Syndicalism's decline coincided with the rationalisation of industry during the First World War which swamped remaining skilled workers with *ouvriers spécialisés* who did not share their aspirations to shop-floor control. However, one should beware of linking its trajectory too closely to technological changes. By 1900 syndicalist leader Griffuelhes, a skilled leather-worker, was encouraging craft unions to amalgamate into industrial federations capable of defending workers in an era of large-scale industry and employers' associations. The syndicalist CGT proved more successful than the American Federation of Labor (AFL) at recruiting members in large metallurgical and chemical plants (Friedman 1998; Vandervort 1996).

At least 40 per cent of syndicalist militants were at some stage socialist party members. Socialists worked alongside syndicalists in *Bourses du Travail*, socialist municipalities aided syndicalist strikers and shielded pickets from police harassment. Socialist orators addressed strike rallies. Levels of unionisation in large industrial plants correlate with local socialist voting. Nevertheless, syndicalism was ideologically and organisationally distinctive. Pelloutier envisaged *Bourses du Travail* as centres of an alternative workerist culture, with libraries, training courses and facilities for workers from different trades to exchange ideas. Pouget was editor of the anarchist *Père Peinard*, built around the figure of an irascible cobbler forever ridiculing capitalists and hypocritical Republican politicians. Written in Parisian *argot*, the paper tapped into the popular sub-cultures of the capital and was adept at channelling populist grievances. Exiled in the mid-1890s for alleged encouragement of terrorism, Pouget returned to lend his talents to syndicalism. However, it was strike-leaders Griffuelhes or Yvetot who were the quintessential syndicalists. The former was impatient with intellectual justifications for syndicalism offered by retired engineer Sorel in his *Reflections on Violence*, insisting that he read Alexandre Dumas! By 1902 syndicalists controlled both the CGT and the *Bourses*, allowing them to launch a campaign of strikes whose immediate goal was to raise workers' consciousness, but whose ultimate aim was the revolutionary general strike (Julliard 1971; Mitchell 1987).

Even in its brief heyday in the 1900s, when annual strike rates topped a thousand, syndicalism's critics denied that it was representative of workers, dismissing it as a 'general staff without an army' (C. Bouglé). German and American union leaders warned that revolutionary rhetoric alienated ordinary workers, pragmatists interested in achievable wage gains, not class warriors. This judgement was reiterated by Stearns, who dubbed syndicalism a 'cause without rebels' backed by a minority of that minority – perhaps 15 per cent – of workers who were unionised. Larger, better-funded unions – mining, rail, print and textiles – were led by reformists who avoided rash strikes. These kept aloof from the CGT, whose domination by syndicalists was the result of manipulation of a number of small unions. Syndicalists' revolutionary rhetoric was bluster born of impotent frustration. Eulogy of militant 'active minorities' reflected their tenuous hold on the rank-and-file. When they did persuade labour's poor bloody infantry to go over the top, the results were a series of demoralising defeats. Syndicalist unions charged low dues, were unable to collect these regularly and lacked the funds to sustain strikes. Reformist printers charged union-dues five times higher than syndicalist unions (Stearns 1971).

Stearns (1971) exaggerates his case. His claim that most strikes were wage-orientated ignores the rise in job-control and hours disputes. He ignores the quasi-messianic mood of the 1906 strike wave and the range of workers attracted to syndicalist-led mobilisations, which included breakaway minorities from reformist mining and rail unions. Perrot's (1987) magisterial study of strikes provides the essential prelude to an understanding of the syndicalist years. During the 1880s Depression, newly legalised unions were weak, strikes often ill-organised, 'defensive' reactions against wage cuts. Yet by 1890 annual strike levels of 300 were double the average of the previous two decades. Skilled workers' strikes remained better organised and more successful, but two-thirds of strikers were now unskilled or semi-skilled. In the absence of unions, their disputes were coordinated from local *Bourses*. Barely 4 per cent of strikes involved serious violence, but some foremen and managers were armed. Strikers' often threatening rhetoric was redolent more of 1789 than of Marxism! Employers were parasitic *seigneurs* exploiting industrial serfs. Strikes were 'happenings' – lived experiences which stayed in the memory of those involved, 'days of hope' eroding workers' sense of fatalism and isolation. Rituals of street demonstrations with red flags and singing of the *Internationale* developed. Labour leaders addressing mass rallies were evangelical preachers spreading a message of the historic 'mission' of the working class to build a New Jerusalem, and evoking a future revolutionary *Grand Soir*. May Day strikes planned by labour organisers after 1890 for the international

Eight-Hour Day campaign escalated out of control as Nord rioters attacked mill-owners' homes and Gard miners attempted to dynamite pitheads (Perrot 1987; Tilly and Shorter 1981).

Unions organised 30 per cent of strikes in 1890, 75 per cent by 1906. Union growth between 1884 and 1913 was concentrated in five years of major strike outbreaks. Strikers flooded into unions during disputes. Many drifted away once conflict ended, but membership stabilised at a higher level. *Bourses du Travail* widened support for strikers. Their broader role was to nurture an autonomous workerist culture. They demanded shorter hours to give workers chances for self-education and family life. It was hours strikes which were most stubbornly resisted by employers. *Bourses* campaigned against alcoholism, arguing that drinking wrecked families, diverted workers from the class struggle and lined the pockets of brewers and distillers. They spread birth-control propaganda, urging a *grève des ventres* which, by reducing birth rates, would deprive capitalists of a reserve army of labour and militarists of cannon fodder for Imperialist wars. But activists agreed with Griffuelhes that strikes were 'worth more than the content of libraries' – teaching the values of solidarity, 'exposing' the repressive nature of the state. The only gains worth making were won through struggle, not 'conceded' by reform from above (Mitchell 1987; Julliard 1971).

Syndicalism benefitted from the post-1896 economic upturn which strenthened labour's bargaining position. Strike failures fell from 46 per cent to 33 per cent between 1895 and 1904. But syndicalism also relied on the 'space' permitted to it by a Republic which it professed to despise. Republicans relied on workers' votes and mistrusted reactionary elements of big business which wished to crush unions. The strike wave of 1899–1900 was triggered by hopes raised by Millerand's cabinet appointment. 'Successful' syndicalist-led strikes often saw intervention by bureaucrats who pressured employers into concessions; 50 per cent of state mediation resulted from workers' requests, only 3 per cent from those of employers. At the apogee of syndicalist influence, annual strike levels regularly exceeded a thousand. In 1906, 68,000 troops were mobilised in Paris and CGT leaders arrested to break the May Day general strike which, like one-third of strikes since 1904, demanded shorter hours. Syndicalist-led unions were more successful at running strikes than reformist rivals, recruiting a range of workers including many in large-scale industry. Catholic Mazamet wool workers and Besançon watchmakers established unions during syndicalist-led strikes. One unlikely bastion of syndicalism was the Parisian food-workers' union (*Fédération de l'Alimentation*) which mobilised an eclectic mixture of chefs and pastry cooks, journeymen bakers, hotel and café workers, grocery assistants and female sugar workers in strikes against exploitative job-agencies and for implementation of the weekly rest-day. The surprise here is less the union's decline after 1907 than the scale of its activity among such workers in the previous years.

By contrast, construction workers, whose *Fédération du Bâtiment* (FB) was strongly syndicalist, had a tradition of militancy. They clashed with big construction firms which ignored established pay-scales and safety regulations on Paris *Exposition* or Metro construction sites. Carpenters and joiners, resentful of the introduction of power saws and concrete and steel girders, were prominent in strikes, but navvies and bricklayers were also recruited into an industrial union. There were 47 major strikes in Paris in 1906–08. One on the Metro lasted eleven months. These demanded the Eight-Hour Day, fixed pay-scales and safety regulations. Violence between pickets and 'yellows' – and hired gunmen – was frequent. The climax of FB militancy came in 1908 when four demonstrators were killed and 67 wounded as cavalry charged a demonstration at Villeneuve-St-George called to protest at police shootings into the strike headquarters at a nearby quarry dispute. With the state supporting the employers, the FB faced crisis. Leaders were arrested for anti-militarist propaganda. Latent tensions between craftsmen and navvies and between native and immigrant workers exploded.

The trajectory of the *Fédération des Métaux* (FM) illustrates syndicalism's weaknesses. In 1905–06 union leader Merrheim acted as roving strike organiser, pointing to the use of troops against strikers as evidence of the Republic's true nature. But strike defeats prompted him to rethink his strategy. By 1914 the FM had 25,000 members, 3 per cent of the workforce – a paltry level of unionisation compared with that of its British counterpart the Amalgamated Society of Engineers (ASE). Events in 1912 epitomised the union's dilemmas. Confronted with craftworkers' protests against time-and-motion studies, Renault locked out his workers, went to the Riviera, then returned to sack 400 activists and replace them with semi-skilled workers. In 1914 the FM had 50 members in Renault's 4000 workforce – and none among the 2000 at Berliet's Lyon car plant! The FM's future lay in organising new semi-skilled strata. But union activists were craftsmen contemptuous of such neophytes for lacking skills and professional pride. Despite sharing such sentiments, Merrheim argued for a new approach which found favour with Jouhaux, the new pragmatic CGT leader. Faced with government collusion with employers' associations, one had to jettison outmoded strategies of militancy and provocative anti-militarism and construct industrial federations with large, dues-paying memberships. 'We are *for* active minorities', Jouhaux insisted, 'but these grow weary if their efforts are futile.' One had to reject craftsmen's quixotic efforts to resist industrial rationalisation and demand that workers reap the benefits – shorter hours, greater leisure, higher wages – of productivity gains achieved via scientific management and technological innovation. This became the strategy of the 'new realists' of the CGT during and after the war. Syndicalist discourse had always identified the worker as producer rather than as citizen. The new policy exposed an Achilles heel in this discourse, for union leaders risked seduction by the productivist rhetoric of neo-St. Simonian, 'progressive' businessmen and technocrats offering the beguiling vision of an 'American' high wage/high productivity utopia (Tucker 1996).

Conclusion: integrating the workers?

Despite anti-militarist demonstrations in the run-up to the war, workers rallied to the *Union Sacrée* of August 1914, albeit more with a resigned sense of duty than real enthusism. Contingency plans to arrest thousands of militants were not implemented. This did not necessarily signify workers' integration into the bourgeois social order. The Communards were revolutionaries *and* patriots. Among the most fervent of patriots in 1914–18 were neo-Blanquist workers in Belleville who viewed defence of France – or perhaps of Paris – as defence of the world's revolutionary epicentre! Socialist leader Jaurès, assassinated by a nationalist fanatic on the eve of the war, insisted on the compatibility of internationalism and Jacobin patriotism. Comparative studies of levels of integration of European labour place French workers in an intermediate position, more reconciled to their society than those in southern or eastern Europe, rather less than those in Britain or Scandinavia. Eugen Weber's trinity of railways/barracks /schools gave peripheral regions a sense of national identity largely absent in parts of Italy or Russia. Despite syndicalists' critique of French capitalism's lack of dynamism vis-à-vis the US, workers enjoyed material fruits of capitalist Imperialism denied to workers in parts of Europe where per capita productivity was two-thirds lower. Unlike Italy in 1896 or Russia in 1904–05, France had suffered no very recent military or colonial humiliation. Many jobs depended on trade with the Empire. Some socialist discourse even portrayed colonialism as part of France's progressive civilising mission! The army was far from universally popular. Workers detested reactionary, upper-class Catholic officers and resented army strike-breaking. Yet syndicalism's *Sou du Soldat* campaign to keep young conscripts in touch with the labour movement had limited success. The laic school taught pupils to do their military duty, and conscripts' experiences of military service were less brutalising and alienating than elsewhere in Europe. Working-class autobiographer G. Navel portrayed his father, a Lorraine steelworker, as nostalgic for the barracks – remembered as a period of escape from the constraints of family and steel mill, of camaraderie, drinking and brothel escapades. *Romans feuilletons* portrayed life in the colonial army, particularly the Legion, as exotic and heroic. Military service strengthened many young workers' sense of the 'foreigner' as 'alien other'.

Except in areas of maternity and childcare, the French welfare system lagged behind that in Germany. The proportion of workers covered by accident, insurance or pension provision was between two-thirds and three-quarters lower than in the Reich. Nevertheless, the growth of welfare provision after 1890 contributed to a sense of national identity. *French*, not immigrant, workers became eligible to be mine-safety delegates or receive free medical care. Immigrants were now excluded from municipal and civil service employment. Crucially French workers were citizens of a democratic Republic. Male German workers had the vote, but within a semi-authoritarian Reich, where parliament's powers were limited and local franchises biased in favour of property owners. Britain had a 'liberal' parliamentary system and union rights, but excluded 30 per cent of male workers from the franchise. In southern and eastern Europe the franchise was much more restricted.

A study of Roanne, a south-eastern textile town, emphasises the importance of workers' incorporation into municipal sociability. Workers showed signs of class consciousness. They voted socialist after 1896 and joined consumer cooperatives which supported frequent textile strikes – despite modest union-isation levels. However, they also joined non-class voluntary associations – music societies, sports clubs, former pupils and ex-conscript groups – where they rubbed shoulders with bourgeois and petty bourgeois. These were active in municipal festivals and concerts. In 1914 such workers had a sense that they were defending a democratic Republic which did not exclude them. In 1915 a Gard miner, none too keen on the war, insisted that 'if Germany had a Republic, even one as bastardised, uncaring and crass as ours, there would never have been a war!'. This was clearly an endorsement, of sorts, of the French system. Yet the industrial unrest of 1917–20, culminating in the foundation of the Communist Party, was not just a product of the war. France had revolutionary strands – Marxist and syndicalist – in its labour movement much stronger than those in Britain. These were a legacy of its post-1789 political heritage and of unresolved social and industrial tensions (Van der Linden 1988; Milner 1990; Howorth 1985; Turner 1999).

Bibliography

Introductory
Berlanstein, L. 'Working with language: the linguistic turn in French labour history', *Comparative Studies in Society and History* 1991.
Berlanstein, L. *Rethinking Labor History* (Urbana: State University of Illinois, 1993).
Berlanstein, L. 'The distinctiveness of the French labour movement', *Journal of Modern History* 1992.
Judt, T. *Marxism and the French Left: 1830–1981* (Oxford: Oxford University Press, 1986).
Kaplan, S. and Koepp, C. (eds) *Work in France* (Cambridge: Cambridge University Press, 1986).
Katznelson, I. and Zolberg, A. (eds) *Working-Class Formation* (Princeton, NJ: Princeton University Press, 1986).
Magraw, R. *A History of the French Working Class*: Vol. I *The Age of Artisan Revolution: 1815–71*, Vol. II *Workers and the Bourgeois Republic* (Oxford: Blackwell, 1992).
Noiriel, G. *Workers in French Society in the 19th-Century* (New York: Berg, 1990).
Vincent, K. Steven *P-J Proudhon and the Rise of French Republican Socialism* (Oxford: Oxford University Press, 1984).

1780–1871
Accampo, E. *Industrialisation, Family Life and Class Relations: St Chamond 1815–1914* (Berkeley, CA: University of California Press, 1989).
Agulhon, M. *Une Ville Ouvrière au temps du Socialisme Utopique: Toulon 1830–51* (Paris, 1970).
Amann, P. *Revolution and Mass Democracy: the Paris Club Movement in 1848* (Princeton, NJ: Princeton University Press, 1975).
Aminzade, R. *Ballots and Barricades: Class Formation and Republican Politics in France* (Princeton, NJ: Princeton University Press, 1993).
Auslander, L. 'Perceptions of beauty and problems of consciousness: Paris furniture makers', in L. Berlanstein (ed.) *Rethinking Labor History* (Urbana: State University of Illinois, 1993).
Berenson, E. *Populist Religion and Left-Wing Politics in France 1830–52* (Princeton, NJ: Princeton University Press, 1984).
Berlanstein, L. 'Growing up as workers in 19th-century Paris', *French Historical Studies* 1980.
Bezucha, R. *The Lyon Uprising of 1834* (Cambridge, Mass: Harvard University Press, 1974).

Calhoun, C. 'Industrialisation and social radicalism: British and French labor movements in the mid-nineteenth century crisis', *Theory and Society* 1983.

Cottereau, A. (ed.) *Le Sublime* (Paris, 1980).

Dalotel, A., Faure, A. and Freiermuth, J.-C. (eds) *Aux Origines de la Commune 1868–70* (Paris: F. Maspero, 1980).

Elwitt, S. *The Making of the Third Republic* (Baton Rouge: State University of Louisiana, 1975).

Faure, A. 'Mouvements Populaires et Mouvement Ouvrier à Paris 1830–34', *Le Mouvement Social* 1974.

Faure, A. and Rancière, J. *La Parole Ouvrière* (Paris, 1976).

Fitzpatrick, M. 'Proudhon and the French labour movement', *European History Quarterly* 1985.

Gaillard, J. *Paris, La Ville: 1852–70* (Paris: H. Champion, 1977).

Geiger, R. *The Anzin Mining Company: 1800–33* (Newark, Philadelphia, 1974).

Gordon, D. *Merchants and Capitalists* (Alabama: University of Alabama Press, 1985).

Gould, R. *Insurgent Identities: Class, Community and Protest in Paris from 1848 to the Commune* (Chicago IL, University of Chicago Press, 1995).

Haine, W. Scott *The World of the Paris Café: Sociability among the French Working Class* (Baltimore, MA: Johns Hopkins University Press, 1996).

Hanagan, M. *Nascent Proletarians: Class Formation in Post-Revolutionary France* (Oxford: Blackwell, 1989).

Harrison, C. 'The organisation of labor: laissez-faire and marchandage in the Paris building trades through 1848', *French Historical Studies* 1997–98.

Harvey, D. *Constructing Class and Nationality in Alsace: 1830–1945* (Dekalb, IL: North Illinois University Press, 2001).

Heywood, C. *Childhood in 19th-Century France* (Cambridge: Cambridge University Press, 1989).

Huard, R. *Le Mouvement Républicain en Bas-Languedoc: 1848–1881* (Paris: FNSP, 1982).

Hunt, L. and Sheridan, G. 'Corporation, association and the language of labour 1750–1850', *Journal of Modern History* 1986.

Jacquemet, G. *Belleville au XIXe Siècle: Du Faubourg à la Ville* (Paris, 1984).

Johnson, C. *Icarian Communism in France: 1839–51* (Ithaca: Cornell University Press, 1974).

Johnson, C. 'Economic change and artisan discontent: the tailors' history', in R. Price (ed.) *Revolution and Reaction in France* (London: Croom Helm, 1975).

Johnson, C. *The Life and Death of Industrial Languedoc, 1700–1920: the Politics of De-Industrialisation* (Oxford: Oxford University Press, 1995).

Johnson, M. *The Paradise of Associations: Political Culture and Popular Organisations in the Paris Commune of 1871* (Ann Arbor: University of Michigan, 1996).

Kulstein, D. *Napoleon III and the Working Class: A Study in Government Propaganda* (Los Angeles: California State Colleges, 1969).

Liebmann, R. 'Repressive strategies and working-class protest: Lyon 1848–52', *Social Science History* 1980.

McWilliam, N. 'Peripheral visions: class, cultural aspiration and the artisan community in mid-nineteenth-century France', in S. Kemal (ed.) *Politics and Aesthetics in the Arts* (Cambridge: Cambridge University Press, 2000).

Ménager, B. *Les Napoléon du Peuple* (Paris, 1988).

Moss, B. *The Origins of the French Labor Movement: the Socialism of Skilled Workers 1830–1914* (Berkeley, CA: University of California Press, 1976).

Moss, B. 'Republicanism, socialism and the making of the working class', *Comparative Studies in Society and History* 1993.

Papayanis, N. *The Coachmen of Nineteenth-Century Paris: Service Workers and Class Consciousness* (Louisiana: State University of Louisiana, 1993).

Perrot, M. 'Les ouvriers et les machines en France', in L. Murard and S. Zylberman (eds) *Le Soldat du Travail* (Paris, 1978).

Pierrard, P. *La Vie Ouvrière à Lille sous le Second Empire* (Paris, 1965).

Price, R. 'Poor relief and social control in mid-19th-century France', *European Studies Review* 1983.

Prothero, I. *Radical Artisans in England and France: 1830–70* (Cambridge: Cambridge University Press, 1997).

Rancière, J. 'The myth of the artisan', *International Labor and Working-Class History* 1983.

Rancière, J. *The Nights of Labor: the Workers' Dream in 19th-Century France* (Philadelphia: Temple University Press, 1989).

Reddy, W. *The Rise of Market Culture: the Textile Trade and French Society 1750–1914* (Cambridge: Cambridge University Press, 1984).

Reid, D. 'The night of the Proletarians: deconstruction and social history', *Radical History Review* 1984.

Reid, D. *The Miners of Decazeville* (Cambridge, Mass: Harvard University Press, 1985a).

Reid, D. 'Labour management in rural France: the Aubin Miners' Strike of 1869', *Social History* 1988.

Rougerie, J. *Le Procès des Communards* (Paris, 1964).

Rougerie, J. 'Remarques sur l'Histoire des Salaires à Paris au XIXe Siècle', *Le Mouvement Social* 1968.

Rudé, G. 'Cities and popular revolt: London and Paris 1750–1850', in J. Bosher (ed.) *French Government and Society: 1500–1850* (London: Athlone Press, 1973).

Schulkind, E. *The Paris Commune: the View from the Left* (London: Cape, 1972).

Scott, J. 'Men and women in the Parisian garment trades', in G. Crossick and P. Thane (eds) *The Power of the Past* (Cambridge: Cambridge University Press, 1974).

Sewell, W. 'Social change and the rise of working-class politics in Marseille', *Past and Present* 1974.

Sewell, W. *Work and Revolution: the Language of Labour from the Old Regime to 1848* (Cambridge: Cambridge University Press, 1980).

Sewell, W. *Men and Women of Marseille: 1820–70* (Cambridge: Cambridge University Press, 1985).

Sewell, W. 'Uneven development and the autonomy of politics: dockworkers of Marseille', *American Historical Review* 1988.

Sheridan, G. *The Social and Economic Foundations of Associationism Amongst Silk-Workers in Lyon: 1852–70* (New York: Arno Press, 1981).

Sibalis, M. 'The mutual aid societies of Paris 1789–1848', *French History* 1989.

Stewart-McDougall M.-L. *The Artisan Republic: Lyon 1848–51* (Montreal: McGill-Queens University Press, 1984).

Stewart-McDougall M.-L. 'Popular culture and political culture in Lyon 1830–50', *Historical Reflections/Réflections Historiques* 1981.

Strumhinger, L. *Women and the Making of the Working Class: Lyon 1830–70* (Montreal: McGill-Queens University Press, 1978).

Thomas, R. and Rifkind, A. (eds) *Voices of the People: the Social Life of 'La Sociale' at the End of the Second Empire* (London: Routledge, 1988).

Tilly, C. 'How protest modernised France', in W. Aydelotte (ed.) *Dimensions of Quantitative Research in History* (Princeton, NJ: Princeton University Press, 1972).

Tilly, L. 'Coping with company paternalism: family strategies of coalminers in 19th-century France', *Theory and Society* 1985.

Tilly, C. and Lees, L. 'The people of Paris in June 1848', in R. Price (ed.) *Revolution and Reaction* (London: Croom Helm, 1975).

Tombs, R. *The Paris Commune* (London: Longman, 1999).

Traugott, M. *Armies of the Poor: Determinants of Working-Class Participation in the Paris Insurrection of June 1848* (Princeton, NJ: Princeton University Press, 1985).

Traugott, M. *The French Worker: Autobiographies from the Early Industrial Period* (Berkeley, CA: University of California Press, 1993).

Truant, C. *Rites of Labor: Brotherhoods of Compagnonnages in Old and New Regime France* (Ithaca: Cornell University Press, 1994).

Weissbach, L. 'Artisanal response to artistic decline: cabinet-makers of Paris', *Journal of Social History* 1982.

1871–1914

Berlanstein, L. *The Working People of Paris: 1871–1914* (Baltimore, MA: Johns Hopkins University Press, 1984).

Berlanstein, L. *Big Business and Industrial Conflict in 19th-Century France* (Berkeley, CA: University of California Press, 1991).

Cross, G. *Immigrant Workers in Industrial France: the Making of a New Working Class* (Philadelphia: Temple University Press, 1983).

Elwitt, S. *The Third Republic Defended: Bourgeois Reform in France* (Louisiana: State University of Louisiana, 1986).

Friedman, G. *State Making and Labor Movements: France and the United States 1876–1914* (Ithaca: Cornell University Press, 1998).

Gordon, D. *Liberalism and Social Reform* (Westport, CT: Greenwood, 1996).

Gras, C. 'La Fédération des Métaux en 1913–14', *Le Mouvement Social* 1971.

Green, N. *The Pletzl of Paris: Jewish Immigrant Workers in the Belle Epoque* (New York: Holmes and Meier, 1986).

Hanagan, M. *The Logic of Solidarity* (Chicago: University of Chicago, 1980).

Hilden, P. 'Women and the Labour Movement in France: 1869–1914', *Historical Journal* 1986.

Howorth, J. 'French and German workers: the impossibility of Internationalism', *European History Quarterly* 1985.

Humphrey, G. *Taylorism in France 1904–20* (New York: Garland, 1986).

Jennings, J. 'Syndicalism and the French Revolution', *Journal of Contemporary History* 1991.

Julliard, J. *Fernand Pelloutier et les Origines des Bourses du Travail* (Paris, 1971).

Lebovics, H. *The Alliance of Iron and Wheat: the Origins of the New Conservatism: 1860–1914* (Baton Rouge: State University of Louisiana, 1988).

Lequin, Y. *Les Ouvriers de la Région Lyonnaise: 1848–1914* 2 vols (Lyon: Lyon University Press, 1977).

Linden, M. van der 'The National Integration of European Working Classes', *International Review of Social History* 1988.

Magraw, R. 'Management, labour and the state in France: 1871–1939', in R. Mathias and J. Davis (eds) *Enterprise and Labour from the Eighteenth Century* (Oxford: Blackwell, 1996).

Marty, L. *Chanter pour Survivre: Culture Ouvrière, Travail Technique dans le Textile Roubaix* (Lille, 1982).

Merriman, J. *The Red City: Limoges and the French Nineteenth Century* (Oxford: Oxford University Press, 1985).

Michel, J. 'Syndicalisme Minier et Politique dans le Nord/Pas-de-Calais', *Le Mouvement Social* 1974.

Milner, S. *The Dilemmas of Internationalism* (Oxford: Berg, 1990).

Mitchell, B. *The Practical Revolutionaries: A New Interpretation of Revolutionary Syndicalism* (Westport, CT: Greenwood Press, 1987).

Moch, L. *Paths to the City: Regional Migration in 19th-Century France* (Beverley Hills, CA: Sage, 1983).

Moss, B. 'Radicalism and social reform: progressive employers and the "Comité Mascuraud"', *French History* 1997.

Noiriel, G. *Longwy: Immigrés et Prolétaires: 1880–1980* (Paris, 1984).

Papayanis, N. A. *Merrheim: the Emergence of Reformism in Revolutionary Syndicalism* (Baton Rouge: Louisiana State University Press, 1985).

Perrot, M. *Workers on Strike: 1870–1914* (Leamington Spa: Berg, 1987).

Perrot, M. 'Three ages of industrial discipline', in J. Merriman (ed.) *Consciousness and Class Experience* (New York: Holmes and Meier, 1979).

Reid, D. 'Industrial paternalism: practice and discourse in French mining and metallurgy', *Comparative Studies in Society and History* 1985b.

Schneider, W. *An Empire for the Masses* (Westport CT: Greenwood Press, 1982).

Schöttler, P. *La Naissance des Bourses du Travail* (Paris, 1985).

Scott, J. *The Glassmakers of Carmaux* (Cambridge, Mass: Harvard University Press, 1974).

Shapiro A.-L. *Housing the Poor of Paris: 1850–1914* (Madison: University of Wisconsin Press, 1985).

Smith, T. 'The plight of the able-bodied poor and the unemployed in urban France: 1880–1914', *European History Quarterly* 2000.

Smith, T. 'Assistance and repression: rural exodus, vagabondage and social crisis in France 1880–1914', *Journal of Social History* 1999.

Stearns, P. 'Against the strike threat: employer policy towards labor agitation 1906–14', *Journal of Modern History* 1968.

Stearns, P. *Revolutionary Syndicalism and French Labor: A Cause without Rebels* (New Brunswick, NJ: Rutgers University Press, 1971).

Stein, M. 'The meaning of skill: The case of French engine drivers 1837–1917', *Politics and Society* 1979.

Stone, J. *The Search for Social Peace: Reform Legislation in France 1890–1914* (Albany: State University of New York, 1985).

Stuart, R. *Marxism at Work: Society and French Socialism 1882–1905* (Cambridge: Cambridge University Press, 1992).

Tilly, C. and Shorter, E. *Strikes in France: 1830–1968* (London: Cambridge University Press, 1981).

Trempé, R. *Les Mineurs de Carmaux* 2 vols (Paris, 1974).

Tucker, K. *French Revolutionary Syndicalism and the Public Sphere* (Cambridge: Cambridge University Press, 1996).

Turner, P. 'Hostile participants?: working-class militancy, associational life and the "distinctiveness" of the pre-war French labor movement', *Journal of Modern History* 1999.

Vandervort, B. *V. Griffuelhes and French Revolutionary Syndicalism: 1895–1922* (Louisiana: Louisiana State University Press, 1996).

Willard, C. *Le Mouvement Socialiste en France: Les Guesdistes 1893–1905* (Paris: Editions Sociales, 1965).

117

Chapter 3

The peasantry

Introduction: peasant France

Nineteenth-century French rural society was highly distinctive. Britain was dominated by capitalist estates farmed by tenants and employing landless labourers. Serfdom persisted in central and eastern Europe until mid-century, and Junker domination persisted in East Prussia long after 'emancipation'. Italy and Spain had areas of huge latifundia. Peasant farming did persist in south-west Germany and northern Spain. But France was *the* bastion of a *free* peasantry. This overthrew seigneurialism in 1789, was enfranchised in 1848, owned 40 per cent of the land and clung tenaciously to the soil. Thomas Hardy contrasted 'Hodge' – the demoralised, deferential agricultural labourer of southern England, his land and communal rights long since lost – with the sturdy, independent peasant across the Channel. Rural exodus was slow and migrants retained stakes in family farms. Peasant reluctance to enter heavy industry, allied to the spread of birth-control practices to avoid subdivision of small farms, forced industrialists to import immigrant labour. There was no rustic idyll. Small farms often relied on supplementary resources and pluri-activity for survival. There was endless debate about the 'crisis' of the countryside, the exodus of the young, *la terre qui meurt*. Yet there was no inexorable, unilinear peasant 'decline'. Economists, casting envious eyes across the Channel, described peasant farming as inefficient per se and anticipated its demise. Marx noted ironically that peasants looked to Louis Napoleon as a Messiah, unaware that Bonapartist political 'stability' would boost agrarian capitalism which would hasten the decline of peasant farming. Such predictions proved premature. The *fin des paysans* came only after 1950. Paradoxically falling land prices and agricultural profits during the late-nineteenth-century depression allowed some peasants to consolidate farms by purchasing land cheap.

Attitudes towards the peasantry were ambivalent. After 1945 peasant archaism was cited as symptom and cause of economic stagnation. Yet by the 1980s there was nostalgia for a peasantry which had incarnated the values of *la France profonde*. Such changes of perception were not unprecedented. Many nineteenth-century observers viewed peasants as savage 'others'. Balzac's *Les Paysans* (1844) portrayed them as greedy, rodent-like quadrapeds on two legs. The image in Zola's *La Terre* (1884) was equally unflattering. The agrarian unrest of 1848–51 reminded aristocrats of the horrors of the *jacqueries* of 1789. Liberals viewed peasants as prone to violent revolt or to deference to reactionary landowners and priests. Republicans blamed peasant electors for supporting authoritarian Bonapartism. Socialist leader Jaurès attributed the Vendée's counter-revolutionary tradition to the brutality of its peasantry. Yet both Left and Right sometimes offered more sympathetic images. Catholic-Royalists portrayed peasants as salt of the earth, immune to the vices, scepticism and artifice of city life. Conversely, Michelet suggested that hardworking peasants' devotion to the soil made the *petit pays* the cradle of Republican patriotism. Neo-Jacobin novelist Eugène Le Roy praised peasants of his native Dordogne as instinctive foes of *seigneurs*. In the 1890s Méline justified tariffs to protect small farms by portraying the peasantry as a repository of France's true values. Its survival was imperitive if France was to avoid class polarisation. Rural exodus engendered nostalgia for rustic traditions, prompting folklorists, ethnographers and cultural regionalists to record folksongs and proverbs at risk from a homogenising mass culture (Lehning 1995).

Was the peasantry a 'class'? Marx's answer was ambivalent. The millions who owned or rented small farms and faced similar problems constituted a 'class-in-itself'. However, because literacy and involvement in market agriculture were low, they were insular and lacked wider perspectives. Class-consciousness and capacity for class mobilisation were weak. Ironically this analysis is shared by liberal historian Eugen Weber, who argues that only the widening of horizons by railways, schools and conscription after the 1860s enabled peasants to become conscious national 'actors'. Others insist that peasant identity was constructed by a sense of difference from, exploitation by – and inferiority to – the towns. Hence their instinct was to rally behind landed *notables* in an agrarian bloc – a countryside alliance – to defend all-class rural interests (Weber 1977; Barral 1968). Weber portrays an 'urban' state imposing its agenda on to the peasantry in order to integrate it into 'France'. Others propose more interactive, less unilateral, processes. Peasants, whether through direct action or the ballot-box, proved adept at negotiating with state and elites. Indeed the idea of the peasantry was an integral part of that 'national identity' which was being constructed. There could be no 'true' France without its peasants! McPhee (1992) argues that memories of the mobilisations of the 1790s nurtured a vigorous rural political culture. Peasants proved quite capable of reflecting upon their own problems without reliance on urban 'culture brokers' (McPhee 1992).

It remains difficult to know how peasants made sense of their experiences. Written sources derive largely from priests, prefects and notables who asserted, in patronising tones, that '*nos paysans*' were parochial, credulous, ignorant of and apathetic about politics. Historians may accept such stereotypes unthinkingly. Balzac portrayed peasants as ferocious individualists, wedded to their plots of land, suspicious of everyone. Yet in an economy of scarcity, survival depended on mutual aid and collective action. Villages had communal shepherds or road-repairers, agreed patterns of crop-rotation and harvesting dates. Loire valley peasants formed work-teams to shore up river banks to prevent flooding. Networks of 'instrumental' voluntary associations developed in some regions – fire-brigades, mutual aid societies, livestock insurance associations

119

and cooperatives. These nurtured forms of participatory village democracy and represented grass-roots incarnations of the associationist ideology sponsored by the Left in 1848 and by Solidarists in the 1890s (Baker 1999).

No single 'key' can explain the enormous variety of local peasant cultures. After 1789 both Revolution and counter-revolution developed fierce peasant support. In 1950 French peasants divided their votes equally between three Left-wing and three Right-wing parties. Peasant conservatism flourished in regions with a high proportion of tenants, sharecroppers and landless labourers, in areas of dispersed habitat rather than large nucleated villages and where religious practice was high. Cereal or livestock farmers tended to be less radical than *vignerons*. Some invoked the strength of regional cultures in 'peripheral' areas to explain specific local *mentalités*. Memories of, or 'myths' about historical conflicts such as the persecution of Cévenol Huguenots in the 1690s or the 'genocide' of Catholic Vendéen peasants in the 1790s could create local political traditions which survived across generations despite changes in local economies. Anthropological analysis of family structures may explain regional political cultures. The 'liberal' France of the North-East correlates with 'individualism' fostered by nuclear families practising partible inheritance, which encouraged children to set up their own farms. Conservative, hierarchical values in the West were nurtured by inegalitarian stem-families within which paternal authority over resident children was maintained and only one child inherited. Conversely, egalitarian stem-families in parts of the Midi underpinned Left-wing rural cultures. There are exceptions to all such (useful) generalisations. Beaulolais *vignerons* were less radical than those in the Midi. Allier sharecroppers's militancy in the 1900s suggests that dependence on large landowners may generate resentment and revolt – not just deference. Châtillonnais was an area of small peasant property, few notables and low religious practice, yet it was consistently more conservative than the rest of the Côte d'Or (Brustein 1988; Lagrange and Roché 1988; Lévêque 1980).

Post-modernists warn that all historians are storytellers who use a variety of literary tropes. Weber (1976) related a success story in which a 'backward' peasantry was 'modernised' by economic and cultural change and 'progress' was charted by rising literacy, market agriculture and integration into national politics (Weber 1976). Alternative narratives are more tragic. These present the inexorable erosion of a once-vigorous peasant culture with the toil required to make a living from small farms and the lure of the cities leading to an exodus of the young. Intrusion of urban values led to the wisdom of the old being mocked rather than respected. As villages shrank and populations aged, a diluted variant of faceless urban mass-culture imposed itself on those who remained. Yet perhaps it is the *ironic* trope which ought to inform narratives about the peasantry. It is misleading to assume that cities simply reconstructed the countryside in their own image and nationalised the peasantry. Urban France was *itself* in flux because of the inflow of rural migrants, and immigrants. Peasants appropriated elements of modernity for their own purposes, took what they wanted from schooling in order to preserve the rest of their way of life. Peasant revolts in 1789 forced the Revolution down paths which bourgeois politicians had not planned to take.

Peasant enfranchisement in 1848 meant that governments ignored peasant voters at their peril. Protectionist tariffs after 1880 were framed to safeguard peasant farming. It would be misleading to label the France of 1914 a 'peasant democracy'. But it was Europe's largest Republic – and a century of peasant struggles did much to shape its character.

The peasantry and the French Revolution

Rural conflicts of the 1790s both revealed and accentuated divisions within the peasantry and generated experiences, myths and memories upon which identities of Catholic-Royalist and Republican peasants were constructed. Yet the *cahiers de doléances* of 1788–89 had suggested that peasants shared a range of grievances and aspirations. Seigneurialism and tithes were denounced. There were demands for fairer taxation and a consensus that communal lands should not be acquired by the rich. English landed elites expropriated peasants via enclosures. Their French counterparts had opted to keep peasants on the land, using seigneurialism to extract surplus value. Seventeenth-century peasant revolts had been provoked by royal taxation, but it was seigneurialism that now fuelled peasant resentments. Around 40 per cent of Upper Burgundy *cahiers* complained of seigneurial exactions. Demographic pressure on land and food supplies made peasants vulnerable to 1780s harvest failures which drove-up food prices and reduced demand for wine and proto-industrial products. Inevitably the act of compiling the *cahiers* politicised peasant grievances by offering a forum for discussion and raising hopes of some 'great change'. Although the seigneurial burden varied between regions it was the general hostility towards the system which explains the scale and intensity of revolt in 1789–90. Wholesale destruction of seigneurial records was the culmination of localised revolts which had been occurring since the 1760s (Jones 1988).

However, myriad divisions within rural society were soon exposed. 'Peasant' France consisted of large peasant-proprietors and tenants, small owners, sharecroppers, landless labourers and village artisans. By 1792 landless labourers around Amiens alarmed local peasant proprietors by organising strikes. Abolition of the seigneurial burden won the Revolution less gratitude in Brittany, where it had been relatively light, than in Burgundy where it had been onerous. Peasant loyalty to the Revolution was consolidated in some areas by acquisition of church lands (*biens nationaux*). Elsewhere urban bourgeois purchasers thwarted such peasant aspirations. Catholic regions might view the Revolution as a threat to their religion. Some peasants were angered by attempts to enforce redemption payments for seigneurial dues. Meanwhile conflicts erupted *within* villages. Small peasants demanded limitations on the size of tenancy holdings. Conflicts over common lands and usage rights were endemic and highly complex. Some viewed their retention as essential for the survival of village 'small men'. Others argued that the real beneficiaries of the existing system were larger peasants whose herds dominated local grazing. Hence commons ought to be distributed among villagers. But some insisted that the village poor should be given priority, others that commons be allocated in proportion to the size of existing landholdings or auctioned to the highest bidders.

The peasantry's role in the counter-revolution was long ignored by Marxist historians, who emphasised manipulation by clerical and aristocratic reactionaries. But *chouan* peasant rebels who invaded western towns had their own grievances against a 'revolutionary bourgeoisie' – identified in their minds as urban parasites, 'usurers', godless acquirers of church lands and agents of an alien bureaucratic state. Around Cholet bourgeois had acquired 53 per cent of church lands, peasants only 9 per cent. Efforts of *Armées Révolutionnaires*, composed of urban artisans, to requisition grain or enforce conscription further alienated some peasants. Draft evasion became endemic in the Southern Massif. Anti-conscription rebels drifted into 'brigandage'. Jacobin contempt for 'backward', 'patois'-speaking peasant culture provoked resistance in peripheral regions. The *mentalités* of such areas were deeply marked by memories and myths of persecution by godless, alien, Revolutionary forces. Republican historian Michelet portrayed counter-revolutionaries as 'dependent' sharecroppers, deferential to aristocratic landowners, and 'fanatical' rustics duped by priests. Such stereotypes ignored the 'redneck' populism of such mobilisations. Nothing confirms the bourgeois nature of the Revolution more clearly than the hostility of its peasant opponents to intrusion of urban bourgeois into the countryside. But rural counter-revolutionaries of the West or the Southern Massif did not represent the entire peasantry. Images of Revolutionary *fêtes* with peasants parading proudly behind the local National Guard were not simply propaganda. In Saumur, on the fringes of the West, peasant acquisition of church lands underpinned rural Republicanism. Regions where seigneurial burdens had been heavy – Burgundy, Dordogne, Dauphiné – feared a resurgence of aristocratic power. The sheer scale of the antiseigneurial revolts of 1790–93 was striking. Jacobin abolition of redemption payments created village *sans culottes*. In Provence, a region of relatively egalitarian social structure, village assemblies had contested domination of landed elites even before 1789.

Restoring stability to a countryside ravaged by civil war was the priority for Bonapartism. The regime guaranteed *biens nationaux* holders' acquisitions and used military courts to repress Catholic-Royalist peasant 'brigands' who were terrorising the Midi. The Revolution's agrarian settlement bedded down. The Rural Code allowed a proprietor to dispose freely of 50 per cent of his land, but the remainder had to be shared among his heirs. A comprehensive land-survey (*cadastre*) was begun. But the image of these years as a rural 'golden age' was a product of subsequent Bonapartist myth-making. Labour shortages, due to conscription, pushed up agricultural wages, but created problems for family farms already burdened by war taxation. Bad harvests in 1810–11 forced the regime to recognise that the free market in grain benefited only large producers, and controls on grain prices and supplies were reintroduced. Worsening relations between Bonapartism and the Papacy prompted Catholic-Royalists to encourage army desertion and rural brigandage. The scale of distress emphasised that many rural aspirations remained unfulfilled. Peasants lacked the franchise. Most church lands had gone to bourgeois purchasers. Jacobin promises to reform sharecroppers' contracts had not been carried out. The Rural Code still recognised gleaning and grazing rights, and governments were wary of advocating immediate abolition of communal rights – yet the overall thrust of post-Revolutionary legislation had been towards agrarian individualism.

The impact of the Revolution on the peasantry and on agrarian capitalism was complex. Some portray the Revolution as harmful to agricultural development. Aristocrats had been eroding communal resistance to modernisation of estates and enlightened bureaucrats like Turgot attempting to free the grain trade. Because peasants lacked the capital and expertise to adopt new agricultural methods, and clung tenaciously to routines and communal practices, the 'price' paid for their partial victory in 1789 was survival of quasi-subsistence farming and low productivity. This interpretation is less than persuasive. It exaggerates the scale of agricultural innovation before 1789. Most aristocrats had been concerned simply to squeeze additional seigneurial dues out of the peasantry. It underestimates the long-term impetus which the Revolution gave to agrarian capitalism. Internal tolls were abolished. Free trade in grain was introduced, albeit subject to reassertion of controls in crisis years. Abolition of tithes meant that farmers retained more of their crop for sale. Some were now free to concentrate on livestock-rearing rather than being obliged to produce grain for monastic tithe-owners. Above all it ignored peasants' capacity to become effective cash-crop commodity producers. Many combined residual loyalties to the 'moral economy' and communal rights with a willingness to adapt to changing market realities, just as eighteenth-century peasants had seized opportunities opened up by proto-industrial rural textiles. Agricultural production rose in the 1800–20 period. Often, as in the Pyrénées Orientales, it was small peasants rather than large landowners who were diversifying into cash-crops such as wine or olives (McPhee 1989; Root 1987).

The peasantry were net beneficiaries of the Revolution. The end of seigneurialism and the tithes removed impositions which often amounted to 30 per cent of income. Rural death-rates fell. If around Paris or Dijon most *biens nationaux* went to bourgeois, in the Nord peasants' share of the land rose from 30 per cent to 42 per cent – and one-third of those acquiring land hitherto owned little or none. Less tangible psychological gains resulted from participation in revolt. Not only were seigneurial justice and hunting-monopolies abolished but deference was shaken and a sense of independence generated. The fall in the birth-rate, from 36 to 32 per thousand between the 1780s and 1810, indicates a resort to birth-control strategies reflecting declining fatalism, a heightened sense of agency. Peasants had struggled for a better life in their own villages. But many also fought in armies which had challenged feudalism in Europe. Peasants in eastern France rallied to Bonaparte's 'Hundred Days' because his claims to be the 'People's Emperor' standing between France and the seigneurial yoke sounded plausible. *Grande Armeé* veterans perceived Bourbon subservience to the Holy Alliance as a betrayal of their crusade to liberate Europe. Mass conscription had widened horizons, creating a sense of French identity beyond the confines of the *petit pays*. Peasants paying modest levels of taxation secured the municipal franchise and gained electoral experience and an apprenticeship in local

123

democracy. The Revolution disappointed the utopian hopes of 1789. But it brought real material gains to many peasants and raised peasant conscious-ness. Attempts to portray the countryside as archaic and unchanging must be viewed with some suspicion.

Apogee and crisis of a peasant society? (1815–48)

Although some peripheral regions were locked into quasi-subsistence polyculture, claims that peasant agriculture was routine-bound and under-capitalised and that no significant change occurred until the advent of the railways appear dubious. Agricultural productivity grew at 1.2 per cent per annum between 1820 and 1860 – a rate similar to that of industry. Nor was growth confined to capitalist estates of Picardy or the Paris basin. The spread of maize and of the potato fed expanding populations. Wheat was replacing rye. Doubs peasants increased wheat yields by 25 per cent between 1836 and 1850. The area of land under cultivation and its quality were rising. Revolu-tionary legislation strengthening property rights facilitated irrigation and drainage projects. Diffusion of fodder crops allowed a 50 per cent increase in livestock between 1815 and 1835 – providing manure for fertiliser. The 1830s saw increased funding of rural roads and bridges. Improved nutrition cut rural mortality rates. Peasant conscripts were taller and healthier than their industrial counterparts. Agrarian structures were complex. The number of landholders grew from 5.4 million to 6 million between 1815 and 1842. However, 1 per cent of proprietors owned 28 per cent of the land. In all, aristocrats and bourgeois controlled some 60 per cent, leasing it to 0.9 mil-lion tenants (*fermiers*) and 0.5 million sharecroppers (*métayers*), the latter mainly in the Centre and South-West. Aristocratic estates were prominent in the West, but islands of aristocratic landholding existed in many regions. The Morvan had 21 noble estates of over a thousand hectares. Urban bourgeois had extensive holdings in Beaujolais, Burgundy and Bordelais vineyards. Fertile plains around Paris and northern towns had fully developed capital-ist agriculture. Fertilisers and threshing-machines boosted wheat yields and labour productivity in Île-de-France and Soissonnais. The Normandy country-side was dominated by livestock rearing, parts of Flanders by sugar-beet.

Hierarchical social relations engendered by capitalist farming are exem-plified by the power of the tenant farmers of Artois (Pas-de-Calais). Although under 5 per cent of the population, these *fermiers* farmed two-thirds of the land before 1789. They used the Revolution for their own ends. Freed from payment of tithes, they dominated new *mairies*. They faced challenges in 1793–94, when their grain hoarding aroused popular suspicions. Small peas-ants and artisans filled some municipal offices and urged subdivision of communal lands. However, by 1800 *fermiers'* dominance had been reimposed, and remained largely unchallenged thereafter. Although some acquired church lands, most remained tenants, hence potentially subordinate to their landlords. But their expertise was vital to the success of their farms and they enjoyed long, secure leases. They lived in impressive farmhouses, were ad-dressed deferentially as *Sieur* and had ornate family pews. Their sons attended Catholic secondary colleges and either inherited the tenancy or became merchants; 50 per cent of the region's mayors were *fermiers*. They were flourishing commercial farmers who owned 70 per cent of horses – which they *loaned* to smaller neighbours – and provided employment for farm-servants and labourers. This *'fermocratie'* were clearly the fulcrum of rural life – above and yet part of village society. They took part in *fêtes*, acted as godparents, wrote references. Enjoying 'respect' as well as socio-economic power, they were 'natural' community leaders, protectors against the out-side world. They espoused an 'agrarian' ideology which denied that class tensions existed within the hierarchical village community. Indeed after the 1790s there were few significant conflicts in the region (Jessenne 1987).

Much of the agricultural proletariat remained quiescent. There were four million rural labourers. Pay was low, seasonal lay-offs long. Many slept in farmers' barns. Few solidarities developed, for employers developed effective divide-and-rule strategies. Farm servants lodged with the farmer and, though 'dependent', were relatively secure. Those hired on an annual basis had higher status than seasonal harvesters. In some areas labourers clung tenaciously to gleaning rights, but there was little collective protest. Any resistance tended to be individualistic – punching the foreman, stealing chickens, cattle-maiming or, as during the 'Normandy fires' during and after the 1830 Revolution – arson (Hubscher and Farcy 1996).

In central and southern France small peasant owners were more promi-nent. Weber (1982) portrayed their world as one of isolation, economic autarchy, ignorance, illiteracy, patois-speaking, poverty, superstition, fear and brutality. The need for child labour meant that families saw little use for education. Popular religion was intertwined with fear of witches and were-wolves and resort to sorcerers. Houses, shared with livestock, were dark, since window-tax was not abolished until 1914. Hard black bread, vegetables and in some regions chestnuts were the staples of the diet. Chickens, eggs and similar delicacies were sold to raise cash to pay taxes. Violence was endemic, whether expressed in punch-ups with youths from neighbouring villages or, within the family, against wives, children or the unproductive old. Envy and feelings of inferiority engendered suspicion of and resentments towards 'para-sitic' towns. The 'French' state appeared alien, incarnated by gendarme, tax-collector and recruiting-sergeant. Conscription evasion, localised brigandage, smuggling and poaching remained endemic in peripheral and frontier regions into the 1840s. What passed for 'politics' was merely the loyalty of peasant 'clients' to (rival) local notables or atavistic inter-village feuds (Weber 1982).

Though undeniably some regions – the Massif Central, Pyrenees, inland Brittany – exhibited such characteristics, Weber's generalisations are too sweep-ing. The peasant economy was not one of unchanging, semi-subsistence poly-culture. France had a thousand small towns (*bourgs*) of up to 3000 inhabitants which held markets or fairs, were centres of networks of cash-crop farm-ing and of proto-industry. Around Beaune (Burgundy), vineyards occupied 80 per cent of the land. *Vignerons* sold wine to Paris. Alpine peasants pro-duced 'industrial' crops – raw silk, madder – for Lyon. In wheat-growing Beauce, market production was dominated by a politically moderate, if anti-clerical, middling peasantry employing farm servants. But since all peasants required some cash to purchase essential items and pay taxes, small peasants were drawn into cash-crop specialisation. In Rodes (Pyrénées-Orientales) peasants, not large landowners, pioneered market-orientated wine and olive production (Farcy 1990; Lévêque 1980; Vigier 1963; McPhee 1989).

Many peasant farms were economically precarious. The Midi, short of livestock and of manure, had grain yields often 70 per cent lower than those of the north. Scarcity of draft animals precluded introduction of heavy Dombasle ploughs. Short-term leases offered little incentive for sharecroppers to improve farms. Some innovations were received suspiciously by peasants and rural labourers. There was resistance to replacement of sickles by scythes, since the latter cut close to the roots and reduced stubble for gleaning. Poor transport led many to persist with polyculture to ensure local production of subsistence crops. And 1846–47 harvest failures were a reminder that France was not yet immune to Malthusian crisis, as demographic growth threatened to push against the limits of agricultural output. The rural population had reached its all-time peak; 75 per cent of France's 35 million inhabitants lived in the countryside. Population pressures drove up land prices. However, sixteen rural departments were already losing inhabitants. The crisis marked a watershed in rural society as birth-rates fell and rural exodus accelerated.

Various strategies were employed to combat problems of scarce land resources and to avoid the subdivision of farms into unviable units. Strict implementation of the Code was evaded by ceding inheritance of the family farm to one brother. The 'clerical' southern Massif sent 'surplus' offspring into the church. Celibacy and late marriage became commonplace. The average age of Corrèze groom was thirty-one. The birth-rate remained above 40 per 1000 in Catholic Brittany, but around Meulan (Seine-et-Oise) the proportion of families practising birth-control rose from one-sixth to one-half between 1789 and the 1820s. Yet the number of small owners was still growing – by 46 per cent in the Morvan between 1835 and 1852. Proliferation of 'micro-properties' threatened dreams of independence; 10 hectares – or 4 hectares of vines – was required for economic viability. Three-quarters of peasants owned less than this. In the Alps small-ownership rose by 1 per cent per annum after 1830, as rising crop prices encouraged borrowing to purchase land. When raw-silk prices collapsed after 1846 peasants were unable to afford the high interest rates on these loans. Expropriations doubled, while thousands faced the threat of losing their farms. The problem of usury stalked the countryside. Creuse peasant-stonemason Nadaud recalls in his autobiography how a medical bill, a daughter's dowry and a bad harvest forced his father to take out a crippling loan at 30 per cent interest. Excluded from urban credit networks, peasants relied on unofficial lenders – *notaires*, millers, grain-merchants and even *curés*. The usurer might buy-up peasant crops cheap after the harvest to sell later when prices had risen. Marx admired Balzac's *Les Paysans* for illustrating the illusory nature of 'independence' won by peasants after 1789. As they gnaw away at the estates of a declining aristocrat, the novel's Burgundian peasants fall in debt to *notaire* Rigoult. In the Pyrenees usurers accumulated credit of up to 500,000 francs from loans to peasants. Desire for cheaper credit was widely recorded in the 1848 parliamentary agricultural enquiry and anti-usurer hatreds fuelled the volatile politics of the Second Republic (Corbin 1975; Lévêque 1980; Soulet 1987; Vigier 1963).

An equally emotive issue was the threat to commons and usage rights. These had been eroded before 1789 by seigneurs, capitalist farmers and larger peasants; 20 per cent of Artois commons were privatised in the 1770s. However, *intendants*, fearful of eroding the peasant tax-base and provoking rural unrest, had restricted this process. The 1791 Rural Code favoured individual property rights. Successive regimes took a hard-headed free-market stance, arguing for sale of communal lands or distribution to local proprietors in proportion to size of existing landholdings. Private exploitation of such resources, it was assumed, would boost productivity. Such thinking was reflected in the 1813 Law and the 1827 Forest Code. In 1835 the Picardy *Conseil Général* proclaimed *vaine pâture* – customary rights to graze livestock on harvest stubble – 'a servitude (for landowners) which is no longer tolerable given the (need for) agricultural progress'. Yet *actual* erosion of such rights occurred only gradually. There were differences of opinion within the bureaucracy and among rural *notables*. Some landowners argued that commons retained social utility. By permitting the poor to stay in the villages they maintained a reserve army of labour, useful at harvest time, and reduced the burden of welfare provision. However, by 1845 only a dozen of eighty *Conseils Généraux* still voiced such opinions (Vivier 1999). Opinions within village communities were complex. Many clung to the status quo to graze an odd sheep on communal land or to continue to glean. Others protested that it was bigger peasants who used the rhetoric of 'defence of communal rights' in order to swamp commons with their herds. Some retained fond memories of Jacobin promises of an egalitarian *partage* of the commons. The more entrepreneurial favoured their privatisation. Orleanist officials encouraged municipalities to lease out commons, arguing that this would stimulate agricultural innovation while providing villages with funds for roads and welfare; 113 Côte d'Or villages approved leasing-out schemes. It proved impossible to find a formula to satisfy such diverse local interests. It was unclear in law whether prefect, *Conseil Général* or municipality had the final say in disputed cases. As population pressures intensified, survival of the remaining 4.71 million hectares of commons – 9 per cent of total land area – remained a crucial issue. Villagers petitioned municipalities to reassert control over commons. In the Lyonnais uplands, where 40 per cent of commons had been sold off, they resorted to violence.

The 1827 Code tightened controls of *Eaux et Forêts* officials over grazing and wood-collection rights in state woodlands. Orderly projects for planned felling and regular rotation of planting were now envisaged. Peasant overgrazing and unsystematic *jardinage* (cutting of branches and shrubs) were blamed for soil erosion and flooding in the Pyrenees, which had lost 70 per cent of woodland since 1730. But sale of forests to charcoal-forge owners caused peasants to query authorities' supposed environmental concerns. Resistance to the Forest Code, and to private forest owners, became endemic. In Provence, Republican lawyers courted popularity by defending peasants who reasserted usage rights in forests owned by legitimists. In the Allier, Jean Roujot became a local 'martyr' when executed for killing an aristocrat who prosecuted intruders on to former communal woodlands. By the 1840s there were 135,000 prosecutions annually for Code infringements. The most spectacular disputes occurred in the Ariège, a region of the Pyrenees where one-third of land was forested and population grew 37 per cent between 1800 and 1846. As wood prices rose, forests were leased to owners of Catalan forges. The Code granted villagers two years to prove customary usage rights, but courts disregarded medieval charters which villagers cited. From 1829 onwards peasants responded by illegal grazing, wood theft, harassment of forest guards and threats to forge-masters and (aristocratic) landowners. Despite inter-village feuds over disputed communal boundaries, police could find no witnesses either from the peasantry or from mayors and petty notables. Troops and gendarmes were sent to restore a semblance of order. It was the form of this revolt which fascinated contemporaries. Its rhetoric and symbolism suggested more than just pragmatic resistance to the intrusion of the state and capitalist practices.

Despite threats against forest guards and forge-owners, decades of conflict saw only two fatalities. Although women were prosecuted for wood theft, the revolt was dominated by young men whose *corps de jeunesse* organised *fêtes* and annual Carnivals. It was they who organised *charivaris* (rough-music) against those who offended against communal norms – dominant wives, widows who remarried, outsiders. The revolt played with gender codes and symbols. It adopted a macho tone, ascribing to its leaders military ranks. Yet those harassing forest guards dressed in white 'female' clothing – hence the name '*Guerre des Demoiselles*'. This attire, and their blackened faces, were not just a device to avoid identification. Forests were viewed as communal, as sites where village men had right of entry. But they were also 'female'. Trees symbolised fertility and forests were the home of 'fairies' – *demoiselles* in local parlance – who wore white and punished those who harmed them. Intrusion by outsiders was thus a violation. Moreover, cross-dressing was a feature of the 'misrule' of Carnival when, briefly, the world was turned upside-down. The 'war' was thus a *révolte carnavalesque* – and woodlands the site of 'ritual inversion' as control was re-exerted over the 'female' forest. This interweaving of ritual and revolt also constituted a gigantic *charivari*, protesting at the mismatched 'marriage' of forest and alien intruders.

The timing of protests, in January/February and May, supports such anthropological readings. These months correlated with the festive cycle. Winter Carnival was a period of gastronomic excess, scatological humour, inversion of social, age and gender hierarchies and mock trials of clergy and notables. May was the month of rituals of fertility and female sexuality revolving around the May Queen and May Tree, now 'stolen' from the forest in defiance of the Forest Code! The wider significance of all this remains problematic. Functionalist anthropologists suggest that 'tolerated licence' acts as a safety-valve which strengthens the status quo. After Carnival excesses the clergy dominated Easter Mass. Yet the authorities had long sought to control such rituals which, potentially, posed a real challenge to the social order. These struggles were not isolated from national politics. '1830' was a window of opportunity when state power briefly collapsed. Rebels were prompted to use the rhetoric of anti-feudalism, since landowners engaged in lawsuits to exclude villagers from woodlands included ex-seigneurs. Peasants learned to manipulate the rhetoric of 'rights' and 'liberty'. Threatening letters to forge-owners ended 'Long live freedom!'. 'The word "Republic" has deep resonance in the spirit of the populations, because it immediately translated into a capacity to (act) with impunity and to (become) masters of the forests', lamented one official. This was no 'archaic' peasantry locked into 'traditional' mentalities, rather one capable of playing with its folkloric culture to enact ritualised protest and also to appropriate political rhetoric for its own ends. Nor was rural politics reliant on culture-brokers. Influences could travel in both directions. The *demoiselles* captured the imagination of urban Republicans, and featured in Parisian stage plays. A Republican satirical journal *Le Charivari* was founded, and Dijon and Grenoble radicals appropriated the *charivari* to mock clerical opponents. This was a rare Rabelaisian moment in which festive folk traditions came to occupy a place in 'high' politics and art (Sahlins 1994).

As many as 20 per cent of peasant families resorted to temporary migration. Massif Central villagers sought harvest work in the Midi wine plains. Pyreneans specialised as *colporteurs*, hawking Almanachs, woodcuts and trinkets around France. From hilly Creuse, 35,000 building workers tramped each spring to Parisian construction sites. Survival strategies in remote regions were not dependent on autarchy. Pluri-activity was widespread. Small-owners' children did day-labouring for landowners or acted as carters. Their wives might, as in the Morvan, act as wet-nurses for urban babies or sell their hair to wigmakers. Thousands were involved in proto-industry – linen around St. Quentin, silk-spinning in the Gard. Rouen spinning mills relied on thousands of female weavers in the Pays de Caux. Rural forges in Périgord, clock-making in the Jura and ribbon-making in the Stephenois all provided supplementary income (Corbin 1990; Moulin 1991). But harvest failures in 1846–47 exposed the vulnerability in the pre-railway age of grain-deficit regions. Wide regional variations in grain supply and prices emerged. Deficiency diseases such as rickets remained prevalent in remote regions. Even in the prosperous Beauce grainlands, peasants exported wheat and ate black bread. Despite advances in agricultural productivity and cash-crop farming, peasants had few resources on which to fall back in crisis years. Erosion of communal rights, chronic indebtedness and demographic pressures were creating economic pressures and acute social tensions.

The politicisation of rural protest? (1846–51)

During the Second Republic peasants, ravaged by agrarian crisis, acquired the vote and made their debut in electoral politics. It was once assumed that they acted as a conservative force, first by voting for neo-royalist *notables* in April 1848 and then by electing Louis Napoleon as president December 1848. Were not peasants obsessed with safeguarding their farms against urban 'reds', reluctant to pay increased land-taxes to keep unemployed urban workers in 'idleness', deferential towards village priests, sufficiently credulous to imagine Louis Napoleon as a charismatic 'saviour'? Were not there reasons aplenty here for progressives to dismiss peasants as ignorant, selfish, myopic – to share Marx's verdict that they were 'the class that represents barbarism within civilisation'? However, the story of the countryside is more complicated, and interesting, than this. In the 1960s historians (re-)discovered the 'Republican peasant' – a figure until then almost unthinkable. If the Left played its cards ineptly in 1848, it compensated by skilful exploitation of peasant grievances in the following years, even if handicapped by its inability to make headway in the countryside of northern and western France and by the appeal of Bonapartist populism.

Initial responses to harvest failures in 1846–47 showed parallels to 1816–17, when thirty food rioters had been executed in the Lyonnais. Moulin portrays protests as 'reactions of an ill-educated peasantry for whom violence was the sole means of expression' – symptomatic of 'archaic' mentalities rather than of authentic 'popular political opinion' (Moulin 1991). Transport inadequacies were exposed as prices rose much faster in grain deficit areas such as Alsace. Agricultural labourers, facing lay-offs and bread shortages, became reliant on the uneven, semi-charitable welfare provision of *Bureaux de Bienfaisance*. Vagrants roamed the countryside, millers were intimidated, grain-barges attacked and grain was seized at markets, as in the 1770s 'flour war'. Rumours circulated of landowners hoarding grain. A sensational trial attracted attention to events at Buzençais (Indre). Agricultural labourers and artisans had pillaged grain-mills, destroyed threshing-machines, and sold grain at a 'just price'. A usurer had been killed after shooting two men attempting to hand him a petition. Three of the accused received death sentences. George Sand expressed disgust at the spectacle of 'men gorged with money (refusing) necessities to fellow humans and rubbing their hands saying "this is an excellent year for profits"'. Rioters, she added, had exhibited 'rare discernment' in their choice of targets. Their defence lawyer reappeared as a socialist deputy in 1849. Such disturbances were more than spasms of a distressed 'pre-political' peasantry. Protesters invoked the Jacobin price maximum and denounced the regime for protecting bourgeois speculators. Endemic rural unrest – including resistance to the Forest Code and protests against wine-taxes – meant that beleaguered Orleanism could not turn to the countryside for support in the political crisis of 1847–48.

Rural politics in the period between the collapse of the Orleanist regime (February 1848) and the May 1849 elections were volatile, complex and confused. Social tensions were fuelled by ongoing economic distress, ironically now exacerbated by *good* harvests, oversupply and falling cash-crop prices which intensified problems of indebtedness. Many peasants welcomed the Republic, hoping for policies to ease their plight. Meanwhile, as in 1830, they seized opportunities offered by the change of regime to invade forests, destroy enclosure fences and attack wine-tax offices. Faced with financial deficits, due to subsidies of grain imports since 1846, the Provisional Government shrank from alienating financial elites by introducing progressive income tax. Fatally it retained unpopular wine and salt taxes and increased by 45 centimes the tax on land, giving conservative elites the chance in the April elections to denounce 'urban' Republicans' indifference to rural problems and willingness to tax an overburdened peasantry to keep unemployed proletarians in idle luxury. When the new conservative government provoked

Parisian workers into revolt by closing down the National Workshops, de Tocqueville rejoiced at the zeal with which tenants from his Normandy constituency rushed to Paris to help suppress the rising.

However, the crisis persisted. Many peasants refused to pay the land tax and troops were mobilised to protect towns from bands of tax protesters. This was the context of Louis Napoleon's presidential campaign. He promised 'order' to the more prosperous peasantry of areas like Normandy who felt threatened by urban socialism. But it was Bonapartist populism which carried the wider appeal. In the Dordogne and Burgundy, Bonapartism was perceived as a bulwark against the return of the seigneurs. Its propaganda promised cheap credit, relaxation of Forest Codes, reduced wine-taxes. Limousin and the South-West, bastions of the tax revolt, voted heavily Bonapartist. Electors in Alsace marched from polling-booths behind a figure in Napoleonic uniform to tear down fences erected around local forests! Marx described Louis Napoleon's victory, with 74 per cent of the vote, as a 'peasant revolution by proxy'. Peasants went to the polls chanting 'Down with the rich! Aristocrats to the guillotine!'. Bonapartism did least well in the Catholic West and in the Midi. Yet despite Bonapartism's ability to tap the frustrations and anxieties of peasant voters, its hold on the countryside was challenged in 1849–51. Louis Napoleon's strategy involved both wooing angry peasants and cultivating the elites. His ministers and prefects were mainly tough ex-Orleanist conservatives. Unwilling to challenge the propertied elites, they maintained the land and wine taxes and Forest Codes and failed to introduce rural credit. Unable to stand in the elections of May 1849 and lacking his own 'party', the president was obliged to allow ex-Royalist notables to dominate his election lists. In the West and North, where the Right won 202 of 214 seats, this strategy was effective. Elsewhere there were real shocks for conservatives. Inspired by the *Solidarité Républicaine* electoral organisation, the Left reinvented itself as a broad coalition capable of addressing problems of rural 'little men' whom it had hitherto neglected. Its 'democratic socialist' programme was couched in associationist rhetoric. It promised state aid for peasant cooperatives, cheap rural credit, abolition of Forest Codes and wine-taxes, progressive income-tax, free education and cheaper rail freight-rates. Peasants and workers, it claimed, shared common enemies – financiers, speculators – and common interests. Only prosperous workers could afford peasants' produce! With 53 per cent of the vote and 450 seats the Right won the elections. Moderate Republicans, reduced to a 11 per cent of the vote, were the clear losers. The real surprise was that the *Dem-Socs*, with 36 per cent of the poll and 220 seats, were the majority party in one-third of departments.

The 1849 electoral map reflects the influence of local history and memory, of social structures and social relations of production. Some regions had shifted political orientation since the 1790s. The Paris basin, an area of low religious practice, had supported the Revolution but now rallied to 'order'. However, there were historic continuities. Radical Burgundy and Dordogne had strong anti-seigneurial traditions. In the Cévennes and the Drôme, radical voting patterns in 1849 closely followed the contours of 'dechristianisation' in the Year II or of Protestant communities (McPhee 1992). The countryside was now the strategic battleground. Left-wing by-election gains prompted a new electoral law (May 1850) disenfranchising 30 per cent of voters – seasonal migrants and those with a 'criminal record', a category which included much of the population in forest areas. Despite draconian bureaucratic repression, conservatives feared defeat in the 1852 elections, for which Louis Napoleon, as president, was ineligible to stand. Such fears prompted the 2 December, 1851 coup which met little resistance from heavily garrisoned towns but provoked an insurrection involving over 100,000 in rural areas of the Centre and South. The Second Republic had given the countryside a crash course in participatory democracy. After first looking to landed notables to protect them against urban radicalism and then to a charismatic Messiah, sections of the peasantry had learned how to use their vote in local and national elections.

The *Dem-Socs* became adept at exploiting peasants' economic grievances. Small peasant-owners engaged in cash-crop farming and hit by the price collapse of 1849–51 were their key constituents. 'Middle peasants' have consistently featured in rural mobilisations. Exposed to volatile capitalist markets, they are perennially insecure and anxious. But ownership of (small) farms provides an independence which sharecroppers and tenants lack. Their capacity for mobilisation is increased because market agriculture brings contact with culture-brokers with access to ideologies – originating it is assumed, in cities – which offer analysis of the contradictions of existing society and solutions to these. Denunciation of usurers, who profited from exorbitant interest rates charged to indebted peasants, and proposals for rural credit struck a chord with peasant voters. Alpine prefects emphasised the distress of peasants who had borrowed to buy extra land but who were vulnerable when prices for industrial crops and wine collapsed. In the Drôme, *Dem-Soc* gains were in the cash-crop farming central belt. They did poorly further south where sharecroppers leased farms from legitimist landowners. Mass meetings in the *bourgs* applauded orators denouncing 'financial feudalism' which profited from peasant misery. Although under 2 per cent of peasants in central Drôme were expropriated for inability to repay loans, a handful of expropriations had a serious psychological impact on a village. In Burgundy, 'official' records of indebtedness reveal only the tip of the iceberg. Peasants took out unofficial loans at even higher interest rates to clear existing debts. Hatred of Jewish usurers nurtured antisemitism in Alsace, just as Catholic-Royalist populism fed on the association of money-lending with Protestant financiers in the Midi. Although the Left occasionally flirted with antisemitism, in general it targeted the financial system itself, emphasising that most usurers were Catholics! In the Ardèche, hitherto the site of sectarian Catholics/Protestant rivalries, *Dem-Socs* captured six seats in May 1849, and Catholic peasants joined the insurgents who in December 1851 marched on Privas to 'burn the prefecture, the mortgage office and the tax bureaux . . .' (Vigier 1963; Lévêque 1980; Margadant 1979).

There *were* peasant farming areas the left failed to secure a foothold. The key to the conservatism of small peasants in the Doubs was the strength of rural Catholicism. However, even here *Dem-Soc* support for cooperative and cheap credit schemes did win support. Jura cheese producers faced price falls of 30 per cent in 1848–49. Inspired by local watch-makers' cooperatives, they established a network of *fruitières* – cooperative storage schemes which allowed small producers to avoid sales in the autumn on a glutted market. Credit notes were issued on the security of this stored produce, permitting peasants to secure goods and services without cash. Such schemes were praised by *Dem-Soc* propagandists as practical 'associationist' socialism in action (Magraw 1978).

Vignerons proved the Left's most fervent rural supporters. *Dem-Socs* won 50 per cent of the vote around Beaune in the Côte d'Or *vignoble* – a region with a tradition of opposing wine-taxes (*droits réunis*) and with a vibrant anti-clerical Republican culture among the small-town petty bourgeoisie which supplied the movement's cadres. Since vines needed careful tending, wine-production was labour-intensive. *Vignerons* lived in large villages, alongside carters and barrel-makers. Obliged to sell wine to acquire cash to pay for food, they were peculiarly vulnerable to market fluctuations. With export prospects hit by tariff policies designed to protect industry and large grain-producers, urban consumption of *vin ordinaire* restricted by the flat-rate wine tax and wine prices collapsing, *vignerons* had particular reasons to blame governments for their plight. Socialists promised to abolish wine taxes and sought to strengthen urban/rural solidarities by persuading *vignerons* that higher industrial wages would increase wine consumption. The sociability and relatively egalitarian culture of wine villages created an exception to the norm of low levels of mobilisation among labourers. In Lower Languedoc, vineyard workers lived alongside *vignerons* in large villages on the coastal plain. Day-labourers were a high proportion of the *Dem-Soc* rank-and-file around Narbonne and Béziers (Lévêque 1980; Margadant 1979; Loubère 1968). The *vigneronnage* sharecropping system in the Beaujolais may explain the subordination of winegrowers there to the landed elite. The social geography of the Left confirms Brustein's (1988) correlation of sharecropping and tenant farming with conservatism. In the Allier, hostility to ruthless estate-managers who supervised the farms of absentee aristocratic landowners did provoke occasional protest, but short leases and threats of eviction kept most sharecroppers deferential. Sharecroppers were relatively sheltered from the price collapse because they paid rents in kind, as a fixed proportion of their crop, and because many remained quasi-subsistence polyculturalists with limited market exposure (Brustein 1988; Garrier 1973).

However, neither economics nor social relations of production, by themselves, provide the key to political geography. Rural mobilisation also had cultural roots, though these have to be analysed with care. The Vendée's dispersed habitat has been cited to explain that region's Catholic-Royalism, yet similar habitat patterns correlated with radical voting in the Limousin. Regionalist sentiment in Flanders or Brittany expressed hostility to Jacobin centralisation, yet *occitan* or Catalan areas of Languedoc-Roussillon became 'red' bastions. The battle for control of the countryside was explicitly one to define rural culture. Joigneaux, the Left's rural propagandist, did advocate cooperatives as practical organisations allowing peasants to pool limited resources, share draft animals, purchase in bulk, eliminate 'parasitic' middle-men. But he also insisted that such 'practical socialism' was in tune with the communal culture of the countryside, with an age-old, doctrine-less village communalism. The peasant was not a 'natural' bourgeois individualist. Villages clung obstinately to communal rights, tilled the fields of their sick neighbours and established voluntary associations – fire brigades, mutual aid societies, insurance schemes (Berenson 1987; Magraw 1978; Baker 1999).

Weber (1976) portrayed peasant culture as irredeemably 'archaic', ill-suited to 'modern' politics. What passed for 'politics' in the Second Republic resembled age-old *jacqueries*. In 1848, peasant columns, summoned by drums and bells, invaded market-towns and burned tax-records, thereby exorcising the mysterious powers of the written word, before getting drunk and staggering home. Subsequent mobilisations, culminating in the 1851 rising, were further manifestations of archaic violence. Radical peasants were simply clients of Republican *notables* – lawyers, doctors, wine-merchants – just as conservative peasants were part of the patronage networks of Royalist elites. Many 'red' peasants exhibited visceral hatred of the towns and a susceptibility to the lure of Bonapartist populism. Weber's model may 'fit' the 1848 tax-revolts. Yet only nine of the three hundred centres of tax protest participated in resistance to the coup. Assumptions about cultural and economic isolation scarcely fit with evidence of an expanding rural market economy. Hatred of towns was stronger in Normandy, where conservative peasants feared 'red' Parisian or Rouen proletarians, than in the Midi. Historians' current obsession with 'rural violence' – exemplified by Figes's notorious study of revolutionary Russia – led to rejection of interpretations of popular protest in terms of collective solidarities in favour of Taine-ite anxieties about 'primitive' rustic 'brutes'. Though one can find 'reds' gloating at the prospect of playing bowls with skulls of their 'white' opponents, much of this was ritualised rhetoric. Actual levels of violence were surprisingly low. Conservatives 'justified' the coup for saving 'civilisation' from pillage by rustic hordes. But official reports of resistance to the coup around the river port of Clamécy (Nièvre) admitted that the socialist leader had impressed on his followers that 'probity is the first duty of a Republican'. The atrocities came from troops who behaved 'as if in Africa'.

However, correlations of rural radicalism with indices of 'modernisation' are little more persuasive. Margadant (1979) claimed that the Left's heartlands were marked by market agriculture, rising literacy, falling birth-rates and declining religious practice. Yet if conservative Brittany had low literacy, so too did radical bastions such as the Allier, Gâtinais or Ariège. The most persuasive analysis of culture and politics remains Agulhon's (1970) study of 'modernity' and 'archaism' in the Var. Here peasants involved in a cash-crop economy of wine and olives were exposed to 'politics' via the 'cultural brokerage' of fellow-inhabitants of large villages – artisans, café-owners and Republican lawyers. Peasant *chambrées*, imitating bourgeois *cercles*, acted as centres of sociability where newspapers could be read aloud and as a focus for mutual aid and resistance to the wine-tax. Democratic patronage was less hierarchical than the vertical patronage of the Royalist West. Conservatives sought refuge from urban class conflict in a consoling myth of rural social harmony, yet became aware that this myth had little substance. The furore which greeted Courbet's *Burial at Ornans* at the 1851 Salon stemmed from the painting's oblique suggestion of the complexity of rural social relations.

The rural bourgeois might be hated, as outsider, usurer or parasitic middleman. Yet the lawyer, doctor or city-educated son of a well-to-do peasant might become a key figure in local radical politics (Margadant 1979; Agulhon 1970; Mayaud 1999; Clark 1973).

There was a complex dialectic between elements of modernity and traditional culture. Far from being obstacles to the spread of politics into the villages, carnivals, *charivaris*, *fêtes* or folk songs could serve as vehicles of expression or transmission of political ideas. While cultural brokerage widened horizons and provided a political goal, the 'democratic and social Republic', attachment to village communities gave peasants something to defend. Rural culture could be adapted to mount such a defence. *Charivaris* were used to humiliate priests or Royalist landowners. The mannequin ritually beheaded at the climax of the Carnival procession showed a striking resemblance to the departmental prefect! Folk songs about thieving millers or evil seigneurs acquired political overtones. The innocuous verse 'Let us plant the thyme/And the Mountain will flower' could appear subversive at a time when '*La Montagne*' denoted the neo-Jacobin Left. Pierre Dupont, village-born son of a Lyon silk-weaver, was the Left's most popular songwriter. But in Pyrénées-Orientales 'reds' adapted Catalan folk-songs. The Second Republic witnessed an ephemeral marriage between emerging radical politics and a still-vital folkloric and festive culture. Alarmed by the Left's success in channelling the 'tolerated license' of the *fête*, police banned Carnival processions and confiscated 'seditious' red flowers at weddings – actions viewed as absurd and arbitrary and which proved counter-productive (McPhee 1992). Joigneaux's *Feuille du Village* praised the *veillée* as an opportunity for older villagers to remind the young of the horrors of the seigneurial past. It argued that 'socialist' fraternity and solidarity, denounced by the clergy, were the values of the Jesus who had driven usurers from the temple. Statues of 'Christ the Carpenter' mingled with texts of Pierre Dupont's *Chant des Vignerons* in the repertoire of *colporteurs* who, subject to police harassment, hawked their wares round fairs and markets. Joigneaux adapted the *Almanach*, the peasantry's staple reading matter, by augmenting its agricultural tips, medical remedies and tales of knights and monsters with stories about 'social bandits' who lived in forests and robbed the rich to help the poor! (Berenson 1987; Magraw 1978; Vigreux 1987).

Margadant (1979) disputes the correlation between 'pre-political' forest rights disputes and *Dem-Soc* networks which organised resistance to the coup. Certainly forest regions lacked the radical secret societies which spread in the Mediterranean coastal plain. Yet forest disputes did engender support for the Left. Ariège voted heavily for the *Dem-Socs* in 1849. In the Ardèche, gun battles between poachers and forest guards led to the imposition of a state of siege. The radical press denounced the 1844 Law which had introduced a 25-franc hunting permit and portrayed poachers as culture heroes. Forty-eight Var villages with forest disputes participated in the 1851 rising. The Morvan in northern Burgundy was a hilly region of low literacy. Yet it had its culture brokers – wood-floaters (*flotteurs*) who took logs down-river to Paris and petty bourgeois of small towns like Château-Chinon. Peasants were convinced that forests were a natural resource which belonged to everybody and should be reclaimed. Arson attacks were mounted in retaliation against aristocrats who were eroding usage rights. In 1848 Republican authorities urged landowners to make concessions and peasants to refrain from violence. Louis Napoleon, perceived as the 'antiseigneurial' candidate, attracted 90 per cent of the vote in a region which had rallied to Napoleon's 'Hundred Days'. But in May 1849, the Left won 60 per cent of the vote in central and eastern Morvan. Peasants invading aristocratic forests shouted 'Long Live Robespierre! Down with the *Chouans*!'. Aristocrats were denounced as 'traitors' who had allied with France's enemies. Radical lawyers researched villages' historic titles to the forests. A notorious poacher was elected to a municipal council. Peasants showed some solidarity with *Dem-Soc* cadres as they were picked off by police repression in 1850–51. But they remained vulnerable to the lure of Bonapartist populism, for Louis Napoleon was still perceived in forest villages as a protector against the seigneurs (Vigreux 1987).

The Left faced sustained harassment which weakened its capacity for effective mobilisation before the coup. Radical mayors were dismissed, municipal councils dissolved, newspaper editors jailed. *Colporteurs* caught distributing radical propaganda had their licences revoked. Mutual aid societies were harassed and dissolved; 1500 *instituteurs* had been sacked by early 1851. The net result, Merriman (1978) suggested, was to undermine the movement's capacity to sustain urban/rural ties. In the Ariège, petty bourgeois cadres who had linked forest protests with national politics were picked off by the police. The relative quiescence of such regions in December 1851 reflected the demobilising impact of such repression (Merriman 1978). Yet piecemeal repression sometimes provoked further resistance. Radical mayors in the Hérault were acquitted by juries, then re-elected, causing prefects to demand appointed mayors and trials without jury. In the Midi there was a positive correlation between villages which suffered municipal purges and resistance to the coup. Police manpower was insufficient to enforce effective control. *Gardes-Champêtres* were untrained, and often embroiled in local factions. Police commissaires, based in market towns, were 'outsiders' whose attempts to control cafés, *bals* and festivals were bitterly resented. Patrols of paramilitary gendarmes were sent to troublesome villages, but could not stay indefinitely. The Nîmes *Procureur-Général* insisted that heavy-handed policing was counter-productive. To send gendarmes to investigate a red scarf found in a tree was to invite ridicule. 'Men who are harmless find themselves treated as if guilty. In their irritation they enter the current of opposition to government . . .'. Police found themselves, McPhee observes, 'lost in a chase through popular culture' (McPhee 1992).

The May 1850 electoral law posed strategic dilemmas for *Dem-Soc* leaders. Most opted for a mass protest petition which attracted 500,000 signatures. A minority, the 'New Mountain', argued that direct action was now needed. Alarmed by talk of violence, some bourgeois Republicans backed away from the movement. Weber's (1977) emphasis on the reliance of peasant 'politics' on notables is unconvincing at this point. Peasants and village artisans were active in the network of 700 secret societies which developed in central and southern regions; 48 per cent of secret societies in four Midi departments had peasant leaders. As urban cadres were picked off by the police, leadership in the Yonne passed to peasants and rural clog-makers. Secret societies were organised in small cells, with blindfolded 'novices' initiated by swearing an oath on a dagger to defend the 'social and democratic Republic'. Agulhon (1970) interprets this clandestinity, and sporadic local violence, as a regrettable, if explicable, regression from the 'apprenticeship' in electoral politics. Yet were alternative paths still open? Grass-roots frustration and anger found expression in rhetorical violence. Durin's *Chant des Paysans* urged Limousin peasants to take guns and pitchforks to the polling-booths. The *Carmagnole des Paysans* began

Let us dance the *Carmagnole*/Mortgage offices will be burned/
Usurers will be hanged/Their goods and châteaux given to the poor.

The date of the next elections, '1852' assumed quasi-millenial overtones. On the 'great day' the 'social and democratic Republic' – *La Belle* – would be installed. The secret societies illustrated peasants' political commitment and organisational capacity. Though bureaucrats' overheated fantasies swelled 'plots' to implausible proportions, they were not 'inventing' a red peril in order to justify a coup. They faced real threats, albeit partly of their own making. Their rhetoric became increasingly 'medicalised'. An 'occult army' was spreading 'like a plague'. Hitherto 'healthy' villages were becoming 'gangrened'. The *Montagnard* cadres were physically and morally deformed *déclassés* – 'seducing' and 'infecting' the (female) rural masses. Fortunately salvation was at hand. For the masses respected virile firmness. A timely 'surgical operation' would restore France to robust health (Merriman 1978; McPhee 1992; Margadant 1979).

Arrests of urban militants meant that coordination of resistance fell to village and small-town cadres. This occurred in seventeen departments and involved 900 communes and 100,000 insurgents. Most marched from villages to the local town, before eventually fleeing in face of army fire. To justify the coup, Bonapartists portrayed the rising as a *jacquerie* of rape, pillage and confiscation of property, emphasising an episode at Clamécy in which gendarmes were killed. The official Republican version, outlined in Ténot's *La Province en Décembre 1851* (1867), presented insurgents as citizens outraged by the threat to Republican legality. Survivors were given medals by the Third Republic and memorials erected to the 'martyrs'. Socialists shared Ténot's view that insurgents had political convictions and rejected accusations of brutality. However, their goal was to establish '*La Belle*', the social and democratic Republic, which would usher in a world without wine-taxes, usurers or forest guards. Many secret societies had multiple social functions, acting as centres of sociability and mutual aid. It had been their wider socio-political aspirations, not just their willingness to fight, which had led bourgeois 'moderates' to withdraw from the movement, as at Cuers (Var) where *vignerons* and barrel-makers had assumed the leadership in 1850.

There were 27,000 arrests and 5400 peasants were prosecuted. Of the detainees in the Vaucluse, 46 per cent were peasants, yet many rank-and-file rural insurgents escaped arrest. Many peasants who were arrested escaped punishment on the grounds that they had been 'led astray' by lawyers, teachers, village artisans and café-owners, some 2000 of whom were arrested.

Some *procureurs* urged leniency, either through legalistic scruples or because they considered harsh repression counterproductive. To bolster his (tarnished) populist reputation, Louis Napoleon commuted the sentences of many about to be transported to penal colonies and announced a reprieve for forest offenders. In the Gard, 33 per cent of convicted teachers were deported – only 14 per cent of peasants. Some peasants astutely played up to their image as credulous 'misguided rustics'. They 'acted dumb', claiming that they joined secret societies because ordered to do so or because they thought they were drinking clubs! Historians who accept them at their word are being misled, just as were the Bonapartist prosecutors! Republican lawyer E. Reclus observed that Pyrenean peasants were adept at adopting a mask of naive bewilderment, at 'playing the Andorran' (McPhee 1992; Margadant 1979).

The relationship between Louis Napoleon and peasant electors was complex and ambiguous. His neo-Royalist ministers had failed to deliver on his populist electoral promises, disenfranchised 30 per cent of the rural poor and clamped down on embryonic village democracy and peaceful rural co-operatives. The agrarian depression had continued. And yet he was an astute political operator. Touring Burgundy in 1850 he distanced himself from his own government, blaming the May law on his ministers. He posed as friend of religion in the Catholic West, defender of property in conservative Normandy and as bulwark against the return of the seigneurs in Burgundy! In December 1851, some peasant insurgents imagined that they were defending the president against a royalist coup! After the coup he made populist gestures – confiscating and distributing Orleanist family estates, repealing the May 1850 law. The massive Bonapartist vote in 1852 owed much to fear and intimidation; 31 departments remained under a state of siege. With prisoners still on trial, Basses-Alpes – a stronghold of the rising – voted 74 per cent for the government. But some 'red' areas – Morvan, Isère, Dordogne – remained susceptible to Bonapartist 'seduction'. Conversely, parts of the Midi never forgave the 'people's Emperor' for consolidating his power by crushing a peasant insurrection.

What was the significance of the Second Republic's rural politics? Was this an 'archaic' peasantry given to 'atavistic' hatreds of seigneurs, usurers or urban dwellers. Are Left-wing historians too keen to sanitise rural violence, portraying it as 'community solidarity' in defence of the 'moral economy'? Yet much rural violence was rhetorical or symbolic. Tilly (1972) characterised conflicts of these years as poised between 'archaic' forest, tax and grain riots and 'modern' political organisation and electoral politics. Realities were more complex than such models suggest. Many political loyalties had been forged in the 1790s. Protestant insurgents in the Drôme portrayed themselves as heirs of the Camisards. Also the rural history of twentieth-century France, from the winegrowers' revolts of 1905–07 via Dorgères's peasant fascism of the 1930s to the *maquisard* resistance of 1942–44, is scarcely devoid of violence (Corbin 1975; Tilly 1972). Although the coup abruptly terminated a brief flowering of participatory democracy, the long-term impact of these experiences should not be underestimated. Traumatic events can prove as influential as *longue durée* structures beloved of *Annalistes*. Certainly these years did mark a demographic watershed, as birth-rates fell, rural out-migration accelerated and the Alps or Pyrenees began to lose the young and the marginal. Yet the electoral map of 1914 or of the Popular Front resemble that of 1849. Despite demographic and economic changes, Saône-et-Loire, which voted for the *Dem-Socs* in 1849, elected six socialist deputies in 1936. The Second Republic implanted, or consolidated, democratic values in parts of rural France. Elderly Allier peasants in the 1960s still associated '1852' with the promised advent of '*La Belle*'. In central Drôme, where indebted peasants resisted the coup, oral tradition kept alive memories of Republican martyrs dragged through village streets in chains, hunted in the woods and imprisoned in the 'tower of Crest'. In 1944 a *Maquis* leader reminded his group that they were heirs of the proud tradition of peasant insurgents of 1851, and the Nazis destroyed a memorial erected in their honour. Local myths recalled that peasants had carried forks and sickles. But this was seen not as proof of 'rustic savagery' but of their courage in confronting armed troops! These myths were transmitted and preserved within family oral traditions, and by stories linking insurgents to the local landscape, rather than by official Republican historiography. The 'tower of Crest', or forests where rebels had sought refuge, became parts of local identity (Pierre 1981).

Bonapartist domination and rural prosperity? (1852–75c)

The following decades saw relative calm return to the countryside. Tight controls on village life were imposed by the Bonapartist 'police state'. Many 'reds' were deported or in exile. But stability owed much to a change in the economic *conjoncture*. A period of relative agrarian prosperity coincided with, and was nurtured by, the advent of the railways which facilitated import of fertilisers and exodus of marginal elements in rural society. The transport revolution was deepened by construction of canals and low-interest loans to municipalities for local roads. Grain could now be moved rapidly to deficit areas, thereby reducing regional price variations which had marked crisis years. This permitted concentration on market crops best suited to local soils and climate. Vineyards grew 13 per cent between 1852 and 1875, but wine production rose 71 per cent, and 152 per cent in Lower Languedoc which became a monocultural region. Per-capita income in the Hérault almost reached that of prosperous Ile-de-France. Urban wine consumption rose and wine exports doubled. Lower Normandy now concentrated on livestock-rearing for the Paris market, the Beauce on wheat and the Charentes on dairy produce. Many such changes were within peasant farming. Demographic pressures were eased by an acceleration of the rural exodus. Between 1851 and 1856 Burgundy lost 3 per cent (29,000) of its population as landless labourers and micro-proprietors sought urban jobs. Annual rural out-migration averaged 110,000 in 1851–56 and 70,000 in the 1860s. Sixty-five departments were losing population at a rate faster than the natural increase due to excess of births over deaths.

Migration was in stages. Villagers went to local *bourgs* before moving on to larger cities. The shift to livestock rearing or the advent of harvesting machines cut demand for labour. Declining sales of goods produced by rural artisans, as in the Beauce, prompted their decision to leave the villages. Agricultural labourers and farm-servants fell by 650,000 between 1860 and 1880. Indeed localised labour-supply bottlenecks produced wage rises in a few regions. A Beauce landowner claimed that only farm mechanisation could 'end the despotic stranglehold excercised by the labouring classes'. Threshing-machines quintupled between the 1850s and 1880 to reach 310,000. Resistance to mechanisation was sporadic and localised. Poor villagers claimed that the scythe, now replacing the sickle, cut crops too close to the root, depriving gleaners of their customary straw (Duby and Wallon 1976; Price 1983; Farcy 1990).

Small owners increased 15 per cent in the 1851–70 period, though the average size of a peasant holding fell 12 per cent. By 1880, 87.5 per cent of farms, covering 22.7 per cent of the total area, were smaller than 5 hectares. As Midi vineyard wages rose during the wine boom, workers purchased plots and became small *vignerons*. In Cruzy (Hérault) their numbers grew from 31 to 185. Limousin peasant-masons used earnings from the Paris construction boom to expand their farms. In the Nièvre, extended families of share-cropping polyculturalists metamorphosed into nuclear families of livestock-rearing tenants. Disapproving clergy lamented the 'corruption' of parishioners by a spirit of 'hedonism', exemplified by the proliferation of cafés in Languedoc wine-plains. While one should discount the moralising tone of such accounts, there is evidence – quantitative and impressionistic – of rising rural living standards. Diets were improving. Per-capita potato, flour and meat consumption increased 30 per cent between 1852 and 1870, and that of wine by 20 per cent. Beaujolais farms began to have 'private' rooms. The percentage of rural conscripts rejected as too small fell from 16 per cent in 1839 to 10 per cent by 1870. Rural death rates fell from 23.1 to 21 per thousand. Birth rates remained high in the Catholic West and in sharecropping areas, since sharecroppers had larger farms, requiring family labour.

Elsewhere, falling birth-rates indicated the spread of birth-control techniques. In the South-West newly weds were advised that after one child one should 'do as the miller does, unload the cart at the door!' If fewer pregnancies benefited women's health, it is unclear whether their lives improved in other ways. The diversity of the rural economy and the wide range of family strategies which evolved make generalisation about the relationship between women's work and their status hazardous. Certain trends in the rural economy posed potential threats to women's work. Scythes were too heavy for most female harvesters. Regional markets, visited largely by men, were replacing local markets which women had attended. Some 'female' proto-industrial jobs were in decline. Hence there may have been temptations to assign to peasant women the roles prescribed by bourgeois domesticity ideology. Rising school attendance, literacy and French-speaking were welcomed by some as evidence of rural 'progress'. But parents worried that literate children might rebel against their authority or no longer wish to work on the land. 'Regionalists' worried that rural exodus and the spread of 'French' culture were undermining linguistic diversity and eroding local costumes, folk songs and dances. Agricultural specialisation and monoculture created ecological

problems. Chemical fertilisers led to soil erosion and degraded water supplies. Although re-afforestation projects began in the Landes and Vaucluse,
excessive felling of trees for fuel produced soil erosion and flooding to adjacent lowlands in Pyrenean and Alpine regions. Forest wardens sought to
restrict peasant livestock on the uplands and preserve woodlands, though
village communities fought tenaciously to retain their grazing practices
(Whited 2000). The decline of rural industries made some areas more
dependent on agriculture than in the past. Monoculture regions like the wine-
growing Midi were likely to prove highly vulnerable to market fluctuations.

The regime won the support of most peasant voters, citing this as proof of
'democratic' legitimacy. Peasants in parts of the Centre and the South-West
remained loyal to Bonapartist candidates beyond 1870. Some still perceived
Bonapartism as a guarantee against the seigneurs' return. In one village in
Haute-Vienne the Bonapartist mayor, a former Republican, was a wine-seller
with a hearty populist style who clashed with the *curé* over communal expenditure and was slapped in public by an aristocratic former mayor whom
he insulted. He controlled the village for two decades until his popularity
was eroded by his authoritarianism and suspicions that he was rigging elections – and diluting his wine! (Vallin 1985). Although fear of socialism led
Royalists to support the coup, relations between Bonapartist prefects and
landed *notables* were often strained. The latter saw it as their role to be
paternalist benefactors of rural communities. But Bonapartist administrators
sought to convince peasants that rewards for voting for government candidates would come in subsidies for local roads and schools, channelled into
villages via sub-prefect and mayor. When Catholic elites turned against the
regime in the 1860s, prefects proved capable of appealing to peasant voters
with a populist rhetoric against the seigneurs. Conversely, when alarmed
by the Left's resurgence in 1869 the regime sought to rebuild fences with the
Royalists, it found Isère peasants reluctant to vote for 'clerical' Bonapartist
aristocratic candidates. Paradoxically Bonapartism prepared the ground for
subsequent rural Republicanism because it allowed the habit of voting to
become established in the countryside, eroded the autonomous power of
landed notables and accustomed peasant electors to look to the administration for 'favours'.

A combination of repression, Bonapartist populism and prosperity meant
that when Republicanism did finally revive, its geographic base had shrunk.
In central regions, the South-West, Dordogne and the Limousin, and in Basses-
Alpes, Republican voting in 1869 was largely urban. Many peasant *Dem-Soc*
electors of 1849–51 proved to be 'recidivists', still addicted to their earlier
Bonapartism. In the Nièvre and Basses-Alpes, the rural exodus eased demographic pressures which had fuelled earlier unrest. Radicalism had also
declined in forest areas of scattered habitat. In the Pyrenees there was
still conscription evasion, endemic poaching and occasional forest invasions.
But younger peasants voted with their feet and joined the rural exodus,
and Bonapartist authorities 'relaxed' enforcement of the Forest Codes. Some
Republicans dismissed peasants as ignorant, credulous, indifferent to the democratic values, easily seduced by 'bribes' of 'pork-barrel' politics. Yet the
legacy of the *Dem-Socs* was not entirely dead. Municipal politics remained

lively in Dauphiné or the Midi, where anti-clerical peasants resented the clergy's attempts to impose Catholic schools or determine village expenditure priorities. One-third of villages in Loir-et-Cher experienced significant conflicts over such issues in the 1860s. Sizeable anti-Bonapartist rural votes were registered in 1869–70 in the Rhône valley, Mediterranean coastal plain, Burgundy and east of Paris. There were Republican gains in a crescent stretching from the Jura via the Loire valley into Upper Normandy and in areas – Franche-Comté, the Burgundy *vignoble* and the Saône-et-Loire valleys – of concentrated habitat where peasants had contacts with Republican petty bourgeoisie (Salmon 1993).

The February 1871 elections, contested with Prussian troops occupying much of France, saw a rural vote for Royalists promising peace and protection from Prussian reprisals. Even the Aude in the Languedoc wine-plain elected six conservative deputies. Yet Republicans won 100 of 120 by-elections in the next two years. In the Creuse, a fief of popular Bonapartism the massacre of hundreds of migrant peasant-masons in the Commune re-kindled the embers of earlier radicalism and allowed Nadaud, the *Dem-Soc* exiled during the Empire, to rally support for the Republic. Narbonnais *vignerons* mobilised in the 'struggle for the Republic', petitioning for secular education and waving red flags at funerals. Republicans penetrated the Doubs, Aube and Ardennes, areas hitherto outside their spheres of influence. In a bid to stifle rural democracy prefects conducted wholesale administrative purges. In the Vaucluse, 103 mayors were sacked, 46 municipalities dissolved, 35 village teachers dismissed and 92 cafés closed down. The 1877 election showed that the Republic had finally put down roots in peasant France. But this was not the 'Republic' of 1849–51. Some social tensions had eased, though Republicanism retained a 'red' tinge in the Midi, Limousin and the Centre. Gambetta's Republic promised stability, defence of small property, education for peasant children, protection against 'clericalism', lower freight rates and protective tariffs. This was a vision to which even Normandy or the fringes of the Catholic West might respond (Vigreux 1987; Corbin 1975; Salmon 1993).

Peasants and the bourgeois Republic

Weber (1976) claimed that it was after 1870 that a quasi-autarchic peasantry was finally integrated into a wider national society. The agents of transformation were railways, schools and universal conscription. The extension of the rail network from 18,000 to 65,000 kilometres, and a 60 per cent increase in the local road network, accelerated the transition to commercial farming. Confronted with balance-sheets and the need to keep accounts, peasants awoke to the importance of literacy and numeracy. Backed by a regime which made primary education a priority, schoolteachers became village notables. By teaching in French, not in the various patois still spoken by half the population in 1860, and by emphasising French history and geography, they created a sense of national identity. The cult of the *patrie* taught in schools prepared peasant boys to accept their future role as conscripts. Hitherto under 10 per cent – those who drew a *mauvais numéro* in the annual *tirage au sort* – had been obliged to do military service. Some peripheral regions had traditions of conscription evasion and the army was seen during the tax revolt of 1848 as an alien, occupying force. Gradually such hostility waned. Conscripts spoke French in the barracks, ate meat, drank wine and learned urban dances. The need to write to conscript sons illustrated the uses of literacy. In Emile Guillaumin's novel *La Vie d'un Simple* illiterate share-croppers obliged to ask the grocer's daughter to read their conscript sons' letters find that 'ignorance appeared hard because we were more disadvant-aged by it than usual'. Conscript illiteracy fell from 15 per cent to 4 per cent between 1887 and 1914, while the average annual number of letters per capita trebled. Returning conscripts brought urban cultural values with them, although the Doubs was not alone in finding that nearly half peasant conscripts never returned to live on the farm. Conscription and the trans-port revolution accelerated the rural exodus. In 1861 only 11 per cent of the population lived outside their native department. By 1914 this figure had risen to 25 per cent (Weber 1976; Moulin 1991; Duby and Wallon 1976).

A way of life was being transformed. Diets became more varied. White bread from bakers, a symbol of civilisation, replaced hard black bread. Vil-lages now boasted groceries selling spaghetti and coffee. Abolition of the wine-tax after 1880 stimulated rural consumption. Dark, heavy clothes lost ground to urban fashions – colourful cotton prints, white wedding dresses, blue work blouses. A Cognac *vigneron's* daughter was seen on Royan beach reading mail-order catalogues from Paris department stores! Replacement of thatched roofs by tiles reduced the incidence of fires. Modest Breton peasant farms acquired kitchen cabinets and large clocks. Indeed precise 'clock-time', already triumphant in city and factory, completed its conquest of the coun-tryside. Village schools and *mairies* acquired clock-towers, rural rail-stations had printed timetables, pupils received watches as rewards for their school-leaving certificate. Concepts of 'leisure' (*loisirs*) emerged. Hitherto work and free-time were interwoven. During winter *veillées* women sewed and men mended tools as stories were told. Children played as they tended animals. Women chatted while doing the laundry in the stream. Neighbours held dances to flatten land for newly weds to construct a house. Market-day trans-actions were an occasion for male sociability. Celebrations were communal – *fêtes*, Carnival, collective dances. Farmers had less free time than urban dwellers, indeed working and living often appeared synonymous.

However, mono-culture was less labour-intensive than polyculture and working hours of agricultural labourers did decline. Leisure patterns became more individualistic. Beaujolais *vignerons* took excursions to spa centres. The affordability of bicycles by 1890 allowed peasants to cycle to dances in local *bourgs*. Young men frequented cafés which offered *boules* terraces and newspapers. Cafés mushroomed after liberalisation of licencing laws in 1881. *Veillées* were abandoned to women, children and the old. 'All the life went out of the villages. Everything now took place in the café in front of a bottle', laments Guillaumin's Père Tiennon. Mid-summer St. Jean bonfires died after 1860, and Carnival by the 1880s. Stalls and amusements at village fairs were now supplied by travelling commercial 'professionals' selling cheap consumer goods. The *fête nationale*, 14 July was 'official', organised and (relatively) decorous. Dubious pastimes such as cock-fighting, bear-baiting and *soules* – a rugby-type game which provided the excuse for inter-village punch-ups – gave way to organised gymnastics, archery, *boules* in Anjou. Brass bands, fanfares and choirs multiplied. By 1900, 17 per cent of villages in the Aude plain possessed a band. Since such groups were organised by teachers and municipal officials one might view them as part of a process of bourgeois encadrement of the peasantry (Goujon 1981; Farcy 1997).

Weber (1976) portrays these changes as 'progressive'. Passivity and fatalism were being eroded. Vaucluse peasants 'copied' birth-control from village teachers as a rational strategy to avoid subdivision of small farms. Fertilisers had more impact on crop yields than crucifixes placed in corners of fields. Nadaud rejoiced that Limousin migrants took the train to Paris rather than tramping three hundred miles on foot. Education and the decline of *veillée* storytelling meant, Guillaumin claimed, fewer peasant children raised in terror of werewolves and witches. Some regretted that a rustic cultural harmony was being wrecked. Breton or Provençal regionalists lamented the threat to peripheral cultures. Legitimist aristocrats and clergy collected and catalogued folk songs, fairy tales and dances. Such defenders of the old culture were romantics from declining strata of the elites – who viewed national culture as a threat to their local hegemony. But Occitan or Breton peasants often abandoned old ways with little hesitation, rejoicing in their newly acquired command of a French language which opened up employment opportunities. The 'regional consciousness' of the Auvergnat colony in Paris was essentially the selective nostalgia for rural roots of a community already established in the city's wine trade and cab industries. Weber acknowledges accusations that alien values of a bureaucratic, centralising state were being imposed on peripheral regions, that peasant culture was treated as 'backward' and 'patois' as a sign of imbecility. However, he questions whether this constituted 'internal colonisation'. Wide inequalities in wealth, literacy, diet and health between regions began to decline. Certainly Algerian workers in inter-war Parisian car-plants were dubbed 'brown Bretons'. Yet not only could Bretons become 'French', many desired to do so (Weber 1976).

Weber's (1976) thesis has not gone unchallenged. His claim that 'national' politics became relevant to peasants only after 1870 seriously underestimates the scale of peasant mobilisations in 1789 or 1848. Some regional cultures and patois proved more resilient than he claimed. Hélias' memoirs of his Breton childhood tell of his parents' desire for him to receive a 'French' education to broaden his employment prospects. Yet his warmest recollections are of his grandfather who tended him when he was a child and imparted the 'old' peasant wisdom. Even if one accepts Weber's (problematic) 'modernisation' metanarrative, his chronology of change remains suspect. Was there really a unilinear shift from poly-culture towards cash-crop monoculture and greater cultural and economic contact with the towns? Some rural areas long involved in proto-industrial production saw this decline in the face of factory competition. The consequent fall in numbers of rural spinners and weavers, clog-makers and barrel-makers – allied to the simultaneous decline of village artisans – eliminated many literate culture-brokers central to earlier rural politics. Weber's model of 'integration' is too conflict-free. He plays down the vulnerability of cash-crop agriculture to the ravages of the Great Depression, neglects continuing class conflict in the countryside and under-estimates regionalist resistance to cultural change.

Republicans sought to consolidate their hold on the countryside just as the agrarian depression gathered pace. They knew that they had to be seen to do something to protect the peasantry or else risk a haemorrhage of votes to the Right, which could invoke the prosperity of the 1850s and 1860s or the socialist Left. The 1884 parliamentary enquiry into the rural economy com-piled statistics, gathered opinions and conducted surveys of family budgets. Although resultant policy decisions were influenced by protectionist demands from powerful industrialists and large landowners, the government insisted that peasant problems were central to Republican concerns and that their voices were being heard (Liebowitz 1993). Ironically it was areas dependent on market agriculture which proved most vulnerable. The construction of local rail lines had increased regional specialisation. Land under the plough declined in 70 departments freed from the need to produce their own grain. A quadrupling of chemical fertiliser use increased grain yields by 30 per cent. Refrigerated wagons boosted Charente dairy farming. Market-gardening of fruit and early vegetables developed in Provence and coastal Brittany. Normandy and the Charolais concentrated on beef production. As many as 81 per cent of respondents to the 1884 enquiry claimed that their sector or region was in crisis, and 45 per cent blamed free-trade. However, 93 per cent of responses from northern France acknowledged the depression. Only 25 per cent of sharecroppers, less involved in cash-crop farming, complained of falling sales and low prices, but 60 per cent of tenant farmers did so. Many called for protective tariffs. Initially livestock and dairy sectors remained rel-atively sheltered from a crisis which began with localised problems, before these merged into a wider price collapse. Although rain in the late-1870s ruined successive cereal harvests, the main threat to this sector came from Transatlantic and Russian competition, producing a 27 per cent decline in prices between the 1870s and 1895; 20 per cent of wheat was now imported compared to 1 per cent in 1855. Livestock prices tumbled after 1885, again due to overseas competition. The South-East was hit particularly hard. In the 1860s raw-silk had been devastated by pebrine disease. Then, as Lyonnais silk manufacturers turned to South-East Asia for raw materials, raw-silk prices fell 40 per cent. Meanwhile, 'industrial' crops such as garance and madder, staples of the Alpine peasant economy, were undercut by artificial dyestuffs. Olive-oil producers were undercut by Mediterranean producers. To compound the region's woes, vines were then devastated by the *phylloxera* blight which marched inexorably through French vineyards between 1865 and the 1890s (Moulin 1991; Duby and Wallon 1976).

Wine was France's second most valuable export and railways now trans-ported cheap table-wines to northern consumers. But as *phylloxera* spread from the Midi to Burgundy, the Bordelais and the Loire in the 1880s, vine-yards contracted by 25 per cent. Initial remedies – planting vines in sandy soil or submerging roots in water – proved ineffectual. Sulphuric acid, pro-moted by chemical companies, was costly. Eventually tough-rooted Amer-ican vines proved resistant to the disease, but grafting these on to native plants was a slow process costing 3000 francs per hectare. By 1894 one million hectares had been re-planted, but the value of the wine crop had fallen by 40 per cent. Reconstruction proved too costly for many. *Vignerons'* dreams of independence and modest prosperity had briefly been realised in the boom. Now their precious vines were uprooted and burned. In Lower Languedoc, the monoculture region, production shifted towards large capitalist estates on the coastal plain. Although economists welcomed this rationalisation, a combination of industrial production of *vin ordinaire* and wine imports from Algeria led to massive overproduction and price collapse (Pech 1975).

Small *vignerons* were clearly 'victims'. But the overall impact of the Depression on structures of rural society was complex. There was no unilinear trend against small peasants. Many who swelled the rural exodus were day-labourers, whose numbers fell from four to three million. Others were rural craftsmen. Such departures led to localised labour shortages. In Seine-et-Marne, farm wages rose by 50 per cent 1892–1912. Tenants and sharecroppers might benefit from the Depression. Average rents had fallen 30 per cent by the 1890s. Thereafter a combination of low rents and recovering prices saw tenant incomes rise by 70 per cent in Loir-et-Cher in the 1900s (Liebowitz 1989). Falling rents and profits persuaded some rentiers to sell off estates and switch investments to stocks-and-shares which promised higher returns than the 3 per cent now the norm in agriculture. Land held by owners of 40 hectares or more fell by only 2.4 per cent in the 1880s, but there were areas such as the Toulousain grain-lands where land was sold to peasants. There was no marked proletarianisation except in Midi vineyards. Indeed the position of some peasant-owners was consolidated. Average incomes eventually edged upwards. Depression, though prolonged, was less severe than that of 1846–51.

However, rural society was affected. Agricultural incomes had fallen by 20 per cent in Loir-et-Cher by the 1890s. A sharp fall in birth rates was one response to economic uncertainties. A combination of demographic stagnation and falling agrarian purchasing power reduced consumer demand. The out-migration of the young deepened a sense of gloom and cultural anxiety in peripheral regions, which felt that a way of life was dying. Yet small cash-crop farmers often adapted flexibly and imaginatively. Vaucluse suffered in the 1870s from pebrine, which destroyed 50 per cent of raw-silk production, *phylloxera*, which hit 30,000 hectares of vineyards, and from the collapse of markets for madder which had occupied 10 per cent of the land. Yet peasants moved into market-gardening of fruit, potatoes and asparagus, and their small-holdings were more productive than rentier-owned large estates in the department. They initiated irrigation projects and found market niches for quality wines. But these enterprising 'petty-capitalists' remained loyal to their cultural and political traditions. They were anti-clerical, established cooperative cellars to store their wine and voted consistently on the Left – radical until the 1890s, sometimes socialist thereafter (Mesliand 1989). Yields rose in labour-intensive market-gardening farms on the Breton coast. When the collapse of weaving deprived Stephenois peasants of supplementary income, they switched to dairy-farming. The modest annual agricultural growth-rates in France of 0.9 per cent between 1880 and 1914 was marginally above the European average. Surveys undertaken by students at *Instituts Agronomes* presented encouraging evidence of peasant farmers diversifying, increasing yields, and marketing an increased proportion of their crops (Hubscher 1985). It is usually claimed that governments offered peasant electors little but protective tariffs and Méline's rhetoric praising them as the backbone of French society and claiming that the 'national genius' was to 'balance' industry, commerce and agriculture. Yet Republicans did take initiatives to bolster crisis-hit peasant farming. The *Banque de France* underwrote state-aid for rural credit. Irrigation schemes were financed, departmental *Professeurs d'Agriculture* appointed and a *Service des Améliorations* established – although it employed only 50 engineers. Tax exemptions were offered to mutualist insurance schemes. Some measures were largely palliatives, but they do suggest a degree of 'interventionism' from governments generally committed to laissez-faire.

In the context of agrarian depression 'modernisation' was not conflict-free. Claims that there existed an all-class unity of interests and values in rural France – a 'countryside alliance' – are implausible. Certainly the dominant discourse about the countryside was that of '*agrariens*'. Both Republicans and Catholic-Royalist talked endlessly of a mythical countryside, bedrock of all national virtues. In *Le Retour à la Terre* (1907), Méline insisted that peasant farming remained the 'root' of national prosperity and that peasants provided France with its soldiers. Yet socialism, denounced as a threat to rustic values, made electoral gains. By 1914 eight of the twelve departments where the SFIO secured over 20 per cent of the vote were rural. The electoral map resembled that of 1849, although former Leftist bastions such as Burgundy were now on the Republican centre-Left. But what type of socialism was offered to peasant voters? Engels criticised French socialists for electoral opportunism – offering a diluted programme from which all mention of the peasantry's inexorable decline or of collectivism had been expunged. Some socialists warned that the logic of supporting peasant farmers involved acceptance of Protectionism, hence of dearer food for working-class consumers. But most argued that in a society where industrial workers remained a minority, peasants were an essential component of any progressive bloc. Jaurès reprimanded those who portrayed peasants as irredeemably selfish and brutal, insisting that harsher traits of their culture could be modified by education. Peasant individualism would decline as they realised that only collective action could save them from market fluctuations and competition from capitalist estates.

Rural protest took many forms. The very different grievances of Allier share-croppers, Cher lumbermen, *vignerons* and landless labourers made it difficult to construct a coherent rural strategy. In the Isère, peasant exposure to rural industry gave the Left a foothold. Lyon silk-merchants, searching for a docile labour force, transferred work to the city's rural hinterland. In a department where 80 per cent of holdings were under 5 hectares, income from female employment in the silk diaspora underpinned peasant farms. Some villages lost 30 per cent of inhabitants after 1870, but in textile villages rural exodus was halted. Peasants' wives worked part-time in small local mills utilising water-power from Alpine streams. But employers' dreams of harmony were soon shattered. Isère had five socialist deputies by 1914, in part due to the militancy of rural textile employees. During strikes in the 1880s and 1890s women occupied public space with *charivaris* against employers. Their demands for a tarif – a region-wide minimum wage – was supported by their peasant fathers and husbands. Socialists, conscious that women lacked the vote, targeted these male electors, addressing them as 'workers of the field' and assuring them that small farms were the equivalent of an artisan's tools and workbench and would be respected in a socialist society (Jonas 1994).

Socialist voting in rural Limousin had rather different causes. In a remote, hilly region of scattered habitat and low literacy, mistrust of the towns was discernible in accusations that Limoges 'stole' water from surrounding villages. Bonapartism had tapped antiseigneurial sentiments, and the Parisian construction boom had benefited the region's peasant-masons. However, the deaths of hundreds of these in the Commune caused distress and anger, and their role as storytellers in winter *veillées* made them important radical culture-brokers. This was a region of strong communal solidarities and relatively egalitarian social structures, where peasants clung to surviving communal lands. Harsh terrain and scattered habitat made mutual aid essential for survival. Neighbours exchanged ploughs and draft animals, tended the fields of the sick and assumed collective responsibility for care of the young. All community solidarities are built on suspicion of 'the other'. But whereas in hamlets of Royalist Vendée the 'other' was incarnated by urban bourgeois who had acquired local church lands, in the Limousin he was the seigneur or capitalist usurer. As peasants migrated to industrial Limoges, suspicion of that city declined. Indeed it was now perceived as bastion of a socialism whose discourse of 'justice' and social solidarity appeared to correspond with villagers' communal values. The existence of a Socialist party gave reassuring proof that an organisation 'out there' was championing threatened village culture and sustaining the dream that 'one day' the poor, the exploited, the perennially ignored might achieve justice. Village voting was performed collectively, not individually, as an act of communal solidarity (Vallin 1985).

By 1914 socialists won 30 per cent of votes in the Var. The wine boom had eased social tensions and the exodus of village artisans peasantised villages, removing some radical activists. But *phylloxera* destroyed 60 per cent of vines by 1890, then wine prices fell 80 per cent by 1905. Although the population declined by 10 per cent, the response to these crises revealed the strength of community solidarities built upon shared mistrust of middlemen, wine-merchants and usurers. Profits from money-lending allowed the Trucs of Arcis to construct substantial wine estates. Small peasant proprietors, unable to utilise the strike weapon, looked to socialist municipalities and deputies to defend their interests. But what did they understand by 'socialism'? Judt (1979) denied that it was simply merely a vague, non-ideological, reheated radicalism. The socialist *Cri du Var* denounced the 'mushy spirit of 1848'. Socialist deputies were Guesdist Marxists and sometimes argued that only collectivisation of big estates would solve the wine industry's structural problems and chronic over-production. Some hitherto 'conservative' villages moved directly to socialism as the crisis deepened. However, socialist deputies' were essentially champions of wine co-operatives. Draguignon was the heart of a network of 35 cooperatives which stored 16 per cent of Var wine, avoided sales on glutted markets just after harvest and organised bulk fertiliser purchase and insurance. Cooperatives flourished in the context of strong communal identities, in egalitarian villages with a vigorous sociability built around cafés and *cercles*. Statues of Marianne next to village fountains symbolised a particular style of peasant democracy. *Vignerons* retained loyalties to a (radical) Republic which had reduced the power of priests and introduced secular schooling. But they wanted tougher regulation of rail freight charges, and resentment at losing sons to conscription made them responsive to socialist antimilitarism (Rinaudo 1982; Judt 1979).

Agricultural labourers played only a minor role in struggles in the Var, where large wine-estates were rare. However, there were union-led strikes on capitalist coastal estates. In 1904 vineyard labourers mobilised thousands of red-flag waving demonstrators and forced landowners to concede a labour charter. Such 'explosions' were short-lived, any gains ephemeral. Many Var labourers were Italians, allowing employers to practise crude but effective divide-and-rule strategies, either inciting locals against foreign 'trouble makers' or importing immigrant blacklegs. Union organisers faced similar problems elsewhere. Many potential rural militants voted with their feet by migrating to cities. Around half of the remaining 1.2 million labourers owned small plots or were sons of peasant farmers who hoped to inherit some land. Some were seasonal harvest migrants. Many were immigrants – Spaniards in Lower Languedoc, Belgians in Île-de-France. If the likelihood of such a workforce developing the solidarities required for coherent collective protest was slim, strikes did increase after 1900, even among hitherto docile workers in the Valois region of the Paris basin in 1906–07. Some strikes made ambitious demands, seldom achieved, for union control of hiring rotas comparable to those of contemporary workers in the Po valley. Militancy was higher where workers had a firm identity, as with the lumbermen (*bûcherons*) of central France, whose bastion was the Cher. At its peak their *Fédération Nationale* had 20,000 members in 170 branches. *Bûcherons* had a fierce sense of autonomy and solidarity. They worked in teams, fixed wage rates collectively and clung tenaciously to 'customary' perks such as a share of deadwood. Their economic future was darkening as coal replaced wood fuel, iron ships reduced naval demand for wood and Norwegian imports drove down prices. Employers reduced *bûcherons'* perks and cut the work-days offered. Strikes, coordinated by syndicalist-led Bourges *Bourse du Travail*, made sophisticated demands, for a closed-shop, union control of hiring and accident compensation. The Cher elected two socialist deputies and 230 lumbermen were elected to municipal councils. Their union was the backbone of the *Bourses* in central France, organised cooperatives, libraries and May Day festivals. Yet despite ambitious calls for nationalisation of forests under workers' control, actual union practices were pragmatic and corporatist, levels of dues-paying patchy. *Bûcherons* were isolated from farm workers who viewed them as a privileged labour aristocracy (Pigenet 1993; Hubscher and Farcy 1996).

Nevertheless, *bûcherons* influenced the belated revolt of Allier sharecroppers, hitherto cowed by rapacious *fermiers généraux* who managed the estates of absentee landowners. Faced with falling prices and profits during the Depression, owners shortened leases and increased rents. After paying the *impôt colonique* for the farm and garden, sharecroppers were left with barely 25 per cent of their crop. The sharecroppers' union, *Fédération des Travailleurs de la Terre* (FTT), claimed 1800 members by 1900. It demanded longer leases and compensation for farm improvements. Sharecroppers' struggles are charted in two novels by Émile Guillaumin, himself a working share-cropper and advisor to FTT leader Martin Bernard. *La Vie d'un Simple* recounts the hardships and subordination of his parents' generation. Wives feel obliged to provide laundry services and poultry for *fermiers généraux*. Men touch their caps to '*Not maître*'. Despite underlying class resentments, there is little overt conflict, merely everyday forms of resistance, occasional refusals or ruses. It is a world of incessant toil, where the death of a horse can spell disaster. Inability to speak 'proper' French causes growing humiliation, since bour-geois children mock sharecroppers' patois. Women appear silent, fatalistic, sullen, yet capable of tenderness to a sick child or tears at the departure of a conscript son. *Le Syndicat de Bougignoux* analyses the explosion of open confrontation as sharecroppers struggle to establish their union. The hero's illiterate father, a lifelong Republican, rejoices that his son's literacy, acquired at the *école laïque*, enables him to read aloud for him from the radical news-paper to which he dutifully subscribes. The father concedes that white bread, bacon soup and the odd glass of wine suggest that some material progress is occurring. Yet despite the advent of the Republic, 'we are still treated like dogs'. Republican *notables* show little interest in the sharecroppers' plight. The Republican mayor, a wine-merchant, is a 'pork-barrel' politician who uses his contacts to ensure that the railway passes through the *bourg*, writes letters for peasants and allows them to delay payments of bills. But faced with the FTT his social conservatism becomes clear. In a Republic, he insists, strikes are unnecessary. 'No one today is a slave', all contracts are freely en-tered into. Abandoned by the Republican 'establishment', the union turns to the socialists. The militancy of the book's hero, modelled on Guillaumin himself, derives from anger at injustices suffered by his father, the widening of horizons by schooling and military service and from lumbermen's inspi-ration. He is angered by witnessing the humiliation and eviction of a share-cropper who refuses to apologise to a bourgeois hunter who has stumbled over an obstacle on his farm. He writes a pamphlet portraying *fermiers généraux* as heirs of seigneurial oppressors, a classic example of invocation of 'anti-feudal' memories to mobilise protest. The FTT establishes a fertiliser coop-erative and contacts with Midi wine cooperatives. Yet habits of deference die hard. The father is alarmed by the transition from covert dissenting thoughts to actions. The hero's Catholic wife resents time 'wasted' on the union. The Right-wing press portrays FTT organisers as half-educated *déracinés* under-mining local traders by selling Jewish products in their cooperative. Catholic landowners sponsor a 'mixed' *Syndicat Agricole* bringing together land-owners, sharecroppers and small peasants. Letters to the union newspaper complain that its rhetoric of 'fraternal solidarity' is too high-flown for rural readers. Dispersed habitat makes coordination of activity difficult. Tensions surface between sharecroppers and day-labourers. The hero urges gradualist tactics, but others favour 'direct action', although the strike weapon is ill-suited to sharecroppers since it harms their own livestock and crops. Struggles raise local consciousness sufficiently for socialists to capture the *mairie*, but the union disintegrates. The hero retires to his farm, reads in the evenings and dreams 'utopian' dreams of a future when the château will be a people's clinic and village assemblies will make local decisions! By 1914 Allier voted more strongly socialist than any other department and its sharecroppers provide an exception to general correlations between sharecropping and rural conservatism. Yet many rural Left-wing votes came from peasant-owners and lumbermen. The position of sharecroppers was ambiguous. They were always vulnerable to threats of eviction. Yet their farms were quite large. In 1920 they comprised 20 per cent of the rural population of the department, yet farmed 50 per cent of the land. Hence they often used some hired labour, and were thus employers as well as exploited tenants (Sokoloff 1980).

The crisis which shook Lower Languedoc in the 1900s provoked a massive mobilisation. An 'all-class', cross-party regionalist alliance to defend the wine industry emerged which, briefly, transcended social and ideological divisions. The collapse of wine production in the *phylloxera* years prompted various expedients by large wine producers, including expansion into Algerian vineyards and wine 'sugaring' to increase its alcohol content. Reconstruction of vineyards with American vines then led to a wine glut. Between 1899 and 1905 wine prices fell 70 per cent, land values by two-thirds. Small *vignerons* and the Left argued that overproduction was the fault of industrial coastal vineyards like *Compagnie des Salins du Midi* whose production rose 13.5 per cent per year after 1893. Conversely, larger wine producers and Republican and Legitimist politicians claimed that northern sugar-beet interests, close to government, were fraudulently 'sugaring' wine stocks to the detriment of Midi wine producers. Social conflicts remained close to the surface. Small *vignerons* established cooperatives. One was established by socialist Elie Cathola at Mauressan, a village which had resisted the 1851 coup. But many *vignerons*, unable to meet the costs of re-planting after the *phylloxera*, were forced to work on the big estates; 50 per cent of land around Béziers was now controlled by 3.4 per cent of owners. Four Mediterranean coastal departments now had 163,000 agricultural labourers, 56 per cent of the wine workforce. In Cruzy (Hérault) labourers rose from 9 per cent to 46 per cent of the workforce between 1876 and 1911. However, 60,000 retained tiny plots on which they tended a few vines. Embittered by their recent expropriation and living in villages with strong community solidarities, 'red' in 1848, they hired themselves to the big estates in collective work-gangs (*colles*). Pruning and grafting work was highly skilled. However, management sought to reduce their 'privileges' – introducing tough foremen and tighter time-keeping, forcing them to spray vines with toxic chemicals, importing cheaper Spanish labour. Wage cuts provoked a wave of strikes in 1904–05, involving 44,000 workers, organised by the syndicalist *Fédération des Travailleurs Agricoles du Midi* (FTAM). Since many estates were owned by anti-Dreyfusard Royalists, strikers expected sympathy from Republican authorities, but troop protection of blacklegs provoked antimilitarist rhetoric. At Coursan (Aude) the estate manager shot two demonstrators, and syndicalists flew red flags from the church steeple. At Cruzy the socialist municipality initiated road construction schemes to provide jobs for strikers and established soup kitchens.

However, in 1905 local elites seized the initiative, directing the simmering anger of the region against 'northern' sugar-beet interests and their 'Parisian' political allies. They succeeded, for two years, in constructing an alliance to 'save the vine'. Tax-boycotts were organised and mass demonstrations held. A strange alliance of Radical politicians, wine-merchants, socialists and legitimist landowners emerged. Protest banners had slogans in *occitan* and a regionalist consciousness permeated the movement. Dr Ferroul, enigmatic socialist mayor of Narbonne, was the unlikely spokesman of an all-class wine lobby, the *Confédération Générale des Vignerons du Midi* (CGVM). 'The interests of rich and poor are *not separate*', he claimed. 'We are no longer Opportunists, Radicals, Socialists . . . , merely *southerners* demanding the right to live.' The crisis climaxed in 1907. The Perpignan prefecture was burned down, demonstrators shot in Narbonne, local conscripts mutinied at Agde. Three-quarters of Hérault municipalities resigned. Clemenceau defused the crisis. In return for CGVM disavowal of any desire for southern independence and promises to assist unemployed labourers, he offered tax concessions to winegrowers and a clampdown on 'fraud'. As wine prices gradually improved, aided by poor harvests, 'normality' returned. Although their local politicians, to preserve credibility, had flirted with the *révolte*, Radicals were essentially the party of the status quo. Their leaders included wine-merchants who maintained their populist credentials by gestures of support for peasant cooperatives and progressive taxation. The socialists won 15 per cent of votes in the region. Their flirtation with the CGVM confirmed them as defender of wine interests, particularly of *vignerons* whose cooperatives they encouraged. But it exposed their lack of concern with the interests of the rural proletariat. FTAM membership had tumbled from 15,000 to 2000 between 1905 and 1907 before reviving. Its leader, Ader, denounced the CGVM as a front for capitalist interests and criticised socialist 'betrayal'. The *révolte* could, he claimed, provide useful lessons in direct action once its obfuscatory all-class rhetoric had been jettisoned. Syndicalist *Bourses du Travail* coordinated a strike-wave after 1910. Although the union had few women members, it dropped its earlier insistence that women were biologically 'unsuited' to tasks in the vineyards such as using heavy chemical equipment. Women, their solidarities nurtured by the 'sociabilities' of the village community and by working in collective gangs, made up 33 per cent of strikers in 1913. During strikes they ran soup-kitchens, hounded blacklegs, sat down in front of cavalry sent to break picket lines and sang to the tune of the Internationale:

If, one day, we are victorious/We'll show our dear husbands/
That all the women have fought/For the lives of our poor little ones.

The role of regionalist consciousness in these conflicts was complex. The dominant regionalist discourses were those of the Catholic Right, hostile to Jacobin centralisation, and of Mistral's cultural *Félibrige* movement. Support for regional autonomy was limited. Midi wine needed northern consumers. *Occitanie* was too ill-defined a concept to be the basis of a real identity. Many workers and peasants viewed *occitan* as a symbol of their inferiority and, as Jaurès perceived, took pride in their growing command of French which opened up wider career prospects. Many in the region did resent both conscription and army's role in suppressing protest, but ideological anti-militarism had only a limited appeal and anxieties about mass refusal of mobilisation by southerners in the event of war were exaggerated. However, a 'regional class identity' did exist, constructed around perceptions of reliance on a cash-crop vulnerable to overproduction crises, and on a conviction that the French state was more concerned to defend interests of organised northern capitalist landowners than those of *vin ordinaire* producers. There was a sense of solidarity between vineyard workers and *vignerons*, for the former often owned a few vines and the latter sought additional income by working part-time on the big estates. Ironically an 'alternative', dissenting version of regional heritage was spread by anti-clerical teachers who encouraged pupils to view themselves as heirs of Albigensian heretics who had resisted Rome and 'northern' Catholic kings. Banners in 1905–07 demonstrations, as in those of the 1970s, proclaimed winegrowers' determination to live and die *'al Païs'*. Oral histories confirm that *vignerons* viewed French as the language of the elites, *occitan* as that of the people (Loubère 1968; Pech 1975; Frader 1991; Smith 1975; Lem 1995).

Class tensions in the French countryside were less acute than in Italy or southern Spain and generated open conflicts only in a few regions. Peasants were told that there were distinct agrarien interests which they shared with landowners. The bourgeois Republic consistently flattered peasant voters. Ferry insisted that *'la République sera paysanne ou elle ne sera pas'*. Méline argued that for a 'balanced' society peasants could not be left at the mercies of the free market. From the 1880s onwards, fearing that the depression might drive peasants to the Right or the far Left, they sponsored *Syndicats Agricoles* (SAs), which lobbied for peasant interests and organised bulk purchase, insurance and credit schemes. These were challenged by a rival Catholic-Royalist organisation, the *Union Centrale des Syndicats Agricoles de France*, better known after the site of its headquarters as the Rue d'Athènes. This was led by landowners, but 58 per cent of members were peasant owners, 28 per cent tenants and sharecroppers. Although strong in Catholic heartlands, it boasted 125,000 members in ten south-eastern departments, some Leftist strongholds. Clergy organised voluntary associations and sports groups. Catholic SAs proclaimed the all-class unity of the countryside against the cities, the role of paternalist landed elites as protectors of the peasantry and the importance of regional identities (Barral 1968). Since Republican and Catholic SAs had a million members between them, one might conclude that the countryside remained under the control of rival notables. Are depictions of France as a 'peasant democracy' therefore naïve or disingenuous? Nearly 60 per cent of land was owned by aristocratic or bourgeois landowners. Although peasants constituted the largest single class, there were only 10 peasant deputies in parliament in 1889. Republican gains in the countryside did not necessarily entail significant 'democratisation'. In prosperous livestock-rearing Calvados the transition from Bonapartism to Republicanism was merely an exchange of one brand of pragmatic conservatism for another. The Southern Massif 'converted' to the Republic later. It was a region where the parish had been the focus of social life. Birth rates were high and inheritance practices inegalitarian. Eldest brother inherited family farms, while younger siblings remained unmarried, worked as day-labourers or entered the Church. However, these patterns gradually broke down. As younger family members demanded a share of inheritance or migrated to Paris, the Republic was perceived more favourably – as a source of schooling, jobs and administrative favours. Dependence on traditional notables gave way to a democratic clientalism in which peasants turned to accessible bourgeois for conscription exemptions or civil service jobs (Jones 1985).

Yet rural Republicanism was not simply bourgeois manipulation revolving around 'pork-barrel' politics. An argument can be made for some democratisation of the countryside. In the Morvan, peasants held municipal office by the 1880s. Mayors of larger communes were now elected, not appointed. By 1912, 50 per cent of mayors and 75 per cent of deputy-mayors (*adjoints*) were drawn from the peasantry. The bust of Marianne at the town hall, the fountain in the square were – alongside the new purpose-built laic school – symbols of a village democracy. This democratic culture was rooted in voluntary associations which flourished in the countryside. The *citoyen vigneron* evoked in Goujon's study of Saône-et-Loire was a member of musical and singing groups, of gymnastic and shooting societies. He helped organise the 14 July *fête*. A former pupil of the *école laïque*, he joined the *Amicale Scolaire*. Similar 'expressive' male associations multiplied in viticultural areas of the Loire Valley where crown-green bowling (*boules de fort*) flourished. As the Republic fulfilled its promise to cut the price of hunting, the number of peasants with hunting permits trebled between 1876 and 1900.

Of course some of this could plausibly be dismissed as a process of extension of bourgeois hegemony into the villages. Organisers of such associations included lawyers, doctors or schoolteachers. Annual Republican banquets spread the bourgeois art of *savoir manger*, with peasants fined for 'coarse' behaviour. Trips were arranged to industrial centres to give villagers pride in France's economic dynamism. The chronology of the creation of associations coincided quite closely with the political history of Republicanism, with surges in the late-1860s, early 1880s and in the aftermath of the Dreyfus crisis. And yet even if the cadres of mutual aid societies in the Allier countryside were largely from the *bourgs*, a strong current of fraternalist associationism existed in rural France. This helped to underpin Republicanism, but it also ensured that its ethos was often closer to that of the *Dem-Socs* of 1849 than to that of bourgeois individualism. The solid bedrock of village Republicanism in Burgundy, the Jura or the Charentes was a network of 'instrumental' voluntary associations. Baker's study of Loir-et-Cher has shown how such associations emerged as a form of secular risk management. Peasants were neither fatalistic and locked into habitual routine, nor were they 'petty-bourgeois individualists'. They were a 'class of survivors' – forced to adapt to a world of scarcities and endless difficulties. As pragmatists they were aware that mutual aid and solidarity were prerequisites for survival. Village fire-brigades had been established by the 1830s. Mutual aid societies emerged in the 1840s and constituted a dense network by the 1860s. Anti-*phylloxera* associations emerged in the 1870s, livestock insurance associations multiplied after 1900. Republican politicians claimed that government sponsorship helped erode peasant routine and narrow individualism, and undoubtedly Republican cadres in departmental *chef-lieu* Blois had a role in organising associations. However, the impetus came 'from below'. The department's first *Syndicat Agricole* emerged from a peasant-run participatory association. In short, Baker (1999) argues, to a pragmatic system of mutual aid, born of peasants' own experiences and from their own culture, was added a theoretical 'justification' as the national political discourse of Republican Solidarism filtered into day-to-day lives. Inevitably associationism was stronger in some areas than in others. In Loir-et-Cher its heartlands were in the western parts of the department – in the 'open' cultures of river valleys, among *vignerons*, in villages with the remnants of Protestant culture.

French rural society was thus more 'democratic' than that of contemporary Britain or Germany. This is not to deny the power of Catholic landed elites or the skill of new Republican notables in manipulating the rhetoric of a 'little man's' *République des Paysans* for their own purposes. But village politics was often lively and passionate. Electoral turnouts of 90 per cent were common in Vaucluse villages. Peasants were elected to municipal councils. Mutual aid societies and cooperatives both allowed peasant farmers to adjust flexibly to the problems of the Depression and provided 'schooling' in democracy. Through this vigorous, participatory democratic culture, peasants were, to some degree, able to 'make their own history' (Goujon 1981; Baker 1999; Mesliand 1989).

Bibliography

General
Barral, P. *Les Agrariens Français de Méline à Pisani* (Paris: A. Colin, 1968).
Brustein, W. *The Social Origins of Political Regionalism: France 1848–1981* (Berkeley, CA: University of California Press, 1988).
Duby, G. and Wallon, C. *Histoire de la France Rurale* Vol. III (Paris: Editions du Seuil, 1976).
Lagrange, H. and Roché, S. 'Types familiaux et géographie politique en France', *Revue Française de Science Politique* 1988.
Lehning, J. *Peasant and French* (Cambridge: Cambridge University Press, 1995).
Margadant, T. 'Tradition and modernity in rural France', *Journal of Modern History* 1984.
Mayaud, J.-L. *La Petite Exploitation Rurale Triomphante* (Paris: Belin, 1999).
Moulin, A. *Peasantry and Society in France Since 1789* (Cambridge: Cambridge University Press, 1991).
Price, R. *The Modernisation of Rural France* (London: Hutchinson, 1983).
Weber, E. *Peasants into Frenchmen: the Modernisation of Rural France 1870–1914* (London: Chatto and Windus, 1976).

1789–1851
Agulhon, M. *The Republic in the Village: the People of the Var from the French Revolution to the Second Republic* (Cambridge: Cambridge University Press, 1970).
Baker, A. *Fraternity Amongst the French Peasantry: Sociability and Voluntary Association in the Loire Valley: 1815–1914* (Cambridge: Cambridge University Press, 1999).
Berenson, E. 'Politics and the French peasantry', *Social History* 1987.
Clark, T. *Image of the People* (London: Thames and Hudson, 1973).

Corbin, A. *Archaïsme et Modernité en Limousin: 1845–80* (Paris: M. Rivière, 1975).

Jessenne, J. *Pouvoir au Village et Révolution: Artois 1760–1848* (Lille: Lille University Press, 1987).

Jones, P. *Politics and Rural Society: the Southern Massif Central 1750–1880* (Cambridge: Cambridge University Press, 1985).

Jones, P. *The Peasantry and the French Revolution* (Cambridge: Cambridge University Press, 1988).

Lévêque, P. *La Bourgogne de la Monarchie de Juillet au Second Empire* 5 vols (Lille: Lille University Press, 1980).

Loubère, L. 'The extreme Left in Lower Languedoc 1848–51', *American Historical Review* 1968.

Magraw, R. 'P. Joigneaux and Socialist Politics in the French Countryside 1849–51', *French Historical Studies* 1978.

Margadant, T. *French Peasants in Revolt: the Insurrection of 1851* (Princeton, NJ: Princeton University Press, 1979).

Mayaud, J.-L. *Les Paysans du Doubs au Temps de Courbet* (Paris, 1979).

Mayaud, J.-L. *Courbet: L'Enterrement à Ornans, Un Tombeau pour la République* (Paris, 1999).

Merriman, J. *The Agony of the Republic: 1849–51* (New Haven: Yale University Press, 1978).

McPhee, P. 'The French Revolution, peasants and capitalism', *American Historical Review* 1989.

McPhee, P. *The Politics of Rural Life 1846–52: Mobilisation in the French Countryside 1846–52* (Oxford: Oxford University Press, 1992).

Pierre, R. *Ah! Quand viendra la Belle? Résistants et Insurgés de la Drôme, 1848–51* (Valence: Edits Notre Temps, 1981).

Price, R. (ed.) *Revolution and Reaction* (London: Croom Helm, 1975).

Root, H. *Peasant and King in Burgundy* (Berkeley CA: University of California Press, 1987).

Sahlins, P. *Forest Rites: the War of the Demoiselles in 19th-Century France* (Cambridge, Mass: Harvard University Press, 1994).

Soulet, J.-F. *Les Pyrénées au XIXe Siècle* 2 vols (Toulouse: Éché, 1987).

Tilly, C. 'How protest modernised France: 1845–55', in W. Aydelotte (ed.) *The Dimensions of Quantitative Reseach in History* (Princeton, NJ: Princeton University Press, 1972).

Vigier, P. *La Seconde République dans la Région Alpine: 1848–51* 2 vols (Paris: PUF, 1963).

Vigreux, M. *Paysans et Notables du Morvan au XIXe Siècle* (Château Chinon, 1987).

Vivier, N. *Propriété Collective et Identité Communale: les Biens Communaux en France 1750–1914* (Paris: Sorbonne, 1999).

Weber, E. 'Comment la Politique Vint aux Paysans', *American Historical Review* 1982.

Whited, T. *Forests and Peasant Politics in Modern France* (New Haven: Yale University Press, 2000).

1851–1914

Corbin, A. 'Historiography of violence in the French countryside', in R. Aldrich (ed.) *France: Politics Society, Culture* (Sydney: University of Sydney, 1990).

Farcy, J.-C. *Les Paysans Beaucerons* 2 vols (Chartres, 1990).

Farcy, J.-C. 'Le Temps libre au Village', in A. Corbin (ed.) *Le Temps des Loisirs* (Paris, 1997).

Frader, L. *Peasants and Protest: Agricultural Workers, Politics and Unions in the Aude 1850–1914* (Berkeley, CA: University of California Press, 1991).

Garrier, G. *Paysans du Beaujolais et du Lyonnais: 1800–1970* 2 vols (Grenoble: Grenoble University Press, 1973).

Goujon, P. 'Associations . . . dans les Campagnes au XIXe Siècle: le Cas du Vignoble de Saône et Loire', *Cahiers d'Histoire* 1981.

Gratton, P. *La Lutte des Classes dans les Campagnes* (Paris: Anthropos, 1971).

Hubscher, R. and Farcy, J.-C. (eds) *La Moisson des Autres: Les Salariés Agricoles au XIXe et XXe Siècles* (Paris: Créaphis, 1996).

Hubscher, R. 'La petite exploitation en France: reproduction et competivité', *Annales ESC* 1985.

Jonas, R. *Industry and Politics in Rural France: Peasants of the Isère 1870–1914* (Ithaca: Cornell University Press, 1994).

Judt, T. *Socialism in Provence: 1880–1914* (Cambridge: Cambridge University Press, 1979).

Lem, W. 'Identity and history: class and regional consciousness in rural Languedoc', *Journal of Historical Sociology* 1995.

Loubère, L. *Radicalism in Mediterranean France: 1848–1914* (Albany: State University of New York, 1974).

Liebowitz, J. 'Tenants, sharecroppers and the French agricultural depression', *Journal of Interdisciplinary History* 1989.

Liebowitz, J. 'Parliamentary support for protectionism: the parliamentary enquiry of 1884', *French History* 1993.

Mesliand, C. *Paysans du Vaucluse: 1860–1939* 2 vols (Provence: Université de Provence, 1989).

Pech, R. *Entreprise Viticole et Capitalisme en Languedoc* (Toulouse: Le Mirail, 1975).

Pigenet, M. *Ouvriers, Paysans nous sommes: Les Bûcherons du Centre au Tournant du Siècle* (Paris: L'Harmattan, 1993).

Rinaudo, Y. *Les Paysans du Var: Les Vendanges de la République* (Lyon: Lyon University Press, 1982).

Sagnès, J. 'Le Mouvement de 1905–07 en Languedoc-Roussillon', *Le Mouvement Social* 1978.

Sagnès, J. *Le Midi Rouge: Mythes et Réalités* (Paris: Anthropos, 1982).

Salmon, F. 'La Gauche Avancée en 1849 et en 1870', in L. Harmon (ed.) *Les Républicains sous l'Empire* (Paris: MSH, 1993).

Smith, H. 'Work routine and social structure in a French village', *Journal of Interdisciplinary History* 1975.

Sokoloff, S. 'Sharecroppers and politics in central France', *European Studies Review* 1980.

Vallin, P. *Paysans Rouge du Limousin* (Paris: L'Harmattan, 1985).

Chapter 4

Religion and anti-clericalism

Introduction

Secularisation or religious revival?

The authors of an authoritative religious history of modern France claim that the historiography of French Catholicism is overdependent on a discredited metanarrative which assumes that 'modernisation' entails secularisation (Cholvy and Hilaire 1985–86). Secularists once rejoiced at the prospect of science, education and democracy consigning 'obscurantist' religion to richly deserved oblivion. Zola depicted the last priest saying the last Mass in the last church. It is struck by lightening, the curé crushed by a falling crucifix. His body turns to ashes, which blow away in the wind! By 1950, with the Catholic hierarchy discredited by collaboration with Vichy and workers voting Communist, sociologists assumed that the Church had 'lost' the popular classes. Worker-priests blamed their own church for this, arguing that its alliances with the wealthy rich and its reactionary politics had betrayed the poor and ignored aspirations for social justice (Pierrard 1984). Ironically, Marxism, not Catholicism, now risks consignment to the rubbish heap of history. Unilinear narratives of secular progress are no longer in vogue. Too many historians, it is now claimed, assumed that a decline in religious practice in a particular region at a particular moment constituted the watershed – that thereafter ongoing decline was inevitable. Studies of dioceses such as Orléans were taken to show that 1830, or 1848, marked decisive moments in the rise of popular anti-clericalism or religious indifference (Marcilhacy 1964).

The new orthodoxy accepts that Catholicism suffered blows in the 1790s and in the early Third Republic, but sees no definitive victories for the forces of secularisation. The decades after 1810 witnessed a religious revival, marked by the post-Concordat reconstruction of the Church, a rise in vocations, expansion of Catholic education, 'ultramontane' piety and the emergence of a more 'personal' religion involving frequent communion. In some dioceses the nadir of religious practice was reached in the 1900s, after which indices of religious vitality pointed upwards. The 'new social history' exhibited little sympathy for religion, treating it as an expression of 'false consciousness' or an instrument of social control. Younger historians suggest that religion offered positive 'resources' for the weak and powerless. Feminists claim that it provided a 'site' of 'female agency' in a society which denied women access to the public sphere. Regionalists have emphasised its contribution to the vitality of peripheral cultures struggling against centralisation.

158

A divided France?

Religion was the most divisive issue in French society. The counter-revolution's fervour stemmed less from loyalty to King or seigneurs than from villagers' determination to defend local religious cultures against a dechristianising Revolution. In the Gard, revolutionary conflicts, culminating in massacres of Protestants by Catholic-Royalist gangs in the 1815–16 'White Terror', re-volved around atavistic feuds going back to the Wars of Religion. Catholics viewed the Revolution as an anti-Christian conspiracy hatched by *philosophes*, Freemasons and Jews. Conversely, anti-clericalism was almost obligatory for liberal or radical heirs of the Enlightenment. Republican historian Michelet identified two 'actors' on the nineteenth-century stage – Christianity and Revolution. The anti-clericalism of the emerging labour movement, in-herited from the *sans-culottes*, grew more virulent when bishops' support for the 1851 Bonapartist coup confirmed the myth of the alliance of 'the sword and the holy-water sprinkler'. The ferocity of these hatreds eased after 1914. Catholics and anti-clericals rallied to the *patrie* during the Great War and socio-economic conflicts dominated inter-war politics. Yet into the 1960s religion remained the best single indicator of voting habits. A Catholic worker was less likely to vote Communist than an atheist businessman. In the 1970s film-comedy *Cousin, Cousine* old men sit on a bench outside a church during a family wedding. Asked by his little granddaughter why he is not inside the church, the grandfather replies 'What's the point? We live in a Republic'. During the bicentenary of the Revolution, 10,000 Vendée Catholics attended a commemoration Mass for the 'martyrs' of Jacobin 'genocide'. 'Of course (they) learn French history at school', one commented, 'but we parents have explained to our children that the teachers never explain that the Revolu-tion was, *above all else*, directed against Catholicism.' Vendéen Republican minorities had kept alive their culture with ceremonies at 'sacred sites' to their 'martyrs' massacred by Catholic *chouans*. Midi Protestant communi-ties assimilated victims of the White Terror into the tradition of martyrs going back to the Cévenol Huguenots of the 1690s *Guerre des Camisards* (Lewis 1978).

After 1816, intercommunal sectarian violence in the Gard – France's Ulster – did decline. In the West there was no Catholic insurrection to reverse the July Revolution, merely violent sermons and paramilitary drilling. The Con-cordat of 1801 was a pragmatic success. Despite predictable criticism from Catholic ultras, including the intransigent Vendéen *Petite Église*, and from anti-clericals, it calmed the worst of sectarian hostilities. It acknowledged Catholicism as the majority religion, while tolerating Protestant and Jewish minorities and providing state funding for their clergy. It insisted on free-dom of conscience and refused to recognise the 'crimes' of heresy, blasphemy and sacrilege, even though dossiers on Protestants in episcopal archives *still* classify them as '*hérétiques*'! Although Catholics criticised the Organic Articles appended to the Concordat for 'shackling' the clergy, a modus vivendi between Church and state was largely achieved, despite tensions in the 1830s, 1860s and after 1880. The *Police des Cultes* monitored clerical conduct, withholding salaries of priests whose behaviour was 'unacceptable'. The system functioned best with 'Gallican' bishops willing to cooperate with the Administration while resisting 'excessive' interference. Hence the rise of an 'ultramontane' episcopate created real problems. Conflicts over religion remained bitter, but were now largely conducted in rhetorical and symbolic ways. Catholics and anti-clericals 'fought', but for votes in the ballot box. Male suffrage after 1848 allowed Catholics to elect neo-Royalist deputies sympathetic to their culture. Perhaps, in time, this integrated them into the post-Revolution world. Catholics threw secularist textbooks on to bonfires – not teachers! Many 'battles' were *guerres des boutons*, gang-fights between pupils of adjacent Catholic and laic schools. Possibly this long-term decline in religious/sectarian violence reflected revulsion against public violence in the aftermath of the bloodletting of the 1790s and of 1815–16. Sixteenth-century 'Warriors of God' believed that violence was sacralised because one's opponents were 'enemies of God'. Now violence of all types was coming to be viewed as 'uncivilised', atavistic. Public branding was ended, slaughter-houses relocated on the margins of towns (Langlois 1998).

One cannot push this argument too far. The official Restoration policy of *oubli* urged Catholics not to seek violent revenge for the Revolution's 'martyred' victims. Yet revivalist missions portrayed regicides as Christ-killers, arguing that only the executioner could save post-Revolution society from anarchy. In the 1890s Catholics instigated riots against synagogues and Jewish businesses. Catholic antisemitism, playing on themes of the Jew as 'usurer' and Christ-killer, portrayed Jews as 'reptiles' or a 'plague' (Sorlin 1967). Religion still dominated the 'violence of the imagination'. Normandy peasant Pierre Rivière, who slaughtered his mother and siblings in the 1830s, explained his actions by evoking the Old Testament. Anti-clericals reacted violently to intrusion of religious symbols – Mission crosses of the 1820s or Marian statues of the 1870s – into 'their' urban space. Several Catholics were killed 'protecting' their processions and religious orders in the 1900s. The 'feminisation' of religion inflamed anti-clerical violence, as myths of priests as 'satyrs' preying upon irrational women aroused male sexual anxieties.

The legacy of the Revolution
Until 1789 the clergy were the 'first estate'. The Church owned 10 per cent of the land and collected tithes. Protestants and Jews could not hold public office or worship in public. Evangelising missions showed that counter-reformation zeal was not extinguished. The lower clergy were better educated than ever before. In regions such as the Southern Massif, the 'Catholic parish' remained the focus of communal identity, the *curé* the culture-broker. Though a decline in bequests for payments for services for souls of the dead marked a decline in 'baroque piety', this was symptomatic less of secularisation than of a shift towards enlightened piety, since more money was bequeathed to charity (Aston 2000). Yet Catholicism did face serious problems. A combination of 'clerical' arrogance, killjoy puritanism and intolerance of 'folk religion' made parish clergy unpopular in some regions. The Enlightenment, more anti-clerical in France than elsewhere, disseminated secular values – utility, reason, happiness, health. Recruitment to religious orders was falling. Religious practice was declining among young males, strata of the bourgeoisie and artisanate and in some regions. Many lower clergy resented

exclusion from decision making in the Church and aristocratic domination of promotions to the hierarchy (Gibson 1989).

Hopes of a modus vivendi between Revolution and Church were soon dashed. While lower clergy favoured reforms to improve their prospects within the Church, few welcomed the toleration of Jews and Protestants or the weakening of their hold on parishes. Many had misgivings about the Civil Constitution of the clergy to which they were required to swear an oath – in part because it was imposed unilaterally, without agreement from Rome. Proposed reforms went beyond those limited measures which many priests accepted as necessary. Dioceses were to be reduced from 137 to 80, to correspond with the new departments. Church lands were to be auctioned off, tithes abolished – making clergy dependent on state salaries. Parish clergy were to be elected and 'useless' contemplative orders abolished. The Civil Constitution proved the watershed of the Revolution, uncovering a seismic 'fault line' in French society. As many as 50 per cent of priests – 'jurors' – swore the oath. In the Paris basin, Centre and parts of Provence, where there were already signs of declining practice, 90 per cent were jurors. Conversely, a France of greater religious fervour emerged in the West, Flanders and the Southern Massif, where 90 per cent refused the oath.

Religion became the issue around which opposition now coalesced. Identification of Catholicism with emerging counter-revolution, in turn, nurtured ferocious anti-clericalism. By 1793, Republican authorities showed little sympathy even for constitutional clergy who rallied to the Revolution. Thousands succumbed to pressures to abjure the priesthood or to marry. Robespierre, denouncing atheism as 'counter-revolutionary', sought to establish a deistic 'Cult of the Supreme Being'. But some Jacobins favoured 'dechristianisation' and *sans-culottes* exhibited visceral contempt for the clergy. The Revolutionary calendar introduced a ten-day week, replacing Sunday with *décadi* as the day of rest. *Armées Révolutionnaires* sent out from the cities subjected villages to a crash course in ritual demystification, smashing saints' effigies, urinating in Communion vessels, melting down church bells and drinking the Communion wine. Non-jurors were forced into hiding; 2000 clergy fell victim to the Terror. By 1794, 25 per cent of parishes celebrated the Cult of Reason and only a few hundred held regular Catholic services. Alternative cults failed to take root, but habits of religious observance were weakened and the Year II left its mark both on popular, 'vulgar' anti-clericalism and on secularist 'free-thought' ideology and practice.

Anti-clericalism provoked a backlash. Three 'types' of counter-revolutionary regions can be identified. In Brittany tithes and seigneurial burdens had been relatively light. A locally recruited clergy tolerated Breton 'folk-religion', with its processions to 'holy rocks', 'healing saints' and 'Cult of the Dead'. In isolated villages with poor communications and little commercial agriculture in the Vendée or Southern Massif, the parish church remained the focus of sociability and the priest the local notable. Emancipation of Protestants provoked a violent Catholic backlash in the Gard, where the aristocracy incited the Catholic *petit peuple* against Protestant business elites who were consolidating local economic and political power. However, the religiosity of popular counter-revolution created dilemmas for the Catholic hierarchy.

With priests in hiding or exile, laymen assumed control of local worship, allowing a resurgence of elements of 'folk religion' which post-Tridentine clergy had sought to eliminate, and giving powers to the laity which counter-reformation clericalism had never tolerated. Those most active in sustaining worship were *women* – fanatical 'whores of the priests' according to the revolutionaries. The Church hierarchy was torn between praise for their fidelity and courage, and alarm at the dangers posed by abandonment of 'natural' feminine passivity and submissiveness (Tackett 1988; Lewis 1978; Hufton 1983; Aston 2000).

A Catholic revival? (1815–75c)

After the traumas of the 1790s, the years from 1810 to the 1870s were a period of religious reconstruction – even revival. An upsurge of popular religiosity had fuelled the culture of the counter-revolution. Although the Church found itself at odds with particular governments, in general it could rely on sympathy from most regimes until the Third Republic. Virulent anti-clericalism was given a free hand during revolutionary upheavals in 1830–31, 1848 and 1870–71. In more 'normal' times periods of prickly State–Church relations alternated with warm collaboration. Relationships between Bonapartism and the Church were never close. The regime signed the 1802 Concordat with the Papacy, abandoned the anti-clericalism of the 1790s, salaried the clergy, funded the upkeep of church buildings and acknowledged Catholicism as the religion of the majority of French citizens. Yet although a modus vivendi was achieved, many Bonapartist officials and supporters remained sceptics. The regime maintained the Revolutionary land settlement, guaranteed rights for Jews and Protestants, maintained divorce and imposed the 'Organic Articles' which restricted contacts between French clergy and Rome. The *Université*, established to control state education, was secular. Napoleonic armies in Italy contained militant anti-clericals. High-handed treatment of the Pope outraged mainstream Catholic opinion which, associating Gallicanism with clergy who had compromised with Revolution, was increasingly 'ultramontane' in tone.

Catholics welcomed the Restoration, if disappointed by the *Charte's* maintenance of religious pluralism. During his 'Hundred Days' Napoleon rallied popular support by evoking the spectre of the return to clericalism and the tithes. In 1815–16 the 'White Terror' swept the Midi. Royalist élites, exploiting the socio-economic and sectarian grievances of peasant and artisan co-religionists, encouraged Catholic gangs to murder or forcibly 'reconvert' hundreds of Protestants and purchasers of church lands. The Restoration was the classic alliance of throne and altar. It created thirty dioceses and raised clerical salaries. It appointed Mgr Freyssinous to head the *Université*, abolished divorce, sought to reimpose compulsory Sunday observance and encouraged revivalist missions which held public burnings of books by Voltaire. Charles X, crowned in medieval pomp in Rheims Cathedral, claimed powers, as God's anointed, to cure scrofula with the 'royal touch'! A largely symbolic Sacrilege Law of 1825 introduced the death penalty for blasphemy (Lyons 1996).

The Orleanist regime began with outbursts of popular and bourgeois anti-clericalism. The Paris archbishop's palace was ransacked, priests feared to walk the streets in *soutanes* and mission crosses were destroyed. The new regime was heir to the 'liberalism' of 1789. Guizot, its leading figure, was a Protestant Sorbonne history professor sacked in the 1820s. His co-religionists in the Gard reasserted the control over local politics which they had lost in the White Terror. Orleanist prefects kept aloof from episcopal palaces and banned church processions. There were clashes with Rome over episcopal appointments. Official support for the *Université* and imposition of limits on Catholic colleges fostered conflicts with Catholic pressure groups, which demanded that the regime conform to its 'liberal' pretensions by granting 'freedom of education'. Yet the regime's anti-clericalism was nuanced. Guizot admired Catholicism as 'the holiest school of respect the world has ever seen'. Social conservatism or Romanticism led sections of the bourgeoisie towards a reconciliation with Catholicism. Relationships between Paris and Rome, and between Orleanist officials and bishops, became more cordial. But Catholics shed few tears in 1848 when the regime fell.

Because not closely associated with the fallen regime, the clergy suffered less anti-clerical violence than in 1830. Catholicism soon emerged as a rallying point for conservatives alarmed by the red peril. While Louis Napoleon was no *dévot* – and was capable of flirting with anti-clericalism in some regions – his ministers viewed alliance with Catholicism as a strategic necessity. The 1850 Falloux Law offered educational concessions to Catholics. Bishops disciplined the minority of 'democratic' priests and celebrated the 1851 coup with *Te Deums* – to be rewarded with increased salaries and creation of new Western dioceses. In the 1850s Bonapartist officials supported the clergy in disputes with municipalities and with primary teachers. However, this remained a marriage of convenience. Many clergy retained pro-Bourbon sympathies. And Bonapartism was essentially a post-revolutionary regime, its bureaucrats former Orleanists. After 1859 the threat to Papal Temporal Power unleashed by French intervention in Italy soured Paris/Rome relations. The regime's response to sermons denouncing its foreign policy was to cut support for Catholic education, keep ultramontane extremists under surveillance and tolerate the anti-clericalism of a reviving liberal press. In the West, prefects sought to woo peasant voters away from the control of clergy and legitimist notables. After an upsurge of popular anti-clericalism in 1870–71, the years of 'Moral Order' (1872–77) were dominated by a Catholic triumphalism, memories of which fuelled subsequent Republican anti-clerical mythology. A Royalist-dominated parliament urged prefects to clamp down on anti-clerical municipalities, civil funerals and lay teachers. Funds were collected to construct the Sacré Coeur, designed to dominate the skyline of the 'Paris-Babylon' in expiation of the 'sins' of the Commune. Thousands of pilgrims travelled to Marian visitation sites such as Paray-le-Monial to demand a Christian monarchy (Jonas 2000; Harris 1999).

Hence Catholicism was functioning in a reasonably favourable national political climate, under generally sympathetic regimes. Outbursts of anti-clericalism were intense, but brief and quickly contained. The Restoration and 'Moral Order' governments were sympathetic to clerical aspirations.

Orleanism and Bonapartism, though 'blue' regimes suspicious of excessive clericalism, were socially conservative and keen to preserve a modus vivendi with the Church in the interests of social control.

Indices of a Catholic revival?

The reconstruction of the clergy
With the Concordat system providing adequate financial support, the Church reversed the long decline in recruitment and rebuilt a well-trained secular clergy. New parishes were created. An extensive building programme produced impressive neo-Gothic churches. Many drawn to revivalist Missions in the 1820s became regular communicants. Within the elites there was evidence of 're-christianisation' of repentant aristocrats, chastened by revolutionary traumas, and conversion of some Voltairean bourgeois. If popular religious practice was highly variable, dioceses where clergy had earlier lamented widespread indifference – Bordeaux, Montpellier and Périgeux – witnessed rising Mass attendance after 1830. The Church emerged from the Revolution with a manpower crisis. Priests in the Grenoble diocese declined by 30 per cent in the 1790s. An 1819 report labelled 99 of 268 Dordogne parish clergy old, incompetent or 'immoral'. Southern dioceses had filled vacant parishes with Spanish or Italian clergy lacking empathy with their parishioners. The first requirement was to rebuild structures of recruitment to the parish clergy. Between 1815 and 1830 *petits séminaires* (training colleges) rose from 53 to 144, annual vocations doubled to 2400. They fell to 1000 after 1840, but by then there were 30 per cent more parish clergy than in 1814. In 1821, 42 per cent of parish priests were 60 or older, by 1848 6 per cent. In response to villagers eager to enhance their commune's prestige with a resident priest, the number of parishes had been expanded. The diocese of Belley created 117 new parishes between 1815 and 1880 and its priest/ population ratio improved from 1:770 to 1:526 (Boutry 1986). In devout dioceses such as Rodez in the Southern Massif this ratio was 1:350. The national average of 1:657 in 1877 was 20 per cent better than in 1815. Only after the 1870s was the trend towards more vocations reversed, because of the hostile climate of the Republic and the growth of alternative white-collar career opportunities (Gibson 1989).

The Restoration revived earlier patterns of episcopal appointments, with 82 per cent of new bishops from aristocratic families. But 1830 proved a watershed. Barely 10 per cent of Orleanist or Bonapartist appointments were aristocratic. By 1870 only 6 per cent of bishops came from noble families, whereas 53 per cent were from lower-middle-class backgrounds and had risen through administrative or seminary teaching skills (Gadille 1967). No longer beneficiaries of wealth from church lands and tithes, they were more pious and dedicated than their predecessors. Nevertheless there were conflicts within the episcopate and between bishops and lower clergy. The Concordat allowed the state a consultative role in Rome's nominations to vacant sees. Governments after 1830 favoured Gallicans or 'liberal' Catholics willing to compromise with 'modernity'. But currents within Catholicism drew clergy and laity towards Roman rites and liturgy, 'ultramontane piety', rejection of compromise – and 'Papal Infallibility' (1870). Although France's greatest ultramontane, Lamennais, came to espouse 'advanced' democratic views, most ultramontanes were virulently hostile to modern 'heresies' – religious toleration, educational pluralism, liberal democracy. Ultramontane clergy were encouraged by Right-wing populist journalist Veuillot of *L'Univers* to disobey Gallican/liberal diocesan bishops. Their disciplinary powers were limited. *Desservants* could be moved from a parish at the bishop's whim, but *curés* were tenured. The balance within the episcopate shifted towards intransigent ultramontanes. At Montpellier Mgr de Cabrières, scion of the ultra-Royalist aristocracy, succeded cautious Gallican northerners who had hitherto controlled the diocese but had been out of sympathy with their lower clergy. By 1870 a rump of Gallicans remained to voice objections to Papal Infallibility. One, Mgr Darboy of Paris, was – conveniently for the Vatican – executed by the Communards (Cholvy 1973; Gough 1971).

The social origins of the lower clergy changed after 1789. The Church's reduced wealth made a clerical career financially less attractive. Recruits came increasingly from the peasantry or small-town petty bourgeoisie. Between 1812 and 1837, 52 per cent of recruits in La Rochelle diocese were urban, by 1877–1911 27 per cent. Cities like Bordeaux had low vocation rates. Some were pushed into the priesthood by parents who viewed it as a 'safe' career – avoiding conscription and manual labour and guaranteeing a pension. In the Lozère uplands the priesthood was 'the only industry of our countryside'. Salaries were modest, but higher than those of primary teachers. Some clergy continued to collect local variants of the tithe, dubbed *quêtes*. All derived income from the *casuel* – charges levied for services and rites of passage. These were more lucrative in regions of high practice. Observers agreed that clergy were generally well-disciplined, austere, chaste. Recruited from pious families in 'clerical' regions they avoided 'scandals' which had dogged their predecessors. Their besetting weakness, Lamennais claimed, was ignorance. Seminary training, through surveillance of mind and body, nurtured docility not intellectual curiosity; 95 per cent of Périgueux seminarists were classified as 'good' for 'application' and 'morality' – only 24 per cent for 'intellect' or 'talent'. Responses to Mgr Dupanloup's 1850 Orléans diocesan enquiry reveal banal errors of spelling, grammar and reasoning. In 1900 abbé Baudrain lamented that 'during the whole of the century just ended the French clergy has remained stranger to the progress of human knowledge'. Clergy were ill-equipped to cope with the jibes of local sceptics. Few played a serious role in debates over Darwinism or Biblical criticism. 'Intellectuals' in the hierarchy were masters of a theology which appeared quaint in a 'scientific age'. The legacy of seminary training was a fundamental mistrust of 'modernity' in all its guises (Gibson 1989; Marcilhacy 1964).

An early sign of secularisation had been declining recruitment to regular orders. Cloistered, contemplative ideals affronted Enlightenment concepts of 'utility'. Reversal of this trend after 1800 may signify a genuine religious revival. Since men could enter the parish clergy, the growth of male orders was modest. Jesuits, Capuchins, Benedictines and Dominicans were all re-established by 1841. These prestigious orders recruited from sons of army officers, landowners and professionals, although Assomptionists, founded to contest Protestant domination in the Gard, had some popular recruits. Fastest expansion was among largely unordained teaching *frères*, from modest social backgrounds. The personnel of the male orders grew by 66 per cent to 30,000 between 1850 and 1878. Expansion of female orders – from 12,300 in 1808 to 135,000 by 1875 – was spectacular. By the latter date seven Frenchwomen in every thousand were nuns (*réligieuses*) – in orders such as Carmelites or Ursulines – or *soeurs*. The majority of 'religious' females were either *congréganistes* – in teaching, nursing or industrial supervision – or *tertiaires*. These took no permanent vows but ran catechism classes and crèches and taught lace-making. Recruitment was strongest in Catholic bastions of the West and the Southern Massif. There were social distinctions in patterns of recruitment. Carmelites had to bring a dowry with them. 'Little sisters' were largely drawn from peasant or artisan families (Turin 1989; Mills 1991; Langlois 1984). Membership of religious orders offered women denied access to electoral politics and to careers forms of solidarity and sociability. In Brittany, where birth rates remained high, the orders provided employment for 'surplus' daughters of pious peasants. Intelligent, restless daughters of educated families joined the Ursulines who offered a 'career', a measure of independence, a chance to wield influence and do something 'useful', and an alternative to stultifying bourgeois marriage. In a culture where girls were taught to regard carnal pleasures – indeed the body itself – as sinful, and marital intercourse a distasteful duty, the 'sacrifice' of sexual relationships may not have appeared a loss. Since few orders were now cloistered, members could play active roles administering orphanages or training workshops or as warders in women's prisons. By the 1870s two-thirds were involved in education. Despite secularisation of some city hospitals, there were still 12,800 in nursing in 1912.

Winning back the 'repentant' elites?
Clergy blamed the Revolution on 'infection' of the elites by ideas of the *philosophes* which had, in turn, corrupted the lower classes. The 'excesses' of Restoration clericalism rekindled the anti-clericalism of the liberal bourgeoisie. Twelve editions of Voltaire's works were published between 1817 and 1824. Students rioted against compulsory Mass attendance and revivalist missions. Theatregoers flocked to Molière's *Tartuffe* to applaud its depiction of religious hypocrisy. Montalembert claimed that at college in 1826 he was the only believer among one hundred and twenty mocking *incrédules*. In Cahors in 1840 one male bourgeois was present at Easter Mass. In small towns the *chapeaux noirs* remained the rivals of the clergy in the struggle for local hegemony. In Erckmann-Chatrian's *Maître Gaspard Fix* the eponymous hero – a small-town brewer – belongs to a club whose library is stocked with copies of Voltaire and scorns his wife's Mass attendance. Orleanist *grand bourgeois* such as the Périers died refusing final sacraments (Gibson 1989; Kroen 2000). Elderly aristocrats often assumed a façade of conformity only because 1789 had impressed on them the dangers of irreligion. Anti-clerical pamphleteer P.-L. Courier sneered that 'these friends of the altar scarcely go near

it themselves'. The nobleman torn between awareness of the importance of Catholicism to his class interests and personal indifference was evoked by H. Gazeau in the person of an Anjou landowner who 'never misses Mass – and it's not his fault if he falls asleep during the sermon. "God's Truth", he tells his servants, "we mustn't blaspheme, tomorrow we're doing our bloody Easter Communion". . . . He harbours solid resentments against the "blues" of the canton, who provide him with names for his hounds which – without the slightest evil thought – he's housed in an old chapel. *For his time* he is a good Christian'. But younger aristocrats, often Jesuit-educated, exhibited genuine piety. *Châtelains* sought to 'set an example' to their sharecroppers. Comte de Diesbach, Legitimist founder of the *Société d'Agriculture de France*, displayed an ostentatious piety and carried a banner at the Marian apparition site at Paray-le-Monial. There was a vein of quasi-millenarian visionary religiosity among ultra-Royalist aristocrats. They were obsessed with 'rumours of God' – heavenly apparitions which came to simple peasants to relay messages that the Revolution signified God's anger at the impieties of French society. Aristocrats patronised such 'visionaries', circulating prophecies that the 'true' King's return would be prefaced by conversion of the Jews and herald the Second Coming! (Gibson 1989; Guillet 1994). Aristocratic piety did not necessarily mean harmonious relations between Legitimist landowners and parish clergy – whom they often treated as social inferiors, fit to eat with the servants. Though they were 'allies' against the forces of secularisation, their alliance could eventually crumble as the clergy asserted some independence (Ford 1993). Yet priests were quite aware that, deprived of tithes and income from church lands, they relied on donations from Royalist notables to fund church buildings or charities.

Some bourgeois returned to the Church in search of 'gendarmes in cassocks'. Alarm at worker unrest prompted a religious revival among anxious bourgeois in the Nord after 1830; 1848 turned a trickle of such 'converts' into a flood. After a century of scepticism, Proudhon noted sardonically, the middle class now prayed for a religious revival! The once anti-clerical *Journal de Rouen* discovered that 'without religion family ties are broken, property lies defenceless, moral order lacks any basis'. Ozanam observed that 'today there is not a single Voltairean with an income of a few thousand per year who does not want to send everybody to Mass'. Not all bourgeois were such *chrétiens de la peur*. Solid, provincial Catholic cultures already existed. In Lyon descendants of ancien régime *robe* families and business dynasties shared a sober, individualistic 'Tridentine' Catholicism. Romanticism encouraged sensitivity to religious sentiments. Until the 1830s Parisian bourgeois made little provision in wills for religious bequests. Then Dominican preacher Lacordaire made 'going to the sermon' fashionable. In 1842 Hugo reported that 'the Good Lord is in vogue . . . amongst us. Young men run from church to church, admire the preachers, eat no meat on Fridays, go to confession and take communion'. Students joined the paternalistic St Vincent de Paul society. In Brest, 5 per cent of naval students attended Easter Communion in 1843, 19 per cent in 1846. Expansion of Catholic colleges after 1850 accelerated such trends (Gibson 1989; Cholvy and Hilaire 1985–86).

The clergy, popular piety and 'folk religion'

> There is something dreadful in the thought that superstition is the only religion
> open to the peasant, that *all* worship is reducible to practices that he doesn't under-
> stand, that 'God' is for him no more than an idol who protects the . . . crops of
> those who offer him a candle. Coming here this morning, I met a procession stopped
> by a spring to end the drought. I asked why they prayed there and not elsewhere. A
> woman replied by showing me a little plaster statue in a niche. 'It's because *that*
> Good Lady's the best for rain.'
>
> (George Sand; see Cholvy and Hilaire 1985–86)

Catholicism always existed in a symbiotic relationship with pre-Christian
folk-beliefs and practices. Evangelisation gave these a Christian veneer. The
outcome was a pagano-Christian syncretism verging on polytheism. Post-
Tridentine clergy aspired to an austere religion purged of 'superstitious' rituals. Educated priests felt uneasy at processions to 'holy' rocks or springs, once
focal points of Druidic worship, at mid-summer fertility rites such as St. Jean
bonfires, or when obliged to ring bells to ward off thunderstorms. Parishes
without a priest during the Revolution had been left to their own devices,
and folk religion received a new lease of life. In St. Chinian (Herault), an
anti-clerical commune where priests were killed in 1793, priestless processions to pray for rain were conducted. The first instinct of the post-Concordat
clergy was to return to Tridentine orthodoxies. The bishop of Arras instructed
clergy to reduce involvement in livestock-blessing rituals which caused contempt for religion and 'gave ammunition to the *philosophes*'. One compromise was to urge participants in such rituals to take Communion, another to
purge the more 'dubious' local practices and tolerate, *without encouraging*,
the remainder. Local saints' *fêtes* were changed to fit the liturgical calendar,
but villagers celebrated both new and old dates! Clergy emphasised their
control by transferring healing-saints' effigies to niches inside parish churches.
They lamented that popular religion involved little personal piety, but consisted of attempts to manipulate the physical world. They 'only pray . . . when
they are ill, when they believe themselves . . . under a spell, when cattle are
sick. They call on God for worldly goods, never for spiritual blessings . . .',
lamented one cleric.

However, clergy were less disapproving of folk religion than their predecessors. Drawn from humbler social strata they were closer in culture to their
parishioners. Less well-educated they were less inclined to compromise with
Enlightenment rationalism. Veuillot, their favourite journalist, trumpeted
his humble origins and delighted in shocking 'scientific' anti-clericals and
fastidious 'liberal Catholic' intellectuals by exulting in the 'absurdities' of
miracles and 'superstitions' which formed the bedrock of popular piety. Aware
that popular religiosity had sustained the Church in the dark days after 1789,
clergy were reluctant to criticise 'unorthodox' beliefs and practices. Renan
claimed that the Breton clergy preserved a delicate balance, avoiding open
endorsement of folk beliefs yet refraining from challenging them. They calculated that it was safer for peasants to retain such stepping-stones to orthodox piety than to risk sliding down the slope to unbelief. Clergy decided that

earlier campaigns against local saints had proved a strategic error. Religion was more resilient for being rooted in the seasonal routines of village life. There was no agreed official strategy. Diocesan authorities and individual priests struck their own balance between participation, turning a blind eye and disapproval. Where a *curé* disowned local rituals, his successor might revive clerical participation. Usually a modus vivendi was achieved. Clergy led processions to secure rainfall, protect crops or bless livestock at St. Eloi's feast. Some tied garters to bell-ropes to secure marital fertility, or tolerated the cult of St. Grélichon, which involved women rubbing themselves against the private parts of the saint's statue for the same purpose! They allowed veneration of St. Roch – protector against cholera and rabies. Parishes possessed relics of local saints. The *curé* d'Ars assiduously collected 500 relics – before *becoming* one, as the faithful collected and venerated strands of his hair! The rise of the cult of St. Philomena, a virgin martyred resisting the sexual advances of Roman legionaries, led to relics of 400 saints from Roman catacombs finding their way to France, some acquired at auctions in job-lots by Périgueux clergy! Mgr Pie of Poitiers championed the cult of the Sacré Prépuce (Holy Foreskin) – the part of Christ's anatomy not to have risen to Heaven (Weber 1988; Marcilhacy 1964; Gibson 1989; Cholvy 1973).

The goal after 1850 was to wean parishioners from battered effigies of local saints on to a standardised 'ultramontane piety', concentrated on the Marian cult. Transition from local Marian statues to the Virgin of Lourdes was unsettling. After one sermon a woman was heard to mutter, 'did you hear that imbecile claiming that it was *the same "Our Lady" everywhere*?'. Chartres clergy had elided belief in Marcou, the 'seventh son' with magical powers, with the cult of 'Saint Marcou'. Now they replaced the latter's *fête* with that of the Virgin. In such ways, Gibson (1989) wryly observed, were peasants being transformed into Frenchmen! In a culture with little medical or welfare provision, apparently 'credulous' behaviour gave psychological reassurance to many who felt it wiser to deal with 'supernatural' forces than to ignore them. The dead were buried with sweets, to pay the Styx boatman to transport them to the next world. Those involved in processions to healing saints might tell the priest that they 'hadn't come here for *your* good God but for the saint'. Even sceptical peasants argued that if such processions did little good, then they did no harm. Such saints were a focus of local identity, and were insurance agents, security guards, marriage-guidance counsellors. Yet a saint who failed to 'deliver' rainfall or protect crops might find his effigy smashed! When Renan was taken to visit a healing saint in his Breton village, the blacksmith threatened the effigy with a hot poker. 'If you don't lift this child's fever, I'll shoe you like a horse . . . !'. It was reassuring to believe in witchcraft or spells, for these explained misfortunes which might be reversed if one consulted a *leveur des sorts* to lift a curse. Priest and sorcerer were 'in the same trade' – arousing similar fears and hopes and fulfilling similar functions. Sorcerers blended 'magic' with Catholic symbols and rituals – candles, *Aves* and bones from cemeteries. Victims of a 'spell' were advised to wear an amulet containing a religious text, even to swallow it. Bread – 'the body of Christ' – had magic powers if treated with due respect and not turned upside down (Devlin 1987; Weber 1988).

The 'feminisation' of Catholicism?

We require a *vicaire*: our young women have need of one.

(Mayor of Viriey, Bellay diocese)

It is the honour of women everywhere to seek a haven for their weakness and shame close to the altar.

(Mgr Dupanloup)

A significant development was the 'feminisation' of practice, piety and recruitment. The 'gender gap' widened after the Revolution and only narrowed after 1914. It explains the reluctance of (male) Republicans to enfranchise women until emancipated from subordination to priests. Would not women voters return France to the clerical-Royalist yoke from which Republicans were fighting to liberate her? Feminists dismiss such reasoning as a fig-leaf to disguise misogyny. Did not Republicans enfranchise 'backward' male peasants in 1848, ensuring their own electoral defeats? Were not male intellectuals seduced by the Catholic-Romantic mood of the 1830s or anti-positivist Catholic irrationalism in the 1890s? Was not male church attendance in Brittany higher than female practice in central France? Was it not Republican support for domesticity which denied women access to political experience and career opportunities? Did not anti-clerical *pères de famille* treasure the piety of wives and daughters as a guarantee of fidelity and chastity? In short was not female religiosity less the inevitable outcome of women's 'irrationality' – as Enlightenment discourse argued – than a product of Republicans' own misogyny and patriarchalism? Since women were denied the vote and largely excluded from cafés and *cercles*, what tolerated outlet for female sociability existed outside the Church?

Yet the scale of the feminisation of Catholicism remains striking. The reconstruction of the Church was dependent on an enormous expansion of female orders. In 1808 there were 14,000 *religieuses*, by 1878 127,000. In 1830 women constituted 41 per cent of church personnel, in 1880 60 per cent. Nationally compiled statistics may underestimate this trend, since they omit groups like the *béates* of Haute-Loire who did not take full vows. In Brittanny, where female celibacy was high due to male migration to Paris, a 'job' as a nun was an opportunity for dowry-less peasant daughters. For bourgeois girls with some education it offered the prospect of a 'career' of responsible and challenging administrative work in education, charity, nursing or pilgrimage organisation.

The gender gap in religious practice widened, particularly in dioceses where overall levels of practice were mediocre. This pattern was discernible earlier in many regions. Mgr Dupanloup's enquiry into practice in Orleans diocese in 1850 revealed 60 per cent girls and 20 per cent adult women attending Easter Mass, but only 3.8 per cent adult men (Marcilhacy 1964). There were often acute tensions between priests and male parishioners. Clergy lamented men's taste for politics and cafés, deplored their obsession with *respect humain* – their conviction that men forfeited independence, virility, self-respect and the respect of others if they were subordinate to a priest. Men resented

Adults taking Easter Communion (c. 1900)

Diocese	Men	Women
Nantes	91%	97.4%
Nancy	23%	55%
Nevers	6.9%	30.5%
Bourges	4.3%	24.8%
Sens	2.2%	11.0%

confessors' controls over 'their' womenfolk and were alienated from confession because *coitus interruptus, the* method of birth-control, was blamed
on them. Wives who 'submitted' – through 'conjugal duty' – to husbands'
sexual practices were exonerated from responsibility. Young men ran penitent
groups whose boisterous behaviour during *fêtes* incurred clerical disapproval.
As such male associations declined, women and girls were recruited into
Enfants de Marie societies. It is difficult to know whether the Marian Cult was
cause or consequence of the feminisation of Catholicism. The capacity of
the figure of Mary – 'Mary always, Mary everywhere' – to symbolise Virgin,
Wife *and* Mother, was crucial to the new Catholic ideology. Hitherto the
Church had presented itself as a 'gendered' hierarchy. The supremacy of a
male pope and bishops reinforced the monarchical order and the patriarchal
family. Since Eve was the original sinner, women required firm control. But
the Revolution modified Catholic perceptions. Seduced by Enlightenment
scepticism, revolutionary chimeras and hedonism 'fathers and sons now fight
under the banner of indifference and sensuality', claimed abbé Gaume.
Women were the potential saviours. They had sheltered priests from godless
Jacobins. Although men made laws, mercifully women forged morals. The
femme forte, capable of rescuing France from materialism and atheism, came
in two versions. One was the non-cloistered nun educating future generations.
The second was the wife and mother – 'the priest of the home' – ensuring
the faith and morality of her offspring and devoting her spare energies to
Catholic charities, a tolerated form of 'public' activity. No longer was marriage
and motherhood a 'fallen' state, inferior to celibacy. Mgr Bouvier of Le Mans
warned against alienating women by 'rash rigour'. 'The question is of immense
importance. The rising generation is in the hands of woman; the future
belongs to her. If woman eludes our grasp . . . with her everything could
disappear.' 'Chaste Motherhood' *à la* Virgin Mary became a path to virtue to
which all wives could aspire (Mills 1991).

Mariolatry had once been suspect in the Church. But the nineteenth century became the 'century of Mary'. Pius IX's enunciation of the doctrine of
the Immaculate Conception (1854) threw down a gauntlet to the modern
world; 40 per cent of new congregations were dedicated to Mary, and 48 per
cent of paintings exhibited at the Paris Salon from 1828 to 1850 portrayed
Mary, female saints or feminised angels. Previous Marian visitations had been
witnessed by adult males, but as her visits to France became more frequent
both visionaries and the messages received changed. Having appeared in the

Vendée to support the counter-revolution, she was seen in Périgord in 1816 by peasant children whose parents duly died for ignoring her warning to cease Sunday work! Thereafter her most celebrated appearances were to a novice nun – later beatified – in Rue du Bac in Paris (1830), to peasant children at La Salette in the Alps (1846), at Lourdes (1858) and at Pontmain during the Franco-Prussian war. Catholic-Royalists were delighted by her messages, urging repentance of revolutionary apostasies, and by evidence that despite appearances at Knock in Ireland, Marpingen in South-West Germany and elsewhere, France was her favoured destination! She chose 'marginal' communities in peripheral regions – poor villages whose menfolk migrated in search of work and whose inhabitants were envious of adjacent villages with flourishing markets or prestigious shrines. An accredited Marian miracle could, as cynical journalists and shrewd locals were aware, boost local economies by offering opportunities to provide café and hotel facilities and religious souvenir shops for pilgrims.

The Virgin arrived in troubled times. Her apparitions were symptomatic of a broad eschatological current in a Europe aware of God's anger at the modern world. Divine apparitions and prophecies were central to Restoration politics. Peasant Thomas Martin was idolised in ultra-Royalist salons after visions in which warnings of disasters about to befall an unrepentant France were tempered by tantalising promises that 'Louis XVII' was poised to return to undo the Revolution's crimes. As Romanticism drew elite culture and popular culture closer, such rumours were disseminated via Almanachs and evangelical missions. Shining crosses in the sky suggested that God might forgive France for its crimes. Marian apparitions belong in the context of such *rumeurs de Dieu*. At La Salette the weeping Virgin prophesised that crop failures would continue until the Bourbons and Sunday observance were restored. The typical visionary was a young peasant from a mountain village and female. Bernadette Soubirous of Lourdes was one of six children of a bankrupt miller, an asthmatic mistreated by her foster-mother. For her the Virgin was surrogate mother, vision of beauty in a harsh world and fairy-godmother. Fantasies of revenge against abusive step-parents figure in many fairytales. Visionaries became the focus of attention, acquiring power to 'turn the world upside-down' by contradicting or insulting mayors or notables. One Pontmain visionary informed a noblewoman that 'next to the Virgin, *you* are ugly'. Such populism suited the ultramontane Right more than cultured Gallican liberal Catholics seeking compromise with 'modernity'. Veuillot exulted in Marian miracles precisely because poor women, scorned as 'superstitious' by urban intellectuals, were shown to be favoured by God. Lacking education, they were uncorrupted by Enlightenment scepticism. Just as Joan of Arc was a peasant selected to be France's saviour, so now God was ignoring sinful cities with their sophisticated sceptics and godless proletarians, such as Ain textile workers who in 1871 jeered at faithful women waiting on a hillside for a Marian apparition! (Boutry 1986; Blackbourn 1993; Kselman 1983). 'Miracle cures' at Marian sites challenged doctors who promoted 'scientific' medicine as key to a world freed from the scourge of disease. Pilgrims flouted Pasteurian warnings by drinking and bathing in Lourdes water. Even

Zola expressed grudging admiration for nuns who tended sick pilgrims and accepted that the world's suffering was not amenable to scientific cure and that suffering should be embraced. La Salette visionary Melanie proclaimed her 'love of suffering'. Young nun Thérèse of Lisieux was beatified for describing ways in which the terminal stages of TB brought her closer to God (Harris 1999).

Before Lourdes became a site of 'authenticated' miracles it needed official recognition. Grenoble's diocesan authorities were initially sceptical about the La Salette 'apparition'. However, although concerns about local cults and shrines persisted, clergy now accepted that it made strategic sense to recognise within folk beliefs a kernel of healthy spirituality which might be channelled into large-scale national Marian pilgrimages under clerical supervision. Missionary orders were keen that 'miracles' at Marian sites should be associated with the official Church. New, uniform statues of the Madonna, produced at St. Sulpice, gradually ousted battered, idiosyncratic, weather-beaten *madonnes du terroir*. Of participants in mass pilgrimages which developed after 1870, 90 per cent were women, mostly from the popular classes. The West and Nord supplied many Lourdes pilgrims – the adjacent Midi few. Pilgrimages provided a 'female space'. Women whose lives were dominated by domestic burdens and restrictions enjoyed the trip of a lifetime, companionship, the thrill of participating in Eucharistic processions and witnessing 'miracles'. The success of Lourdes, which attracted half-a-million pilgrims annually by 1900, relied on that modernity which the Catholic Right deplored. Pilgrimages were sponsored by the Assomptionists' mass-circulation paper *La Croix* – and the railway made the Pyrenees accessible to thousands of long-distance pilgrims. The Marian Cult phenomenon was less the remnant of a traditional, rustic past than the construction of a new national, and international, community of the Catholic faithful (Gibson 1989; Harris 1999; Kselman 1983). State authorities – Orleanist, Bonapartist or Republican – reacted with the mixture of distaste, derision and anxiety exhibited by Bismarckean bureaucrats towards the Marpingen Marian cult in newly annexed Catholic south Germany. Public displays of peasant 'credulity' and female 'hysteria' appeared atavistic in an age of science and undercurrents of populist protest discernible in the Virgin's utterances were worrying. In Bonapartist France, as in Bismarckean Germany, secularist liberals – critics of authoritarian regimes – found themselves supporting policing measures to control outbursts of popular religiosity (Blackbourn 1993).

Was Marian piety part of that transition from a religion of fear to a religion of love which some have discerned in mid-century Catholicism? In Zola's *La Faute de l'Abbé Mouret* the older priest incarnates 'Tridentine' severity, threatening villagers with God's wrath and eternal damnation. Young Mouret is gentle, devoted to the Virgin. Typically Zola has him collapse with nervous exhaustion because of erotic fantasies about Mary's statue, then sleep with the niece of a freethinking woodman who nurses him back to health! The Marian phenomenon raised issues of female 'space' and 'agency'. In a society otherwise dominated by male urban elites, female visionaries attracted attention. The pilgrimage industry provided opportunities for Catholic ladies to carve out a role. They staffed *Notre Dame du Salut* which raised funds for pilgrimages, in which they participated, albeit travelling first-class on the train! They perceived no contradiction between the Catholic Right's domesticity ideology and their active 'public' role as organisers. Anti-clericals' disapproval would have been even stronger if they had secured access to the correspondence between Catholic *grandes dames* and charismatic priests such as Père Picard, since the barely disguised erotic charge in the relationships would have confirmed their worst suspicions about the clergy's seductive appeal! Republicans denounced commercial exploitation of pilgrimage sites which allowed Bernadette's siblings to prosper from the sale of effigies and holy water. But their obsession was with sinister clerical plotters whose orchestration of pilgrimages constituted blatant political manipulation of female 'credulity'. *La Croix* spearheaded the antisemitic campaign which threatened the Republic during the Dreyfus crisis. Marian pilgrimages reached their apogee during the Catholic crusade against laic education laws and the conflicts which followed Separation of Church and State in 1905 (Harris 1999).

Happenings in Morzine, in the Savoyard uplands annexed to France in 1860, illustrate female religiosity of a different type. An epidemic of 'possession' saw women blaspheme, demand 'luxuries' such as chocolate, make sexually suggestive remarks and ridicule priests who failed to exorcise their 'demons'. Finally the government sent an 'alienist', Dr Constans, accompanied by troops. The crisis was contained by interning women in hospital, detailing troops to help with harvest work and increasing subsidies for schools and roads. Historians once concentrated on the psychiatrist's control strategy and the encounter between the 'coercive', modernising state and the women's 'atavistic' behaviour. Harris insists that only by comprehending the women's worldview can one discern how they used their culture, including pre-Christian folk beliefs, to express anxieties and discontents. Their community was being disrupted by the absence of migrant menfolk and cultural contacts with the urban world. They resented burdens imposed on them by the men's absence. Yet dreams of return to a 'whole', self-contained community mingled with yearnings for exotic luxuries of the city and a sense of guilt for such desires. Their possession stemmed from internalising unresolved conflicts. It was a region the proximity of which to Calvinist Geneva had inspired counter-reformation missionary activity, and religious practice remained high. The catalyst for the possessions was a sermon about Satan and Hellfire. Soon women were 'speaking' – in French not patois – and demanding chocolates and *eau de vie*! 'Devils' urged them to make animal noises, insult priests, play cards. Refusing to sleep with their husbands they insisted that devils were their masters. They were constructing, from fragments of folk culture, a 'demon world' where they could act in a transgressive way against constraints of gender and class codes while denying responsibility for their actions. Constans, the incarnation of positivistic knowledge/power, viewed such fantasies of 'hysterical' women as typical of a peripheral region with a history of witchcraft where heredity and milieu created conditions mercifully absent from modern cities. Labelling this behaviour 'irrational' is unhelpful. Faced with inexorable socio-cultural changes the women experienced unresolved tensions. They aspired to some fruits of 'modernity', yet felt guilty for so doing. Their *mal* was a symptom of otherwise unarticulated, partly gender-specific, peasant distress (Harris 1997).

The forces of opposition

Anti-clericals and *libres-penseurs*

Catholics and their Republican rivals perhaps shared more values, assumptions and 'real' interests than either cared to admit. Ferry defined the values of the Republican school as 'the good old values of our fathers'. Catholics and Republicans alike espoused an ideology of domesticity. There was a de facto consensus before 1914 on colonialist, protectionist and social-Imperialist strategies to contain the working class. Yet Republicans sometimes inflated the menace of clericalism to frighten popular electors into voting for 'progressive' bourgeois candidates. Republican notables who evoked the spectre of the return of tithes included usurers to whom peasants were in debt! In 1904 the anarchist *Assiette au Beurre* featured a cartoon in which a child was offered choices between crucifix and tricoleur, Sacré Coeur and Eiffel Tower, Virgin Mary and Marianne. Either set of choices, it was implied, led workers to the capitalist factory and to the barracks.

Yet although one might claim that such squabbles were largely irrelevant to workers, they were more than mere shadow-boxing. Many bourgeois did believe that clericalism was the enemy, religion the obstacle to progress. In the Arras diocese lawyers, *fonctionnaires* and heirs of *biens nationaux* purchasers were often anti-clerical. Some industrialists came to view Catholicism as an outmoded, ineffectual tool of social control, and clerical education as unsuitable for France's economic requirements. Positivist medical students found bishops' influence within the *Université* intolerable. Petty notables of rural *bourgs* were the priest's natural rivals. As Gibson (1991) observed, there were 'progressive' bourgeois who simply 'couldn't stand' Catholics or Catholicism (Gibson 1991; Hilaire 1977). Had clergy been liberal Gallicans, then a modus vivendi might have evolved. But the tone of contemporary Catholicism was set by ultramontane piety, Marian miracles and Papal Infallibility (1870). Clerical influence within higher education stifled debates over Darwinism or German biblical criticism. The Syllabus of Errors (1864) placed the Church in defiant opposition to 'liberal' intellectual and political currents. Republicans, and many Bonapartists, who believed in mankind's potential to harness reason to achieve 'progress' viewed the Syllabus as a calculated insult to the modern world. Catholicism, claimed the *Journal de Rouen*, appeared 'an insult to the progress of science and an outrage to human reason'. It undermined efforts of the 'liberal' Mgr Dupanloup to revive the clergy's influence and credibility in his Orleans diocese. The 'clericalism' denounced by Republicans was the product of a specific style of Catholicism. This raised funds to construct the Sacré Coeur to dominate the Paris skyline in expiation of the sins of 'Paris/Babylon' – capital of materialism, secularism and socialism. Liberal Catholic Montalembert deplored *L'Univers*'s influence. Its editor was 'the most redoubtable enemy of religion' – his provocative extremism supplying ammunition to the Church's enemies. Veuillot retorted that *his* brand of intransigence expressed ordinary Catholics' gut-feelings more accurately than did liberal-Catholics' decorous nuances. Veuillot enjoyed baiting intellectuals, ridiculing their 'rationalism', championing 'credulous' peasants' faith in miracles. When in power liberals tolerated him – that was *their* principle. Given the chance he would persecute them – because that was *his*!

This was a *Kulturkampf* – a war of rival worldviews. Many who repudiated Christianity needed alternative beliefs, rituals and secular saints to provide a purpose to life. The eponymous hero of Zola's *Doctor Pascal* proclaimed a defiant credo. 'Humanity's future lies in the progress of Reason . . . The pursuit of Truth through Science is the "divine" concept that mankind ought to propose for itself.' Saint-Beuve, denouncing clerical interference in education, invoked that 'greater diocese that exists throughout the world, . . . made up of spirits emancipated from blind submission – a great intellectual province (with) neither pastors nor bishops'. The resulting ethic, derived from an eclectic blend of Kant and liberal Protestantism, was stern and austere. E. Salvat's message was uncompromising: 'We say to the Church, to the monster that has devoured so many generations, "your time has passed!" The struggles and the blood of our fathers have delivered us from your yoke. Get back sinister phantom! Now you scare only children and imbeciles.' Freethinkers 'failed' in their goal of replacing supplanting with secularism. Catholicism remained the 'most acceptable form of religious indifference' (Anatole France). Yet they were rarely the fanatical 'priest-eaters' depicted by Catholics. They helped to weaken deference to organised religion and championed egalitarian and secularist values.

The first *libre-pensée* societies emerged in 1848 to organise secular funerals. Their apogee came after 1900, when the number of groups doubled to over a thousand. Bastions included Isère, the Rhône valley, the Languedoc coastal plain, Burgundy, Seine-et-Marne, Haute-Vienne and Charente-Inferieure. In the Yonne, free-thought societies flourished in Auxerre and Sens, former Jansenist strongholds. Its implantation in the south-east correlates with support for the Cult of Reason in the 1790s. Its rank-and-file were small-town petty bourgeois, students and skilled workers. Republican and socialist freethinkers shared a common pool of ideas. Christianity was antisocial because it encouraged selfish preoccupations with personal salvation. 'Science' promised liberation from disease and poverty and underpinned a moral code built around reciprocal obligations. *Libre-penseurs* had 'Liberty, Equality, Fraternity' inscribed on their tombstones or gave offspring 'revolutionary' names such as Maximilien, though some criticised Robespierre's refusal to espouse atheism. They kept alive anti-clerical insults of the 1790s against '*la prêtraille*', and used the Revolutionary calendar because 'free men emancipated from the yoke of superstition cannot continue to measure time according to the incarnation of Christ'. Day-to-day *libre-pensée* activity consisted of minor insults to Catholic susceptibilities, eating sausages at Good Friday banquets, mocking Christian dogmas to 'kill Christianity with laughter', campaigning to 'de-baptise' street names and ban Catholic processions. Some received a religious burial to avoid a 'sectarian' insult to family and community traditions. For others the secular funeral became the touchstone of their cultural identity and commitment. Haunted by fears that in a moment of weakness they might summon a priest to their deathbed, or that pious relatives would insist a religious funeral, many signed declarations that 'I, the undersigned, forbid any priest from entering my home when I am sick, *even if I request it*, because any such request could only be the result of delirium'. Prefects sometimes insisted that secular funerals be held before dawn, and suspended teachers for attending them. An 1887 Law recognising the right to choose one's funeral was a symbolic victory. Substitute rituals, designed to assuage any sense of emptiness or futility, were constructed to permit a 'good death'. Affirmations that in a godless Universe a life derived meaning from its contribution towards a future just society buttressed stoic acceptance of death without sacraments or hope of an afterlife. Funeral orations proclaimed that an exemplary, priest-less death bore witness to courageous conviction. Red flags or tricoleurs were draped on the coffin, to the strains of the *Internationale* or *Marseilleise*. Such funerals were the touchstone of civic virtue. A socialist was reprimanded for criticising Gambetta and Ferry for 'betraying' the workers. 'These men founded the Republic . . . and socialists cannot doubt their Republicanism *because they had secularist funerals*.' Special rituals commemorated secular deaths. The Society for Mutual Autopsy (SMA) preserved organs for scientific analysis, including the brain, the size and structure of which was viewed by materialists as linked to intelligence. Gambetta's sadly small brain was displayed at the 1889 Paris *Exposition*! SMA members – medical students, anthropologists and Left-wing activists – compiled autobiographies 'locating' their life within a progressive historical narrative. One insisted that 'the perspective of unlimited progress . . . is a modern faith – (replacing) the mirage of a lost paradise. It sustains and consoles us in our public and private trials . . . We regard ourselves as labouring in an always uncompleted task . . . to which all can lend a hand. The cruelty and injustice of the present (are) mere accidents on the voyage of Humanity toward a better life'.

Libres-penseurs confronted Catholic hegemony head-on in the sensitive area of rituals of death. Secularist rituals remained fairly rare outside laic bastions – working-class Paris and Limoges, a few mining towns and Yonne or Lower Languedoc *bourgs*. But minor victories were won. Accusations of nuns pressurising patients to receive the last sacraments allowed the Paris municipality to secularise the city's hospitals. And 1880s legislation proclaimed the 'neutrality' of cemetaries. Yet the real beneficiaries of changing funeral cultures were not austere freethinkers but commercial funeral companies offering elaborate coffins and tombs to bourgeois consumers (Lalouette 1997; Hecht 1997; Kselman 1993). Not all faced death with the stoicism of committed *libres-penseurs*. Spiritualism attracted those craving contact with deceased loved ones. Seances and 'table-turning' became fashionable, despite denunciations from Catholics *and* scientists. The 'Romantic generation' was often sceptical of religious orthodoxy, disillusioned by the failure of 1848 yet unable to contemplate a universe where death had absolute finality. Victor Hugo, seeking contact with his dead daughter, was one of several Republican luminaries convinced by guru A. Kardec that spiritualism was a 'science' where contact with the dead could be monitored by positivistic techniques!

Anti-clericals and Catholics battled for control of women. Republicans resented clergy prying into their families. The Church blamed men for *coitus interruptus* – the standard method of birth-control. One bishop observed in 1842 that 'young husbands feel offended when the confessor questions the manner in which they use their matrimonial rights. They respond by abandoning the sacraments'. Priests who eroded male authority by worming their way into the confidence of wives and daughters obsessed successive generations of Republicans. In *La Conquête de Plassans*, Zola attributed the collapse of Republicanism in a Provençal town to infiltration of homes of Voltairean bourgeois by a feline young priest who extracts intimate secrets from their wives! Behind political concerns lay sexual anxieties. Men were alarmed by confessors' access to marital secrets. Michelet, denied access to his dying mistress by her confessor's influence, was made paranoid by thoughts of priests' privileged knowledge of details of sexual intimacy. 'How humiliating to meet in the street someone who knows your private marital weaknesses *better than you do*, who salutes you humbly, turns away – and *laughs!*' Many shared his concerns. Priests were portrayed as bisexual, using their 'softness' to win women's confidence. Genin talked of the confessor 'sliding into bed between wife and husband'. How could weak, sensual women resist whispered intimacies of a priest taking confession in an empty church? (Zeldin 1970).

The Jesuit incarnated the seductive priest. The 'myth' of a Jesuit plot was a mirror-image of conspiracy theories underpinning the Manichean worldview of the Catholic Right. The 1884 encyclical *Humanum Genus* denounced Freemasons as agents of Satan. Catholic newspapers serialised the fantasies of hoaxer Leo Taxil about a global Judeo-Masonic conspiracy centred on caves under the Rock of Gibraltar! Mgr Fava of Grenoble urged boycotts of Jewish shops. Freemasonry's 'blasphemous rituals' allegedly parodied those of the Church and its spirit permeated Republican politics and laic education. Republicans' portrayals of the 'Jesuit peril' were very similar. Anti-clericals sometimes distinguished relatively benign, homely parish priests from sinister Jesuits – 'disloyal to their earthly *patrie*' – who encouraged ultramontane clergy to appeal to Rome against 'liberal' bishops. They were foes of all progressive forces – Huguenots, p*hilosophes*, 1789. 'Ask the man in the street who the Jesuits are and he'll reply "the Counterrevolution"', Michelet claimed. Justifying their expulsion in 1879 as an 'unauthorised Congregation', Ferry insisted 'that which I honour most (i.e. freedom), they degrade'. Jesuits ran 30 colleges with 11,000 secondary pupils. Former pupils' 'pilgrimages' to legitimist pretender Chambord confirmed fears about the influence of their teaching. *Lycées* were austere, rationalist. Jesuits cultivated the senses. Their chapels had perfumed, boudoir-like alcoves. Their pupils emerged as facile, vaguely bisexual sensualists. Béranger's song *Les Révérands Pères* hinted Jesuits' delight in caning 'pretty little boys'. Jesuits practised casuistry and deception. Trained to lie, spy and adopt disguises, they were perfect agents of police surveillance. In Sue's *Le Juif Errant* the Jesuit conspiracy is incarnated by seductive, worldly d'Aigrigny and reptilian Rodin, whose sexual energies are sublimated into the bid for world domination. Anti-Jesuit and anti-Masonic myths were central to the Manichean worldviews of both sides. Post-Reformation history was an ongoing battle between progress and obscurantism – or God and Satan. Anti-Jesuitism, a feature of French culture before 1789, provided anti-clericals with a repertoire of stereotypes on which to draw. Whereas the village *curé* was a target of mockery, the occult figure of the Jesuit was to be feared (Cubitt 1991).

Rural France: *'chrétientés'* and anti-clerical 'badlands'
The huge geographical variations in church attendance and vocations mapped by religious sociologist Boulard in 1947 were already discernible in the nineteenth century, or even earlier. Three types of region can be identified. In *'chrétientés'* almost all women and many men practised regularly. In intermediate zones many women and a substantial minority of men practised. But in 'badlands' (Gibson 1989) female practice was mediocre, male practice negligible. Clerical regions included the Breton West and adjacent Vendée and Lower Normandy, Flanders, Lorraine, the Southern Massif and the Basque country. Areas of 'de-christianisation' – later dubbed *pays de mission* – included the Paris basin, Limousin, the Charentes and the Mediterranean coastal plain. But can historians measure religious beliefs and mentalities through crude quantitative data on church attendance? Many attended church to conduct business transactions, to show off new clothes, or from habit or social conformity. Ignorant of basic rudiments of Catholic doctrine, they were often impatient with the priest's concerns. Dupanloup's diocesan enquiry revealed parishioners coughing, spitting, chatting and yawning their way through Mass. Even if positivistic quantification of religious practices has some value there is the problem of which statistics to emphasise. Tridentine Catholicism prioritised Easter Mass as the thermometer of religious vitality. The faithful were expected to signal acceptance of priestly authority by taking Communion.

Yet perhaps for that reason Easter attendance was lower than that for a Sunday Mass. Many adhered to festive practices such as *fête patronale* processions. But this did not necessarily denote individual 'piety' or commitment to orthodox doctrines. In Sens diocese in 1912, 23 per cent attended *fêtes*, only 9.7 per cent Easter Mass. Observance of rites of passage offers one index of religious fidelity. This rose in the period 1820–70. Via school catechism classes, the young learned by rote the 'duties' of a Catholic. In Orleans diocese in 1870, 14 per cent attended Mass, but 75 per cent took the Last Sacraments. Yet substantial minorities in the Limousin were abandoning rites of passage. By 1900, 22 per cent of marriages and 17 per cent of funerals in the Sens diocese were civil (Marcilhacy 1964; Pérouas 1985).

There is a lack of systematic runs of easily comparable statistics. Random 'snapshots' produced by episcopal enquiries into the state of religion in dioceses depend on the zeal and competence of clergy who filled in questionnaires. Clergy made qualitative judgements on styles of religiosity. Breton peasants exhibited a 'Celtic' mysticism illustrated by their 'cult of the dead'. In Lower Normandy, priests discerned a 'calculating' attitude: 'The Norman is *not* a mystic. He intends to save his soul. Just as he would get a lawyer to defend his material interests, so he goes to a priest to look after his spiritual ones.' The *méridional*'s love of processions reflected an 'external', shallow piety. Historians of the nineteenth century struggle to explain *longue durée* religious 'temperaments'. Behind the façade of enforced conformity, there is evidence of varied vocational rates before 1789. Some later 'badlands', such as the area around Saintes, had been forcibly 're-converted' from Protestantism. Others, such as the Limousin, were never properly evangelised. Dioceses around Paris suffered from absentee bishops and 'outsider' priests unsympathetic to village culture. Auxerre experienced a popular backlash against excessive *rigorisme* of clergy trained in local Jansenist seminaries. Wealthy, tithe-collecting monasteries like Cluny engendered local antipathies discernible in low rates of practice in the nineteenth century. One Creuse priest in the 1890s blamed derisory Mass attendance of 0.2 per cent on bitter memories, transmitted across generations, of the seigneurs of a local abbey (Gibson 1989; Pérouas 1985; Cholvy and Hilaire 1985–86).

As many as 90 per cent of clergy were 'non-jurors' in regions which emerged as 'clerical' bastions. Acceptance or refusal of the oath both reflected pre-existing differences and, in turn, widened the gulf between regions. 'Juror' clergy were in a difficult position, both despised by Rome and the Catholic faithful and pressured by anti-clericals to abandon the priesthood. As some villages were left without a priest for years, habits of practice and catechism classes were eroded precisely where the hold of religion was already relatively weak. A variety of explanations have been suggested for Catholicism's hold on its heartlands. The challenge from Dutch Protestantism had stimulated counter-reformation missionary evangelisation in Flanders, just as Protestant enclaves in the Gard and Aveyron kept alive the zeal of adjacent Catholic communities. In the Southern Massif clergy invoked the hilly terrain to explain how parishioners were sheltered from 'corruption' by Enlightenment ideas. Rodez and Mende dioceses formed a 'Brittany of the Midi', 'exporting' priests to less pious regions. Mass attendance approached 90 per cent and birth-rates were 50 per cent above the national average. In an area of scattered habitat it was the parish which acted as the focus for community identity. Twenty dioceses stretching from Franche-Comté in the east to the Basque region formed a 'Catholic crescent' in which Republican *instituteurs* had to show respect for a dominant clergy. Religious practice was lower in the Rhône Valley, and by 1880 churchgoing peasants in the Cahors diocese or in Franche-Comté were defying their priests to vote Republican (Cholvy and Hilaire 1985–86). In 'those unhappy dioceses which had Paris as their neighbour' (Dupanloup), a shortage of priests persisted beyond 1830. By 1900, 1.5 per cent of adult males attended Easter Mass in Chartres. Evangelist missions to the Oise in 1840 found undisturbed spiders' webs in confessional boxes! Mission crosses were torn down in the region in 1830 and priests feared to appear in public in clerical garb. However, there were signs of an upturn thereafter. Dupanloup improved seminary training at Orleans, drew on resources of clerical personnel and money from Paris and nurtured village *oeuvres*. Practice in his diocese rose modestly (Marcilhacy 1964; Cholvy and Hilaire 1985–86).

Clergy blamed anti-clericalism on the attacks of their 'enemies' or on social changes, rather than enquiring whether *they* were to blame for their own unpopularity. The roles of a village priest were varied and demanding. He was expected to be advisor, ombudsman, poor relief administrator. He might supervise the school or organise the agricultural syndicat and youth club. He could be local historian or folklorist. The 'good priest' was the repository of 1001 virtues – 'simultaneously pastor, father, friend, JP and doctor to his parishioners. In his village no divisions . . .' (Boutry 1986). Such a paragon might leave few archival traces for historians, who use agitated correspondence between mayors, prefects and bishops to learn of local conflicts. Clergy faced new challenges after 1789, including rivals for local hegemony in mayors and municipal councillors. Loss of church lands and tithes left them dependent on funding from governments or landed notables. Because clerical recruitment was concentrated in areas of high religious practice where priests were influential and respected, young priests experienced a culture shock when appointed to villages where their beliefs were challenged by sceptical petty notables – pharmacists, vets, café-owners, artisans. Seminary training failed to equip them for such problems, merely instilling 'an aversion to modern ideas', as one Limousin prefect claimed. Many *curés* combined nostalgia for a lost age of religious conformity, conviction of their own 'superiority' by virtue simply of being a priest and a Manichean vision which labelled critics agents of Satan or Revolution. The post-Tridentine model of the priest set apart from and superior to his flock persisted. The *curé* d'Ars insisted that a priest was a 'man who takes the place of God, who is regaled with all the power of God'. One Le Mans priest told his parishioners, 'the Gospel gives clergy the *right to command* – and imposes on you the *duty to obey*'. Where deference was no longer automatic, such attitudes proved provocative. In 1848 a petition against a priest in Belley diocese claimed that 'the population, faced with his haughty, vindictive character, has grown weary of his tyranny . . .'. Faced with criticism priests became abusive and obstinate. The rise of Republicanism and declining church attendances left many isolated and beleaguered, hence their paranoia about Masonic or Jewish plots. The *curé* of Châtelus (Limousin) lamented that his parishioners were freethinkers who never set foot inside a church. However, he added, most were hardworking, living decent lives according to their own moral code. Such tolerance was singularly rare in the rural clergy. Too many exhibited a killjoy puritanism which denounced as 'sinful' and 'hedonistic' pleasures such as dancing, particularly 'satanic' modern dances such as polkas and waltzes which were performed by couples not in groups! (Boutry 1986; Pérouas 1985; Faury 1980).

The clergy's alliance with Royalist notables made anti-clericalism virtually obligatory for village Republicans. Diocesan catechisms asserting that nonpayment of the tithe remained a sin, compounded by localised attempts to collect a form of tithe, aroused alarms. Bonapartism promised to protect peasants' against a return to the ancien régime. In the Dordogne in 1867 peasants rioted when seigneurial insignia reappeared on church pews. *Biens nationaux* holders in southern Pas-de-Calais feared that a clerical regime might reverse the Revolution's land settlement. Priests who denied burial services to *biens nationaux* purchasers or those married by juror priests sparked conflicts. Their critics claimed that the cemetery was a *communal terre de repos*, that all villagers had an equal right to a decent burial. In 1861 an Ain schoolteacher conducted a service for an unbaptised infant to whom the priest had denied a Christian funeral. Similar disputes occurred when clergy treated suicides as 'rebels against God'. Controversy over Courbet's notorious *Burial at Ornans* (1850) arose in part because its ambiguous portrayal of sinister-looking rural bourgeois alarmed conservatives in the atmosphere of class-war that prevailed in the Second Republic. The painting portrayed the funeral as a key site of village tensions. In contrast to traditional reassuring artistic images of devoted priests and attentive mourners, Courbet offered no comforting images. The priest looks red-faced and overfed. The 'mourners' turn their heads away and avoid each other's eyes. A skull protruding from the soil evokes the 'Dance of Death'. The message of the painting is one designed to subvert the clergy's control over the meaning and rituals of death (Boutry 1986; Kselman 1993; Hilaire 1977; Gibson 1989).

Political conflicts between clergy and villagers peaked around 1830 during the Second Republic and in the 1860s and 1870s; 70 per cent of serious disputes in Belley diocese occurred after 1860. Indeed *anticléricalisme* was a neologism coined in the 1860s. The 1877 Republican election triumph allowed anti-clericals to take revenge for decades of humiliation by banning religious processions, removing crucifixes from village schools and erecting statues of 'Marianne'. Clergy's attempts to sabotage 14 July festivities or boycott 'godless' schools proved counter-productive. The Limousin clergy, claimed one prefect, were 'entirely hostile to Republican institutions (and) would fight ardently against them *if they did not feel so completely impotent*'. Rivalries between priests and mayors, who claimed legitimacy as representatives of popular suffrage, were endemic. Priests had kept village records and acted as intermediaries with the outside world. Now it was the mayor who became the distributor of state patronage – a 'pork-barrel' dealer in jobs, scholarships, hunting permits, building contracts or conscription exemptions. He claimed control over poor relief or the 'municipal' cemetery. Expenditure priorities were a source of friction. (Re)building churches, symbolic of recovery from revolutionary iconoclasm, was an obsession of rural priests; 49 per cent of churches in Belley diocese were reconstructed between 1815 and 1870. Funding came from notables and sympathetic governments in the 1820s and 1850s. Even 'indifferent' villages viewed an impressive church as a prestige symbol. But such projects often led to financial bickering. Escalating construction costs, fuelled by priests' taste for elaborate neo-Gothic architecture, provoked clashes with municipalities more concerned to build roads or bridges. In the Isère in the 1860s women barricaded themselves inside a church to prevent the mayor demolishing 'unauthorised' repairs carried out by the priest. The balance of power tilted against the clergy. The power of the Republican mayor, agent of democracy, incarnation of 'progress', reached its apogee after 1880 (Singer 1983; Magraw 1987; Silver 1980; Boutry 1986).

Accusations of clerical greed were widespread. Courbet's *Retour de la Conférance* (1863), depicting red-faced clerics on donkeys mocking a peasant as they return inebriated from an ecclesiastical gathering, captured popular perceptions of the priesthood as pensioned sinecure. In 1849 villagers of Chenel (Ain) petitioned to remove a *curé* whose activities as miller and moneylender made him 'more industrialist than priest'. Donations from Royalist notables made it appear that clergy were in the pockets of the rich.

Overcharging for the *casuel* – fees for rites of passage – was resented, causing the bishop of Belley to urge his clergy to 'forget the *casuel*'. Limousin parishes turned to Protestant pastors who were cheaper and whose God was one 'who loves us (not one) who holds us to ransom' (Boutry 1986; Pérouas 1985).

A de-christianised working class?

Pius XI's lament that 'the Church has lost the working class' was long accepted as accurate. Nor was this just a matter of worker indifference, for priests were shot by the Communards. However, recent scholarship, influenced by the implosion of Marxism and signs of a global religious revival, has questioned assumptions of the 'de-christianisation' of industrial France (Cholvy 1994). Too often falling religious practice in a particular city in a given decade was cited as if this marked a 'watershed moment', after which recovery was impossible. But an ebb-and-flow model, allowing for periodic resurgence in practice, is more plausible. Even in the Paris *banlieues* priests established nuclei of practising workers around social *oeuvres* and youth and sports groups. Le Play's studies of workers' families revealed mothers sending children to catechism classes and in touch with Catholic charities. Clergy 'sensed that one should start with the woman – that alongside a deeply Catholic wife, the husband would not remain for long a dangerous socialist'. Norbert Truquin, a radical silk-weaver, submitted to a Catholic wedding to appease his future mother-in-law, while suspecting women of passing militants' secrets to the clergy! Male workers who refused to take communion often observed rites of passage. In that sense working-class culture in 1914 remained largely christianised. No department outside the Paris conurbation had more than 10 per cent of children unbaptised until 1960. There were bastions of working-class Catholicism where male practice reached 30 per cent. In Tourcoing the legacy of Counter-Reformation missionary activity was 'a race . . . "catechised" for generations'. Even Lille had 15 per cent male practice in 1860. Like the Irish in Britain, Flemish-speaking Belgian immigrants clung to Catholicism as a badge of cultural identity (Pierrard 1984). Patterns of urban religiosity often mirrored the rural hinterland from which workers were recruited. Decazeville, drawing upon the pious Southern Massif, had male practice of 40 per cent. Protestant enclaves in the Midi fuelled sectarian rivalries which caused Catholic workers to identify strongly with their religion. In Mazamet (Tarn), where textile employers were Protestant, 3000 Catholic workers petitioned in 1883 to defend religious schools.

The clergy were never uniformly sympathetic towards industrial capitalism. Few priests came from the urban bourgeoisie. Many espoused paternalist values, were suspicious of industrialists' 'individualism', found laissez-faire ideology distasteful and rapid industrialisation dangerous. Precisely because many clergy 'refused to accept the nineteenth century', their attitudes towards capitalism were ambivalent. Taught in seminaries to mistrust 'materialism', many priests criticised industrialists who disrupted family life by employing women and children and operating factories on Sundays. At Aubigny in 1820 an anti-clerical employer, an ex-Bonapartist officer, provoked the priest by making Monday the weekly rest-day! The bishop of Arras beatified an eighteenth-century beggar in calculated defiance of bourgeois norms of property, hygiene and work. Many hard-headed businessmen were not practising Catholics. Sunday working imposed by rail and gas companies in the Paris *banlieue* contributed to declining religious observance (Heywood 1991). Conversely, Catholic industrialists sometimes retained their employees' 'loyalty'. The classic 'good' Catholic employer was Léon Harmel who blamed social conflicts on fellow industrialists' lack of compassion, viewing the 'Catholic *patronat*' of the Nord as authoritarians acting like miniature Louis XIVs in their mills. Harmel's 'christian' factory at Val-des-Bois, near Rheims, organised medical and pension schemes and mutual aid societies. Factory councils allowed workers to express grievances. There was no Sunday work, but workers were free not to attend the factory chapel. The workforce of 800 appears to have been stable and loyal. Although Harmel was a paternalist, his 'third way' between laissez-faire and collectivism foreshadowed elements of later Christian Democracy.

In a France 'noted for its unbelief', Engels was amazed by the religiosity of some 1840s militants. Furniture-maker Perdiguier claimed that fellow workers mistrusted priests and rarely attended church, yet viewed Christian values as the basis of their cooperative ideals. Abbé Chatel, who broke with Rome to establish a 'French Catholic Church', insisted that priests should be elected, charge lower fees and emphasise God's compassion rather than Hellfire and Damnation. They should tolerate workers' pleasures such as dancing or theatregoing. People wanted an egalitarian religion which accepted the Enlightenment and the Revolution, not one obsessed with miracles and Rome's reactionary agenda. At its peak his church controlled thirty parishes. Chatel preached in Left-wing clubs in 1848. His supporters included June Days barricade fighters (Prothero 1999). Responding to a question in the 1848 *Enquête* about the 'state of religion', St. Etienne workers claimed that all depended on the definition of 'religion': 'If one means . . . external practice, there is plenty amongst women but little amongst men, (but) if one means sentiments of God's existence, love of one's fellows and of justice we will reply that there is lots of religion.' In 1860 artisan Corbon claimed that in Parisian workshops the 'very few faithful that the Church can muster are exposed to no less sarcasm than the few opponents of democracy'. Yet few were atheists. Workers cherished 'Christian values' abandoned, they believed, by the Church, and invoked a working-class Christ – a carpenter's son who evicted usurers from the temple and preached a social gospel (Berenson 1984). Autodidacts flirted with a range of alternative beliefs. Suspicious of both Church and academic science, they sought a 'democratic epistemology' which synthesised the 'spiritual' and the 'scientific'. Silk-weaver Benoît was converted to socialism after debates with Swiss Swedenborgians who believed in 'equal sharing'. Chatel's followers flirted with phrenology, theosophy, homeopathy, mesmerism and spiritualism. Much of this recalls William Blake's 'alternative London' of the 1790s. Individual artisans oscillated between rationalism, idiosyncratic spiritual beliefs and the heterodox religiosity of Lamennais' *Livre du Peuple* which advocated a Christ-centred social gospel freed from clerical control. As Prothero argues, in the 'popular underbelly of the Enlightenment a variety of rational mysticisms, enchanted rationalisms and parallel religions flourished', which rejected both Original Sin and the Voltaireanism of educated liberals (Prothero 1999).

This radical religious sub-culture declined after 1851. By 1881 socialist B. Mâlon insisted that 'neither Rousseau's God nor the Jesus of the 1848 socialists has . . . attracted my political faith'. This was rooted in positivism and 'modern materialism'. Catholic support for the Bonapartist coup fuelled worker anti-clericalism. The few priests sympathetic to emerging social democracy were marginalised by the hierarchy. International comparisons suggest that French workers were more anti-clerical and de-christianised than their European counterparts. Rhineland workers supported the Catholic Centre party. The presence of Irish Catholics fuelled the 'Orange' Protestantism of native workers in Lancashire and Glasgow. Methodism or Non-Conformity attracted workers in the north and the Celtic fringe, and London workers were indifferent to religion rather than ideologically hostile. Yet Adolphe Blanqui was already struck by the weak hold of religion on French workers by 1849. Paris had 3 per cent of adult males at Mass in 1826, and a male believer was viewed as an 'archaeological curiosity'. In Brest, a town with a clerical rural hinterland, port and dockyard workers were 'irreligious' – as were Limoges porcelain workers. In Marseilles, once a bastion of popular Catholic-Royalism, Easter practice declined from 47 per cent to 16 per cent between 1841 and 1901. Some attributed falling churchgoing to the reluctance of successive regimes to sanction new urban parishes. Church officials estimated that no parish ought to have more than 10,000 inhabitants, yet the average Parisian parish by 1870 had 35,000 inhabitants. The significance of such factors is questionable, for churches in densely populated workers' quartiers remained empty. Clerical *attitudes* were of greater significance. The workers' world remained closed to the clergy, Péguy claimed, because 'the clergy's minds are closed to the workshop' (Gibson 1989). Recruited from rural France, priests saw the liturgical year fitting 'naturally' with seasonal agricultural rituals. Industry, which used technology to master nature, was per se detrimental to belief and practice and 'killed the soul'. In the Ain, priests explained their pessimism about the future of religion by invoking the construction of a railway repair workshop at Villars-de-Dombes, whose workers would be frequenters of *bals*.

Insistent on their right to dignity and social justice, artisans shared Proudhon's view that clergy insulted workers by offering charity. A Lyon weavers' newspaper insisted that the working class could 'no longer resign itself to suffer whilst hymning psalms to the Virgin to pray her to send good works'. The paternalistic tone of most 'Social Catholicism' was typified by the response given to Lille workers in the 1870s who requested a say in running their social club. 'I *know* the *true* Christian worker. He does *not* ask to be treated as an equal nor to leave his modest sphere.' De Mun's workers' *cercles* attracted white-collar employees, but few proletarians. *Abbés démocrates* in the 1890s were less patronising, but by then the damage had been done. Workers resented the clergy's failure to accord them dignity even in death. A lucrative funeral industry developed offering a choice of funerals and a range of ostentatious coffins and tombs. But workers found themselves marginalised to cut-price, rushed funeral services in side-aisles, and saw loved-ones dumped in communal graves. The 'men in black' were selling religion. Clergy faced the problem of workers' feelings of *respect humain*. Many male workers perceived churchgoing, let alone Communion or confession, as a sign of loss of independence. Harmel was told by one worker that if rumours spread round the factory that he was a churchgoer he would have 'lost everything'. Workers perceived clergy to be allies of employers, as the *curé* of Notre Dame de la Croix admitted in his response to an 1889 Paris diocesan enquiry. His fellow clergy were content to blame the 'usual suspects' for their unpopularity – the influence of Freemasons, Jews, radical municipal councillors, dance-halls and 'bad books'.

Some industrialists were keen to use priests as 'gendarmes in cassocks', agents of industrial discipline and social control. In company towns the regular orders ran schools and operated moral surveillance systems. At Blanzy miners' Mass attendance was monitored, and promotion depended on it. At Montceau-les-Mines in the 1880s miners were sacked for arranging a secular funeral. In response pit-shafts were sabotaged, the church dynamited, crosses torn down and church schools attacked. The strike was broken and militants arrested. Two decades later miners gathered to jeer and gloat at the expulsion of the 'unauthorised' congregations employed by management. By then the edifice of Catholic company-paternalism was crumbling elsewhere. Carmaux miners voted for Jaurès and championed laic schools and secular funerals (Heywood 1989; Pierrard 1984; Trempé 1971). Convent-workshops were a feature of the Lyonnais silk diaspora. Nuns supervised dormitories, workshops and leisure-time of girls recruited from Lyon orphanages and Ardèche peasant families. It proved an effective strategy. Jujurieux mills experienced no strikes for sixty years. Isère women-workers resisted Republican expulsion of 'their' nuns in the 1880s. Denunciation of the system came primarily from male workers and only after the 1900s was there a belated revolt of women themselves against clerical discipline. The congregations trained seamstresses for the 'sweated' garment sector which supplied Parisian department stores. Nord textile patrons used nuns of *Notre Dame de l'Usine* to conduct Mass in the factories, ensure sexual segregation of the workplace and monitor the 'family morality' of charity applicants. Guesdists claimed that anti-clericalism was an issue inflated by the Republican bourgeoisie in order to divert workers from the 'real' struggle against capitalism. Yet they admitted that such activities were a serious threat to workers' independence – and some joined *libre-pensée* societies (Stuart 1998).

The largest anti-clerical explosion occurred in the Paris Commune. Priests were taken hostage and archbishop Darboy executed. 'Social gospel' rhetoric and evocation of Christ the Carpenter – features of the 1848 revolution – had largely disappeared. The clergy's support for Bonapartism ensured, one observer claimed, that 'hatred of the *robe noire* is now a rooted social hatred'. A priest lamented that the 'working population is ... becoming atheist. Hatred is firm and persistent and will soon explode. Listen to the echoes of the workshops ... (and) the rumours of the streets. You priests will soon find that you top the target list of working-class scorn'. Though workers respected the welfare work of some nuns and a few dying Communards requested the last sacraments, many Communards did share the militant atheism of the Blanquists. They resented the treatment which they had experienced in Catholic primary schools and clerical pressures to force them to 'regularise' sexual relationships. Seamstresses disliked the nuns' role in organising sweatshops. The number of baptisms in Paris fell 50 per cent in 1870–71. The tone of the Commune is captured in its mock prayer.

'Mother of Liberty, Deliver us From Kings!
Mother of Equality, Deliver us from Aristocrats!
Mother of Fraternity, Deliver us from Troops and Gendarmes!

Virgin of Truth, Deliver us from Diplomats!
Deliver us from the Stock Exchange!

Bourgeois Republicans' helped to defeat the Commune. Yet they shared certain secularist values with the labour movement. Both were children of the Enlightenment. Workers found the ultramontane piety of the 1870s both absurd and threatening. The laic education pressure group Ligue de l'Enseignement recruited artisans. Labour culture was not only virulently anti-clerical but increasingly anti-religious. A song by E. Pottier, composer of the *Internationale*, began:

There is no Supreme Saviour
Neither God, nor Caesar nor Politics
Producers, Let us save ourselves!
Let us decree the Salvation of all Mankind!

(Gough 1971)

While much anti-clericalism consisted merely of a litany of insults against the 'black crows', some was 'ideological'. Members of *libre-pensée* groups in the Nord were mainly working-class. Printers' leader Keufer was a positivist. In the1890s Blanquist municipal councillors in Paris spent, or wasted, much energy 'debaptising' street names. The threat from the Catholic Right in the Dreyfus crisis prompted workers to abandon rites of passage. In Limoges unbaptised children rose from 2 per cent to 25 per cent, civil funerals from 5 per cent to 23 per cent; 47 per cent of Carmaux miners' children went unbaptised. Red flags flew at secular funerals, the deceased were praised for dying without sacraments, and the 'God of Capitalism' was denounced. In Paris unbaptised infants rose from 11.9 per cent in 1875 to 39 per cent by 1908, civil marriages from 12.6 per cent to 39 per cent. Already in 1889 pastoral visits revealed Mass attendance below 10 per cent in all popular quartiers. And 42 per cent of workers in the XXe Arrondissement, in the shadow of the Sacré Coeur, chose secular funerals (Trempé 1971; Boulard 1971). Working-class anti-clericalism permitted secularist Republicans to pose as 'progressive' and win popular votes without offering fundamental social reforms. Yet virulent anti-clericalism also contributed to workers' consciousness. Syndicalist Monatte insisted that 'amongst (numerous) defects, the French worker possesses some valuable, deep-rooted qualities. These include a distaste for everything to do with the Church, eternal accomplice of the rich. Take the most indifferent worker, the most aloof from the class struggle. He will treat the clergy with instinctive mistrust which nothing can cure'.

187

A Catholic country?

An article in *Revue des Deux Mondes* in 1892 portrayed the typical *curé* as 'banished from the school, regarded with malicious distrust by mayor and teacher, (ostracised) as a compromising neighbour by minor officials, spied on by the innkeeper, exposed to anonymous denunciation in the local press. He spends his mornings reciting prayers to empty pews – and afternoons planting cabbages'. Renan claimed that 'there *are* no more believing masses. Religion has become irrevocably a matter of personal taste'. Republicans justified Separation of Church and State by citing empty pews and taunting Catholics with the imminent collapse of their religion. Catholics sensed that their influence was waning as schools were secularised and divorce reintroduced. Municipalities banned church processions and changed street names. The Combes administration cited Catholic involvement with anti-Dreyfusards to justify dissolution of the regular orders – a policy backed by 45 of 53 deputies from Burgundy and adjacent regions. The end of the Concordat raised doubts about payment of clerical salaries. Vocation rates immediately fell. Rejection of rites of passage was spreading rapidly. Within Catholicism there appeared little coherent attempt to analyse these problems or engage in a self-critique. Instead secret Judeo-Masonic conspiracies were blamed by the mass circulation Assomptionist newspaper *La Croix* – a leading purveyor of antisemitism.

Yet Catholic historians deny that there is clear evidence of religious 'decline'. The eponymous hero of Roger Martin du Gard's *Jean Barois* is a 'progressive' intellectual alarmed by a resurgence of Catholicism – and bellicose nationalism – among his students in 1900s Paris. In 1900, 6 per cent of *École Normale Supérieure* students went on Easter retreat – by 1914, 60 per cent chose to do so. Catholic schools retained 20 per cent of primary and 40 per cent of secondary pupils. The long-term expansion of Catholic education ensured, one cleric noted, that 'the rising generation *understand* and *practise* their religion *better* than those born in 1850'. Catholic bastions remained largely intact. In the Southern Massif male practice was above 50 per cent and female 90 per cent. Migrants from this region formed nuclei of Catholic associations in Paris. In Rodez diocese vocations peaked around 1900. Lyon's business community was strongly *pratiquant* – and the decline of radical silk-weavers ensured that only 1 per cent of the city's funerals were secular. The 'trough' of religious practice around 1900 in some 'indifferent' towns was followed by a perceptible revival by 1914 (Cholvy and Hilaire 1985–86).

Significant changes in theology – and tone – of French Catholicism were now bearing fruit. In Anjou, sermons preached before 1850 warnings of Hellfire outnumbered promises of Heavenly rewards by three to one. The world was a place of corruption, where sinners were the majority. Catechisms defined Hell as 'as the place where the evil (burn) for eternity'. *Le Miroir des Pécheurs* portrayed their agonies in graphic detail. Yet already a God of Love and a Religion of Hope were being promoted by preachers like Lacordaire. By 1860 sermons emphasised the joys of Heaven. The image of God preached in Brittany changed as clergy perceived that Hellfire sermons drove away a generation of peasants beginning to believe in 'progress'. Heaven became a big 'happy family' reunion! (Gibson 1988; Lambert 1985; Kselman 1993) The Church was promoted as 'a good mother who has renounced her earlier severity'. Where once the faithful were required to 'engage in long fasts, tears and prayers, *we* – by a single ejaculatory prayer – can pay all our debts and escape Purgatory'. Adapting to the consumer age, clergy introduced catalogues offering indulgences for souls in Purgatory. Abbé Claquet's *The Easiest Indulgences* urged purchasing indulgences for friends as both a selfless act and a Pascalian wager on the future of one's soul – guaranteeing 100 per cent return on one's investment!

A further 'softening' of doctrine came with the embrace of the ideas of theologian Alphonse de Liguori (1696–1787) – canonised in 1839. Rejecting *rigoriste* doctrines which urged severity towards the 'sinful', Liguori argued that confessors should not be Inquisitors driving parishioners to despair by inflexible imposition of 'moral law'. His ideas won Papal support and were adopted by Mgr Devie of Belley in 1840, then disseminated in the Midi via missions. The main beneficiaries were wives absolved of 'blame' if husbands practised *coitus interruptus*. A loving God became central to 'ultramontane piety'. This was characterised by flamboyant processions, incense and 'St. Sulpician' art. In place of local, often grotesque effigies came mass-produced statues in crude pinks and pale blues, wearing fixed, saccharine expressions whose mawkish insipidity offended secularists *and* Catholic intellectuals (Gibson 1989). Feminisation of piety was accentuated Marian cult. Republicans tried to appropriate the cult of Joan of Arc at Donrémy, portraying her as a patriotic peasant girl betrayed by clergy and elites.

Catholics claimed that faith was being 'deepened', with individual commitment replacing a religion of habit conformity and seasonal *fêtes* in which communion was a 'reward' for virtue and rarely taken. A new 'eucharistic' piety, championed by Mgr Dupanloup, encouraged men to take communion. Its success was among the bourgeoisie, for peasants, clergy lamented, appeared to 'lack the Eucharistic sense'. 'Personal piety' nurtured the committed laity required to sustain Catholic social networks. French Catholicism no longer simply revolved around relationships between the parish priest and his congregation. Facing the challenge of secularism it rebuilt contacts with youth. By 1914 Catholic sports federations had 150,000 members, *L'Association Catholique de la Jeunesse de France* 140,000 – some in southwestern *bourgs* outside Catholic heartlands. Despite Papal insistence that the post-Separation parish must be under clerical control, the *Association Catholique des Pères de Famille* collected funds for Catholic schools and participated in parish councils. The largest female organisations in France were the *Catholic-Royalist Ligue des Femmes Française* – a promoter of the cult of Joan of Arc – and the (slightly) more moderate *Ligue Patriote des Françaises*.

Some Catholics were aware of the need to move beyond the elitist/paternalist Social Catholicism dominant since 1850. The encyclical *Rerum Novarum* (1892) – if reluctant to accept trade-unions and nostalgic for a lost corporate world – urged Catholics to engage with social issues of the industrial age. Some simply paid lip-service to it. But *abbés démocrates* accepted the Republic and the need for social legislation, agitated on behalf of 'sweated' labour and even, as in the Limoges bakery strike of 1910, supported industrial action. The roots of post-war Catholic trade-unionism were being planted. But embryonic Catholic (social) democracy was fraught with tensions. To differentiate themselves from socialists, some *abbés démocrates* flirted with 'anticapitalist' antisemitism. Yet their radicalism provoked criticism from Catholic industrialists and bishops who refused to countenance any *rapprochement* with the Left. Marc Sangnier's *Sillon*, which had 10,000 members by 1905, attracted students, young professionals and white-collar workers. It was open to 'modernist' ideas within Catholic theology, sympathetic to Republicanism and social reform and engaged in public debate with freethinkers and syndicalists. But conservatives within the Church persuaded Rome to demand Sangnier's 'submission' (Cholvy and Hilaire 1985–86)

Catholics identified with forces seeking to preserve regional identities and cultures. The counter-revolution's strength in Brittany and the Midi confirmed Republicans' conviction that 'fanaticism spoke patois'. They saw 'reactionary' priests sustaining their local hegemony by resisting the spread of French – language of reason and progress. But, reluctant to risk open confrontation, they turned a deaf ear to use of patois in catechism classes and sermons. A Finistère school inspector in 1863 warned that imposition of linguistic uniformity would provoke resistance: 'For good or ill . . . most clergy think that without Breton one would see the disappearance of faith and the religion of our peasantry.' Ferry avoided coercive measures, but tensions rose as Catholics mobilised opposition to the laic laws. Not all Catholic regionalists were linked to the far Right. Abbé Lemire, a Flemish cultural regionalist, urged Catholics to fight for rights within the Republic. However, Mgr de Cabrières of Montpellier, who championed Mistral's *Félibrige* Provençal cultural movement, was a legitimist. Proto-fascists Maurras – himself a Provençal – and Barrès sought to destabilise the liberal Republic by cultivating a nationalism rooted in the soil of *petits pays*. 'One will never love one's country so much', Barrès insisted, 'as when one is rooted in a region.' In Barrès's native Lorraine, Royalist clergy collected and preserved folktales and songs. Republicans became more intransigent. The 'Republican nation', conceptualised since 1789 in terms of citizenship, rights and consent, was redefined in terms of a uniform language imposed through state schools. Use of Breton in catechism classes was now banned because existing catechisms defined it a 'sin' to vote for 'enemies of God' (i.e. Republicans). Twenty Finistère priests had salaries suspended for refusal to comply. Yet a 1902 enquiry found two-thirds of catechism classes still in Breton.

Republicans viewed the West as a region where reactionary *hobereaux* kept sharecroppers and day-labourers in subordination, aided by clergy who ruled the minds of ignorant, credulous rustics. This world would remain untouched by Republican civilisation for as long as priests propped up Breton as a barrier against progressive ideas. There was some truth in this 'myth'. One Breton bishop admitted his reliance on aristocratic landowners: 'My diocese is not a parish, but *150 manors* which provide money for my Catholic *oeuvres*.' This was a region of intense religiosity whose 'incense, organs, prayers and stained-glass windows' inspired post-Impressionist painter Emile Bernard to 'become a Catholic again, capable of fighting for Christianity'. Mass attendance remained above 90 per cent. Re-evangelised by Counter-Reformation missions, Brittany had long recruited local clergy sensitive to the peasantry's 'cult of the dead' and – Druidic? – beliefs in healing rocks and springs. Defence of the 'good old religion' had fuelled peasant resistance to Revolutionary conscription, Jacobin centralisation and bourgeois outsiders who acquired church lands. Outraged by revolutionary iconoclasm, and bolstered by visits from the Virgin, *chouan* peasant bands fought a protracted guerrilla war, the heroic myths of which informed local mentalities into the twentieth century. In a region of scattered habitat and poor internal transport, the church remained the focus of rural sociability and priests the culture-brokers. Money from payments for well-attended rites of passage services, private masses and *quêtes* – 'voluntary' tithes – meant that Breton priests were not dependent entirely on state salaries or on donations from landed notables.

But Brittany was more diverse than Republican stereotypes suggested. The road system was patchy, railways arrived only in the 1860s and the textile industry was in decline. The dominant tenancy system – *domaine congéable* – stifled initiative, since landowners had no obligation to reimburse tenants for farm improvements. However, a market agriculture was developing based on market-gardening of spring vegetables and fruit. Aristocrats with deferential tenants did exist around Quimper or Morlaix, but elsewhere there were many peasant farmers. Breton mobilisations were, as Republicans feared, strongly Catholic, but they were not necessarily 'archaic' or tied to reactionary projects of Legitimist aristocrats. By the 1890s some villages with high Mass attendance and devoted to their saints elected Republican municipalities. Christian-democracy made a dramatic debut with the 1897–98 electoral victories in Brest of abbé Gayraud over a Royalist aristocrat. Gayraud, pointing to a crucifix, told journalists 'we are not Jacobins. But there is on the one side the bishops and the châteaux, and on the other the people and the Republican lower clergy. A class war? Exactly! We've had enough of leaders by right of birth'.

Protesters against the laic laws, against Combes' assault on the religious orders or against inventories of Church property in the aftermath of Separation included neo-Royalists. Yet the tone of this resistance was populist not elitist. Breton Catholics mobilised their cultural resources – Almanachs, *veillées*, folk songs. Their leaders included Christian democrats who accepted a Republic, but one that did not discriminate against Catholic schools. Local Republicans warned governments not to impose neo-Jacobin policies 'repugnant to this region's independent temperament'. The clergy's influence was strengthened by their role in building cooperatives and *Syndicats Agricoles* to support depression-hit peasants. Finistère villagers who resisted troops who were dispersing the female orders chanted 'long live the sisters! Down with Combes! Long live the Republic!'. The *soeurs* were important to local society because they gave employment opportunities for girls in a densely populated region. As teachers, paramedics and child-minders they provided multiple services to communities. This was not reactionary resistance to Republican democracy nor archaic obstruction of modernisation. Nor was a 'backward' region being 'assimilated' to 'France'. Rather some Breton priests were mediating between periphery and centre – seeking a third way between

Catholic-Royalism and secularist Republicanism. However, tensions between the Right's 'integral Catholicism', the liberalism of the emerging *Action Libérale Populaire* party and the social concerns of *abbés démocrates* prevented the formation of a single Catholic party on the model of the German *Zentrum* (Ford 1993).

The prominence of 'religious sensibility' in society's response to the traumas of the First World War confirmed the limits of secularisation. Wartime *Union Sacrée* signified a truce between Catholics and anti-clericals. A religious revival, of a sort, took place as populations drew on the resources of their Catholic culture. Mass attendance rose. The ideas of Catholic and nationalist intellectuals found a wider audience, though Germans now played the role of Satan hitherto reserved for Freemasons and Jews! War became a sacred experience. France would be purified through sacrifice as its people, civilians *and* soldiers, were brought closer to the experiences of the suffering Christ. Medallions, *ex-votos* and sacred charms proliferated. Cults which expanded as people sought intercession included the Sacred Heart and Joan of Arc, but also Ste Thérèse of Lisieux who exemplified the sanctity of daily suffering. After 1918 there was a commemorative 'cult of the fallen' expressed in monuments, cemeteries, ossuaries, stained glass, sculptures and paintings – and in chalices for fallen aviators engraved with propellers and machine-guns! In short the war led to an intensification of a range of practices – many unofficial and unstructured – which blended the religious and the patriotic and which helped many to sustain years of personal suffering and national crisis (Becker 1998).

Bibliography

Aston, N. *Religion and Revolution in France: 1780–1804* (London: Macmillan, 2000).

Atkins T. and Tallett, T. (eds) *Religion, Society and Politics in France Since 1789* (London: Hambledon, 1991).

Becker, A. *War and Faith: the Religious Imagination in France 1914–30* (Oxford: Berg, 1998).

Berenson, E. *Popular Religion and Left-Wing Politics in France 1830–52* (Princeton, NJ: Princeton University Press, 1984).

Blackbourn, D. *The Marpingen Visions: Rationalism, Religion and the Rise of Modern Germany* (Oxford: Oxford University Press, 1993).

Boulard, F. 'La "déchristianisation" de Paris', *Archives de Sociologie des Religions* 1971.

Boutry, P. *Prêtres et Paroisses au Pays du Curé d'Ars* (Paris: Cerf, 1986).

Cabanis, J. *Michelet, le Prêtre et la Femme* (Paris: Gallimard, 1978).

Cholvy, G. *Religion et Société au XIXe Siècle: le Diocèse de Montpellier* (Lille: Lille University Press, 1973).

Cholvy, G. 'Sociologists, historians and the religious evolution of France from the 18th-century to the present', *Modern and Contemporary France* 1994.

Cholvy, G. and Hilaire,Y.-M. *Histoire Religieuse de la France Contemporaine: Vol. I 1800–1880, Vol. II 1880–1930* (Toulouse: Privat, 1985–86).

Corbin, A. *Village Bells: Sound and Meaning in Nineteenth-Century France* (New York: Columbia University Press, 1998).

Cubitt, G. *The Jesuit Myth* (Oxford: Oxford University Press, 1991).

Devlin, J. *The Superstitious Mind: French Peasants and the Supernatural in the 19th Century* (New Haven: Yale University Press, 1987).

Faury, J. *Cléricalisme et Anticléricalisme dans le Tarn: 1848–1900* (Toulouse, 1980).
Ford, C. *Creating the Nation in Provincial France: Religion and Political Identity in Brittany* (Princeton, NJ: Princeton University Press, 1993).
Ford, C. Religion and popular culture in modern Europe', *Journal of Modern History* 1993.
Ford, C. 'Violence and the sacred in 19th-century France', *French Historical Studies* 1998.
Gadille, J. *La Pensée et l'Action Politique des Evêques Français: 1870–83* 2 vols (Paris, 1967).
Gibson, R. 'Hellfire and damnation in 19th-century France', *Catholic Historical Review* 1988.
Gibson, R. *A Social History of French Catholicism: 1780–1914* (London: Routledge, 1989).
Gibson, R. 'Why Republicans and Catholics couldn't stand each other in 19th-century France', in T. Atkins and T. Tallet (eds) *Religion, Society and Politics in France Since 1789* (London: Hambledon, 1991).
Gough, A. 'Reflections on the death of an archbishop', in E. Kamenka (ed.) *Paradigm for Revolution* (Canberra: Australian National University Press, 1971).
Guillet, C. *La Rumeur de Dieu sous la Restauration* (Paris, Editions Imago, 1994).
Harris, R. 'Possession on the Borders: the "Mal de Morzine" in 19th-century France', *Journal of Modern History* 1997.
Harris, R. *Lourdes: Body and Spirit in a Secular Age* (New York, 1999).
Hecht, J. 'Scientific materialism and the liturgy of death: the invention of a secular version of Catholic last rites', *French Historical Studies* 1997.
Heywood, C. 'The Catholic church and the formation of an industrial labour force in 19th-century France', *European History Quarterly* 1989.
Heywood, C. 'The Catholic church and the business community in 19th-century France', in T. Atkins and T. Tallet (eds) *Religion, Society and Politics in France Since 1789* (London: Hambledon, 1991).
Hilaire, Y.-M. *Une Chrétienté au XIXe Siècle: la Vie Religieuse des populations du Diocèse d'Arras* (Lille, 1977).
Hufton, O. 'The reconstruction of a church 1796–1801', in G. Lewis and C. Lucas (eds) *Beyond the Terror* (Cambridge: Cambridge University Press, 1983).
Jacquemet, J. 'Déchristianisation, structures familiales et anticléricalisme: Belleville', *Archives de Sociologie des Religions* 1984.
Jonas, R. 'Restoring a sacred centre: pilgrimages, politics and the Sacré Coeur', *Historical Reflection/Réflexions Historiques* 1994.
Jonas, R. *France and the Cult of the Sacred Heart* (Berkeley, CA: University of California Press, 2000).
Kroen, S. *Politics and Theatre: the Crisis of Legitimacy in Restoration France* (Berkeley, CA: University of California Press, 2000).
Kselman, T. *Miracles and Prophecies in 19th-Century France* (New Brunswick: Rutgers University Press, 1983).
Kselman, T. 'Funeral conflicts in 19th-century France', *Comparative Studies in Society and History* 1988.
Kselman, T. *Death and the Afterlife in Modern France* (Princeton, NJ Princeton University Press, 1993).
Lagrée, M. *Religion et Culture en Bretagne: 1850–1950* (Paris, 1994).
Lalouette, J. *La Libre Pensée en France* (Paris: A. Michel, 1997).
Lambert, Y. *Dieu Change en Bretagne* (Paris: Cerf, 1985).
Langlois, C. *Le Catholicisme au Féminin: les Congrégations Françaises . . . au XIXe Siècle* (Paris, 1984).
Langlois, C. 'Catholics and seculars,' in P. Nora (ed.) *Realms of Memory I Conflicts and Divisions* (New York, 1996).
Langlois, C. 'La Fin des Guerres de Réligion: la Disparition de la Violence Réligieuse en France au XIXe Siècle', *French Historical Studies* 1998.

Le Goff, T. and Sutherland, D. 'Religion and rural revolt in the French Revolution', in J. Bak and G. Benecke (eds) *Religion and Rural Revolt* (Manchester: Manchester University Press, 1984).

Lewis, G. *The Second Vendée* (Oxford: Oxford University Press, 1978).

Lyons, M. 'Fires of expiation: book-burning and Catholic missions in Restoration France', *French History* 1996.

Magraw, R. 'Rural anticlericalism in 19th-century France', in J. Obelkevich, L. Roper and R. Samuels (eds) *Disciplines of Faith* (London: Routledge, 1987).

Marcilhacy, C. *Le Diocèse d'Orléans au Milieu du XIXe Siècle* (Paris, 1964).

McLeod, H. *Secularisation in Western Europe: 1848–1914* (London: Macmillan, 2000).

Mills, H. 'Negotiating the divide: women, philanthropy and the public sphere in 19th-century France', in T. Atkins and Tallet (eds) *Religion, Society and Politics in France Since 1789* (London: Hambledon, 1991).

Pérouas, L. *Refus d'une Religion, Religion d'un Refus en Limousin Rural: 1880–1940* (Paris: EHESS, 1985).

Pierrard, P. *L'Eglise et les Ouvriers en France* (Paris: Hachette, 1984).

Prothero, I. *Radical Artisans in France and Britain: 1830–70* (Cambridge: Cambridge University Press, 1999).

Silver, J. 'Peasant demands for popular leadership in the Vendômois', *Journal of Social History* 1980.

Singer, B. *Village Notables in 19th-Century France: Priests, Mayors and Schoolmasters* (Albany: State University of New York, 1983).

Sorlin, P. *'La Croix' et les Juifs* (Paris, 1967).

Stuart, R. 'A 'de profundis' for Christian socialism: French Marxism and the critique of political Catholicism', *French Historical Studies* 1998.

Stuart, R. 'Jesus the Sans-Culotte': Marxism and religion during the French fin-de-siècle', *Historical Journal* 1999.

Tackett, T. 'The West in France in 1789: the religious factor in the origins of the Counter-Revolution', *Journal of Modern History* 1988.

Turin, Y. *Femmes et Religieuses au XIXe Siècle: Le Féminisme en Religion* (Paris: Nouvelle Cité, 1989).

Weber, E. 'Religion and superstition in 19th-century France', *Historical Journal* 1988.

Zeldin, T. (ed.) *Conflicts in French Society: Anticlericalism, Education and Morals in the 19th Century* (London: Allen and Unwin, 1970).

Chapter 5

Education and the uses of literacy

Primary education

Government policies and educational ideologies

'Who controls the school, controls the world', claimed Republican Jean
Macé of the *Ligue de l'Enseignement* (LE) – a conviction shared by his liberal
Orleanist, Bonapartist and Catholic Legitimist opponants. Guizot insisted
that education must be a government concern, for 'the key problem of modern
societies is the government of minds'. Liberals vaunted education's civilising
mission. Successive regimes viewed education as central to nation-building,
to cultural unity and social cohesion, to 'moralisation' of the masses or to
the creation of a productive workforce. Some have argued that the evolution
of popular schooling owed more to *longue durée* demand for basic literacy
and numeracy than to education laws framed in Paris. Increases in literacy
and school-attendance pre-dated the 1833 Guizot Law, often stemming from
voluntary local initiatives. Certainly the real impact of education must be
understood in terms of complex interactions between schools and the wider
society. One must analyse the 'agency' of 'consumers' of education – pupils
and parents – as well as the ideologies and practices of politicians, educational bureaucrats and teachers.

Nevertheless, analysis of the impact of primary schooling should
begin with the legislation of 1833, 1850 and 1879–86. Even historians concerned with 'reception' of education, uses of literacy and relationships between
teachers and communities accept that state policies remain significant. Official
ideologies and policies exhibited a complex blend of continuity and change.
The Guizot, Falloux and Ferry Laws did reflect the different priorities and
goals of successive conservative-liberal, authoritarian-Catholic and Republican
regimes – and thus diverse strategies of rival segments of the elites. Yet there
were some underlying continuities. Perhaps similarities between Guizot and
Ferry reflect shared liberal-Enlightenment convictions that education was
the vehicle for the spread of reason and civilisation. Possibly both were
essentially strategists of bourgeois social control, concerned to ensure that
the masses were taught just enough to equip them for their subordinate
socio-economic roles and to ensure that they internalised values congruent
with the dominant social order.

Before 1789 a patchy school network existed, run by Catholic orders or by
private lay teachers. There was some demand for basic literacy and numeracy,
particularly in northern and eastern regions. Overall literacy, higher among
men than women, reached 50 per cent by the 1790s, better than in southern

and eastern Europe but below levels in largely Protestant northern and western Europe (Furet and Ozouf 1982). Jacobins advocated free, secular and obligatory schooling and set a target of a school for every village. Abbé Gregoire's enquiry, worried by patois-speaking in peripheral regions, urged schooling in French as a prerequisite for national and Republican unity. But as with hospitals and welfare, the Revolution in practice disrupted existing Catholic and charitable provision without having time or resources to provide an effective statist alternative. Only 6800 village schools were established. Subsequent regimes afforded primary schooling low priority. The Napoleonic *Université* (1808) had powers to inspect primary schools and vet syllabuses, but it established only one training college (*École Normale* – EN) for primary teachers (*instituteurs*). Teaching orders were permitted to return and expanded rapidly. The Restoration's modest contribution to primary education was the 1816 Ordinance encouraging communes to establish boys' schools, supplemented by an 1818 Law allocating a little funding to assist these. While the Catholic teaching orders resented the new *Université*-monitored teaching certificate (*brevet de capacité*), their position was strengthened when Bishops were authorised to appoint public teachers. Yet if the 'system' remained a patchwork-quilt of religious, municipal, charitable and 'clandestine' provision, more change was occurring at local level than bare outlines of official policy suggest. Demand for schooling was rising and official statistics certainly underestimate the number of pupils. Communes with a 'school' – of some sort – rose from 17,000 to 24,000 between 1817 and 1820, though this left one-third of villages with none.

Nevertheless, the Guizot Act (1833) remains the key moment in primary education provision, and a symbol of the priorities of the liberal Orleanist elite (Gontard 1976). Its main provisions were:

1. Every commune should possess a (boys') school.
2. Each department would establish an *École Normale* (47 already existed).
3. All teachers – including the religious orders – should possess the *brevet*.
4. Teachers were guaranteed a (modest) minimum annual salary of 200 francs.
5. Financial assistance was provided for poor families. By 1834 29 per cent of pupils had assisted places.
6. 'Higher' primary schools (*Écoles Primaires Supérieures* – EPS) were established to train future lower cadres – clerks and foremen.
7. A corps of *Inspecteurs Primaires* (IPs) would monitor standards.

Guizot compromised with conservatives. Respecting 'freedom of choice' of *pères de famille*, he rejected compulsory schooling. He permitted Catholic regulars to teach in the public sector. Religious textbooks and catechism were to occupy a central role in the classroom. Whatever the precise impact of the Act on school attendance and literacy, it was clearly a watershed. The new corps of *instituteurs* attracted Catholic suspicion well before Education Minister Carnot attempted, with modest success, to mobilise teachers as Republican activists in 1848. As radical ideas 'infected' the countryside, teachers were blamed for corrupting peasants. Catholic *frères*, former Voltairean Thiers insisted, were best suited to teach that 'suffering is a condition of life'. Henceforth, he hoped, 'when the poor catch a cold, they will no longer think that it is the rich who gave it to them'. Their children would be taught basic numeracy, literacy and religion. 'That is all that is necessary for them to learn. The rest is superfluous.'

The Falloux Law (1850) was an outcome of this backlash. Catholic regulars with a 'letter of obedience' from their superiors could now teach without a *brevet*. *Curés* could inspect village schools. 'Subversive' subjects were pruned from EN syllabuses and 'higher' primary schools were abolished for fuelling 'excessive' ambition. Several thousand *instituteurs* were purged, some for wearing beards or for visiting village cafés. Catholic schools expanded, and by 1875 taught 60 per cent of girl pupils and over 20 per cent of boys. Falloux insisted that all communes with 800 inhabitants should have a girls' school. In Pas de Calais girls' schools doubled to 585 – two-thirds taught by nuns. Working in pairs and doubling as nurses or pharmacists, nuns fitted village gender-norms better than lay teachers (*institutrices*). Many of the latter were trained by nuns in departmental *cours normaux* – fulsomely praised for producing pious, docile teachers. 'It is through these girls', claimed one Inspector, 'who come from the countryside and who return there conscious of the grandeur in God's eyes of their modest tasks, that one can hope to spread the healthy doctrines (on which) society rests.'

Meanwhile *instituteurs* found their schools beleaguered or closed down. Pupils in Catholic boys' schools trebled between 1850 and 1863. But growing tensions between Bonapartism and the Church weakened government support for religious schools. Education Minister Duruy encouraged the lay sector. He increased the percentage of 'free' places, encouraged adult classes and supported his inspectors who deplored Catholic schools' reliance on catechism and rote-learning. Meanwhile, the reviving Republican movement founded the *Ligue de l'Enseignement* whose campaign for free, obligatory, secular schooling won support, in departments such as the Yonne, from artisans and peasants. During the 'Moral Order' years (1873–76) its mass petitions were ignored by Catholic ministers. But the Republican electoral triumphs of 1876–77 paved the way for the Ferry Laws (Auspitz 1982).

Republican ministers were 'moderates' who jettisoned the radical elements of Gambetta's 1869 Belleville programme. Yet they saw themselves as secularist democrats and viewed religion as anachronistic and an ineffectual tool of social control in a society where the popular classes, rural as well as urban, were increasingly suspicious of clericalism. Catholic education was 'obscurantist' in a world of science and industry and divisive in a society where the traumas of 1870–71 had emphasised the need for social and national unity. Ferry's rhetoric called for the mixing on the school-bench of those who would later be 'thrown together under the flag of the Republic'. Key measures of his 'Laic Laws' included:

1. Departmental Training Colleges for lay *institutrices* (1879). Only 11 existed in the 1870s. Ferry denounced 'primitive' training courses provided by nuns for *institutrices*. These received public subsidies, yet the state had little control over them. On their rare visits inspectors complained of poor quality of pedagogy. Secular colleges would train 'real schoolmistresses' – not just those capable of teaching lace-making!

2. Free, compulsory, secular schooling. Free (*gratuit*) education was introduced in June 1881, compulsory, laic schooling in March 1882. The 'Goblot Law' (1886) decreed the phasing-out, over five years, of Catholic teaching personnel in boys' schools – and over an indefinite period in girls' education. Catholic orders would be permitted to teach in the 'free' (*libre*) private sector.
3. Substantial additional state funding. The state's contribution to educational expenditure had fallen in the 1850s and 1860s but now it rose to above 66 per cent. In 1889 the state took over from municipalities direct payment of teachers' salaries.

The next phase of this project came after 1900. In the intervening years the Catholic sector clung on tenaciously. It still taught 38 per cent of girls, 10 per cent of boys. It also directed a barrage of abuse at Ferry's 'school without God'. In the aftermath of the Dreyfus crisis Combes sought to phase out all teaching by Catholic orders, though many congregational teachers quit their orders and continued to teach in the still-sizeable Catholic private sector.

The priority assigned to primary education by successive regimes is shown by the fact that each, in turn, legislated shortly after consolidating power. All believed that moulding young minds held the key to society's future. There was a growing consensus that leaving the masses ignorant and illiterate was to invite disorder, immorality and indiscipline. Some Catholic-Royalists continued to warn of the greater dangers posed by extension of literacy, which bred dissatisfaction, nurtured unrealistic dreams of social promotion, tempted semi-educated rustics towards the big cities and swelled the audience for subversive propaganda and cheap novels (*romans feuilletons*). Calling for abolition of *Écoles Normales*, one Legitimist insisted that 'ignorance, with its honest rusticity, is far better for a society's happiness than an instruction corrupted by evil passions'. Eugènie de Guérin's *Journal* records her alarm when a peasant on her Tarn estate disputed with the *curé* the significance of the Council of Trent! The only books fit for rustics, she insisted, were prayer-books (Lyons 2001).

Legitimists claimed that departments with low literacy had the least crime. 'Happy ignorance' was the best safeguard of morality. The 'best' villagers read nothing. Such attitudes explain Ferry's denunciation of his clerical opponents: 'For us the book – and I mean *all* books whatever they are – is the fundamental instrument for emancipating the intellect. *Your* attitude is that it is better not to read rather than to read books that are not "good" – in other words, which don't conform to (your) principles *We* believe in knowing how to read – even if it means reading the Marian Rosary. We say that because we believe in the soundness of the human spirit and in the final triumph of Good over Evil, in Reason and Democracy – whilst you don't believe such things at all.' Republicans agreed that education must inculcate morality and social discipline. However, in an age of science, industrialisation and gradual democratisation it was neither possible nor desirable to achieve this by restricting children to the catechism. They admired British Mechanics Institutes and sponsored cheap editions of self-help manuals and selected 'classics' and local lending libraries.

Guizot's education project had admirers among Republicans, and even worker activists such as Nadaud critical of his wider conservative agenda. Guizot was a 'man of order', with no sympathy for Jacobinism which had 'legislated for the free and universal education' while producing a society 'without schools or teachers'. Yet he did not want schooling left to private initiatives. Reluctant to abandon education to the marketplace, he admired the Prussian state's role in the modernisation of schooling 'from above'. He attempted to balance tradition and innovation, religion and liberalism. His schools shared features of de la Salle's seventeenth-century 'schools of the people' which emphasised literacy, social discipline and religious texts. Yet as a child of the Enlightenment, Guizot believed that an 'ignorant' people could be 'civilised' by reason, that education nurtured self-discipline and civic virtues. His advice to those demanding the franchise – *'enrichissez-vous!'* – was less a crude exhortation to make money than a call for cultural self-improvement and for maximising one's talents. He contributed, like Roussseau and Ferry, to the 'cult of the school'. His project involved more than simply social control in defence of bourgeois privileges. He favoured question-and-answer methods to cultivate reasoning, not rote-learning, and emphasised self-discipline as the prerequisite for the future adult citizen (Rosanvallon 1985).

Guizot sought to appease Catholic critics by siting *Écoles Normales* in small towns, away from the temptations of big cities, cultivating a quasi-monastic ethos within them and making religion central to the school syllabus. Worker unrest in 1831–34 intensified his overt concern with 'moralisation'. Policing the *peuple barbare* took priority over enlightening the *peuple ignorant.* He told *instituteurs* that only 'by teaching deference and respect for one's social betters' could an 'enlightened population, one of the guarantees of social stability', be constructed. He later reiterated that education's mission was 'to resist . . . not simply evil . . . but the *principle* of evil, not only disorder but . . . *ideas* which engender disorder'. Only thus could oscillations between revolutionary anarchy and repression be ended. The spectacle of vagrant children wandering the cities and a popular culture of violence pushed Guizot towards emphasising social control. Ferry placed greater emphasis on the right of autonomous individuals to develop their talents. Guizot rejected free, compulsory schooling for ideological *and* pragmatic reasons. Property-owners were reluctant to pay taxes to fund state education, while lauding the virtues of voluntary educational provision and of self-help. Parental responsibilities and rights of fathers were emphasised by Catholics suspicious of a Jacobin 'teaching state'. Guizot praised education's capacity to liberate children from brutal fathers and superstitious mothers, but lauded the *paterfamilias* who saved prudently to pay for his children's schooling. Education was valued if sacrifices were needed to acquire it. Orleanists, despite lip-service to 'careers open to talent', wanted to limit social mobility, feared 'over-education' of subversive *déracinés* – and retained a 'realistic' awareness of child labour's contribution to family economies.

Similarities between Guizot's education project and those of liberal Bonapartists and of Ferry support Max Weber's claim that 'with all the changes of master in France since the First Empire, the power-machine has remained essentially the same' (Rosanvallon 1985). Yet the Republican elites were less dominated by financiers and big landowners – and Ferry's discourse *sounds* rather different from that of his predecessors. The blend of progressivism and bourgeois class interest in Ferry's project reflects his own upbringing, experiences and ideology. Son of a Republican lawyer, he was a vocal opponent of Bonapartism, critical of its authoritarianism, of Haussmann's 'corruption' and of concessions made to Catholicism. Married into a Vosges textile dynasty, he accepted the social inequalities of the capitalist order, yet believed that class conflict had benefited Bonapartism by fragmenting Republicanism in 1848–51 and divided Frenchmen in 1870–71 in the face of foreign invasion. An efficient society required elites to accept obligations to pay taxes to fund mass education. From Littré's positivism he derived his conviction that industrial society, reliant on social interdependence, could be built neither on archaic Catholicism nor on narrow individualism. Only secular education could assure social cohesion through inculcation of a 'scientific' morality, self-discipline and a sense of civic duty. Mature citizens would accept a meritocratic social hierarchy. Using religion to inculcate deference and morality was futile in a society where religion was in decline. Credulity was an obstacle to scientific and social progress. Education's function was to teach a civic morality of *virtu* – based upon social interdependence and duties (Stock-Morton 1988). Education was not a market commodity, 'an industry like any other' with 'the consumer (as) the only judge of its products'. Government could not allow those who taught to have 'either the freedom to be ignorant or the freedom to poison'. The *école laïque*'s moral code was, despite the absence of explicit religious underpinnings, fairly 'traditional'. Hard work, sobriety, thrift and self-discipline were emphasised. Civics textbooks taught respect for the complementary contributions made by parents to stable households. Buisson, architect of teacher-training and school inspection systems, learned from his Protestant upbringing how to control children by playing on a sense of guilt. Laic ideology offered a narrative in which the Republican school facilitated the transition from ignorance, superstition and injustice to a secular, rational future. It presented a 'solidaristic' variant of liberalism, utilising a secularised version of Catholic family values combined with emphasis on self-control, duty and obedience.

The traumas of 1870–71 explain the urgency of the quest for national unity and social integration. Once Prussian reformers had borrowed from the victorious French. Now the French – viewing the war as a 'victory of the Prussian schoolmaster' – sought to appropriate elements of a system which had nurtured national pride, literacy and numeracy and generated efficient soldiers and productive workers. Republicans admired Prussian concepts of the teacher as a model for civic behaviour, of a national history taught to provide examples of moral and patriotic conduct. French should replace patois in regions where, it was feared, linguistic particularism underpinned cultures which obstructed a firm sense of French identity. Bruno's textbook *Tour de France par deux Enfants* (1878) – 8 million copies of which were distributed by 1900 – portrayed two orphans from Alsace-Lorraine travelling through the diverse regions of the 'hexagon'. In one village they find themselves in an *auberge* where patois is being spoken. But, as a symbol of hope for the future, when the landlord's children arrive home they are French-speaking! (Ozouf and Ozouf 1984). Despite Republicans' proclaimed devotion to ideals of humanity and peace, the laic school was to inculcate a sense of military patriotism. School cadet corps (*bataillons scolaires*) were established in some departments. 'If the pupil does not become a soldier who loves his gun, the teacher will have wasted his time', insisted Lavisse, the leading author of history textbooks. Maps of Alsace-Lorraine were coloured purple on school walls in mourning.

Ferry feared that France's endemic social conflicts would reduce her to the level of a Poland – 'madder and more tragic – and no less justly punished'. The 'real danger', he insisted, 'is within ourselves. It is the spirit of class division – the agitation of the proletariat'. Only laic education could integrate workers by persuading them of the contrast between parasitic landed and clerical elites and the Republic's meritocrats – doctors, engineers, scientists. The First Republic rescued peasants from seigneurialism. The Second enfranchised the people. Now the Third was offering secular schooling and equality of opportunity. Pupils who achieved the school-leaving certificate (*Certificat d'Études Primaires*) would be fêted. This was a 'people's *baccalauréat*' – holding out the promise of white-collar careers. Yet the limited social mobility promised by the laic school existed within the framework of a two-tier system. Only 5 per cent of boys attended secondary schools. There was no 'ladder' between primary and secondary sectors other than a few token annual scholarships. Ferry insisted that 'democratisation' could not be extended beyond the primary sector. There were few Horatio Alger-style stories of social promotion in school textbooks. Most emphasised that one should be content with, and proud of, one's existing occupation. A 'well-constructed Republic', Ferry argued, needed forces of conservatism. 'To moderate and restrain democracy (was a) noble role' – only possible if elites dominated post-primary schooling.

Schools, pupils, literacy

The diffusion of education: interpretative models
Some claim that schooling met with popular indifference, even resistance, because book-learning was viewed as irrelevant to a 'real' world of work and subsistence. Child labour was essential on family farms. Grandparents, who transmitted know-how and culture to young children, saw teachers as outsiders and schools as a threat. Martin Nadaud's father, a Creuse stonemason who worked in Paris in the summer, paid for his son to acquire basic literacy and numeracy from an 'irregular' teacher. His family were sceptical, for none of them had attended school, yet they had 'managed to eat all the same'. Hugo claimed to love the people, but despaired of their wilful, impenetrable ignorance. Ferry cited the appeal of Boulangist populism and the gullibility of Lourdes pilgrims as evidence of the credulousness of the uneducated masses. Thabault's (1971) study of his native village in the South-West showed that the school was long attended only by artisans' and shopkeepers' sons. When the railway made commercial dairy-farming possible, the need to keep accounts convinced peasants of the value of literacy. The *instituteur* became

more respected than the *curé*. Hence Weber identified the 1860s and 1870s as the moment at which a transport revolution, an emerging national market and military service encouraged acceptance of schooling by peasants wishing to write letters to conscript sons or aspiring to white-collar employment. Labour-saving machinery reduced reliance on child labour, thereby 'freeing' children to attend school. However, where local economies remained reliant on youthful workers, employers and parents colluded to evade school and factory inspectors seeking to enforce the 1874 and 1892 laws regulating child labour. Truancy in Paris's 13th Arrondissement was above 20 per cent in the 1910s. In the Auvergne, agricultural work reduced summer school attendance until after 1945 (Thabault 1971; Heywood 1989).

However, the chronology of Weber's seductive model is dubious. Areas around towns and along river valleys and coasts were drawn into market economies much earlier. *Longue durée* studies of literacy discern a popular demand for some education – not necessarily for 'official' schooling – in the eighteenth century (Furet and Ozouf 1982). In 1806, a prefect in the 'backward' Massif Central observed that 'mental horizons' had been broadened by 'great events (which) this generation has witnessed'. Once his curiosity was stimulated, the peasant, 'to satisfy these (new) needs has to be able to read and write. Once schools opened, inhabitants of the countryside have rushed to them'. *Annaliste* historians' disdain for 'politics' has led them to downplay the role of state education policies. Schooling is portrayed as having its own momentum and dynamics, driven by local needs and virtually independent of government action. A growth in schooling occurred in the years before the Guizot Act. Attendance of nearly 90 per cent was achieved before the Ferry laws. In the 1820s thousands of unofficial schools existed, lacking state approval but supported by families and municipalities. In the 1830s some municipalities preferred 'clandestine' teachers, whom they could pay in kind, informing them of the impending arrival of the school inspector! Guizot's enquiry into schooling largely ignored 'unofficial' – particularly girls' – schools. Unthinking elite contempt for popular culture led to a myopic disregard for informal rural education given by village autodidacts like Père Fourchon in Balzac's *Les Paysans* – cobbler, postman, letter-writer and unoffical teacher. The 'school-form' of education was that most conducive to eventual state control. But the history of literacy is not identical with the history of formal schooling. Peasants aspired to utilisable skills while wary of official schooling. Traditions of seasonal migration led to a precocious awareness of the value of basic literacy in Alpine villages. Migration from the Breton uplands led to peasants welcoming teaching in French at a time when Breton elites were hostile to this. In 1840, 141 Vosges villages had 'clandestine' schools. Peasants selectively accepted facets of schooling which they found useful, while remaining suspicious of those which threatened local cultural values.

Measuring the growth of popular education
Quantitative analysis of records compiled by nineteenth-century bureaucrats led Grew and Harrigan (1991) to conclude that long-term educational trends were largely independent of official education policies. Growth in schooling was faster in the 1850s than after the Ferry Laws. Critics of attempts to 'reify'

	'Schools'	Communes without school	Pupils	Catholic sector pupils
1829	36,000	13,900	1.35 mn	
1832	42,000			
1837	52,000	5,600	2.69 mn	
1847		4,000	3.52 mn	
1851	60,000			1.1 mn
1863	68,000	800	4.33 mn	
1877	71,500	300	4.77 mn	2.1 mn
1881	75,000		5.34 mn	
1886–7	80,000		5.52 mn	
1910	83,000			1.10 mn

education insist that such statistics are as problematic and difficult to use as crime figures (Grew and Harrigan 1991; Luc 1986). They might provide a crude guide to certain major trends. But interrogation of their compilation and 'production' is required. To qualify as a 'pupil' does a child have to appear once on an annual school register, or does (s)he need to attend regularly? Does a barn or back room of a café qualify as a 'school'? What qualifications are necessary to be a 'teacher'? Guizot recommended class registers, but these were kept systematically only after 1860. The corps of inspectors was thinly spread. 'Attendance figures' which it compiled were ad hoc 'constructions', compromises between numbers present on inspection day, names on the register and teachers' estimates of average daily attendance. One inspector in 1866 claimed that 90 per cent of children appeared on registers, yet barely 70 per cent attended regularly. Calculation of percentages of children of 'primary school age' attending school assumed that the relevant cohort was that from 7 to 13 years of age. In practice, some younger and older children attended. Estimates of annual attendance were inflated by counting all present in a calendar year, thereby including both those who left in July and those who joined in September. 'Attendance' in the 1850s was inflated by counting infants in kindergardens (*salles d'asiles*). In the Doubs, daily register-keeping after 1880 detected hitherto disguised levels of absenteeism (Gavoille 1986). The 'penumbra' of unofficial establishments – *garderies* for mill-workers' children, Catholic catechism classes – eluded official records. It is difficult to 'prove' claims that rural schools' summer attendance averaged 50 per cent of winter attendance in the 1850s but 80 per cent by 1875. Quantitative analysis thus offers 'scientific' measurement in an area where claims for precision must remain presumptuous. More specifically, Grew and Harrigan's methodology leads them to overestimate growth in the 1850–75 period, while underestimating that of the 1830s and 1880s (Grew and Harrigan 1991; Luc 1986).

Several observations can be made about these statistics. Clearly the Guizot Act triggered rapid expansion. Pupil numbers grew at 8 per cent per annum in the late-1830s and many communes acquired their first school. Growth rates were highest in 'intermediate' departments such as the Nièvre, where the number of schools rose from 86 to 197, rather than in the more 'backward'

West. More contentious is the claim by Grew and Harrigan that periods of rapid expansion in the 1820s and 1850s and 1860s were unrelated to any significant stimulus from government policy – and that the Ferry laws came at the tail-end of a growth period and had minimal impact on the school/ population. 'French society', they concluded, had already provided the schools required for universal education 'more by way of local initiative and internal momentum than as a direct result of the most famous measures of governmental compulsion'. After 1880 education 'gains' were measurable less by rising pupil numbers than by smaller class-sizes, separate classes for different age-groups, single-sex village schools and improved *Certificat d'Études* Primaires (CEP) results (Grew and Harrigan 1991). This analysis overestimates expansion rates in 1850–63 by failing to note that France's acquisition of Nice and Savoy added some 2 per cent to the potential school population. Conversely, it underestimates the impact of Duruy's 1860s provision of additional free places in state schools and encouragement of hamlet schools – 'hidden' by the loss of Alsace-Lorraine in 1871 which cut 5 per cent from pupil numbers. Its assessment of the Catholic contribution to mass education is misleading. Undeniably the educational network, which permitted over 80 per cent of children access to schools by 1875, was heavily dependent on the Catholic orders. But one cannot 'explain' this by 'Catholic initiatives' and socio-cultural demand without emphasising the role of the state which purged thousands of lay teachers, passed the Falloux Law exempting Catholic teachers from the *brevet* and tolerated the dubious tactics employed by Catholics to harass, close down and replace existing lay schools. One cannot divorce educational trends from governmental strategies, which in this case favoured the Catholic sector.

Nevertheless, even critics of 'obscurantist', pedagogically inadequate Catholic schooling accept that the construction of a national network owed much to Catholic efforts. Revitalised Catholic teaching orders increased school provision during the Restoration. Many 'lay' *institutrices* were trained by nuns. By 1850, 1.1 million pupils (28 per cent) were already in Catholic schools. Their bastions, the Rhône region and Brittany, were rural areas with lowish overall school attendance. Five departments, in the 'advanced' east and anticlerical west-central France (Creuse, Charente), had under 15 per cent of pupils in Catholic schools. The boom came between 1850 and 1875, when 80 per cent of new schools were in the Catholic sector. Its pupils increased 117 per cent, those in lay schools by 12 per cent. In 1875, at its apogee, it taught 2.1 million pupils – 44 per cent of the total. It made three particular 'contributions'. By 1870 over 60 per cent of *female* pupils were in Catholic schools. Catholic spokesmen emphasised that control of girls' minds was the prerequisite for influence over future generations. Secondly, Catholic schools served 'deprived' regions. Finally they provided many free places. Duruy failed in his bid to introduce *gratuité* into state schooling in the 1860s. Two-thirds of Catholic places were free, only one-third in the lay sector. Anti-clerical Republican municipalities seeking in the 1860s to secularise schools found the costs prohibitive. Not all former Catholic pupils were grateful for their schooling. Working-class children felt humiliated and stigmatised wearing heavy smocks of the *classes des pauvres*. Often 'free' places in nuns' schools were subsidised by the sale of lace produced in sweatshop conditions by girl pupils. Working-class militants claimed that their atheism was a reaction against the absurdities of Catholic textbooks. The tide turned after 1875 as Republican municipalities laicised schools. Thereafter clergy and Catholic parents conducted a stubborn rearguard action against 'godless' Republican schools. By 1901 Catholic pupils had declined to 26 per cent of the total. Over 80 per cent of these, as against 66 per cent in 1875, were girls. Paternalist mining companies financed nuns' schools to produce 'docile', pious wives and mothers who would 'moralise' their menfolk. Otherwise Catholic schools were now concentrated in the West and Southern Massif, having fallen away sharply in the Rhône (Grew and Harrigan 1985).

The rise of 'literacy'

Literacy rates provide rough indicators of regional cultural differences and of the rise of popular education. However, sources from which these are calculated remain crude and potentially misleading. The proportion of conscripts signing their names – or brides and grooms filling in marriage registers – says little about levels of functional literacy. Many Catholic schools taught reading but not writing, regarded as too 'independent' an activity. Peasants might simply learn to sign their name. In the 1860s officials advised Duruy that one-third of school-leavers were virtually incapable of reading or writing. Bureaucrats were fascinated by the 'St. Malo–Geneva' line dividing an 'advanced' North and East from a 'backward' South and West – a division 'proved' in the 1870s by former Bonapartist education official Maggiolo. He purported to show, utilising marriage registers from the 1690s onwards, that literacy rose under the Ancien Régime, well before the Republicans' beloved Revolution. However, his statistics simply reinforced long-held stereotypes portraying inhabitants of the South and West as physically smaller and living shorter, more criminal, more violent lives. There were pockets of greater literacy in backward regions – Protestant enclaves in the Cévennes or areas of Brittany around Rennes. But literacy was below 20 per cent in much of Brittany in 1820, and below 15 per cent in Corrèze. Conversely, in rural Doubs in Franche-Comté, literacy was 80 per cent. Factors invoked to explain these contrasts ranged from levels of urbanisation, involvement in a market economy and proximity to high literacy cultures in Holland, Germany and Switzerland, to 'racial' contrasts between northerners and mongrel/Latin peoples of the Midi. Stendhal evoked a 'fatal triangle' – its apexes Brest, Bayonne and Valence – within which superstition and ignorance ruled. After 1830 parts of the Midi closed the literacy gap, but in Brittany or Limousin advances were slow. The St. Malo–Geneva line gradually lost significance. Yet in 1880, 21 of 31 departments north of the line had literacy rates above 90 per cent, and only 6 of 51 below the line had reached 80 per cent. The gender gap narrowed steadily. Unsurprisingly literacy had been much higher in urban areas. However, child labour in textile mills meant that it was lower in Lille than in surrounding rural areas, and literacy among Le Creusot industrial workers was below that in the Saône-et-Loire countryside. Cash-crop farmers, villagers in areas of concentrated habitat or with traditions of temporary migration had higher literacy than agricultural labourers or inhabitants of

Conscript	Conscript/literacy	
1831–35	47%	
1846–50	64%	
1866–70	78%	
1871–75	82%	

% signing names on marriage registers

	Grooms	Brides
1700	29%	14%
1780	47%	27%
1850	68%	52%
1880	84%	75%
1913	98.4%	97.3%

bocage, forest or mountain areas. Sharecroppers might be discouraged by their landlords from sending children to school (Furet and Ozouf 1982).

The teaching corps: from social pariahs to 'Black Hussars' of the Republic
In France the 'real' history of teachers is difficult to disentangle from heroic myths in which they figure as selfless 'lay apostles' of Ferry's crusade – carriers of Enlightenment, democracy and progress to 'backward' provinces. Survivors of the first generation of laic teachers, interviewed in the 1960s, had internalised the values of devotion and self-sacrifice central to this myth (Ozouf and Ozouf 1992). There were always 'contradictions' in their role. Many did not share the priorities of their political masters. Many were covert Republican sympathisers under Orleanist and Bonapartist regimes. Some of their successors' syndicalism fitted uneasily with the official Republican patriotism of the pre-1914 years. The carnage of 1914–18 converted many inter-war teachers into integral pacifists.

If teachers in Ferry's schools remained vulnerable to humiliations by *notables*, mayors and school-inspectors, their situation was preferable to that of their predecessors. In the 1820s wages and status were so low that one report claimed that 'schoolteacher and beggar are almost synonyms'. The first *École Normale* fell victim to the anti-Jacobin backlash. After 1810 a few departments copied Strasbourg's German-influenced training college, but most teachers simply learned on the job. Some were hired at agricultural fairs, wearing two feathers in their cap if they taught both reading and writing. Some were disabled or itinerant ex-soldiers or doubled as barbers or café-owners. 'Schools' were often in barns. The Guizot Law would clearly have been a watershed had it merely insisted that each department establish an *École Normale*. Everything was done to ensure that new *instituteurs* would not become ambitious, radicalised *déracinés*. Colleges were situated in small towns and had Catholic chaplains. *Normaliens* – 'pupils' not 'students' – would imbibe just sufficient knowledge and pedagogic skill to fit them to impart necessary numeracy, literacy and morality to schoolchildren. They were expected to adopt a deferential stance towards *notables* and clergy, and serve as choirmasters and sacristans. By 1846, 9000 *normaliens* were in post. Recruitment was not easy. Salaries were low. Recruits were viewed as rough diamonds, scruffy dressers too keen to spend their evenings in cafés. Applications fell in the conservative backlash after 1849, with even Dijon college, in 'advanced' Burgundy, choosing from barely sixty applicants per year as against over a hundred in 1845.

Bald macro-statistics fail to capture the qualitative differences between *normaliens* and their predecessors. Essays written by trainee-teachers at the Rhône college in the 1840s reveal stirrings of an embryonic 'professional' mentality. Written for the eyes of inspectors, even the 'fictions which they elaborate are of historical interest'. Some dutifully echoed Guizot's rhetoric, claiming that a teacher's 'glory' was to 'seek for nothing but his obscure and difficult position and to work for mankind and not to expect any recompenses save from God'. Others were proud that college training was raising them from ignorance and creating a teaching corps with a sense of *camaraderie*. Some foresaw careers which would bring self-fulfilment in the vital task of popular Enlightenment. Such essays hint at convictions which encouraged teachers to subscribe to the *Echo des Instituteurs*, which campaigned against low salaries and demeaning subordination to the clergy and, by 1848, for free secular education (Gemie 1988).

Brittany was inhospitable terrain for the new teachers. It was largely Breton-speaking, its politics nurtured by myths of counter-revolutionary *chouans*. Two-thirds of communes in 1832 lacked an official school. If *instituteurs* could make it there, they could make it anywhere. Yet by the 1850s they were establishing themselves – and exhibiting a commitment which made them recognisable precursors of Ferry's laic teaching corps. Recruits to Rennes *École Normale* came from more literate areas and 'liberal' towns such as Brest. Their fathers were artisans, shopkeepers, minor *fonctionnaires* and small-peasants. The college was adorned with crucifixes and its director insisted that they must be submissive and sober. Its Catholic chaplain gave the *normaliens* a foretaste of future difficulties in the Breton countryside, denouncing the college as the godless invention of an illegitimate Voltairean regime! Yet training provided for teaching French, applied mathematics and agriculture fitted *normaliens* well for their future careers. Initial implantation was in coastal regions, but by the 1850s they had footholds in the hinterland. They held Sunday classes at which they offered advice on pruning, grafting, new ploughs and livestock breeding, thereby, inspectors claimed, attaching themselves 'closely to the preoccupations of the populations amongst whom they are called to live'. They taught peasants to calculate the area of fields and fill-in tax forms. Many stayed for decades in the same village, 'rooting' lay schooling in the countryside through their dedication. School inspectors rated 70 per cent 'good' teachers, claiming that the practical skills which they imparted gave them an edge over their Catholic rivals. They faced fierce competition from *Frères de l'Instruction Chrétienne* who viewed 'godless', 'French' *normaliens* as a threat to their regional hegemony. Some quit the profession because they felt isolated in 'clerical' villages, under the constant scrutiny of their private lives. Any hint of scandal involving an *instituteur* was ruthlessly exploited. Some achieved a pragmatic modus vivendii with local priests, but many were denounced from pulpits as 'atheists', or lost their posts in the 1850s as *frères* poached their pupils. Many became 'professional anti-clericals', seeing themselves as beleaguered agents of 'progress' in a countryside swept by 'Jesuit reaction'. 'I like to think', said one, 'that this bitter warfare is limited to our region, that other parts of France have better understanding of the interests of public education and don't sacrifice this to petty political rivalries. I congratulate my fellow teachers for being happier than their Breton colleagues.' By the 1860s, as relationships between the Bonapartist regime and its erstwhile clerical allies soured, prefects and inspectors offered them firmer support (Nicolas 1993).

Instituteurs were rarely politically active. Most kept a low profile in 1849–51 as suspected radicals were purged from the teaching corps. In all, eight training colleges were shut down. In the remainder the syllabus was pruned of 'non-essential' elements. Quasi-military regimes were introduced, with pupils proceeding from one activity to the next accompanied by a roll of drums! Most teachers spent the grim 1850s struggling to survive, outwardly conformist. Nevertheless, as one sub-prefect reported, many 'spoiled' their sound (professional) qualities by covert Republican sympathies: 'They only *appear moderate* out of fear.' Teachers *were* permitted a moment of self-expression in 1861. Education Minister Rouland requested them to describe their conditions, aspirations and grievances. The resulting 5940 essays constituted a *'cahiers de doléance* of the teaching profession's Third Estate'. Prize-winning entries were conformist in tone. More interesting were the 80 per cent of essays which voiced complaints. Articulate and well-written, they confirm the inspectorate's favourable impression of the teaching corps' quality. A sense of 'mission' and professional pride is evident. A high 88 per cent complained that low salaries necessitated demeaning auxiliary jobs. Guizot's claim that 'the teacher's glory (was) to work for mankind and receive his reward from God' ignored the fact that 'his family must still eat'. Lack of a garden was frequently cited, both as symbolic of inferiority to the priest and because it precluded growing food or giving pupils practical botanical or agricultural lessons. Complaints over school buildings and equipment were relatively rare, but 20 per cent lamented being 'teachers only in name' because they were obliged to be 'liege-men' of the priest – to ring church bells or take pupils to choir practice. The 'wisdom of Solomon' was required to keep in with rival village factions. They aspired to spread 'Enlightenment' to the villages, yet be part of local culture – to encourage love of the countryside and of farming and slowing the rural exodus. They urged the state to 'recover' its schools from the clergy. And 42 per cent – mainly from North and East – urged obligatory schooling, insisting that fathers no more had the right to deprive children of education than to beat them. They favoured nursery schools, libraries, agricultural and adult classes, and teachers' conferences to allow debates on pedagogy and contact with 'brother teachers'. Guizot's Act was praised as a milestone, the decisive moment in the emergence of their profession (Day 1983).

Some attention was paid to these opinions. Duruy raised starting salaries to 700 francs, increased free places, encouraged adult classes and school libraries and relaxed discipline and broadened the syllabus in training col-leges. The emergence of Republican educational pressure groups made teachers feel less isolated and impotent. There was a Catholic backlash in the 1870s, when teachers were purged, including one in the Drôme who attended the secular funeral of her uncle, a Republican doctor who had delivered her baby! Ferry enhanced teachers' public standing. State expenditure on primary schooling was boosted. The purpose-built school-house, next to the *mairie*, became the civic monument to the Third Republic. Salaries were increased. Teachers could now earn over 2000 francs and dispense with demeaning odd-jobs undertaken to make ends meet. Henceforth in disputes with Catholic *notables* they could (usually) rely on support from the educational hier-archy. Even in Brittany teachers now became local notables. Cropped hair, dark suit and polished shoes gave an appropriately dignified air. Avoiding open displays of anti-clericalism, and seeking a modus vivendi with local Catholic opinion, teachers expanded the role of all-purpose village expert which they had cultivated since the 1840s – advising on land surveying, legal problems and wills. They ran seed nurseries, introduced guano ferti-liser, and organised mutual aid societies. By 1911, 20 per cent of all teachers acted as secretary to the *mairie*, which kept their finger on the pulse of the community. They gave hygiene advice and ran adult evening classes. Despite pockets of Breton cultural resistance to 'French' education, many parents regarded literacy in the French language as essential to children's career prospects. In his autobiographical account of his Breton childhood, Hélias (1978) notes that his mother kept a copy in Breton of the *Lives of the Saints* in a trunk, while a French Larousse dictionary was placed prominently on the window-sill. The *Certificat des Études Primaires*, achieved by 40 per cent of pupils, became a source of pride to families, who framed it to hang alongside wedding photos (Singer 1977; Hélias 1978).

The heroic 'myth' of teachers as 'lay apostles' has been questioned. Yet the moving impression to be derived from oral testimonies of former teachers is that they *did* view their lives as incarnating this myth. 'My occupation (*métier*) was my entire life', one claimed. 'If I had my life again', another insisted, 'I would become a schoolteacher once more. It is an exalting job when one is convinced that moral values count in life.' Many were saddened by the failure of the world to take the paths of peace, tolerance and social justice along which they had aspired to guide the young generation in their charge. The carnage of the First World War, in which colleagues and loved ones perished, fascism, colonial wars, the revival of religiosity, the hedonism of consumer society and decline in social solidarity all distressed them. Some saw that their own youthful misconceptions contributed to these disasters. It took the shock of 1914–18 to question naïve confidence that Republican patriotism and international peace were easily reconcilable. Many had accepted France's 'civilising' mission, viewing emancipation of Arabs from Islamic superstition as equivalent to spreading secular education to 'backward' Breton peasants. Some admitted that by educating village children they had encouraged them to seek careers in the cities, thereby unwittingly accelerating a rural exodus which undermined the vitality of village communities. They were not the arrogant sectarians of Catholic legend. Few had believed that education could

Social origins of primary school teachers

	Peasant	Petty-Bourgeois	Artisan	Working-class
Ozoufs' survey (4000)	15%	33%	17%	13%
Sample of 620 in ENs				
(1840–70)	27%	34%	25%	
Vosges (1862–92)	61%	28%		
Manche (1883–4)	53%	28%	3.4%	
Manche (1900)	28%	10%	34%	

Note: It is difficult to compare local studies. Some group shopkeepers with artisans, others place them with minor *fonctionnaires*. Some have separate sections for children of teachers.

create a utopia. They were aware of their own limited cultural capital and of the obstacles posed by insensitive bureaucratic superiors, clerical opponents and non-malleable pupils. Most repudiated the far-Left critique that they were agents of social control – remoulding popular culture so that conformist masses would accept capitalist hierarchies and fit smoothly into prescribed roles in the labour force. They felt gratitude to their own teachers and parents who had made real sacrifices both to educate them and for the cause of popular education. Because the school could not *unilaterally* construct a brave new world, this did not mean that it played no useful role. Children could be taught core values of solidarity, fraternity and social justice. They could and should be taught to be self-reliant, critical, to know their rights but accept their social duties. Only a schooled people could be a free people (Ozouf and Ozouf 1992).

It would be churlish to deny these teachers' sincerity or real achievements. There is a stark contrast between the arrogant Prussian teachers, seeking to inculcate loyalty to the *Kaiserreich*, portrayed by German workers' autobiographies and the *instituteurs* affectionately evoked by their French counterparts. The latter were portrayed as overworked, under-resourced, struggling to cope with large classes. But they were fundamentally decent, committed to instilling democratic values and encouraging children to think. Even future Communists viewed the humble *instituteur* not as an agent of bourgeois social control but as a man of the people genuinely attempting – in a Europe still dominated by authoritarianism – to nurture a democratic people prepared to live in a world freed of Kings and priests (Maines 1995). As oral testimonies make clear, many teachers came from families for whom the Republican heritage was 'lived' as part of an ongoing struggle for popular emancipation. They came from peasant, petty bourgeois, artisanal and, to a lesser extent, working-class backgrounds.

Most came from villages and small towns, possibly because urban artisans often took technical courses and sought careers as foremen or industrial cadres. Children of minor civil servants and white-collar workers were more prominent in training colleges in the Midi than the North; 95 per cent of their parents were literate in a period when overall literacy rates were around 80 per cent, and 28 per cent of their fathers had received some post-primary schooling. Having a teacher – with 'white hands', guaranteed salary and pension – in the family was perceived as a symbol of social promotion and status. Pas-de-Calais miners viewed teaching as a chance for a son to escape the 'hell' of the pit. Illiterate parents often exhibited valued education as offering offspring a chance to avoid the frustrations of their own lives. Some possessed prized copies of books – Walter Scott, Hugo – and had been delighted when their children read these aloud to them. Village and small-town artisans felt passionately that the Republic could be a 'people's Republic' – long-promised, often postponed. As many as 30 per cent of teachers in the Ozoufs' oral history sample had relatives in teaching. Their 'piety' towards the school was intensified by a sense of affinity with struggles of older generations – grandfathers purged after 1848, uncles disciplined for informing the *curé* that the doctrine of the Immaculate Conception was nonsense! Of the same sample, 47 per cent viewed teaching as a 'calling', an 'apostolate'. One dedicated his own career to the memory of his own Breton *instituteur* who 'had witnessed the birth of the laic school (which) was incarnated in him. He bequeathed the best of himself, concern for a job well done, a social and civic sense, a scrupulous respect for the convictions of others'. Former *institutrices* eulogised their own fathers – teachers who had scrupulously treated daughters as equals and encouraged them to take up the career. Family traditions and personal experiences nurtured their conviction that the Republic, for all its faults, could be a regime of social progress. Popular education was the path to popular Enlightenment; 48 per cent admitted an interest in politics, yet 'apolitical' *institutrices* noted that 'of course' (*évidemment*) they were Republicans. They admired a 'socialism' of mutual aid and solidarity identified with the 'fraternity' of 1789 and incarnated in the generosity of spirit of Jean Jaurès, who had 'come from the bourgeoisie to the people' and was the laic teachers' champion. Their political views were shaped by formative years at their *École Normale*, where discussions about the threat to the Republic posed by the Dreyfus crisis broadened their horizons.

Anti-clericalism – ideological and 'professional' – was a key component of their coherent cultural universe. Only 11 per cent described themselves as Catholic, 38 per cent as 'freethinkers'. Many, with 'melancholy resignation', had submitted to a church marriage to avoid offending their wider family or 'scandal' for their school. Rejecting assertions that there could be no morality without God, they insisted that there could be no civic morality without laic education. Religion had once played a civilising role, Christ was a 'great man' with fine ideals. Religion gave some 'poetry' to existence. But it was now 'science' that explained the universe. Their 'laic faith' comprised a belief in universal, humanistic values and social justice. If only 6 per cent confessed to being masons, 22 per cent expressed positive views of freemasonry which championed the laic school and encouraged intellectual debate in small towns. Some anti-clericalism stemmed from family traditions, some from personal experiences of being taught by religious orders who had sought to stifle pupils' intellectual curiosity. But it often derived from professional experiences – from the endless 'war of pin-pricks' to which they had been subjected. In the Vendée, an *institutrice* might be unable to find a horse-and-cart to transport her from the station or a midwife to deliver her baby. Stones were hurled at her windows by unseen but pious hands. Sharecroppers faced eviction for daring to send children to her school. Catholic *institutrices* in 'clerical' villages felt driven to adopt a fiercely laic stance to defend the Republican school. A few had made provocative gestures of defiance, playing the *Marseillaise* on the violin during religious processions! But most in clerical areas sought to compromise with local opinion – even if this felt like 'a sort of treason towards oneself' (Ozouf and Ozouf 1992).

Poor material conditions and a lowly place in the education hierarchy led some teachers to espouse Left-wing views which led to conflict with the Republican administration. Despite salary increases in 1889, incomes remained modest. By 1914 a mature male teacher could earn 2500 francs per year, 70 per cent of the salary of a junior sub-lieutenant. Those resisting teachers' trade-union demands pointed to their 'privileges' – pensions, job-security, holidays. Teachers ridiculed talk of their 'leisure'. Class sizes could exceed sixty. Schools were often damp or airless. Levels of stress were high, headaches and respiratory complaints endemic. However, it was their sub-ordination which they most resented. Appointed by prefects on the recommendation of inspectors, teachers were vulnerable to transfer on political grounds. They might, like the eponymous hero of the novel *Jean Coste*, be required to 'deliver' votes for a local politician to secure promotion. Young teachers were subject to surveillance by school directors who imposed specific teaching methods or counted the chalk stubs. Faced with irate Catholic fathers who viewed the laic school as an abomination – and whose children were offered gold medals by *La Croix* for burning textbooks – it was not reassuring to be warned by 'moderate' Republican politicians to 'avoid politics' and to ask oneself if 'one single father could refuse to approve what you are saying were he present in your classroom'. When 'peasants treat us like thieves and *curés* like atheists, Jews and corrupters of youth', beleaguered teachers expected firmer backing!

Ministers denied that teachers were 'workers' with rights under the 1884 trade-union Act. '*Amicales*' were encouraged – anodyne socio-cultural associations patronised by prefects and school inspectors which raised salary issues as matters for debate within the 'great Republican family'. When teachers demanded a genuine trade-union, governments resorted to threats. Teachers' class identity was ambiguous. Yet modest Left-ish sympathies, low salaries and work-related grievances generated some affinities with the labour movement. A 1905 manifesto asserted that 'having taught the children of the people in the daytime, we wish to join the men (sic!) of the people in the evening'. Inspired by syndicalism, some urged rebellion against bourgeois Republicans who wanted them to teach workers' children to submit to the new God, Capital. The union newspaper *L'École Émancipée* moved beyond issues of wages and condition and 'administrative tyranny' to demand 'democratic rights'. It denounced the official history syllabus as an apologia for bourgeois individualism, militarism and social hierarchy. School inspectors stifled innovative teaching methods, hence an alternative pedagogy was needed to stimulate pupils' creativity and critical independence. The government whipped up press hysteria against militants – portrayed as unrepresentative of that mass of teachers selflessly devoted to developing France's 'priceless national capital', the minds of her young. Teachers were not 'workers' and had no 'rights' to unionise or to question the national consensus. Educational expenditure – 261 million francs per year – was a 'budget of national defence' to produce literate and patriotic conscripts. It should not be squandered on antimilitarists, allied to CGT 'anarchists', bent on corrupting the young. Most teachers remained loyal to the *Amicales*. Village teachers involved in local battles against clericalism found issues raised by militants largely irrelevant. Most of the Ozoufs' respondents joined the union after 1918, arguing that it had been tactically unwise to demand one before 1914 since this soured relations with the administration, alienated more timorous teachers and played into the hands of the laic school's enemies. Lyonnais union activists were teachers whose fathers were silk-weavers or militants in railway workshops whose identification with organised labour was a matter of filial piety. Yet even they were hesitant about strikes and conceded that for all its faults the Republican school was preferable to its rival. Had not Jaurès himself proclaimed workers would be emancipated 'only through the *école laïque*, the school of progress and reason'? (Ozouf and Ozouf 1992; Feeley 1989).

The 'contradictions' of the Republican school were peculiarly acute for women teachers, of whom there were 55,000 by 1906. They were lauded as dedicated professionals. *École Normale* training provided them with skills superior to those of nuns who taught catechism and sewing. Their mission was to challenge Catholic domination of girls' education and train future Republican wives and mothers to nurture democratic citizens. Only monarchies wished to see children's heads filled with superstitions, prejudices and mystical ramblings. Radical-feminist Madeleine Pelletier saw *institutrice* as symbolising rejection of assumptions that 'a woman could never know too little', as subversive of accepted gender stereotypes. Nevertheless, their status and conditions of employment were scarcely those of emancipated women. At the bottom of a gendered hierarchy they were vulnerable to the whims of male superiors. They were paid 20 per cent less than male teachers. The handful of female inspectors were resented by some male teachers who viewed such posts as one of the rare chances of promotion available to them. Female inspectors were, allegedly, too 'emotional' to make dispassionate assessments, too 'fragile' to tour the villages, too 'gentle' to impose requisite discipline. Their defenders retorted that 'female' sensitivity gave them empathy with the problems of young *institutrices*. Female training colleges were run like secular convents. Pupils wore drab uniforms. Their recreation consisted of supervised Sunday walks through deserted streets of small towns where colleges were located. Talking in dormitories was banned. There were signs of covert resistance by the girls to the austere regime imposed upon them. Illicit love-letters were smuggled out of college – and fashionable clothes and make-up smuggled in! (Gemie 1995; Clarke 1989).

Institutrices were expected to be competent but not pedantic 'bluestockings', smart but not 'fashionable' in dress, firm yet gentle, zealous yet docile, 'feminine' yet sexless. Their 'natural' maternal instincts were invoked to explain their empathy with children. They were urged to 'love' pupils 'like a mother' – without showing 'excessive' affection. After the cloistered environment of training college, the difficulties of the job came as a shock. *Curés* kept them under surveillance, complaining to the authorities if they wore fashionable clothes, took walks alone or exchanged letters with men. As 'outsiders' and 'professional' women they were viewed with suspicion in village culture. Marriage to a fellow teacher could provide psychological support but, despite the introduction of maternity leave in 1910, combining career and family was difficult, not least because of the problem of finding posts for husband and wife in the same commune. *Institutrices* often 'infantilised' relationships with school inspectors, making fulsome gestures of 'gratitude' for their 'paternal' concern. Applications for transfers cited 'natural' desires as loyal daughters to be close to ageing parents. By acting as 'helpless' females seeking compassion, they failed to develop a discourse of women's independence. Their ambiguous identity, neither conventionally 'feminine' nor yet accepted as 'professional', imposed emotional strains. Though most remained politically cautious, some were dragged willy-nilly into village conflicts and used, perhaps internalised, Republican rhetoric. In time the creation of a corps of women teachers did pave the way for a female professional identity. An embryonic 'feminist' awareness of the 'contradictions' of their position did develop. They were agents of a 'progressive' Republic which denied to them the vote which it conceded to bigoted Catholic *pères de famille*. Only a few followed activists like Hélène Bron into feminist organisations. Yet the Ozoufs' interviewees admired Communarde Louise Michel and confessed to a surge of pride at news of the first female doctors. Although more co-opted into the Republican project than really 'liberated', their experiences had some long-term emancipatory potential (Ozouf and Ozouf 1992).

Schooling and gender roles
Successive regimes favoured separate girls' schools and sought to inculcate specific gender roles. Most Republicans viewed 'female liberation' as freeing girls from the clutches of 'obcurantist' nuns – and did not present the *institutrice* as the model of an emancipated career woman. Republican textbooks maintained their precursors' emphasis on training girls for domestic duties. A schoolmistress's goal, claimed one 1840 manual, was to produce 'the Christian, respectful child, the virtuous woman, the faithful spouse, the tender but not weak mother and the thrifty housewife'. By deleting 'Christian' one could insert this sentence into a Republican textbook of 1890. The orphaned heroine of Marie-Robert Holt's *Suzette* – which sold two million copies after 1890 – selflessly cooks and cleans for her father and brothers to hold the family together after her mother's death. The hero of Zulma Carraud's *Maurice ou le Travail* (1855) uses the Tour de France to hone skills learned from his wheelwright father, prospers through hard work and serves his village as deputy-mayor. A companion volume, *Jeanne ou le Devoir*, locates the 'duty' of its peasant heroine within the family. While working as a farm-servant Jeanne, through her moral example, reforms her employer's wanton daughter. Once she becomes a selfless wife and mother she avoids employment outside the home. Women, such texts insist, have duties to diffuse 'new' values – hygiene, literacy, awareness that 'time is money' – while upholding 'good old virtues' of respect and deference. Carraud's explicitly Christian textbooks were phased out after 1890. But her Republican successors propagated similar values. Alice Marie Céleste warned her little readers that

'a woman with no taste for household duties cannot long remain virtuous'. The eponymous heroine of *Cécile* opens a family savings account, persuades her son to fulfil his military service and her husband to refuse to join a strike. A survey of 76 textbooks found not one girl going on to secondary school. Of six references to female suffrage, five are hostile (Clarke 1984). Textbooks thus offered a consistent, prescriptive ideology which doubtless had some impact. Analysis of pupils' exercise books suggests why inspectors were confident that pupils were imbibing 'correct' values. Emulating the 'qualities of a man', girls wrote, could only spread unhappiness. Cleanliness was 'the wealth of the poor'. Girls claimed to enjoy sewing because it was useful to their families. Amidst this plethora of worthiness, one's heart warms to the girl who drew the moral lesson from the late arrival in class of a fellow pupil who tended her family's cows that 'work is the mother of all vices'! (Strumhinger 1983).

The influence of such indoctrination on actual gender attitudes is difficult to determine. Peasant families had ways of inculcating gender roles which owed little to schools or bourgeois ideology. Hélias derived many of his values from his peasant grandfather. Boys learned tool-making by copying male relatives, while their sisters were learning to sew and tend farmyard animals. Misogynist proverbs – 'Women stay at home like cats, men take to the streets like dogs'; 'Run-around wife, cold soup' – both reflected and reinforced gender roles within the family economy. Yet peasant and working-class parents must have been puzzled by schools' attempts to preach a domesticity which bore no relation to the actual working lives of thousands of young women in mill towns, 'sweated' industry or peasant farms. France had a higher percentage of women in the workplace than any of her European neighbours. Some girl pupils questioned the relevance of the ideology fed to them by school textbooks. Peasant suspicions about schools and teachers, persisting into the 1980s according to one study of the Auvergne, may have been confirmed by the 'unrealistic' visions of their future lives presented to girl pupils (Reed-Donahay 1996; Heywood 1991). Where textbooks did discuss female employment they emphasised 'traditional' workers – seamstresses, servants, lace-makers. Yet increasingly girls used school qualifications to secure jobs in the tertiary sector as postal employees, typists, clerks – even as teachers! Girls made up 29 per cent of those securing the CEP in 1877, 46 per cent by 1906. By 1910, girls comprised 40 per cent of pupils at *Écoles Primaires Supérieures*. Yet in their concern to perpetuate the domesticity myth, schools wilfully ignored their own contribution to equipping girls for new types of employment (Alaimo 1994; Chapoulie 1992).

Schooling and linguistic and cultural integration

Weber presented a model of belated but unilinear linguistic and cultural change in which schools imposed French language on peripheral regions after 1870. History and civics lessons conveyed explicative and mobilising 'myths' – and encouraged a selective amnesia – to persuade children that they were 'French' and should be proud to be so. Abbé Grégoire's 1790 survey found six million speaking no French and a further sixteen million 'bi-lingual' – using patois among family and friends. In 1863, 11 per cent could still speak no French and 39 per cent could write none. The Guizot Law demanded teaching in French, though in practice teachers used some patois to make themselves understood. Viewing French as the language of Voltaire, clergy championed patois culture to shield 'their' peasants from corrosive secularist values and the lure of the cities. For the elderly, the poor and women patois culture appeared familiar, 'natural', reassuring. It was part of one's identity and met pragmatic daily needs. There were others – the young, migrants, those involved in market activities – who valued French as the language of 'progress'. The balance tilted towards French in Burgundy by 1840, in larger villages around Toulouse before 1860. By the 1900s Breton parents, despite their attachment to the 'old ways', were sufficiently concerned for their children's prospects to acquiesce to the teaching of French in the schools. Parents might converse in patois but speak French to their children. Patois was appropriate to talk about the weather or farming, but French became the language of public discourse and abstract debate. The Provençal *Félibrige* movement was one of many attempts to preserve – or revive – regional cultures. But Mistral's 'purified' literary Provençal was incomprehensible to Midi peasants.

Teachers supported the spread of French. Some later apologised for their naïve, youthful support for France's colonial 'civilising mission' and the cultural arrogance implicit in assumptions that francophone education would 'rescue' Arabs from backwardness – but few perceived spreading French to peripheral regions as 'internal colonialism'. They saw difficulties involved as largely technical and pedagogic. Some who taught in Brittany were proud of knowing no Breton, sharing Grégoire's assumption that patois were 'coarse idioms which (merely) prolong the infancy of reason and the old-age of prejudice'. Children had the right of access to a language which permitted rational thought and communication and which expanded career prospects. Yet policies and practice were rather more nuanced and complex than is sometimes recognised. Republican education officials conceded that the best way to nurture sentiments of national identity might be to begin by encouraging love of the local *pays*, the *petite patrie*. Geography lessons might begin with local topography, agriculture and flora and fauna. *Instituteurs* who taught in their native region dabbled as local historians or folktale collectors. One 'message' of the classic textbook *Tour de France par deux Enfants* was that France comprised countless diverse, yet mutually complementary, *petits pays*. And linguistic policy was actually flexible in practice. In 1873, Collège de France professor M. Bréal argued that failure to use patois as a vehicle for teaching French would delay pupils' assimilation of the national language. Although neither government nor school inspectors officially adopted his proposals, teachers – who recalled their own struggles at school to learn French – got pupils to recite verbs in both French and patois. Inspectors tacitly condoned this approach. Some teachers were active in the Breton folklore movement or in Mistral's *Félibrige*. It is ironic that by the 1920s the Republican school, which began with a mission to assimilate the peasantry into 'modern' urban culture, was itself becoming a bulwark of France's threatened rustic cultures – with village schools establishing little museums to preserve local folkways! (Chanet 1996; Ozouf and Ozouf 1992).

The process of linguistic integration proved less rapid than Weber suggested. In Windhoek (Pas-de-Calais) the retreat of Flemish was a protracted process which slowed in the decades after 1860. Flemish-speaking villages fell from 105 to 80 between 1806 and 1930, but more than half of this decline had occurred by 1856. This 'cultural conservatism' occurred not in some remote economic backwater but in an area of flourishing market agriculture producing wheat, sugar-beet and tobacco, with good communications. However, many of its economic and cultural ties were with Belgium. Thousands of Belgian migrant labourers came in each year and there was much cross-border investment, trade and smuggling. Laic teachers faced an uphill task in a region with the highest percentage of Catholic pupils in France. Even Flemish-speaking teachers were instructed by inspectors not to use the language in class. But successive bishops encouraged clergy to give catechism classes in Flemish – 'language of Heaven'. Catholic resistance to the Ferry laws created problems for *instituteurs*. In one village eight teachers requested transfers in two years! There was more to the Republican school's integrationist strategy than just its linguistic agenda. Teachers enjoyed some success with history lessons in which, in line with the model proposed by Lavisse, a 'constructed memory' of a seamless national past of heroes – from Clovis to the giants of 1789 – was invented. The laic school benefited from outside factors – the influence of the barracks on Flemish conscripts, awareness that wages were higher in France than in Flemish areas of Belgium, and migration from Windhoek to factory jobs in French-speaking Lille. The Flemish regionalist movement remained socially and culturally elitist and failed to develop a mass base (Baycroft 1995).

However, social anthropologists still identify in rural inhabitants of 'peripheral' regions such as the Auvergne, forms of 'everyday resistance' to alien 'urban', 'French' culture of which the *instituteur* is seen as the representative. Peasant families apparently comply with school requirements, even encourage children to acquire skills like bookkeeping useful to family farms. But they remain fearful that if children imbibe the school's ethos they will aspire to 'too much' education and leave the village for the city. Geographical and social mobility is thus viewed as a 'threat' to the survival of the family economy and of the community. Hence family culture encourages children to view teachers as outsiders – to be treated with suspicion and tricked with ruses (Reed-Donahay 1996).

Two cheers for the *École Laïque*?

How should one evaluate the impact of the Republican school? In a Europe where traditional elites and clergy remained all too powerful, did it help to 'root' democratic values – making the peasantry and petty bourgeoisie more resistant than their counterparts elsewhere to the lure of clerical and, later, Fascist parties? The zeal with which the Vichy regime hounded 'masonic' teachers may be a testament to the school's 'progressive' credentials. Did not peasants and workers – even Left-wing militants suspicious of Republican patriotism – express gratitude for the dedication shown by humble teachers to their task of 'educating the people'? Was not the school-house the civic monument to the Third Republic? Or was the project seriously flawed and ultimately ill-equipped to prepare its pupils for the harsh realities of the twentieth century?

Teachers accepted Hugo's dictum that only an educated people could be truly free. They were proud and moved when former pupils recalled lessons on civic duty and social responsibility which had stayed with them into their adult lives. Their teaching methods were more effective than those of their predecessors. In the Doubs, where mass schooling and literacy had been achieved before 1880, the Ferry laws did little to boost attendance, and child labour and truancy persisted. But there was less mechanical rote-learning and greater efforts made to get children to reason and to capture their attention through imaginative use of stories. Teachers attended *conférences pédagogiques*, subscribed to pedagogic journals, and discussed innovative methods for improving literacy. They took children on trips, held classes in the woods, even portrayed the classroom as a miniature self-governing Republic (Gavoille 1986). However, the system's weaknesses have been analysed by M. Crubellier (1993), who suggests that a simplified version of elite culture was being 'passed down' in an effort to eradicate 'undesirable' elements of popular culture. This project was doubly problematic. 'Elite culture' was, itself, an (uneasy) amalgam of Catholicism, humanism, Enlightenment rationalism and positivism. An effort was made to 'freeze' a cultural consensus at a moment of rapid cultural and technological change. Inevitably this was outflanked by the mass commercialised culture of popular newspapers, cheap novels, advertisements and, later, of cinema and radio. One academic inspector claimed that school would 'lead the child from savagery – the savagery of all primitive peoples – to the one, true Civilisation, that of the West, which is close to its zenith'. The multiple arrogance of this statement derives, Crubellier observes, from its simultaneous contempt for popular culture, its 'Orientalist' dismissal of non-European cultures, its blithe assumption of a single 'Western culture' and its myopia about the new 'mass' culture. Schooling could produce cultural dislocation and loss. 'Old' time had been polychronic – that of the annual work-cycle, the liturgical year, seasonal *fêtes*. 'Modern' time was set by clocks, railway-timetables. It was a 'commodity' to be 'spent' not 'wasted'. Peasants had called the river 'Aude' – not *the* Aude – as though it were a person with qualities. They had measured lengths in 'thumbs', distances in terms of 'a day's travel'. Maps now de-personalised the landscape and the metric system standardised distances. French became the sole vehicle of rational discourse. 'In France the language of the people is *incorrect*', insisted one school Inspector. 'We will not tolerate anything radically contrary to the rules of language and we will begin the process of correction as soon as we receive the child from the hands of its mother.' Yet 'school French' remained a foreign tongue, mastered only in a stilted, wooden fashion. Letters sent home by Midi conscripts suggest how difficult it was for them to use French to express emotion or intimacy. Books used in class were often mediocre. Most who left school at thirteen abandoned reading or read mainly *romans feuilletons*. Loans of 'serious' books from Doubs school libraries were stagnant in the years before 1914.

The philosophical basis of the 'good old morality of our forefathers' – recommended by Ferry as the foundation of civic morality – was left unexplored.

Christ remained a figure symbolising compassion and peace. When the children in Bruno's *Tour de France* rescue a drowning sailor he promises to do for others what has been done for him. But at the heart of the school's civic ethos was an obsessive work ethic, derived from the liberal-Protestant culture of many Republican leaders. Benjamin Franklin's was quoted, but with emphasis on passages praising industry and thrift, *not* 'American' social mobility. The *Tour de France* textbook is a hymn of praise to *'la France travailleuse'* – with rail stations, factories and ports receiving favourable mention. Yet attitudes to the modern world were ambiguous. The school's discourse favoured the solid virtues and occupational stability of village and *bourg* over the cultural flux of the city. A favoured text was Daudet's *Lettres de mon Moulin*, with its nostalgia for a rustic world that was being lost. Ferry's initial concern with promoting industrial skills was largely forgotten. The 'gaps' in the Republican school's vision of the world remained striking. Rituals surrounding death remained ubiquitous in rural society, yet no one died in a textbook except gloriously for the *patrie*. Churches were absent from the landscape of later editions of Bruno's textbook. There was little place for aesthetics. Art was perceived as dangerous because it had pretensions to access 'mysterious' and 'deeper' truths. The body was suspect as a potential site of hedonism and corruption. Sport, other than quasi-militaristic gymnastics, was largely ignored. Attitudes to 'play' were negative. The teacher was viewed as suppressor of the 'anarchic' mischief of childhood. In L. Pergaud's *La Guerre des Boutons* the schoolchildren conceal their feelings from the teacher and seize every opportunity to pursue their agenda of play. Union activist G. Dumoulin's autobiography evokes an 1880s childhood of truancy and gang-warfare with children from neighbouring pit-villages. Gangs had their own *argot* and codes of honour. Those who 'grassed' to teachers were ostracised. These were not the malleable creatures of educational blueprints. The educational crusade of the 1880s and 1890s occurred against a background of alarm about juvenile delinquency. With school ending at thirteen and apprenticeships in decline, there were real fears that adolescents would be exposed to the lure of commercialised mass culture, 'bad' books and cafes, or to the expanding network of Catholic youth groups. For an 'elite' of the popular classes there were *Écoles Primaires Supérieures*. Laic youth clubs, *Petites Amicales*, were introduced to channel adolescents' energies.

Republican efforts to use school to equip children for the 'modern world' were thus flawed. They did deepen the sense of Republican-patriotic identity which contributed to the cross-class unity which sustained France in the Great War. Yet the carnage turned some teachers into inter-war pacifists. In retrospect many teachers were uneasy at their role in transferring 'sacrality' from religion to *patrie*, from saints to national heroes. They were made queasy by Lavisse's exhortation to pupils 'let us make our wishes together – I *was going to say* "Let us pray together"' – that France remain strong amongst nations, by force of arms if necessary'. In provincial France in 1880 the laic school may, indeed, have appeared a vehicle for democracy and modernity. Yet whatever the subjective sincerity of the convictions of many teachers, the worldview projected by the school system soon appeared distinctly quaint faced with the harsh 'realities' of the twentieth-century world (Crubellier 1993).

Reading and popular culture

There was no consensus about the implications of the spread of print-culture which resulted from schooling and the advent of mass literacy. Catholics hoped that with firm guidance literate peasants could be kept in line by the pious literature churned out by religious publishers. But they feared that cheap editions of Voltaire and pornographic 'bad books' were flooding into the villages, 'poisoning' popular culture and swelling the ranks of the undeferential and the criminal. Liberals shared fears about sensationalist, immoral or subversive *romans feuilletons* and were alarmed by the cultural deprivation of migrants to cities. They hoped that subsidised cheap editions of simplified versions of classic texts and 'improving' literature and provision of carefully monitored municipal and school libraries, might 'moralise' the people. Labour activists approved aspects of the liberal project – applauding Guizot's Act, if critical of his wider political agenda. Radical craftsmen were often puritanical autodidacts, sharing bourgeois distaste for Rabelaisean aspects of popular culture. Many socialist militants, however critical of Ferry's Imperialist projects, praised the Republican school for widening popular cultural horizons. However, there were dissidents on the Left who claimed that the school sought to inculcate bourgeois values by offering simplified, selective, hand-me-down extracts from 'high' culture. There were healthy components of popular culture which workers should not abandon. Folksongs, *fêtes* and café sociability were vital to living communities. Pelloutier's project for the syndicalist *Bourses du Travail* envisaged labour nurturing its own culture of skilled work, establishing its own libraries and cultural space (Lyons 2001).

Radicals hoped that literacy, by broadening access to knowledge, would underpin democratic citizenship. The credulousness, insularity and brutality of the countryside would be eroded and the cultural deprivation of the industrial towns alleviated. What actually emerged, pessimists argued, was a 'mass' culture dominated by sensationalist newspapers and cheap *romans feuilletons*. Popular readers were fed a diet of crime, sensational *faits divers*, serialised pulp romance and adventure and crime fiction, fostering a culture of escapism, conformity and xenophobia. The 'masses' were 'culturally integrated', but into the values of a corrupt consumer capitalism. Such a reading of popular culture may be too monolithic. Cultural theorists claim that popular audiences 'appropriate' the products of mass culture in ways which may subvert the conformist ideology of those who produce them.

Before 1789, *Almanach* stories about brigands like Mandrin nurtured fascination with 'Robin Hood' figures that defied seigneurs. Printed literature was already widely available. Peasants and artisans possessed didactic *Lives of Saints*, La Fontaine fables and lives of heroes – a genre boosted by hagiographic books on Napoleon which disseminated the Bonapartist myth after 1815. Almanachs combined agricultural tips, astrological forecasts and stories of knights, princesses and dragons. These might be read aloud in *veillées*, though much story-telling was oral. Works of coarse humour such as mock-sermons represented a Rabelaisean strand in the popular cultural repertoire, though produced by educated authors plagiarising pagan classics. *Colporteurs* from the Pyrenees, who disseminated this material, found their main markets in culturally 'intermediate' regions of central and south-eastern France – not the 'backward' West or the 'advanced' East. Alarm at the spread of radical propaganda led to tighter controls on *colportage* after 1849. The advent of the rotary press, declining printing and publishing costs, rising school attendance and literacy and the advent of the railway, which distributed published materials and provided retail outlets at station kiosks, made the 1850s a watershed decade for dissemination of print-culture. The real price of Paris-published newspapers fell 20 per cent between 1851 and 1870, then a further 40 per cent by 1889. *Le Petit Journal*, launched in 1863, was selling 1.4 million copies by 1914. Press baron Soubeyron – a *Crédit Foncier* director – had financial interests in 64 dailies. Worried by the diet of crime trials and serialised pulp-fiction offered to readers of the mass-press, conservative and Republican elites sought to impose their cultural agendas. Catholic publisher Hachette multiplied its output of pious novels. The *Ligue de l'Enseignement* sponsored *Bibliothèques Populaires* and 'useful' literature to promote technical skills and civic values. Yet ironically the real consolidation of bourgeois hegemony came precisely through that mass press of which the elites were so dismissive. Escapist and conformist trivia fed to its readership did much more to remould popular culture in line with the values of emerging consumer capitalism than any number of earnest moralising tracts (Lyons 2001; Crubellier 1993).

A petty-bourgeois audience for *romans feuilletons* had emerged in the 1830s with the serialisation of novels in *La Presse*, the use of advertising revenue of which enabled them to cut prices and boost circulation. By 1900 this audience had swelled enormously. Women readers favoured love stories and historical romances, men favoured *romans policiers*. Women cut out, sewed together and bound serial episodes, swapping these with neighbours who subscribed to a different paper. The tone of this literature was conformist and escapist. Socialist papers encouraged politically conscious *feuilletons*, but radical authors showed little flair for the genre. The growing conservatism of the petty bourgeoisie was reflected in their taste for *revanchiste*, vaguely antisemitic novels. Most novels were depressingly banal in style and dubious in ideology, set in a Manichean world where heroines seek lost children while evading the clutches of evil seducers before finally marrying handsome, upper-class paternalists. Others featured a gallery of arrogant Germans, oily Latin Americans, savage or childlike blacks and sinister Arabs scheming against heroic legionnaires. This last stereotype, perpetuated in inter-war French cinema, helped instill an unthinking popular acceptance of colonialism (Thiesse 1984).

Yet the spread of print culture also nurtured dissent. In Weber's model peasants are passive recipients of the forces of modernisation – either the pawns of strategies of cultural integration or involved in 'archaic' resistance to these. Absent from such analysis are independent, semi-autonomous popular 'uses of literacy'. These could be pragmatic and utilitarian. In his autobiography, Allier peasant H. Norre thanks the school which gave him the skills needed to fill notebooks with 'useful' information – copied from newspapers – on hygiene, horticulture, fertilisers and estimating the weight of a bull from a few simple measurements of its dimensions! Norre was a founder member of a village *Syndicat Agricole*. Conservative fears that literacy might undermine deference were not entirely fanciful. In the 1860s the sub-prefect of Bourges lamented the diffusion of 'Hugo, Sue, Sand . . . and a series of more or less useless books'. Many *instituteurs* recalled borrowing novels of Zola from teachers, which expanded their youthful horizons. An interviewee in Thiesse's (1984) study of popular reading recalls how, as a young worker in Marseilles, he devoured papers and *romans feuilletons* but also his parents' bound school copies of Hugo and, eventually, anarchist pamphlets and books on Esperanto! One Cévenol teacher achieved a miniature 'cultural revolution' by loaning villagers copies of Tolstoy! Although Republicanism became part of the 'establishment', in regions still dominated by Royalist landowners or authoritarian industrialists 'the Republic' retained overtones of dissidence. In Guillaumin's *La Vie d'un Simple* the illiterate old sharecropper takes a Republican paper as a gesture of defiance against his landowner – and has pleasure in hearing his son, educated in the laic school, read it aloud to him. It is in the context of such experiences that one can appreciate why many labour militants continued to identify with the *école laïque* (Thiesse 1984; Lyons 2001).

Secondary and higher education

Extention of primary schooling was justified by reference to the needs of an emerging democratic society. Yet access to post-primary education expanded scarcely at all in the early Third Republic. Historiographical debate has focused on two questions. Just how elitist was the system? And which strata of a highly diverse elite had their values, priorities and interests most strongly reflected within secondary and higher education?

An elitist system?
By mid-century many agreed, reluctantly, with Tocqueville's insistence that the march towards 'democracy' was now inexorable. Privileges of rank and birth were declining, deference eroding, the franchise had been extended and literacy was expanding. Even semi-authoritarian Bonapartism, as Royalist notables lamented, flirted with 'vulgar', populist practices. Yet precisely *because* the masses now had access to politics and because reading and writing were no longer accomplishments confined to the elites, cultural distinctions and barriers appeared all the more necessary. To safeguard 'culture' against 'American' mass mediocrity required preservation of educational distinctions. 'The more elementary education is disseminated . . . amongst the poorest classes, the greater the need to maintain an aristocracy of intelligence', insisted Orleanist Education Minister Villemain. Many moderate Republicans agreed with Taine that only educational distinctions could prevent a disastrous 'levelling down'. The *École Libre des Sciences Politiques* was established to train a cohort of technocrats to guide the new Republic. Even Gambetta emphasised the need to keep decision-making from the 'immature' masses.

The *culture générale* of the *lycées*, which emphasised classics, philosophy, rhetoric and linguistic nuances, was designed to furnish elites with a 'cultural capital' distinct from that of their 'inferiors', whose education favoured the mechanical and the instrumental. One analysis of secondary-school prize-day speeches detects a gradual increase in references to 'meritocracy' and the need for science qualifications to compete in the modern world. The culture heroes of some French conservatives became Yankee businessmen rather than British gentry. Yet there remained an emphasis on qualities of 'taste'. Alarm was expressed at threats to classical education from modernity. The sub-text was that though France appeared to be falling behind cruder, brasher industrial rivals like Germany or the USA, its prestige as a Great Power rested on its higher levels of general culture. One significant, if apparently trivial, example of the importance accorded to the curriculum is the role of 'school grammar' in secondary education. Its inventor, 'grammarian-entrepreneur' Chapsal, purchased a château with profits from his textbooks! Enlightenment grammarians had wrestled with issues such as the logic of grammatical structure. Chapsal's concerns were 'correct' spelling and formulation of increasingly byzantine, abstruse grammatical rules. 'School grammar' was obsessed with clause composition and codification of parts of speech. English elites were identifiable by their class accent, their French counterparts by mastery of grammatical phrases and complex, formulaic public rhetoric. Use of the subjunctive became the functional equivalent of polite table manners – a badge of membership of the bourgeoisie. Grammatical hegemony underpinned class power (Cherval 1978).

Attempts to widen access to post-primary schooling, in the name of democratic or meritocratic principles, aroused alarm at 'threats' from 'overeducated' *déracinés* with thwarted career ambitions. *Écoles Primaires Supérieures* were invented by Guizot to divert children of the popular classes away from secondary education. Carnot's career was cut short in 1848 because his plans for meritocratic entry to secondary education outraged conservatives. Duruy insisted that it was absurd and dangerous to have peasants' sons reciting – badly – Greek verbs. His 'special' technical schools were designed to channel pupils of modest social origins away from *lycées*. *Écoles des Arts et Métiers* (EAMs) had been set up to provide 'practical' training for petty-bourgeois pupils. A 'revolt' at one of these in 1826 was blamed on its 'lax' syllabus. The education minister insisted that 'insurmountable barriers' must be erected between such pupils and literature and philosophy, suitable only for authentically bourgeois students (Gildea 1983). Elites feared the spectre of an 'excess of educated men'. In 1890, Radical Léon Bourgeois still insisted on restricted access to the *baccalauréat* to avoid 'overcrowding' the professions. During the 1880s depression, 'overeducated', underemployed young men could be found writing cheap *romans feuilletons* and, swelling the ranks of Boulangist, antisemitic or anarchist malcontents. Such anxieties were not new. Bohemian student radicals haunted conservative nightmares in 1848. It cost at least 2000 francs per year for a student to survive in Paris. Inevitably university students were, with rare exceptions, a privileged minority of that already narrow cohort with access to full secondary education. Yet any student unrest in Paris was potentially dangerous. For Paris was, uniquely, the political and administrative centre of a centralised state, Europe's major artisanal city and home to two-thirds of France's higher-education students. Many students struggled to cope on modest parental allowances, augmented by income from tutoring. Many of the 3000 law students in the annual intake had little chance of acquiring a lawyer's practice, a *notaire's cabinet* or a bureaucratic post. As the eponymous hero of Louis Reybaud's *Jérome Paturôt* discovers, nepotism and 'contacts' were essential. Balzac identified frustrated careerism as the factor 'pushing youth towards Republicanism' in the 1846 depression. 'Hooked' on Paris life, reluctant to return to the provinces, they were the potential cadres of revolution. Michelet hoped that the youthful idealism of those whose horizons were broadened by education – and the fact that 'the son of a rich man is not yet himself a property-owner' – might make students agents of political change, culture-brokers between the liberal middle-class and artisans with whom they mingled in Left Bank cafés and *bals populaires*.

Student unrest was endemic during the Restoration, when 'the generation of 1820' was confronted by dismissal of liberal professors and abolition of 'subversive' courses. Students consorted with dissident Bonapartist veterans in Rue Mouffetard bars, sang Béranger songs, applauded Molière's *Tartuffe* and joined Carbonarist secret societies. By the 1830s the image of the radical student had been consolidated. He was bearded, had long hair, wore a cap and a red tie. He despised bourgeois materialism, hypocrisy and corruption, and consorted with working-class girls (*grisettes*). Guizot lamented that such creatures typified the 'deplorable . . . youth pouring out of our *Grandes Écoles*'. Such fears were exaggerated. By 1840 apathy and political conformity were the norm. Many students shared the taste for fashion of Balzac's Rastignac. They spent their leisure time at Right Bank *bals* or frequenting prostitutes (*lorettes*). Their contempt for a 'philistine' bourgeoisie was the ephemeral posing of *fils à papa* soon to be ensconced in provincial law firms, family businesses or bureaucratic careers. A few flirted with reformist politics in 1847–48, but they were marginal to the conflicts of the Second Republic. When a few student radicals attempted to arouse popular resistance to the Bonapartist coup, a quizzical worker responded 'Young bourgeois! Was it your father or your uncle who shot us down in the June Days?' (Caron 1991; O'Boyle 1970; Spitzer 1987) Nevertheless, conservatives retained a stubborn conviction that 'overeducated' *déclassés* were responsible for 1848. Education Minister Fortoul reduced *lycée* scholarships awarded to *instituteurs'* sons. Although a few Blanquist medical students participated in the Commune, socialist novelist Vallès noted bitterly that, as in 1848, Latin Quarter students stood 'on the side of the assassins'.

Access to secondary education was available only to a small minority. Yet there remains some debate as to just how narrowly elitist the system was and about the degree of upward – or lateral – social and occupational mobility which it permitted. Some 2 per cent of boys attended secondary schools in the 1830s, and only 5 per cent by 1914. During the entire nineteenth century only 439,000 candidates passed the *baccalauréat*, of whom 127,000 took the science variant. And it was the *baccalauréat* which remained the passport to higher education, and to bureaucratic, professional and, increasingly, managerial careers, as well as a badge of legitimation of a certain style of bourgeois culture. It has been argued that close scrutiny reveals the system to be less exclusive than such statistics might suggest. Analysis of 27,000 pupils in 1864–65 indicates that 27.7 per cent were sons of petty bourgeois and 12.3 per cent of peasant families. Although fees for boarders were high,

Table A   *Male pupils in secondary education*

	State lycées and colleges	*All secondary pupils*	*% of age cohort 13–18*
1809	51,000		1.67%
1830	33,000		
1850	50,000	119,000	3.75%
1896–1900	89,000	176,000	5.0%

Table B   *Baccalauréat*

	Successful candidates
1820	2000
1840s	3500
1856	4600
1900	6000

Table C   *Secondary pupils per thousand in population*

1830	21
1854	33
1876	41
1910	38

Table D   *University students*

1840s	7000
1870	11,000
1890	17,500
1914	42,000 (women admitted after the 1890s)

those for day-boys were as low as 100 francs in some colleges (Harrigan 1980). Even the exclusive *Lycée Condorcet* drew 20 per cent of its pupils from the petty bourgeoisie; 10 per cent of places were occupied by scholarship pupils, though scholarships often went to notables' sons as election bribes. Was this system more 'open' and accessible to modest social groups than its British or German counterparts, and did it facilitate social mobility? One might argue that Harrigan's statistics are skewed by the omission of exclusive city *lycées* and that he underestimates the bourgeoisie's determination to perpetuate its privileges. Wealth and 'cultural capital' gave middle-class pupils advantages. Very few non-bourgeois pupils took the full lycée syllabus. In most colleges 70 per cent of pupils dropped out by the age of 16. And there was a hierarchy within the *lycée* sector. Douai *lycée* had many bourgeois boarders, that of nearby Condé admitted traders' and peasants' sons. In Brittany those who 'rose' via the *baccalauréat* were mainly sons of 'comfortable' commercial families. Mobility remained 'lateral' or highly circumscribed, with grocers' sons becoming primary teachers, or peasant boys minor *fonctionnaires*. *Lycée* teaching remained a poorly remunerated profession, with modest social prestige; 86 per cent of the 9000 *professeurs* in 1900 came from 'below' the authentic bourgeoisie.

Recruitment to the *École Normale Supériere* (ENS), the training college for university and *lycée* teachers, reveals a pattern of some upward mobility over three generations. Sons of peasant or upper-artisan families became *instituteurs* or employees, and *their* sons secured access to higher education. Yet although the ENS claimed to embody meritocratic Republican ideals, social mobility via education remained very restricted. Gambetta's 1869 promise of free scholarships for 'children of intelligence' remained unfulfilled. Republican discourse replaced references to 'God' who wished the poor to remain in their humble station with 'destiny' – which, apparently, ensured that children followed naturally and happily in parental footsteps. In the 1900s some 4000 pupils per year – 0.5 per cent of the 13-year-old cohort – were 'promoted' to the secondary sector. 'Success stories' like that of Charles Péguy, son of a widowed cane-chair repairer, who won a *lycée* scholarship and entered the ENS, provided a meritocratic veneer to an essentially closed system just sufficiently flexible to allow renewal of elites by assimilation of a thin trickle of 'talent'. The issue of providing a 'ladder' between primary and secondary education, raised by the 1899 Ribot Commission, was not addressed.

However, emphasis on the gulf between 'mass' and 'elite' education may obscure evidence that this was a three-tier system. A diverse, shifting, intermediate sector provided post-primary training for those who could not afford, or did not desire, 'academic' courses. It included *Écoles Primaires Supérieures* (EPSs) and 'special' classes in 'practical' subjects run by *lycées* for those leaving at fifteen. Catholic colleges adapted courses to employers' local needs, attracting pupils for whom *lycées* were too exclusive. EPS pupil numbers trebled to 54,000 between 1880 and 1914 as Republicans wrestled with problems of declining apprenticeships and juvenile delinquency. Some argued that the EPS should offer non-vocational courses in history or literature and encourage pupils to enter teaching or the civil service. Others claimed that pupils should be given spades, chisels and planes, not books, in order to learn to love, rather than flee, manual trades (Gildea 1983; Alaimo 1994).

Education for an industrialising society?

Wilhelmine Germany's industrial success has been attributed to technical high-schools and faculties of applied science, while Britain's relative industrial decline after 1850 has been 'blamed' on the 'seduction' of industrialists' sons by the cultural values of the public schools and Oxbridge – generating contempt for technology and science and aspirations to 'escape' from 'vulgar' business into the City, the professions or colonial administration. A similar model has been suggested for France. Here Napoleon provided the structures for a 'modern' secondary- and higher-education system by establishing a centralised state system, controlled by the *Université*, which drew up syllabuses, set examinations and inspected teaching. State grammar schools (*lycées*) and

	State lycée pupils	Lay private college pupils	Catholic college pupils
1855	48,000 (42%)	40,000 (36%)	25,000 (22%)
1867	65,000 (46%)	41,000 (28%)	36,000 (25%)
1899	82,000 (51%)	10,000 (6%)	68,000 (43%)

colleges prepared pupils for the *baccalauréat*, the prerequisite for entry to university faculties or for the competitive *concours* for the prestigious *Grandes Écoles*. However, it is alleged, this system was concerned to train bureaucrats and army officers. Its ethos was that of 'older' strata of the elites, not of a capitalist class whose hegemony was incomplete. Education was to smoothe the rough edges of sons of *parvenu* businessmen and assimilate them into the rentier class. The most prestigious *lycée* stream was the 'classical' *baccalauréat*, which valued the 'rounded' *honnête homme* with non-utilitarian cultural values. It emphasised verbal games-playing and the ability to pronounce intoxicating rhetorical generalisations. Only 9 per cent of pupils in one Parisian *lycée* in 1860 aspired to a business career. Unsurprisingly some French industrialists were scathing about such a system (Anderson 1971).

In the 1850s, Fortoul introduced a science *baccalauréat*. 1848 had heightened fears about 'overproduction' of arts graduates and Bonapartism's industrialisation projects required more technical cadres. However, Fortoul met resistance from *lycée* teachers, with vested interests in the status quo, and from parents worried that the new qualifications lacked status and that their sons would be regarded as cultural inferiors. Fortoul's problems were compounded by the expansion of Catholic colleges. Before 1848 Catholics complained at the limit of 20,000 pupils imposed on their secondary sector and at *Université* control of syllabus and examinations. In a 'liberal' society, they argued, all had the 'right' to teach. After 1850 bishops were placed in the *Université* and anyone with a *baccalauréat* could open a secondary school. In the wake of the upheavals of 1848, bourgeois parents were persuaded of the virtues of 'faith schools', while free-market ideologists claimed that competition between state and Catholic schools would raise academic standards. Though the initial impetus to the expansion of Catholic colleges was provided by the alliance between Bonapartism and the Church in the 1850s, it was to be sustained for the remainder of the century.

Growth was most rapid in regions with an existing Catholic network – the West, Massif Central, Pas-de-Calais, Lyonnais and Lorraine. In Brittany the only parents loyal to state schools were naval officers, bureaucrats and liberal doctors. Bonapartist officials, alarmed by the *haemorrhage* of pupils, told anecdotes of building contractors warned that commissions from the Cathedral would cease unless they transferred their sons to Catholic colleges. These proved adept at carving out niches in the educational market. Jesuit colleges attracted snobbish, *bien-pensant* bourgeois keen that their sons 'acquire an aristocratic perfume'. At Avignon the liberal bourgeoisie used the *lycée*, Royalist landowners the Jesuit college. Diocesan *petits séminaires* functioned as colleges for sons of petty bourgeois and peasants. Congregational teachers, with no families to support, had modest salaries which allowed Catholic colleges to keep fees low and attract pupils for whom *lycée* fees were prohibitive (Gildea 1983; Padberg 1969).

Even during the 1850s honeymoon between Bonapartism and the Church, ultramontanes did not hide their contempt for the *Université* or their goal of a Catholic educational monopoly. Even liberal Catholic Montalembert said that he would rather his son were taught by a cabin boy than by godless *lycée* professors! Bonapartist officials aimed for a modus vivendi between Church and *Université* – whose ethos, they insisted, was respectful of religion and philosophically eclectic. Most *lycée* professors were cautious conformists eager to prove their respectability. Within *lycées* religion was treated with respect – pupils were taken to Mass and bishops made inspection visits. Yet Catholic ultras resented state control of syllabuses and examinations. Abbé Gaume, Vicar-General of Nevers, campaigned against Greek and Roman 'pagan' classics, the rediscovery of which in the Renaissance had proved a fatal prelude to subsequent disasters of European civilisation – the Reformation and the Enlightenment! Such fanatics were unimpressed when Fortoul clamped down on discussion in *lycée* philosophy lessons, for all philosophical debate engendered scepticism. In a Europe threatened with moral collapse 'scepticism will not save us'. The 'liberal' Mgr Dupanloup banned Voltaire and Molière from his seminary library, and expurgated Racine. Clergy on *Université* committees purged references to Darwin from scientific theses. Unsurprisingly, *lycée* pupils protested that in an era of science and industrial change such absurdities were intolerable. Protestant parents complained when their sons' classes were inspected by bishops and Dijon *lycéens* in 1869 refused to attend Mass (Gerbod 1968). Meanwhile Catholic college pupils lived sheltered lives in 'well-arranged hot-houses with chinks carefully stopped up against modern draughts' (Taine). Critics dismissed them as priggish, self-righteous young men who were suspicious of, and felt superior to, the sinful modern world. Since Catholic teachers had no family responsibilities, they could devote all their energies to their pupils. They took them on excursions and pilgrimages. In contrast to the cerebral emphasis of *lycées*, they aspired to educate the 'whole man' and, like English public schools, saw sport as 'character building'. The impact of Catholic schooling on its pupils alarmed Bonapartist officials who looked to education to reconcile the various segments of a fragmented elite. Rivalries between state and Catholic school pupils escalated, sometimes, as at Auxerre, exploding into physical violence. Anxieties that the Catholic sector was 'stifling' state schools in Brittany were exacerbated when over a hundred former pupils from a single Vannes Catholic college enlisted in the Papal *zouaves* to defend the Temporal Power. Did these youngsters' loyalty lie with Paris – or with Rome? The spectre of *deux jeunesses* – of French youth polarised between the mutually incompatible value systems of two rival school systems – haunted the official mind.

Although *lycées* achieved better overall academic results, families who sent sons to Jesuit or Assomptionist colleges expected examination success which gave access to higher education and the professions. Catholic pupils aspiring to enter St. Cyr officers' college required mathematics and science. Around 20 per cent of *Grandes Écoles* entrants by 1870 were from Catholic colleges. Catholic teachers sought to avoid debate in (compulsory) *baccalauréat* philosophy classes, lest this contaminate pupils' minds with the seeds of scepticism. They provided model answers to be churned out unthinkingly in exams, a practice not altogether unknown in the state sector! Catholic colleges appealed during the Third Republic to conservative parents who suspected *lycées of* encouraging secularist ideologies and 'promiscuous' social mixing. Such stereotypes were cultivated by Right-wing novelists such as Bourget who denounced the disastrous moral and social consequences of the dry, 'godless' positivism allegedly purveyed by *professeurs* in *le lycée corrupteur*. Expansion of the Catholic sector, however well-adapted to the social interests and prejudices of its diverse clientèle, was not helpful to the needs of an industrialising society. *Lycées* were not stimulated to 'modernise' their syllabus by competition from rivals more conservative than themselves. Duruy was inhibited from pushing through *lycée* reform by fears of driving pupils into the Catholic sector. Rivalries between the *Université* and its opponents sapped energies better devoted to more productive activities.

Nevertheless, the supposed 'anti-industrial' ethos of French education has recently been questioned. Fortoul's science *baccalauréat* did find support from businessmen and from parents, and not merely in industrial Mulhouse or Lille. By the 1860s Latin was in decline in Nancy *lycée*, with two-thirds of older pupils taking the science option. Duruy's 1865 *enseignement spécial* was designed to attract businessmen's sons to courses combining modern languages and science. The stereotype of a uniform, centralised system is something of a myth. Education was adapted quite flexibly to meet local demands and economic needs. Gard Protestant businessmen sponsored silk-design classes, courses in chemistry and a mining college. Catholic colleges provided navigation classes in Breton ports and trained pupils for entrance to the *Écoles des Arts et Métiers* (Gildea 1983).

Claims that it was German universities' science faculties that had 'won the war' in 1871 stimulated attempts to restructure French higher education. Until 1860, 85 per cent of students were studying law or medicine. Duruy complained that while 'all of Paris is being reconstructed, Higher Education buildings alone remain in a state of decay'. The Sorbonne science faculty was located in a disused basement. In 1868 the *École des Hautes Études* was established to boost a fragile research culture. Genuine progress was made in scientific and technical education. Parisian colleges were established to train chemists and electrical engineers (1894). Parisian engineering graduates increased 50 per cent to 300 per year between 1900 and 1910. The fastest expansion in higher education occurred in science, technology and social science. Standards in provincial science faculties were high. Grenoble specialised in hydro-electricity research, Nancy in chemistry. Although their emphasis on applied science perpetuated beliefs that such institutions were 'inferior' to 'theoretical' departments in Parisian *Grandes Écoles*, the dynamism of faculties such as Lille – where Pasteur did bacteriological research for local breweries – stemmed from their symbiotic relationship with regional industry. Besançon University laboratories collaborated with Franche-Comté watch-making firms. Toulouse chemistry faculty produced a Nobel prizewinner in 1912, although it remained underfunded and still lacked the prestige of the law faculty (Day 1992). Some cultural and social constraints on 'modernisation' persisted. Duruy's project of 'special' secondary education was designed to attract the clientèle of the *lycées'* special classes and woo the *classes moyennes* away from Catholic colleges without diluting the *lycées' baccalauréat* stream, thereby risking an outflow of bourgeois pupils into the Catholic sector. His goal was a four-year course which could provide practical training for future intermediate *cadres* of industry and commerce. It proved only a qualified success, despite attracting pupils in industrial towns. The *École Normale Spéciale*, established in the former monastery of Cluny, was treated with supercilious condescension by the educational hierarchy and produced more clerks and accountants than industrial technicians (Day 1992; Fox and Weisz 1980).

The role of the *Grandes Écoles* reveals much about the priorities of the education system. The *École Polytechnique* was criticised for recruiting exclusively from the *grande bourgeoisie* – notably pupils from elite Parisian *lycées*. Its syllabus was 'theoretical' and it favoured examinations over research. Its graduates, destined for careers in the army and the upper bureaucracy, shunned provincial industry. The prestige of the *Grandes Écoles*, which attracted 3000 high-quality applicants for 800 places in 1880, contributed to the neglect of provincial faculties. And yet was it not significant that the most prestigious French educational institution should be entitled the 'Polytechnic School'? Together with the *École des Ponts et Chaussées* and the *École des Mines* it produced a cohort of technocratic bureaucrats who planned the railway network and framed the industrial strategies of the Second Empire. *Polytechnique* graduate Charles Dupin established industrial design centres in Nîmes and Rennes. After 1850, 25 per cent of Nord industrialists' sons studied at the *Grandes Écoles* – and returned to the family business. Dynamic industrialists and managers such as Cavillier of Pont-à-Mousson or Louis Renault were *Grandes Écoles* graduates. In the science-based industries of the Second Industrial Revolution – automobiles, steel, electronics, chemicals – *pantouflage*, the interpenetration of the personnel of state bureaucracy and industrial management, expanded rapidly. France's often-underestimated successes in the Second Industrial Revolution depended on a sophisticated higher-education system (Shinn 1980).

Many weaknesses remained unaddressed. Access to secondary education remained much too narrow. Integration of primary and secondary education was not debated until the inter-war period. Although one-third of 7500 successful candidates in 1900 took the science option, modernisation of the *baccalauréat* was incomplete. The Catholic sector's vitality indicated the strength of 'traditional' cultural values within the bourgeoisie. The examination successes of elite Catholic colleges could not hide the poor quality of that sector's long 'tail'. The three *Écoles des Arts et Métiers* – at Angers, Châlons and Aix-en-Provence – were distant from industrial heartlands. A fourth, at Lille, was founded only in 1900. Training of personnel for local industries involved a haphazard mix of local employer initiatives, government-backed *Écoles Pratiques* – such as that for rail-fitters in Nîmes – and municipal 'professional schools' such as Vierzon. Such courses involved only a minority of skilled workers. Intermediate-level technical training, much needed because of the decline of apprenticeships, remained weaker than in Germany.

Bibliography

General
Anderson, R. *Education in France: 1848–1870* (Oxford: Clarendon Press, 1975).
Baker, D. and Harrigan, P. *The Making of Frenchmen: Current Directions in the History of Education in France* (Waterloo, Ontario: Historical Directions, 1980).
Gildea, R. *Education in Provincial France 1800–1914* (Oxford: Oxford University Press, 1983).
Prost, R. *L'Enseignement en France: 1800–1967* (Paris: A. Colin, 1968).
Rosanvallon, P. *Le Moment Guizot* (Paris, 1985).
Stock-Morton, P. *Moral Education for a Secular Society: the Development of Morale Laïque in 19th-Century France* (Albany, State University of New York, 1988).

Primary education and popular literacy
Alaimo, K. 'Adolescence, gender and class in educational reform in France: the development of the *École Primaire Supérieure*: 1880–1914', *French Historical Studies* 1994.
Auspitz, K. *The Radical Bourgeoisie: the 'Ligue de l'Enseignement' 1865–85* (Cambridge: Cambridge University Press, 1982).
Baycroft, T. 'Peasants into Frenchmen: the Flemish in the North of France', *European Review of History/Révue Européenne d'Histoire* 1995.
Bertrand, M. (ed.) *Popular Traditions and Learned Cultures in France* (Saratoga: Anima Libri, 1985).
Briand, J.-P. and Chapoulie, J.-M. *Les Collèges du Peuple: L'Enseignement Primaire Supérieure sous la Troisième République* (Toulouse, 1992).
Chanet, J. *L' Ecole Républicaine et les Petites Patries: 1879–1940* (Paris: Aubier, 1996).
Clark, L. *Schooling the Daughters of Marianne* (Albany: State University of New York, 1984).
Clark, L. 'The Battle of the sexes in a professional setting: the introduction of *Inspectrices Primaires*', *French Historical Studies* 1989.
Crubellier, M. *L'Ecole Républicaine: 1871–1914* (Paris: Editions Christian, 1993).
Curtis, S. 'Lay habits: religious teachers and the secularisation crisis of 1901–04', *French History* 1995.
Day, C. 'The rustic man: the rural schoolmaster in 19th-century France', *Comparative Studies in Society and History* 1983.
Emiliana, J. 'La littérature de l'École Primaire', in M. Yardeni (ed.) *Idéologie et Propagande en France* (Paris, 1987).
Feeley, F. *Rebels with a Cause: Revolutionary Syndicalist Culture Amongst French Schoolteachers: 1880–1919* (New York: P. Lang/American University Studies, 1989).
Furet, F. and Ozouf, J. *Reading and Writing* (Cambridge: Cambridge University Press, 1982).
Gavoille, J. *L'Ecole Publique dans le Département du Doubs: 1870–1914* (Paris: Les Belles Lettres, 1986).
Gemie, S. 'A danger to society'? Teachers and authority in France 1833–48', *French History* 1988.
Gemie, S. 'Marianne as schoolmistress? Female teachers and the construction of French nationhood 1815–1914', in M. Kelley (ed.) *France: Nation and Regions* (Southampton: University of Southampton, 1993).
Gemie, S. 'Docility, zeal and rebellion: culture and subculture in women's teacher training colleges 1860–1910', *European History Quarterly* 1994.
Gemie, S. *Women and Schooling in France: 1815–1914* (Keele: Keele University Press, 1995).
Giolitto, P. *Histoire de l'Enseignement Primaire au XIXe Siècle: les Méthodes d' Enseignement* (Paris: Nathan, 1984).

Gontard, M. *Les Ecoles Primaires de la France Bourgeoise: 1833–75* (Toulouse: Centre Régional de Documentation Pédagogique, 1976).
Grew, R. and Harrigan, P. 'The availability of schooling in 19th-century France', *Journal of Interdisciplinary History* 1983.
Grew, R. and Harrigan, P. 'The Catholic contribution to universal schooling in France', *Journal of Modern History* 1985.
Grew, R. and Harrigan, P. *School, State and Society: the Growth of Elementary Schooling in 19th-Century France* (Ann Arbor: Michigan University Press, 1991).
Harrigan, P. 'Women teachers and the schooling of girls in France', *French Historical Studies* 1998.
Hélias, P. *The Horse of Pride* (New Haven: Yale University Press, 1978).
Heywood, C. *Childhood in 19th-Century France* (Cambridge: Cambridge University Press, 1989).
Heywood, C. 'On learning gender roles during childhood in 19th-century France', *French Historical Studies* 1991.
Leblond, M. 'La scolarisation dans le Département du Nord', *Revue du Nord* 1970.
Luc, J.-N. 'La scolarisation en France au XIXe Siècle: l'Illusion Statistique', *Annales ESC* 1986.
Lavergne, A. *Jean Coste* (Paris, 1902).
Lyons, M. *Readers and Society in Nineteenth-century France: Workers, Women, Peasants* (Basingstoke: Palgrave, 2001).
Mayeur, F. *L'Education des Filles en France au XIXe Siècle* (Paris: Hackette, 1977).
Maines, M.-J. *Taking the Hard Road: Life Course in French and German Workers' Autobiographies* (Chapel Hill: University of North Carolina, 1995).
Ménager, B. *La Laïcisation des Ecoles Communales dans le Département du Nord: 1879–99* (Lille: Lille University Press, 1971).
Meyer 'Professionalisation and societal change: rural teachers in 19th-century France', *Journal of Social History* 1976.
Moch, L. 'Government policy and women's experience: the case of teachers in France', *Feminist Studies* 1988.
Nicolas, G. *Instituteurs entre Politique et Réligion: la Première Génération de Normaliens en Bretagne* (Rennes: Editions Apogée, 1993).
Nora, P. 'Ernest Lavisse: Son Rôle dans la Formation du Sentiment National', *Revue Historique* 1962.
Ozouf, J. and Ozouf, M. 'Le Thème du Patriotisme dans les Manuels Primaires', *Le Mouvement Social* 1964.
Ozouf, J. and Ozouf, M. 'Le "Tour de France par Deux Enfants": Le 'Petit Livre Rouge' de la République', in P. Nora (ed.) *Les Lieux de Mémoire La République* Vol. I (Paris: Gallimard, 1984).
Ozouf, J. and Ozouf, M. *La République des Instituteurs* (Paris: Gallimard, 1992).
Quartararo, A. *Women Teachers and Popular Education in 19th-Century France* (Newark, NJ: University of Delaware, 1995).
Reed-Donahay, D. *Education and Identity in Rural France* (Cambridge: Cambridge University Press, 1996).
Singer, B. 'The teacher as notable in Brittany: 1880–1914', *French Historical Studies* 1977.
Singer, B. *Village Notables in 19th-Century France* (Albany: State University of New York, 1985).
Strumhinger, L. *What are Little Girls and Boys made of?: Primary Education in Rural France* (Albany: State University of New York, 1983).
Thabault, R. *Education and Change in a Village Community* (London: Routledge, 1971).
Thiesse, A.-M. *Le Roman du Quotidien: Lecteurs et Lectures Populaires à la belle Epoque* (Paris: Le Chemin Vert, 1984).

Secondary and higher education

Anderson, R. 'Catholic secondary education in France 1852–70', in T. Zeldin (ed.) *Conflicts in French Society* (London: Allen and Unwin, 1970).

Anderson, R. 'Secondary education in mid-19th-century France', *Past and Present* 1971.

Bush, J. 'Education and social status: Jesuit colleges in the early Third Republic', *French Historical Studies* 1975.

Caron, J.-C. *Générations Romantiques: les Etudiants de Paris et le Quartier Latin 1814–51* (Paris: A. Colin, 1991).

Cherval, A. *Et il Fallait apprendre à Lire à Tous les Petits Français* (Paris, 1978).

Citron, S. 'Enseignement Secondaire et Idéologie élitiste: 1880–1941', *Le Mouvement Social* 1976.

Day, C. 'Education, technology and social change in France 1866–9', *French Historical Studies* 1974.

Day, C. 'Science, applied science and higher education in France: 1870–1945', *Journal of Social History* 1992.

Fox, R. and Weisz, G. *The Organisation of Science and Technology in France* (Cambridge: Cambridge University Press, 1980).

Fox, R. *Science, Industry and the Social Order in Post-Revolutionary France* (Great Yarmouth: Varorium, 1995).

Gerbod, P. *La Vie Quotidienne dans les Lycées . . . au XIXe Siècle* (Paris: PUF, 1968).

Gerbod, P. 'The baccalauréat and its role in the formation of French elites', in J. Howorth and P. Cerny (eds) *Elites in France* (London: Croom Helm, 1981).

Harrigan, P. *Mobility, Elites and Education in French Society of the Second Empire* (Waterloo, Ontario, 1980).

Margadant, J.-B. *Madame le Professeur: Women Educators in the Third Republic* (Princeton, NJ: Princeton University Press, 1990).

Mayeur, F. *L'Enseignement Secondaire des Jeunes Filles sous la Troisième République* (Paris: PFNSP, 1977).

O'Boyle, L. 'The excess of educated men in Europe 1815–48', *Journal of Modern History* 1970.

Padberg, J. *Colleges in Controversy: the Jesuit Schools in France 1815–80* (Cambridge, Mass: Harvard University Press, 1969).

Shinn, T. *Savoir Scientifique et Pouvoir Social: L'Ecole Polytechnique 1789–1914* (Paris, 1980).

Spitzer, A. *The French Generation of 1820* (Princeton, NJ: Princeton University Press, 1987).

Weisz, G. *The Emergence of Modern Universities in France 1863–1914* (Princeton, NJ: Princeton University Press, 1983).

Chapter 6

Crime and punishment

'Societies have only the criminals they deserve' (A. Lacassagne, criminologist)

'When we open a school, we close a prison' (V. Hugo)

'For each new school opened, there are five more arrests' (C. Lombroso, criminologist)

'A well-administered prison should seem more like a factory than a place of coercion' (L-R Villermé)

'"*Police*": Are always wrong' (G. Flaubert *Dictionary of Received Ideas*)

'The hero surging forward with his rifle carries the signs of the galleys on his face and certainly the stench of the assize Courts on his disgusting clothes' (H. Heine, commenting on Delacroix's *Liberty Leading the People*)

'Criminal dossiers are but "fragments of the real"' (Arlette Farge)

'There are no "facts" about crime, only a judgemental process that institutes crime by designating as "criminal" both certain acts and their perpetrators. In other words there is a-discourse on crime which reveals the obsessions of a society' (Michelle Perrot)

Introduction

Since the 1970s crime and punishment, once left to lawyers and jurists and to popular writers fascinated by sensational trials, has become a major research topic in French provincial universities. Colloquia are held to pool the expertise of sociologists, criminologists, anthropologists and historians. Explanations for this belated upsurge in interest are complex. The dominant historical schools of the 1950s and 1960s largely ignored the topic. *Annalistes* were largely preoccupied with *longue durée* economic and demographic structures and with *mentalités*. Neo-Marxist 'social history from below' was concerned with working-class or peasant militants rather than with the 'criminal', and viewed justice, penal and police systems simply as part of the super-structure of the (capitalist) state. However, changes in focus did occur *within* these two schools. *Annaliste* fascination with quantification led to attempts to utilise the serial national crime statistics compiled from 1826 onwards by the *Compte Générale de l'Administration de la Justice Criminelle* (CGAJC). Meanwhile, building on Hobsbawm's (1969) pioneering studies of 'social banditry', E. P. Thompson (1975) explored 'crime' as a form of social protest and law and

234

rituals of punishment as a key site of ruling-class hegemony. In particular they emphasised ways in which erosion of traditional and communal rights criminalised the everyday behaviour of the poor.

However, the main inspiration for new approaches to the history of crime came from elsewhere. In France the events of 1968 and subsequent prison riots focused attention on the centrality of the penal system to capitalist oppression. Foucault's *Discipline and Punish* (1975) identified the prison as central to disciplinary and surveillance systems developed since the Enlightenment, and a model for barracks, schools and asylums. As the Marxist metanarrative about the 'rise of the working class' crumbled, so historians shifted their focus from labour movements to even more marginalised groups – single-mothers, gays, vagrants and criminals and convicts. They sought to 'retrieve' their experiences without necessarily fitting these into any broad historical narrative. Crime, and discourses about it, appeared to offer insights into the role and nature of the state, into social and cultural values and into society's anxieties and fantasies. Analysis and control of crime was perceived as a field of 'expertise' for strata of the professional bourgeoisie – lawyers, criminologists, penologists and psychiatrists. The significant recent development has been the revolt against positivism and quantification. *Annalistes* insisted that the only place to begin a 'serious' social history of crime was an analysis of the CGAJC statistical records. These would establish a framework for plotting long-term trends in criminality and begin to offer 'scientific' answers to basic questions. Did crime increase inexorably with industrialisation and urbanisation? Has society become more violent? Did the growth of 'materialistic' consumer society lead to a growth in property crime? Were certain social groups or regions more 'criminal' than others? Yet G. Désert (1981) was forced to confess that study of official statistics led to conclusions that were more descriptive than analytical or explanatory. He could suggest certain 'probabilities', but left basic questions unresolved. Abundant yet incomplete national records generated statistical averages which failed to capture – or could not explain – regional variations. Concluding, sadly, that 'we know, in fact, little about criminality or about criminals', he called for monographs to explore and explain localised crime patterns. Yet when these are undertaken one found, as with Chatelard's (1981) study of St. Etienne, that their authors fell back on the a priori assumptions and stereotypes, indeed prejudices, of the bureaucrats who had compiled the statistics and attempted to utilise them (Farcy 2001; Désert 1981; Chatelard 1981).

Post-modernists, feminists, sociologists and anthropologists warned against attempts to derive 'hard truths' from crime figures. Michelle Perrot (1975) urged historians to be deaf to their siren song. They are chimeras, reliant upon constantly shifting definitions of 'crime', on policing levels and police priorities, on variable levels of crime reporting. Judicial and police archives present but 'fragments of the real' because they are themselves 'constructed'. Dossiers are slanted by ways in which suspects are interrogated and the terminology in which testimonies are recorded (Perrot 1975). Historians now address *discourses about* and *representations of* crime, ways in which 'crime' and 'criminals' are constructed by legal and penal systems. They analyse how actions come to be labelled 'criminal', and why labelling of deviancy changes

235

over time. They chart 'moral panics' which reveal societies' anxieties. At various times French 'public opinion' was obsessed with the 'dangerous classes', with biologically programmed 'born criminals', with 'recidivists' and with female and juvenile delinquents. Shifting obsessions were amplified by an emerging mass press. *Faits divers* columns and trial reports of *Le Petit Parisien* nurtured fascination with criminal 'monsters' and sensational murders. It disseminated vulgarised versions of already crude criminological theories about 'degeneration'. Media coverage peaked in periods of socio-economic tension such as the 1840s, 1880s and 1900s. Press obsessions were significant not for any correlation with 'real', verifiable trends in criminality but for revealing – and accentuating – public anxieties. *'Fantomas'*, a master criminal of infinite disguises, became a cult-figure in the literature of the Belle Epoque.

A 'progressive' narrative of the nineteenth century might emphasise abolition of torture and branding and removal of public executions from city centre to outer *barrières*, in tune with growing squeamishness about bloodshed which led to controls on blood-sports and relocation of slaughterhouses away from residential areas. Yet popular culture retained a fascination with blood and violence. Illustrated supplements of Parisian popular newspapers contained colour pictures of thrusting knives and bleeding corpses. *Romans policiers*, police memoirs and underworld exposés were staples of popular and petty-bourgeois literature. The mass press deluged its readers with graphic depictions of horrendous crimes, while urging them to tremble and recoil from 'unspeakable' horrors 'beyond understanding' or description. It claimed that its effects were cathartic. Because 'all of Paris' felt 'moved' by such crimes, then 'decent' people were bonded into a community of revulsion. Conservatives criticised such voyeurism as morally corrupting, since it might induce readers to imitate these crimes. The gullibility, morbid bad taste and hysteria exhibited by readers of the mass press marked it as essentially 'female'. Socialists argued that such journalism was designed to divert working-class readers from 'real' social issues. Artificially created moral panics undermined serious public debate. Ironically abandonment of attempts to quantify crime trends has led historians back to micro-studies of individual crimes or sensational trials in order to tease out their cultural 'meanings' and the perceptions and sensibilities of those involved.

Historiographical debates reflect the lack of consensus within our own society about causes of crime, and echo arguments which raged in nineteenth-century France. Liberals and the Left insist that crime is related to social deprivations and social dislocation. Rates of theft soar, as in the 1980s, in periods of mass unemployment. As capitalist consumer society advances theft due to absolute deprivation may give way to that prompted by *relative* deprivation, by a sense of being denied access to goods which have become 'necessities' during periods of economic expansion. Stealing 'luxuries' flaunted by the affluent may represent a personalised 'revolution' of frustrated rising expectations. Indeed some 'crime' is a form of social revolt, flowing from rejection by the poor of the norms of a society which denies their legitimate aspirations. Durkheimians see 'crime' as a product of *anomie* – the dislocation of social norms by processes of urbanisation and migration. This approach influenced the 1930s Chicago school of criminology, and also L. Chevalier's study of the Parisian 'labouring and dangerous classes' (Chevalier 1973). Conservatives mistrust such approaches, emphasising individual choice and moral responsibility. Since not all the unemployed become thieves, clearly the jobless retain the capacity to choose to be law-abiding! Talk of economic 'causes' of crime, emphasis on rights rather than duties, encouragement of moral relativism – all systematically erode an individual's sense of responsibility, blur distinctions between right and wrong and deny links between material success and individual effort. By weakening religion, the family and sexual controls, Left-wing and secularist ideologies deprive the poor of the 'policeman in the head' necessary for social discipline. Such emphasis on individual moral responsibility is often combined with the conviction, supported by one influential strand of criminological thought, that certain sub-groups are biologically disposed to criminality and aggression. Such thinking, liberals retort, ignores complex interaction between social environment and biological predispositions, and fails to ask whether there exists a bourgeois gene that predisposes middle-class men to commit large-scale financial fraud!

Such debates were foreshadowed by those in nineteenth-century France. Enlightenment liberals saw crime as a product of the injustice, ignorance and poverty of ancien régime society. They argued that economic expansion, education and equality before the law would, in time, reduce delinquency. When no such reduction occurred, liberals clung, forlornly, to hopes that penal reform would achieve some 'rehabilitation'. Socialists insisted that the 'formal' legal freedoms and equality of post-Revolution society were inadequate as long as capitalist exploitation and social inequalities persisted. It was no accident that the 1846–47 economic crisis saw an explosion of petty theft. With 80 per cent of all prosecuted offenders from the popular classes and magistrates and jurors from the propertied elites, class justice was inevitable. Conservative *notables* insisted that liberals refused to take account of 'human nature' and man's fallen state. The Revolution had weakened religion – foundation of all social morality – the family, social discipline and deference. Urbanisation was further undermining social cohesion. Slowing the rural exodus and reconstructing religious and family values were the first steps to the return to an organic society. After the traumas of 1848 conservative discourse was given a 'scientific' veneer by the rise of positivistic criminology. Why, Gabriel Tarde enquired, was the economy expanding and educational provision increasing and yet, contrary to liberal predictions, crime still rising? The answer was provided by theories of hereditary degeneration which portrayed criminality as the outcome of a combination of the biological predispositions of a hereditary criminal sub-class with 'pathological' urban milieux. Such theories never achieved total dominance yet were sufficiently pervasive to influence the entire debate on crime from 1860 onwards. They suggested that attempts to rehabilitate 'born criminals' were futile. A cultural climate was created favourable to draconian penalties for certain types of offenders. Hence one paradox of French society in this period is that political trends towards a more 'liberal', 'democratic' society apparently coincided with tougher attitudes towards delinquents and a harsher penal regime.

Measuring criminality

The compilation, after 1826, of annual crime figures was typical of an era fascinated by possibilities of using quantification in the service of social morality. Disciples of Belgian statistician Adolphe Quetelet sought correlations which might uncover 'laws' of criminality. Maps were made charting the nation's 'moral geography'. The key was to study social groups not individuals, to eliminate 'chance', to frame 'laws' based on observed generalisations. Bureaucrats supplied ministers with rolling five-year comparisons of crime figures in order to identify trends and to offer plausible explanations for these (Emsley 1983). Sceptics insist that the problematic nature of all crime statistics rendered such projects chimerical, that explanations provided by bureaucrats simply reflected their assumptions and prejudices. Ironically, when bureaucrats later faced graphs of falling delinquency rates, which correlated poorly with their continued anxieties, they began to talk of a 'black figure' of unreported and unprosecuted crime! Neo-positivist historians who continue to insist that crime statistics remain the foundation stone of any serious social history of nineteenth-century crime now admit that before they can be utilised a series of 'adjustments' must be made.

Policing

In 1907 the head of the criminal statistics bureau confessed that increases in arrests for drunkenness reflected less a 'real' upsurge in such offences but a decision to enforce the 1873 Act against public drunkenness with greater zeal. This was a belated official recognition that the nature and priorities of policing determine levels of reported crime and types of offences – and offenders – highlighted. Police numbers did expand, particularly after 1848. Standards of training and expertise improved gradually, yet critics argued that the police remained deficient in both personnel and in quality. Eighteenth-century 'free-born Englishmen' viewed the Paris Lieutenant-General of Police and the mounted rural *maréchaussée* as evidence of a 'police state'. Yet with only 3500 men to police provincial France, the *maréchaussée* was spread very thin, and serious law-and-order problems such as the food-riots of the 1770s necessitated army intervention (Emsley 1983). After 1789 progress towards a large-scale 'professional' police force proved slow. Contrary to Bonapartist mythology, it was the Directory which did most to contain the wave of rural brigandage and conscription evasion which followed the conflicts of the Revolution. But the resultant 'security state' was constructed more on tried and trusted methods of military repression and courts-martial than on any new police system (Brown 1997–98). The ubiquitous power of Napoleon's Minister of *Police Générale* became legendary. Yet Fouché confessed that 'the power of the police lies in the *general belief in* its omnipotence and omnipresence'. Limited manpower and rivalries between different types of police made this an illusion difficult to sustain. Rural *gardes champêtres* were ill-trained and subservient to village factions. *Commissaires* in provincial towns were torn between loyalty to municipal authorities and to the Interior Ministry, while the paramilitary *gendarmerie*, which patrolled the countryside, reported to the War Ministry. Paris bourgeois, fearful of property crime and social unrest, cast envious eyes across the Channel to the Metropolitan Police (1829). Uniformed *sergents-de-ville* were introduced for 'preventive' policing and to patrol regular beats, but numbered only 330 by 1846 (Emsley and Weinberger 1991).

1848 proved a watershed. Bourgeois nightmares in the spring were fuelled by the spectacle of a 'police of conciliation', under radical Caussidière, manned by ex-political detainees and barricade insurgents from the February rising (O'Brien 1975)! A reliable, effective police force became a priority. By 1855 the Bonapartist regime had created 392 new *gendarmerie* brigades, raised the number of *gendarmes* to 24,000, established 23 chief *commissaires* – modelled on the Paris Prefect of Police – in major cities and increased provincial *commissaires* by 82 per cent. The Paris beat-system was extended as the number of *sergents de ville* rose to 3000. A Railway Police was established. Police pay increases strengthened the regime's 'law-and-order' credentials. Yet the Bonapartist 'police state' remained modest by subsequent standards. Cities such as Lille and Rouen still had a police population ratio as low as 1:1000. Plans to group *gardes champêtres* into rural brigades were shelved. Police numbers grew only gradually. By 1892, Paris, with a population of over 3 million, had only 7000 police. Policing levels were high in Lyon and frontier regions, but surprisingly low in the industrial Nord.

The Republic inherited Bonapartism's police personnel and system and showed little embarrassment at so doing. Radicals were suspicious of the paramilitary gendarmerie, whose numbers were allowed to decline by 8 per cent and Left-wing municipalities clashed with Interior Ministers over control of *commissaires* and policing of strikes. Despite anxieties about crime, taxpayers proved reluctant to fund more police. Nor was efficiency helped by endemic *guerres des polices* – above all bureaucratic rivalries between *Prefecture de Police* and *Sûreté Générale* in Paris, which systematically refused to exchange information (Martin 1990). Nevertheless, steps towards 'professionalisation were taken. 'Modernisers' insisted that recruitment of ex-army personnel was a serious weakness. 'Nothing', complained Lyon police chief Locard, 'is more harmful to the police than the *obligation* to have NCOs. I accept that the Army is a school of courage. But it is *not* a school of police . . . (Ex-soldiers) bring with them three unutilisable qualities to their new careers – insolence, habits of revelry and laziness'. Entrance examinations, training courses and promotion by merit were all advocated. As public fascination with detective fiction (*romans policiers*) suggests, policing was acquiring a new 'scientific' image. 'Experts' like Bertillon were identified with detection techniques based on photography, finger-printing, centralised record-keeping and 'anthropometric' data such as skull-size! Migrants were obliged to carry a *carte anthropometrique* recording such data. New 'mobile brigades' were established to adapt policing to the age of the automobile (Emsley and Weinberger 1991; Martin 1990).

Changes in policing influenced crime statistics. *Sergeants de ville* were introduced in Paris after 1830 in response to bourgeois anxieties about theft, yet even 600 daily patrols caught few thieves. Disturbances in the city still required army repression. In order to prove its worth the police force needed 'targets' and began to arrest those with visible street presence whose activities were a nuisance to bourgeois pedestrians – street-traders, rag-pickers, drunks and unregulated prostitutes (*filles insoumises*). Some 'flexibility' in enforcing such controls was needed, since the 'economy of makeshifts' of the marginal poor relied on such street activities. Police thus issued warnings and settled some disputes by arbitration. *Commissaires* closed their eyes selectively to some activities in order to manage, as best they could, the 'established disorder'. In short, a crime was less an act transgressing the law than one which police or public prosecutor decided to prosecute. 'Criminals' were a selected proportion of *actual* offenders. Arrests in Paris fell sharply during Caussidiere's regime of spring 1848 – only to rise 50 per cent in the following year. Increased police resources then resulted in an upsurge in arrests. Minor crimes (*délits*) 'rose' 21 per cent in 1851–55, petty offences by 69 per cent. In 'red' Lower Languedoc the presence of more police led to a rise in arrests of café customers – for insulting the police! An unpopular police force might actually provoke certain types of offences rather than deter crime. At best, one bureaucrat conceded, 'our police are *tolerated*, as an army of occupation, from fear of greater evils; but they are viewed with a certain contempt . . .'. In *Dictionary of Received Ideas*, Flaubert's ironic entry for 'Police' simply reads 'are always wrong!'. In *La Police* (1884) G. Guyot was more brutal: 'There is a man . . . whom nobody calls by his name but by his title. The Administration chose him from absinthe-drinkers, chasers of skirts and those whose habits prevent them from participating in social life. Pushed out of the Army, good for nothing . . . This villainous, boastful, cowardly, aggressive . . . and superfluous being, detested by everyone, this representative of authority, moral order, family and property is – the police *commissaire*.' 'Cogne', a slang term for 'cop', derived from the verb 'to thump'. Such unpopularity was not hard to explain. Unlike New York's 'citizen cop' or London's unarmed 'bobby', the French policeman was viewed as an agent of political repression, whether harassing student liberals in the 1820s or spying on the labour movement. Experience of Bonapartist repression gave middle-class Republicans cause to mistrust the police. French police, claimed Balzac, 'are, in political matters, as partial as the Inquisition'. By 1890 hundreds of 'special' inspectors were involved in surveillance of the labour movement. Official police numbers omit the informers (*mouchards*) and *agents provocateurs* paid from secret slush-funds to infiltrate unions. Police arrogance angered workers who were neither labour militants nor 'criminals'. Police-chief E. Reynaud's autobiography emphasises that in popular *quartiers* police who broke-up disputes or protected bailiffs would attract jeering, hostile crowds (Guiral 1979).

The police force remained too small to function without a degree of popular consent. 'Respectable' artisans criticised Sue's novels for romanticising crime and insisted that they supported policing of drunken brawls and jailing of 'real' criminals. By the 1880s, as the working class became more 'settled', there was support for tighter policing of marginal 'others' – vagrants, beggars, gypsies and immigrants. Clemenceau's government won applause for its tough stance against juvenile delinquents. The image of the police improved slightly as police chief Hennion advocated policing by consent and as *romans policiers* fostered the myth of the detective.

Measuring 'crime'

Use of annual statistics to establish crime trends is problematic because acts classified as 'criminal' change over time. The 1827 Forest Code criminalised everyday actions of villagers for whom access to forest resources was essential for survival. In the 1830s annual prosecutions for forest offences averaged 132,000 – 60 per cent of all *délits* tried by lower-courts. Prosecutions still averaged 75,000 per annum in the 1850s, before plunging to 18,000 in the 1860s and to 2200 by 1900. This long-term trend reflected lessening demographic pressures due to out-migration. But the precipitate fall in prosecutions after 1859 stemmed from a new strategy encouraging 'transactions' between forest authorities and minor offenders designed to keep the latter out of court. By itself this change almost accounted for the 'decline' in crime for which Bonapartist propaganda took credit when it claimed that its brand of tough law enforcement had subdued the 'evil passions' of 1848. Similar fluctuations in crime rates occurred when hunting laws were amended. The 25-franc hunting permit, introduced in 1844, trebled poaching prosecutions to 27,000 per annum by 1855–59. The most ferocious repression of 'crime' in Hanoverian England occurred when employers and the state clamped down on traditional 'perks' of groups of workers. Similarly rights of miners to scavenge for coal or of dockers to appropriate a small proportion of goods in transit were suppressed. Boundaries between different levels of offences – 'crimes', *délits* and minor offences – shifted constantly. An apparent reduction of 40 per cent in serious 'crimes' in the Second Empire was due to a reclassification of offences such as 'minor woundings' as *délits* in 1863. Judicial authorities felt acquittal rates in higher courts were too high because jurors perceived sentences to be too harsh, hence chances of securing convictions in lower courts might be better. Shifts in official priorities influenced the zeal with which particular offences were pursued. 'Natalist' anxieties about falling birth-rates led to more prosecutions for abortion and infanticide, though juries remained reluctant to convict the women involved.

Expansion of the railways produced a plethora of new *délits* – ticket evasion, damage to carriages, trespassing on the track. In 1846–50 there were 256 prosecutions annually for such offences, by 1913 12,500. State tobacco and match monopolies led to prosecutions for smuggling and evasion. Food-safety laws introduced after 1850 led to 8400 prosecutions per annum by 1860. Tougher regulations in 1905 prompted a new wave of convictions. It is difficult to know whether the fall in convictions in the interim was due to improved food hygiene, fading of initial enthusiasm for enforcement of hygiene laws or ruses to evade detection. In short, sceptics argue, fluctuations in levels of policing and changes in the law and in classifications of offences render all attempts to utilise crime statistics as a guide to the 'moral state' of French society – or that of particular regions – problematic. Possibly statistics are more reliable for major crimes (e.g. murder) than for endemic petty theft. Yet it was the sheer volume of such minor offences which determined overall averages.

Correlatations of crime with occupation and class must be treated with due caution. The format of the annual statistics is unhelpful because it lumps together in 'Category A' peasant proprietors, farm labourers and miners.

Prosecutions per annum (approximate figures)

1820s	100,000
Mid-1840s	180,000
Mid-1850s	200,000
1860s	100,000
1880–90s	200,000
1900s	170,000

Unsurprisingly migrants, vagrants, immigrants and street prostitutes occupy a prominent place in crime statistics. In Seine-Inférieure, 20 per cent of arrests between 1860 and 1890 were of migrants. In Toulouse between 1835–54, 2.2 per cent of bourgeois were prosecuted, 3.3 per cent of artisans, but 19.2 per cent of the poor and unskilled. While material deprivation doubtless made such groups prone to petty theft, there remain questions about their precise role in 'criminality'. Although prosecutions for fraud and embezzlement did rise by 600 per cent, much 'white-collar' crime went undetected. Bourgeois taxpayers were preoccupied with theft and street disorder. To assuage such anxieties police targeted limited resources on specific popular quartiers and visible groups and arrested the 'usual suspects' – a process accentuated by the advent of 'scientific' methods. Photography and fingerprinting facilitated compilation of files on those with 'a record'. Policing strategies 'constructed' the class of 'recidivists' which came to preoccupy criminologists and public alike as the century progressed (Martin 1990; Désert 1981).

The consensus of official and public opinion was that crime was an ever-growing problem. Crime statistics cannot be used in any straightforward way to substantiate, or refute, such assumptions. Heightened anxieties about crime sometimes flew in the face of falling numbers of court cases. Prosecutions rose markedly between 1820 and the mid-1850s, then fell sharply in the 1860s, in part due to relaxation of the forest régime, in part because *Procureurs'* reluctance to prosecute cases where evidence was thin. Prosecution rates then rose sharply from the 1870s to the 1890s, before declining slightly in the 1900s.

Property crime

Though property crime has been little studied by historians, it was the perceived rise in theft which preoccupied contemporaries. It was the crime par excellence in a society with many peasants and petty bourgeois wedded to private property. Juries, drawn from such strata, proved harsher on thieves than on offenders involved in worker-on-worker violence. In 1851–53 acquittal rates in theft trials (26 per cent) were lower than in cases involving violence (33 per cent) – and this gap widened steadily. Utilisation of prosecution numbers to 'measure' property crime remains a hazardous exercise. Trials for theft increased 60 per cent between 1830 and the 1900s, but reported theft trebled. Apparent falls in theft rates sometimes reflected victims' fatalistic perception of the futility of reporting endemic petty-theft. There do appear to be close correlations between economic fluctuations and theft rates until the 1850s. The graph of petty theft, vagrancy and begging offences shadows those of grain prices and unemployment. Cases of 'simple' theft rose from 25,000 per annum in 1841–45 to over 41,000 in 1847, while prosecutions for begging trebled to 10,600 between 1845 and 1847. In St. Etienne in 1847–48 one-quarter of cases involved women, many seeking to feed their children. In 'normal' years women comprised barely 10 per cent of offenders. Jobless migrants were charged in Normandy with taking clothes from washing lines or vegetables from fields. In Cherbourg in 1847–50, 44 per cent of money thefts were under 10 francs (Désert 1981; Zehr 1976).

Individual theft of food should be placed in the wider context of collective grain-riots, market-pillaging and *taxation populaire* of these years. There were 11 such incidents in 1841–45, but 530 in 1847 alone. Correlations between grain-prices and petty-theft weakened after 1854, whereas in Germany they remained strong into the 1880s. In Calvados the proportion of thefts involving food fell from one-third to one-fifth after the 1850s. Models of 'absolute deprivation' fit property crime patterns until mid-century, but a 'relative deprivation' model becomes more persuasive later in the century – as expectations were raised and 'new needs' created by the relative prosperity of the 1850s and 1860s and of the post-1896 period (Zehr 1976). Nevertheless, an overview of trends in property crime across the century suggests a degree of economic determinism. Thefts rose steadily during the difficult years until mid-century – then fell 12 per cent in 1855–69. The rapid rise in theft prosecutions after 1875 correlates with the 'Great Depression', while an 18 per cent fall in 1896–1914 coincides with the economic upturn of the Belle Époque. Vagrancy and begging offences rose most sharply in the 1880s in relatively 'developed' departments – Seine-Inférieure, Hérault – where the jobless hoped to find better-funded welfare provision. Some allegedly headed for Rouen where the newly refurbished jail 'served ragoût daily'! In the late-1850s annual vagrancy and begging prosecutions averaged 11,000. In 1885 they reached 34,000, prompting criminologist Joly to confess that many were unfortunate 'casualties of the industrial struggle'.

By 1900 highest theft rates were in Marseilles, St. Etienne and Paris. The thirty departments with highest urban densities had theft levels 68 per cent above the national average. Explanations for high urban theft-rates offered by contemporaries – and by historians – are banal, plausible and difficult to prove. Towns contained a high percentage of young adult males, the most 'crime-prone' group. They attracted jobless migrants who comprised one-third of those arrested for theft in 1850. Seaside resorts with affluent tourists and large hotels became a target for thieves – some, like the Pollet gang in the Nord, 'professionals'. Cities contained concentrations of mobile wealth offering opportunity for and incitement to theft. They also displayed glaring contrasts between affluence and poverty – in a context of 'anonymity' and of weak social controls. Hence crime statistics reinforced bourgeois anxieties about urbanisation, although these were compounded by the fact that towns appeared and sounded more threatening because of a visible and audible petty 'criminality' of café-brawling, drunken shouting (*tapages nocturnes*) and insults to the police.

	Reported violent offences	Per 100,000 in population	Prosecuted violent offences	Per 100,000 in population
1830	21,000	69	17,000	57.8
1840	28,000	81	22,000	63
1870s				
1900s	60,000	152	40,000	109

Crime and violence

One-fifth of studies of French crime since 1970 have been of violent crime. Levels of both reported and prosecuted violent offences did increase steadily, although at a slower rate than theft. However, relationships between violence and urbanisation appear more complex than for theft. The contradictions apparent in analyses by contemporary criminologists are echoed by those of neo-positivist historians seeking to explain their statistical findings. Much of this confusion derived from the contradictory, but often simultaneously held 'myths' of the countryside as both 'rustic idyll' and as a Jurassic park where savage, atavistic brutes roamed. The relative strength of these two images fluctuated as threats of rural disorder rose or waned. One can thus find claims that a low rate of violent crime in rural areas reflected remoteness from big city corruption – or, conversely, that high rates of violence stemmed from rustic brutes unacquainted with civilised mores!

Identification and quantification of criminal violence is complicated by the persistence of collective violence in popular protest and politics. Were tax and grain rioters – or 1848 insurgents – 'criminals'? The status of statistics which label as 'violence' both murder and the 1851 insurrection is problematic. Elite alarm at such unrest sustained fear of 'popular violence' of all types. At times officials waxed lyrical about rural 'tranquillity'. Recalling the murder of a widow, an ex-police chief noted that suspicion fell 'naturally' on her son, who consorted with Parisian rag-pickers, 'because country people in France, as elsewhere, are usually law-abiding'. Yet criminologists often discerned 'atavistic' savagery in country-dwellers. In 1890 Tarde, lamenting that 'civilising' influences had made little impact on the 'still brutal brain of our peasants', described the murder of a shepherd-girl as typical of 'our *arrières couches sociales*'. The new social history of the 1960s, fascinated by its (re)discovery of collective rural social protest, shied away from individual violence in the countryside, merely hinting euphemistically that 'indocility' was still more frequent than in our day.

Recently there has been a tendency to portray violence as endemic in the countryside, from the family feuds and vendettas uncovered in the Southern Massif in the late ancien régime onwards (Corbin 1991; Chauvaud 1997). Historians sometimes discern in forms of violence an underlying logic and a function as a cornerstone of village 'order'. It served to affirm identities and clan loyalties, to claim 'respect' and status. Much violence was tolerated within the community. Youths' punch-ups were affirmations of virility. Bonapartism's macho/military image undoubtedly tapped rustic admiration for 'tough guys'! Villagers won respect because of their reputation as fighters. Bullying of farm-servants and wife-beating were accepted as 'normal'. Family feuds smouldered for generations. Insults launched as a prelude to physical violence often began 'your family has always been . . .'. Neighbours fought over unpaid debts or unreturned borrowed tools. Arson or animal-maiming were 'anonymous' crimes carried out during such feuds – or expressions of the impotent social resentments of landless labourers against landowners (Chauvard 1995). An 1860s Doubs police report spoke of 'divisions and pro-found hatred (that) reign amongst the inhabitants of certain communities'. Only if 'everyday' violence escalated out-of-control did the law become in-volved. Villagers often resented intrusion of external authorities. In the Gers in 1850, in a period of political tension, gendarmes who intervened in a café dispute were manhandled by a crowd of several hundred. Within villages it was accepted that 'abnormal' behaviour – including 'excessive' marital brutality – would be controlled and punished by youth groups and *charivaris*. Elderly lechers might be mocked in song as '*vieux macquérous*'. Village identity and cohesion were cemented by aggression directed at outsiders – migrants, gypsies, seasonal harvesters, Jewish pig-slaughterers in Alsace. 'For the traveller theft is a condition of his being, like poison to a toad', insisted a Pyrenean mayor. Shepherds from adjacent villages fought to protect 'their' territory. Residents of neighbouring villages would be insulted in song ('There are more whores in "x"/ Than there are milking cows'). Youth groups clashed at *fêtes* or at the annual conscription lottery (*tirage au sort*) in the local *bourg*. Ariège forest rights disputes sometimes 'balkanised' into boundary conflicts between adjacent villages. Infringement of game-laws led to clashes between poachers and forest guards and gamekeepers. Shoot-outs between poaching-gangs and gendarmes were commonplace in Sologne and Hurepoix in mid-century. At Ramboullet in 1841 a poacher was shot dead by a guard in a 'duel' outside a café. A forest guard was buried alive by poachers who watched ferrets eat his face! Public prosecutors dubbed poaching 'a school of violence'. Many poachers had the rebellious aura of 'social bandits'. The target of poachers around Cherbourg was the estate of General Dumourcel – notorious for making profits by selling rotten grain in 1846–47. Others were brutal men who terrified fellow villagers. In frontier regions smuggling was a way of life. And although local 'brigandage' by army deserters and conscription evaders never again reached levels witnessed in the Revolutionary decade, it persisted in parts of the South until mid-century. Sometimes villagers admired and protected such characters, but might turn to the *gendarmerie* for protection against those who preyed on local farmers. In this, as in much else, rural attitudes to the state remained highly ambivalent.

Calculating trends in 'rural violence' is fraught with difficulty. Much 'every-day' violence went unreported. National statistics indicate that in the 1830s, 38 per cent of rural offenders were charged with violence, as against 24 per cent of urban accused. In 1830 nine of the thirteen 'most violent' depart-ments were in the Midi. Murder rates were high in Corsica, the Var and the

Alps. Until 1880, 80 per cent of village brawls resulting in prosecutions were south of a line from the Jura to Gascony. Criminologists made unconvincing attempts to correlate rural violence with alcohol, suggesting that 'hot-blooded' *méridionals* had access to cheap wine. The fastest growth of alcohol consumption appears, however, to have been in the cider-drinking West. But whereas Calvados had a per capita rate of prosecutions for alcohol-related violence three times higher than the national average, Breton alcoholism appears to have produced less violence.

In July 1870 a noble was murdered on market-day in Hautefaye (Dordogne) by a crowd who had first subjected him to prolonged torture. Corbin (1991) locates the episode in the context of anxieties about the war and of rural Bonapartism, with its populist hostility to the aristocracy and folk-memories of émigré support for the Prussians in 1793 and 1814–15. But he also evokes a brutal countryside where infanticide, casual cruelty to the unproductive old ('useless mouths') and sexual violence were endemic. Public revulsion stemmed, he suggests, from the fact that urban bourgeois culture increasingly shrank from manifestations of violence. Public executions were no longer widely attended, cruelty to animals was outlawed, and slaughterhouses relocated to city outskirts. When bourgeois society felt obliged to resort to mass slaughter for its own survival and reproduction – to suppress workers or colonial revolts – it entrusted this to the army and portrayed victims as sub-human. Many bourgeois had cause to thank the 'rural hordes' who helped suppress the Commune. The gruesome killings of young children in the South-East in the 1890s by the 'monster' Vacher did revive discourses about primitive rural 'atavism'. But observers claimed that the countryside was becoming less savage, its behaviour more 'gentle' and civilised, with residual violence confined to remote regions (Corbin 1991; Chauvaud 1991). The relative prosperity of the countryside after 1851, the exodus of 'surplus' population, the establishment of electoral politics and the 'civilising' role of schools reduced rural violence, although an unsuccessful candidate in rural Seine-et-Oise in 1869 attacked tenants who failed to vote for him with an axe! By the 1900s a visitor to central France claimed that village brawls were being supplanted by football – 'a vigorous but not a brutal game'. Possibly village culture became less willing to tolerate persistent sexual molestation. In the 1860s *gendarmes* reported complacently that although a Calvados mayor, a large farmer, molested, impregnated and sacked a series of young farm-servants, he was 'very well thought of by honest people and entirely devoted to the Emperor's government'. By the 1900s in rural Normandy both victims and neighbours were increasingly prepared to report incidents of sexual assault and child abuse.

Calculating trends in urban violence remains a problematic exercise. Police often ignored worker-on-worker violence within slum areas, becoming involved only if this threatened surrounding 'respectable' quartiers. Much urban disorder involved *rixes* between rival *compagnons* or drunken brawls at *guinguettes* at the city outskirts. The ratio of violence to theft in cities, which stood at 0.69:1 in the early 1850s, rose to 0.94:1 by 1855–70. Northern industrial towns appear to have overtaken the rural Midi as the most violent areas. Such violence was, perhaps, a 'transitional' phenomenon as *déraciné* migrants adjusted to a new urban environment in a period of rapid industrialisation. In St. Etienne there were 80 recorded cases of violent assault annually in the 1840s, 300 by 1905. Over half of those prosecuted were recent migrants (Zehr 1976; Chatelard 1981). After 1880 there was a growing correlation between ethnicity and violence, with immigrant workers three times more likely than 'natives' to be prosecuted for assault. The extent to which this pattern reflected police prejudices or was an outcome of xenophobic provocation by French workers is unclear.

By the 1900s France averaged approximately seven hundred murders annually, an increase from 450 in 1890 which aroused alarm and a vigorous law-and-order debate. Despite such sudden upturns – a previous one had occurred in the 1870s – the overall per capita rate declined slightly across the century. By 1900 it stood at 1.7 per hundred thousand – one-third higher than in modern Britain. Murder rates were high in Bouches-du-Rhône (6.27%ooo) – with Italian immigrants often held responsible – and above average in Paris (2%ooo). They were lower in industrial St. Etienne than in some southern rural departments. The rate in the industrial Nord was well below average. Here the 'pattern' of murder across the century changed. The 'typical' killing in 1820 was the result of a café fight between strangers or of a feud over family inheritance. By the 1870s, after a half-century of industrialisation, many murders occurred within working-class households, possibly a symptom of increased tensions within proletarian marriages generated by new factory work patterns (Parella 1992).

Désert (1981) concluded his analysis of national crime statistics with a plea for regional studies whose nuances might illustrate and explain trends discernible in his macro-statistics. However, even such regional studies remain 'prisoners' of the juridical and spatial categories of the official sources which they utilise. Despite this, Santucci's (1986) study of the Hérault is of interest because it analyses a socially and geographically diverse department experiencing considerabe socio-economic change. Its interior was hilly, forested, thinly populated, with declining textile towns. The densely populated coastal plain became dominated by wine monoculture. 'Traditional' crime in the uplands was dominated by feuds, insults and violence, and by forest and poaching offences – some committed by textile-workers who shared peasants' conviction that access to forests was a 'right'. The focus of crime shifted to the 'urbanised' wine plains. A 151 per cent rise in *délits* between 1851 and 1885, double the national average, marked the department as a 'blackspot'. Theft rose sevenfold in per capita terms, and 'insults to the police' by 1750 per cent! Urban theft, mostly opportunistic, rose from 60 per cent to 87 per cent of all prosecuted petty offences. The booming wine economy created rising expectations and a demand for migrant labour after 1851, with a lively sociability built round cafés and brothels in the *bourgs*. Clergy viewed this 'materialist' culture with suspicion and linked it to political volatility, 'immorality', de-christianisation and crime. During the post-*phylloxera* wine depression in the 1880s the department came third in the table of vagrancy and begging offences. Half of those prosecuted in Montpellier were of 'no fixed abode'. Crime figures by the 1900s were dominated by workers – rail navvies, Sète dockers and unskilled labourers.

Chatelard's (1981) study of St. Etienne, which trebled in population to become France's seventh-largest city, explores relationships between industrialisation and criminality. Between 1840 and 1880 the number of offenders per capita rose from 2.5‰ to 6.17‰. Urban crime levels in the Loire were four times higher than in rural areas. Contemporaries linked crime to the grim environment of an ugly industrial city plagued by bad housing, industrial accidents and high TB rates, whose economy suffered in the Great Depression. Alcohol consumption was two-thirds above the national average. Serious assaults rose to 300 per year in 1905, most involving unskilled, less literate strata of the working class. Violent clashes with the police trebled to 159 per annum. Police who intervened to break up workers' brawls found themselves attacked by both sides. In 1850, 36 per cent of prosecutions were of miners, unskilled and unemployed. By 1900 this figure was 49 per cent. Theft, which rose faster than violent crime, remained small-scale and opportunistic, though one miners' gang used its tunnelling skills to burrow into bourgeois villas! Miners were prosecuted for poaching and coal-pilfering. 'Recidivism' rose, in part because police surveillance made it difficult for ex-convicts to find employment. Official rhetoric portrayed workers as atavistic 'zoological freaks – and then we flatter them'. A medical report on a child delinquent described her as 'flat-nosed, mongoloid. The daughter of an alcoholic, (she is) cynical, foul-mouthed and smutty – with the malevolent cunning of a monkey'. Such 'biological' rhetoric about the urban underclass increasingly dominated bourgeois discourses about crime (Désert 1981; Santucci 1986; Chatelard 1981).

Moral panics – myths and perceptions of crime

France was plagued by recurrent anxieties over crime 'epidemics'. Bourgeois nightmares were haunted successively by the 'dangerous classes', the female criminal, the 'recidivist' and the juvenile delinquent (*apache*). Positivist criminology existed in symbiotic relationship with such 'moral panics'. It nurtured and exacerbated them by offering 'scientific' evidence of 'threats', then trumpeted its role in diagnosing and offering 'therapies' for them. Both bourgeois fears and criminologists' theories are indicators of public obsessions rather than accurate indicators of verifiable trends in criminality. Crime had a central place in the wider cultural anxieties of late-nineteenth-century France. Concern with national degeneracy drew on theories of Italian criminologist Lombroso about 'born criminals', neo-Lamarckean biological theories about degenerative consequences of transmission of acquired characteristics, natalist obsessions with France's declining birth-rate, venereal disease, infanticide and alcoholism, and social-Imperialist concerns about 'unfit' conscripts. Once 'fields of fear' had been generated, figures such as the 'recidivist' assumed inflated significance as symptoms of wider national decline. Resultant 'panics' had little correlation with actual incidence of crime. Fear of crime essentially floated free of the 'facts' of criminality. Hence it is misleading to assume that what *really* matters are actual levels of crime. Fluctuating perceptions of crime are structured by class and gender relations, medical discourses, and national self-image (Nye 1984).

The myth of the criminal and 'dangerous classes'

Although fears about a Parisian 'criminal class' are discernible in the 1780s, the classic era of paranoia lasted from around 1830 to 1871. The term 'dangerous classes', coined in 1840 by police bureaucrat Frégier, was popularised by journalists. Attempts were made to locate these strata, define their characteristics, quantify them and explain their emergence. Historians remain sceptical about such efforts, arguing that the 'dangerous classes' were a 'construct' of a discourse about the popular classes – which labelled them in order to justify surveillance and control. Historiographical debate has centred on Louis Chevalier's (1973) flawed classic – a blend of quantitative demography, Durkheimian sociology, literary evidence and idiosyncratic political views. The Paris which he evoked was a 'sick city' whose pathological demographic and hygiene problems, described in biological metaphors, resulted in a volatile blend of crime and social revolt. The population doubled – to 1.2 million – between 1800 and 1850 through the in-migration of young males. Resultant gender imbalances produced sexual tensions, weak family ties and prostitution. By 1840 one-third of births were illegitimate, one-quarter of babies abandoned. Yet the city's economy was too underdeveloped to offer secure employment for migrants. Inadequate housing provision led to overcrowding and rent increases. Archaic water and sewage systems led to periodic water-shortages and to pervasive filth and stench in an era when the bourgeoisie exhibited an increasing distaste for strong odours. Cholera, which devastated the popular quartiers, gave a biological twist to endemic class hatreds (Chevalier 1973).

Crime and social revolt, Chevalier implies, were the twin consequences. Insurrections stemmed from a brutalised, criminalised popular culture. Even artisans were often dragged down by job insecurity into a subculture of petty criminality alongside *déraciné* migrants, semi-rustic brutes living dozens to a room in lodging houses (*garnis*) which housed some 50,000. These lower depths encompassed workers in marginal trades such as rag-pickers, street-sellers, juveniles from broken homes and prostitutes – many of them unregistered *filles insoumises* (Harsin 1985) – seamstresses and *déclassé* bohemians. Crime became all-pervasive and threatening, no longer picturesque as it had once appeared to élite voyeurs. And it drew in the entire labouring class, not just a marginal stratum. Crime fascinated and appalled the public. The *Gazette des Tribuneaux* reported sensational trials. Eugène Sue's *Mystères de Paris*, the knight-errant hero of which Rodolphe plumbs the lower depths, was a serialised best-seller. Hugo's *Les Misérables* features a convict (Valjean), a street-urchin (Gavroche) and a working-class girl turned prostitute (Fantine). Parent-Duchâtelet estimated that 12 per cent of 15,000 regular prostitutes in Paris were under twelve. Obsessive fear and loathing dominated the mood of the city. Proudhon confessed 'it is getting too much for me living in this city of masters and servants, thieves and prostitutes . . .'.

Anxieties about the 'dangerous classes' were not confined to France. Liberals in post-Risorgimento Italy blamed problems of unification on the criminal poor of the *Mezzogiorno* (Pick 1988). Similar rhetoric was used in Victorian Britain. But elision of the 'criminal classes' with the wider working class and of threats from criminality with those from political radicalism was less pervasive. Anxieties faded in the years of 'mid-Victorian prosperity', despite resurgences during the 1866 Hyde Park riots or 1880s unemployment demonstrations. One Manchester policeman concluded that a 'dangerous class' did exist, but 'it must *not* be confounded with the working class'. It was a hereditary pariah stratum, located in specific areas distinct from 'respectable' labourers. Police 'targeting' of vagrants, street-traders and the Irish served to 'construct' a deviant sub-group. Surveillance of ex-convicts sought to shield the 'honest' poor from contact with and contagion by them. By 1890 Charles Booth proclaimed that 'there *are* barbarians, but they are a handful – a disgrace but not a danger'. The 1867 and 1884 Reform Bills enfranchised 'respectable' artisans while excluding this 'residuum'. In France the threat of popular insurrection persisted. Fear of crime remained more directly linked to politics. One may question claims about a 'real' upsurge in urban crime and 'actual' links between criminality and revolution. But pervasive fears about rising crime and social revolt did haunt the bourgeoisie. Such anxieties in themselves constituted important 'social facts', irrespective of their plausibility. There was no one theory of the dangerous classes. Rather there were constant oscillations between labelling (almost) all workers as (potentially) criminal – and embryonic revolutionaries – and defining particular strata as 'dangerous' in order to use policing and penal strategies to isolate these from the mass of workers. Marx talked of a *lumpenproletariat* forming 'a mass *sharply differentiated from* the industrial proletariat'. His originality was to invert established stereotypes, insisting that this stratum could play a reactionary role as hired tools of the bourgeoisie. Some 'respectable' artisan radicals were concerned to distance themselves from the criminal dregs with which bourgeois rhetoric sought to identify them. Chevalier (1973) blends problematic positivist statistics and impressionistic literary hyperbole to reiterate contemporary prejudices. Since élites feared both crime and social revolution, what could be more 'natural' but that they should perceive socialists – who challenged private property – as criminals?

In his *Recollections*, Tocqueville talks of a drunken wife-beater in his quartier as a socialist by birth and by instinct! 'We are dealing here', Tombs (1989) observes, 'less with coherent theories than with a "myth", a body of shared prejudices and automatic reactions', shared, he adds, 'not only by policeman but by many middle-class revolutionaries.' One-third of Communards, police claimed, were recidivists. One army commander claimed that their 'very faces reveal *at once* what one could expect of them were they free to commit evil . . . Their physiognomies are as revolting as could be imagined'. Mass executions and transportations were essential measures of social hygiene. Le Gaulois insisted that just as 'we take a murderer to the scaffold without asking his opinion on the death penalty . . . so France will pack off to Cayenne 20,000 scoundrels without asking them about the legitimacy of their so-called social ideas'. Troops simply shot vagrants, rag-pickers and labourers from 'dirty' industries of the XIIIe Arrondissement on the assumption that such insalubrious specimens must be criminal and insurrectionary. Similar prejudices permeated the rhetoric of trial judges. 'Never doing any work, believed to live off immoral earnings – a raving Communard . . .' was a typical judicial summing-up (Bailey 1993; Tombs 1980).

Chevalier's implicit elision of revolutionary social protest with criminality is highly dubious. Few Communards had criminal records for offences other than indebtedness or breach of the peace, and most were artisans. Communard National Guardsmen patrolled to prevent looting. In February 1848 insurrectionary crowds who invaded the jails liberated political detainees and prostitutes, but not the 'dregs of the prisons' (Perrot 1980). The statistical basis for Chevalier's claims about Parisian criminality are slim. Many of the relevant records were burned in the siege of 1870–71. Correlations between urbanisation and crime are much more nuanced than Chevalier implies. One analysis of rural and urban crime in France concludes that 'urban growth, population growth and socio-economic change *may* cause tensions but . . . we do not believe that they (necessarily) cause crime' (Tilly and Lhodi 1973). Violence was as often a *rural* phenomenon. Correlations between migration, *déracinement*, anomie and crime are less clear-cut than Chevalier assumed. Police, bureaucrats and criminologists regarded as suspect anyone who moved – *colporteurs*, seasonal migrants, tramping artisans. Yet many migrants to towns contacted pre-existing social networks from the same village or region. Paris was a 'city of villages'. Auvergnats settled in specific quartiers as café-owners, wine-sellers and coachmen, known for their taste for the occasional drink and the odd strike but not really for criminal violence. Limousin migrant building-workers were rarely involved in anything worse than a tavern brawl. Many migrants to Marseilles were industrious, talented and determined to make a success of careers in small business or white-collar occupations. The city could offer chances to escape stifling village constraints or grasp opportunities. Corsicans who migrated from their vendetta-ridden island were viewed as 'criminogenic' by criminologists. Murder rates in Corsica were eight times higher than the national average. Yet whereas French-born migrants and foreign immigrants were accused of over two-thirds of crimes in Marseille in the 1860s, crime-rates among Corsicans were low. By 1890 most of the city's 25,000 Corsicans were *fonctionnaires* or white-collar employees, products of a culture on the island which had come to view education made available by the Guizot Act as the path to social promotion and 'escape' from a violent rural background (Donavan 1984–85).

The Chevalier model is now largely discredited. It talks more of the 'barbarity' of the poor than about their poverty, more about 'pathological' urban milieux than about capitalism. It echoes contemporary élite obsessions with immorality, hygiene and foul smells. Such discourses should not be taken as an 'innocent', accurate mirror of the 'criminality' of the big-city poor (Ratcliffe 1991). Yet the alternative model of urban protest dominated by skilled artisans rooted in families, crafts and communities is too 'decorous'. There *were* areas of Paris, around the Hôtel de Ville before Haussmann, where artisans lived alongside migrant navvies and the poor. Popular disturbance of 1830–34 *did* involve *garnis*-dwellers, migrants, vagrants, and pimps angered by police crackdowns on prostitution. At customs *barrières guinguettes* housed a popular culture in which drinking and rowdiness were endemic, and where police surveillance covered *compagnons'* brawls, the 'Saint Monday' drinking of artisans, planning of strikes and the world-turned-upside-down of Carnival revelry. Most migration was initially to outskirts of cities. There, on the 'margins of city life', police surveillance may, paradoxically, have created a perverse sense of pride and identity (Merriman 1991). The Paris inter-war *banlieue* developed into the notorious 'red belt' because its inhabitants developed solidarities based on exclusion from the bourgeoisifed city centre. Belleville expanded during the Second Empire through an influx of rural migrants, industrial workers and artisans displaced from the centre. Initially notorious for a volatile culture of dance halls and petty crime, it emerged as the bastion of radicalism in 1869–71 – an evolution similar to that of Faubourg St Antoine in the 1780s. This metamorphosis from being viewed as 'dangerous' because of perceived criminality to being notorious for revolutionary politics meant that young workers with a history of petty crime eventually achieved a degree of 'class identity' by fighting in units of the Belleville National Guard first against the Prussians, then as Communards. Some were grasping a unique opportunity to seek revenge on landlords and police (Ratcliffe 1991; Tombs 1980).

Such processes were not confined to Paris. In Rouen, bourgeois rhetoric conflated perils from crime with those from suburban textile proletarians. Ingouville, on the outskirts of Le Havre, was notorious as a haunt of sailors, dock-workers and unlicensed prostitutes before becoming a 'red' bastion in 1848–51. Justifying the May 1850 electoral law, which disenfranchised migrants and those with criminal records, Thiers insisted 'it is *the mob, not the people*, that we wish to exclude – the heterogeneous mob so mobile that they cannot be "pinned down" and who have not succeeded in establishing any regular home for their families'. After the Bonapartist coup police received wider powers to control such suburbs. Transportation was now used against political suspects and 'hardened' criminals. The 'dangerous classes' myth which conflated criminality and socio-political protest proved tenacious not merely because of élite paranoia but because there was just sufficient evidence constantly to reconfirm its plausibility. Some insurrectionaries did come from occupations and neighbourhoods with a 'dangerous' image. Hence, Tombs (1980) concludes, 'it is the *half-truth* of the "myth" of the dangerous classes that *some* of them *were* prone to riot, the streets of Paris into which they were crowded *were* dangerous – (and) not only for passers-by but for the security of the State' (Tombs 1980).

After 1871 the 'myth' assumed new forms. The post-Commune mood is graphically illustrated by responses to Zola's *L'Assommoir* (1877), written to illustrate how insecurities of workers' lives pushed some to the consolation of drink. Conservatives, who viewed the Commune as an outburst of proletarian alcoholism, took the novel as evidence that workers were poor and violent because they drank. After the 1873 Law on Public Drunkenness police arrested some 60,000 per annum for alcohol-related offences, targeting specific urban quartiers (Barrows 1981). Thereafter anxieties focused sometimes on 'juvenile delinquents', sometimes on '*apache*' gangs descending from Belleville to terrorise bourgeois central Paris. 'Greasy', 'knife-wielding' Italian immigrants became a target for police surveillance, and were three times more likely to be arrested than native workers. Like the Irish in Britain, they served a useful function of dividing the working class by acting as scapegoats, targets

for the xenophobia of 'respectable' native workers. Undoubtedly the experiences of the Commune gave greater clout than in Victorian Britain to
the biological positivism of emerging 'scientific' criminology with its emphasis
on the 'born criminal' nurtured by a combination of flawed heredity and
pathological social milieu.

The female criminal

The spectre of the female criminal haunted the social imagination of fin-
de-siècle France, even though statistics suggested low and declining female
delinquency. Women comprised a mere 14 per cent of defendants, were
convicted of 6 per cent of violent thefts and 13 per cent of murders, and
comprised only 12 per cent of convicts by 1914. Certainly crime per se
obsessed the mass media. Readers had the choice of serialised crime novels,
vivid details of crimes in *faits divers* columns of newspapers, memoirs of
celebrity criminals and vulgarised versions of criminological theories. These
provided vicarious thrills and illusions of insights into the pathologies of
contemporary society. But it was the female offender, 'a titillating figure poised
on the cusp of cultural change', who excited 'experts' and the press (Shapiro
1996). She tapped into a range of anxieties. By her violation of social and
gender codes she incarnated a profound national sickness in a period when
a sense of decadence generated anguished debates on crime, gender and degeneration. The dominance of the old *notables* was waning, cities were growing,
the masses were enfranchised. The rise of syndicalism, and the threat of
anarchist bombers, indicated the difficulties of integrating the working class.
Alcoholism and venereal disease nurtured fears of 'degeneration'. Crime, in
particular recidivism, appeared to be rising again after levelling-off in the
1850–60s. A cluster of concerns about the family, the birth-rate and feminism were elided together. It appeared that processes of social destabilisation
and national decline were nurtured by a 'gender slippage'. Feminists' concerns with educational and career opportunities suggested that marriage and
motherhood were now relegated in importance and that the decline on the
birth-rate would accelerate, threatening France's future as a Great Power and
the survival of the 'race'. Debate about women's 'right' to sexual satisfaction
in marriage was blamed for the spread of adultery and divorce and alarming
evidence of male sexual anxiety and impotence (Nye 1984). Fascination with
the figure of the 'insatiable' nymphomaniac 'stood at the intersection of male
fantasy, myth, anxiety and medical science'. The duel, which enjoyed an
apparently anachronistic revival under the democratic Republic, signified
a desperate attempt to reassert virile masculine values on the face of the
devouring sexual demands of the new woman (Nye 1984).

In this anxiety-ridden, emasculated culture 'female criminality' symbolised both gender disorder and wider social disintegration. Distinctions
between the feminist and female criminal blurred. In *Les Femmes qui tuent et
les femmes qui volent* (1873), Alexander Dumas *fils* portrayed murderesses as the
vanguard of the feminist crusade, prepared to act to secure rights for their
sex. The woman with a knife or a vial of acid was a feminist with a bargaining chip! The world was being turned upside-down, as women pursued careers,
sought 'sterile' sexual pleasures, practised birth-control or lesbianism. Was

not 'the story of sapphism the story of emancipated women?'. In such discourse all independent women in the city were potential prostitutes, and taken to incarnate wider urban pathologies. The eponymous heroine of Zola's *Nana* is the daughter of alcoholic proletarian parents who wreaks class revenge on her rich lovers by spreading venereal disease. 'With her', Zola commented, 'the rottenness which was allowed to ferment amongst the lower classes was rising to the surface.' Zola shared, perhaps unconsciously, assumptions of Right-wing 'crowd theorists' such as Le Bon about the 'irrationality' of the female crowd. In *Germinal*, a crowd of wives of striking miners castrate the local grocer. One academic study of 'crime and debauchery' in 1890s Paris saw fit to insert an appendix listing women who had gained university degrees! The author of a study on women convicts claimed that 'in this time of feminism this book had found its moment!'. These issues were analysed by criminologists and psychiatrists, male 'experts' who collected 'social facts', diagnosed society's pathologies and offered prophylactic knowledge. The medical/criminological consensus was that all women, not just the 'criminal' minority, were potentially 'hysterical'. 'All women', Lombroso insisted, 'fall into the *same* category, whereas *each* man is individual to himself.' Republican historian Michelet, a close observer of his partner's menstrual cycle, had insisted that woman was 'almost always in a state of relative incapacity' because of her reproductive biology. Some doctors argued that this might trigger degeneration, others that the reproductive cycle was per se pathological. Such theories were endlessly malleable. 'Hysterical' behaviour might be triggered by late, or early, puberty, by a period or the non-arrival of a period. The menopause might end years of menstrual problems, or precipitate menopausal mania! Irrational violence might stem from suppression of periods by pregnancy, or by their return after childbirth. An analysis of 104 'kleptomaniacs' diagnosed 35 suffering menstrual tension and 10 from menopausal mania!

Such discourses systematically blurred distinctions between 'criminal' women and *all* women. They were portrayed as suggestible, prone to copy what they read in newspapers, susceptible to hypnotic suggestion and capable of committing crimes under the sway of lovers (Harris 1989; Shapiro 1996). Experts identified a cluster of superficially contradictory 'female' characteristics. Natural gossips, women were prone to reveal the secrets of their crimes. Yet because adolescent girls learned to hide menstrual blood from their first periods, women were deceitful, capable of tricking psychiatrists attempting to analyse them. The 'secretive' female crime was poisoning. Male poisoners were assumed to possess 'female' characteristics. One newspaper proclaimed that 'suddenly poisoning is on the scene again, speading horror, multiplying suspicions, creating stories more terrifying than truth itself'. Though recorded poisoning cases were rare, the press sensationalised cases such as that in Bouches-du-Rhône where wives allegedly purchased poisons from a female herbalist to kill their husbands and 'give themselves over more fully to libertinage'!

The net impact on women's treatment by the criminal justice system was paradoxical. The female criminal aroused the spectre of 'unruly' women rejecting their role as passive victims. Yet female offenders were treated with increasing leniency. Acquittal rates of 50 per cent contrasted with 30 per cent for male defendants. Many 'female' crimes were reclassified as *délits* and sent to the lower courts. However, such 'leniency' developed because women were deemed 'irrational' – not fully 'adult' nor fully 'responsible' for their actions. Indeed, in 'crime of passion' cases they became 'victims', deserving pity from male jurors. Defence lawyers adopted a paternalistic tone, posing as protectors of the defenceless, urging (male) jurors to be compassionate. Leniency was easier for bourgeois jurors to contemplate in cases of violence between working-class women and husbands or lovers. Violence within the working class posed less of a threat to the social order.

Female defendants were expected to play their prescribed role in the 'script' of courtroom cases – formulaic dramas in which victims of seduction, betrayal or brutality had been unable to control their passions. Assize Courts attracted large crowds. Trials were theatrical 'happenings'. Defendants' courtroom 'stories' were constructed through complex interaction between stereotypes of femininity borrowed from literary genres, particularly melodrama, criminological and psychological theories, and the mass media. Graffiti in men's prisons evoked hatred and pride. Those in women's cells, it was claimed, spoke of love, religion, regret. Acquittals occurred if women internalised and acted out a part – loyal wife and mother, credulous and betrayed lover and contrite wrongdoer. Such defendants emerged as 'victims' of their 'female' frailties and of male betrayal. Defence lawyers appealed to courts to 'close the Codes and open our hearts!'. As one sardonic jurist remarked, 'just as . . . socialism has claimed the right to insurrection . . . for the poor . . . , so novels and modern drama have invented rights to vengeance for forsaken love'. Some defendants put themselves beyond the pale because unable or unwilling to act out prescribed roles. Marie Lerondeau alienated the court by citing her husband's sexual inadequacies as justification for not doing housework ('*You* don't do *your* duty, so I won't do mine!'). Marie Charrier regularly contradicted her husband in public. Eugènie Belligand aroused anxieties of male jurors by killing a man who had rejected her paternity claim against him.

To comprehend the implications of such cases, Shapiro (1996) insists, one must view these as 'stories in tension', marked by internal contradictions and possibilities of alternative narratives. Some defendants claimed to have attacked husbands or lovers who had squandered savings or defrauded them in business deals. As such trials attracted media headlines, a public forum was created in which critiques of women's subordinate legal and economic status could be voiced. Male irresponsibility was placed in the spotlight. Men were exposed evading paternity claims, neglecting illegitimate children, squandering family money, evoking the 'double standard' to justify their own infidelities. A 'crime of passion' trial became a 'social text' within which gender relations were played out. It was no accident that on the eve of 1914 women won the right to seek paternity of illegitimate children. As courtroom 'theatre' merged with the *faits divers* columns of the mass press and with cheap crime novels, distinctions between fiction and reality blurred. Zola's *La Bête Humaine*, in which a wife and lover murder the husband, was based on a newspaper *faits divers* story. 'Expert' witnesses cited novels to support their evidence. Critic Talmeyr deplored such trends: 'The *roman feuilleton* is able to create that dangerous thing, a *mentalité populaire*. It is said that a man's life ends by resembling his dreams. Will the life of the people end by resembling its fiction.' Perhaps women were throwing vitriol in lovers' faces because they had read about such acts in newspapers or in novels. Lawyers were worried that the agenda of justice was slipping out of official control – that the meaning of trials was being determined by groups beyond the courtroom who were articulating narratives about the crimes appropriate to their own concerns and codes. Trials involving women who killed abusive husbands or lovers became eloquent pleas for legal reforms which might give women a greater say in household finance or question sexual double standards. Acquittals by jurors signified acceptance, de facto, of women's right to carry out personal acts of justice (Shapiro 1996).

Unsurprisingly a backlash developed. Novels and plays featured scheming women who learned to play the role of repentant wronged lover to secure acquittal. The jury system was criticised, as were 'scientific' orthodoxies about women's biological frailties which, allegedly, undermined courts' ability to insist on women's personal responsibility. 'Today with vulgarised theories . . . spreading everywhere and announcing determinism, the corrupting influence of social milieu, *how* is it *possible* for juries to declare with any assurance "this person is guilty", asked Baradez. By 1900 some psychiatrists, alarmed that their testimonies were leading to acquittals, tightened definitions of 'insanity'. There were disturbing implications to claims that all women were ruled by their reproductive cycles. If they felt and acted differently not only was it difficult to apply the same principles of justice to them but also to draw a demarcation line between the 'criminal' female and the respectable bourgeois wife. How could one regenerate French society around domesticity and the family unit if, in effect, wives were granted *carte blanche* to murder husbands and if male jurors regularly acquitted women accused of infanticide or abortion?

Hence the female-in-court appeared to incarnate feminism in action. By dramatising a range of women's grievances, such cases nurtured the climate in which divorce was reintroduced (1884) and women began to secure wider legal, financial and educational rights. The role of *romans feuilletons* and *faits divers* in these processes may suggest that standard accusations about their 'conservative' cultural impact must be nuanced (Schapiro 1996). Rather than being either 'conformist' or 'subversive', their effects should be viewed as multivalent – for 'subaltern' groups could appropriate them to articulate alternative values. Their meaning was not fixed by the ideology or authorial intent of their often mercenary and reactionary authors. For they drew wide audiences into debates about female crime which raised fundamental questions about women's rights and gender relations.

'Juvenile delinquents' of the Belle Époque
With the birth-rate collapsing it appeared vital that the educational system should deliver dutiful, patriotic youngsters – future citizen-soldiers. Hence juvenile delinquency aroused real anxieties. And there was statistical evidence for such fears. Gabriel Tarde claimed that juvenile crime had quadrupled between 1830 and 1880 and Interior Ministry figures in 1890 suggested that

prosecution rates of males in their late-teens were four times higher than the national average. Rates of 'recidivism' among former detainees of juvenile agricultural colonies established since 1850 stood at 75 per cent.

Most juvenile crime was petty, and figures were inflated by arrests of truants and by police clampdowns on street culture. But gangs of youthful *apaches* 'descended' from Belleville to prey on tourists in central Paris. Between 1890 and 1894, 39 juveniles were charged with murder. The murders in July (Yonne) of a farmer, his wife and three employees, including a servant-girl whose head was found floating in the river, led to the arrest of two teenage cowherds, described by the press as of 'a type that one has *never* seen in *any* society at *any* time'. One was an orphan treated 'too leniently' by an over-indulgent uncle. The other had been born prematurely – a sure recipe for a 'vicious and unbalanced' personality! Comparative evidence might have suggested to such commentators that juvenile delinquency was a Europe-wide phenomenon. Prosecutions of juveniles rose 51 per cent in Germany between 1881 and 1892. But it was treated as if a peculiarly French problem. The Right's analysis drew on a bizarre blend of Lombroso, degeneration theory and religious moralism. It came as no surprise to Catholics that 90 per cent of juveniles incarcerated in the Petite Roquette jail had attended laic schools. If the young carried the mark of the beast on their foreheads, it was the fault of *l'école sans Dieu*. A 'defence' of *instituteurs* from charges of corrupting the nation's youth by criminologist G. Tarde was unlikely to reassure Republicans, for he denounced the whole of contemporary culture: 'It is in the parental home that the pupils first drank in the poisoned well of religious and moral scepticism, of precocious greed, of alcoholism. When it is not in the home, it is from the workshop, the café or the press that the microbes of this virus have penetrated the child's heart.' The left countered with critiques of privately run, Catholic 'agricultural colonies' for juveniles. High rates of recidivism among detainees showed that it was the Catholic sector, with its brutal discipline, forced marches, under-trained staff and rumoured sexual molestations, which was the 'school of vice.' Agricultural skills which they purported to inculcate were totally irrelevant to the urban job-market (Faure 1980; Perrot 1979; Lefaucheur 1996).

Some Republicans accepted that juvenile offenders were often victims deserving care, training, rehabilitation – *not* incarceration alongside hardened offenders. The Radical *Dépêche de Toulouse* dared suggest that had the Yonne orphan-murderer had adequate welfare support he might have been 'saved'. An 1889 Act facilitated removal of children from 'brutal' parents, although respect for paternal authority it was invoked in only 1200 cases annually. In 1898 'delinquents' were bracketed with abused and molested children as needing protection not punishment, although local authorities complained that *Assistance Publique* lacked the funding to care for juvenile delinquents who risked 'corrupting' their regular child charges. A 1905 Law followed Scandinavian examples by raising the age of majority in criminal cases to 18 – provoking predictable howls from conservatives about excessive leniency for younger offenders. A 1908 law forbade incarceration of under-age prostitutes. Finally, following the German model, juvenile courts were established and instructed to adopt a conciliatory and 'psychological' rather than punitive approach. Extra skill training was provided in juvenile colonies, since the decline of apprenticeships contributed to the 'rise' of delinquency. A 'hard core' of offenders was identified and placed in segregated camps, denounced by the Left as *bagnes d'enfants*. Progressives praised the new initiatives but criticised persistent under-funding, for 'in the education of young delinquents there are economies which cost dear and are (themselves) criminal'. Inevitably, given the savage tone of law-and-order debates, the Right denounced this 'soft' approach. The *Petit Journal* complained that 'never have criminals begun at such a precocious age. And, as if to fly in the face of common-sense, (politicians) are . . . making penal sanctions softer and . . . removing the one remaining fear that these (young thugs) had – that of the *gendarme*'. It urged restoration of flogging.

Discipline and punish . . .

The penal system has recently become the focus of empirical research and vigorous ideological dispute. Liberal historians offer a 'grand narrative' telling of humanitarian progress, albeit erratic and gradual. The Ancien Régime's overstretched police forces apprehended a tiny proportion of offenders, but inflicted exemplary brutality on those caught. Suspects languished in dungeons, confessions were extracted by torture, public executions and dismemberment were key rituals of royal power. Criminals were whipped, branded, hauled through streets in chains and consigned to hard labour in *bagnes* in naval ports or galleys. The Enlightenment's humanitarian and utilitarian critique of this barbaric system was one of its achievements. Following the Italian Beccaria, reformers demanded greater certainty of punishment, but punishment to fit the crime. Judicial torture was both cruel per se and produced false confessions. Such methods brutalised popular culture. Equality before the law, access to a defence lawyer, open court procedures, clear penalties proportionate to the crime were prerequisites of any 'civilised' system.

Actual use of torture was declining and younger magistrates were sympathetic to reforms. More radical voices were heard suggesting that crime was not the product of free-will of flawed individuals but of a society of inequalities and mass ignorance. Education and social reform would reduce crime, and a penal régime built around training could 'rehabilitate' offenders. From 1789 till 1848, liberals argue, the general thrust of official policies was broadly in tune with such ideas. The 1791 Penal Code insisted that punishment serve purposes of retribution and deterrence but also of rehabilitation. A maximum sentence of 24 years was fixed to allow prisoners to 'retain hope'. Accused were assumed innocent until proven guilty and had the right to jury trial. Torture was abolished, needless severity in punishment forbidden. The goal was to replace *bagnes* and galleys with purpose-built prisons (Wright 1983; Petit 1990). A minority argued for abolition of the death penalty, but fears of popular unrest and of counter-revolution led the majority to insist that social defence required its retention.

Violent political oscillations meant that consolidation of a liberal judicial and penal system proved difficult. The period 1791–1810 witnessed fewer capital sentences and less forced labour, with more offenders fined or jailed.

However, the Jacobin Terror resorted to arbitrary arrest and the guillotine, invented as a 'humanitarian' alternative to older methods of execution. The Directory and Bonapartist régimes used military courts and summary executions to control counter-revolutionary brigands and army deserters in the Midi and the West, arguing that justices of the peace and juries were intimidated by, or in collusion with, local armed gangs. Bonaparte, determined to deal with men 'as they were' and not as liberals would have liked them to be, increased public-prosecutors' powers, introduced a tougher Penal Code (1810), restored corporal punishment and branding and maintained the surviving *bagnes* – in short built a 'security state' (Brown 1997–98). Between 1815 and 1848 there was a vigorous debate among liberals and 'philanthropists' keen on a system of model prisons. Statistics were gathered, reports compiled and visits made to American 'penitentiaries', with their segregated prisoners, small cells and disciplined work-routines. Some favoured isolation of prisoners, others – such as prison inspector Charles Lucas – viewed this as inhumane and advocated shared work systems. Gains were made. The 1831 Penal Code introduced the concept of 'extenuating circumstances'. Branding was ended, corporal punishment phased out. A reduction in capital offences led to a decline in executions, henceforth held at the outer *barrières*, no longer in the city centre, and at dawn not midday. Chain-gangs en route to the *bagnes* were no longer to be paraded for public view. Cell prisons were built in Bordeaux, Tours and – for juveniles – at Petite Roquette. An 1839 circular endorsed age and gender segregation of prisoners, fixed daily routines, regular work, silence and close supervision. It appeared that a reformist coalition of Protestant and Catholic 'philanthropists', bureaucrats and 'scientific' experts was winning official backing for the extension of such policies. Yet governments were reluctant to build costly cell-prisons. Hence most prisoners were still held in dark, overcrowded buildings, often ex-convents or *dépôts de mendicité*, and slept in dormitories. Prisoners' survival rates were higher in *bagnes* than in older jails such as Limoges. Rising recidivism allowed conservatives to argue that emphasis on 'rehabilitation' was making the system too 'soft' to act as a deterrent.

Marxists, suspicious of 'humanitarian' penal reformers, suggest that the new system reflected the priorities of emerging capitalism. Perceiving the ancien régime's arbitrary system as a threat to their own freedoms, the bourgeoisie wanted the 'rule of law'. However, the rise of agrarian and commercial capitalism was changing the nature of popular crime. By defining traditional popular activities – gleaning, use of forests, 'perks' on the docks – as 'theft', capitalism pushed peasants and workers into crime, thereby increasing the need for discipline and punishment. Meanwhile property-crime expanded as the commercial revolution increased the visibility of commodities. Economic crisis in the 1780s pushed the poor into petty theft, so that the percentage of galley-prisoners convicted of food theft rose from 5 per cent to 15 per cent (Petit 1984). Reformist projects were a quest for a more efficient method of controlling property crime. Magistrates favoured a larger mounted constabulary to clamp down on vagrancy. The goal was to punish not less but more systematically and effectively. Moreover, since the new capitalist order multiplied social inequalities and injustices, and was incapable of delivering its rhetorical promises of freedom and opportunity, it pushed the poor into delinquency. By 1840 there were over 100,000 prisoners in French jails, a per capita rate three times higher than in modern Britain. Prisoners were used as cheap labour, undercutting wage levels of 'free' labour and providing profits for private entrepreneurs. Convicts were moulded to become a suitably docile and productive labour force. Torturing prisoners made less economic sense than tapping their labour power. The incarcerated population swelled in the depressions of the 1840s and the 1880s, when capitalism faced the problem of controlling masses of 'surplus' unemployed. By the 1840s, as debates over 'recidivism' attest, reformers knew that prison was failing in its ostensible purpose of 'rehabilitation'. Yet by then this system appeared essential for preserving 'order'.

This Marxist analysis overlaps with that of Foucault, who is equally suspicious of liberal reformers' humanitarianism and views creation of *homo docilis* – the obedient, industrious being essential for a disciplined labour force – as a goal of the system. But Foucault insists that to ask why prison failed to rehabilitate or eliminate recidivism is to ask misconceived questions. The system's real purpose was never to reduce crime but rather to 'construct deviance', to create the 'habitual criminal' by a process of jailing and categorisation. It was a divide-and-rule strategy designed to widen the gulf between honest workers and criminals and create a manageable criminality which produced both police informers and blacklegs (Foucault 1977; Petit 1990). Foucault's methodology is not easily assimilated by empiricist historians or Marxists. An attempted 'encounter' in the 1970s between Foucault and social historians produced an ephemeral dialogue of the deaf (Petit 1996; Perrot 1975). Foucault despised the historians' 'true little facts'. For all its critique of bourgeois humanitarianism, Marxism – a child of the Enlightenment – shared with liberalism a 'progressive metanarrative', and had its own vision of a progressive future, albeit one beyond capitalism. Foucault, by contrast, was an anarcho-Nietzschean *enfant terrible* for whom the Enlightenment meant not potential human emancipation but rather power and control. The logical outcome of Enlightenment projects was the dystopia of a disciplinary society based on surveillance. The 'knowledge' of experts and reformers was directed to the construction of a 'carceral society', of which prisons, alongside asylums, hospitals, schools, barracks and factories, were pillars. The *modus operandi* of the penal system was no longer to torture bodies of transgressors against the King, but to exert systematic control over prisoners' bodies and minds. Having broken the social contract these would be forced to accept that they deserved punishment and to understand the logic of their punishment. Bentham's Panopticon – the 'all-seeing-eye' – thus symbolised a project the ultimate goal of which was to persuade prisoners to think and behave as if under constant surveillance. Dark dungeons thus gave way to 'transparent' cells. 'Micro-penalties' were imposed for lateness, swearing, talking, dirtiness. Some prisoners expressed a preference for the *bagnes* where 'at least one can chat'.

Foucault was a brilliant gadfly, a stimulating provocateur. The Enlightenment *did* have its dark side. Post-Revolutionary régimes, liberal as well as Bonapartist, had disciplinary projects. Modernity has meant in practice, all too often, not liberty and equality but bureaucratic efficiency. Possibly the 'power' of liberal-humanitarianism is insidious because it denies its own will-to-power. Foucault's emphasis that 'power' does not reside just in the hands of 'capitalist state' or economic bourgeoisie is useful. 'Power' is often diffuse, located in multiple sites, in multiple 'micro-powers'. In the penal system it resides with prison governors, warders, the discourses of penologists, criminologists or architects who design model prisons. It derives from 'knowledge', 'expertise' and the ability to label some as 'criminal' or 'insane', to establish 'regimes of truth' where they set the norms and compile the dossiers. Anarchist Proudhon was already aware that 'to be governed is to be surveilled, spied upon, regimented, indoctrinated'. But how should the social historian approach Foucault's *Discipline and Punish*? Although this appears to be a 'history' of the French penal system from 1750 to 1850, it is described as a 'chapter in the history of penal reasoning'. Can one subscribe to Foucault's critique of the Enlightenment? Were Beccaria's French followers simply seeking more effective methods of control? Did the Revolution destroy the Bastille only to construct more efficient *gulags*? Or should one not acknowledge that, despite very real configurations of class power and coercive cultural traits, real efforts to create a freer, more equal society were being made? Was not the post-1789 system a blend of remnants of the old cruelty, utilitarianism, bourgeois class prejudice and genuine humanitarianism? Social historians remain uneasy with Foucault's condescending insistence that their quest for 'causes' is a symptom of intellectual immaturity. Penal policy remains, in Foucault's account, a 'strategy without generals'. There appears to be a 'project' of surveillance and control. But who is devising the strategy? Are the processes described a product of human agency? Foucault's cavalier attitude to 'facts' cannot but worry empirical, not just 'empiricist', historians. He shows little interest in the contingencies of 'actual' history. He largely ignores the Revolution and omits the 1810 Penal Code, which reintroduced some 'brutal' procedures. He implies that the old system was swept away once the 'epistemological break' had occurred. Yet *bagnes* and chain-gangs persisted till 1848. While cell-prisons epitomised new ideals of surveillance, bourgeois taxpayers proved reluctant to fund construction of these. St. Lazare women's jail, still in use in 1940, was a seventeenth-century building. Foucault largely ignores prisoners' 'agency' and capacity for action. While he championed prisoners' rights in the 1970s, his analysis appears to assume that prisoners, like hospital patients or company-town workers, were passive pawns of strategies and discourses of power which, per se, exerted a normative impact. However, as J. Léonard warned, 'The historian's nineteenth-century is *neither* a mechanism for crushing individuals *nor* a Machiavellian plot – but an assortment of political and social struggles' in which bourgeois 'normalisation' was vigorously contested (Léonard 1980; Petit 1996).

After a brief libertarian moment in 1848 the penal system appeared to become *harsher* as the century advanced. During the 1840s advocates of cell-prisons increasingly argued in terms of isolating and disciplining dangerous offenders rather than of rehabilitation. In Fresnes jail, cells were used in an essentially punitive way. In February 1848, crowds invaded jails and freed prisoners. Capital punishment was abolished, as was prison labour. The latter had been a target of protest from 'free' workers for undercutting wage-rates. Cholet textile merchants utilised prisoners in Fontevraud jail. Entrepreneurs bribed warders to turn a blind eye to abuses, and operated a truck-system whereby convicts were obliged to spend the tiny wage they received buying food at a prison company store. A scandal at Clairvaux, where 709 convicts died in 1845–47, many from polluted food supplied by such a store, discredited the system. Investigators found survivors emaciated and vermin-covered. In the aftermath of February 1848, workers demonstrated against prison-labour schemes and prisoners, 'infected' by the mood beyond the prison walls, rioted and sang the Marseilleise.

The 1848 reforms were jettisoned as the conservative backash gathered pace. Prison governors claimed that bored convicts welcomed reintroduction of prison labour. Capital punishment returned. A major casualty was the penitentiary model, jettisoned without ever having been properly tested. The dominant reactionary discourse insisted that rehabilitation was a mirage. Penal systems had to be harsh in order to deter. Unless prisoners were kept hungrier and more miserable then industrial workers, recidivism would rise inexorably. Liberal Lamartine supported transportation, for all 'civilised nations' felt the need 'to disgorge their scum, if I may use the phrase, on some distant shore'. Thousands of June Days insurgents and many who resisted the 1851 coup were to die of disease in tropical penal colonies. Transportation, introduced just as Britain was phasing out her system, lasted until the 1940s. In 1854 it was extended to some recidivists. Anyone sentenced to eight years' hard labour would now serve this in a penal colony and remain there for a further eight years as 'free' labour. The Emperor praised the policy for furthering 'the advance of French colonisation' (Wright 1983).

This shift to tougher penal strategies was influenced by the rise of positivist criminology and 'degeneration theory'. Orleanist liberals accepted free will and individual responsibility, but urged that 'deserved' punishment should contain rehabilitative components. Medicalisation of the discourse on crime led to questioning of offenders' capacity to reform. The 'born criminal', with low-forehead, thick-skull, imperviousness to pain and absence of remorse, was perceived as a product of hereditary determinism and the corrupting influence of pathological milieux. Though French doctor Morel anticipated some of Lombroso's ideas on degeneration, these ideas never achieved undisputed hegemony within French penal discourse. Liberals still argued for 'free will', Catholics for restoration of religious and family values. Criminologist Lacassagne claimed that the social milieu provided the environment in which criminal 'microbes' reproduced. Public opinion remained eclectic and confused. But politicians assumed that a majority favoured tough policies. If 'free will' did exist, criminals *chose* to offend and deserved punishment. If heredity and biology determined actions, then 'social defence' and public safety required draconian penalties. 'When a mad dog bites', Le Bon commented, 'I do not ask whether it is *responsible*. It is shot.' This 'logic' led inexorably to the belief that elimination of criminals – via guillotine, castration, eugenicist policies or transportation – was the only viable option (Pick 1988).

This climate may explain the contrast between the Republic's liberal rhetoric and its penal strategies. Republicans criticised Bonapartist authoritarianism and inherited a prison-system which, even liberal neo-Orleanists admitted, needed reform. In 1875 d'Haussonville introduced a Bill to restore the cell-prison model to reduce recidivism. However, a study of the 'Republican prison' by R. Badinter – who as minister in Mitterand's 1981 government abolished the death-penalty – concludes that the régime lived in 'permanent contradiction', maintaining a penal system which flouted its supposed ideals. Governments were tougher on crime than on the causes of crime. An 1885 Act introduced transportation for a second identical offence, for a third offence meriting a sentence of more than three months, or for any fifth offence. Politicians were aware that transportation, the 'dry guillotine', was a virtual death-sentence; 66 per cent of convicts sent to Guiana died before their sentence was completed. 'Freed' convicts who survived their term were kept on in the colony to work the land. Embarrassed by similarities between their policies and those of the Bonapartists, Republicans coined the euphemism 'relegation'. By the 1890s some 1700 'relegations' occurred annually.

Badinter (1993) concedes that, if Republican judicial humanism halted at the prison door, efforts *were* made to reduce the numbers incarcerated. Convict labour was phased out. Non-custodial sentences were introduced for first and minor offenders. A parole system released nearly 2000 annually after 1885 into the care of largely private patronage networks. Suspended sentences, probation and youth-courts further reduced numbers in custody. Yet the overall climate was harsh. Republicans eulogised hard-work and honesty and appealed to an electorate dominated by 'little men' – peasants, white-collar employees, small businessmen. It was tempting to portray 'criminals' as parasitic 'others' – good-for-nothing children to whom 'Marianne' had every justification for refusing her breast. Lip service was still paid to the cell-prison, but there were only nine of these. Taxpayers were reluctant to 'waste' money on prison refurbishment. Myths persisted of five-star jails where prisoners were lodged and fed better than honest workers. The result was a prison system of extraordinary heterogeneity, with overcrowded jails and departmental prisons notorious for their 'promiscuous' mixing of different types of prisoners (Badinter 1993; Wright 1983). Some 'settled' workers now felt distant from and unsympathetic towards 'marginals' and 'deviants', and vagabonds and beggars whose numbers swelled in the 1880s depression and who faced transportation. The rise in recidivism above 50 per cent by the 1880s was influenced by police surveillance strategies which forbade ex-convicts from returning to their native department, which constructed habitual criminals by cutting them off from working-class communities. Rather later than in Victorian Britain, elites were splitting the 'respectable' from the 'rough'. Tough penal policies were also a product of parliamentary in-fighting. Short-lived cabinets were reluctant to alienate voters by appearing 'soft' on crime. Clemenceau, who had savaged the 'relegation' Act, metamorphosed into France's 'Top Cop', wasting much of his 1906–09 Radical government's reforming potential on 'law-and-order' initiatives. Juvenile delinquency and a rise in the murder rate nurtured a near-hysterical mood. Radical deputies, who had once denounced capital punishment as a 'stone-age' policy, abused socialists for seeking its abolition. Fewer than 20 executions now occurred annually. There was one full-time executioner (*bourreau*), rather than one per department as in 1800. Executions were now largely hidden from public gaze. Yet they continued to fascinate the popular press, which gave them gruesome coverage. Republican politicians were too wary of offending the *Petit Parisien* to risk supporting abolition.

We know less of prisons and prisoners than of the projects of those who ran the penal system. However, it is misleading to view prisoners as simply trapped in the discourses of those in power. Convicts developed their own prison culture and resistance strategies, even if we lack information about the scale of protest. At its apogee the penal system housed some 108,000 prisoners – 1 in 300 of the population. Transportation and selective leniency cut numbers after 1860; 90 per cent were male, and two-thirds aged between 21 and 40. A rising percentage were urban dwellers, often unskilled and frequently unemployed when arrested. Illiteracy among prisoners did decline, but remained well above the national average. Whereas acquittal rates for those with secondary education reached 70 per cent, 50 per cent of illiterate accused were convicted. For all reformers' enthusiasm for rehabilitation, few resources were devoted to prison education, despite an increase after 1873. This reflected not only endemic penny-pinching but also a growing scepticism about Hugo's dictum that when a school opened, a prison closed. Criminologist Tarde insisted that education raised expectations among the popular classes, thereby generating more, and more sophisticated, criminals. Since successive régimes lacked the will to fund cell-prisons, the dream of total surveillance never came close to fulfilment. Prisoners were no more passive guinea-pigs of disciplinary projects than miners in company-towns were the 'tireless little workers' of paternalist discourse. There were at least 37 revolts in Parisian jails between 1815 and 1848 (Petit 1990). Prisoners ran black-markets in contraband goods, often with the connivance of ill-paid and ill-trained warders. Tattooing with a variety of images, symbols and slogans – sexual, patriotic, military, political, occupational, defiant – was endemic, as was use of prison *argot*. While this was taken by criminologists as confirmation of the 'atavism' of hardened criminals, it served to assert individuality and refuse submission to the prison régime. Hence rather than being a 'total system' of control, prison was a complex system of dominance and resistance, with its own complex rituals of exchange (O'Brien 1988).

Prison did help to construct a class of 'hardened criminals' and to inflate the problem of recidivism which so preoccupied the authorities. As liberal lawyer Faucher – later a hard-line Bonapartist – observed in 1844, 'prison takes a robust constitution and weakens it, takes the occasional criminal and turns him into a habitual one. Instead of dispersing offenders, it encourages the need in them to associate with one another'. While hardships of working-class life led to a delinquent's first offence, it was prison culture which turned him into a 'criminal'. Recidivism was the logical outcome of a convict culture nurtured by resistance to the technologies of power. Ex-convicts were kept under police surveillance and denied access to their native commune and to industrial centres where jobs were available. Once stigmatised as 'criminal', they were stuck with the label. They were banned from begging, and threatened with transportation if they breached regulations. Over 60 per cent of recidivists in the 1870s and 1880s began as short-term prisoners convicted of minor *délits*. The system's logic pushed them inexorably towards a career of multiple petty offences. Finger-printing, photography and centralised dossiers made police surveillance more efficient. In the decades when peasants were being turned into 'Frenchmen', the penal system was excluding recidivists from the nation. Criminologists contributed to this by emphasising the atavistic savagery of born criminals and the need for 'social defence'. By explaining crime in terms of the personality of the criminal or by hereditary biological characteristics, criminology also served usefully to deflect blame away from the bourgeois social order.

Bibliography

General
Farcy, J.-C. *Histoire de la Justice Française de la Révolution à nos Jours* (Paris: PUF, 2001).
Lévy, R. 'Crime, the judicial system and punishment in modern France', in C. Emsley and L. Knafla (eds) *Crime History and Histories of Crime* (London: Greenwood, 1996).
Martin, B. *Crime and Criminal Justice Under the Third Republic* (Baton Rouge: Louisiana State University Press, 1990).

Crime and policing
Bailey, V. 'The fabrication of deviance: "dangerous and criminal classes" in Victorian England', in J. Rule (ed.) *Protest and Survival* (London: Merlin Press, 1993).
Barrows, S. *Distorting Mirrors: Visions of the Crowd in Nineteenth-Century France* (New Haven, CT: Yale University Press, 1981).
Blanc, D. and Fabre, D. *Le Brigand de Cavanac: Le Fait Divers, le Roman et l'Histoire* (Lagrasse: Éditions Verdier, 1982).
Brown, J. M. H. 'From organic society to security state: the war on brigandage in France 1797–1802', *Journal of Modern History* 1997–98.
Carrol, A. *Le Maintien de l'Ordre en France* 2 vols (Toulouse, 1984).
Chatelard, C. *Crime et Criminalité dans l'Arrondissement de St Etienne au XIXe Siècle* (St. Etienne: Centre d'Etudes Forèzienne, 1981).
Chauvaud, F. 'La garde chasse et la société rurale dans les forêts d'Yveline', in *Révolte et Société* (Paris, 1988).
Chauvaud, F. *De Pierre Rivière à Lendru: La Violence Apprivoisé au XIXe Siècle* (Paris: Éditions Brépols, 1991).
Chauvaud, F. *Les Passions Villageoises au XIXe Siècle* (Paris: Publisud, 1995).
Chauvaud, F. 'Les Violences Rurales au XIXe Siècle', *Cahiers d'Histoire* 1997.
Chauvaud, F. *Les Criminels de Poitou au XIXe Siècle* (La Crèche: Geste Editions, 1999).
Chevalier, L. *Labouring and Dangerous Classes in Paris* (Beverley Hills, CA: Sage, 1973).
Choquette, L. 'Degenerate or degendered? Images of prostitution in the French Third Republic', *Historical Reflections/Réflexions Historiques* 1997.
Corbin, A. L'Histoire de la violence dans les Campagnes Françaises au XIXe Siècle', *Ethnologie Française* 1991.
Corbin, A. *Village of the Cannibals: Rage and Murder in France, 1870* (Cambridge, Mass: Harvard University Press, 1992).
Désert, G. 'Aspects de la criminalité en France et en Normandie au XIXe Siècle', *Cahiers des Annales de Normandie* 1981.

Donovan, J. 'The uprooting theory of crime: the Corsicans of Marseille', *French Historical Studies* 1984–85.

Donovan, J. 'Justice and sexuality in Victorian Marseille', *Journal of Social History* 1987.

Donovan, J. 'Infanticide and juries in France: 1825–85', *Journal of Modern History* 1991.

Emsley, C. *Policing and its Context: 1750–1870* (London: Macmillan, 1983).

Emsley, C. *Gendarmes and the State in Nineteenth-Century Europe* (Oxford: Oxford University Press, 1999).

Emsley, C. and Weinberger, B. (eds) *Policing Western Europe* (London: Greenwood Press, 1991).

Faure, A. 'Enfance Ouvrière, Enfance Coupable', *Les Révoltes Logiques* 1980.

Guillais, J. *Crimes of Passion: Dramas of Private Life in 19th-Century France* (Oxford: Polity Press, 1993).

Guiral, P. 'Police et Sensibilité Française', in J. Aubert (ed.) *L'Etat et sa Police en France: 1789–1914* (Geneva: Droz, 1979).

Harris, R. *Murders and Madness: Medicine, Law and Society in Fin-de-Siècle France* (Oxford: Oxford University Press, 1989).

Harsin, J. *Policing Prostitution in Nineteenth-Century Paris* (Princeton NJ: Princeton University Press, 1985).

Hobsbawm, E. *Bandits* (London: Weidenfeld and Nicolson, 1969).

Hobsbawm, E. *Primitive Rebels* (Manchester: Manchester University Press, 1971).

Johnson, F. and Cohen, D. 'French criminality: urban and rural differences in the 19th century', *Journal of Interdisciplinary History* 1982.

Lefaucheur, N. 'Dissociation Familiale et Délinquance Juvenile', in M. Chevalier (ed.) *Protéger l'Enfant* (Rennes: University of Rennes, 1996).

Léonard, J. 'L'Historien et le Philosophe: Apropos de Surveiller et Punir', in M. Perrot (ed.) *L'Impossible Prison* (Paris: Seuil, 1980).

Merriman, J. *The Margins of City Life* (Oxford: Oxford University Press, 1991).

Mucchelli, L. *Histoire de la Criminologie Française* (Paris: L'Harmattan, 1994).

Nye, R. *Crime, Madness and Politics in Modern France: the Medical Concept of National Decline* (Princeton, NJ: Princeton University Press, 1984).

O'Brien, P. 'The revolutionary police of 1848', in R. Price (ed.) *Revolution and Reaction* (London: Croom Helm, 1975).

Parella, A. 'Industrialisation and murder in Northern France: 1815–1914', *Journal of Interdisciplinary History* 1992.

Perrot, M. 'Dans la France de la Belle Epoque: Les "Apaches", Premières Bandes des Jeunes', in *Les Marginaux et les Exclus de l'Histoire Cahiers Jussieux* No. 5 1979.

Perrot, M. 'Faits Divers et Histoire au XIXe Siècle', *Annales ESC* 1983.

Ratcliffe, B. 'Classes Laborieuses, Classes Dangereuses à Paris? The Chevalier Thesis Re-Examined', *French Historical Studies* 1991.

Santucci, M. *Délinquance et Répression au XIXe Siècle: L'Example de l'Hérault* (Paris: Economica, 1986).

Shapiro, A.-L. *Breaking the Codes: Female Criminality in Fin-de-Siècle Paris* (Stanford: Stanford University Press, 1996).

Schnapper, B. 'Le Récidive: Une Obsession Créatrice', in *Le Récidivisme* (Paris: PUF, 1983).

Taithe, B. 'Consuming Desires: Prostitutes and "Customers" in France and Britain 1836–85', in M. Arnot (ed.) *Gender and Crime in Modern Europe* (London: UCL Press, 1999).

Thompson, E. P. and Hay, D. (eds) *Albion's Fatal Tree* (New York: Pantheon, 1975).

Tilly, C. and Lodhi, A. 'Urbanisation, crime and collective violence in 19th-century France', *American Journal of Sociology* 1973.

Tombs, R. 'Crime and the security of the state: the "dangerous classes" and insurrection in 19th-century France', in V. Gatrell (ed.) *Crime and the Law* (London: Europa, 1980).

Wagniart, J.-F. *Le Vagabond à la Fin du XIXe Siècle* (Paris: Belin, 1999).

Zehr, H. 'The modernisation of crime in Germany and France 1830–1913', *Journal of Social History* 1975.

Zehr, H. *Crime and the Development of Modern Society: Patterns of Criminality in 19th-Century Germany and France* (London: Croom Helm, 1976).

The penal system

Badinter, R. *La Prison Républicaine: 1871–1914* (Paris: Fayard, 1993).

Bouchat, M.-S. *Enfance et Justice au XIXe Siècle* (Paris: PUF, 2001).

Foucault, M. *Discipline and Punish: the Birth of the Prison* (London: Penguin, 1977).

O'Brien, P. 'Crime and punishment as an historical problem', *Journal of Social History* 1978.

O'Brien, P. *The Promise of Punishment: Prisons in Nineteenth-Century France* (Princeton, NJ: Princeton University Press, 1988).

Perrot, M. 'Délinquance et Système Pénitentiaire en France au XIXe Siècle', *Annales ESC* 1975.

Perrot, M. (ed.) *L'Impossible Prison* (Paris: Le Seuil, 1980).

Petit, J.-G. *La Prison, le Bagne et l'Histoire* (Paris/Geneva: Librairie des Méridians, 1984).

Petit, J.-G. *Ces Peines Obscures: La Prison Pénale en France 1789–1870* (Paris: Fayard, 1990).

Petit, J.-G. 'Les Historiens et la Prison de Michel Foucault', *Sociétés et Représentations* 1996.

Petit, J.-G. 'Assistance ou Châtiment: Le Travail Pénitentiaire en France au XIXe Siècle', in *De la Charité Médiévale à la Sécurité Sociale* (Paris, Le Seuil, 1992).

Petit, J.-G. and Castan, N. *Histoire des Galères, Bagnes et Prisons: XVIII–XXe Siècles* (Toulouse: Privat, 1991).

Wright, G. *Between the Guillotine and Liberty* (Oxford: Oxford University Press, 1983).

Chapter 7

The medicalisation of nineteenth-century France

Introduction

Until recently the history of medicine, dominated by medical insiders, combined the narrowly technical or institutional with the anecdotal. It recounted the rise of a profession that was 'scientific' and 'humanitarian'. Its tone was hagiographic. It told of the progress of medicine from the theory of humours and charlatans' 'quackery' to the 'scientific' methodologies of nineteenth-century research hospitals and clinics, and of widening access to healthcare as medical networks expanded public provision. The 'new medical history', which questions this teleology, is less developed in France than in Britain. The *Annales* school, despite aspirations to 'total history', marginalised a field of practitioners who struggled to secure niches within French universities. Inspired by 'social history from below', the 'new' history analyses experiences and perceptions of patients and the role of the unofficial medical 'penumbra' which, it claims, cannot be divorced from that of the 'core' of 'official' doctors. It has been influenced by recent critical analyses of the medical profession from differing, if complementary, perspectives. Studies of the bourgeoisie increasingly focus on the professions. The emergence of consumers of medical goods and services has been identified as one facet of the rise of commercial capitalism. The 'heroic myth' of Western medicine has been questioned. Ivan Illich claimed that modern, technocratic medicine is characterised by a ruthless exercise of power, ignores generations of folk-wisdom and know-how and dispossesses the sick of their bodies. Feminists portray doctors and psychiatrists as wielders of male power intent on discrediting and marginalising female practitioners – 'wise-women', midwives, nursing nuns – and to subject the female body to the 'male gaze'. For Foucault medicine was a site of knowledge/power. Doctors' rhetoric of care, science, professionalism and humanitarianism disguised their 'real' project – categorisation, surveillance and control of the 'sick'.

Periods before the 'heroic' nineteenth century have been re-evaluated, no longer simply dismissed as a quaint prelude to the era of 'scientific' medicine. The medical world was already in disarray before the hothouse atmosphere of Revolution and the pressures of the nation-in-arms accelerated developments such as the rise of surgery. The 'established' medicine of the ancien régime was based on the medical ideas of Galenism and the theory of humours and on corporate institutions in place since around 1600. Medical personnel were divided between physicians, surgeons and apothecaries and organised into quasi-independent guilds recognised by the state. However, with Galen's ideas losing credibility, medical theories were in flux, though no coherent alternative medical paradigm had emerged enjoying widespread acceptance. Some advocated a more empirical approach to medicine and emphasised the importance of dissection. Advances were being made in surgery. Yet clearly eighteenth-century physicians were modest men because they had much to be modest about. Educated opinion was increasingly sceptical of doctors' claims. As one ironic 1780s pamphleteer remarked, 'All the learned faculty doctors will put on a good face in professing that medicine is a real science, based upon the principles of certainty and the experience of centuries. And they will do so without blushing'. Some came to believe that self-medication or a 'natural' lifestyle or a healthier milieu would be more beneficial than consulting physicians. The Paris Medical Faculty, hitherto regarded as the repository of medical knowledge, was losing control of medical discourse, as became apparent during the 1780s vogue for Mesmerism. Mesmer, an Austrian physician, claimed that the universe was bathed in invisible fluids and magnetic forces and that illness could be cured by restoration of the balances of these forces in the body. Established doctors denounced him as a 'mountebank', hinting that his techniques of touching (female) patients had erotic overtones and produced orgasmic convulsions. The Mesmerist controversy became a 'site' of the crisis of the corporate medical world, with Court factions, Freemasons, pamphleteers and some physicians supporting Mesmer. Mesmerist propaganda, produced by figures on the peripheries of the 'official' medical world, hinted that while Mesmer might indeed be a 'charlatan', so too were most of the elite of the medical faculties and corporations!

Mesmer's formation of a joint-stock company to market his 'product' exemplified a trend within contemporary medicine. In a world of commercial capitalism and embryonic consumerism a marketplace for medical goods and services, a 'greater chain of buying', was appearing. As commercial prosperity grew with the Atlantic trade, and death-rates fell with improvements in diet, at least until the 1770s, the world of baroque piety and fatalism was giving way to secular hopes for a healthier life on this earth – and to the conviction that non-fatal diseases and complaints could be 'mended'. Official physicians responded to growing consumer demand, as did many so-called 'empirics'. Newspapers featured adverts for patent medicines, hernia trusses, medical mail order catalogues. Some in this 'medical penumbra' were not easily distinguishable from official physicians. They included Montpellier medical faculty graduates unable to secure a niche in the corporate medical hierarchy. Many diagnoses and remedies offered by 'illicits' derived from orthodox medicine, albeit of a slightly outmoded type. 'Consumers' of medicine felt, like Mercier, that 'empirics' provided treatment that was just as effective, and cheaper, as that of physicians: 'How much do physicians owe to "empirics"? The latter, *by experience*, have remedies . . . which, by achieving cures, disconcert the vain eruditon of the Faculties.' Faced with the uncertainties of an incomplete paradigm-shift in medical ideas and the rise of commercialised medicine, the hierarchical medical world was crumbling.

Within the corporate world, surgeons challenged the supremacy of physicians, claiming that *they* possessed the most valuable blend of knowledge and 'hands-on' skills. Surgeons outside the corporation demanded the 'right' to practise. The idea of a new surgery within a reformed hospital system gained support. A growing belief that a 'strong state' required a healthy population led reformers to establish the *Société Royale de Médecine* (SRM) to oversee public health and hygiene, map epidemics, collect statistical data and license remedies.

The Revolution made major restructuring of the medical world possible. There were several possible blueprints. One was a reformed neo-corporate system. A second, briefly attempted in the 1790s, was a deregulated medical free-market in tune with the Revolution's liberal anti-corporatism. A third involved an extension of the 'statist' model implicit in the SRM. The fourth, favoured by the Jacobins, was a proto-Welfare State, with salaried citizen-physicians providing healthcare as a right to all citizens. After a decade of flux, the 1803 Ventôse Laws settled for a state-sanctioned neo-corporatist system. This abandoned the free-market experiments which had abolished the 'aristocratic' corporate hierarchy, including medical faculties. Alarm as the 'excesses' of unqualified 'empirics' led to a consensus that deregulation led to chaos. But in a liberal climate, statist and Jacobin social-medicine models appeared excessively *dirigiste*. Revolution and war acted as catalysts for change. Whereas the mood of the 1780s had been critical of medical 'expertise', there was now an enthusiasm for medical students to receive comprehensive training in anatomy and in chemistry. The experiences of war surgeons in military hospitals acted as a forcing-house for new surgical techniques and emphasised the need for hygiene. There was an emphasis on the hospital as the site for medical research, dissection, anatomy, the 'clinical gaze', compilation of medical statistics and the development of new standards of hygiene (Jones and Brockliss 1997).

The 'heroic' rise of the medical profession

Professional groups are now viewed as central to middle-class identity. Zeldin's *pointilliste* disaggregation of the bourgeoisie portrayed doctors as a distinct stratum with their own interests, viewpoint and agenda. They were a 'success story' – a group who in the nineteenth century achieved, with state support, recognition of their 'expertise', increased status, income and power, and a near-monopoly of medical provision. The discrediting of free-market and Jacobin social medicine agendas during the 1790s paved the way for the Ventôse Laws which provided the structural framework for medical profession's 'rise'. Framed by Interior Minister Chaptal, a Montpellier medical graduate, these abolished distinctions between physicians and surgeons. Henceforth doctors were to be trained in one of three medical faculties – Paris, Montpellier or Strasbourg. Pharmacists required qualification from pharmacy schools. *Officiers de santé*, in effect second-rank doctors, would receive an apprenticeship and then be licensed by a departmental medical committee to work in that department, particularly in rural areas. Midwives would receive training and be licensed. 'Official' practitioners would enjoy a monopoly, with 'unofficial' competitors – 'charlatans', local healers and homeopaths – forbidden to practice. The model envisaged was a hierarchical, state-sanctioned neo-corporatism. Doctors were members of a liberal profession, not state bureaucrats. But their expertise was guaranteed by qualifications acquired in state-supported medical faculties. In 1820 an Academy of Medicine was established, on the model of the SRM, to license 'secret remedies' and oversee medical research and public hygiene (Ramsey 1988).

It took time for this 'profession' to establish itself. The Ventôse Laws contained lacunae, and were laxly enforced. Article 23 allowed those already practising to continue to do so, as some did for decades. Some local authorities were so keen to acquire any medical provision that they turned a blind eye to the dubious qualifications of *officiers de santé* or midwives. One Beaujolais *officier* escaped with a 50-franc fine in 1820 for causing 24 deaths by excessive bleeding. Doctors' status remained below that of lawyers. Fewer medical than law students were sons of the land-owners or rentiers. The image of medical students before mid-century was often one of poorly dressed, anticlerical and radical semi-bohemians. If peasants viewed doctors as notables, many bourgeois viewed them as rather vulgar 'tradesmen', decidedly not respectable suitors for their daughters. Aristocratic patients of the distinguished Paris physician Laënnec – inventor of the stethoscope – both valued his expertise and treated him as a social inferior. Barely one-third of doctors in 1844, and only 20 per cent in Brittany, qualified for the franchise. Few became deputies. Status anxieties fuelled debates at the 1845 medical congress, as did issues of low incomes, paucity of patients, competition from 'illicits' and the 'glut' of doctors. There were calls for reform, or abolition, of the *officier de santé* category (Sussman 1977). Concentration of doctors in cities and the high fees which they charged exacerbated difficulties. Lyon had serious health problems, many private doctors, but few patients sufficiently affluent to afford their services. It was left to charities to supply funding to allow the poor some access to 'official' medicine. Lyon contained 40 per cent of the Rhône's population, but 85 per cent of its doctors (Faure 1977). Upland areas were thinly served by *officiers de santé*. In the 1840s France had 11,000 doctors and 750 *officiers* – a ratio of one 'official' practitioner to 1898 in the population. The map of medical provision reflects levels of urbanisation, wealth and literacy. There were low densities in the Massif Central. In Brittany French-speaking doctors were concentrated on the coast, with provision in the Breton-speaking interior left to folk-healers, pharmacies staffed by nuns, and healing-shrines. The official medical ratio here was 1:5736. The Midi was better served by this medical network than the urbanised Nord, thanks to Montpellier Medical Faculty. Also medicine appeared a more attractive career here than in dynamic industrialised regions (Léonard 1978a).

Doctors' surgeries, with their solid furniture and medical tomes and diplomas on display, sought to convey an impression of respectability and scientific expertise. But a slump in medical recruitment in the 1840s suggested a crisis in a profession whose members sometimes accepted payment in kind – eggs, poultry, even horse-feed – from rural clients. Between 1850 and 1880 the number of official practitioners declined, due to a two-thirds fall in the numbers of *officiers*. The inability of many to afford 'official' medicine limited the numbers who could derive a steady income from the profession. Yet these decades also witnessed consolidation of doctors' professional status and influence. Many doctors remained very modest. Annual incomes were below 6000 francs in Brittany. But in Lyon income levels and marriage patterns suggested that many were established members of the bourgeoisie. More were now sons of *notables* or *notaires*, with landed estates, vineyards, stocks and shares. The *Association Générale des Médicins de France* (AGMF), founded in 1858, recruited 50 per cent of doctors by 1880. It negotiated fees for members who tended patients whose expenses were paid by mutual aid societies and established a pension fund. By the early 1880s it was supplemented by the *Syndicat* – a tough lobbying organisation. Claiming to speak for provincial general practitioners, it criticised the 'elitist' AGMF, medical faculties and big-city hospitals. The *Syndicat* was not consulted by government on the important 1890s medical legislation. Its recruitment was predomintly in small towns; 90 per cent of Creuse doctors became members, but only 10 per cent in the Paris region. There were quarrels over use of the strike weapon and tensions between local branches and the national union. Yet its achievements were considerable. It campaigned to enforce fee-payment, mediated in negotiations between public authorities and doctors, and gave legal and insurance advice. Members derived income from acting as school medical inspectors, court witnesses and departmental health advisors. But the *Syndicat* insisted that they remained private doctors, not functionaries of an emerging public health bureaucracy, who should be well remunerated for care provided for the poor or aged. It lobbied for the Chevandier Law (1891) which achieved the long-standing goal of phasing-out *officiers de santé* – on the (spurious) 'egalitarian' grounds that 'equality of the patient before science is a democratic right which the Republic must recognise'! It campaigned for tighter controls on 'illicit' medicine and supervision of midwives. It warned that the annual intake of medical students – three times higher in 1890 than the pre-1860s average – was creating 'overcrowding' in the profession and declining incomes. But it sought to dispel stereotypes about 'greedy' doctors by promoting an image of the devoted GP friend of the family willing to brave snowstorms to attend patients, and provider of caring support which contrasted with hospitals' cold, 'scientific' ethos (Hildreth 1987).

The profession's enhanced reputation owed less to corporate organisation than to the congruence between Republican ideology and the myth of the 'progressive' doctor. Republicans, seeking to heal social divisions by commitment to reform and social 'solidarity', portrayed professional groups as disinterested, public-spirited, devoted to the general good – 'outside' the divisions of a polarised class-society. Not all professions fitted this image. Engineers and managers were viewed by workers as agents of capitalism rather than as 'social technicians'. Doctors were more promising Republican culture-heroes. In *Un Médecin de Campagne* (1834), Balzac offered in Dr Benessis an example, albeit Catholic, of a paragon 'on whom depend progress and civilisation (and) the well-being of the masses'. Zola's Doctor Pascal offered a Radical-Solidarist variant of this model. The altruistic, devoted 'people's doctor' was a key figure of Left-Centre politics, epitomised by Dr Guépin, whose civil funeral in Nantes in 1873 attracted huge crowds. But the doctor-politician came into his own in the Third Republic. The French Parliament of 1893–98 boasted 71 medical deputies and senators, the British and German legislatures each contained under 10; 11 per cent of all Third Republic deputies were doctors. Most sat on the Centre-Left – 38 per cent were Republicans, 45 per cent Radicals, 5.7 per cent socialists. Successive Radical prime ministers, Combes and Clemenceau, trained as doctors. Whereas only 10 per cent of deputies came from petty-bourgeois families, 41 per cent of doctor-deputies had modest social origins. Many shared positivist views disseminated in the medical faculties in defiance of the 'clerical obscurantism' of the Bonapartist years. Dr Bourneville's *Le Progrès Medical* presented sagas of heroic hospital doctors obstructed by nun-nurses who imposed confession on the dying, placed crucifixes on hospital walls, insulted Protestant and Jewish patients and discriminated against single mothers and VD patients. Its readers were left in no doubt of the need for municipal councils to secularise hospital personnel or for 'scientific' medicine to combat the credulity typified by belief in Lourdes 'miracle cures'. Of doctor-politicians, 24 per cent were Freemasons, many members of the *Ligue de l'Enseignement*. Their electoral manifestoes emphasised commitment to popular health – their role in vaccination campaigns or school hygiene inspectors. They rarely mentioned that they might earn 5000 francs per year for such official functions! But some were much-loved slum doctors, campaigners against the dangers of lead-paint to building workers or advocates of 'social medicine' and public hygiene. These were 'humanitarian' issues, but essential to ease social tensions and assure the future of the 'race' through reduced infant mortality. Epidemic threats from water pollution were invoked to justify *some* public and collective interventionism. A range of legislative measures from Roussel's 1874 Act controlling wet-nursing, via support for infant-clinics and medical provision for the poor (1893) to the 1902 Public Hygiene Act 1902 strengthened the image of the Republican doctor-politician as humanitarian culture-hero (Ellis 1990).

Alternative narratives

A range of critics – Catholics, feminists and Foucauldians – have questioned doctors' role in post-Enlightenment Europe. There *was* a 'dark side' to the bio-medical discourse which came to permeate French culture, the potency of which is sometimes underestimted by empiricist historians. However, the best recent research does provide both empirical data and a loose framework to allow one to probe the 'heroic' metanarrative without necessarily succumbing to Foucault's seductive model. Jacques Léonard (1981) questions Foucault's vision of a totalising medicalisation 'project' designed to increase doctors' powers by subjecting the population to the surveillance of the medical gaze and the discursive control of medical categories. 'The historian', he insists, 'does not have the right to project a fictitious clarity on dense and complex reality which he can only know via contingent and debatable documents.' The 'real' medical world was too diverse to share any single 'project'. Provincial GPs were at odds with the elites of the faculties and big-city hospitals. Doctors had to contend with differing priorities of strata of the elites and also with the 'agency' and potential resistance of patients, 'customers' and unofficial medical rivals (Léonard 1981).

Professional status and 'scientific' pretensions

There was a chronological gap between improvements in doctors' professional status and their acquisition of the ability to offer adequate diagnosis, let alone effective treatment, for disease. This had to await the 'Pasteur Revolution' of the 1880s, which identified bacteria as carriers of infection. Hence there was little obvious correlation between doctors' professional success and the scientific status, diagnostic capacity and therapeutic efficacy of the medicine which they provided. Perhaps the social myth of the scientific, humane doctor-hero was required precisely to enable the profession to bluff its way through the years when its achievements singularly failed to match its promise to rid the world of the threat of disease, exemplified in Gross's portrait of Napoleon and a physician offering the protection of Occidental medicine to Egyptian plague victims in 1798. Doctors benefited from state recognition and from its rhetorical concerns with public hygiene. Here, Léonard conceded, Foucault correctly highlighted the power/knowledge relationship. Only later, when 'scientific' medicine began to deliver on some of its promises, could doctors begin to justify their own mythology. Until Pasteur, 'medical science' lacked an agreed paradigm within which to fit its findings. There were ongoing skirmishes between advocates and opponents of 'contagionist' ideas, or between 'Parisian' materialists and the Montpellier school of 'vitalism' which argued for a holistic approach to medicine incorporating philosophical and 'moral' dimensions (Williams 1994).

Some 'progress' *was* made in the first half of the century. A patchy vaccination campaign, eventually covering 70 per cent of new-born babies, reduced the incidence of smallpox, despite epidemics in 1824–28 and 1870. Quinine was introduced to calm fevers, tisanes to rehydrate fever victims and cod-liver oil to reduce childhood rickets. The Paris Medical School was the centre of world medicine until the 1840s – a Mecca for foreign students. Paris hospitals, once a dumping ground for the aged poor, the insane and vagrants, and perceived as antechambers of death, became centres for clinical medicine and research. A plentiful supply of corpses allowed surgeons to practise dissection. An 'intern' system put some students on a fast-track towards the medical elite. Laënnec's stethoscope enabled monitoring of patients' internal organs. Microscopy was developed, albeit with few immediate practical results. Statistics were compiled to provide a database for analysis and explanatory theories. Hygiene in the wards was emphasised and after 1850 anaesthetics such as chloroform were used for operations. Moves towards 'specialised' wards and hospitals began as attempts to segregate 'marginals' – prostitutes, venereal patients – but came to reflect emerging medical specialisation, once dismissed as the preserve of 'charlatans'. Specific centres were established for children, the deaf, maternity patients and others. Specialised medical journals emerged in the 1830s for obstetrics, orthopaedics and venereal diseases (Ackerknecht 1967).

The international reputation of Parisian medicine boosted doctors' prestige and encouraged provincial emulation of the clinical and research hospital model. In Lyon the results were initially patchy. Surgeons' projects ran up against problems of reliance on Catholic charitable funding and the resistance of nursing-nuns to male medical power. And critics emphasised a variety of weaknesses in hospital medicine and medical training. There was overuse of opium and bloodletting – France imported 40 million leeches annually in the 1840s! A relative neglect of chemistry meant that France lost ground to German medicine after 1830. Until the advent of cocaine in the 1880s there was no effective pre-operation anaesthetic. Medical training remained theoretical, with students given little hands-on practice. A newly qualified GP might feel at a disadvantage in his practice faced with the experience and know-how of 'illicit' competitors. Above all, despite advances in clinical anatomy and diagnosis, clinical hospital medicine made few advances in therapy or cure. TB, cancer and syphilis remained intractable enemies. Even the pasteur Revolution, which brought vaccination for rabies and diphtheria and the bacteria paradigm, had only limited impact. Some remained unconvinced by the new paradigm, but even those who accepted it recognised that Pasteurism offered no universal panacea. Its insights needed to find application through fusion with traditional techniques of medical diagnosis and therapy. Nevertheless, Pasteurism's obsession with hygiene and disinfection, sterilised equipment, rubber gloves and washing facilities *did* improve the success rates of internal operations.

The gulf between medicine's pretentions and actual medical competence – diagnostic and therapeutic – was exposed by cholera epidemics in 1832, 1849 and 1853–54. One doctor admitted in 1849 that 'medicine is *powerless* today, as it was during the first epidemic'. Yet, ironically, these episodes consolidated doctors' claims to be 'experts' who could and should manage crises. Cholera became a major 'actor' in the West after 1820 as epidemics spread via trade routes from the East. Although the death toll in France – 100,000 in 1832 – was modest by comparison with perennial killers such as TB, cholera was peculiarly terrifying. It killed, often within twenty-four hours, 50 per cent of those who contracted it, and up to 20 per cent of affected communities. Its symptoms – a blue face, burning stomach pains, dehydration, vomiting and diarrhoea – were particularly distasteful to a bourgeoisie growing prudish about bodily functions and odours and complacently confident that the 'civilised' West was no longer vulnerable to 'Oriental' diseases. Until the work of Koch in the 1880s medicine lacked any agreed diagnosis of the agency of cholera's dissemination – a bacillus which spread via victims' faeces and infected food and water, was ingested and then lodged in the digestive tract. Popular 'common-sense' deduced, correctly, from the clustering of victims that it *was* contagious. This view was shared by some doctors, and by Prussian bureaucrats who imposed quarantine controls. However, until the 1860s medical consensus was that it was not contagious but linked to foul air, damp soil and '*miasmas*' prevalent in overcrowded popular neighbourhoods. Some 'anti-contagion' doctors took this stance primarily because the 'ignorant' populace believed the opposite! Debates were as much ideological and cultural as medical, cholera as much 'textual construction' and metaphor as organic disease. Anti-contagionism appealed to 'liberal' elites – in Orleanist France and commercial Hamburg – because it justified resistance to 'authoritarian' quarantine measures which disrupted international trade. Since doctors had no explanation for the causes or spread of cholera, their advice was banal, absurd or clearly 'ideological'. A 'healthy diet' was advocated, and workers chided for eating 'indigestible food'. Hot tea, garlic, vinegar and rubbing with *eau de vie* were recommended! Avoidance of 'indulgence' was deemed to offer protection. With 'official' medicine so ineffectual, 'charlatans' profited from the sale of patent remedies – violent purges, ether, ammonia.

The timing of cholera prompted agonised debate about epidemics and revolution. An 1832 cartoon portrayed cholera as a Polish vagabond embracing 'Marianne', and thanking 'dear Revolution' for allowing him to enter France. The disease *was* carried westward by political refugees and counter-revolutionary armies, just as Jewish refugees from 1890s Tsarist pogroms carried cholera to Hamburg. Similarly it was not coincidental that the war years 1814–15 and 1870–71 coincided with typhus and smallpox epidemics. But whereas medieval plagues led to scapegoating of 'marginals' – Jews, witches – in post-Revolutionary Europe ruling elites were disconcerted to find themselves denounced as epidemics exacerbated class tensions. Landowners and government officials were attacked in Western Russia in 1832. The Parisian *grande-bourgeoisie* was appalled at the 'savage credulity' of crowds who believed that cholera stemmed from a plot by the rich to poison the wells. Images of the rich fleeing the city fed popular disquiet. Heine commented that 'certain *parvenus* should not be blamed for fleeing, since they probably thought that cholera, which has come such a long way from Asia, does not know that *they* have grown rich on the Stock Exchange and, mistaking them for poor scum, will force them to bite the dust'! Ragpickers rioted to defend their livelihood against attempts, on hygiene grounds, to centralise garbage collection and disposal. Crowds besieged hospitals, accusing doctors of dissecting corpses of the poor to save the rich. Initially the elites had been complacent about an epidemic concentrated in popular quarters; 70 per cent of victims were workers and the poor. Hence a journalist reported '*le Tout Paris*' in celebratory mood. 'Drink champagne when you're thirsty! *Voilà* the way to avoid cholera!'. Cholera helped to consolidate class identities. A bourgeoisie fragmented along lines of religion, politics and culture could agree that not catching cholera was a badge of common identity, that the 'diseased other' was proletarian, much as white, middle-class heterosexuals in Reagan's America dismissed Aids as the scourge of blacks, homosexuals and drug addicts. The cholera-infested poor of central and eastern quarters provided a clear image of what the bourgeois was not. What the cholera proved, argued one doctor, was that 'vice accompanies misery'. The poor were to blame for the pathological state of their neighbourhoods. Some enjoyed the irony that cholera functioned as a *guillotine ambulant*, spreading panic to popular quarters where *sans-culottes* had applauded the Terror. Others portrayed a 'pathological' city, 'sick' with both plague and revolution.

Cholera marked a stage in ongoing struggles for dominance within the elites, raising the issue of which group(s) would control the 'narrative' of epidemics. With '1830' still fresh in their minds, Legitimists talked of 'God's Punishment' on 'Paris-Babylon'. Why else would cholera be 'oozing' into the capital while sparing the provinces? Legitimists portrayed Louis Philippe seated on a chamber-pot defecating *sans-culottes* – for cholera *and* revolution were in the new regime's guts. Once, Catholics claimed, epidemics led to full churches and repentance. 'What is to be said of a people who, in the face of death, know only how to seek help in pharmacies' – or of a society 'which finds itself abandoned to the wisdom of doctors (who) treated it as if it had a body not a soul?'. Yet doctors lacked the prestige to monopolise epidemic management. The prefect of police assumed responsibility for order, moving corpses and inspecting buildings. Bureaucrats 'controlled' the disease by mapping and quantifying its spread, listing names, occupations and addresses of victims. Doctors chafed at their dependence on the administration for equipment and First Aid posts. Nevertheless, their profile was rising. They sat on the Hygiene Committee which directed the 'medical gaze' onto popular quartiers. Medical bulletins implicitly blamed the poor for their own filth by urging them to clean latrines and avoid living and sleeping in the same room. Despite doctors' inability to offer coherent diagnosis or effective cures, the episode led to increased acceptance of the status of medical surveillance, definitions and advice. However, empirical evidence does question a Foucauldian emphasis on faceless, clinical medical 'control'. Epidemic doctors were overworked, overwhelmed by the scale of the problem, often distressed and scared. Cholera in 1849 killed 20,000 in a city whose demographic, social and hygiene problems had worsened since 1832. This second epidemic caused less elite anxiety and aroused less debate. Kudlick (1996) explains this by claiming that intra-class friction within the elite was now substantially reduced. Catholics were less wedded to legitimism, less eager to use cholera to score points against the 'liberal' bourgeoisie, who, in turn, had become less anti-clerical and less hostile to Catholic charity. The medical profession had become more prestigious, tensions between doctors and bureaucrats less acute. And elites showed less willingness to blame popular 'immorality' for the pathologies of the 'sick' city. Not all these arguments are entirely persuasive. Perhaps the experiences of 1848 suggested that many Parisian workers now espoused socialist ideas, and blamed capitalism, not the poisoning of the city's water supply, for popular misery. Conservatives talked of socialism as the real plague, 'one thousand times more dangerous then Asiatic cholera' (Kudlick 1996; Delaporte 1986; Bourdelais and Raulot 1978; Corbin 1986).

Medicine in the marketplace: consuming and selling medicine

Cholera highlighted discrepancies between doctors' rising prestige and power and the inadequacy of their 'scientific knowledge' and diagnostic and therapeutic competence. After 1880 they could bask in the reflected glory of the Pasteurian Revolution. Germ-theory provided medicine with a central paradigm. Yet many doctors remained ambivalent about implications of the 'pasteurisation' of France. What if disinfected streets and pure water supply reduced disease – and patient numbers and incomes? What if bourgeois patients deserted family doctors for hospital clinics and Pasteur institutes? This raises doubts about 'heroic' narratives of a profession dedicated to the disinterested task of spreading healthcare to superstitious and fatalist masses – wedded to 'illicit' healers and entrenched in their unsanitary lifestyles. It is difficult to draw clear distinctions between 'official' and 'illicit' medicine – the 'core' and the 'penumbra' – and one should probably avoid a teleology which portrays folk-healers, empirics, charlatans and doctors as successive stages in the rise of 'modern' medicine. Medicine must be located in the marketplace, where doctors competed with 'unofficial' rivals to sell goods and services to patients who were eclectic consumers, willing to 'shop around' pragmatically. Unofficial medicine was not part of some 'timeless', autonomous popular culture. Rather it existed in symbiotic relationship with 'official' medicine, borrowing in piecemeal, eclectic fashion from out-of-date medical textbooks and orthodoxies. Emetics and purgatives, 'popular' because of their dramatic effects in 'clearing-out the system', had been a staple feature of Galenist medicine, the goal of which was to evacuate 'corrupt humours' from the body. Use of charlatans was, perhaps, a significant step towards 'medicalisation' of society, habituating peasants to resort to medical assistance for minor ailments.

Charlatans, travelling medical salesmen, were entrepreneurs in a world of commercial capitalism, operating on the urban–rural 'frontier', opening up the countryside to a version of 'modern medicine'. Some claimed 'certificates' from medical schools. Most required payment in cash not kind. The inventor and vendor of 'Leroy's vomi-purge' – a best-selling emetic containing sal ammoniac blamed for deaths in the Loiret in 1817 – had been an *officier de santé*. He defended his 'freedom' against the pernicious 'medical monopoly'. Giraudeau, who acquired rights to the notorious '*rob* Laffecteur', a vegetable syrup supplied to the army as a cure for syphilis, had a Parisian medical doctorate. Charlatans used 'vulgarised' medical textbooks, such as *Le Vrai Médecin des Pauvres*. The *Académe de Médecine* tested and licensed 'secret remedies'. It took this task seriously, rejecting 95 per cent of remedies investigated in 1825–27. However, medical mandarins' efforts to regulate the market in medicines and remedies remained, Ramsey (1988) insists, 'an island of disapprobation in a sea of commercialism'. Millions of 'customers' continued to buy concoctions of animal greases to treat hernias, of rhubarb, brandy and saffron to calm their nerves, and a variety of 'rubs' against cancer, rabies and syphilis. These proved no more ineffective than most 'official' treatments. They purported to deal with complaints for which orthodox medicine could as yet offer no cure. Prosecuted 'illicits' expressed contempt for doctors: 'Who are these tyrants crushing me?', enquired one. 'They have a diploma – and that's all. With that they can "cut and kill". There is no jail for them' (Ramsey 1988).

Resort to 'unofficial' medicine made sense in a society where 'official' medicine remained costly. 'Illicit' practitioners offered options of payment in kind, or a sliding scale correlated with a client's wealth. Doctors appeared condescending, unable to conceal their sense of cultural and social superiority to patois-speaking patients. In Givors in 1855 there was sympathy for a prosecuted 'illicit' who failed his qualifying exams as an *officier de santé* but had given devoted service to the local poor. Many illicits specialised in bonesetting, extracting teeth, hernias or corns. 'Sedentary empirics' – shepherds and blacksmiths – might come from 'dynasties' who transmitted skills across generations. Some doctors expressed guarded admiration for such expertise. If taken to court, empirics often found local *notables* willing to testify for them in court. A statue was erected to commemorate the skills of a Lozère bonesetter whose 'real' job was as a roadmender. Some empirics were 'marginals' – widows for whom medicine offered an opportunity for making money within an 'economy of makeshifts', or the variety of sorcerers, *leveurs de sorts*, magic-healers (*maiges*) and *guérisseurs* who flourished in remote regions. Some claimed the 'gift' or 'power' to heal by touch. Others knew magic words, gestures and rituals which lifted evil-spells. Such powers may have been granted because they were the seventh-son, because – as a blacksmith – they could harness St. Eloi's fire. J. X. Texier in the Vaucluse in 1815 was 'sent by God' to make the crippled walk – and to support ultra-Royalism! Some cured diseases unknown to medical nosology – 'twisted liver' or 'the hunes' (a nervous complaint) – by slitting patients' tongues or getting them to drink urine. Ethnographers delighted in uncovering such beliefs and practices, assuming that they were timeless and unchanging. Social historians are sceptical about such claims. Calculation of the numbers of such folk-healers and their 'customers' and providing a chronology of decline of belief in or use of them remains extremely difficult (Devlin 1987).

The Ventôse Laws standardised midwives' training while restricting their functions and subordinating them to doctors. However, in the Rhône uplands midwives were prized by villagers and municipalities for their care, conviviality and patois-speaking, and for practising bloodletting and vaccination. In practice, many doctors left delivery of peasant babies to them (Faure 1993). 'Alternative' medicine was, in part, a female counter-culture. Pharmacists complained about competition from nuns but prefects turned a blind eye to their activities, dismissing pharmacists' complaints as self-interested, albeit technically justified. Nuns were ubiquitous in the mid-century countryside. The attraction for municipalities in employing *soeurs* to run schools was that they were cheap, came in pairs, had no family responsibilities, ran *Bureaux de Bienfaisance*, visited the sick and provided an unofficial pharmacy. They also staffed hospitals and acted as private nurses for bourgeois families. Many Catholic wives were ambivalent towards 'modern' medicine. Bourgeois families in Lyon were interested in health issues, passed hygiene advice to their children, curtailed social contacts during periods of infection and used family doctors, usually Catholics, as confidants. Yet they retained religious doubts about 'scientific' medicine, believing that preoccupation with the body was symptomatic of a godless age. Disease was an expression of God's will, prayers to the Virgin a protection against cholera, and a Papal benediction under the pillow a guarantee against heart problems. Catholic wives had qualms about inspection by male doctors: 'My dear wife has a violent repugnance towards being subjected to that type of medical scrutiny', noted one businessman. One alternative towards which some were drawn, despite or because of doctors' disapproval, was homeopathy. A Catholic homeopathy clinic was established in 1869 (Pellissier 1997). Upmarket spas – Uriage, Dax and Cannes – providing hydrotherapy at private clinics became fashionable. Some spas catered for less exclusive clienteles. Some were communally owned, and villagers protested – as at Charbonnière (Rhône) in 1827 – when commercial companies gained control. The trade in mineral and spa water expanded rapidly. Lyon alone had twelve water-bottling firms in the 1830s. The Loire exported millions of bottles by 1860, its sales boosted by the rail network which was to prove crucial to the commercial success of Lourdes after 1858.

The Ventôse Laws provided training, exam qualifications and, in theory, a guaranteed monopoly for pharmacists. Pharmacies quadrupled to 5000 between 1803 and 1850 and reached 11,600 by 1914. Pharmacists sought to enforce their legal monopoly and maintain their 'professional' status, while embracing commerce and advertising. By 1850, 75 per cent of products sold by Lyon pharmacists were supplied by big pharmaceutical companies. Hence the history of pharmacy is that of successful medium-scale commercial enterprise in a competitive market. Pharmacists complained about threats to them, and to patients' health, from illicit competitors – nuns, perfume-sellers, *limonadiers* and herbalists. One Rhône grocer-pharmacist displayed laudanum and strychnine in his window! However, municipalities, appreciative of the lower prices of such 'unofficials', obstructed efforts to close them down (Faure 1996–97).

Demand for medicine thus reflected pragmatic, eclectic consumer tastes. Many patients retained older medical beliefs about the need to purge the body of humours, but combined these with perceptions of the body as a machine to be tinkered with by medical mechanics. They tried 'official' medicine if they could afford it – or if all else failed. But they found the treatments and 'cures' of illicits less painful, and unofficial practitioners less judgemental and less supercilious. The stereotype of the popular classes as fatalistic, scared of, or hostile to modern medicine, was often a self-serving myth peddled by doctors. Hospitals had once been shunned on the quite sensible grounds that they were dirty, disease-ridden places where the marginal went to die. But as hospitals became more hygienic, workers were prepared to go there, often in search of shelter as much as therapy. The limited success of early vaccination campaigns was attributed by doctors to popular superstitions and prejudices. Rumours did circulate that vaccination was introduced to make people ill and require treatment from fee-charging doctors! Some, fatalistically, viewed smallpox as inevitable, or held the traditional view that it was beneficial because it purged the body of bad humours. Yet some popular doubts were quite rational. How could doctors guarantee that vaccination would not harm babies or spread syphilis or that vaccine from infected animals was safe? Few doctors admitted that the obstacle to success of vaccination campaigns stemmed from reluctance to fund or administer them adequately. Private doctors proved unwilling to devote time and energy to activities for which they were offered only small fees. Lyon hospitals exhibited 'spectacular ill-will' when requested to store and distribute vaccine. Mayors failed to compile vaccination lists or keep statistical records. It took the 1870–71 smallpox epidemic and 'natalist' alarms to convince the Third Republic to use schools to encourage and monitor a comprehensive child vaccination campaign (Faure 1993; Darmon 1985).

Doctors, public health and 'social medicine'
Laissez-faire objections to 'Statism' and the corporate selfishness of a profession committed to the 'private' doctor were major obstacles to the provision

of 'social medecine' and improvement of public health. Radical governments, rhetorically supportive of 'Solidarist' projects and 'national efficiency', were reluctant to risk confrontation with corporate interests. Hence accounts of the public health movement which adopt a 'whiggish', optimistic tone are unconvincing (La Berge 1991). Building on projects of 1780s bureaucrats, a hygienist lobby emerged in the 1820s based around the Paris Health Council and the *Annales d' Hygiène Publique*. Recruiting bureaucrats, engineers, scientists and doctors it published investigative reports, with the goal of sanitising 'pathological' cities by provision of pure water, sewage systems and healthy dwellings. Little was accomplished. The scale of environmental and health problems necessitated substantial state intervention. But where the *dirigisme* of a Parent-Duchâtelet clashed with the laissez-faire instincts of a Villermé, it was the latter which found government favour. There was stiffer resistance to interventionism in France than in Chadwick's Britain. The Insanitary Dwellings Act (1850) was resisted by landlords and laxly enforced. Eventually bourgeois anxieties about correlations between proletarian revolution, crime, sewers and epidemics *did* overcome resistance from cess-pool contractors to a comprehensive sewage system (*tout à l'égout*). Removal of excrement became a metaphor for the restoration of order to Paris. By the 1860s tourists could take boat-trips in the new sewers to observe how the netherworld had been tamed! Outside Paris, health and hygiene committees were singularly inactive in the years after the major cholera epidemics. In 1902 a Public Health Act was finally passed, despite obstruction from bishops – outraged at 'sacrilegious' threats to move cemeteries – landlords and slaughter-houses. Most doctors, alarmed by recurrence of typhus and cholera in the 1880s and evidence that unhygienic barracks killed many French conscripts, supported requirements on municipalities to inspect buildings, check water supplies and disinfect public spaces. Disinfection and bottled water contained Le Havre's 1891 cholera outbreak. Purified water supplies, together with Republican fountains in public squares, symbolised the laic answer to Catholic 'holy water' (Shapiro 1985; Reid 1991; Faure 1993). Yet there was some medical disquiet. Would not preventative medicine and disinfection deprive the private doctor of patients? Would not an intrusive public health bureaucracy and compulsory reporting of contagious disease threaten patients' privacy and the sanctity of the doctor–patient relationship? Among the 1902 Act's critics was Dr Treille who illustrated the threat to fundamental liberties from creeping medical interventionism by evoking lovers 'sharing tender intimacies' just as 'the sanitary inspector storms in with a court order . . .'!

In the 1770s Dr Tissot's pamphlets, addressed to a reading public of country doctors, midwives and charitable ladies, offered medical advice to be passed on to the poor, who would be encouraged to take charge of their own health. The ideal of the right for all to receive medical care was articulated clearly by radical Jacobins. While recognising that the 'utopia' of medical care for all was not achieved in the Revolution, Weiner (1994) has argued that the ideal of the 'citizen-patient' informed official thinking into the Napoleonic period, even if he had commensurate duties of personal hygiene and had to accept that he should be inspected and have his corpse dissected for science!

Much of this is questionable. The reformers of the 1790s were more concerned with the indigent poor than with the wider popular classes. Official thinking was marked more by notions of elite philanthropy than by radical concepts of 'rights' to medical provision. The disruptions of war and the cutting of hospital funding after 1794 worsened medical services to the popular classes, although the Napoleonic period witnessed some improvement in Parisian hospital services and in provision of care in the home for poor families (Weiner 1994).

The idea of medical care as a 'social right' was tarnished by association with Jacobinism. After 1815 a few doctors advocated the 'Bas-Rhin model' of salaried cantonal doctors providing services to the poor, a scheme adopted by a few eastern departments by the 1840s. Official opinion regarded this as costly to taxpayers and insufficiently remunerative for doctors. In 1847 the Senate blocked a Bill to generalise the cantonal-physician scheme. Funding for medical care for the poor remained thin and patchy. In Lyon after 1830 a 'General Dispensary', dependent on Catholic and lay philanthropists, treated 10,000 indigents annually. During the Second Empire, mutual aid societies whose membership trebled to 794,000 increasingly used their resources to purchase medical care for members. But mutualist membership was largely confined to (male) artisans and excluded the 'lazy', 'immoral' unskilled. Although doctors complained at the paltry fees offered for treating mutualists, whose numbers had risen to two million by 1902, such payments did accustom them to the idea that treating workers might be compatible with professional dignity and with their material interests. 'Paternalist' firms funded medical schemes for employees, although Loire miners claimed that company doctors were management stooges and demanded access to 'independent' medical treatment. Such 'third party' funding did allow gradual expansion of doctors' popular clientele. Bonapartism encouraged departmental authorities to subsidise medical provision for the poor, although barely half of them did so. In the West there is little evidence of such provision before 1890. In the shoemaking town of Fougères, the population doubled between 1850 and 1890, while the number of doctors fell from 11 to 6 (Faure 1984; Faure and Dessertine 1994).

Doctor-deputies sponsored the 1893 and 1903 Acts guaranteeing state-subsidised medical care for the indigent and the aged poor. But most doctors proved keener to utilise the 'Pasteur myth' of scientific medicine to strengthen their status than to deliver 'social medicine'. Whereas 28 per cent of all doctors resided in cities of more than 50,000, 64 per cent of doctor-deputies represented rural and small-town France. The 'social medicine' rhetoric utilised by a few Left-wing city doctors, and by some from the medical faculties, was drowned out by the wider profession, inside and outside parliament, which refused to be confused with *fonctionnaires* and insisted on being well-remunerated for medical services provided for the poor. Patients should have a 'free choice' of doctors. They should be treated at home rather than in clinics or hospitals, by doctors who would be recompensed on a payment-per-visit basis. Doctors obstructed the establishment of rural dispensaries. Their *Syndicat* threatend strikes to force departments to accept the payment systems they wanted (Hildreth 1987).

By the 1890s the social status of doctors had risen. Viewing themselves as new notables, many affected 'scientific' disdain for popular ignorance and contempt for the working class. Some doctor-politicians ran private clinics or spa centres, purchased vineyards or married into capitalist dynasties. Some prospered by accumulating posts in both public sector and private companies. One St. Nazaire doctor held consultancies for the hospital, *Bureau de Bienfaisance*, vaccination committee, law courts and naval base – and for a rail company, the Penhoët shipyard, a shipping company and for workers' mutualist societies! 'Who could ask for anything more?', he enquired.

Even had they agreed on an agenda for the 'medicalisation' of society, doctors would have been inhibited by 'realities' of health politics, and of wider class relations, from undertaking initiatives which challenged prevailing conventions and practices. Public hygiene and social health programmes constantly confronted the medical profession's obsession with its independence and suspicion of creeping statism. Where the medical establishment desired to regulate 'secret remedies' or tighten public hygiene regulations, it ran up against free-market dogmatism, powerful landlord and business lobbies and cost-cutting government – national and local. For good or ill, French medicine was too diverse and individualistic to fit the model suggested by those who claim that there was a monolithic, 'medicalisation' agenda (Faure 1993).

The 'dark face' of medicalisation

If the 'heroic' narrative of the medical profession must be questioned, one should heed empiricist historians who warn that the social realities of French medicine were too complex to fit neatly with notions of a sinister medicalisation project. However, critics of Foucault's empirical 'errors' concede that he offered brilliant insights, hinted at new interpretive frameworks and posed serious questions about the 'dark side' of the 'Enlightenment project'. Doctors in medical faculties or research hospitals justified their claims to status and influence by presenting their work as the prerequisite for a society freed from unnecessary disease and suffering. Yet experiences of medically directed eugenicist sterilisation projects, conducted not merely in Nazi Germany or deepest Alabama but in 'social democratic' Sweden, have taught historians to be wary of accepting medical rhetoric at face value. For Foucault the 'progressive' discourse of – male, bourgeois, European – doctors serves to justify monopolistic power. 'Scientific' medicine claims to define 'normality', to distinguish the 'sick' from the healthy. 'Power' does not reside merely in the 'bourgeois state' nor with the 'capitalist' class. It is ubiquitous and multi-centred. In a medicalised society it lies in the capacity of the psychiatrist to diagnose the 'insane' and the 'hysterical', in the authority of the hospital consultant, in dissection of bodies and corpses by the surgeon, in the 'medical gaze' of doctors, in the surveillance by the dispensary or the medical social worker of working-class families.

Empiricist historiography, typified by a valuable recent study of rural Seine-et-Oise, tends to dismiss the 'grand dream of a medicalised social order' as an intellectual fantasy of a few medical theorists or medical professors – of little relevance to the 'real' world of medical practice in a France where peasants still used empirics, local authorities were reluctant to fund hygiene schemes, nursing-nuns obstinately obstructed the authority of hospital consultants and Catholic rural GPs disliked the pretensions of medical elites (Ackermann 1990). Nevertheless, it is unwise to underestimate the impact – political, social or cultural – of medical discourses and projects. It was in medical metaphors that debates about society were conducted. Revolutionaries in 1789 talked of 'regenerating' a decomposing body politic, and of 'purging' political charlatans offering quack remedies for the Nation's ills. After 1830 debate centred around the pathologies of cities where cholera and revolution appeared intertwined. After 1848 bureaucrats sought to 'quarantine' 'healthy' sections of rural society against 'infection' by migrant 'carriers' of the socialist 'plague'. The traumas of 1870–71, as Taithe has shown, generated a range of medicalised discourses abourt French society. War produced thousands of military and civilian casualties. The siege of Paris increased death rates from malnutrition and TB and a smallpox epidemic broke out. Many contrasted 'sick', 'syphilitic', 'ageing' France with 'healthy', vigorous, 'young' Germany. Thereafter anguished debates about national decline were conducted in a rhetoric which assumed a bio-medical model of national/social 'degeneration'. This bio-medical discourse, conflating fears of 'hereditary' criminality and labour unrest with anxieties about falling birth-rates, infant mortality, VD, TB and declining racial 'virility', was central to the 'cognitive heuristic' of the wider society. There was a gulf between discursive projects for national 'regeneration' through systematic 'medicalisation' and actual policies. But one must emphasise how pervasive this way of analysing problems became, in areas of crime but also of gender, sexuality, the family, welfare, race and labour relations. Moreover, delays in implementing favoured schemes of medical 'experts' merely heightened those anxieties which had initially generated them (Nye 1984; Taithe 1999).

Of the founder members of the *Société Française Eugénique* (SFE) in 1913, 15 per cent were doctors, the highest proportion of any national eugenics association. Far from being an eccentric project of the Radical Right, 'scientific' eugenicism was one logical culmination of a mainstream bio-medical discourse beginning in the Enlightenment and attracting some socialists. Enlightenment projects for a healthy humanity such as those of Cabanis echoed a utopian tradition going back to Plato. Eighteenth-century writers advised parents how to produce healthy children. But the focus shifted to fantasies of collective breeding projects. Robert Le Jenne in 1801 envisaged selective breeding by elites to produce a race of 'great men'. Anxieties about the nation's future were nurtured by the demographic losses of the Napoleonic Wars and by concern that war had denied procreation opportunities to the most vigorous elements in society. Colonial contacts with non-European races raised fears about racial miscegenation, while the first evidence of a marked decline in birth-rates was taken as proof of declining national 'virility', caused, according to disciples of the eighteenth-century masturbation expert Dr Tissot, by loss of precious bodily fluids and vitality due to semen loss. To remain a great power the French would have to learn Anglo-Saxon habits of sexual self-control and sublimation of sexual energies into productive military and colonial activities (Schneider 1992).

Anxieties about 'pathological' problems of growing cities led to identification of a degenerate urban underclass and proposals for medical inspection of future spouses in order to limit breeding by the 'unfit'. A 'scientific' bio-medical model was provided in 1857 by Dr Morel's *Traité de Dégénérescence*, drawing on a tradition of medical thought, still influential in Montpellier, which emphasised 'anthropological' medicine, reciprocal physical-moral relations and a 'holistic science of man'. Morel purported to show how pathologies of individual 'degenerates', partly a product of a 'tainted' milieu, could be transmitted via heredity to their families and to the 'race'. The biology of the lower classes could be invoked to explain social dislocation, crime and disease. Degeneration theory was popularised by journalists and novelists. Hence Republican progressivism was constantly being dragged down by the deeply pessimistic, fatalistic undertow of hereditary biological determinism. The new disciplines of anthropology and criminal anthropology were similarly affected (Pick 1989). Fears of 'degeneration' assumed differing emphases in national contexts. In Italy positivist doctors distinguished honest northern workers from criminal degenerates of the newly annexed South. In France the 'master pathology', identified as symptomatic of wider national degeneration, was demographic stagnation and the collapsing birth-rate. 'Natalist' obsessions about the 'quantity' of the race were compounded by concern that TB, syphilis, alcoholism and 'nervous' complaints proved that the 'quality', too, was declining as the hereditary transmission of acquired defects led to a vicious, counter-evolutionary spiral of degeneracy (Taithe 1999; Schneider 1990).

As bio-medical categories colonised most fields of debate, doctors stepped forward as 'experts' to diagnose national decline and to formulate policies to halt it. One outcome was the vogue for '*puériculture*' – a term for 'cultivation' of small children popularised in the 1890s by Dr Pinard of the Paris Medical School obstetrics department. He saw doctors' mission as safeguarding the quantity and quality of French babies via supervision of procreation in the interests of national repopulation. In practice, Pinard's projects, which gave a particular 'flavour' to the embryonic French welfare state, included worthy efforts to supervise nursing of babies, advise on diets and rest for pregnant women and new mothers, encourage breast-feeding and the use of sterilised milk and bottles for infants, and establish crèches. But Pinard, a founder member of the SFE, was drawn towards preventing 'defective' groups from breeding. He criticised 'humanitarian' colleagues who 'wasted' resources keeping alive premature babies in efforts to rescue 'nature's rejects'. Alcoholics, the sexually 'abnormal', mental 'defectives' and those with TB should be 'persuaded' to avoid procreation. There were calls to increase medical surveillance of prostitutes. A *Société de Prophylaxie Sanitaire et Morale* sought to prevent marriage or procreation by those not vetted for venereal disease. Evoking the dilemmas raised by intellectually gifted but physically deformed individuals, Dr Charles Richet admitted that precise identification of those to be subject to breeding prohibition was difficult, though he favoured killing malformed babies. The logic of this discourse led to more extreme positions. In 1918 Dr Binet-Single portrayed a utopia where unproductive 'defectives' were gassed and selected superior males encouraged to impregnate 103 women annually! Some doctors welcomed the war as a chance for a racial cull by sending the degenerate to the front (Schneider 1992; Pick 1989).

One instructive, and depressing, intellectual trajectory was that of Jules Soury, whose career illustrates how medical theories of pathology could slide into biological racism. Soury was a linguist and student of ancient religion. He took a doctorate in biology, lectured to large audiences at the *École Pratique des Hautes Etudes* and published a major work on the central nervous system. Soury began as a Republican atheist, holding a classic Enlightenment view that all religions were superstition. His Dreyfusard opponents attributed his subsequent 'apostasy' to frustrated careerism, since he failed to secure a chair at the *Collège de France*. Yet his racial views were not really a 'betrayal' of his 'science'. Republicans complacently assumed that science's findings were congruent with the values of liberty-equality-fraternity – that medicine was the natural ally of progressive politics and antisemitism the product of Catholic bigotry or the frustrations of a struggling petty bourgeoisie. Yet Soury's biological racism stemmed 'logically' from trends in medical science, ethnography and anthropology. Initially Soury claimed that 'Aryan' culture was creative, Jewish culture parasitic. But he lost interest in philological and cultural explanations. His 'scientific' anti-semitism flowed from his medical epistemology with its reductionist insistence that everything was determined by the central nervous system and that dissection of the brain could establish racial characteristics. Soury had observed Charcot's research at Saltpetrière hospital which purported to show that Jews, not just women, were prone to 'hysteria'. Jews' distinctive nervous systems made them immune to alcoholism, but peculiarly prone to neurological disorders as a result of generations of intermarriage. Soury was more than just a maverick proto-Nazi. His biological-medical reductionism made him a widely admired intellectual figure. He acted as 'mediator' between the frontiers of medical science and the world of cultural politics. His admirers included both proto-fascist Barrès and Dreyfusard Maurice de Fleury, Zola's advisor on medical matters! (Gelfand 1994)

By 1900 there was a convergence in 'advanced' medical thinking around eugenicist premises and support for imposition of premarital medical tests to prevent hereditary 'degeneration'. Only in 1926 was a Bill debated requiring medical certificates for prospective spouses, a measure implemented in diluted form under Vichy (1942). Ironically the very anxieties about population stagnation which prompted eugenicist modes of thought precluded extreme eugenicist solutions. While there was alarm about 'quality', the striking statistics were those which showed France's birth-rates plunging below those of her rivals. Eugenicist controls on 'degenerate' breeding would reduce birth-rates yet further. Hence 'natalism', with its focus on birth-rates, became the dominant medical current, spearheaded by Bertillon's *Alliance pour l'Accroissement de la Population* (1886). By contrast the pro-birth control, neo-Malthusian movement led by Paul Robin was small, and suspected of antipatriotic, anarcho-syndicalist tendencies because it urged workers to support a 'strike of the wombs' to deprive militarists of cannon-fodder and capitalists of a reserve army of labour. Yet Robin also flirted with eugenicism. Others on the libertarian Left found eugenics sinister and authoritarian, as did those doctors who believed that 'Republican' medicine involved pity for the weak and support for disability and insisted that, in time, it might be possible to treat major diseases, rather than resigning oneself to the view that they were incurable and hereditary. 'Liberty, Equality, Fraternity' remained a better slogan than 'Determinism, Inequality, Selection'. Ironically their distaste for eugenicist ideas was shared by Catholic doctors, whose numbers are often underestimated, for whom eugenicism was as distasteful as birth control or abortion because all God's creatures, 'healthy' or otherwise, deserved love (Schneider 1992; Nye 1993; Carol 1997).

The social practices and professional ethos of family doctors were an obstacle to eugenicist projects. Those elements in the medical profession which obstructed progressive steps towards healthcare for the popular classes also blocked the eugenicist aspirations of some medical mandarins. In the last resort the medical system involved more than scientific ideas, disease etiology, diagnosis, therapy, medical agendas of the state or medical elites or 'bio-medical' discourse. It also involved doctor–patient relations in their social context. While doctors were happy to see their status and prestige grow in the reflected glory of Pasteur, their role as intermediaries between 'scientific' medicine and the patient was fraught with difficulties. For, as patients became aware, implications of medical theories were often less than reassuring. There were anxieties, shrewdly exploited by Catholic writers, about medical mandarins' projects. Leon Daudet's *Les Morticides* (1906) portrayed a dystopia where all are 'ill' and subjected to experiments by a medical elite. In F. Carel's *La Nouvelle Idole* the doctor remains unrepentant when a patient whom he has injected with cancer cells dies: 'If it is permitted to lose a whole regiment to save a country', he asks, 'why cannot a *grand savant* sacrifice a few lives for a sublime discovery?' Public opinion was uneasy when medical researchers justified aggravated skin-cancers suffered by patients subjected to pioneer X-ray treatment by invoking long-term benefit to humanity.

More worrying for the GP was the problem of remaining a reassuring family confidant when 'scientific' medicine propounded degeneration theories about which, thanks to the press, patients were well informed. Implications of theories suggesting that defects – and 'sins' – of parents might be visited on succeeding generations were disturbing. Since syphilis was considered to be hereditary, not simply contagious, might not even 'cured' syphilitics transmit the disease to their offspring? This theme fascinated and horrified writers. In *L'Avarié* (Damaged Goods), Eugene Brieux presented theatre audiences with the dilemma of a family doctor who, respecting patient confidentiality, fails to warn a woman of her fiancé's syphilis. Following the birth of three deformed children, the wife goes insane (Harsin 1996–97). Meanwhile the doctors' *Syndicat* constructed a distinctive image of the family GP as more understanding and caring than 'cold' medical elites. Such doctors viewed themselves less as members of a scientific priesthood with grandiose 'medicalising' pretensions than as members of a trade whose livelihood depended on serving clients' interests. They were less concerned with national genetics than with doctor–patient relations and appearing loyal family friends to whom one turned in moments of stress. Eugenicist modes of thought raised the spectre of a bureaucratised medical machine and implied the shattering of doctor–patient confidentiality, since hereditary 'defects' would have to be declared. It raised prospects of doctors having to refuse medical approval for marriage and procreation, and being sued by parents if new-born infants were 'defective'. Eugenicism was the project of a segment of a rising professional class eager to show that their expertise was necessary for vetting and control of efficient reproduction of humane capital. It made less sense for the day-to-day practice of a GP in a liberal-bourgeois society. The constraints on eugenicist programmes suggest that the fate of medical ideologies can be dependent on the social history of medical practice.

The net impact of medical ideologies on public opinion is difficult to assess. Some saw implications of new medical orthodoxies as depressing: 'Science has replaced God as the Higher Authority', observed L. H. Dejust, 'Science is all powerful. But Science is not God. It cannot perform miracles'. Others, under the sway of neo-Lamarckean ideas, gave a more optimistic twist, arguing that transmission of acquired characteristics need not imply acceptance of hereditary degeneration. Perhaps medical science could apply itself to controlling 'defects' rather than eliminating the 'defectives'. Perhaps pessimistic neo-Darwinian views of inexorable hereditary decline were best left to Germans like Weismann.

The 'war against TB'

The eugenics debate was conducted largely within medical elites, even though its implications were wider and did attract public interest. Tuberculosis was of more than academic interest. It was a 'social disease', responsible for one-quarter of all deaths in France. Identified as a national scourge, it became the target of a 'crusade' after 1898. TB was a killer elsewhere in the industrial world, but its annual mortality rate of 4‰ in France was substantially higher than the 2.5‰ to 3‰ in Britain or Germany. After 1882 there was a consensus that the 'Koch bacillus' carried the disease. International congresses pooled data and experience and co-ordinated strategies against it. However, treatment of TB displayed national 'peculiarities' (Barnes 1995).

In the 1820s Laënnec had insisted that although 'the common people and doctors in certain . . . countries believed TB to be contagious, *informed* opinion viewed it as the product of inherited predisposition . . . and of certain types of passionate sentiments'. Playwrights portrayed the 'typical consumptive' as a 'fallen woman', as in *La Dame aux Camélias*, whose death constituted a moment of redemptive suffering. Some doctors claimed that masturbation caused excessive semen-loss and placed an exhausted body at risk from the disease. However, the public hygiene movement provided empirical data which changed the debate. Villermé's investigation of correlations between ill-health, residence and occupation questioned claims that TB could be correlated with wind-direction or altitude. Differential mortality was explicable by differences of income. When, in 1868, Dr Villemim claimed that the disease was contagious, his findings were greeted with scepticism by experts such as Pidoux who found the concept naïve, vulgar and 'medieval'. However, Pidoux did admit that it was linked to low living standards of workers 'freed from serfdom but not yet from wage labour'. He added that if contagion were to be proved, it would have to be whispered quietly to avoid ostracism of victims. In 1882 Koch proved that the disease spread via a bacillus which could be inhaled from droplets expelled by coughing or spitting. This might lodge in the respiratory tract, or spread to lungs and bones.

One could write the subsequent history of the disease as a progressive narrative of transition, in the words of one recent survey, 'from despair to salvation' – a victorious combat waged by 'intrepid' men of science. This echoes the 'story' promoted by the Third Republic, which lauded medicine's success in diagnosing the causes of the disease and introduction of measures to curb its threat. The Paris medical establishment launched the 'war' on TB, Republican *notables* sat on a parliamentary TB commission. In 1905 Paris hosted an international TB congress. Yet France's treatment of the TB shows how the 'scientific' etiology of a disease can be ideological and medical 'knowledge' socially conditioned. It offers ammunition for Foucauldian and Marxist critiques of 'bourgeois' medicine, whose 'narrative' was remarkable both for its 'bacillocentrism' and for blaming workers for their own ill-health by systematic downplaying of poverty's role in the disease's social distribution.

The medical model of cultural crisis exercised a conceptual hegemony which precluded other ways of viewing the national condition. TB was viewed as a 'truly national peril' in its own right but also as a metaphor for wider socio-cultural ills. The war on TB peaked in the 1900s, with 35 books per year published on the disease. This correlated neither with any medical break-through nor with an upsurge in the disease, but rather with anxieties related to the Dreyfus crisis, labour unrest and crime. The official 'story' of TB provided a sense of order, causality and moral significance, with workers as both victims and villains. It was their filthy habits, domestic squalor and propensity for vice which threatened their own lives and those of hygiene-conscious bourgeois. Official TB etiology was 'bacillophobic' not just 'bacillocentric'. Combating the contagious dissemination of the Koch bacillus became the focus of the medical crusade. Spitting, once an accepted habit, was now viewed as a working-class monopoly. 'Homicidal spittle' – *le crachat homicide* – figured in all accounts of the disease's dissemination. The proletarian spitter had an alarming tendency to spit everywhere. One meticulous medical researcher counted 875 *crachats* on a short stretch of pavement, omitting those on café terraces! A single spitting worker might contaminate an entire factory, a servant a bourgeois household. Hence 'who can claim, whatever his social position, never to receive in his home someone . . . who deposits the fatal germ?'. Public library users were at peril from infected volumes. Provision of sanitary spitoons became an element in the crusade.

Workers' housing was a second target. By 1905, 200 *foyers de TB* were maked on the Paris map as responsible for one-third of deaths from the disease. This was a classic case of 'ecological slippage', attempting to explain and control pathologies by mapping them geographically. Medical reports juxtaposed 'scientific' phraseology with visceral aversion for proletarian squalor evident in lurid descriptions of stench, lack of ventilation, urine leaking through ceilings from blocked latrines. Overcrowded dwellings were associated with lack of hygiene and sexual immorality. The 'ravages of promiscuous cohabitation' explained why entire families succumbed to TB.

Philanthropists visited workers' homes to give wives their 'womanly advice' on the dangers from microbes dwelling in dust. However, actions undertaken by authorities remained modest. Thousands of Parisian buildings were now disinfected. Demolition of unhealthy dwellings encountered the twin problems of landlords' property rights and providing shelter for displaced tenants in the absence of a public housing strategy. Republican rhetoric about the need for affordable working-class housing remained largely hot-air, with an ineffectual Housing Act (1894) merely encouraging private builders to construct cheap housing by offering tax concessions.

Workers' 'immorality' was the third 'cause' of the social distribution of TB. Interrelated seductions of alcohol and prostitution to migrants were endlessly cited in an etiology whose moralistic and ideological content was blatant. 'The young peasant, healthy and robust, dazzled by what he saw of the city during military service, deserts hearth and home and comes to swell the incalculable numbers of malcontents and have-nots. He begins to perceive that life is not all rosy. Poverty, alcohol and TB catch up with the stragglers and rip them apart without mercy', claimed one medical thesis. Workers contracted TB through a culture of vice. Only a Republic built around 'Cleanliness, Sobriety, Prosperity' could halt such degeneracy. Evidence that men were more prone to catch the disease suggested that 'alcohol made the bed for TB'. Doctors ridiculed syndicalist claims about the beneficial effects of leisure for workers, arguing that workers spent free time boozing in cafés and discussing revolutionary politics. Dr Lancereaux claimed that 1229 of 2192 TB patients were alcoholics. The *cabaret* stood 'at the confluence of several social pathologies'. Drinking led to sexual liaisons with barmaids and exposure to venereal disease, which weakened resistance to other diseases. By the 1890s prostitutes, treated not as victims of economic pressures but as carriers of infections, became a focus of the anxiety, incarnating the interlinked threats of VD, TB, alcoholism and moral and physical degeneration. There were calls to close down Latin Quarter brasseries where barmaids infected *Grandes Écoles* students. Absence of firm medical evidence linking syphilis and TB did not deter Alfred Fournier from asserting that the former formed 'fertile soil' for the latter. Professor Brouchard claimed that TB was 'acquiring the *character* of a veritable venereal disease'. Prostitutes should face obligatory tests for both diseases. But doctors faced dilemmas when advocating measures to combat TB. Republicanism was ideologically incapable of demanding massive public expenditure for affordable popular housing projects. Publicising the threat from TB might, in the absence of any cure or vaccine, create panic or despair among those already infected, whose incentives for ceasing to spit would be minimal! Doctors faced ethical dilemmas about disclosure. Where bourgeois patients exhibited symptoms of TB, neither their families nor their GPs would admit this in writing! Disclosure not only risked breaching doctor–patient confidentiality but could lead to TB sufferers being ostracised by neighbours, sacked by employers, or evicted by landlords.

The outcome was a system which created illusions of care for victims, but whose priorities were to identify and isolate them in the interests of public hygiene. The rhetoric and actions of medical authorities 'searching out and isolating vectors of contagion' lend themselves to a Foucauldian reading.

Deaths per 1000 in population from TB

	1887	1913
Paris	4.6	3.6
Le Havre	5.4	4.8
26-city average	3.6	3.4

Municipal authorities 'tracked down' the infected, constructed 'finely-meshed nets' to filter out 'suspects' in order to 'render them incapable of harming the community'. TB dispensaries were established in working-class areas. Le Havre authorities sought to utilise space in a bourgeois district for a dispensary, but surrendered to residents' complaints and relocated it in a popular quartier! Dispensaries' ostensible purpose was to wash patients' linen, provide spittoons and food coupons. Doctors' less public rhetoric resembled that of agents of a would-be collective Panopticon designed to ensure surveillance of workers' *quartiers* and isolation of suspects. These were to be 'educated' – taught to wash daily, use spittoons, breathe through the nose – for 'the consumptive who is taken in, educated, kept in check . . . becomes perfectly harmless'. Sanatoriums provided before 1914 were, one doctor insisted, designed for the 'isolation of bacillus-spitting *tuberculeux*' and for their unobtrusive deaths rather than for cure. One should leave such patients 'the *illusion* that they are going to recover'. TB experts demanded powers to intern those who, during periods of temporary remission, tried to return home. Dr Jules Héricourt, a friend of crowd theorist Le Bon who advocated the killing of 'hereditary criminals', equated the TB sanatorium with a leper colony, designed to shield the economically productive against the useless.

The efficacy of the war on TB is not easily measured. Contemporary statistical sources do not always give precise causes of death, but recent estimates suggest that TB deaths were declining, albeit slowly, between 1880 and 1914. One-fifth of all deaths remained TB-related – a higher proportion than in Germany or Britain. The long-term decline pre-dated the war on TB and reflected improvements in wages and diet more than medical measures. The rapid surge in TB deaths in Paris from an average of 8000 per year in 1865–69 to 12,000 per year in 1870–71 had been due to food shortage during the siege (Taithe 1999). Doctors derived prestige from their identification with the discoveries of Koch and Pasteur as well as political clout from their role in the Republic. Yet despite their high profile as 'experts' in the anti-TB crusade, their bacillocentric and moralising diagnoses were not accompanied by any effective cure. In this pre-streptomycin era their therapies were largely ineffectual.

The field of medical 'knowledge' remained contested terrain. Though there was an alternative 'narrative' about the etiology of the disease, it struggled to make itself heard. Even after the Koch bacillus was accepted as the agent of contagion, some insisted that uneven incidence of the disease stemmed not so much from differing levels of exposure to the bacillus but from some groups' weakened resistance. Left-wing doctors highlighted long work-hours, factory conditions and poor diets which made workers vulnerable. If there were alcohol/TB correlations, these occurred because capitalist exploitation drove exhausted workers to seek sustenance in drink. Such views, expounded by syndicalist Pelloutier, were taken up by socialist deputy Dr Vaillant who sought recognition for TB as an occupational disease qualifying sufferers for industrial compensation. Proposed legislation was, predictably, rejected. Prosyndicalist doctors, with fewer illusions about legislative reforms, were more outspoken, denouncing the anti-TB crusade as a charade, a smokescreen designed to observe real issues. 'Low wages go hand in hand with prolonged workdays and intense labour. These are marvellous conditions for the blossoming of TB. What are we supposed to do about it?', asked Dr Pierrot. 'Avoid spitting on the ground? Create dispensaries? Elect better deputies?'. Even if workers could afford rest cures in sanatoriums, what would happen to their health when they returned to unchanged home and work conditions? One doctor wrote an ironic prediction of the outcome of the 1905 international congress. Wives of the medical great and good would go shopping in department stores. There would be self-congratulatory speeches on medicine's scientific and humanitarian mission, erudite lectures on esoteric aspects of the Koch bacillus. There would be calls for further government commissions. Champagne would flow. These predictions proved only too accurate. However, there was a speech from a doctor from the Lille dispensary, claiming that 98 per cent of his patients were overworked, 68 per cent undernourished. It was ignored. Returning to Lille he wrote that existing anti-TB strategies were futile half-measures designed to buy-off workers' unrest. The only sure cure for TB was social revolution (Barnes 1995; Cottereau 1978).

Bibliography

Ackerknecht, E. *Medecine at the Paris Hospital: 1794–1848* (Baltimore, MD: Johns Hopkins University Press, 1967).
Ackermann, E. *Health Care in the Paris Countryside: 1800–1914* (New Brunswick: Rutgers University Press, 1990).
Bardet, J. P. (ed.) *Peurs et Terreurs face à la Contagion* (Paris: Fayard, 1988).
Barnes, D. *The Making of a Social Disease: Tuberculosis in 19th-Century France* (Berkeley, CA: University of California Press, 1995).
Bercé, Y.-M. *Le Chaudron et la Lancette: Croyances populaires et Médecine préventive 1798–1831* (Paris, 1984).
Bourdelais, P. and Raulot, J.-Y. *Une Peur Bleue: Histoire du Choléra en France 1832–1854* (Paris: Payot, 1978).
Carol, A. 'Médecine et Eugénisme en France', *Revue d'Histoire Moderne et Contemporaine* 1997.
Coleman, W. *Death is a Social Disease: Public Health and Political Economy in Early-Industrial France* (Madison: University of Wisconsin, 1982).
Corbin, A. *The Foul and the Fragrant: Odor and the French Social Imagination* (Cambridge, Mass: Harvard University Press, 1986).
Cottereau, A. 'La Tuberculose: Maladie Urbaine ou Maladie de l'Usure du Travail?', *Sociologie du Travail* 1978.
Darmon, P. *La LongueTraque du Variole* (Paris, 1985).
Delaporte, F. *Disease and Civilisation: the Cholera in Paris, 1832* (Cambridge, Mass: MIT, 1986).

Dessertine, D. and Faure, O. *Combattre la Tuberculose* (Lyon: Lyon University Press, 1988).

Devlin, J. *The Superstitious Mind: French Peasants and the Supernatural in the Nineteenth Century* (New Haven, CT: Yale University Press, 1987).

Ellis, J. *The Physician-Legislators of France: Medicine and Politics in the early Third Republic* (Cambridge: Cambridge University Press, 1990).

Faure, O. 'Physicians in Lyon during the 19th century', *Journal of Social History* 1977.

Faure, O. *Genèse de l'Hôpital Moderne: Lyon 1802–45* (Lyon: Lyon University Press, 1982).

Faure, O. 'La Médecine gratuite au XIXe Siècle', *Histoire, Economie, Société* 1984.

Faure, O. 'The social history of health in France', *Bulletin of the Society for the Social History of Medicine* 1990.

Faure, O. *Les Français et leurs Médecins au XIXe Siècle* (Paris: Belin, 1993).

Faure, O. *Histoire sociale de la Médecine: XVIII–XXe Siècles* (Paris: Anthropos, 1994).

Faure, O. 'Les Officines Pharmaceutiques de la Réalité au Mythe', *Revue d'Histoire Moderne et Contemporaine* 1996–97.

Faure, O. and Dessertine, D. *La Maladie entre Libéralisme et Solidarité: 1850–1940* (Paris: Mutualité Française, 1994).

Gelfand, T. 'From Religious to Bio-medical Antisemitism: the Career of Jules Soury', in A. La Berge and M. Feingold (eds) *French Medical Culture in the 19th Century* (Amsterdam: Rodopi, 1994).

Goldstein, J. *Console and Classify: the French Psychiatric Profession in the 19th Century* (Cambridge: Cambridge University Press, 1994).

Guillaume, P. *Médecins, Eglise et Foi* (Paris: Aubier, 1990).

Harsin, J. Syphilis, wives and physicians: medical ethics and the family in late-19th-century France', *French Historical Studies* 1996–97.

Hildreth, M. *Doctors, Bureaucrats and Public Health: 1888–1902* (New York: Garland, 1987).

Hildreth, M. 'Doctors and families in France 1880–1920', in A. La Berge and M. Feingold (eds) *French Medical Culture in the 19th Century* (Amsterdam: Rodopi, 1994).

Jones, C. 'The new medical history in France', *French History* 1987.

Jones, C. 'The great chain of buying: medical advertisement, the bourgeois public sphere and the origins of the French Revolution', *American History Review* 1996.

Jones, C. and Brockliss, L. *The Medical World of Early-Modern France* (Oxford: Clarendon Press, 1997).

Knibiehler, Y. and Fouquet, C. *La Femme et la Médecine* (Paris: Hachette, 1983).

Kudlick, C. *Cholera in Post-Revolutionary France: a Cultural History* (Berkeley, University of California Press, 1996).

La Berge, A. *Mission and Method: the Early 19th-Century French Public Health Movement* (Cambridge: Cambridge University Press, 1991).

La Berge, A. and Feingold, M. (eds) *French Medical Culture in the 19th Century* (Amsterdam: Rodopi, 1994).

Latour, B. *The Pasteurisation of France* (Cambridge, Mass: Harvard University Press, 1988).

Léonard, J. 'Femmes, Réligion et Médecine', *Annales ESC* 1977.

Léonard, J. *La France Médicale au XIXe Siècle* (Paris: Gallimard, 1978a).

Léonard, J. *Les Médecins de l'Ouest au XIXe Siècle* 3 vols (Paris: H. Champion, 1978b).

Léonard, J. *La Médecine entre les Pouvoirs et les Savoirs* (Paris: Aubier Montagne, 1981).

Murard, A. and Zylberman, P. (eds) *L'Haleine des Faubourgs* (Fontenay-sous-Bois, 1978).

Nye, R. *Crime, Madness and Politics in Modern France: the Medical Concept of National Decline* (Princeton, NJ: Princeton University Press, 1984).

Nye, R. 'The rise and fall of the eugenics empire', *The Historical Journal* 1993.

Nye, R. 'Honor, impotence and male sexuality in 19th-century French medicine', *French Historical Studies* 1996–97.

Pellissier, C. 'La Médicalisation des Elites Lyonnaises au XIXe Siècle', *Revue d'Histoire Moderne et Contemporaine* 1997.

Pick, D. *Faces of Degeneration: 1848–1918* (Cambridge: Cambridge University Press, 1989).

Ramsey, M. 'History of a profession, Annales-style: the work of J. Léonard', *Journal of Social History* 1983–84.

Ramsey, M. 'The Politics of Professional Monopoly in 19th-century Medicine', in G. Geison (ed.) *Professions and the French State* (Philadelphia: University of Pennsylvania Press, 1984).

Ramsey, M. *Professional and Popular Medicine in France: 1770–1830* (Cambridge: Cambridge University Press, 1988).

Ramsey, M. 'Academic medicine and medical industrialism: the regulation of secret remedies in 19th-century France', in A. La Berge and M. Feingold (eds) *French Medical Culture in the 19th Century* (Amsterdam: Rodopi, 1994).

Reid, D. *Paris Sewers and Sewermen: Realities and Representations* (Cambridge, Mass: Harvard University Press, 1991).

Schneider, W. *Quality and Quantity: the Quest for Biological Regeneration in 19th-Century France* (Cambridge: Cambridge University Press, 1990).

Schneider, W. 'Towards the improvement of the human race: eugenics in France', *Journal of Modern History* 1992.

Schulteiss, K. *Bodies and Souls: Politics and the Profesionalisation of Nursing in France 1880–1922* (Cambridge, Mass: Harvard University Press, 2001).

Shapiro, A.-L. *Housing the Poor of Paris: 1850–1902* (Madison: University of Wisconsin, 1985).

Sussmann, G. 'The glut of doctors in mid-19th-century France', *Comparative Studies in Society and History* 1977.

Taithe, B. *Defeated Flesh: Medicine, Welfare and Warfare in the Making of Modern France* (Manchester: Manchester University Press, 1999).

Weiner, D. *The Citizen-Patient in Revolutionary and Imperial Paris* (Baltimore MD: Johns Hopkins University Press, 1994).

Weisz, G. 'The development of medical specialisation in 19th-century Paris', in A. La Berge and M. Feingold (eds) *French Medical Culture in the 19th Century* (Amsterdam: Rodopi, 1994).

Williams, E. *The Physical and the Moral: Anthropology, Physiology and Philosophical Medicine in France 1750–1850* (Cambridge: Cambridge University Press, 1994).

Chapter 8

The birth of a consumer society?

Introduction

Studies of the 'industrial revolution' once emphasised technological change and production. It is no accident that historians' focus has now shifted towards consumption, for consumerism is central to the culture of our age. With the decline of clear 'class' identities built around work has come an emphasis on those constructed around consumer taste and lifestyles. Choice in the market-place, it is assumed, defines one's true essence. I shop, therefore I am – and I am what I buy! 'Trickle-down' economics revitalised once fashionable, but briefly discredited, assumptions that élite consumption produced benefits for the poor. Insisting that expensive silk gowns should be worn at Court in the 1857 industrial recession, Empress Eugènie explained that 'when those *above* are spending, there is no unemployment down below'. During the 1847 depression etiquette magazine *Le Counseiller des Dames* observed that 'government, in the interests of the labouring population, wants celebration parties, gatherings of the fashionable set – for they are precious sources of work for all industries' (Vanier 1960). Because our own 'underclass' allegedly dreams of Armani fashions and Porsches, the Industrial Revolution has been re-conceptualised as a consumer-driven process during which elite tastes in furniture, porcelain, fashion and colonial goods were aped by rising 'middling classes', then by the populace as servants coveted their employers' cast-off fashions and workers emulated the servants (Fine and Leopold 1990). Certainly British workers developed a taste for cheap colonial goods such as tea and tobacco, and wore bright-coloured cotton clothing, though some remain unconvinced that a 'bleak-age' of worker immiseration can be reinvented as an era of popular consumerism on the strength of the poor acquiring the second-hand clothing of their social superiors. Emerging 'consumerism' has been discerned in Holland and in the American colonies, where the 1770s revolt was symbolised by a boycott of imported British consumer goods and the Boston Tea Party was an elaborate 'ritual of non-consumption'! There is evidence that flourishing colonial trade and proto-industrial production were expanding the world of material goods in pre-1789 France. Parisian artisans were being drawn into a *culture des apparences* – acquiring a taste for clothing, furniture and household utensils. Indications of an emerging market culture have been discerned in sales of medical services and products, and in the alacrity with which an astute entrepreneur transformed the Bastille into a lucrative heritage site by selling historical memorabilia from it within months of July 1789 (Roche 1989; Jones and Spang 1999)!

This burgeoning literature on embryonic consumerism is underpinned by new theoretical assumptions. Marx's assumption that economics determined culture has been countered by claims that taste and cultural priorities may influence production – that, for example, French bourgeois wives' preference for 'quality' goods helped perpetuate artisanal modes of production. Max Weber's claim that the capitalist ethos was 'puritanical' – austere, based on hard work and thrift – has been challenged by assertions that an 'Arminian' spirit of self-indulgence was equally central to bourgeois identity. Possessions and fashion choices are symbols and signifiers which can be de-coded to gain insights into (changing) bourgeois values. Pessimistic assumptions of the Frankfurt school that mass consumers are passive, manipulated by forces of commercial capitalism, have been questioned. Just as the (female) consumer of fashion magazines and TV 'soaps' is now construed not as an imbiber of conformist values but as an active agent, capable of constructing her own meanings, so historians claim to discern consumer 'agency' in earlier centuries. Even within the home women were not simply birds in gilded cages, but rather 'ministers' controlling the budget for household consumption, arbiters of domestic taste (Walton 1986; Tiersten 1993). Hence the world of consumer goods, its rules codified in etiquette and fashion journals, becomes an arena of female 'empowerment'. Housewives are viewed as just as important to the Nord's bourgeois culture as their textile-manufacturer husbands (Smith 1981).

France and the consumer revolution

Economic historians once relegated France to the status of 'also-ran' – outstripped by Britain in the First Industrial Revolution and failing to match Germany and the USA in the Second. However, emphasis on marketing, 'taste' and fashion has presented France in a different guise, as a pioneer in a modern retailing revolution. Although brightly lit shopfronts, fixed prices and advertising were features of some eighteenth-century British cities, it was Paris which became the world's shopping capital. *Nouveauté* shops like *Belle Jardinière* emerged after 1830. But it was Haussman's reconstruction of the city that launched the era of the department store. Paris became the hub of the rail network. Department stores stood on broad boulevards flanked by bourgeois apartments and served by omnibuses and cabs. Prominent in the crowds portrayed in early Impressionist paintings were shoppers, 'shop-girls' – in fashionable dresses – and male strollers (*flâneurs*) (Clark 1985). By 1878 the *Louvre* store had branches in Tokyo and Latin America. However, it was to Paris – the global symbol of leisure and shopping – that tourists were drawn, as the 1878 diary of young American Hattie Crocker suggests.

July 15   Mama and I went shopping . . . to Bon Marché and Louvre.
July 16   Went shopping – same as yesterday.
July 17   Went to Exposition – very interesting but tiring.
July 18   Went shopping all day.

After shopping for eight further days, they departed for the provinces, only to return for eighteen days' consecutive shopping (Davis 1989)!

By 1910, *Bon Marché*, with an annual turnover of 230 million francs, was three times larger than *Au Printemps* and *Galeries Lafayette*. Founded in 1852 by hatter's son Boucicaut, its turnover reached 20 million francs by 1867. Its Rue de Sèvres store became a Parisian landmark and a model for competitors. By 1900 it employed seven thousand. It was, an admirer claimed, the retailing equivalent of an Oldham smelting works! It made striking use of new technologies and material – steel-frames, sweeping marble staircases, plate-glass windows. Gas, then electric lighting illuminated exotic window displays, transforming perceptions of the city at night from the sinister shadows and darkness of the 1830s to a world 'shining like the sun' (Schivelbusch 1988). It had bureaucratic managerial structures and utilised economies of scale. Its owners exercised 'paternalistic' controls over sales assistants – lodged in dormitories, subjected to curfews and obliged to take classes in elocution and etiquette (Miller 1981). The firm's image seamlessly blended 'tradition' and 'modernity'. It emphasised 'family values' and respect for traditions of French handicraft production, yet utilised an army of 'sweated' Parisian and provincial workers, dealt in bulk with suppliers, had fixed prices, wide stock range and rapid turnover. The 'choreographed confusion' of the store's interior was designed to make it difficult to locate the exits, obliging customers to walk past more goods. Prices were a 15 per cent 'mark-up' on wholesale rates, as against 50 per cent in small shops. Bargain racks near entrances enticed casual passers-by into the store. Browsing was encouraged. There was a cycle of quasi-liturgical seasonal rituals – 'sales', spring collections, and Christmas lights. Illuminated adverts for the store dominated the city skyline (Crossick and Jaumin 1999). The store's elegance endowed its goods with an aura which not all merited. Indeed the store itself became an attraction, advertised alongside cathedrals and museums in guide books and open for guided tours. Mail-order catalogues became a key to stores' success. *Au Printemps* distributed one million annually by 1900, some in foreign languages. Department stores were 'imperialists', viewing the provinces as colonies to be conquered. Goods were dispatched within twenty-four hours. There were Sunday delivery services for the Paris *banlieue* (Miller 1981). Stores embodied Max Weber's bureaucratic rationality, while peddling fantasies. They relied less on economically 'rational' customers than on those seduced by window displays. 'One came', a critic noted, 'less to purchase a particular article than simply to visit – buying in the process because it was part of the excitement.' Inevitably there were critics. Zola, fascinated by their dynamism, worried that they signalled doom for small retailers. This view was echoed by the populist Right and by small shopkeeper associations in the 1890s Depression, although by attracting more potential customers to city centres, department stores possibly provided small retailers in side-streets and arcades with extra trade (Nord 1986).

As Hattie Crocker's diary suggests, Paris *Expositions* became complementary attractions to department stores, existing in a symbiotic relationship with them. *Expositions* became, one fashion magazine observed, 'a solemn commercial occasion and every elegant and economic woman (wants) to be there'. They were designed to boost national prestige and pride in France's revived colonial empire (Silverman 1989). The 1878 *Exposition*, which attracted 16 million visitors, symbolised a burgeoning renaissance under the Third Republic after the disasters of 1870–71. A France regenerated by consumption was rejoicing in her global prestige as the centre of world shopping! Luxury goods on display were not 'frivolities' but 'art'. And, one fashion writer recalled, 'every department of Art [at the Exposition] bore witness to women's beauty and their influence inspired the industrial and artistic revival of the nation' (Davis 1989). Whilst *Expositions* retained their original pretence of being 'educational' showcases of technology and science, their tone became more blatantly commercial. By the 1890s commentators noted the incongruous juxtapositions of new machinery, belly-dancers, silk fabrics, peep-shows, Menier chocolates, camels and automobiles on display.

Zola's *Au Bonheur des Dames* celebrated the department store as the embodiment of capitalist dynamism and embryonic consumerist culture (Zola 1992). However, it is important to assess who 'consumers' were – to 'marry' emerging discourses about and images of consumerism with data on actual affordability and diffusion of material goods and spending power and priorities of social groups. There is no historiographical consensus about the chronology of popular consumerism. Some locate its origins in the 1770s, a period no longer viewed as one of falling living standards but marked by flourishing colonial trade and proto-industrial production. Analysis of inventories shows Parisian artisans furnishing rooms with decorative wall-tapestries, stoves, chests of drawers, flowered bed linen and bed-curtains, so the 'luxury of crepuscular well-being and sexual privacy filtered down from the elites'. Wall mirrors facilitated shaving and symbolised an era of narcissism. Watches and snuff-boxes became regular purchases. People had access to a range of clothes made from brightly coloured, lighter cloths. They revelled in frock-coats, stockings, muffs, bonnets, waistcoats and 'imitation beaver' (rabbit) fur-hats. 'For the first time', Roche (1989) claims, 'a huge consumer system – based on the ephemeral and allowing for some excess – emerged. The popular classes aspired to better living standards – authenticated by more frequent changes of clothing – and showed a new flare for sartorial taste.' However, Roche's concern is not just with what people actually bought but also with a mental shift – from an Ancien Régime where one wore what one's social position dictated, to a 'culture of appearances' where anyone could aspire to buy what he or she as an individual chose to wear. 'Civilisation' became associated with cleanliness and decent clothing. This transition alarmed traditionalists, who saw it as symbolising the breakdown of the socio-political order and demanded reinforcement of established dress-codes (Roche 1989).

Despite evidence for the emergence of a *populuxe* market for affordable versions of elite products, some remain sceptical that servants wearing employers' cast-offs or artisans buying these from second-hand clothes dealers (*fripiers*) necessarily constitutes evidence of a consumer revolution (Fairchilds 1993). *Sans-culotte* rhetoric emphasised the struggle for 'bread' and hostility to hoarders and speculators and portrayed revolutionaries as austere Spartans who despised *chétives marchandises* and luxury-loving, 'effeminate' aristocrats. However, this concern with 'bread' and 'subsistence' was partly a rhetorical trope. Paris artisans were regular purchasers of sugar, tobacco and coffee. The term '*sans-culotte*' – literally 'without knee-breeches' – alluded more to a fashion choice, a preference for straight trousers, than to abject poverty! Revolutionary 'austerity' was already swimming against the cultural tide, as yesterday's 'luxuries' became daily 'necessities' because commercial capitalism was generating new 'needs' (Jones and Spang 1999). Economic dislocation caused by two decades of warfare then led to a prolonged stagnation in popular living standards. Hence in *Le Peuple* (1846), Michelet claimed that only the recent advent of factory cotton-production had allowed workers to replace heavy, dark, long-lasting clothes with light, bright alternatives. He welcomed this as evidence of 'civilisation'. For the worker fashion was, he claimed, 'an initiation into art' and appreciation of the aesthetic (Magraw 1993). The growth of a ready-to-wear clothes industry (*confection*), based on division of labour and, later, on the sewing-machine, and of *nouveauté* stores encouraged *Le Figaro* to claim during the 1855 *Exposition* that class tensions were declining: 'A man of *whatever* social class wants to be well-dressed.' Popular violence 'declined as the taste for the wardrobe has gained ground' (Vanier 1960). Despite such claims, it may be safer to locate the emergence of mass consumerism – at the earliest – in the decades after 1880 (Williams 1982). Worker delegates to the 1867 *Exposition* reacted sourly to the goods on display – made by exploitation, de-skilling and 'sweating' of labour: 'The worker', they claimed, 'is essentially a *producer* and *consumes* little. In consequence low-price products can *only* be established at his expense' (Rancière 1988).

Studies of family budgets undertaken by disciples of social-Catholic Le Play suggested that up to 70 per cent of expenditure was still on foodstuff (Dauphin and Pézerat 1975). The phrase '*chez nous on vit bien*' – 'at our house we live well' – meant, in effect, 'we eat well'. French workers spent most extra income on food. Many celebrated Carnival as an excuse for a 'blow-out' on eating and drinking, a festival of burping, farting and vomiting! With popular housing cramped, expenditure on furniture was restricted. French workers spent, on average, 40 per cent less than British counterparts on clothing. Barely one-in-ten workers in the 1870s devoted more than 10 per cent of their income to their wardrobes, whereas American workers spent over 15 per cent. Attitudes to clothing were complex. A 1905 survey talked of the 'desire of (provincial) workers to imitate bourgeois lifestyles in their external manifestations. Clothes, fashion magazines and goods of all kinds absorb . . . their attention'. Yet Parisian skilled workers were less fashion-conscious than semi-skilled workmates. And when Le Play did locate well-paid artisans who owned stylish clothes, and enjoyed theatre and books, they proved to be political radicals whose goal was to 'exacerbate class hatreds'! The percentage of workers owning a suit rose from 10 per cent to 50 per cent between 1850 and 1890. Yet workers rejected top hats, straw boaters, canes and gloves as effete and 'bourgeois', and took pride in their class 'uniform' of blouse and cap.

Real wages did rise after 1880. As prices fell during the agricultural depression, expenditure on food declined to 60 per cent of the average family budget, as against under 50 per cent in Britain (Crane 2000). As spending patterns changed, Dufayel downmarket chain-stores, offering hire-purchase and credit facilities for skilled workers and white-collar employees, gained a foothold (Furlough 1991). They sold imitations of elite fashions, toys, kitchen utensils and metal bedsteads. Advertising strategies for sewing machines emphasised their usefulness to housewives and seamstresses, but hinted at escapist fantasies with images of women astride sewing-machines flying above Paris (Coffin 1994)! Chain-store grocer Felix Potin (1859) and stores such as Docks Rémois specialising in cheap clothing and utensils emerged in popular quartiers, despite protest from small retailers and consumer co-operatives. Shorter working-hours and the emergence of 'leisure' and of mass sports boosted a popular market for fishing tackle and bicycles (Holt 1985; Corbin 1995; Furlough 1991).

A peasantry increasingly 'Malthusian' in its fertility patterns slowed the development of a rural consumer market. Yet peasants involved in proto-industry were purchasing from *colporteurs* in the eighteenth century and there was a rural market for medical services. Although in 1830 banker Laffitte claimed that 'we still have only the poverty and stricken France of the *fourteenth* century to consume the produce of the ingenious France of the *nineteenth*', rural consumption expanded after 1850 as agricultural prices rose. In the Nièvre wives of larger peasants received mail-order catalogues, and inventories show villagers possessing rubber rainwear, metal bedsteads and cutlery (Thuillier 1977). Falling agricultural prices in the 1880s and 1890s depressed rural purchasing power again, yet studies of *fêtes foraines* suggests that itinerants continued to sell porcelain, crockery, coffee-sets and clothing at village fairs, as well as offering lottery prizes and fairground rides. However, the slow growth of a mass consumer market did not prevent a proliferation of *discourses about* consumerism. A culture of consumerism began – via advertisements, images and rhetoric – to infiltrate popular culture before the rise in mass purchasing power which could translate it into 'reality'. In 1855 Taine cited crowds attending the Paris *Exposition* as reassuring evidence that the masses were 'on the move to look at merchandise, (to) learn the lesson of objects'. Prosaic economic calculation, claimed *Le Figaro*, was giving way to an 'infinitely sunnier perspective – because everyone (sic!) is rich and has leisure . . . Sound production at low prices, that is what intelligent democracy, not to be confused with demagogy, consists of . . .' (Williams 1982; Vanier 1960).

Individual department stores targeted different clienteles. The *Bon Marché* attracted 'solid' bourgeois purchasers. Those of the *Louvre* were more elitist, those of *Au Printemps* younger and more stylish. As yet few customers were working-class. And yet discourse about department stores emphasised the social mixing that they encouraged, evoking a world where 'the working woman finds her fine woollens . . . , the honest bourgeois her simple, rich silk, the *grande dame* the most aristocratic designs that caprice can imagine'. All Parisiennes, fashion magazines claimed, regardless of class, shared an innate sense of style, a unique *savoir-vivre*. They formed a 'sisterhood of shoppers', a sorority of chic consumers. By using their instincts for bargains and sewing skills to make dresses from patterns, Parisian housewives or shop-girls could dress almost like a lady (Tiersten 2001). By the 1890s conservative

social observers argued that 'democratisation of luxury' proved that socialism was irrelevant in a society where consumerism permitted equality of
enjoyment without the need for further equalisation of income (Williams
1982). Economists argued that large-scale capitalism, by reducing production costs, was allowing consumption to spread down to the lower classes.

Debates about mass consumerism cannot obscure the primacy of the middle-
class shopper. Bourgeois consumer patterns – in particular women's tastes –
moulded the characteristics of French industry. By insisting on quality and
good design, they sustained 'craft' industries – porcelain, silk, furniture, jewellery, bronze, wallpaper and fashion – which enjoyed a 'second wind' after
1850. At the Crystal Palace Exhibition (1851) France secured around a thousand prizes, a tally second only to Britain, and won, Cobden acknowledged,
'universal recognition of (its) supremacy in matters of art and taste'. By comparison, British designs were 'brash', German 'heavy' and Italian 'gaudy'.
Economists suggested a global division of labour where America fed the world,
Britain supplied it with cotton goods and coal, but France supplied niche-
markets with 'embellished', tasteful products in sectors not monopolised by
mass-production (Walton 1992). But only one-sixth of French furniture or
clothing were exported. The key market for 'quality' products was French,
bourgeois and female. Wives of Nord manufacturers had once helped run
their husbands' businesses and lived frugally. By mid-century, however, these
'ladies of the leisure class' retreated into a domestic world of reproduction
and consumption. Their role was to make the home comfortable and stylish.
Their aesthetic mentors were editors of those fashion and etiquette magazines perused by Flaubert's Emma Bovary when still playing the model
provincial housewife. 'The mistress of the (bourgeois) household', observed
Audiganne, 'was like the Finance Minister of a Great-State (who) has capital
to apportion.' But she was also custodian of 'taste', with a patriotic role of
maintaining appreciation of quality craft production vital to the national
economy. Such magazines conflated 'fashion' and 'art', insisting that a housewife's instinct for colour co-ordination was comparable with that of a great
colourist. Fashion magazines sponsored exhibitions. By 1890 their adverts
were plagiarising Impressionism (Tiersten 2001). Shopping was more than a
utilitarian practice, it was a way of life and a social ritual. Group identities,
fashion guru Louise d'Alq insisted, were established not by equality of income but by shopping at the same store! With the husband a sober, rational
producer-provider, his wife became organiser and embellisher of the home.
Emma Bovary, having perused the mail-order catalogues, 'wanted two blue
vases . . . for her mantelpiece. The less Charles knew of such refinements, the
more they seduced him. They added, somehow, to the pleasure of the fire-
side'. The aesthetic tastes of these women – their avoidance of machine-made
British wallpaper or American shoes – bolstered artisanal production in Paris
and Lyon (Gaillard 1977). As Audiganne insisted, 'to triumph before (such)
feminine taste . . . is worth much more than to succeed before the most
thoughtful of Exhibition juries' (Walton 1986).

Among 'artisans' who survived were Fauborg St Antoine furniture-makers,
albeit often reduced to performing repetitive tasks, to operating labour-
saving machines or to assembling furniture made in the provinces (Auslander

301

1996). Bric à brac and furniture became key expressions of an authentic bourgeois style. Balzac recognised furniture as an accurate depictor of social class and character. 'Life', Madame Vauquer concludes in *Père Goriot*, 'is nothing without furniture.' Inventories of apartment-dwelling Parisians in mid-century suggest that the role of the wife as 'artistic designer' involved creative eclecticism, a capacity to juxtapose harmoniously the modern and the 'best of the past' (Walton 1990; Tiersten 2001). The aim was to create an appearance of affluence via selective 'borrowing' from historic styles – from Renaissance to Louis Quinze. Velour-backed sofas, *armoires*, heavy wall-tapestries and carved mahogany were favoured. Public display took precedence over private comfort. Functional metal-framed beds were bought for servants and children, but married couples had four-poster beds with decorative carvings and a visible, thick woollen mattress covering a modern, iron, box-sprung mattress underneath. Stoves – cheap and practical – were viewed as prosaic and vulgar and confined to kitchens and servants' quarters. Apartments of Haussman's Paris featured ornate fireplaces, symbols of 'hearth and home' but also focal points for displays of bellows, gilded bronze-fenders, ornate shovels. Mantelpieces were adorned with clocks, statuettes, porcelain vases, and electrolytic-plated 'silverware', a new speciality of the Paris semi-luxury industry. Ornate candlesticks provided atmospheric candle-glow at bourgeois dinner-parties. Painted porcelain oil-lamps remained fashionable despite the advent of electric lighting. It was as *soirée* hostess that the wife could display her expertise as conspicuous consumer. Etiquette literature instructed her on how to entertain and attain the correct blend of taste, material comfort and polite behaviour. Louise d'Alq advised on judicious placements of screens, plant-stands and sofas: 'Everything in the apartment *must* offer English comfort and French grace. Perfect order, elegance which easily passes for sumptuousness, must distinguish the dwelling and the furniture . . .'. The husband's role was self-abnegation personified – leaving the hostess to direct dinner-conversation towards her tasteful decorative skills. Guests such as 'Caroline B . . . ', whose diary has just been edited, were duly impressed: 'How well it is decorated! Salon especially delicious. Curtains of sky-blue; furniture of same with Louis Quinze medallions; the small console on which are scattered many gracious things . . . Everything is chosen with taste . . . Returned home filled with enthusiasm . . . ' (Walton 1990). With the outside world potentially chaotic and threatening, careful arrangement of material goods within the house symbolised stability and order. The wife's main contacts with the world beyond the *foyer* was as a consumer on expeditions to department stores. But her activities in this 'public' space aroused anxieties which reflected the ambivalence of bourgeois responses to emerging consumerist culture.

This ambivalence became apparent in the area of clothing. Cultural historians are experts in the 'semiotics of the wardrobe', decoding the socio-cultural meanings of changes in dress (Perrot 1994; Crane 2000). The gap between male and female fashions widened. The all-purpose dark suit, badge of post-Restoration bourgeoisie, represented an assertion of the industrious practicality of the newly hegemonic class. It filtered downwards to petty-bourgeois strata, thanks to confection which enabled purchase of cheap, off-the-peg suits from *Bonhomme Richard* by 1840. *Confection*, insisted the jury at the 1867 *Exposition*, 'is the true child of the century'. Bespoke tailors, who lamented the sobriety of Orleanist dress codes, were encouraged when the Bonapartist regime revived elaborate uniforms. But men's styles changed little across the decades. Space devoted to men's fashion in mail-order catalogues did double to 10 per cent between 1880 and 1910, but this was due to changes in accessories, as top-hats were challenged by caps and straw-boaters. Balzac (1998), lamenting the lack of style in men's clothing, complained that 'the grocer epitomises our age. He is civilisation in a shop, life itself distributed in . . . jars and jackets'. Dandies exhibited their distinction by the cut of their cloth, the elegance of their knotted tie, expressing distaste for the boring conformity of bourgeois attire and the mediocrity of those who wore it. By adopting the pose of (mock) heroic rebellion against new machine-culture, they sought to subvert it. They cultivated an esoteric elegance of dress which elevated them above the shopping-crowds with whom they mingled – and whose eyes they used as a mirror which reflected back their own exquisite aesthetic tastes. Disdaining vulgar mass consumerism, they were themselves the ultimate shoppers (Crane 2000; Tiersten 2001; Gilloch 1992).

Meanwhile, women's clothing became an outlet for vicarious male consumption, a symbol for the husband's status. 'When one is rich one must provide business for the shopkeeper', remarks the husband in Paul de Kock's novel when spending 1200 francs – the annual wage of a Paris craftsman – on a wedding dress (Constant 1986). Etiquette magazines insisted, however, that choice of clothing allowed women to construct themselves. Ten thousand Parisians in 1860 worked in the corset industry and *couturiers* quadrupled between 1830 and 1860; 800 Parisian firms manufactured a range of accessories – ribbons, bows, feathers, artificial flowers. Peugeot's Besançon works based its expansion on production of crinolines (Vanier 1960; Magraw 1993). Fashion magazines urged ladies to change clothes eight times per day! *Confection* came later to female than to male fashion, but by 1880 sewing-machines, improved yarns and cheaper 'mixed' Lyonnais silks allowed department stores to offer similar-looking garments at varying prices for differing female clienteles. The Duc de Gramont expressed his irritation that the Franco-Prussian war should have been launched in July 1870 when 'everybody (sic!) was at Deauville!'. Significantly, *Au Printemps* chose this Normandy resort to launch its first provincial branch. As the vogue for the seaside – Biarritz in the 1850s, the Côte d'Azur by 1880 – spread, fashion catalogues responded by featuring beachwear costumes – dark, heavy and unerotic – and a range of shorter skirts, practical shoes and lighter shawls appropriate for rail-travel (Crane 2000; Corbin 1995). Contemporary interest in tennis, cycling, mountain-climbing and ski-ing and automobiles were similarly reflected in the catalogues.

Consumerism, hedonism and bourgeois cultural anxieties

The middle-class housewife's role in burgeoning consumer culture was perceived by some as symptomatic of a 'corruption' of bourgeois values. As

Hobsbawm's (1987) analysis of Europe's 'long nineteenth century' suggests, the 'heroic' virtues of the bourgeoisie were austerity, thrift, sobriety and industriousness. The dark suit symbolised rejection of the narcissism of an idle aristocracy. Wives of Nord textile manufacturers had kept the firm's accounts, lived in Spartan accommodation close to the mill and eschewed silk-dresses (Smith 1981). After the 1830s there was a tug-of-war in Paris between such values and an emerging taste for 'luxury'. Yet despite evidence of a shift in the balance between 'frugality' and 'hedonism', clearly these two always coexist within bourgeois culture. Although Rousseau advocated simplicity, the Romantics' advocacy of self-expression and self-fulfilment could be channelled into conspicuous consumption. Proliferation of colonial consumer goods undoubtedly influenced the material culture of the middle classes. Port merchants displayed their trading successes through building town-houses and employing local craftsmen. The press of the 1770s carried adverts for cosmetics, furniture and jewellery – and some bourgeois purchased carriages in order to ape the aristocracy. After the austerity of the early Revolution, the fall of Robespierre launched a tidalwave of gluttony and conspicuous consumption. 'Restaurants' of the 1760s had been places to 'restore' oneself by sipping water, eating lettuce and parading one's abstinence. Now they became sites of gargantuan public meals and flaunting of opulence. The bourgeoisie displayed its mastery of the subtleties of gastronomic taste. Game, once an 'aristocratic' preserve, appeared on the menu. Rituals developed to consecrate eating as the bourgeoisie defined itself and displayed its discreet charm at the dinner-table. Balzac's Monsieur de Beauseart 'like many other sophisticated men, no longer indulged pleasures except good food'. Second Empire Paris was notorious for ostentatious, multi-course banquets. The Third Republic celebrated the Revolution's centenary with a huge Parisian banquet for 18,000 provincial mayors. The advent of gas allowed the bourgeois dinner-party to flourish. *La Cuisinière Bourgeoise* instructed housewives how to plan a meal. *L'Art Culinière* (1892) introduced the aspiring lower-middle-class to gastronomic refinements, for 'today everyone aspires to eat well. But one must also eat quickly . . .' (Aron 1975).

The advent of running water after 1850 increased 'comfort' within bourgeois households. A literature emerged to advertise the wares of industries which catered for the luxuries of the bathroom. Bidets ceased to be the preserve of upmarket brothels. Hot-water boilers, showers, bath-salts and scented perfumes proliferated. Women were urged to 'pamper' their bodies, relish the 'sensuality' of warm baths. The spread of individual mirrors encouraged narcissism. Since the consensus remained that hair should be brushed rather than washed regularly, shampoo's triumph lay in the future (Goubert 1989). As successful bourgeois moved to leafy suburbs, there was a relaxation of strict accounting practices hitherto observed by middle-class families. Indulgent husbands sometimes expected wives to be deficient in a sense of economy. 'My mother had very refined tastes', wrote one daughter. 'She loved clothing, beautiful furniture, lavish dishes. She knew *nothing* of the value of money.' Gestures of budgetary austerity were largely symbolic. Small economies and 'sacrifices' were made, which then justified extravagant refurbishment of the home (Smith 1981).

Yet many worried about this culture of comfort. Obsession with shopping, the vogue for extravagent, often erotic ladies' fashions, the decline of 'older' values rang alarm bells. Zola, whose *Au Bonheur des Dames* (1883) offered a dazzling portrait of the world of the department store, was typically ambivalent. He admired its dynamism and was fascinated by contrasts between its bright lights and seductive window-displays and the drab, old-fashioned shops in the side-streets. His department store owner is a creative, thrusting figure whose ruthlessness is eventually tempered by the love of a warm, compassionate young shop assistant – a perfect Third Republic marriage between productive capitalism and the people (Bowlby 1985)! Zola's anxieties went beyond concern at the decline of small retailers and the 'sweating' of the department store's army of outworkers. His main worry was with the impact of consumerism on bourgeois values. Was not shopping an intoxicant? The department store might typify capitalist efficiency. But its success depended on transforming itself into a fantasy palace, a 'dream world'. It was designed to lure (female) shoppers from the mundane monotony of daily life. Its internal layout was planned so that exits were impossible to locate without passing through seductive departments which one had not intended to visit. It persuaded the woman that she was 'queen in the shop'. A 'cathedral of consumption', the store was replacing the church in women's lives. Were it to shut, would not streets 'echo to the cries of *dévotes* whose temple had been suppressed'? Indeed, as one journalist noted, since women now went to Mass to display their fashionable dresses, had not churches themselves become 'the theatre of the world conflict between silk, satin and lace'? (Zola 1992; Bowlby 1985; Crossick and Jaumin 1999).

Zola's crowds of female shoppers were deeply irrational. They were flies drawn into a spider's web. The wife's veneer of decency was tossed aside as she succumbed to harem-like displays of lingerie, perfumes, oriental rugs and fetishistic gloves – awakening 'new desires', presenting 'immense temptations'. 'Pale with desire' she 'fatally succumbed'. Since the department store was outside her normal domestic sphere, she might, in her fevered state, fall prey to seductive men whom she encountered. Journalists claimed that stores closed their eyes to 'amorous intrigues'. Store detectives mistook elegant bourgeois shoppers for *filles publiques* (Bowlby 1985). Tempting displays lured women into extravagance. Zola portrayed the 'crazed shopper', Madame de Marty, in the process of ruining her teacher-husband. 'Incarnate in her' was the 'madness of impulse shopping, the growing desire for luxury instilled into the petty bourgeoisie by the department store'. Uzamme depicted such women 'dressed with exquisite grace, buying without purpose, without need, by whim or ill-defined caprice . . . because of the idleness and ennui of the home, in search of distraction and oblivion' (Williams 1982). Zola shared the widespread conviction that the stores' hot-house atmosphere was pathological. Shoppers, psychologists claimed, developed dilated pupils and irregular pulse-rates. Menstruating or menopausal women were prone to forms of hysteria which transformed the most respectable into 'kleptomaniacs' (O'Brien 1983–84). Shopping was an addictive drug. One sweated in anticipation at the 'fix'. The resultant pleasure proved ephemeral, but the subsequent sense of emptiness led to a compulsion to make yet further purchases . . .

Consumerism was a Pandora's box unleashing uncontrollable forces which might ravage the bourgeois household. A wife who intended to make responsible household purchases was soon won over to 'coquetry', then devoured by it (Zola 1992). Some accepted that women's obsession with shopping was a logical consequence of exclusion from education, careers and politics. The piano – ubiquitous in middle-class and even petty-bourgeois homes – became, Taine suggested, an 'opium' allowing wives to accept the 'nullity of the female condition' by whiling away the hours when husbands were absent. The neglected wife in Paul Bourget's *Un Homme d'Affaires* takes a lover and shops compulsively. Zola's Madame de Boves shoplifts because her husband controls the rest of her life. The novel's striking image of headless shop-window dummies (mannequins) with price tags hints at the commodification of the female. Was not the elegantly attired wife endlessly purchasing goods herself in danger of becoming a commodity? In Giffard's *Les Grand Bazaars* (1882) the female shopper becomes the focus of a range of deep-seated cultural anxieties. She is frivolous and spendthrift. Her egoism leads her to neglect family duties. Vain, narcissistic and coquettish, she is ripe for sexual adventures. Her irrationality and lack of self-control evidently make her unfit for responsible citizenship.

Such concerns fed a wider critique of consumerism. Elitists equated it with vulgarity, materialism and mass mediocrity. This critique, echoing denunciations of philistine *parvenus* long fashionable in aristocratic and intellectual circles, was directed at those middling strata who were the backbone of the bourgeois Republic – a lower-middle-class deficient in aesthetic discernment who cluttered their homes with banal bric-à-brac, pillaged the past to plagiarise historic furniture styles. Their concern with 'art' was driven by a mixture of snobbery and crude material calculation that paintings might prove a 'good investment'. Their lack of taste threatened France's aesthetic patrimony. Quality design and production were doomed in a world dominated by pastiche and *faux-luxe* promoted by parasitic advertising agencies. All this foretold an 'Americanised' future of mass mediocrity – a homogenised culture in which the 'same kind of comfort and food, dwellings and clothing bid to win their way through the whole of America and Europe to the rest of the world'. The hero of Huysmans's *À Rebours* retreats into a private world of aesthetic refinement, turning his house into a shrine dedicated to exquisite artifacts.

Republicans were sensitive to such critiques, for they had their own doubts about consumerism. Echoing Rousseau's distaste for 'luxury', many admired austerity, hard work, solidarity, civic *virtu* – 'manly' virtues threatened by consumerist self-indulgence. Some Republicans voiced a 'Jacobin' mistrust of unrestrained economic individualism. The female shopper – extravagent, selfish, frivolous, out-of-control – exhibited 'irrational' behaviour which disqualified her for Republican citizenship because it evoked memories of the (female) moral 'corruption' which had accompanied the authoritarianism of the ancien régime or the Second Empire. Like Right-wing aesthetes, Republicans deplored the impact of crude commercial values on France's position as arbiter of global taste. The 1889 *Exposition* jury denounced the 'bombastic' and 'overdecorative' styles of department store products. A *Fédération des Industries de la Mode* was formed to halt France's descent into the 'age of the fake' under the 'shoddy-goods empire' of the big stores. Craft skills were, allegedly, being eroded as market pressures forced artisans to become 'ingenious copyists' of past styles. Crude mass-marketing lithographs were replacing the artistic wall-posters which French advertisers had once produced. On the horizon loomed a world dominated by mass production and 'American' taste, where French quality industries would have little place.

Others insisted that it was possible to square the circle – that the commercial marketplace could be reconciled with family values and with France's aesthetic patrimony and quality production. Most Republicans perceived a flourishing market economy as vital for France's international position and internal social peace and accepted free-market economists' claims that department stores had widened consumer choice, reduced prices and made central Paris a thriving centre of leisure and consumption and a tourist attraction. A *Bon Marché* pamphlet claimed that since the advent of the stores, general well-being had increased. All branches of national activity benefited from lower retail prices. The alleged participation of all social groups in consumer culture was adduced to buttress claims that workers were being integrated into the national community (Tiersten 2001). Satisfaction of consumer demand was capitalism's historic mission. Republicans sponsored posters such as Steinlein's *La Rue*, portraying a democratic public sphere in which workers and bourgeois, old and young – and a nursemaid with a small child – happily mingle. By forging consensual values, the department store became a commercial equivalent of the Republican school. Workers' contentment was symbolised by images of the housewife using her newly affordable sewing-machine to transform department store dress-patterns into passable approximations of high fashion. A poster portraying bourgeois, workers and children alike fascinated by Peugeot's success in the Paris–Nantes cycle-race emphasised that workers could not only aspire to purchase former 'luxuries' like bicycles but had the leisure to follow commercialised sport (Levin 1993). In 1895, *La Mode pour Tous* claimed that 'in the simple dwelling of the clerk, in the opulent residence of the financier – from top to bottom of the social scale – a sort of elegant and tasteful homogeneity reigns, embodying the general sensibility of our era'. Now that everyone could participate in the great spectacle of the department store, that noble social dream 'beauty for everyone' could be realised.

A new discursive structure was required to reconcile the values of Republican citizenship and the qualities of France's aesthetic heritage with consumerist culture. The project of 'civilising' the marketplace was undertaken by fashion and etiquette journals, 'taste professionals' and Republican officials. Their task was to 'reconstruct' the female shopper as incarnation of family values rather than as home-wrecker. Fashion journalists sought to dispel anxieties about frivolity, extravagence and hedonism by presenting Parisiennes as disciplined, skilful, rational consumers. In his notes for *Au Bonheur des Dames*, Zola characterised Mde Bourdelais as a model family shopper who 'always shopped at the department store, but *shrewdly, without getting carried away*. Takes advantage of sales. Very prudent. Takes charge of her husband for his own good'. The Parisienne, *La Mode Pratique* claimed, 'is economical, she keeps household accounts. She shops to make the house comfortable – though she still dresses well'. Writers sought to channel shopping's pleasures into acceptable outlets. One could derive satisfaction from shopping *en famille* for gifts for loved ones, toys for children. Adverts portrayed parcel-laden married couples emerging together smiling from a store. The responsible housewife need not be stingy or dowdy – indeed she had a duty to her family to be elegant, to avoid the twin faults of parsimony and prodigality. 'The real woman', insisted the *Courrier de la Mode*, knew how to 'run the Great Ministry which we call the *foyer domestique* for the good of everyone, how . . . to play her complex role – as wife, mother and *femme du monde.*' True Parisiennes, of whatever class, had the expertise to combine budgeting with elegance. A woman was permitted to swoon over sensuous lace and velvet – but a 1907 advert avoids overtones of narcissism and eroticism by placing her daughter next to her as she does so! Department stores projected themselves as family institutions: 'I feel so pleasantly *at home* in the Bon Marché', proclaims a wife in one advert. 'The atmosphere is one of honesty, order that comfort without eccentricity which is the charm of the French *foyer*. It is one big family and I am part of it.' Stores provided reading rooms and play areas. Fashion magazines now featured gardening tips, simple recipes and needlework patterns.

Stores also mounted art exhibitions. Presenting shopping as an artistic activity, and commodities as works of art, represented a second discursive strategy. To refute elitist contempt for philistine consumers, claims were advanced that the Parisienne's identity was built around her taste, indeed around her success in constructing herself as a work of art. Fashion magazines contrasted the Parisienne's chic with cruder tastes of provincials and foreigners, though railways, mail-order catalogues and branches of department stores in provincial towns were disseminating taste to the regions. Parisiennes were 'artists in their own way', concerned 'to create new and original combinations of their *toilettes* and homes'. As shopper or domestic interior designer the woman exhibited creativity, often by imaginative juxtaposition of items of clothing or furniture. The worlds of department store and art intertwined. One advert portrayed two chic ladies complimenting each other on their tasteful costumes, and recalling a previous encounter at an art exhibition. Impressionism, with its focus on the 'painting of everyday life' and its rhetoric of 'originality', was readily assimilated by fashion magazines and advertising catalogues. Modernism and consumerism shared a view of urban life as something experienced in a series of disconnected surface sensations – a 'chaos' given order by individual consciousness. Magazines like *L'Art de la Mode* systematically elided 'art' and 'fashion'. Shop-window displays or advertising posters were described as if 'decorative arts'. As active participants in this world of 'taste', consumers safeguarded and developed France's 'artistic patrimony'. The civic role assigned to the chic female shopper was that of nurturing quality production. Rather than passively accepting the department store's prescriptions, she interacted creatively with them, guided by writers of fashion and etiquette journals who posed as disinterested aesthetic 'experts' while 'recommending' that readers buy certain products from specific stores!

Hence a model female consumer had been discursively constructed, combining the virtues of the rational, family-orientated, budget-conscious shopper with 'French' – or Parisian – chic and artistic sensibility. This paragon was compatible with Republican civic values and could create a 'civilised' marketplace. A 1904 *Pygmalion* advert for a silk sale thanked the store's customers: 'It is *you Parisiennes* who, through your taste for refined luxury, have combined the useful with the beautiful and performed a true act of patriotism by supporting a national industry which employs thousands of workers.' The Republican vision of a reformed marketplace had distinctive features. It valued personal vision and innovation, not the fixed aesthetic values of classical, aristocratic culture. It sought to combine sales potential and the functional and the practical and with 'traditional' French design. Rejecting Second Empire 'opulence', it aspired to a 'democratic' simplicity. And it envisaged a world where the popular classes were drawn into a world of consumption without undermining France's 'artistic' heritage. One advert for the *Bazaar de Hotel de Ville* portrayed a mother wearing a Republican *cocarde* handing gift-tokens to her three sons – a bougeois, a policeman and a worker (Tiersten 2001).

An alternative ethos: consumer co-operation

There *were* potential alternatives to individualistic consumer capitalism. Not all workers had yet been drawn into the world of the department store. By 1912 the consumer co-operative movement – united as the FNCC after a merger between 'socialist' and 'reformist' groups – had 865,000 members and over two million customers. Its roots lay in the 'associationist' culture which underpinned the emerging labour movement of the 1830s. Initial bastions included Paris, Lyon and Lille. Early consumer co-operatives were part of networks of mutual aid societies, job agencies, popular bakeries and producer co-operatives. During the Second Republic activists like Jeanne Deroin focused on co-operation as a peaceful path to socio/political change, though many co-operative activists were jailed in 1849–51. In the Second Empire co-operatives were sponsored by Bonapartist officials, paternalistic industrialists and moderate Republicans – all seeking to encourage workers' self-help. Although some dismissed consumer co-operation as a retreat from the dream of producer co-operatives, the socialist strand never disappeared. In Paris in 1869, eleven co-operative restaurants were run by affiliates of the First International. Guesdist Marxists, impressed by the Belgian example, praised consumer co-operatives as a valuable 'third pillar' of the labour movement, complementing party and unions and providing an example of 'socialism in daily life'. The Guesdists' Nord bastion, with 450 co-operatives by 1900, was a key regional stronghold. Workers *quartiers* in Paris such as Levallois-Perret boasted vigorous co-operatives, as did small provincial towns such as the pipe-making centre of St Claude (Jura), where a bust of Jaurès presided over the co-operative's courtyard. Co-operatives lay at the heart of networks of popular sociability which sustained the vibrancy of the combative labour movement of the pre-1914 period. Their premises were used for meetings, plays, strike co-ordination and childcare. Their funds supported mutual aid societies and backed strikers. They purchased raw materials from producer co-operatives of Midi *vignerons* and Albi glassmakers. Many labour leaders were 'trained' in consumer co-operative administration.

However, by 1912 the socialist consumer co-operative BCS was, like the wider labour movement, in difficulties and was forced into a reluctant merger with the rival 'reformist' UC federation. The latter had been founded in Nîmes in the 1880s with backing from Protestant businessmen. Its spokesman, radical-solidarist economics professor Charles Gide, argued for a 'third way' between collectivism and the 'excesses' of laissez-faire capitalism. UC rhetoric echoed socialist denunciation of the ethos of department and chain stores with their vision of a world where selfish, greedy, hedonistic individuals worshipped 'Caesar, Jesus and Felix Potin'. Within capitalism, it was argued, customers were nothing. However, they could and should be everything if only they could organise and impose their priorities. UC membership was more diverse than that of the BCS. Its iconography portrayed blue-collar workers, employees, civil servants and bourgeois hand-in-hand (Furlough 1991).

By 1912 co-operatives were aware that they were under challenge. They lacked efficient managerial cadres and an effective wholesale network. Small retailers' organisations, supported by populist radical Right deputies, were demanding more equitable (i.e. higher) taxation on consumer co-operatives (Nord 1986). Chain stores such as Felix Potin had 6400 branches, as against the co-operatives' 3966, more professional managers and the backing of large advertising agencies. Their stores were larger and more brightly lit, their range of goods wider. In the years after the merger which created the FCSS, many existing trends were accelerated. The co-operative movement, drawn into supporting the war effort, jettisoned its remaining 'socialist' ideology. It adopted 'professional' management and commercial techniques and ceased to fund strikes. Images of solidarity such as clasped hands were abandoned. Individual 'dividends' and multiple shares were introduced and higher priced items such as furniture introduced. Adverts for washing machines targeted the 'Taylorised' housewife, an 'expert' in 'domestic science'. Although co-operatives retained two million customers in 1930, they had a mere 3500 stores – whereas new 'dime-stores' like Monoprix had 18,500.

One cause of co-operatives' inability to compete with commercial rivals lay in their refusal to grapple with gender tensions within the movement. Co-operative rhetoric claimed that department stores 'seduced' women into extravagant, frivolous purchases. Hence their strategy should have been to recruit working-class women as the cornerstone of the movement. Yet French co-operatives failed to develop an equivalent of the Women's Cooperative Guild, which placed women's issues on the agenda of the British co-operative movement. The thinking of (male) co-operative activists was tinged with residual misogynistic assumptions. The Consumer Co-operative was presented as an 'extended Proudhonian family' with the male administrator in the role of *bon père de famille*! Although the labour force in the co-operatives' northern bastions was heavily female, cooperative rhetoric assumed that the male was the producer, woman the consumer. Gide praised co-operatives as a 'primary school for the proper (sexual) division of labour', with man the 'tool', woman the 'basket'. Some male co-operators saw women as too frivolous and spendthrift to be trusted with administrative roles. The resulting tensions were captured in an outburst by Clotilde Wegmann at a meeting of the Levallois-Perret co-op: 'You *say* that the progressive march of the co-operative depends on women – yet when we go to the general assembly meetings, a place garnished with insignia symbolising fraternity and mutuality, you say politely that we cannot enter . . . You call this "good administration" – but then the housewife, who alone is responsible for purchasing, is not allowed to give an opinion.' She urged them to allow full female participation. If that occurred, she promised, 'we will not desert the co-operative for the private store'. Co-operatives' efforts to resist the rise of commercial consumerism were not allied to any wider project of gender emancipation. Their depiction of women as 'irrational' consumers echoed that of the wider culture which they purported to challenge. And yet for all their flaws, and despite being obliged to borrow practices from their chain-store rivals, the vitality of the co-operatives in the 1880–1910 period did parallel that of the wider labour movement. Their role in the 'socialism of daily life' suggests that, as yet, consumerism had but a limited hold on workers' culture, that 'forces of consumption (still remained) contested terrain, a forum where political and social contests were fought out' (Furlough 1996).

Bibliography

Aron, J.-P. *The Art of Eating in France: Manners and Menus in the 19th-Century* (London: Owen, 1975).

Auslander, L. *Taste and Power: Furnishing Modern France* (Berkeley, CA: University of California Press, 1996).

Balzac, H. de *Le Père Goriot* (New York: Norton, 1998).

Bowlby, R. *Just Looking: Consumer Culture in Dreiser, Gissing and Zola* (New York: Methuen, 1985).

Clark, T. *The Painting of Modern Life: Paris in the Art of Manet and his Followers* (New York: A. A. Kopf, 1985).

Coffin, J. 'Credit, consumption and images of women's desire: selling the sewing machine in late-nineteenth-century France', *French Historical Studies* 1994.

Constant, E. 'Votre Argent m' Intéresse!: L'Argent dans les Romans de Paul de Koch,' *Romantisme* 1986.

Corbin, A. (ed.) *L'Avènement des Loisirs: 1850–1960* (Paris: Aubier, 1995).

Crane, D. *Fashion and its Social Agendas: Class, Gender, and Identity in Clothing* (Chicago: University of Chicago Press, 2000).

Cross, G. 'Time, money and labor history: encounters with consumer culture', *International Labor and Working-Class History* 1993.

Crossick, G. and Jaumin, S. *Cathedrals of Consumption: the European Department Store 1850–1939* (Aldershot: Ashgate Publishing, 1999).

Dauphin, C. and Pézerat, P. 'Les consommations populares dans la seconde moitié du XIXe Siècle à travers les Monographes de l'Ecole de le Play', *Annales ESC* 1975.

Davis, S. 'Fine clothes to the altar: the commodification of late-nineteenth-century France', *Art Journal* 1989.

Fairchilds, C. 'Consumption in early modern Europe: a review article', *Comparative Studies in Society and History* 1993.

Fine, B. and Leopold, E. 'Consumerism and the Industrial Revolution', *Social History* 1990.

Furlough, E. *Consumer Co-operatives in France: the Politics of Consumption 1814–1930* (Ithaca: Cornell University Press, 1991).

Gaillard, J. *Paris la Ville 1852–70* (Paris: H. Champion, 1977).

Gilloch, G. 'The heroic pedestrian or the pedestrian hero? Walter Benjamin and the *Flâneur'*, *Telos* 1992.

Goubert, J.-P. *The Conquest of Water* (Oxford: Blackwell, 1989).

Grazia, V. de and Furlough, E. (eds) *The Sex of Things: Gender and Consumption in Historical Perspective* (Berheley, CA: University of California Press, 1996).

Green, N. 'Art and industry: the language of modernisation in the production of fashion', *French Historical Studies* 1994.

Hobsbawm, E. *The Age of Empire: 1875–1914* (London: Weidenfeld and Nicolson, 1987).

Holt, R. 'Social history and bourgeois culture in 19th-century France', *Comparative Studies in Society and History* 1985.

Jones, C. and Spang, R. *Sans culottes, sans café, sans tabac*: shifting realities of necessity and luxury in 18th-century France', in M. Berg (ed.) *Consumers and Luxury* (Manchester: Manchester University Press, 1999).

Levin, M. 'Democratic vistas, democratic media: defining a role for public images in industrialising France', *French Historical Studies* 1993.

Magraw, R. 'Producing, retailing, consuming: France 1830–70', in B. Rigby (ed.) *French Literature Thought and Culture in the Nineteenth Century* (London: Macmillan, 1993).

Miller, M. *The Bon Marché: Bourgeois Culture and the Department Store* (London: Allen & Unwin, 1981).

O'Brien, P. 'The kleptomania diagnosis: bourgeois women and theft in late-19th-century France', *Journal of Social History* 1983–84.

Nord, P. *Paris Shopkeepers and the Politics of Resentment* (Princeton, NJ: Princeton University Press, 1986).

Perrot, P. *Fashioning the Bourgeoisie: A History of Clothing in the 19th Century* (Princeton, NJ: Princeton University Press, 1994).

Rancière, J. 'Good Times, or pleasures at the Barrières', in. A. Rifkin and R. Thomas (eds) *Voices of the People* (London: Routledge, 1988).

Roche, D. *La Culture des Apparences: Une Histoire de Vêtements au XVII et XVIII Siècles* (Paris, 1989).

Schivelbusch, W. *Disenchanted Night: the Industrialisation of Light in the 19th-Century* (Leamington Spa: Berg, 1988).

Silverman, D. *Art Nouveau in Fin-de-Siècle France: Politics, Psychology and Style* (Berkeley, CA: University of California Press, 1989).

Smith, B. *Ladies of the Leisure Class* (Princeton, NJ: Princeton University Press, 1981).

Thuillier, G. *Pour une Histoire du Quotidien au XIX Siècle en Nivernais* (Paris: Mouton, 1977).

Tiersten, L. 'Redefining consumer culture: recent literature on consumption and the bourgeoisie in Western Europe', *Radical History Review* 1993.

Tiersten, L. *Marianne in the Marketplace: Envisioning Consumer Society in Fin-de Siècle France* (Berkeley, CA: University of California Press, 2001).

Vanier, H. *La Mode et ses Métiers: Frivolités et Luttes des Classes 1830–90* (Paris: A. Colin, 1960).

Walton, W. 'To Triumph before feminine Taste: bourgeois women's consumption and hand methods of production in mid-19th-century Paris', *Business History. Review* 1986.

Walton, W. *France at the Crystal Palace: Bourgeois Taste and Artisan Manufacture in the 19th Century* (Berkeley, CA: University of California Press, 1992).

Walton, W. 'Life is nothing without furniture': consumer practices of the Parisian bourgeoisie 1814–70', *Proceedings of the Western Society for French History* 1990.

Williams, R. *Dream Worlds: Mass Consumption in Late-19th-Century France* (Berkeley, CA: University of California Press, 1982).

Zola, E. *The Ladies Paradise* (English trans.) (Berkeley, CA: University of California Press, 1992).

Chapter 9

Gender

Writing the history of (French) women

Three decades ago Michelle Perrot launched the first women's history course in a French university with tentative questions. *Do* women *have* a history? *Can* it be written? Her project grew out of the 'new social history', and initial research, building on that of sociologist Madeleine Guilbert, was on women workers in the labour movement. Soon the focus broadened to cover women's work and the family, feminism and girls' education. To uncover experiences of those hitherto 'hidden from history' new sources were explored – diaries, letters, women's novels, etiquette books and oral interviews. Despite real achievements, 'women's history' soon faced a crisis. It had constructed a 'necessary but depressing saga of women's oppression', of women deceived, violated, abandoned, locked up, dying in childbirth. A comprehensive 'inventory of women's miseries' portrayed them as victimised by the Code Napoléon, denied educational and career opportunities. To offset this bleak picture of 'woman as victim', feminist historians presented women as 'agents' making their own history through acts of everyday resistance and self-assertion – with real 'powers', albeit within a society where men held 'power'. Such a relatively optimistic reading of women's past, however inspirational, risked replicating, in the rhetoric of new feminism, an old conservative trope – that (French) women neither *needed* nor *desired* political rights or legal equality because they were already wielding 'petticoat power'.

There was a more fundamental problem. Without *theoretical* underpinnings, empiricist women's history risked marginalisation within the discipline. Exploring experiences of long-dead women might be fascinating. Meanwhile, 'real' history – of wars, revolutions, economic change – proceeded much as before. Hence the transition to 'gender history'. Joan Scott, like Perrot, moved initially from labour history to women's history, co-authoring a study of women's work. 'Sex', she now argued, was a biological 'given'. But 'gender' – characteristics attributed to a sex in a society at a specific time – was *socially constructed*. 'Gender history' made *men* visible by showing how masculinity was constructed and how *its* attributes varied. 'Gender' should be a key category of social analysis – on a par with 'class' or 'race'. Social formations were themselves gendered. The emerging working-class was constructed around the figure of the male artisan. Labour iconography portrayed 'the worker' as tough miner or steelworker. Study of gender relations would, henceforth, be central to analysis of power structures. Gender could be used to reinterpret major 'events', for both the French Revolution and First World War emerged in a new light if interpreted as 'gender crises' (Scott 1986; Perrot 1998).

Gender history borrowed from a post-modernism increasingly in vogue in Anglo/American universities. Emphasising language and discourse, it saw identities as constructed through systems of binary opposites by, for example, juxtaposition of 'rational' male with 'irrational' female. It welcomed post-modernism's fascination with 'marginals'. Marxism privileged a narrative of the 'forward march of labour'. Now emphasis was on localised, everyday struggles of gays, prisoners and, by analogy, women. It accepted Nietzschean epistemological claims that one could never acquire real 'knowledge' about past 'social realities' or experiences. At most one could analyse discourses about and representations of women. Corbin enquired whether there 'can be envisaged any *any other history than* that founded resolutely on the history of *representations?*'. American feminists now wrote as if 'woman' was a construct of discourses of doctors, psychiatrists, demographers. Discursive representations of women's subordination were presented as if these constituted the organising realities of women's lives, as if the working-class family was produced by complementary discourses about 'male' wage labour and the housewife's home-making qualities. The world became text. Language, not material determinants, constructed realities.

Yet as American gender historians flaunted their mastery of theories of French post-modernists Foucault and Derrida, French women historians proved reluctant to abandon women's history. Some professed to find 'French' theory unrecognisable or incomprehensible. Americans worked within a system which allowed women's studies to emerge as an interdisciplinary project. Feminist historians could interact with other disciplines. French universities were less flexible. 'Traditional' disciplines remained dominant, boundaries between them defined and tightly patrolled. History remained a 'male' discipline – long linked to (Republican) nation-building. It proved difficult to establish a niche for women's history or build institutional ties with feminists in other disciplines. Some who assimilated elements of Scott's approach were wary of going too far down that path – arguing that gender cannot be translated into French or that abstruse post-modernist theory might confuse and alienate the potentially large audience interested in women's past. American 'political correctness' and multiculturalism was mistrusted. In a Europe where labour movements were still not (entirely) defunct, perhaps class remained as important as gender. 'Gender history' risked denying the possibility of retrieving women's past experiences, the 'social realities' of their lives and their capacity for meaningful 'agency'. By emphasising representations one portrayed 'woman' as constructed by and trapped within dominant (male) discourses, and wrote history which endlessly recycled these. By accepting post-modernism's 'incredulity towards metanarratives' one ruled out any emancipatory narrative to underpin women's history. Many agreed with

Scott's former colleague, Louise Tilly, that one should continue to use archival research to 'get at' the 'realities' of women's lives (Thébaud 1998).

There were resentments at Americans' misunderstanding of French culture. French women historians belonged to a university system with historic ties to the Republican tradition. They accepted that despite its faults the culture of the (French) Enlightenment and the Revolution (implicitly) promised universal emancipation, whether for black slaves, oppressed classes, subject peoples or women. This culture was suspicious of 'cultural particularisms', whether of Breton Catholic peasants or Romantic Germans proclaiming the virtues of the *Volk*. *If* human emancipation needs universalist values, then (American) feminism's flirtation with the cultural – and moral – relativism of multiculturalism and neo-Nietzschean post-modernism is highly suspect. Their prickly defensiveness was provoked by allegations that French women's movements were 'backward' for failing to secure women's franchise until 1945. American feminists blamed this 'retardation' on the French Enlightenment and the Revolution. The values proclaimed by the Declaration of Rights of Man were, allegedly, those of white, bourgeois male citizens. Women were excluded from France's dominant secular intellectual discourse.

Rejecting this thesis, Mona Ozouf accuses American radical feminism – rooted in puritanism and hatred of men – of failing to comprehend the nuances of French gender relations. French women always recognised that they could play upon real differences between the sexes. Being a woman was an *opportunity* as well as a misfortune. One had a hand to play. Relations between the sexes in France have been less conflictual than in puritanical Protestant or in macho Mediterranean cultures. Rousseau is routinely denounced by American feminists for claiming that women were caring and emotional – hence suited for domesticity. Yet Frenchwomen, including George Sand, warmed to Rousseau for his sensibility and understanding of women, using his *Confessions* as a model for their autobiographical writings. France's gender relations, like her economy, were not 'backward' but different because she synthesised aspects of ancien régime elite culture, in which women framed civilised, polite values, with Enlightenment emphasis on individual rights which underpinned claims for women's emancipation. Ozouf's depiction of French gender relations is doubtless too idyllic. Frenchmen manipulated 'gallantry' as a strategy of domination which kept woman a slave by pretending to place her on a throne. Ozouf relies on clichés of man-hating, politically correct American radical feminists and 'feminine' Frenchwomen. Not all American feminists reject the French Enlightenment's universalist discourse. Ozouf's approach may be appropriated by complacent traditionalists claiming that feminism was never really 'needed' in France. It contains 'contradictions'. She portrays women as carriers of tradition and family, their lives constructed – and constrained – by the cycle of puberty, menstruation, motherhood and menopause. Hence lived experiences meant that even when they demanded 'rights' as equal, rational individuals, they remained aware of biological 'differences'. Yet this claim that *biology* establishes the framework for women's lives and explains their need to balance 'progress' with tradition fits uneasily with insistence on *national cultural* differences (Ozouf 1997).

An ambivalent legacy: women, Enlightenment, French Revolution

Whereas Liberals once assumed that the Enlightenment and Revolution had been beneficial to women's interests and rights, if only because the Ancien Régime was so patriarchal, many feminists now argue that the Enlightenment 'project' was constructed not merely *without* but essentially *against* women, that the outcome of its discourses and practices was a strengthening of male domination. The barest schematic outline can be offered of this debate. Women, it is claimed, had a significant place in the Ancien Régime's emerging 'public sphere'. Intellectual debates were conducted in *salons* where hostesses set the agenda. Their talent for compromise kept discussions civilised by curbing male aggression. Female writers explored women's issues, and painters like Elizabeth Vigée-Lebrun were given recognition. Elite ladies were free to take lovers – and falling birth rates suggested the spread of birth-control practices. Sadly the later Enlightenment marginalised female influence. By prioritising 'reason' and labelling women 'more delicate and spiritual than cerebral' (Diderot), the *philosophes* denied women's capacity for active citizenship. Rousseau's Emile is educated for public life, Sophie trained in submissiveness and household tasks. In *La Nouvelle Héloïse*, Julie accepts her father's choice of husband and dies rescuing a drowning child – a martyr to motherhood and the *foyer*. Rousseau juxtaposed the intellectual and sexual liberties of decadent *salonnières* with provincial housewives' simple virtues. Medical science confirmed *philosophes'* dismissive assessment of woman's capacities. Her 'otherness' was portrayed as biological inferiority, her identity dictated by her reproductive organs. 'Terrible spasms' of the uterus governed uncontrollable mood swings. Woman's place was under male protection in the home, where her qualities of caring, sensitivity and compassion came into their own (McMillan 2000).

The Revolution allegedly consolidated these assumptions into a political discourse which fixed women's exclusion from public life for generations. Initially it appeared to offer women scope for participation. They were active in insurrectionary *journées*, food protests and clubs. Olympe de Gouges demanded the 'rights of women'. Yet revolutionary iconography testifies to their marginalisation. Depicted at first as actors in revolutionary crowds, they became confined to anodyne roles as allegories of the Republic in official festivals – or victims seeking male protection. Jacobin discourse invoked Rousseau to label women 'Republican mothers' not citizens. Ancien régime corruption was exemplified by female *salonnières* and the sexually voracious Marie-Antoinette's manipulation of her 'impotent' husband. A Republic required 'virile' citizens – stoic, virtuous, liberated from the sway of 'effeminate' aristocrats. Jacobin repression of women's clubs in 1793 occurred not because of their support for the ultra-radical *enragés*, but to safeguard a gendered social order. Women in politics were 'viragos' who had abandoned their sex's 'natural' functions. Republicanism, the 'progressive' ideology of modern France and carrier of the Enlightenment's emancipatory promise, stands accused of fundamental misogyny, of defining women as intellectually and biologically inferior. Lacking the capacity for 'reason' required of citizens, they could not share the 'Rights of Man'.

Lynn Hunt has portrayed the Revolution as a 'family romance' in which these gender paradigms were played out. She charts the erosion of the authority of the 'patriarchal' King through literary depictions of ineffectual fathers. Attempts by 'moderates' to reinvent Louis XVI as a 'good father' proved futile. The Queen's 'petticoat power' and infidelities had undermined his reputation. The regicide of 1792 was an act of parricide. Revolutionary culture was dominated by a 'band of brothers' seeking a 'fraternal' Republic. Yet this proved a fine (family) romance with no sisters. The 'brothers', alarmed that the collapse of paternal authority created a void which female power might fill, excluded women from the public sphere. Contemporaries made sense of social upheavals through such familial metaphors, which provide a key to the Revolution's collective unconscious. Meanwhile the Marquis de Sade was questioning certainties about God, Nature and the Family – 'freeing' women from sexual shame and inhibitions only to make them objects of, and participants in, his own sexual fantasies. 'Order' was restored, and the family put back together, only when the Napoleonic Code underpinned the return of the 'good father'. The Revolution is, thus, presented as a 'gender crisis'. Yet questions about the evidential base and methodology of such 'new cultural history' suggest themselves. Was the 'family romance' experienced or perceived by peasants in the same way as by Parisian bourgeois? Were characters conscious of playing roles in this 'romance'? Did people have free will, or were they propelled by forces deep in their (collective) unconscious? (Hunt 1992).

An alternative narrative is possible. Feminists who denounce Enlightenment and Revolution fail to 'distinguish between . . . friends and . . . enemies', writes one woman historian. Neither timing nor language of des Gouges's demand for 'rights of women' were accidental. The Revolution utilised a discourse on rights deriving from the Enlightenment. Counter-Reformation theology, building on centuries of Christian misogyny, portrayed pregnancy as woman's 'punishment' for Eve's sins and eulogised the submissive wife who avoided sensual pleasures. Ancien régime patriarchal discourse automatically subordinated women, that of the Revolution had to be distorted to do so. Radical feminist Madeleine Pelletier later identified herself as a Jacobin egalitarian, despite Jacobins' unfortunate comments about women! Alleged contrasts between 'female' *salons* and the supposedly all-male sociability of Masonic lodges which supplanted them as the locus of enlightened debate are spurious. Some lodges admitted women and permitted them to officiate. Discussion of women's rights and education secured a sympathetic hearing. The catechism of the *Rites Ecossaises* supported equality within marriage. Women members were scarcely dupes of 'masculine reason'. Towns such as Dijon with female lodges developed women's clubs in the 1790s (Burke and Jacob 1996). The Revolution raised women's aspirations vis-à-vis marriage and the family and attempted to deliver reforms. It promoted secular marriage based on mutual consent and introduced divorce on the grounds of incompatibility and mutual consent as well as cruelty in 1792. Soon there were 3000 divorces per year among urban middling classes and artisans – two-thirds instigated by women, often against violent husbands. The law was abolished in 1816 by Catholic-Royalists intent on reconstructing the Christian family as a bulwark against anarchy. The Revolution abolished primogeniture and permitted daughters to inherit. Many women demanded rapid implementation of this 'law of equality which has converted to the Republic many women led astray by the fanaticism of priests'. Women petitioned for reforms to create an egalitarian family. A *Tribune de la Famille*, established to mediate disputes, proclaimed previous laws 'barbarous'; 80 per cent of court decisions in the Midi and Normandy, where hitherto women enjoyed few inheritance rights, favoured sisters over brothers. Women utilised the language of 'rights' and equality – appropriating revolutionary discourses to question paternal and fraternal 'despotism'. 'If we finally accept that the strong no longer impose laws on the weak in the great family of the State, why should we remain enslaved by barbarous customs which allow a father to sacrifice his daughters?'. Some foresaw a 'democratic' family, calling the Republic their 'true' father if real fathers failed them (Desan 1997).

Domesticity and its discontents

Divorce is veritable domestic democracy. In order to keep the State out of the hands of the people it is necessary to keep the family out of the hands of wives and children.
(De Bonald)

We may live in a democracy. But this house is a kingdom, and I am the King.
(Pierre Marot)

Domesticity ideology pervaded nineteenth-century society. The ideal of *la femme au foyer* appealed across barriers of class, politics and religion. Originating in the eighteenth-century bourgeoisie, it was later espoused by Catholic-Royalist aristocrats who saw the 'angel of the hearth as the key to the moral reconstruction of post-Revolution society'. If its relevance to the popular classes was less obvious, many male workers eulogised the *ménagère* (housewife) who created a cosy home as refuge from a harsh factory world. Anticlerical Republicans extolled 'Republican motherhood'. Far from being merely a discourse about women's 'natural' role, 'domesticity' was buttressed by the Napoleonic Code. Reflecting the Emperor's personal misogyny and patriarchal instincts, this aimed to rebuild a stable, gendered order after revolutionary chaos. Strands of Enlightenment culture conducive to nurturing affective family bonds were downplayed. Only a man could be a legal 'individual'. Although the Code retained divorce, incompatibilty and mutual consent ceased to be sufficient grounds. Divorces fell by 90 per cent in Rouen in the decade after 1803 before the Restoration abolished divorce entirely. The Code treated a woman as a 'minor', subject to 'paternal' and 'marital' power. Article 213 insisted on her duty of 'obedience'. Her dowry and income belonged to the husband. She required permission to seek a job. The Code sanctioned 'double standards'. A husband could use violence for the 'legitimate ends of marriage' and was granted *carte blanche* to kill an adulterous wife. Since bourgeois marriage was a property transaction, the bride was expected to be 'undamaged'. The groom was assumed to be sexually experienced, hence to have had sexual relations with lower-class women. Article 340 forbade paternity suits, thereby protecting bourgeois males from maintenace claims by 'unscrupulous' women.

Middle-class girls were instructed in religion, languages, sewing, home management and social accomplishments such as dance in boarding schools. After 1840 Josephine Bachellery argued for a training college for secondary teachers and vocational training to equip girls for careers. But the *dames inspectrices* who monitored schools were unenthusiastic. Their reports were obsessed with maintaining 'safe' distance between girls' dormitory beds and worries that dancing was a 'worldly' accomplishment, more suited to the flippant aristocratic past than to the new order. For girls, they insisted, knowledge was a curse unless accompanied by humility and a moral sense. After the Falloux Law nuns took over many of these schools. A lay headmistress was viewed as a dangerous role model for teenage girls. Domestic skills were now promoted at the expense of intellectual subjects and social graces. Nuns' surveillance over girls within the school was seen as necessary because 'girls teach each other things of which they ought to remain ignorant, (which) excite the senses and lead to knowledge of illicit pleasures – the beginning of depravity' (Rogers 1995).

Outlining the tenets of 'domesticity', its place in the Code and the vehicles for its diffusion does not complete the historian's task. Several questions suggest themselves. Were etiquette books and journals extolling the virtues of *la femme au foyer* descriptive or merely prescriptive? Even if many bourgeoises internalised such values, did not some manipulate 'domesticity' to their own advantage? Victorian bourgeois culture was constructed around the activities and values of middle-class women. Did French bourgeoises tolerate domesticity because they could manipulate it to cultivate genuine 'powers'? Or did domestic constraints provoke proto-feminist sentiments? Did the growth of women's writing develop female networks which nurtured strategies of everyday resistance? The 'angel of the hearth' discourse assumed that women were vulnerable, emotional, yet warm and caring. Etiquette books emphasised marriage as essential for a bourgeois girl. A spinster (*vieille fille*) was an object of pity and contempt, though 12 per cent of women never married. The wife should be a lady of leisure. Family financial strategies dictated 'arranged' marriages in which neither a girl's choice nor romantic attraction played much part, though Catholic confessors reassured brides that love would grow. Etiquette books and 'domestic' novels exalted the status of the wife, and clergy now eulogised 'Christian motherhood' even above chastity. The availability of servants and falling birth-rates eased bourgeois wives' material circumstances. Many participated in charitable *oeuvres*, which provided an arena for activities beyond the home. *Sociétés de Charité Maternelle* emerged, run by *grandes dames* who acquired organisational and negotiating skill in their dealings with local authorities and prefects. In Bordeaux, where hundreds of mothers were aided in the 1840s, they portrayed themselves as 'virtuous ladies, chaste wives, tender mothers (who) feel in their hearts an overabundance of maternal love'. Charitable activities transferred maternal solicitude into the public sphere and attempted to transmit 'correct' familial values to poor mothers. Recipients of their aid should be married, and appropriately 'grateful' women, willing to learn breast-feeding, hygiene and home economy and submit to surveillance by home visits. Some doubtless resented such moralising intrusions. Others may have perhaps imbibed a variant of the elite's domesticity values (Smith 1981; Adams 1999).

Many bourgeois did not share their wives' devout Catholicism. This could generate tensions within the household. In his semi-autobiographical *Les Pères de Famille et les Enfants au XIXe Siècle* (1865), E. Legouvé portrayed a husband who permits his Catholic wife to control their son's upbringing – only to find his own values challenged. Here, in microcosm, was an example of a systematic fault-line in the bourgeois family and in liberal culture. Ironically it was precisely the gender roles prescribed by domesticity ideology which produced this disturbing outcome. Any Jacobin attempt to impose secularism within the family, Legouvé conceded, infringed wives' 'rights' and the doctrine of separate spheres. Religion was viewed as 'fine for women and children', 'flowing naturally like mother's milk'. In Lyon homes boys were exposed to private prayers and Marian devotions in the mother's bedroom with the father absent on business. Mothers corresponded with boys during their army or university careers. In Legouvé's text the gulf between father and son widens when the former refuses to say prayers for his sick wife. Fathers assumed that when the son 'became a man' he would 'put away childish things', including religion. But many adolescents were repelled by the macho culture of *lycées, cercles* and barracks, and too distanced from their fathers to use them as a 'bridge' to the secular world of manhood. Autobiographies reveal them yearning for maternal warmth. At the heart of bourgeois domesticity lay complex, gendered generational dialectics. Middle-class Catholic sons rebelled against their fathers because they were products of a home environment created by pious mothers – able to manipulate powers conferred on them within the *foyer* to subvert their husbands' secular culture (Seeley 1998).

Perhaps such bourgeoises were only carving out a small 'space' within overarching male hegemony. Domestic constraints created frustrations and discontent. Painters were expected to use obligatory family portraits to illustrate domestic harmony to set an example to the lower classes. Yet Dégas' portrait of the Bellilli family reveals only family tensions. Against a background of ornate wallpaper and a decorative mantle-piece a miserable-looking wife singularly fails to interact with her husband. She was the artist's aunt, forced to accept a marriage arranged by her parents for financial reasons. The 'happy family' captured by Dégas' *At the Races* is a 'fraud'. The breast-feeding 'mother' is actually a wet-nurse! Dégas painted brothels as warm and intimate, homes as cold and forbidding (Lipton 1986). Novelists interrogated 'contradictions' of the domestic idyll. Was marriage based on fidelity – or blatant sexual double-standards? Was marriage for 'love' – or a form of high-class prostitution where parents 'sold' daughters to the highest bidder? In Zola's *Pot-Bouille* (1884) the facade of domestic respectability is a masquerade. Family life is stultifying. The husband sleeps with the servants, whose quarters are the moral 'sewer' of the house. Women used diaries, letters and autobiographical novels to articulate grievances, carve out a 'discursive space' and, by communicating with other women, construct informal networks. George Sand or Marie d'Agoult 'reinvented' the home as a 'female space', site for a form of 'work' – writing – which accessed wider public discourses. Claiming time and privacy for activities beyond those of wife and mother was implicitly subversive. Caricaturist Daumier portrayed 'blue-stocking' Madame Sand as someone who 'prevents women from darning socks'. Money earned from publications gave such women dangerous freedoms – to leave husbands, raise children on their own, flirt with politics. Women who read their novels or exchanged letters with them were 'respectable' bourgeois wives who found marriage stifling, 'home' a gilded cage and sexual double-standards offensive. Husbands' control of marital property made many feel intruders in their own homes. In d'Agoult's *Nélida* the husband uses his wife's dowry to re-furbish his family château. Sand's *Indiana* portrays wives oppressed by domineering husbands and seeking their own 'space'. Sand's 'utopian' vision was of 'home' as a base for autonomous activity where one could combine childcare with access – via one's writings – to the public sphere. Both authors were attempting a re-articulation of domestic space through literary representations of women's dispossession and repossession (Walton 1997; Allen 2000).

Sand and d'Agoult became notorious for abandoning husbands, carving out independent lifestyles and flirting with Republican politics. Less celebrated bourgeoises articulated similar preoccupations. Marie-Sophie Leroyer spent her life caring for relatives in her Anjou country house. Viewing marriage under the Code as 'monstrous' slavery, she remained single. A devout Catholic, she lived a life of sexual abstinence which left her deeply frustrated. Her correspondence with Sand expressed admiration for her ideas on girls' education and empathy for her problems. She insisted that 'women desire the *impossible* – because the *possible* cannot satisfy them'. Her novel portrays life for provincial middle-class women as 'deadly to the intelligence'. Geneviève Bréton-Vaudoyer was equally scathing about marriage. She endured marriage to a husband with whom she had no rapport and whose sexual liaisons she tolerated with ill-grace. She resented 'arranged' marriages, sexual double-standards, the tedium of domestic life. 'Education' provided for bourgeois girls was vacuous, fitting them for 'imbecilic (intellectual) slumber'. A liberal Catholic and moderate Republican, she disapproved of feminist antics. Yet she might be viewed as a 'feminist' – even if she would have rejected the label – since her autobiographical writings explored female identity and self-knowledge (Allen 2000).

The diary developed into a Romantic celebration of self. Epistolary novels allowed women authors to share their perceptions with other women. Rousseau's distinction between rational male and sensitive female was embraced – to stake claims for women's importance. Such autobiographical writers were 'proto-feminist' in their awareness that their subordination was socially determined not 'natural', that one should show solidarity with other women and that change was possible. In a culture which valued language, they used it to question male power. They fitted no neat pigeonholes. They were too bourgeois to empathise with working-class women, insufficiently Catholic to be 'christian feminists', insufficiently assertive to make public demands. Little concerned with the franchise, their preoccupations were education, career opportunities and the balance of power within marriage. Such concerns may sound anaemic to modern feminists. But they reflect real discontent with and everyday resistance to 'domesticity'.

Female authors of light romantic fiction were tolerated, although the fate of Emma Bovary suggested that a surfeit of such novels, superimposed on a convent education, might arouse romantic fantasies which made mundane realities of provincial marriage hard to accept! Yet even a publication like *Journal des Femmes* raised disconcerting questions. It was politically conformist and covered 'domestic' issues – food, childcare, fashion. Yet editor Fanny Richomme mocked its potential critics – Republicans contemptuous of yet another publication on jam-making, *grandes dames* who viewed the term *'femme'* as populist and ugly! She denied being a feminist 'blue-stocking'. Yet she speculated about the possibility of the *femme auteur* who would write about domestic issues as a 'professional' career journalist. The paper did debate issues such as divorce and mocked women whose only concern was the 'perfection of their scones'. The paper struggled to survive in the con-servative climate of the mid-1830s, eventually devoting itself to hairstyles and fashion. Yet its project hinted at ways in which even conservative women might exploit loopholes in domesticity ideology to challenge gender ortho-doxies (Morgan 1999).

Women, work and the family

Changes in women's work

The pervasiveness of domesticity ideology appears ironic in a society where many women had paid jobs, including many more married women than in Britain or Germany. In Britain 50 per cent of 'active' women were under twenty-five, in France under 33 per cent. By 1910, 38 per cent of the work force was female. Several issues have dominated debates on women's work. How did employment patterns change? Did such changes widen career opportunities and contribute to women's gradual 'emancipation'? How were such changes received by social observers and experienced by women themselves?

In 1800 most 'working' women were in agriculture. Peasant brides were chosen largely on calculation of their potential as farm assistants. Peasant marriages, Segalen (1983) claimed, were based on complementarity of roles. 'Female' tasks included tending kitchen and farmyard, carrying, doing the laundry and taking eggs and poultry to market. Men worked with plough and sickle – though women helped with harvests and gleaning. Pluri-activity was widespread. In Lower Normandy or the Mauges women wove linen, negotiating with merchants while men worked the farm. Wives and daugh-ters prepared looms or did finishing tasks in family workshops. In clothing, gloves and embroidery women made up a majority of the work force (Segalen 1983; Liu 1994a). Possibly, despite its underlying patriarchalism, this pat-tern of life had certain advantages which industrialisation threatened. Since 'work' and 'home' overlapped, one could combine paid activities with family duties. Lorraine women resisted mechanised workshops and struggled to pre-serve a life which combined farming, embroidery in communal *veillées* and village community solidarities. Women were essential to family economic units and effective functioning of farms or artisanal workshops, making decisions to sell a pig or negotiating with cloth merchants. Le Play portrayed families where the wife kept accounts and doled out spending money to her husband. Such women enjoyed little 'privacy', sharing the farm with servants and animals or workshop with apprentices. Their conduct remained subject to community controls, with dominant wives targets of *charivaris*. But they enjoyed some collective power. The gossip and slander of women gathered in the *veillée* or the washing place was a force in local life.

The significant changes were the advent of factory work, particularly in textiles, then after 1860 the growth of tertiary-sector employment. Women comprised over 80 per cent of one million servants by 1900, and 'sweated' domestic employment, particularly in clothing, also grew. Yet continuities of employment patterns were just as striking; 3.24 million women were still involved in agriculture in 1911. Though use of heavy scythes reduced women's field work, many still picked vegetables and gangs of women sprayed chemicals in Lower Languedoc 'industrial' vineyards (Tilly and Scott 1978). Some claim that expansion of paid female labour signalled a step in women's economic, hence social emancipation, since it allowed wives and daughters unprecedented financial independence thereby altering the balance of power within households. Yet female earnings were viewed as part of a family wage pool rather than for individual use. In Armentières linen mills, women prepared looms for husbands and fathers who received a family wage packet. Girls in Lyonnais spinning mills had workplaces and dormitories controlled by nuns, and their wages were sent direct to their peasant fathers! In the Mauges the collapse of (female) hand-spinning produced a 'retreat' to agriculture. Men did reaping and operated threshing-machines. Women were consigned to (unpaid) drudgery weeding and picking fodder crops for livestock – a sexual division of labour imposed by heads of households. Farm tenancies went to a single male heir. Although 'family solidarities' were eulogised, there were tensions over inheritance and male domination. Men sang of the lost freedom of their adolescence. Women claimed the moral highground because their self-denial kept the family unit viable. Such claims were a form of self-assertion. In a culture imbued with 'magic' practices, brutal – or ineffectual – husbands might fall victim to 'female' spells and bewitchment. Given such gender frictions, notions of 'family interests' remain problematic – even if, to bolster their own self-esteem and prestige, women claimed to embody these (Liu 1994a). There were always some women outside the family. Cities had 'spinster clusterings', groups of women, often widowed or separated, who pooled resources to rent lodgings and support each other. But a 'woman alone' had a precarious existence. Few women could earn enough for real financial independence. Petty crime, or resort to casual, unregistered prostitution, was often the only path to survival (Fuchs 1992).

By 1866, 30 per cent of industrial workers were women, a figure approaching 40 per cent by 1914. From the 1820s it was their role in textile mills that attracted attention. Their wages were barely half those of men doing similar jobs, and in the 1880s they still worked twelve-hour shifts in hot, humid conditions conducive to bronchial diseases. Fewer women worked in metallurgy or mining, though girls did pit-head coal-sorting while their mothers did laundry or took-in lodgers. Women steadily infiltrated printing and hatting jobs. In the tertiary sector female workers quadrupled between 1866 and 1914. Although supervisory posts were dominated by men, women were employed as typists and commercial clerks by banks and the Post Office. The laic laws increased jobs for *institutrices* and female secondary teachers. Such posts attracted daughters of modest bourgeois and 'old' petty-bourgeois families and newly literate daughters of declining artisans who acquired vocational skills in *Écoles Primaires Supérieures*. An 1870s survey of Parisian girls found many aspiring to be schoolteachers, though suspecting that they would become seamstresses! The class status of such employees was ambiguous. Department stores presented their 'young ladies' as stylish and well dressed – the antithesis of vulgar mill-girls. 'Realities' of the job were less glamorous. They lodged in crowded dormitories, subject to curfew, worked long hours and suffered in silence the arrogance of bourgeois customers. Bonus payments systems pushed them into ferocious competition against each other (Tilly and Scott 1978).

The debate on women's work
Women's work aroused passionate debate because it was perceived to flout domesticity norms and produce harmful consequences – for the *ouvrière* herself, the family and the nation's health. Although anxieties were voiced by Catholic traditionalists, canonical texts came from Republicans such as Michelet who proclaimed the term *ouvrière* 'impious, sordid' – one which 'no epoch before this could ever have understood'. By working outside the home the *ouvrière* 'ceased to be a woman'. Jules Simon's *L'Ouvrière* (1863) encapsulated the dilemmas of a bourgeois liberal. Some economists argued that factory work was less arduous than tilling the soil and brought resources into workers' homes. As a free-marketeer Simon accepted that France's international competitiveness relied on using its pool of cheap female labour. Yet he was convinced of the moralising potential of stable families and fixed gender roles. Factory women exposed to sexual harassment and lewd language might slide into immoral ways, even prostitution. Girls failed to learn domestic skills from working mothers. Male workers, deprived of home comforts and well-cooked meals, gravitated to the café – the locus of drinking and seditious conversation. Neglected children roamed the streets. Working women, exhausted by factory labour, were unfit for motherhood (Scott 1986).

Realities of family lives are difficult to disentangle from such ideological narratives. Accampo's study of St. Chamond shows the problems created for working mothers by the factory system. Its economy had been based on family ribbon-weaving and nail-making workshops. By mid-century men worked in metallurgical factories, women did twelve-hour shifts in braid-mills. Combining family duties and paid employment became difficult. Marriage age rose, infant mortality soared and family tensions grew. Mothers depended on mill work to balance family budgets, while maintaining contacts with Catholic charities whose hand-outs were needed in periods of unemployment. It appears unlikely that new work patterns 'liberated' working women. The decline of Lyon silk-weaving disrupted family patterns among journeymen who had once married when about to establish their own workshop. Marriage rates fell as the chances of becoming a small master receded, leaving more young women abandoned as single parents (Accampo 1989; Strumhinger 1979). The 'meaning' of workers' changing sexual relations were rarely those attributed to them by moralists. The *St François Régis* society

325

persuaded some workers to 'regularise' their unions, but many lived in settled *concubinage*, often to avoid the legal costs of a marriage ceremony. As Zola's *Germinal* suggests, parents accepted that teenage daughters might live with their lovers. Such relationships, based on mutual attraction or affection rather than family financial strategy, were more robust than critics allowed. Villermé established the pattern for subsequent *enquêtes* into workers' conditions by juxtaposing 'scientific' statistics with moralising assumptions. The central tropes included lamentations on the 'promiscuity' of factories and workers' cramped housing, with all ages and sexes sleeping together on the same filthy mattresses. Simon inherited this discursive tradition. Faced with the dilemma of reconciling (necessary) female wage labour with 'family values', he offered two solutions. The first, surveillance as operated by nuns in Lyonnais convent-workshops, was ironic, for Simon was an anti-clerical! The second was home-work, permitting women to combine wage-earning with familial duties. St. Etienne ribbon-weaving later attracted praise. Here family workshops were granted a lease of life by electric motors which, by making weaving a less heavy process, allowed replacement of journeymen by masters' daughters, nieces or spinster cousins. Whereas women's factory work signified disorder, the *Guide de St. Etienne* proudly displayed photos of women seated at looms – a reassuring cultural symbol of settled, home-based female employment (Scott 1986; Dubesset and Zancarini-Fournel 1993).

Between 1860 and 1914, clothing workers swelled from 594,000 to 1,380,000; 89 per cent were women, many in the *confection* sector. The spread of the sewing machine, which supplanted the needle as the symbol of working women, facilitated home-work. It was 'sold' to women as a functional tool for one's job, a consumer item affordable through new credit facilities and implausibly as a symbol of personal liberation. Erotic advertising posters portrayed a young woman astride a sewing-machine flying above the Eiffel Tower! Doctors debated whether friction between the legs caused by pedalling caused sexual stimulation! Undeterred by such concerns, Simon agreed with Social-Catholics that the sewing-machine was invaluable for allowing women to combine employment and childcare. Home-workers' stoicism attracted praise: 'They don't strike, they don't make demands. They die of TB and that's that', noted one episcopal admirer. It found supporters on the left. 'If a woman must work', said printers' leader Keufer, 'let her seek an occupation which does not remove her from the home' (Coffin 1996). Yet across the industrial world female 'sweating' was becoming synonymous with capitalist exploitation. In 1910, when male skilled workers earned 8 francs per day, 50 per cent of Parisian female home-workers received under 2 francs. Union activist Jeanne Bouvier recalls fellow seamstresses existing on bread and milk – and sometimes committing suicide. Wages appeared permanently depressed irrespective of their skills or demand fluctuations. Seamstresses paid for their own heating, light, threads and needles. Frantic seasonal rushes involving all-night sessions (*veillées*) alternated with dead seasons. A 1913 survey found 40 per cent of seamstresses unemployed for over three months. The influx of Jewish immigrants into an overcrowded labour market intensified competition and prompted populist xenophobes to champion Catholic *ouvrières* against foreign workers and 'Jewish' capitalism. Home-workers were the labour movement's 'neglected sisters', viewed as atomised, docile, impossible to organise. Factory legislation led employers to switch production into this unregulated sector. Since women worked and slept in the same rooms, dwellings were dirty and dusty. Far from permitting an idyllic reconciliation of work and family, the system violated family space. 'Sweating' provoked impassioned debate. Social Catholics, who applauded the principle of home-work, sought to protect women from exploitative middlemen and from seduction by the labour movement. A Catholic consumers' organisation, *Ligue Social des Acheteurs*, urged shoppers to boycott stores selling 'sweated' goods. If consumption was part of the 'female' sphere, then women should organise action within it. There were campaigns for crèche provision. Despite residual fears about 'creeping socialism', Social Catholic de Mun demanded minimum wage legislation for home-workers, although a Bill introduced in 1909 did not become law until 1915 (Boxer 1986; Coffin 1996).

Office du Travail surveys juxtaposed statistics on low wages, poor diets and irregular work patterns with voyeuristic depictions of suffering bodies of exploited *ouvrières* and processes by which they slipped into part-time prostitution. Doctors warned of the dangers of TB in dusty homes. Union organiser Stéphanie Bouvard denounced stultifying, isolating home-work for depressing wages: 'If the women *must* work, let her do so in workshop or factory.' The future lay with a separation between clean factories and tidy homes. Debates on 'sweated' female labour encapsulated a range of fin de siècle anxieties. International competition and prolonged depression raised questions about the continued viability of the French economic model, the decline of craft skills and erosion of France's reputation for quality goods.

Women's work, maternity and the origins of the Welfare State

Women's work and maternity are issues now viewed as central to the emergence of a French Welfare State once portrayed as 'backward' in comparison to German or British counterparts. Its genesis used to be linked to perceptions of the 'threat' from labour and the need to 'integrate' (male) workers. Feminists question whether this was policy-makers' major concern. Reforms were introduced, largely ignored by labour historians, whose focus was on working mothers and infants. These grew out of anxieties about links between female employment, demographic stagnation and France's 'moral crisis'. French welfare debates became uniquely obsessed with 'depopulation' and 'Republican' motherhood. In the 1870s wet-nursing was regulated and female pit-work and girls' night-work banned. The Paris Municipal Council pioneered programmes to support mothers and infants. Since women and children always comprise a high percentage of welfare clients, France does not, after all, appear a 'laggard'. Much recent research has probed the genesis of the 1892 Act which banned female night-work and limited the hours of adult women factory workers (Stewart 1989).

Malthusian French bureaucrats, long critical of 'feckless' workers who bred like rabbits, welcomed early indications of falling birth-rates. However, defeat in 1870 nurtured anxieties about France's ability to compete with international rivals and altered perspectives. A birth-rate of 33 per 1000 in 1801 fell to 6‰ by 1870 and 19‰ by 1911 – when it was 28‰ in Germany. Infant mortality declined only slowly, from 195‰ to 179‰ between 1800 and 1880, and remained higher than in other advanced countries. 'Depopulation' emerged as the 'master pathology' in diagnoses of national decline, raising the status of 'experts' who could identify and offer 'cures' for the 'problem'. Demography had emerged in the eighteenth century, its function to interpret statistics which the state was now compiling, to indicate 'normal' and 'pathological' levels of births and deaths and to offer policy advice. Demographers invented the 'fertility index' which calculated births to women of 'childbearing age'. For all their 'scientific' pretensions, they were far from 'neutral'. Many joined Bertillon's conservative, 'natalist' *Alliance Nationale pour l'Accroissement de la Population*. Its founder lamented that 'our wives are the least fertile in Europe'. Women were 'blamed' for the low birth-rate – as if husbands' behaviour and attitudes played no role! E. Piot insisted that 'if French wives had the fertility of German women, we would gain 500,000 children per year'. The discourse surrounding the fertility index assumed a duty to procreate. All women from 15 to 50 could, and thus should, be mothers (Cole 2000).

However, because fewer babies were being born and France's cohort of potential workers and conscripts was shrinking, labour needs could only be met through immigrants or married women – nearly 40 per cent of whom had paid jobs by 1911, four times the comparable German figure. Increased female employment reinforced the fears articulated by Simon. Working wives would have fewer babies. Their neglect of the home would drive husbands to the café. Babies would be sickly and their chances of survival lessened by resort to wet-nursing. Demographers claimed that such fears were not fanciful. Infant mortality in St. Chamond increased by two-thirds – to 200‰ – between 1830 and 1880 as women moved into factories. Infant mortality among illegitimate children reached 450‰ in the 1880s depression. The 'problem' of creating 'good' working mothers obsessed contemporary debate. Humanitarian concerns for vulnerable mothers and infants intertwined with 'moral' concerns for the working-class family and patriotic alarm at the (un)fitness of future conscripts. Republicans and Catholics both viewed the mother as a stabilising force in working-class culture. Their natalist and maternalist discourses overlapped, though the former were more concerned with infant and maternal welfare, the latter with birth-rates and paternal authority. Liberals were now willing to accept state policing of workers' homes. Simon, who once claimed that there were bad wives but 'there were only good mothers', supported an 1889 Law enabling 'morally abandoned' children to be taken into state care. Free-market economist Leroy-Beaulieu argued that only state intervention could prevent families undermining French 'virility' by spoiling their single son and making him 'effeminate'! Social Catholics, wary of the tentacles of the secular state, supported legislation to enable working mothers to have dinner ready on the table when the family returned from work!

Debate on the 1892 Act limiting hours for factory women and banning female night-work revealed more about gendered assumptions than about social 'realities'. Its impact was more symbolic than 'real'. Since most *ouvrières* did not work in large factories, its effect was confined largely to northern textile mills. Implicit in the debate were perceptions that nightime was dangerous, sexually and morally, for women. Rouen industrialist Waddington, who framed the Bill, accepted that the *patrie* required female reproductive labour. Yet his own city relied on their factory labour. The goal was to reconcile the *ouvrière* with responsible motherhood. Trade unions urged 'protection' of women workers but their real goal may have been exclusion of women from certain jobs to strengthen a 'gendered' dual labour market and perpetuate women's economic dependency. Radical feminists viewed the Act as discriminatory. Some *ouvrières* protested that consequences of such 'protection' would be their dismissal from better-paid night jobs and relegation to unregulated sweat-shops. Underlying the humanitarian and natalist rhetoric accompanying the 1913 Law on maternity leave lay the 'medicalising' ambition of doctors such as deputy Paul Strauss. As a Parisian municipal councillor he had outraged Catholics by providing assistance to single mothers and illegitimate children. By 1904 this was national policy – in a Europe which habitually aided only married mothers. He campaigned for free child medical care, crèches for children of working mothers, breast- and bottle-feeding centres and child allowances. Unlike 'patriarchal patriots', Strauss rejected tax concessions to fathers of large families as the answer to demographic problems. He denied Bertillon's claim that illegitimate children were 'syphilitic, scrofulous, tubercular', and was refreshingly unmoralistic vis-à-vis single mothers. Yet he was a problematic ally for feminists. He was a eugenicist who framed the 1920 Law introducing tough penalties for abortion and birth control. A Solidarist, he placed the 'needs' of French society above individual women's rights. A woman's body was not fully 'hers' but rather a vehicle of child production for the race – to be protected against the woman herself. 'A woman's life', claimed a colleague, 'does not belong to her. She has a duty to preserve her health for birth.' Malthusian couples were not blamed for demographic stagnation. It was women and their bodies which had to be controlled. Strauss' projects implied surveillance, by bourgeois female inspectors, whose role was a 'natural' extension of 'female' caring functions. Once *grandes dames* had dispensed charity; now health visitors inspected hygiene and childcare routines of working mothers, while doctors policed hospital wards for evidence of attempted abortions. The 1920 Act exposed the dark side of 'Republican motherhood'. It passed by 521 votes to 55 – with serious opposition coming only from Communists who enquired whether priests and nuns should be prosecuted because their lifestyle was not conducive to procreation! (Accampo *et al.* 1995).

The emerging Welfare State thus offered 'protection' for (working) mothers who lacked citizenship rights. Society was portrayed in 'organic', biological terms. Individuals were potential sources of national strength, or weakness, to be 'husbanded' to maximise output, including that of healthy babies. Feminist historians depict concern for 'the social' as a project to control both family – its health, hygiene, fertility, morality, sexuality – and women's bodies. Doctors, a new priesthood, debated whether patient confidentiality should be breached in the war against contraception and abortion. 'Reforms' increased medical surveillance of working-class women and maternity wards. Here was a classic example of interaction between (Republican) state power, consolidation of professions – with their disciplinary power and knowledge – and the social construction of gender. Natalist doctors dominated the extra-parliamentary commission on 'depopulation' which prepared the 1920 Bill. It contained no women. Debates on maternity were debates *about* women. In 1875 Clémence Royer had protested 'until now science, like law made exclusively by men, has considered the woman as a passive being, lacking her own interests. Being always at least half of those involved in reproduction of the species, she *must* play a role in . . . its more or less rapid multiplication'.

The 1920 Law targeted male birth control propagandists while winning support from mainstream feminists. Feminism was dominated by bourgeoises from Republican, often Protestant, families, some involved in philanthropy or health visiting. They shared – or acquiesced to – natalist valorisation of motherhood. If the *patrie* did indeed need babies, then it was women – equal but biologically different – who would provide these. Motherhood was women's patriotic duty – their 'military service'. As a quid pro quo mother-hood should receive status and funding. The Code should be amended to ensure equality within marriage. Falling birth-rates stemmed not from women's hedonism or careerist ambitions but from inadequate support for working mothers. Clémence Royer demanded careers for women, yet accepted that they 'owe the race intelligent and robust children'. Perhaps, given the pervasiveness of natalism, it made tactical sense for feminists to play along with gender stereotypes in order to subvert them. As mothers' status increased, this should raise women's status. But there was a danger of collusion with dominant stereotypes and prejudices of the wider society. 'Maternalist' femin-ists supported the war, and echoed natalists' claims that war losses meant that more than ever it was women's 'duty' to procreate to produce the con-script cohorts of the 1930s! Women's 'reward' for their war efforts was not the franchise but the 1920 law. Feminists colluded with criminalisation of those whose personal choice was to have fewer, or no, babies. Their position was difficult to distinguish from that of the Catholic Right which explicitly subordinated women's indivial rights to their gendered national and social 'duties' (Offen 1984).

Projects to 'protect' and control working mothers divided and confused both the women's and labour movement. Many trade-unionists eulogised the *ménagère* capable of creating a warm, stable home and portrayed factories unsuitable for women – on moral and physical grounds. Absent are voices of women workers themselves and evidence of their aspirations and perceptions. How widespread was their resistance to the 1892 Act? Did working-class mothers resent intrusion of 'meddling' heath visitors? Or, as Canning has suggested for Germany, was it possible for factory women to appropriate natalist discourses about the dangers of factory work for their own purposes – presenting photographs of heavily pregnant women at large machines in order to illustrate capitalist exploitation?

'La femme populaire rebelle'?

Gender History often appears to show women trapped helplessly in dis-cursive webs of bureaucrats or welfare agencies. Yet they did possess 'agency' and developed networks for survival, 'everyday resistance', even sporadic revolt. Possibly electoral politics restricted the scope for these. Based on male suffrage, it denied women a role as citizens and marginalised community-based mobilisations in which they had participated. Since food was a 'female' issue, grain protests were dominated by women. After the 1770s these became endemic as communities resisted the advent of the free market in grain which allowed speculators to export it from their localities. Whereas male urban identities were built around craft and workplace, women's centred on *quartier*, street, shop, laundry and water fountain. Women gathered to protest at police harassment of street traders, resist bailiffs' evictions of tenants, restrain brutal husbands. Women were 'enforcers' of community norms. In October 1789 the crowd which marched to Versailles to return the King – 'baker of last resort' – to Paris included thousands of women who had earlier rioted in food markets. Women supported price controls in 1793 and participated in the final desperate risings of 1794–95 as free-market policies were reintroduced – demanding 'Bread and the Constitution of 1793'. The legacy of women's involvement in revolutionary politics was complex. Republicans were obsessed with the spectre of 'fanatical' counter-revolutionary peasant women, tools of reactionary priests. For 'moderates' the abiding image was of rioters in Parisian *journées* baying for blood. 'Crowd theorists' Taine and Le Bon 'gendered' the urban 'mob' as 'female' – irrational, hysterical, credulous. Female rioters symbolised a world turned-upside-down. Even Jacobins, who expressed guarded admiration for *braves patriotes*, closed women's clubs and sought to limit women's role to that of 'Republican mothers'. The backlash against the Revolution was, in part, a male backlash – triggered by anxieties aroused by women's public activities in the 1790s (Barry 1996).

Women lacked political representation and several processes were underway which were 'privatising' the nuclear family and isolating them in the home. Men had access to clubs, *cercles*, professional associations and café sociablity. Women's survival strategies thus relied on informal support networks which could be mobilised to counter male physical force or legal powers within the home. These empowered women by making 'private' family disputes public and exposing male behaviour to neighbourhood scrutiny. Such networks were, Rachel Fuchs (1992) notes, 'as gendered as an old-school tie' – yet rarely 'visible'. They left few records, yet were ubiquitous and resilient. Jeanne Bouvier, who migrated to work as a seamstress, describes how female kin already installed in Paris found her lodgings and job contacts. Women turned to such 'compatriots' to help with childcare. Midwives acted as character witnesses to allow women access to charity. A subculture of neighbours and midwives put pregnant women in touch with abortionists, a form of female resistance in a society with a dominant natalist ideology. Female neighbours helped women resist eviction, or conduct a 'moonlight flit' to avoid paying rent arrears. Clearly this 'woman's world' had internal conflicts. Concierges or midwives acted as informers for police or welfare agencies. Women were jealous of pretty rivals, or spread gossip against 'stuck up' neighbours. Yet the prevalence of support networks suggests that in popular *quartiers* notions of domestic privacy were largely meaningless. Lives were lived mainly in streets and tenement yards (Fuchs 1992 MacLaren 1983).

Female direct action persisted. Market protests made successive regimes wary of accepting total freedom of the grain trade. Police retained powers to regulate distribution and prices until the 1860s. Until the 1850s there were recurring patterns of poor harvests, localised grain shortages and food riots. In the July Monarchy, 35 per cent of those convicted for obstructing the passage of grain were women. As late as 1911 women participated in *vie chère* riots to protest at food prices. Women were involved in tax-revolts in the 1840s, luddite attacks on textile machinery and endemic wood-pilfering in forests (Tilly 1981; Berry 1996). Parisian protests were fuelled by memories of earlier insurrections, transmitted through oral tradition. They often centred on issues of particular concern to women, such as housing. In 1848 Faubourg St. Antoine rent-strikers hanged landlords in effigy. A prominent protester, furnisher-finisher Elisa Parmentier, was later arrested on the June Days barricades wearing work clothes and carrying a red banner. Quartier solidarities in expanding *faubourgs* were built around women's networks. Women's role in insurrections remains a contentious issue. Did women fight on the barricades in specific groups and for their own agenda? Or was their role as auxiliaries largely symbolic? The decision to hide from public view Delacroix's *Liberty leading the People* – painted after the 1830 insurrection – stemmed from fears that its image of a semi-naked woman surging across a barricade threatened both social and gender orders. Critics perceived the figure, with its powerful erotic charge, not merely as an 'ignoble' 'woman of the people' but as a prostitute escaped from St. Lazare jail! The implications that political freedoms had been achieved through violence involving eman- cipated women were disturbing. Yet there was no uniform response to the concept of the female insurgent. In 1830, as in February 1848, women in- volved in successful uprisings which installed new regimes were sometimes hailed as heroic Joan of Arc figures by the new regimes. In 1830, 52 appli- cants for compensation for wounds sustained in the July Days were women. Corpses of women killed by the army had been exhibited to spur resistance. On Rue St. Denis it was a woman – the model for Delacroix? – who raised the *tricoleur*. Many women were doubtless aiding their menfolk out of family or neighbourhood solidarity. But Louise Bretagne was a Republican who joined the radical *Société des Droits de l'Homme*. In June 1848, 292 (3 per cent) arrested insurgents were women. Most had been lookouts, food suppliers or messengers. Some had shamed 'cowardly' shirkers into fighting – playing the 'female' role of enforcing community norms – or played a 'symbolic' role waving red flags. Forty were convicted for fighting. Seamstresses made up 40 per cent of those arrested. Some had grievances against landlords or employers. A few had participated in earlier insurrections. Many remained defiant, warning that the June rising was the opening round in a war against the 'tyranny of the rich'. Their actions had a wider context of women's clubs and newspapers, franchise campaigns and seamstresses' cooperatives. Women were involved in subsequent *Dem-Soc* mobilisation. In the Loiret, women *vignerons* and café-owners joined secret societies which organised resistance to the 1851 coup (Barry 1996; Tombs 1999). Women also played a 'symbolic' role. In May 1848 a parade of 500 Parisian *ouvrières* took part in the Festival of Harmony – dressed in white, carrying banners proclaiming 'Liberty,

Equality, Fraternity'. National Workshop directors protested that it was 'not suitable for women to involve themselves in a political festival'. Tocqueville, perceiving the women as symptomatic of profound social disorder, made slighting references to the 'virility' of 'muscular' maidens hurling bouquets 'like hailstones' into the crowd!

Women's role in the Commune aroused similar anxieties. Some Communard leaders wanted to end the exclusion of women workers' from the Left's agenda, and there was more dialogue than in 1848. On the Commune's Labour and Education committee, André Leo demanded vocational training for girls and equal pay for *institutrices*. The *Union des Femmes pour la Défense de Paris* (UFDP) insisted that earlier Left-wing defeats had occurred because failure to address women's problems had 'driven half of (the) troops over to enemy'. It liaised between the Commune and women's groups and pressed for women's employment and equal pay. Of 111 identifiable members, 69 were seamstresses. A co-operative was established to make National Guard uniforms, crèches established for working mothers and welfare rights conceded to common-law wives (*concubines*) and single mothers. One male activist claimed that because women identified the Commune as 'theirs', they fought for it: 'Women everywhere! What a great sight!', exclaimed novelist Vallès. Mobilisation was based on quartier solidarities built around female networks. It has been argued that the scale of women's mobilisation was unprecedented and that they had a conscious agenda – as citizens – linking political, social and gender demands. The strident misogyny of the Commune's opponents merely strengthened their attachment to its cause.

Women again participated as 'auxiliaries', erecting barricades, supplying food, acting as lookouts and nurses, sewing uniforms and questioning the virility of local men who refused to fight to shame them into 'doing their duty'. Some were 'mascots' – 'living allegories' wearing red sashes, singing songs such as *La Canaille*. Women figured in Communard iconography. One cartoon, entitled *Trop Petit*, juxtaposed a (sexually) puny Thiers with a Junoesque woman in a red Liberty Cap. Women were shot or bayoneted in the final days and over a thousand arrested. Although those prosecuted were a chance rather than a representative selection, their social identity reveals a predictable pattern: 382 were from the female trades, 269 laundresses. But had there been squads of women fighters defending Place Pigalle and *pétroleuses* firing public buildings? Had women incited massacres of hostages? Images of women warriors fuelled subsequent conservative demonology, and feminist historiography is as interested in myths and representations of female combatants as in their 'reality'. Some remain sceptical about the existence of female brigades or assertions that women's involvement was unprecedently high. They were present on barricades. Many were shot and bayoneted. But most were charged with inciting violence, only five convicted of arson. Women's role in shooting hostages was a myth constructed by conservative photographer Appert, who 'staged' pictures of the Rue Haxo massacre in order to present an 'authentic' image of the Commune which could, in the absence of 'evidence' of *pétroleuses*, serve as an allegory of the threats which it posed. 'Female killers' presiding over a massacre represented an ultimate 'gender transgression'. Yet there is no evidence that Communardes

333

were particularly bloodthirsty. There was none of the mutilation of corpses and celebratory parades with desecrated bodies which had occurred after 1789, though Vallès did admit that women were involved in some hostage killing – 'avenging' sisters seduced by priests or fathers who had died in police custody (Tombs 1999; Barry 1996; Gullickson 1996; Schulkind 1985).

Images of women insurgents dominated the discourse of the misogynst Right. Le Bon evoked the *pétroleuses* when coding the 'crowd' as 'female'. Communardes were denounced as hysterics, lesbians and feminists, though Dumas was disgusted by bourgeois women who stoned female prisoners as they were marched through the streets of Versailles! Courts established, to their own satisfaction, that a quarter of the women prosecuted were convicted prostitutes. These were, Maxime du Camp claimed, 'bellicose viragos' who had 'forgotten their sex' – less *femmes* than *femelles* (she-animals), bitches on heat. Some were appalled by the insolent defiance which they sensed in the women prisoners. 'A woman is *only a woman* when . . . virtuous', claimed one commentator. 'When crazed or criminal she is more horrible than a man.' Criminologists read the 'causes' of the Commune in the head shapes and facial characteristics revealed by photos of women prisoners. One cartoon encapsulated the Commune's subversive meaning in its image of a man holding a baby while a woman brandishes a rifle. Possibly women were punished essentially for being women who threatened a gendered social order, though thousands of *male* Communards were executed for their class identities and political beliefs. And the 'Joan of Arc of the Barricades' of 1830 metamorphosed into the sinister *pétroleuse* not just because women had dared to fight, but because they fought against 'bourgeois civilisation'. After 1871, workers' protest were increasingly channelled into 'organised' politics or trade-unionism. Socialists defended working-class women as innocent victims of repression rather than as activists in a defeated revolution. The scope for women's spontaneous, community-based actions declined. The rapprochement between Commune and women workers proved an abortive brief encounter, and the process of finding a voice for women in the emerging 'labour movement' long and arduous.

Women and the labour movement (1880–1914)

In 1914 women comprised 38 per cent of the labour force, under 10 per cent of trade-union members. The type of jobs performed by women provides one explanation for this. 'Sweated' domestic clothing workers were often isolated. Most female jobs were 'unskilled'. Though many women were single, separated or widowed, women's wages were viewed as a *salaire d'appoint* – a second wage, supplementary to that of a male 'breadwinner'. Wages 50 per cent lower than those of comparable male workers made it difficult for women workers to survive independently of parents, husbands or lovers. Militants perceived women as cheap labour used systematically by employers to undercut established wage levels. 'Today it is via the *ouvrière* that capitalists fight against the working man', claimed one union leader. 'Docile' women lacked the 'virility' to resist management. Artisans criticised women's willingness to operate new machinery which undermined skills. The 1887

Romans hatters' strike was one of many largely abortive rearguard struggles of craftsmen to halt technological change. Young female workers were portrayed as 'hedonistic', lacking concern for traditions of the trade or for social justice. Female wage labour was denounced as capitalism's greatest evil. Factory work harmed women's health and children's physical and moral welfare. Working women were exposed to moral corruption in the factory, obscene language and lewd proposals. The proletarian variant of domesticity ideology eulogised the *ménagère* who created a loving home as a refuge for the working man from the harsh factory world. The 1898 CGT congress voted for a male 'family wage' to permit women to return to the home. Union support for 'protective' legislation for women workers, even for equal pay, stemmed from the hope that employers would feel that there was no point in hiring women (Hilden 1986a; Zylberberg-Hocquard 1978).

This discourse was not simply cynical and misogynistic. Many unionists were subjectively sincere. Women workers *were* clearly exploited by employers who paid them lousy wages for long hours in unhealthy conditions. Some women yearned to return to the home. Male craftsmen writing in the hatters' union newspaper sometimes showed genuine sensitivity to problems faced by women themselves. The 'contradictions' of the labour movement's attitudes are exemplified by the evolution of the Marxist *Parti Ouvrier Francais* (POF). In the 1880s Guesde welcomed women's work as a step towards economic independence and championed female workers in Nord textile mills. The party's emphasis changed in the 1890s when its shift from 'revolutionary' to electoralist tactics led to fears that (male) voters would be alienated by emphasis on women's issues. The Guesdist-dominated textile union described *ouvrières* as 'workers' wives' and defended male strikes against female 'dilution'. Yet POF discourse and strategies were always confused – an incoherence deriving from ambiguities in workers' family lives and lacunae in Marxist theory. The party endorsed emancipation by labour. Only experiences within the factory would give proletarian mothers full awareness of capitalist exploitation, enabling them to share the labour movement's values and transmit these to their children. Yet the party also denounced capitalist exploitation of the female reserve army of labour and demanded emancipation of women from the factory. Ghesquière claimed that a woman 'considered herself happy to marry a young *ouvrier* who can earn enough to get her out of the factory and keep her in the conjugal home' (Hilden 1986a; Stuart 1997).

Factors other than male militants' misogyny inhibited women from joining unions. Because most did unskilled jobs they were easily replaced. Low wages made it difficult to afford union dues. Young women who might leave the factory when they married were less likely to develop strong job-identities. The 'double burden' of waged work and domestic chores left wives and daughters little time or energy to attend union meetings, often held in cafés where the atmosphere of 'male-bonding' was intimidating. Women often resented time and money spent by husbands on 'union business' in bars! With families often dependent on charity, it was wives who were the intermediaries with religious welfare associations which refused aid to those associated with 'red' unions. This, more than clericalism, persuaded many women to maintain good relations with the clergy. Raised from infancy to be unassertive, many women felt ill-at-ease confronting management and reluctant to risk the public ridicule which resulted from involvement in strikes (Hilden 1986a). Nevertheless, women *did* join unions. In the tobacco industry, a state monopoly, the Republic acted as a model employer by recognising unions after 1884. The labourforce employed in large plants was 90 per cent female. Unusually women, many married and middle-aged, filled most 'skilled' posts. Wage-rates were relatively high and jobs secure, sometimes hereditary. By 1910 unionisation stood at 80 per cent – and female delegates attended union conferences. The tobacco union was 'tough' but reformist, relying on deputies and local authorities to pressure management to make concessions. Gains were secured on 'female' issues – maternity leave, and mothers' right to arrive late for morning shifts without incurring fines. The hat industry, now 80 per cent female, provides a sharp contrast. Most work was done in small workshops. Unionisation hovered around 5 per cent. Apart from a few elite milliners, women were poorly paid, lacked job-security and often left the industry in their mid-twenties. Male artisans, who dominated the union, regarded them as 'frivolous', uncommitted to the *métier*, awaiting a Prince Charming to rescue them from the world of work (Zylberberg-Hocquard 1978).

Relations between unions and women workers did improve. In 1900 women comprised under 6 per cent of unionised workers, but 10 per cent by 1914. In 1912 the printers' union expelled a member – Couriau – who had secured a job for his wife at union rates. This became a *cause célèbre*, obliging an embarrassed CGT to disown the union's unreconstructed 'Proudhonist' leader Keufer. The Couriaus received support from radical *institutrices* and female textile workers in the Isère, appalled by the prejudices which the affair revealed. Their leader, Marie Guillot, sought to build bridges between teachers, women workers and the labour and feminist movements. She argued that the correct strategy was to educate women workers, to work to enlighten male unionists on women's issues, but meanwhile to allow unions to wage the social struggle: 'The best way to practice feminism in the trade-unions is to practice trade-unionism' (Sowerwine 1983). Some unionists now accepted that for the forseeable future women were a reality in the labourforce and that efforts must be made to organise them. Entrenched attitudes changed only gradually. The CGT did attempt to 'sell' its campaign for the 'English week' to women workers, but by offering them alluring prospects of spending Saturday afternoons cleaning the house while the husband went fishing! Even outspoken female unionists failed to question the gendered division of labour within the home. Some syndicalists challenged natalism by supporting Dr Paul Robin's 'neo-Malthusian' birth-control campaign, insisting that workers were encouraged to procreate to supply industrialists with cheap labour and the military with cannon-fodder. Police who raided syndicalist *Bourses du Travail* seized birth-control pamphlets – proof of subversive, anti-patriotic plots! Some syndicalists were in tune with radical feminists and aspirations of working women keen to control their own fertility.

Evidence about female militancy remains ambiguous. Women comprised only 14 per cent of strikers in 1890 – only 9 per cent of strikers by 1914. Far from being uniformly 'docile', some women were prone to direct action, hence the effect of the 'discipline' of union membership was to reduce 'wildcat' disputes. Union organisation and collective bargaining remained essentially a male preserve. But women strikers proved highly demonstrative – singing, conducting *charivaris* against foremen, raising their skirts to show their backsides to insult their opponents. Miners' wives mobilised protests against blacklegs and ran *soupes communistes* to feed strikers. During Midi winegrowers' disputes women workers sat down in front of cavalry horses. Female mobilisations were often around community rather than workplace. Working women met around fountains or in the squares of Midi wine *bourgs*, exchanged information at the laundry or corner-shop, and resisted evictions of working-class tenants. The *vie chère* riots which swept the industrial east and north in 1911 were welcomed by the CGT as expressions of the 'splendid fury' of women concerned to feed their children. The labour press's coverage of women's strikes revealed a doubtless unwitting blend of amazement, admiration and condescension. The 'audacity' of *'nos braves ouvrières'* was portrayed as putting to shame male comrades' timidity. What distinguished women's strikes? Textile strikes in northern mill-towns after 1880 were triggered by wage cuts – and such 'defensive' strikes remained typical of women's mobilisations. However, the 1906 Lyonnais strikes, led by Lucie Baud, signalled a belated revolt by young female workers against the convent-workshop system of clerical surveillance and labour discipline. Often strikes involved gender-specific issues downplayed by male trade-unionists. Textile unions showed little interest in protests of female mill-workers against the 1892 law banning female night-work and shortening women's work hours which, they argued, would lead employers to sack women workers or oblige them to work faster in order to maintain piecework wage levels.

Unions were slow to address workplace sexual harassment. Debate was inhibited by tacit awareness that the Code and contemporary mores assumed male control over female bodies. Since (bourgeois) male sexual desire was accepted as a 'given', lower-class women – café-waitresses, opera dancers or servants – were 'fair game'. A bourgeois version of *droit de seigneur* was underpinned by the Code's refusal to endorse paternity searches for illegitimate children and courts' reluctance to disclose identities of employers who seduced female employees. It was assumed that women living alone often survived by part-time prostitution. Managers responded to women's pay-claims by 'joking' that they could always boost their wages in the evenings! Female strikers were dubbed 'whores' by police and press and, during one postal strike, by a government minister. At Rennes in 1909 they were subjected to compulsory VD tests! Women faced a range of bodily degradations in the factory, obliged to work semi-naked in steam-filled mills or face insults because of their smelly work-clothes. Workplace toilets were filthy and inadequate, and management surveillance often denied women privacy.

One standard trope of workers' discourse was that of the *fille perdue* – the working girl seduced and abandoned by her employer. Zola evoked a 'procession of maids made pregnant and sacked in the name of bourgeois virtue'. Of prosecutions for infanticide, 41 per cent involved servants. After 1880 labour and feminist newspapers spotlighted supervisors who behaved as if 'pashas in a seraglio', such as the Troyes foreman who died of a heart attack *in flagrente* with a teenage worker! Renault and Lebaudy were exposed as firms in which securing or retaining a job depended on sleeping with the foreman. And yet there was little 'resistance'. Women remained obstinately tight-lipped on the subject. Brought up to be submissive, to defer to the bourgeoisie and submit passively to sex, many accepted the 'reality' of male power – assuming that complaints would lead to a sacking or being given a worse job. Many feared the 'scandal' of press coverage. Two molested Troyes teenage bonnet-makers committed suicide. To bring a court case was costly and complex. Victims were aware that management might intimidate potential witnesses (Louis 1994) Male workers often colluded in the regime of silence. Husbands or fathers of women workers were fearful of offending management, even complicit in exploiting the sexuality of their womenfolk to secure favours. Some feared the 'shame' of appearing incapable of 'protecting' wives and daughters. In a culture where the 'ladies man' (*galant*) was an admired macho figure, some male workers were aware that they were 'guilty' of sexual harassment – or of sexual violence within their own homes; 80 per cent of women seeking divorce cited marital violence. Some were reprimanded in court because failure to maintain a discreet silence on such issues brought shame on their families! Male workers responded to cases of harassment at work with unease or flippant jocularity. Some women workers resented pretty girls who used their sexuality to win favours. The tobacco workers' union demanded promotion by seniority to eliminate such practices. However, some women workers and unions were prepared to break this conspiracy of silence. Syndicalist Pouget and socialist-feminist Marcelle Capy criticised unions for ignoring the problem. By the mid-1890s, 30 per cent of women's strikes involved 'dignity' issues, and union newspapers devoted columns to them. Anarchists organised direct action to 'name and shame' offending foremen and managers. In Limoges in 1905, serial harasssment by a foreman at De Haviland's porcelain works provoked a strike, backed by the CGT; 30,000 attended the funeral of a demonstrator shot by troops. This was an industry where shopfloor control of male *artistes en porcelaine* was undermined by mechanisation and an influx of female workers. Artisans experienced decline not merely through erosion of their skills but through the humiliation of watching wives and daughters subjected to sexual advances from arrogant foremen. De Haviland was adamant about his 'right to manage', although political pressures led him to transfer the foreman. However, the dispute exposed tensions within the labour movement. Unions praised the 'virile' actions of (male) workers fighting to ensure 'respect for our wives and daughters in the workshop'. But there was an undercurrent of unease caused by guilt about gender relations within the working class. As one union member confessed, 'these women's tales, one can take them or leave them. (The foreman's) morals are no better or worse than those of any other Limoges man!'.

French feminism(s)

'What is a woman?' – No one knows.

'What is her status?' – She has none.

'Is she part of Humanity?' – The Law of the land does not include her as a separate entity nor as a rational creature. The new Constitution denies her the right to vote.
(Jeanne Deroin 1849)

1830–51

Driven underground after 1793, feminism resurfaced after the 1830 Revolution. Early feminism claimed for women the individual 'rights' promised by the Revolution. The *Gazette des Femmes* (1836–38) continued this tradition, demanding rights for wives within marriage and reintroduction of divorce, petitioning for the franchise and arguing that female *commerçants* should have access to the Stock Exchange. Although its editors were jailed for demanding sexual freedoms, their programme was essentially moderate. The most dynamic feminism of these years was indebted to 'utopian' critiques of bourgeois society. St. Simonianism provided inspiration and supportive networks for a genuine 'popular' feminism. The initial St. Simonian project was to create a new social order by replacing 'parasitic' old elites by 'producers' – industrialists, engineers – who would maximise output and wealth and ease workers' distress. But a prerequisite was moral and spiritual change. Only by accepting mutual solidarity and love would people desire a just social order. Early St. Simonians, students at the *École Polytechnique*, saw their careers – as engineers, businessmen, bureaucrats – obstructed by Restoration clericalism. Although sons of bourgeois families, some were Jewish or Protestant and felt 'marginal'. Enfantin, the most charismatic, was illegitimate and unable to marry his fiancée because of family financial difficulties. Such 'hidden injuries' of class and status sensitised them to wider social, and sexual, injustices.

Female 'converts' found three elements of St. Simonian ideology valuable. It offered a critique of (bourgeois) marriage as a system based on male domination, perpetuation of inherited wealth, 'sale' of daughters and sexual repression. It insisted that the qualities – caring, compassion, empathy – designated by Rousseau as 'female' were the qualities needed for a society based upon co-operation and solidarity, not naked competition. And it rejected Christian asceticism, emphasising that carnal pleasures were healthy, Eve's sexuality a quality not a sin. Before women could utilise these ideas they had to disentangle themselves from Enfantin and his male disciples whose preoccupations became a bizarre mixture of Romanticism, religiosity and rehabilitation of the flesh through sexual promiscuity. The new society required an androgynous God – and twin male and female Popes – to represent the qualities of reason and emotion. A quest was undertaken in Egypt for the female Messiah to sit alongside Enfantin! By 1832 such eccentricities had alienated sober male followers such as Cabet and Bazard.

Women members framed their own agenda. The movement had attracted working women through its discussion groups and lectures and support for clinics, pharmacies and co-operatives in popular quartiers of Paris and Lyon. It also recruited several bourgeoises, including E. Niboyet, Protestant wife of a Lyon businessman. Too 'respectable' to remain associated with Enfantin, these were *dames patronesses*, sponsoring educational and charitable projects and giving aid to working women. Some moved into and re-directed the Fourierist movement. Fourier was more hostile than the St. Simonians to the family. 'The extension of privileges to women', he wrote in 1808, 'is the basis of all social progress.' This required abolition of the nuclear family which enslaved women. Since his research convinced him that only 12 per cent of women had a 'natural' affinity for children, he concluded that in model communities (*phalanstères*) child care would be a communal responsibility. Sexual fidelity led to boredom and frustration, so individuals should be free to satisfy 'butterfly passions' with a range of partners. Female 'Fourierists' of the 1840s bowdlerised the master's 'extreme' views which, they insisted, needlessly outraged 'moderate' public opinion. They claimed that a reformed family could protect women. Unrestrained sexual freedom was a licence for male hedonism. St Simonian working women appreciated Fourier's insistence that work was a precondition for female independence, hence that vocational training should be offered to girls and childcare facilities to working mothers.

As the St. Simonian network disintegrated, these women struggled to survive. Suzanne Voilquin, an embroiderer separated from her husband, trained to be a midwife. Jeanne Deroin struggled to acquire the *brevet* which would allow her to teach. Pauline Roland refused maintenance for her illegitimate children and existed on earnings from writing and part-time teaching. Such women were more preoccupied with childcare and job opportunities than with sexual experimentation or the franchise. But they identified their own emancipation with that of the 'working class'. Aware of the class gulf between working women and bourgeois ladies, they resented being patronised by *grandes dames*. Their short-lived *Tribune des Femmes* (1832–34), distributed via the St. Simonian network, was run by and for working women. They signed articles with their first names – for 'if we take the names of men we shall be slaves'. The paper built a consensus around an agreed minimum programme. Rejecting 'domesticity', it portrayed loveless marriage as a source of women's 'slavery'. Denouncing the Code, it called for equality within marriage and restoration of divorce. Rejecting Christian asceticism, it argued that birth-control made sex for pleasure possible. Claire Demar explicitly demanded sexual freedoms, though her suicide indicated the difficulty of living with the stigma created by such outspoken views. Suzanne Voilquin, who had suffered miscarriages and caught VD from an unfaithful husband, was more concerned with women's vulnerability to sexual assault. Espousing an 'equal but different' ideology, they accepted biological differences linked to women's childbearing capacity. Women were less 'rational' than men. However, they appropriated and subverted 'difference' discourse, using it as an argument for women's empowerment. Women were caring, warm, compassionate, peace-loving, altruistic. In a socialist society built on co-operation and solidarity such 'female' qualities would be prized (Pilbeam 2000; Moses and Rabine 1993; Grogan 1992).

The most significant female maverick was Flora Tristan, illegitimate daughter of an emigrée and a Peruvian nobleman. She left her violent husband with her three children in 1826. As illegitimate child, wronged wife and single mother she claimed to have experienced the full injustices of the legal system. In Britain she met Owenite socialists and saw the horrors of industrial cities. She adopted the role of female Messiah, touring industrial regions in an attempt to unite workers into one big union. But she criticised male workers' prejudices, insisting that working-class women were doubly oppressed – by capitalism and by their husbands. Despite some financial support from Fourierist ladies, she was critical of their condescending paternalism – as they were of her free sexual liaisons which possibly included lesbian flirtations. After her premature death, George Sand helped support her daughter (Dijkstra 1992). During the Second Republic many feminists linked their cause to that of social democracy, though critical of insurrectionary violence and uneasy at the Left's secularism. Female clubs flourished in spring 1848, but were soon suppressed. The daily *Voix des femmes* proclaimed that women's 'caring hearts' held the key to the morality of a social Republic. Pauline Roland demanded rights for single parents and backed Crémieux's abortive Divorce Bill which received tepid socialist support but was savaged by the Right. Deported in 1851, she died after imprisonment in Algeria. Desirée Gay campaigned for public works contracts for women workers. Jeanne Deroin stood as a candidate in the May 1849 elections, with support from some *Dem-Soc* leaders and Faubourg St. Antoine workers. Confronting Michelet, who warned against enfranchising priest-ridden women, she argued that unless and until allowed to acquire political experiences, women would always seek solace for their 'slavery' in 'angelic piety'. She supported girls' education, crèches for working mothers and trade unions for seamstresses. Arrested in 1850, she refused to accept the jurisdiction of a 'male' court and was exiled to Britain.

Repression and revival 1852–1900

The conservative backlash after 1851 buried this second wave of feminism. The Church tightened its grip on girls' education. Flaubert's *Madame Bovary* (1858) faced prosecution for its unflattering dissection of bourgeois marriage. The Republican revival of the 1860s was accompanied by a reawakening of feminist debate. Yet just as Republicanism reconstructed itself by jettisoning the socialist baggage of 1848, so many feminists distanced themselves from social and sexual radicalism. Steering clear of 'utopian' dreams, even of suffrage demands, they settled for gradualist legal and educational changes which they hoped, a liberal Republic would introduce. The wisdom of this 'alliance' is questionable. Even Republicans with genuine interests in the 'woman question' accorded it low priority. Many remained strongly misogynist. However, women writers confronted the stereotypes peddled by Left-wing intellectuals. Michelet's *La Femme* (1859) attributed Republican defeats to priests' hold over women. Obsessed with women's menstrual cycle, he was convinced that female irrationality and volatility stemmed from biologically triggered mood swings. Bourgeois ladies were flippant spendthrifts, factory women promiscuous. At best Republicans could look to girls' secular schooling to bridge the cultural gulf between husbands and wives. Proudhon's profound misogyny reflected the anxieties of craftsmen faced with a threat to their trades from female labour. Man was 'complete', his penis signifying power. Women, passive receptacles of semen, were physically and morally inferior, uninterested in issues of social justice. They could be 'saved' only through marriage to a patriarchal male. Proudhon denounced birth control

341

and insisted on a husband's right to kill an errant spouse. In *Les Idées Anti-Proudhoniennes*, Juliette Lambert, daughter of a Republican doctor, insisted that women needed access to employment in order to avoid being driven into prostitution. In many occupations they exhibited impressive skills. And women had to be tough to cope with childbirth. Jenny d'Hericourt, a midwife aspiring to be a doctor, was scathing about Michelet. Women had minds and free will. Menstruation was natural – not a curse or disease. Far from women rejecting the Republic, it had consistently neglected them. Republicans would face defeat until they mobilised female support – though she conceded that it was premature to enfranchise Catholic peasant women. After 1860, Masonic lodges hosted women's debates. Republican culture was now open to ideas of gradualist change. Reform of the Code, girls' education, divorce and companionate marriage were all on the agenda. Leading figures in the new *Association pour le Droit des Femmes*, anti-clerical lawyer Léon Richer and Maria Deraismes, played down the franchise issue (McMillan 2000; Bidelman 1982).

Liberal feminism was stimulated by the advent of the Republic and by economic, social and cultural changes. The Sée Law (1880) establishing girls' *lycées* was not intended as a step towards women's emancipation, rather as an anti-clerical measure to narrow the cultural divide between Republican husbands and Catholic wives. Girls would study for a diploma, not for the *baccalauréat*. Inadequate funding, unsuitable premises and the suspicions of bourgeois parents created real problems for this new sector, whose first pupils were often Protestant or Jewish. However, feminists welcomed the Act and a trained corps of female *professeurs* emerged from the Sèvres training college. Pupil numbers expanded, although many were petty-bougeois girls whose priorities were technical and vocational qualifications. Within a decade clandestine classes in Latin and philosophy did equip some girls for the *baccalauréat*. A thin trickle began to enter universities. The Paris Medical Faculty had 32 female students in 1879, 578 by 1914. The first female lawyer graduated in 1890, though only 0.29 per cent of lawyers were women in 1914. Girls flocked into *Écoles Primaires Supérieures* to acquire vocational qualifications for posts in the expanding tertiary sector. Pressures from anti-clerical city councils accelerated the secularisation of nursing personnel and petty-bourgeois girls acquired nursing skills in training colleges such as Paris's *École de la Saltpetrière*. By 1910 women occupied 97 per cent of nursing posts, though only 3 per cent of doctors and 8 per cent of dentists were female. Employment opportunities for literate and trained women were expanding. Those who embarked on a 'career' were initially cautious. The first cohort of *lycée* teachers were under constant scrutiny from parents and education authorities. Working longer hours for lower salaries than male counterparts, they were conformist in their views. Few identified themselves as feminists. Yet the emergence of a stratum of women who were not working-class yet who sought paid employment did present feminism with a potential clientele. Such women had some education and financial independence – and their growing aspirations were likely to be obstructed by promotion policies and the iniquities of the Code (Margadant 2000; McMillan 2000; Schultheiss 2001).

Limited improvements *were* achieved in legal status. Married women acquired the right to open bank accounts (1886) and to control their earnings (1907). Divorce was reintroduced in 1884. The proposer of the Divorce Bill, Naquet, had to amend his original measure – which permitted grounds of mutual consent – in order to get it through the Senate, which passed it more as a gesture against the Church than from any concern for women. As in the 1790s, two-thirds of those seeking divorce were women, and courts and juries proved receptive to their pleas of serious physical and moral abuse from husbands.

Feminism in the Third Republic

After 1880 feminism became a 'movement' rather than merely a marginal phenomenon tied to the fate of successive short-lived revolutions. The 'new woman' became a figure of public debate and anxiety. Paris hosted international feminist congresses in 1889 and 1900. Ten feminist newspapers were published there. In 1880 a mere handful of provincial towns including Nantes and Nîmes contained women's groups. Most towns had these two decades later. By 1914 a suffrage league claimed 12,000 members and held mass rallies. Yet historical assessment of this era of French feminism remains pessimistic. Feminist organisations were smaller than those in Britain or the USA. In Britain suffragettes made common cause with strata of male workers which still lacked the vote. In France feminism was an essentially urban phenomenon, but the class gulf between bourgeois feminists and working-class women was wide. Mainstream liberal feminists opted for 'respectability', prioritised legal and educational reforms rather than the franchise and were often 'maternalists', making demands on behalf of women as mothers. Yet Republicans, at whom their strategy was directed, gave lukewarm support to their demands. Leading feminists included Protestant *grandes dames* such as Madame Siegfried, whose concerns were philanthropic or – as crusaders against prostitution – moralistic. Radical feminists, voicing critiques of gradualist strategies and 'maternalist' panderings to natalism, were marginalised. The largest women's associations were Catholic patriotic leagues. Because the Commune had linked feminism with 'extremism', liberal feminists espoused 'moderation'. As wives or daughters of Republicans, many shared fears that 'premature' enfranchisement of Catholic women would destabilise a still-fragile regime – and convinced that a Republic remained the prerequisite for any progress. Even some radical feminists shared similar fears. The strategy of *la brèche* – of working steadily to create breaches in the defences of male privileges through piecemeal reforms – was approved at feminist congresses in 1878 and 1889, though in the 1890s the *Ligue Française pour la Défence des Femmes* (LFDF), under pressure from militant anti-clerical *institutrice* Marie Bonneval, hinted at a more radical stance on the franchise (Klejman and Rochefort 1989).

Those sympathetic to mainstream feminism have analysed the 'success' of Marguerite Durand, editor of feminist daily *La Fronde*, in playing with and subverting gender stereotypes and manipulating the fin-de-siècle cultural agenda. *La Fronde* appeared in 1897 in a world where 'serious' journalism, aimed at a politically informed (male) readership, was conducted by hardened male reporters – expert eye-witnesses capable of presenting news 'as it really was'. The emerging 'mass' press was viewed as cheap, corrupt sensationalist. The resultant 'crisis' was depicted in gendered terms. A venal press was being 'prostituted'. Its credulous, irrational and volatile mass audience was coded 'female'. *La Fronde* caused a publishing sensation because its journalists and editors were women and it was produced by female printers who formed a co-operative in order to evade prohibitions on night-work in the 1892 Act! Its austere house-style surprised those who anticipated something 'light', 'typically feminine'. Its journalists aped 'virile' male counterparts by writing analytical political articles – exposing a central contradiction in a Republican ideology which proclaimed democratic values while denying citizenship to women judged incapable of comprehending politics. *La Fronde* published articles by women barristers and doctors. Its journalists took pride in their 'professionalism', braving the ridicule of cartoonists who portrayed them as missing key events because they had returned to the office to find their lip-stick and insinuations that at the Gare de Lyon after dark they resembled 'ladies of the night'! Their pro-Dreyfusard stance won readers among pro-vincial *institutrices*. They made concessions to mainstream values, holding elegant *soirées* in the *Fronde* offices and hosting Christmas parties because 'children hold a special place in women's hearts'. The paper's tone was mod-erate. It aimed to persuade and to woo – to show that the 'New Woman' could be 'feminine'. Was this a 'surrender' to dominant gender ideologies, or was female journalism per se a challenge to such norms? *La Fronde* toyed with contemporary discourses about press venality and credulous, mass ('female') readership, only to subvert them. Its journalists were committed Republicans and dedicated professionals confronting a sensationalist, populist mass press. The paper consciously made itself a 'playground for gender iden-tity' which exposed and parodied accepted norms because its journalists acted out the instabilities of gender identity.

Durand's personal role proved similarly controversial. She courted praise for her 'femininity', yet risked bourgeois disapproval for flouting conven-tions. A career as a *Comédie Française* actress was followed by a marriage to a radical politician, ending in divorce. In 1896 she resisted attempts of *Le Figaro* editor to seize their illegitimate baby. Subsequently she was the mistress of several Republican politicians. Eulogised as the 'prettiest of Parisiennes', she claimed that feminism 'owes a lot to my blonde hair'. Eccentric, deliber-ately ugly 'new women' played into the hands of those eager to brand feminists as lesbian *'hommesses'*. Being elegant, which required dedication, was a duty for feminists since it disarmed critics. She played on her stage experience. Actresses were social 'marginals' who lived 'disorderly' lives, made a public spectacle of their bodies, pleased audiences through role-play and deception. And yet acting was a 'profession' in which a woman could achieve inde-pendence, indeed 'star' status and some power. In 1910, Durand launched a campaign for women's municipal franchise by addressing packed audiences from theatre stages. Just as Sarah Bernhardt played both Joan of Arc and Hamlet, so Durand acted out gender roles. Alert to the age of mass communica-tions, she regarded a striking photo as better publicity than a long speech. On one notorious occasion she was photographed in apparent control of a lioness. In an emerging 'society of the spectacle' she adroitly manipulated the logic of fantasy (Robert 1999). Robert concludes that Durand subverted dominant norms while appearing to accept them, 'confused the codes' by mimicking different models of 'woman' in order to expose the 'artifice of gender identity'. Durand, scarcely a model bourgeois *ménagère*, manipulated images from the conventionally 'feminine' to the transgressive. Not all feminists shared this evaluation. Radical feminists viewed her manipulation of her beauty as pandering to sexual stereotypes and deplored her refusal to reprimand male admirers who referred to other feminists as ugly or dowdy. Working-class women found her a patronising, snobbish *mondaine*. Some viewed her as a self-promoting 'star', hinting that *La Fronde* received Rothschild money. Doubtless she will find admirers among those who categorise Madonna or Princess Di as feminist icons. In advocating maternalism and breast-feeding, Durand was at one with the dominant strand of feminism. Jane Misme, editor of *La Française* – a journal backed by Protestant bourgeois dynasties – proudly advertised babies born to members of her editorial board and urged readers to 'marry, have children, and be (simultaneously) a good wife, a good mother and a good feminist!' (Offen 1984).

Some radicals advocated a 'strategy of assault'. Hubertine Auclert, the leading 'suffragette', was the daughter of an Allier *notable* who revolted against her convent education by becoming a militant anti-clerical and secured nominal support for women's franchise at the 1879 Marseilles socialist congress. She embarked on an agit-prop crusade, risking mockery by haranguing brides on the iniquities of the Code, refusing to pay taxes, standing for election. Ridiculing excuses that it was dangerous to enfranchise 'clerical' women, she denounced Republicans as insufficiently anti-clerical. Why not disenfranchise the clergy, close all Catholic schools, expel the teaching orders? Secular schooling, together with the experience of voting, would broaden women's minds. Auclert was a loner whose Suffrage League had few members. A police report described her as 'an hysteric – an illness which makes her look on men as equals'. When marriage and residence in Algeria took her off the scene after 1890, suffragism was supported by small, ephemeral groups. She returned after 1900 to engage in public burnings of the Code, upturning of voting urns and sponsorship of female electoral candidates. Elizabeth Renaud secured 3000 votes in the Isère, a department with groups of radical *institutrices*. By 1914, the suffragist *Union Française pour le Suffrage des Femmes* (UFSF) claimed 12,000 members, but the caution of its leader Cécile Brunschwig, wife of a Jewish industrialist, alienated activists. Among those who quit was Maria Verone. She began as a flower-maker, was sacked from her teaching post and, after spells as a dancer and *Fronde* journalist, became, by now a divorced mother of two, a barrister specialising in child welfare!

Though feminism and socialism had been intertwined since 1830, relations with the labour movement were strained. Syndicalists, viewing the parliamentary system itself as a fraud, had little use for male workers' votes, let alone those of women! Most socialists argued that women's rights could be addressed only after the overthrow of capitalism. Socialist women were suspicious of an alliance with bourgeois feminists. The *Groupe Féministe Socialiste* was dominated by seamstress Louise Saumoneau, a class warrior

345

who characterised the concerns of middle-class feminists as to how to treat one's servants and control one's dowry! A 1906 conference on women's work arranged by Durand produced vitriolic clashes between feminists and socialist *ouvrières* (Sowerwine 1982). Some who rejected the 'respectability' of gradualist feminism were exasperated at labour's failure to campaign on women's issues. Radical feminism's most coherent voice was that of Dr Madeleine Pelletier who admitted that she was 'decidedly born several centuries too early!'. Her career had been so thoroughly expunged from the record that Simone de Beauvoir appears to have been largely oblivious of her existence. She was the daughter of poor Parisian shopkeepers. Her forceful mother was a Catholic-Royalist in an anti-clerical popular quartier. She decided that her mother's piety did not make her a nicer person, and was alienated from religion by nightmares experienced after hearing a Hell-fire sermon. Informing her mother that she intended to be a general, she was told that women were 'nothing at all. They marry, cook and raise children'. Traumatised by her first period, she was appalled to learn that all women suffered these monthly. She lamented that society eulogised 'wisdom' transmitted from mother to daughter, yet in the sphere of sexuality there was only silence and taboos. Regarding menstruation as a symbol of the biological forces constraining women, she viewed women's bodily functions with distaste and breast-feeding – eulogised by natalists – as animalistic. 'Deciding' not to be a 'woman' sexually, she remained celibate. Her mother's miscarriages convinced her that sex gave ephemeral pleasure at excessive risk and in existing society was a source of debasement for married women and shame for the unmarried. Bourgeois marriage was a form of prostitution where virgin daughters were 'sold' for legalised wedding-night rape. Though mixing with anarchist groups, she rejected their 'free love' ideology as an excuse for male promiscuity. She was angry at professional women such as Marie Curie who gave ammunition to antifeminists by having affairs. Until emancipation was achieved, feminists needed firm self-control. However, feminism did not imply hatred of men. Too many members of the *Solidarité des Femmes* group which she briefly organised were bourgeoises whose husbands squandered their dowries, ran off with younger women or infected them with VD. For them 'feminism' meant a sorority of shared marital woes and a chance to meet to exchange recipes!

Amazingly Pelletier achieved a career in medicine, having taught herself the *baccalauréat* syllabus and won Paris Medical Faculty scholarship. Thwarted in her aspiration to become a medical researcher, she became a GP. She had aspired to disprove Paul Broca's claims that smaller brain size explained women's 'intellectual inferiority', arguing that in relation to body weight women's brains were actually larger! She failed to question the underlying assumptions of positivistic craniometry, accepting that African brain sizes *were* smaller! Her politics fitted the programme of no single party or group. She joined a Masonic lodge and was impressed by its egalitarianism and spirit of intellectual enquiry. She flirted with the Marxist POF, but saw that its quest for votes was undermining its revolutionary and feminist commitments. She parodied the party's new message: 'No feminism! That would displease the worker who rules his wife by kicking her. By seriously demanding votes for women, we might lose the male vote. Citizenesses, the bourgeoisie tore you from your cooking pots and dragged you into the factories! Let your husbands vote for us and, when we're the masters, we'll return you to your kitchens and your brats!'. She joined Hervé's antimilitarist ultra-Left faction which gave her a chance to address socialist congresses, but realised that the party had no intention of acting on women's suffrage resolutions for which it voted. She remained a socialist as well as an 'integral feminist', aware that while she wanted to transform both socio-economic and gender systems, feminist bourgeoises were reluctant to abandon their class privileges. By 1908 she decided to campaign in the labour movement for her revolutionary goals but to fight feminist battles elsewhere. In 1914 she opposed the war, whereas most feminists were Republican patriots. She later joined the Communist party. She claimed to be a Jacobin egalitarian, even though Robespierre 'didn't care much for women'! Conscious of her own intellectual gifts and merito-cratic professional career she was an elitist who saw progress as dependent on intellectual minorities. Most working-class men were unthinking chau-vinists, most women programmed from childhood for submission. Both col-luded in their own oppression. In Nietszchean moments she argued that in a society where war killed millions it was surely permissible to conduct scien-tific experiments on an alcoholic if these led to medical discoveries which help mankind. Pelletier's feminism was distinctive. She deplored Durand's manipulation of 'feminine' beauty and female wiles. Determined not to be a woman 'as society expects', she despised the fashion industry for presenting the female body like 'meat for sale'. She publicised birth-control in working-class areas. Too many babies, she insisted, from her GP experiences, brought misery to overburdened mothers while supplying capitalists with a reserve army of cheap labour and the military with cannon-fodder. Restricting family size could benefit working-class families now. She denounced 'maternalist' feminism's collusion with natalism. A low birth rate, far from being a social disaster, was an indicator of true civilisation. Pregnancies destroyed women's health. She opposed the pro-maternity provisions in welfare legislation. To 'reward' women for fulfilling 'maternal duties' was to lock them into perman-ent subordination. Women should demand equal rights, not plead for special consideration on the grounds of 'differences'. In *Education Sexuelle des Jeunes Filles* she insisted that maternity should be a choice not a patriotic duty. Rough calculations, she noted ironically, showed that France's one hundred leading natalists averaged 0.5 children per household! Her 1913 pamphlet caused a scandal by advocating abortion rights and demanding repeal of Article 317 of the Code under which thousands of women were charged for abortion each year. She probably carried out abortions, and was eventually incarcerated in an asylum for assisting in procuring these. She championed single mothers.

Pelletier blamed girls' upbringing for stifling intellectual curiosity and incul-cating a sense of inferiority. Girls were trained to appear helpless and seek a 'protector'. They were taught 'despicable' qualities, which appeared neces-sary for survival. She deconstructed the social construction of femininity to show how mothers and teachers reproduced women's subordination. Pelletier was shocked by aphorisms of daily conversation. To 'fuck' was perceived as active, 'male'. To 'be fucked' was passive, 'female', and could imply that one had been swindled, 'shafted'. Girls needed to acquire 'virile' qualities, to become assertive. They should have cropped hair, wear 'male' clothes permitting freer movement, and undergo athletic training. They should be brought up communally so that they did not acquire habits of subordination from mothers. Pelletier attended a Hyde Park suffrage rally and admired in the suffragettes a 'state of mind unknown in France'. Dismissing fears that votes for women would imperil the Republic, she insisted that by acquiring and using the vote would women would develop self-confidence, dignity, wider horizons. She stood as a candidate in the 1910 election. Clearly she 'failed'. She came from humble origins, but was not an *ouvrière*. She never 'made it' into the medical and scientific hierarchy. She was never authentically 'bourgeois'. She was active in, but on the fringes of, the socialist movement. She remained a social, professional and sexual marginal. Yet she articulated a sophisticated critique of existing society and mainstream feminism. Natalists expressed reluctant respect for a dangerous adversary. 'Feminism', she insisted, 'should not be a *feeling* – but an *idea* born of *reason*. We do not despise men. We simply demand our rights.' These rights, significantly, she identified as those individual rights promised and fought for in the tradition of the Revolution (Gordon 1990; Bard 1992).

A gender crisis? Male anxieties, misogyny and antifeminism in the fin-de-siècle

> Man is *condemned* to supremacy. If he is not everything he is nothing.
>
> (Joran)

Before 1914 France experienced an acute 'gender crisis'. Feminist demands raised the spectre of women's access to higher education and professional careers. The Divorce Law and married women's control over earnings appeared to herald the crumbling of the Code and husbands' power. Natalist obsessions nurtured 'biomedical' concerns about the birth-rate and the future of the 'race'. Male insecurities fed sexual anxieties and concerns about 'virility'. Though such concerns found their 'natural' home on the Catholic and Nationalist Right, they were perceptible in the discourses of the Left (Bard 1999; Mauge 1987). The 'New Woman', often portrayed as a lesbian, served alongside the Jew and the immigrant as a scapegoat for the fears of the age. Male identity appeared to be in question. In *L'Homme-Femme* (1872), Alexandre Dumas foresaw a 'de-virilised' man. Three decades later Joran's *Le Mensonge du Féminisme* depicted wives abandoning domestic duties to read Ibsen. Some welcomed the coming of war so that the crisis could be resolved by reassertion of warrior values. But war merely compounded the problems. Despite incessant natalist propaganda, birth-rates plummeted. Wounded and shell-shocked soldiers were tended by tough female nurses. Thousands of women performed 'male' jobs in armaments factories. Women's resultant economic and social freedoms produced the iconic figure of *la garçonne* – the independent woman – and a nightmare vision of 'a civilisation without sexes'. This was the context for the 1920 Law against birth-control and abortion.

In antifeminist novels and plays the 'rebellious woman' was consigned to a premature death, or else 'repented' and was reintegrated into decent society. One reason for the 'failure' of feminism was the scale and ferocity of antifeminism. Mobilising 'reasoned' argument, satire and caricature, it appealed to men of different classes and political persuasions – and even to some women. In 1913 feminist Arria Ly discussed '*masculinettes*', those count-less women who internalised dominant values and derived their identity from fulfilling their allotted duties as Catholic housewives. Antifeminism based itself on 'science'. In *Le Féminisme Impossible*, Eduard Perrier insisted that Paul Broca's physical anthropology 'proved' that equality between the sexes was a chimera. Women had smaller brains, hence 'woman is to man what African is to European, and monkey to human'. Only the male brain gener-ated creative thought. Women were biologically programmed to be submis-sive in the sexual act and reproduce the species. The rare woman of talent did exist, Le Bon conceded, but she was a 'monstrosity'. Women were ruled by their wombs, 'hysteria' was merely an exaggeration of 'normal' female characteristics. The female 'hysteric', her body saturated with sexuality, required control by psychiatrists – through hypnosis, cold showers, ovarian compressions and ablation of the clitoris to prevent masturbation. Yet woman was 'feminine' – charming and soft. Sexual relations in France were cour-teous and laced with 'Gallic' flirtatious humour – *gaillarderie*. Some women played up to these stereotypes, perhaps, feminists claimed, because girls were programmed by their upbringing to be pleasing. Antifeminists claimed that they were in touch with sentiments of 'real' French women. France was truly the *pays de la femme* – and men worshipped at her shrine! Such easy sexual relations were the envy of puritanical cultures. Eschewing aggressive rhetoric, this strand of antifeminism simply claimed to appreciate the 'feminine' woman.

Natalists blamed falling birth-rates on feminists' 'selfish' demands for careers. Zola's *Fécondité* (1898) was a hymn of praise to 'Republican motherhood'. Its hero, an engineer turned progressive farmer, is married to Earth-Mother Marianne. Their goal appears to be to people France and her colonies with offspring whose labour will tap the fertility of the soil. The novel ends with the couple having produced 158 children and grandchildren! The full-bosomed Marianne, described by the family doctor as a 'good layer, a good child rearer', is permanently pregnant or breast-feeding. She accepts the pain of childbirth with stoicism. She respects her husband – for 'there is but one *chef*, one patriarch!' The novel's other 'heroes' are a natalist doctor and a single mother who works at home in order to breast-feed her baby. The 'fertile' countryside is contrasted with big city 'sterility'. The 'villains' in-clude a Malthusian rentier family, in which the wife's breast milk is too thin to sustain their single baby. The sexually insatiable *femme fatale*, Serafine, goes insane and castrates the neo-Malthusian doctor who performed a steril-isation operation on her! Years of abortion practice by this doctor, we are told, had caused more casualties than Prussian armies in 1870. Sex for pleasure is sterile – even pathological. A woman is only fully satisfied if intercourse results in pregnancy. Zola was influenced by Lombroso's study of the 'criminal woman', which linked prostitution with degeneracy, perversion and 'nymphomania'. *Fecondité* is laced with typical anti-religious barbs. The Virgin Mary is clearly no match for the fecund Marianne. Clerical celibacy is denounced as a source of France's 'sterility'. Yet the novel's underlying values – natalism, patriarchalism, Imperialism and its preference for 'healthy' countryside above the city and the factory – were those of the Catholic Right, the 'natural' carrier of antifeminism (Bard 1999).

In 1880 Pope Leo XIII insisted that 'man is at the head of woman, just as Christ is at the head of the Church'. Clergy preached that only Mary's maternity had effaced Eve's sins. Latin civilisation was alien to a feminism which was a product of Anglo-Protestant culture, a foreign import imposed on French women. And Naquet and Sée, authors respectively of the divorce law designed to wreck the Christian family and of 'godless' girls' *lycées*, were both Jews. Catholic Theodore Joran won an *Académie Française* prize for *Le Mensonge du Féminisme* in which he insisted that sexual, as well as racial, inequalities were the foundation of all societies. He called on men to rally together in self-defence. But some antifeminism was Nietzschean rather than Catholic. Futurists portrayed feminism, like democracy, as a quest for 'justice' which enfeebled society. Some 'virile' avant-garde intellectuals portrayed women as marginal, if exotic, appendages to life. Feminists' pretensions to enter professional or intellectual life were ridiculed. Antifeminists of the fin-de-siècle included novelists, playwrights and artists resentful of women invading their sphere. The world of the visual arts was constructed around notions of creative male 'genius' and the 'male gaze'. Proposals to admit George Sand to the *Académie* were greeted by observations that 'soon men will be making the jam'. Heavy-handed *gaillardise* remained a staple ingredient of antifeminist discourse. The 'true' French character revelled in the *bonhommie* of *risqué* male jokes. Cartoons portrayed 'feminists' as dried-up spinsters or complete with bicycle – in 'male' *culottes* and smoking a cigarette – instructing exhausted, dish-washing husbands on their dinner requirements. Feminists were assumed to be man-haters. 'Feminist dolls' could be purchased which squeaked '*à bas les hommes!*' if pressed in undefined 'appropriate places'!

The model of the virile male was the powerful, respected *père de famille* and lover – albeit one whose sexual expertise was largely acquired outside marriage. Although the Republican bourgeoisie distanced itself from the values of the aristocratic elites, it developed a cult of the tough 'citizen-soldier'. One odd consequence was the spectacle of middle-class professionals and politicians in the 1890s proving their virility by fighting duels. But beneath such macho posturing were deepseated anxieties. Natalist discourse was informed by fears that falling birth-rates signified a weakening of 'national virility' by comparison with 'younger', tougher nations. Artisans felt disempowered by erosion of their skills by new technologies. Many men now performed sedentary office jobs which 'the most mediocre female brain could learn'. Proto-fascist novelist Barrès, an afficionado of the Spanish *corrida* where 'real', red-blooded men fought bulls, described desk-bound white-collar employees as '*demi-males*'. The cult of sport which produced the Tour de France and the Olympic Games was sponsored by Right-wing ideologists obsessed by the need to provide the increasingly flabby, anaemic urban male with a sun-tan and some 'muscles' (Nye 1993). Perhaps a sense of impotence outside the home required compensation by assurances of male power within it. Male workers – Simon claimed – were 'slaves to regulations in the factory: it is only fair that they should be masters in their own homes'. Contemporary literature portrayed men with career problems who seek solace in home and family, only to be disdained by wives or fiancées. Marcel Prevost's *Les Demi-Vierges* portrays a sex war waged by the 'New Eve', with Adam as impotent victim. 'Crimes of passion' were committed by frustrated husbands unable to control their wives. Anxieties were compounded by an uneasy awareness of sexual ambiguities, the blurring of clear gender distinctions. The figures of the *femme fatale*, the predatory 'nymphomaniac' and the virago/castrator haunt fin-de-siècle literature. Images of feminist-as-lesbian generated anxieties. How did one recognise a lesbian? How widespread was lesbianism? Androgyny and the *péril sapphique* generated both fascination and repulsion. Many appeared to perceive in sexual 'inversion' symptoms of national degeneracy and loss of male control. The emergence of female sport, and the vogue for 'masculine' women's sports' attire, were disturbing signs of the 'masculinisation' of the gentle sex. Pelletier's demand for women to be trained to fence so that they could challenge men to duels was scarcely reassuring! The strident homophobia of antifeminist discourse suggests that prominent antifeminists were worried not merely by an 'effeminacy' sapping the virility of the 'race' but about their own sexuality (Dijkstra 1986; Dean 2000).

France, women, feminism

Failure to win the vote after 1918, the post-war natalist backlash and the crusade against the 'new woman' could be construed as defeats for Belle Époque feminism. When Simone de Beauvoir wrote *The Second Sex* in 1949, key figures of this 'sacrificed generation' remained unknown to her. One explanation for their 'failures' was the power of Catholic women's organisations. By 1918 they boasted a million members. The largest of them, the *Ligue Patriotique des Femmes* (LPF) and the *Ligue des Femmes Françaises* (LFF), both proclaimed their devotion to 'domesticity'. 'Do *not*', the LFF president insisted, 'assume that we are women in politics. We *are*, and only *wish to be*, Christian wives and mothers.' Led by *grandes dames*, they prioritised defence of Catholic schools and charity. However, there *was* a strand of Catholic feminism. If most women were loyal to their priests, might it not make strategic sense for Catholic leaders to embrace women's suffrage? Women, 'by nature' conservative, would vote 'better' than their menfolk. Ultramontane novelist Marie Maugeret viewed liberal-secularist feminism as an alien Jewish/Protestant phenomenon. The task of 'Christian feminism' was to defend marriage and the family. Yet it should accept women's right to work, manage their finances and vote. Why were intelligent Catholic women denied a franchise granted to brutal, anti-clerical, proletarian men? She also urged protection of 'sweated' female workers. Despite support from individual priests, Maugeret failed to convince the Catholic establishment, which feared 'politicisation' of the domestic sphere. Some Catholics argued for a 'family' vote. After 1918 the official Catholic line changed. Women's contribution to the war effort, enfranchisement of women in Germany and Britain, the perceived utility of conservative female voters as a bulwark against Bolshevism and the blessing of Pope Benedict XV contributed to this *volte face*. Ironically this served to delay women's suffrage. By reviving Republican paranoia about the 'clericalism' of potential women voters it contributed to the (narrow) Senate rejection of the franchise bill of 1922 (Hause and Kenny 1984).

Was support for organised feminism simply too small to secure gains? It suffered from ideological fragmentation and from class divisions which made communication between working-class women, radical *institutrices* and bourgeois feminists difficult. The slow pace of cultural change in rural and small-town France may have ensured that the 'woman question' lacked resonance outside the cities. *La Fronde* collapsed, Durand laconically observed, because it was considered 'too bourgeois by socialists, too serious by Parisians and too Parisian by the provinces'. Liberal feminists aimed to be 'respectable'. They distanced themselves from earlier socialist feminism and avoided the 'excesses' of British suffragettes. Feminist organisers included Protestant ladies, close to the Republican establishment, whose natural milieux were philanthropy and moral crusades against prostitution or alcohol. They proposed piecemeal legal reforms, held conferences, lobbied sympathetic deputies. By accepting natalism they secured a say in framing maternalist measures which were a feature of the emerging Welfare State. But Catholics dismissed them as mouthpieces of the Republican elites, while their 'respectability' alienated potential supporters – working-class women, neo-Malthusians.

However, McMillan argues, one should not simply 'blame the victim'. The real problem lies at the heart of a Republican culture which from the Enlightenment onwards had promoted negative images of women. This went beyond fears of credulous Catholic women voting for reactionary clerical candidates. Such Republican apologetics were largely cynical and manipulative. Playing the anti-clerical card proved a useful way to hold together otherwise disparate Centre-Left coalitions – and provided a 'progressive' fig-leaf to disguise the misogyny rooted in the Enlightenment's rationalist and medical discourses. Republicanism was constructed not merely without but allegedly against women. The 'Republican citizen' was a secular, rational, public-minded male whose identity was defined against its Catholic, irrational, domestic female 'other' (McMillan 2000; Reynolds 1986). This thesis should not go unquestioned. Was the 'clerical threat' simply a figment of Republicans' overheated imaginations or invented as a tactical ploy? The Boulangist and Dreyfus crises suggest that fears for the stability of the Republic were not groundless. McMillan claims that 'talk of a clerical threat rings hollow in a situation where churchmen were struggling to stem the tide of de-christianisation'. Yet historians emphasise the continued vitality of French Catholicism – and McMillan himself notes the overwhelming numerical superiority of Catholic women's organisations, with ties to the extreme-Right. The LPF and LFF organised Lourdes pilgrimages, aimed to overturn the laic laws and re-christianise France. Given the clout of such associations, was it surprising that Centre-Left feminists, sympathetic to the Republic's laic ideals, harboured doubts about women's immediate enfranchisement? One might argue, counterfactually, that had mainstream feminism only become less tied to secular Republicanism it might have been better positioned to achieve a modus vivendi with Catholic women. Yet any such rapprochement would have been based on a blend of reactionary patriotism and natalism which, one assumes, modern feminist critics of the Republican tradition would deplore.

French Republicanism had its faults. But it has been unfairly treated by Anglo-American feminist historiography. As Mona Ozouf (1997) emphasises, French feminism was 'born' in 1789–90 precisely because the issue of 'women's rights' had been put on the agenda by the ideals of the Revolution. Divorce was introduced by the Revolution, abolished by the restored monarchy, and reintroduced by the Third Republic. The 'space' for the feminist revival in the 1860s was created within the culture of the Republican movement, including Masonic lodges. Women's suffrage Bills regularly passed the Chamber of Deputies, only to be defeated in the Senate – an upper house created by 'Moral Order' neo-Royalists with an electoral system which favoured conservative rural France in order to block progressive legislation. Feminist ideas found support among lay *institutrices* whose existence as secular teachers derived from the Republican project to secularise girls' schooling. Ozouf's own oral history of these *institutrices* captured their devotion to the Republic. The Sée law, despite its author's conscious intentions, opened access to higher education, making female professional 'careers' a possibility. Doubtless it is difficult for American feminists, seduced by post-modernist critiques of the Enlightenment and inhabitants of a Republic which is the world's most ruthless and exploitative capitalist/imperialist power, to understand that in the European context of the late nineteenth century a French Republic, under challenge from neo-Royalist and proto-fascist enemies, could still broadly stand for 'progressive' values (Ozouf 1997).

There were many different types of feminist. Some emphasised 'equality in difference' or 'relational' rather than individualist feminism. Bourgeois wives and daughters who nurtured proto-feminist sensibilities often were reluctant to be linked with the feminist movement. One doubts that a more radical feminism would have attracted them. There were also women, such as novelist Colette, who viewed feminism as too 'cerebral', alien to their 'femininity'. They claimed that 'Latin' women were 'made for love' and that a 'civilisation without sexes' would be impossibly dreary. Their stubborn false consciousness was astutely cultivated by those fashion designers and romantic novelists who had a vested interest in its survival!

Postscript: from 'discourse' and representation to 'social reality'?

It is easy to portray French women as trapped between the Code, which treated them as permanent 'minors', and dominant (male) discourses of domesticity and natalism. Hence the importance of Sohn's (1996) imaginative use of court records and letters to explore the relationship between these legal and discursive norms and the 'lived realities' of daily lives of 'ordinary' women. Underpinning her approach is an awareness of the 'contradictions' between the pervasiveness of natalist and separate spheres ideologies and the 'facts' that the birth-rate fell inexorably and a high, and rising, proportion of women, including married women, had paid employment (Sohn 1996). The material realities of most French families scarcely fitted neatly with domesticity norms. Issues of dowries and marital property discussed in the Code were largely irrelevant to such households. The ideal of the *femme au foyer* was alien to millions of husbands who wanted an active wife who could bring money into the family; 10 per cent of the population remained trapped in poverty and a culture of fatalism and charity and welfare dependence. But after 1880 material 'progress' – gradual and erratic – did influence millions of lives. Food became cheaper and more varied, real wages rose, the work-day shortened. Medical care became more accessible. Housing conditions improved rather more slowly. Even so, technical changes eased domestic chores. Commercial bakeries meant less reliance on home-made bread. Running water, linoleum floors, plastic table cloths and *eau de Javel* facilitated cleaning the home. Gas and electricity made cooking and lighting simpler and cleaner.

As significant was the emergence of the woman as an 'individual'. The authority of the extended family weakened, even in the 'traditionalist' Southern Massif. The 'family wage economy' gradually eroded, although most female jobs remained too poorly paid to assure any real economic 'independence', most men still refused to do housework and most domestic tasks were still 'female'. Power within the family became less clear-cut, more diffuse and 'negotiated' – increasingly determined by the cleverest or the most manipulative. Husbands wanted to be loved, not just feared or obeyed. With divorce now an option, wives were better positioned to impose some rules on husbands. But the crucial change was that biological fatalism was broken as maternity became a chosen option. The desire to limit reproduction was widespread and deepseated. Having fewer children was viewed as the path to improved quality of life, better health – even social promotion. Taboos once associated with birth-control declined. And there was a veritable 'explosion' of abortions in the 1900s (MacLaren 1983).

Personal 'victories' for individual women perhaps explain the 'weakness' of feminist campaigns for political and legal rights. Women of the popular classes felt, Sohn (1996) suggests, equally distant from bourgeois feminism, official discourses and from the provisions of the Code. Influences on their behaviour and choices were changing. Community pressures, once exerted through *charivaris* or other forms of informal local action, declined. Despite the apparent vitality of Catholicism, the hold of religion on women's personal and sexual behaviour was declining. Even the impact of law on family conduct was problematic. The Code's insistence on inegalitarian marriage was often a dead letter. Women kept their own wages, ran up debts, treated common property in the marriage as their own. Court records indicate that in 90 per cent of cases such behaviour was, de facto, tolerated. Since provisions of the law were regularly flouted, 'it is futile to continue endless glosses on the "antifeminist" character of the Code, or to weep over the fate of the eternal legal minor' (Sohn 1996). Equally one might question the impact of ubiquitous domesticity and natalist discourses. The birth-rate fell relentlessly, even after the 1920 law. As female employment opportunities widened and married women took jobs and had fewer children, the *mère au foyer* ideal appeared bankrupt. Women, in short, acted as if impervious to official discourses and deaf to exhortations and pleading. Conversely medical discourses on hygiene and infant care *were* heeded. Women were persuaded of the advantages of 'medicalised' birth and infant care. They found the 'Pasteurian' message convincing. They were prepared to invest care in those babies which they had chosen to have. It is often assumed that the war marked a watershed in gender relations. But before 1914 a significant, if hidden, cultural revolution occurred. Women with paid jobs were working shorter hours and using birth-control and abortion to limit their fertility. They were dressing in more functional and comfortable styles and, by 1910, some experimented with shorter hairstyles. Changes were most marked among urban workers, petty bourgeois and employees, particularly in 'modern' regions of the East. Here families aspired to greater leisure, had fewer children and developed a secular mentality and 'flexible' moral codes. Peasant migrants, rural wet-nurses and servant girls helped to spread new attitudes into the countryside. In short, Sohn argues, the 'peculiarities of the French' were not located in a 'weak' feminist movement nor in all-pervasive natalist and domesticity ideologies. Rather they resided in the scale of female employment, in precocious use of birth-control and abortion to control fertility, in a family more 'liberal' than that of 'authoritarian' Germany or 'patriarchal' Mediterranean countries – and, above all, in a partly secularised laic culture. Women's history should be concerned with more than elite discourses about women. Rather it should chart women's role as 'agents' – albeit acting within the possibilities and constraints of the material world.

Bibliography

Accampo, E. *Industrialisation, Family and Class Relations: St Chamond, 1815–70* (Berkeley, CA: University of California, 1989).

Accampo, E., Fuchs, R. and Stewart, M.-L. *Gender and the Politics of Social Reform in France 1870–1914* (Baltimore, MD: Johns Hopkins University Press, 1995).

Adams, C. 'Constructing mothers and families: the "Society for Maternal Charity" of Bordeaux', *French Historical Studies* 1999.

Allen, J. *Poignant Relations: Three Modern French Women* (Baltimore, MD: Johns Hopkins University Press, 2000).

Aron, J.-P. (ed.) *Misérable et glorieuse: La Femme au 19e Siècle* (Paris: Fayard, 1980).

Auslander, L. and Zancarini-Fournel, M. (eds) *Différences des Sexes et Protection Sociale* (St. Denis: PUV, 1995).

Bard, C. (ed.) *Madeleine Pelletier (1874–1939): Logiques et Infortunes d'un Combat pour l'Égalité* (Paris: Côté-femmes, 1992).

Bard, C. (ed.) *Un Siècle d'Antiféminisme* (Paris: Fayard, 1999).

Barry, D. *Women and Political Insurgency: France in the Mid-Nineteenth Century* (London: Macmillan, 1996).

Bernheimer, C. *Figures of Ill-Repute: Representing Prostitution in Nineteenth-Century France* (Durham: Duke University Press, 1997).

Bidelman, P. *Pariahs Stand Up! The Founding of the Liberal Feminist Movement in France 1858–89* (Westport, CT: Greenwood Press, 1982).

Boxer, M. 'Protective legislation and home industry: the marginalisation of women workers in late-nineteenth-century France', *Journal of Social History* 20, 1986.

Burke, J. and Jacob, M. 'French Freemasonry, women and feminist scholarship', *Journal of Modern History* 1996.

Coffin, J. *The Politics of Women's Work: the Paris Garment Trades 1750–1914* (Princeton, NJ: Princeton University Press, 1996).

Cole, J. *The Power of Large Numbers: Population Politics and Gender in 19th-Century France* (Ithaca: Cornell University Press, 2000).

Corbin, A. *Women for Hire: Prostitution and Sexuality in France* (Cambridge Mass: Harvard University Press, 1990).

Corbin, A. *Le Temps le Désir et le Horreur* (Paris: Aubier, 1991).

Corbin, A., Lalouette, J. and Riot-Sarcey, M. (eds) *Les Femmes dans la Cité au XIXe Siècle* (Paris: Créaphis, 1997).

Cova, A. *Maternité et Droits des Femmes en France: XIXe et XXe Siècles* (Paris: Anthropos, 1997).

Cross, M. and Gray, T. *The Feminism of Flora Tristan* (Oxford: Berg, 1992).

Darrow, M. 'French noblewomen and the "new domesticity"', *Feminist Studies* 1979.

Dean, C. *The Frail Social Body: Pornography, Homosexuality and Other Fantasies in Interwar France* (Berkeley, CA: University of California Press, 2000).

DeGroat, J. 'The public nature of women's work: definitions and debates during the revolution of 1848', *French Historical Studies* 1997.

Desan, S. 'Wars between sisters and brothers: inheritance law and gender politics in revolutionary France', *French Historical Studies* 1997.

Dijkstra, S. *Idols of Perversity: Fantasies of Feminine Evil in Fin-de-Siècle France* (Oxford: Oxford University Press, 1986).

Dijkstra, S. *Flora Tristan: Feminism in the Age of G. Sand* (London: Pluto, 1992).

Dubesset, M. and Zancarini-Fournel, M. *Parcours de Femmes, Réalités et Représentations: St Etienne 1880–1950* (Lyon: Lyon University Press, 1993).

Frader, L. and Rose, S. (eds) *Gender and Class in Modern Europe* (Ithaca: Cornell University Press, 1996).

Frader, L. 'Femmes, Genre et Mouvement Ouvrier en France au XIX et XXe Siècles', in *Clio: Histoire, Femmes et Sociétés* 1996.

Fraisse, G. *Muse de la Raison: La Démocratie exclusive et la Différence des Sexes* (Paris: Gallimard, 1995).

Fraisse, G. and Perrot, M. (eds) *Histoire des Femmes en Occident: Le XIXe Siècle* Vol. 4 (Paris: Plon, 1991).

Fuchs, R. *Abandoned Children: Foundlings and Child Welfare in 19th Century France* (Albany: State University of New York Press, 1984).

Fuchs, R. *Poor and Pregnant in Paris: Strategies for Survival in the 19th Century* (New Jersey: Rutgers University Press, 1992).

Gordon, F. *The Integral Feminist: Madeleine Pelletier 1874–1939* (Cambridge: Polity Press, 1990).

Gordon, F. and Cross, M. *Early French Feminisms: 1830–1940* (Cheltenham: E. Elgar, 1996).

Grogan, S. *French Socialism and Sexual Difference: Women in the New Society* (London: Macmillan, 1992).

Gullickson, G. *Unruly Women of Paris: Images of the Commune* (Ithaca: New York, 1996).

Hause, S. and Kenny, A. *Women's Suffrage and Social Politics in the Third French Republic* (Princeton, NJ: Princeton University Press, 1984).

Hilden, P. 'Women and the labour movement in France: 1869–1914', *Historical Journal* 1986a.

Hilden, P. *Working Women and Socialist Politics in France 1880–1914: A Regional Study* (Oxford: Oxford University Press, 1986).

Hufton, O. *Women and the Limits of Citizenship in the French Revolution* (Toronto: University of Toronto Press, 1992).

Hunt, L. *The Family Romance of the French Revolution* (Berkeley, CA: University of California Press, 1992).

Klejman, L. and Rochefort, F. *L' Égalité en Marche: le Féminisme sous la Troisième République* (Paris: Des Femmes, 1989).

Louis, M-V. *Le Droit de Cuissage: France 1860–1930* (Paris: Les Editions de l'Atelier, 1994).

Lipton, E. *Looking into Dégas: Uneasy Images of Women* (Berkeley, CA: University of California Press, 1986).

Liu, T. *The Weavers' Knot: the Contradictions of Class Struggle and Family Solidarity in Western France 1750–1914* (Ithaca: Cornell University Press, 1994a).

Liu, T. '*Le patrimoine magique*: reassessing the power of women in rural households in nineteenth-century France', *Gender and History* 1994b.

Maignien, C. *Madeleine Pelletier: L'Éducation Féministe des Filles* (Paris: Syros, 1978).

Margadant, J. (ed.) *The New Biography: Performing Femininity in Nineteenth-Century France* (Berkeley, CA: University of California Press, 2000).

Mauge, A. *Identité Masculine en Crise: 1871–1914* (Paris: Edits Rivages, 1987).

MacLaren, A. *Sexuality and the Social Order* (New York: Holmes and Meier, 1983).

McMillan, J. *Housewife or Harlot: the Place of Women in French Society 1870–1940* (Brighton: Harvester, 1981).

McMillan, J. *France and Women 1789–1914: Gender, Society and Politics* (London: Routledge, 2000).

Moreau, T. *Le Sang de l'Histoire: Michelet, l'Histoire et l' Idée de la Femme au XIXe Siècle* (Paris: Flammarion, 1982).

Morgan, C. 'Unfashionable feminism: designing women writers in the *Journal des Femmes* (1832–36)', in D. de la Motte and J. Przyblyski (eds) *Making the News: Modernity and the Mass Press in 19th-Century France* (Amherst, 1999).

Moses, C. and Rabine L. (eds) *Feminism, Socialism and French Romanticism* (Bloomington: Indiana University Press, 1993).

Nochlin, L. 'A house is not a home: Dégas and the subversion of the family', in G. Pollock (ed.) *Dealing with Dégas* (Pandora, 1992).

Nye, R. *Masculinity and Male Codes of Honor in Modern France* (Oxford: Oxford University Press, 1993).

Offen, K. 'Depopulation, nationalism and feminism in fin-de-siècle France', *American Historical Review* 1984.

Ozouf, M. *Women's Words* (Chicago: University of Chicago, 1997).

Perrot, M. *Les Femmes, ou le Silence de l'Histoire* (Paris: Flammarion, 1998).

Phillips, R. *Family Breakdown in Late Eighteenth-Century France: Divorces in Rouen 1792–1801* (Oxford: Oxford University Press, 1980).

Reynolds, S. (ed.) *Women, State and Revolution* (Brighton: Wheatsheaf, 1986).

Riot-Sarcey, M. *La Démocratie à l' Épreuve des Femmes: Trois Figures Critiques du Pouvoir 1830–48* (Paris: A. Michel, 1994).

Ripa, Y. *Women and Madness: the Incarceration of Women in Nineteenth-Century France* (Cambridge: Polity, 1990).

Robert, M.-L. 'Subversive copy: feminist journalism in fin-de-siècle France', in D. de la Motte and J. Przyblyski (eds) *Making the News op cit* (Amherst, 1999).

Rogers, R. 'Boarding schools, women teachers and domesticity 1800–50', *French Historical Studies* 1995.

Ronsin, F. *La Grève des Ventres: Propagande NéoMalthusianisme et baisse de Natalité Française* (Paris: Aubier, 1980).

Sarti, O. *The Ligue Patriotique des Françaises 1902–32: A Feminine Response to the Secularisation of French Society* (New York: Garland, 1992).

Schulkind, E. 'Socialist women during the 1871 Paris Commune', *Past and Present* 1985.

Schultheiss, K. *Bodies and Souls: Politics and the Professionalisation of Nursing in France 1880–1922* (Cambridge Mass: Harvard University Press, 2001).

Scott, J. *Gender and the Politics of History* (New York: Columbia University Press, 1986).

Scott, J. *Only Paradoxes to Offer: French Feminists and the Rights of Man* (Cambridge Mass: Harvard University Press, 1996).

Seeley, P. 'O Sainte Mère: liberalism and the socialisation of Roman Catholic men in 19th-century France', *Journal of Modern History* 1998.

Segalen, M. *Love and Power in the Peasant Family* (Oxford: Blackwell, 1983).

Smith, Bonnie, L. *Ladies of the Leisure Class: the Bourgeoises of Northern France in the Nineteenth Century* (Princeton, NJ: Princeton University Press, 1981).

Sohn, A.-M. *Chrysalides. Femmes dans la Vie Privée: XIXe-XXe Siècles* (Paris: Sorbonne, 1996).

Sowerwine, C. *Sisters or Citizens?: Women and Socialism since 1876* (Cambridge: Cambridge University Press, 1982).

Sowerwine, C. 'Workers and women in France before 1914: the debate over the Couriau affair', *Journal of Modern History* 1983.

Sowerwine, C. and Maignien, C. (eds) *Madeleine Pelletier: Une Féministe dans l'Arène Politique* (Paris: Les Editions Ouvrières, 1992).

Stewart, M.-L. *Women Work and the French State: Labor Protection and Social Patriarchy: 1890–1914* (Kingston: Queens University Press, 1989).

Strumhinger, L. *Women and the Making of the Working Class: Lyon 1830–70* (St. Albans: Eden Press, 1979).

Stuart, R. 'Calm, with a grave and serious temperament, rather male: French Marxism, gender and feminism', *International Review of Social History* 1996.

Stuart, R. ' "Whores and Angels": Women and the family in the discourse of French Marxism 1882–1905', *European History Quarterly* 1997.

Sussman, G. 'The wet-nursing business in nineteenth-century France', *French Historical Studies* 1975.

Thébaud, F. *Ecrire l'Histoire des Femmes* (Paris, 1998).

Tilly, L. 'Women's collective action and feminism in France: 1870–1914', in C. Tilly and L. Tilly (eds) *Class Conflict and Collective Action* (Beverley Hills: Sage, 1981).

Tilly, L. and Scott, J. *Women Work and the Family* (London: Holt, Reinhart and Winston, 1978).

Tombs, R. 'Warriors and killers: women and violence during the Paris Commune', in R. Aldrich (ed.) *The Sphinx in the Tuileries* (Sydney: University of Sydney, 1999).

Waelti-Walters, J. *Feminist Novelists of the Belle Epoque* (Bloomington: Indiana University Press, 1990).

Walton, W. 'Women's work and the rearticulation of home space', *Women's History Review* 1997.

Zylberberg-Hocquard, M-H. *Féminisme et Syndicalisme en France avant 1914* (Paris: Anthropos, 1978).

Conclusion

C. Charle (1994) concluded his study of nineteenth-century French society on a relatively optimistic note. The France of 1800 was, despite the Revolution, a society of *notables* in which a (diverse) propertied elite sought to preserve its dominance via a narrow franchise system and control of access to education – or, if order was threatened, by imposition of quasi-authoritarian government. Bonapartism was, like Gaullism, in some ways an effective blend of authoritarianism and populism capable of generating widespread support. But the crisis of 1870–71, marked by military defeat and internal civil war, suggested that it was not socially inclusive enough to produce long-term political or social stability. After 1870 a new system of (bourgeois) dominance developed which, at least rhetorically, was more democratic and meritocratic, and which appeared more flexible. The popular classes had the vote, access to free secular schooling and the possibility of white-collar employment. Workers now had trade-union rights. Living standards were rising. If hierarchies persisted they were, perhaps, more acceptable because the system appeared less exclusive. The Republican synthesis was challenged from the Left and far Right. But it avoided destabilising political crisis or, despite the prolonged Great Depression, prolonged social unrest.

As C. Heywood (1999) emphasises, this 'reading' of social development would have appeared Panglossian to two of France's political 'families'. Catholic traditionalists endlessly lamented that society was 'disintegrating'. They saw a world where communities and crafts were being undermined, deracinated migrants were flooding into cities and drifting into crime, the family was in crisis and religious beliefs and practices were being eroded by secularism and pornography. The spread of the forces of scepticism, materialism, socialism and feminism were producing a society of atomised individuals, marked by the decline of deference, divorce, falling birth-rates, child labour and confusion of gender roles. However, these anxieties appear exaggerated if one analyses 'real' social and cultural trends. Despite secularisation of state education and the existence of pockets of free thought, the consensus now is that Catholicism enjoyed a revival in the nineteenth century and remained a vigorous force in 1914. 'The family' was scarcely in the parlous state depicted by Le Play's gloomier disciples; it remained the focus of loyalties and identities. Women and children in factories often worked alongside their kin and paid wages into a family 'pool'. Migrants to the cities relied on contacts with relatives to find lodgings and employment. Although the urban population swelled from barely 20 to 44 per cent in the course of the century, the pace of urbanisation was slow by comparison with Britain or Germany. Two-thirds of those over 45 lived in the department of their birth in 1890. Legitimist landowners and 'paternalist' industrialists sought to pre-serve settled, hierarchic, communities. The expansion of rural cooperatives and mutual-aid societies and cultural and leisure societies – and stubborn resistance to the erosion of communal rights – suggest that village community solidarities were not dead. Even in big city *faubourgs* (suburbs), shops, cafés and informal women's networks developed local solidarities and identities, suggesting that Chevalier's (1973) depiction of urban *anomie* is overdrawn. In short the Catholic Right – nostalgic for a lost golden age of communities and religious conformity – exaggerated the scale of social disintegration and underplayed ways in which religion, family and community still provided the framework for many lives.

Some laments of the traditionalist Right found echoes on the Left. It was not just Marx who portrayed mid-century French society corrupted by the cash nexus and increasingly polarised by class divisions. Though Marx wrote perceptively of the persistence of intermediate social strata – peasants, petty-bourgeois and craftsmen – he predicted the polarisation of society into two warring classes. Similarly, the liberal-conservative De Tocqueville drew the lesson from 1848 that France was descending into a naked class-war which ranged the propertied – 'united in a common terror' – against the propertyless (De Tocqueville 1971). Yet liberal empiricists *and* post-modernists dismiss such class analysis as crude and insufficiently nuanced. The intermediary classes did not disintegrate with the development of industrial capitalism. The bourgeoisie was fragmented along complex lines. Classes themselves, we are assured, were essentially discursively constructed. The 'worker' who was central to the discourse and iconography of the labour movement was essentially male and skilled. The labour movement, which purported to rep-resent the working class, struggled to find a foothold among the unskilled, women workers, immigrants, white-collar employees or Catholics. More-over, as P. Joyce has emphasised for Victorian Britain, alongside the rhetoric of class an older populist discourse persisted that invoked the interests of the '(little) people' against the *gros*, the idle, the parasitic. If class conflicts remained a feature of the France of the 1900s they were, perhaps, less acute than those of 1848. Society had not polarised into two antagonistic classes.

Liberal Republicans presented a more optimistic reading of social develop-ments. They argued that France was becoming a society of free, legally equal individuals with political rights, access to educational opportunity and the chance of upward social mobility in an expanding, increasingly consumerist economy. Belatedly women were securing wider legal, if not yet political, rights and educational and career opportunites. Cheaper and more abund-ant food and widening access to medical care were increasing life expect-ancy. As Charle's (1999) analysis makes clear, there were elements of plausibility in this picture, alongside much wishful thinking and ideological distortion. By comparison with much of Europe France was a peasant de-mocracy with an enfranchised rural smallholding class. Yet 3 per cent of owners owned 50 per cent of the land. Undoubtedly real wages rose after the 1850s, the threat of famine receded, calorie intake increased, and a better bal-anced diet led to a decline in deficiency diseases such as rickets. Nevertheless, the enormous rise in the fortunes of the very wealthy had occurred alongside a sharp relative decline in wealth held by the urban petty-bourgeoisie and the persistence of the pattern whereby three-quarters of urban dwellers died leaving almost nothing. Although Republican ideologists sometimes invoked the ideal of the 'self-made man', in general they were wary of trumpeting the possibilities of upward social mobility – probably with good reason. It was less easy to enter the industrial elite in 1900 than in 1820, and barely 10 per cent of senior civil servants came from outside the *grande* or *moyenne* bourgeoisie. The introduction of free, compulsory primary education was not matched by any real widening of access to secondary schooling. In short, the liberal 'myth' that political democracy, mass primary schooling, legal equality and an expanding free market economy would erode social inequalities and create a genuine meritocracy proved largely illusory – as some Radicals recognised when they began to advocate progressive income tax or extended welfare provision. Marxist and syndicalist claims that the liberal blueprint for French society was deeply flawed were not without foundation.

And yet post-1789 traditions of Republicanism had clearly helped to create a society that was more democratic and secular than its European counterparts. It had enjoyed male suffrage since 1848 and a democratic Republic and secular education since the 1870s. Workers and peasants joined a variety of trade-union, cooperative and mutual aid associations. The Republican vision was one of independent 'little men', and deference towards the clergy and the propertied elites had been eroded, even if it did persist in parts of the West or some company towns. Importantly the gains made by the popular classes stemmed from mass action and protest – they had rarely simply been 'granted'. Workers and peasants had fought for a Republic which was not just the product of the manipulative strategies of the elites. Reformist socialists like Jaurès, and Republican *instituteurs* had reason to take pride in this heritage and to hope that one day they might create a truly 'social' Republic.

Appendix I: Political regimes, 1789–1914

1789   French Revolution; constitutional monarchy
1792   First Republic (Year I); Jacobin government (1793–4) – (notional) manhood suffrage; Directory (1795–99) restricted franchise
1799   Napoleon's coup d'état
1804   (First) Empire – irregular plebiscites
1814   (First Bourbon) Restoration – constitutional monarchy
1815   Napoleon's 'Hundred Days'; (Second) Restoration – constitutional monarchy; very narrow franchise (richest 1 per cent of taxpayers)
1830   July Revolution; Orleanist ('July') Monarchy – constitutional monarchy; narrow property franchise (under 3 per cent of adult males)
1848   February Revolution; Second Republic – manhood suffrage; elected executive president Bonapartist coup (December 1851)
1852   Second Empire – semi-authoritarian pseudo-democracy; manhood suffrage; very weak parliament; powerful executive
1870   Third Republic – manhood suffrage; weak/indirectly elected president

Appendix II: Chronology of events, 1789–1914

1789	Outbreak of the French Revolution; 'Great Fear' in the countryside; abolition of feudalism and privilege; Declaration of Rights of Man; church property nationalised; departments created
1790	Noble titles abolished; Oath to Civil Constitution of Clergy imposed on clergy
1791	Guilds dissolved; Declaration of Rights of Women; Le Chapelier Law outlaws unions; Penal Code
1792	Monarchy overthrown (September); war begins; September prison massacres; (First) Republic proclaimed (December)
1793–4	Jacobin Republic; General Maximum; development of 'Terror'; dechristianisation; erosion of autonomy of 'popular movement'; repression of Counter-Revolution
1794	Fall of the Jacobin government
1795	Final popular risings; directory established; White Terror
1796	Italy invaded; Babeuf conspiracy
1797	Royalist election gains; purge of the Right
1798	Purge of Left-wing deputies; Roman Republic; invasion of Egypt
1799	Coup d'état (November); Bonaparte First Consul
1800	Bank of France founded; prefectoral system established; West 'pacified'
1802	Concordat promulgated; Ventôse laws establish medical profession; Peace of Amiens
1803	War resumes
1804	Civil Code promulgated; Empire proclaimed
1805–9	Military victories for Napoleon's armies across Europe
1808	*Université* established to control education; invasion of Spain
1809	Pope imprisoned
1810	Penal Code becomes more harsh
1811	Economic crisis
1811–14	Military defeats for Napoleon in Spain, Russia and Germany
1812	Food and anti-conscription riots in France
1814	Napoleon abdicates; First (Bourbon) Restoration (May); Constitutional Charter
1815	Napoleon's 'Hundred Days' (March–June); Second Restoration; 'White Terror' in Midi Ultra-Royalist electoral victory
1816	Dissoluton of Ultra-dominated *'Chambre introuvable'*; parliamentary elections
1816–17	Harvest failures/grain riots

1820	Law of 'DoubleVote'; assassination of Duc de Berri
1821	Beginnings of Carbonarist conspiracies; Death of Napoleon; Ultras control government
1824	Accession of Charles X; Ultra-royalist election victory
1825	Sacrilege Law; indemnification of émigrés; Rheims Cathedral coronation
1827	National Guard dissolved; liberal election gains (November); Forest Code
1829	Polignac's Ultra-royalist government; 'Guerre des Demoiselles' begins
1830	Liberal election gains (June); conquest of Algiers; Four Ordinances; July Revolution overthrows Bourbons; Louis Philippe 'King of French People' (September); provincial riots
1831	Municipal election law; elections with wider franchise; First Lyon revolt (October); cholera in Paris
1832	Legitimist rising in Vendée
1833	Guizot Education Act
1834	Law against associations; Second Lyon revolt; Rue Transnonain massacre in Paris
1835	Press controls tightened
1836	Bonapartist attempt (Strasbourg)
1839	Attempted Blanquist rising
1840	Bonapartist attempt (Boulogne)
1842–6	First rail boom
1846	Onset of economic crisis; Virgin Mary appears (in tears) at La Salette (allegedly . . .)
1847	Banquet electoral reform campaign (July–December)
1848	February Revolution overthrows Orleanism; Second Republic proclaimed; provisional government; manhood suffrage; Conservatives win April election; 'June Days' rising crushed; Cavaignac government; Louis Napoleon wins presidential election (December)
1849	French Army in Rome to defend Pope; Right wins parliamentary elections, but Left makes gains in Central and Southern France (May); abortive Left-wing rising in Paris/Lyon provokes repression (June)
1850	Falloux Education Law; Law restricting franchise – after Left-wing election gains (May); Insalubrious Dwellings Act
1851	Bonapartist coup (2 December); (rural) insurrection against coup in Central and Southern France; 35,000 arrests; plebiscite
1852	Second Empire proclaimed (December) after plebiscite; Crédit Foncier/Crédit Mobilier founded
1853	Haussmann becomes Prefect of Seine
1854	Crimean War (1854–56)
1855	Paris Exposition
1857	*Madame Bovary* prosecuted; Algerian conquest completed; legislative elections
1858	Virgin Mary appears to Bernadette Soubirous at Lourdes

1859	France's involvement in the War of Italian Unification alienates Catholic opinion; Saigon occupied
1860	Nice/Savoy annexed; free-trade treaty with Britain
1861	Expedition to Mexico begins
1863	Legislative elections
1864	Papal *Syllabus of Errors*; strikes legalised; Cambodia protectorate
1865	Duruy education reforms begin
1867	Joint-stock company legislation liberalised; Paris Exposition; Crédit Mobilier crisis
1868	Press and public meeting controls relaxed
1869	Opposition electoral gains (May); strike wave (1869–70); 'liberal Empire'
1870	Papal Infallibility; plebiscite on constitutional reforms; military defeats by Prussians (July/August); fall of Empire – advent of Republic (September); Siege of Paris (19 September 1870–January 1871); Government of National Defence
1871	Armistice (28 January); Neo-Royalists win parliamentary elections (February); Alsace-Lorraine ceded to Germany; Paris Commune (March–May); revolts in provincial towns (May); Thiers President (August); Republican by-election gains
1873	*Sacré Coeur* foundation stone laid; government controlled by 'Moral Order' Right (1873–77); indemnity paid to Germans/German troops leave; onset of 'Great Depression' (1873–96); death in exile of Napoleon III; McMahon president
1875	Constitution of Third Republic drawn up
1876	Republican election gains
1877	Republican election victory (October)
1878	Paris Exposition
1879	Marseille Socialist congress; Republican Grévy president; Ferry's 'Laic Laws' (1879–82)
1880	Sée Law (Girls' Lycées); Communards amnestied; Sunday official rest ended; 14 July national holiday
1881	Laws on assembly and press freedom; Tunis protectorate
1882	Collapse of Catholic 'Union Générale' bank (blamed on Jews); Hanoi occupied
1884	Trade Unions legalised; municipal reform – elected mayors; divorce reintroduced; Tonkin and Madagascar invaded
1885	Reverses in Indochina; fall of Ferry; Right's electoral revival
1887	Founding of *Bourses du Travail*
1888	Boulangist electoral campaign
1889	Paris Exposition; flight of Boulanger (April); Centenary of Revolution; Eiffel Tower completed
1890	'Ralliement' (Papacy urges Catholics to accept Republic)
1891	Encyclical 'Rerum Novarum' on 'social question'; army shoots workers at Fourmies
1892	Panama scandal; law banning female night-work
1894	Russian Alliance

1895	Foundation of CGT; radical government of L. Bourgeois
1896	Madagascar annexed; Méline moderate Republican government
1898	Zola's 'J'Accuse' re-ignites Dreyfus Affair; Industrial Accident Compensation Act
1899	Waldeck-Rousseau government of 'Republican defence'; Millerand in Cabinet
1901	Law on Congregations
1902	Public Hygiene Act; alliance of CGT and *Fédération des Bourses du Travail*; Combes Government
1904	Anglo-French Entente
1905	Crise du Midi (1905–07); Separation of church and state
1906	Amiens Charter affirms union autonomy; Paris general strike (May); clashes between army Catholics over 'inventories'; Moroccan crisis; Clemenceau Government (1906–09)
1908	Villeneuve-St-George 'massacre'
1909	Syndicalist strikes
1910	Briand Government breaks rail-strike
1911	Agadir crisis
1912	Protectorate over Morocco
1913	Three-year conscription law
1914	Centre-Left election victory (May); Jaurès assassinated (31 July); outbreak of war (August)

Appendix III: Glossary of terms

Biens Nationaux Church lands confiscated and auctioned off in the 1790s.

Bourses du Travail Labour exchange and meeting point for workers' groups.

Bureaux de Bienfaisance Commune-based welfare bureaux.

Cahiers de doléances Compilation of grievances of various social groups on the eve of 1789.

Charte Constitution of parliamentary monarchy (1814) guaranteeing some of the gains of the Revolution.

Chouans Western (peasant) counter-revolutionaries.

Conseil des Prud'hommes Court to adjudicate industrial disputes.

Gallicanism Strand of Catholicism favouring a degree of independence for the French Church.

Hobéraux Poor provincial nobles.

Jacobins Radical Republicans – supporters of the most 'extreme' phase of the Revolution.

Maximum Price control policy imposed by Jacobins in 1793–4.

Non-Jurors Clergy who refused to swear oath to the Revolution's religious settlement.

Orleanist Liberal-conservative supporter of July Monarchy (1830–48).

Patente Business tax.

Post-Tridentine Practices and beliefs of the Catholic Church after the sixteenth-century Council of Trent.

Prefect Government official with police/administrative powers in the department.

Procureur Général State public prosecutor.

Ralliement Movement of Catholics willing to accept the Republic in the 1890s.

Sans-culottes (Largely artisanal) militants who supported radical revolution in the 1790s.

Terror Phase of the Revolution marked by repression/executions of its opponants (1793–94).

Ultramontanism Strand of Catholicism looking to Rome/the Vatican.

Index